Contents

Contents

Insulation

Electro Mechanical Problems

ML

International Conference on

Electrical Machines - Design and Applications

13 — 15 July 1982

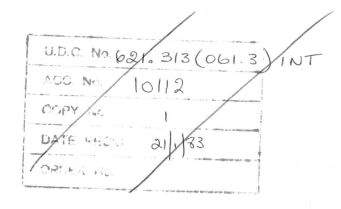
Organised by the
Power Division of the Institution of Electrical Engineers

in association with the
Institute of Electrical and Electronics Engineers
(United Kingdom and Republic of Ireland Section)
Institution of Mechanical Engineers

Venue
The Institution of Electrical Engineers, Savoy Place, London WC2

Organising Committee

W Fairney (Chairman)
Dr K J Binns
J C H Bone
D A Kennedy
Professor P J Lawrenson
Professor J R Smith
Dr M T Wright

Published by the Institution of Electrical Engineers, London and New York, ISBN 0 85296260 6, ISSN 0537-9989.

Printed by MULTIPLEX techniques ltd, Orpington

© 1982 The Institution of Electrical Engineers

Contents

Contents

Contents

Page No

Design

Contents

Page No

List of Authors

List of Authors

STATOR ENDWINDING MOVEMENT - CALCULATION AND MEASUREMENT

P.E. Clark,   I.E. McShane

GEC Large Machines Ltd., U.K.

INTRODUCTION

Most large electrical machines are associated with major capital projects where any failure is of serious consequence with a substantial loss of revenue in any enforced shutdown. The performance of the stator winding is of major importance in the reliability of a machine. Most failures involve significant shutdowns and repairs and extreme practical problems arise in situations such as offshore oil rigs. While diagnostic testing can help to anticipate some problems it is most important that the manufacturer designs on a basis of prevention.

The stator endwindings constitute a complex system which, with suitable bracing is essentially its own structure. It is constantly subjected to oscillatory forces primarily of electromagnetic origin. The forces arising from residual out-of-balance, noise etc. are normally insignificant. The electro-magnetic forcing could cause stresses and movements leading to insulation failure. If the bracing system is inadequate major permanent deformations can occur. Generators would usually be subjected to an occasional short circuit, the transients in synchronising and load variations usually being relatively small. Motors, even large ones up to 20-30MW, are usually direct-on-line started, and where inertias are high (as on some compressor drives), the starting time may be several tens of seconds. Such D.O.L. starts may be encountered several times per day.

There is also an increasing demand for system recovery after a fault requiring reswitching, which place a particularly onerous demand on the winding. Therefore, in general, motors (and obviously some special purpose generators) require particular attention to their endwinding bracing.

The methods of accomplishing a satisfactory support system, are based on the use of various packing systems between the coils in the overhang proper and perhaps at the mouths of slots, together with bracing rings secured back to the stator structure. Total or partial encapsulation is also used by some manufacturers. The bracing requirements and solutions have hitherto emerged generally on the basis of experience. Epoxy systems are almost universally used and there is a choice between the resin rich and vacuum-pressure impregnated systems.

It is therefore important to approach the design of the winding bracing less empirically, and to make detailed calculations. Measurement of stresses and deflections and the assessment of the consequences of these on winding life can be attempted. The advent of good computer programs for electro-magnetic analysis and also finite element mechanical analysis methods have considerably aided these calculations. However care is necessary in the modelling and in the determination of the effective properties of endwindings as they are structures which may not behave in the idealised linear manner.

Aspects of endwinding calculations are considered in this paper using a 3.2MW, 2 pole, 13.8kV motor as an example.

ELECTROMAGNETIC FORCES

The forces on the conductors are caused by the inter-action of the current in the conductors and the magnetic field in which they lie, which is, in turn, created by the same set of currents (3, 7, 12). As both the field and the current vary at supply frequency the forces will, of course, vary at twice this frequency.

The greatest forces will be found when adjacent phase bands carry current of the same magnitude and in the same sense. The usual connection of alternate phase bands requires, therefore, that two line currents are equal and opposite and their magnitude under steady state conditions will be 86.6% of the peak.

Similarly there are maximum "reverse" forces when the two phase bands carry equal currents of unlike sense. The magnitude of these currents under steady state conditions is 50% of the peak.

The maximum "forward" and "reverse" forces are different, not only because the current magnitudes are different, but also because the pattern of current distribution is different. In the former case there are pairs of phase bands carrying like currents separated by phase bands carrying no current, and in the latter case there are pairs of phase bands carrying unlike currents separated by phase bands carrying the peak current.

It can be seen, therefore, that these two peak forces will not be equal (ie the variation of force is asymmetric) and the degree of inequality will depend on the winding type, the size of the machine, the number of poles of the machine and many other factors.

TRANSIENT CURRENTS

When a motor is switched on or re-switched after a line fault, there is an initial transient current which builds up very quickly and then dies away to the so-called steady state starting current. The transient currents are asymmetrical with the degree of asymmetry depending on the voltage phase-angle when the switch is closed.

For example, a motor at the instant of switch-on may be reduced to a single resistance (R) and reactance (X) for each phase and if a voltage

$$v = V \sin (wt + \theta) \qquad (1)$$

is applied at t = 0, where θ represent the switching angle, then the current in one phase is given by

$$i = V/Z . \sin(wt+\theta-\varphi) - \exp(-wtR/X).\sin (\theta-\varphi) \qquad (2)$$

$$\text{where } Z^2 = R^2 + X^2 \qquad (3)$$

$$\text{and } \tan \varphi = X/R \qquad (4)$$

The voltages and currents for the other two phases are obtained by substituting $\theta+2\pi/3$ and $\theta+4\pi/3$ for θ and the largest equal and opposite currents occur when $\theta=\pi/6$ or $(\pi/6 + 2\pi/3)$ or $(\pi/6 + 4\pi/3)$.

MECHANICAL RESPONSE

The behaviour of the overhang is conveniently assessed by finite element methods. Each coil overhang is divided into beam elements (typically about 25) which closely model the structure. The coils are normally considered encastre in the core. Packing blocks are also represented as beam elements. Care is required to select element properties which simulate these correctly and this is discussed later. In some bracing systems, blocks acting only in compression may be used and in this case some additional iteration may be required. Support rings are conveniently modelled as "brick" type elements, with connections to the winding at the appropriate corners. The support rings are normally not considered to be anchored to the frame although in many bracing systems the support rings are so anchored and some degree of support is given. As the anchoring is not usually designed to provide a significant amount of support it is prudent to design on a basis for satisfactory service without it. The net electro-magnetic load on the total endwinding is zero, so the most efficacious bracing systems need not rely on external structures.

For the two pole motor being studied it is sufficient to use half the endwinding for the mechanical model in which the end coils are in regions of zero current and hence zero electromagnetic applied forces. The area of particular interest becomes the centre of the model, where the end effects are not significant. On multi-pole machines, particularly where the coils are stiff relative to the bracing system, a smaller model may be used.

The solution is scanned for the maxima (bending moment, deflections, etc. as desired) and also verified in respect of validity of assumed constraints if non linear elements are involved. The solution obtained is a quasi-static one where an upper bound estimate of the maximum dynamic electromagnetic force is applied as a static load to the mechanical system.

This is an approach which, provided resonance in critical areas is avoided, will give an overall result which is sufficiently accurate for design use. A full dynamic solution becomes prohibitive in computing effort. Bearing in mind the inherent difficulties in matters such as modelling it is hard to justify such increase of complexity. A good design will, of course, avoid such resonances. This is verifiable by calculation or experimental checks on a winding.

MATERIAL PROPERTIES

The correct determination of the effective mechanical properties of the elements used in the model, and the ascribing of fatigue life to them requires detailed consideration of the behaviour of the materials (2, 5, 10).

Stator coils are, of course, a composite material of copper with a surrounding insulation system, the latter having a significant affect on the coil behaviour. The mechanical properties of a flexible resin rich system is very different from those of a rigid or V.P.I. system. The behaviour of some composites is complex, and direct calculation of properties from the constituents may be extremely difficult.

Static tests to determine properties, particularly with the flexible systems, must be used with caution as hysteresis, creep and similar non-linearities may occur. Due to the characteristics of the insulation the mechanical behaviour of the composite will, in general, be temperature and strain rate dependent. Vibration techniques for the determination of properties are particularly convenient as frequencies can be selected to be similar to those of the endwinding forcing.

The vibration tests give the natural frequencies and from a knowledge of the mass distribution of the sample the effective stiffness is found by standard calculation methods. Similar techniques can be used for torsional properties. Fig.1 shows a typical arrangement in which by taking differential signals from probes at each added mass any bending effects are eliminated and the pure torsional signal extracted. For rigid insulation systems impulsive techniques on freely suspended specimens can be applicable.

Items such as packing blocks and connections to supports are more difficult to test. They are likely to be less consistent due to the variations inherent in the winding process. Non-linearities with differences between tensile and compressive behaviour can be expected. Because of the greater experimental difficulties these items were tested only statically in tension, compression, bending and torsion. Experience with coil samples and with the winding itself suggested this would give pessimistic results.

The detailed examination of packing and tying systems to ensure good modelling can itself be valuable in identifying good design methods; the practical detail on large windings is always important.

ESTIMATE OF WINDING LIFE

Having evaluated likely deflections on bending moments, acceptance criteria must be applied. Tests on coil systems have been described in other papers (1, 4, 6, 9, 11), many of these relating to V.P.I. systems and often examining loss tangent or mechanical stiffness during the course of a prolonged vibration test as assessment criteria. A simple high voltage breakdown criteria has been adopted for fatigue testing, supplemented where desirable at the end of the test by interturn, loss tangent and other investigational tests as appropriate.

Coil samples with associated packing blocks, dummy slot etc. have been tested, using the above criteria, as beams at their resonant frequency. A fairly high cycling frequency is required to permit completion of testing within a reasonable time, it being desirable to test to at least 10^7 cycles for motor starting analysis. The cycling creates losses within the material and hence some elevation of temperature above ambient making it representative of service conditions.

Insulation systems which are essentially rigid and homogeneous in the outer layers (HV pressed and VPI coils) will probably behave very much in the manner of metallic materials with crack propogation initiated from the outer surface at or near the points of maximum bending. For these a typical "metallic" life-stress (S-N) characteristic can be obtained, see Fig.(2). The behaviour of a flexible overhang insulation system is very different. It can be very difficult to induce insulation failures by a bending fatigue process. In the example considered amplitudes of the order of 12mm pk-pk on a cantilever 160mm long were required to produce a "failure", and the latter was by copper fracture at 5×10^5 cycles. Subsequent loss tangent and destructive HV and interturn testing showed little significant insulation damage.

Care must be exercised when assessing the deflections and stresses experienced in service. For a motor the currents, and hence stresses vary significantly during every start, see Fig. 3.

Provided the high transient forces do not constitute a gross overload, it will usually be found that the longer period at lower levels of stress will essentially determine winding fatigue life.

MEASUREMENT OF ENDWINDING MOVEMENT

A variety of methods of measuring endwinding movement
have been described by other authors (4, 8). These
include high speed film, strain gauges and optical
interferometry techniques.

The advantages and disadvantages of these methods are
summarised in Table 1.

For the measurements carried out on the 3.2MW motor high
speed film had inadequate resolution (about 1mm movement
was measured) and the unpressed insulation precluded the
use of strain gauges.

An optical technique was considered desirable but as all
degrees of freedom were to be measured the equipment
described below was used as an alternative to
interferometry.

Angular Deflection

This was simply measured by reflecting a beam of
light (from a laser) from a mirror mounted on the
endwinding. As one mirror can only measure the
deflections about two perpendicular axes, two mirrors
mounted at right angles were used. It is not necessary
for the light beams to be precisely perpendicular but it
is desirable in order to remove interference from
translational movement.

TABLE 1 - MEASURING METHODS

High Speed Film

Advantages:-

    No contact with winding,
    Relative movement easily measured,
    Little setting-up required,
    Records many parts of the winding at once.

Disadvantages:-

    Movement must be large (of the order of a
    centimetre),
    Camera shake difficult to remove,
    Immediate review of recording not possible,
    Difficult to correlate movement with current,
    Cannot easily measure all components of movement,
    Special equipment needed to measure movement on film.

Strain Gauges

Advantages:-

    High accuracy and resolution possible,
    Recordings easily made, eg on U-V recorder,
    Can easily correlate movement and current,
    Low mass - inertial effects negligible.

Disadvantages:-

    Not suitable for un-pressed insulation surfaces,
    Difficult to eliminate electrical interference,
    Gauge in contact with high voltage winding,
    Difficult to measure all components of movement,
    Calibration is difficult.

Optical Interferometry

Advantages:-

    High accuracy and resolution possible,
    No contact with winding except for separate
    reflector,
    Recordings easily made, eg on U-V recorder.

Disadvantages:-

    Very expensive apparatus,
    Difficult to measure angular movement,
    Significant interference between angular and linear
    movement.

Linear Deflection

The method for measuring linear deflection is more
complicated and the system is shown in Fig. 4. When the
final lens (which is mounted on the endwinding) is
displaced normally to the beam, the transmitted beam is
deflected through an angle so that it passes through the
focal point of the lens. With the screen a distance L
from the lens (of focal length f) the amplification of
the movement is simply (L-f)/f.

With just one lens the spot on the screen would not,
of course be in focus so a second lens must be added.
Strictly speaking the movement of the lens should be
subtracted from the movement of the spot on the screen
but if the amplification is sufficiently large this may
be neglected.

Small angular movements of the lens do not affect the
beam and to measure movement in three perpendicular
directions two lenses are used, mounted at right angles
to each other.

Mounting the Lenses and Mirrors

It is essential to mount the lenses and mirrors rigidly
on the winding and a combination of adhesive tape to
protect the winding and polyester putty was successfully
used.

Recording the Beam Movements

Opto-electronics offers the most attractive method of
recording the beam movement as hard copies (including
current waveforms) can easily be made on pen-recorders
or U-V recorders. This technique is being used in the
equipment currently being developed (see later) but for
the 3.2MW motor the beam movements were recorded using a
screen, television camera and video cassette recorder.

As the scanning rate of the television system is much
slower than the frequency of oscillation it is only
possible to measure peak-to-peak amplitudes with this
method as each television frame carries several beam
movement cycles. However particularly for the transient
region of a switch on, the results are very useful.

RESULTS

Several measurements were made on the 3.2MW motor. The
measuring point on the winding was on the nose of a coil
and it was found (see Table 2) that the translational
movements compared favourably with the calculated values
whereas the rotational movements were considerably less
than those calculated.

TABLE 2 - Experimental and Calculated movements of spots
on the screen.

Coil Movement	Spot Movement (mm) Calculated	Experimental
Axial translation	69	33
Vertical translation	43	30
Transverse translation	52	73
Rotation about axial axis	44	13
Rotation about vertical axis	22	9
Rotation about transverse axis	53	1

It is likely that the discrepancies in the rotational
movements were due to neglecting some torsional and
bending restraints at the support rings.

Future Developments

The method described above has the following disadvantages:-

a) Lenses mounted on the winding require a through path for the light beams. This limits the positions in which the lenses can be mounted.

b) The recording medium has a limited resolution.

c) The method of recording allows only peak-peak amplitudes to be measured.

An improved system is currently under development which replaces the lens on the machine with a reflector and uses opto-electronics to provide signals suitable for hard copy recorders.

CONCLUSIONS

There remain, and possibly will always remain, theoretical and practical limitations to the calculation and measurement of endwinding properties. Nevertheless techniques such as those described here enable more accurate evaluations of designs than was hitherto possible and thus facilitate their optimisation.

REFERENCES

1. Maughan, C.V., Gibbs, E.E., Giaquinto, E.V., 1970, IEEE Trans, Power Apparatus and Systems, PAS-89, No.8, 1946-1954.

2. Murakami, A., et al, 1974, Mitsubishi Denki Giho, 48, No.3, 315-320.

3. Chura, V., Posmurova, E., 1980, Acta Technica CSAV, No.4 406-430.

4. Ohtaguro, M., Yagiuchi, K., Yamaguchi, H., 1980, IEEE Trans. Power Apparatus and Sysems, PAS-99, No.3, 1181-1185.

5. Ohtaguro, M., Haga, K., Yagiuchi, K., Fuji Electric Review, 25, No.1, 19-26.

6. Futakawa, A., Yamasaki, S., Kawakami, T., 1979, IEE Trans. Electrical Insulation, EI-14, No.4, 193-199.

7. Brandl, P., 1980, Brown Boveri Review, 2-80, 128-134.

8. Futakawa, A., Yamasaki, S., 1981, IEE Trans. Electrical Insulation, EI-16, No.1, 31-39.

9. Mitsui, H., Yoshida, K., Inoue, Y., Kawahara, K., 1981, IEEE Trans. Electrical Insulation, EI-16, No.4, 351-359.

10. Futakawa, A., Yamasaki, S., Kawakami, T., 1981, IEEE Trans. Electrical Insulation, EI-16, No.4, 360-370.

11. Futakawa, A., Hirabayashi, S., Tani, T., Shibayama, K., 1978, IEEE Trans. Electrical Insulation, EI-13, No.6, 395-402.

12. Lawrenson, P.J., 1965, Proc. IEE, 112, No.6, 1144-1158.

5

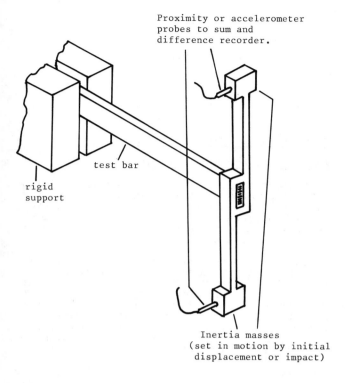

Figure 1.   Natural frequency method for torsional and bending stiffness.

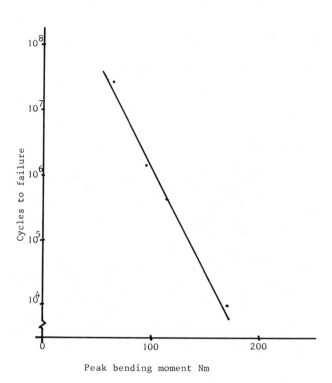

Figure 2.   Typical fatigue behaviour of a pressed coil sample in reversed bending.

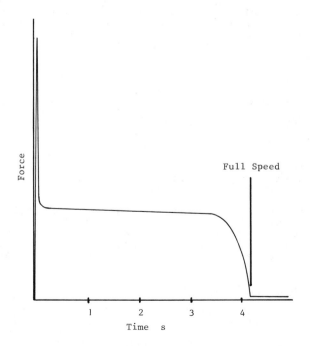

Figure 3.   Typical variation of envelope of endwinding force during motor acceleration.

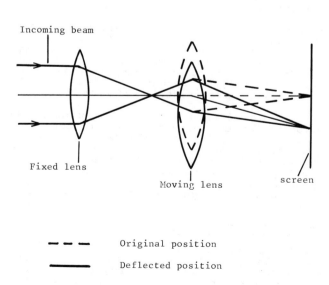

Figure 4.   Linear deflection measuring system.

THE PREDICTION OF TRANSIENT INTERTURN VOLTAGES IN STATOR WINDINGS

M. T. Wright, S. J. Yang,* and K. McLeay

Parsons Peebles Motors and Generators, U.K.   *Heriot-Watt University, U.K.

INTRODUCTION

The distribution of voltage in induction motor stator coils, due to the application of steep fronted switching surges, has aroused much interest in recent years amongst motor manufacturers and users alike. This interest has been prompted by the increased occurrence of winding failure in the interturn mode. The increased use of modern low loss cables has meant that surges are transmitted almost unaltered to the motor. In addition the undoubted advantages of vacuum switchgear have led to their increased popularity in motor control systems. The ability of this type of switchgear to produce repetitive steep fronted transient voltages, however, has in some cases, led to stator coils being subject to more severe surge conditions.

It is well known that steep fronted surges can cause high interturn stressing. Unless stator coils are designed to withstand these surges interturn failures, possibly leading to turn to ground failure, may occur.

The continuing increase in the output coefficients of modern motors has led to a tendency to minimise the size of stator coils. Thus the insulation design of modern coils leaves a less margin for error, although the better quality of modern insulation material has offset this to a considerable extent.

This contribution shows that an accurate method of predicting transient voltage distribution in the coils is necessary.

Following a brief resumé of pertinent work on the topic, it is found that further development of previous analyses would be ineffective and that a completely new analysis is required. The development of such an analysis is outlined here and its validity is experimentally confirmed.

Due to the lack of understanding of surge propagation in stator coils in the past, the insulation testing of coils has been carried out at voltages which were set at levels which may be exceeded in practice. Current test standards are compared with voltage distributions as predicted by the new theory, for various surge shapes and insulation levels.

PREVIOUS INVESTIGATIONS

In the past, voltage distribution has been analysed by an oversimplified model for the winding, i.e. by modelling the winding either as a simple transmission line or as a ladder network. Neither of these methods gives accurate predictions of turn voltages. Further development of existing analyses was not feasible, therefore a new approach to the problem was required.

DESCRIPTION OF THE NEW THEORY

Assumptions and Approximations

A rigorous analysis of electromagnetic fields in and around a stator winding during a transient disturbance is certainly not practicable. Therefore certain approximations and assumptions must be made to enable the analysis to develope.

It has been shown that, at high frequencies, core iron acts as a shield to electromagnetic flux. [3] It can therefore be assumed that over the stator core length, the flux is confined to within the slot. This assumption, together with the assumption that intercoil coupling in the endwinding region is negligible, means that coils can be treated independently since they influence each other only through their series connections.

At the high frequencies associated with the surges of interest here (i.e. surges with front times below 1 us,: frequencies above 1MHz) the surge current in the conductors will be severely skin effect limited. Consequently the internal inductances of the coil can be neglected.

In estimating the copper losses in the coil conductors, both skin and proximity effects must be taken into account. To estimate the skin effect it is assumed that all the current flows in an outer layer the depth of which is found from one dimensional theory, i.e. skin depth, d, is given by

$$d = \sqrt{\frac{2\rho_c}{\mu\omega}}$$

The proximity effect is estimated by multiplying the losses, accounting for skin effect, by a proximity factor, k_p, such that

$$R = k_p R_{a.c.}$$

It can be shown that for the dimensions of stator coil conductors and the range of frequencies in question, k_p is a constant. [2]

Although, in reality, losses are distributed evenly along the coil conductors, it was found to be sufficiently accurate to account for their effect by modelling them as discrete resistances at five points on the coil.

Modelling the Coil

The coil is visualised as comprising five distinct sections as in Figure 1. The five sections are connected to each other at five junctions. Four of these junctions are at the point where a slot section meets an endwinding section. The fifth junction is the terminal junction where the coil terminals join at the coil evolute.

The cross sectional dimensions of all coil sections, at the frequencies involved in analysis, preclude all modes of wave propagation except TEM. Each coil section can therefore be treated as a multi-conductor transmission line. Consequently the five junctions are seen as multiconductor transmission line junctions. The propagation of waves along multiconductor transmission lines is well understood for both lossless and lossy lines. However only lossless multiconductor transmission line junctions have been analysed in the literature.[3]

The relationship between the incident voltage waves on each line and the reflections which are caused to propagate from the lossless junctions is given by Agrawal et al [3] as,

$$(V)^{re} = (S)(V)^{in} \qquad (1)$$

where $(V)^{re}$ and $(V)^{in}$ are the column vectors of the voltages on the conductors.

(S) can be shown to be related to the transmission line admittances and the junction topology by

$$(S) = \begin{bmatrix} -(C_v) \\ (C_i) \quad (Y) \end{bmatrix}^{-1} X \begin{bmatrix} (C_v) \\ (C_i) \quad (Y) \end{bmatrix} \qquad (2)$$

where (C_v) and (C_i) are the voltage connection matrix and current connection matrix respectively and are determined entirely by the interconnections of the conductors at the junction.

Equations (1) and (2) are valid only for lossless junctions. However a further development of the theory which includes discrete loss elements at the junction has now been achieved. Both copper and dielectric losses can be included in this method.

Including the losses in the analysis gives,

$$(V)^{re} = (S_L)(V)^{in}$$

where (S_L) is the lossy scatter matrix for the junction and is found to be:

$$(S_L) = \begin{bmatrix} -(C_v)-(C_v)(R)(Y)-(C_v)(G)(R) \\ (C_i)(Y) + (C_i)(G) \end{bmatrix}^{-1} X$$

$$\begin{bmatrix} (C_v)-(C_v)(R)(Y) + (C_v)(G)(R) \\ (C_i)(Y) - (C_i)(G) \end{bmatrix}$$

where (R) and (G) represent the copper and dielectric losses respectively.

In this way, wave reflections at each junction can be calculated taking account of losses.

Computer programmes were developed to model the coil as sections of lossless multiconductor transmission lines interconnected by lossy junctions. This computer model can be used as a building block to model a complete phase winding. The predictions from the computer model are compared with experimental results below.

EXPERIMENTAL CONFIRMATION OF THE THEORY

Only low voltage tests were practicable because of the necessity to remove some insulation to gain access to the turns.

The results of the tests revealed that the theoretical turn to ground voltages on the line end coil, due to the application of a surge of irregular shape, followed very closely the measured turn to ground voltages.

A more stringent test of the theory is the prediction of interturn voltages. High accuracy is more difficult to obtain for these voltages since they are calculated as the difference between two large turn to ground voltages. Figure 2 shows that the theory is extremely accurate in calculating both the shape and magnitude of the interturn voltages. The theory can therefore be used to investigate the effects of various system parameters on the voltage distribution in the coils and the results of this investigation can be compared to the prevailing standards for coil insulation.

Figure 2 also shows that surge propagation in stator coils is the result of two distinct phenomena. The progression of the voltage peaks shows series surge propagation. The fact that interturn voltages appear at the end of the coil well before the peaks arrive demonstrates that there is also parallel propagation due to interturn coupling.

Since the theory has been shown to be accurate, it can be used to predict voltage distribution due to various surges and on coils with various insulation levels.

EFFECTS OF SURGE RISE TIME ON INTERTURN VOLTAGES

To investigate the variations in voltage distribution due to various surge front times, the theoretical model was used to predict voltages due to surges with front times varying from 25ns - 400ns. Front times below 25ns are unlikely to occur in practice and front times greater than 400ns will not cause severe interturn stressing.

The peak voltage appearing between each pair of turns of the terminal junction of a 13.8kV, 12 turn line end coil is plotted against the turn number in Figure 3 for each surge. These curves clearly indicate that the maximum peak voltage appearing across the turn insulation always occurs towards the neutral end of the line end coil. In the case of surges with rise times below 100ns (0.1µs) the maximum interturn voltage occurs between the final two turns in the coil. This is due to reflection, of the series transmitted portion of the surge at the end of the coil. The result that the maximum interturn voltage (or a voltage of almost equal magnitude) occurs across several interturn spacings at the neutral end of the coil, for the case of the slower rise times, indicates that the surge front and its reflection are spread over a number of the neutral end turns.

It is emphasised that the voltage distribution is due only in part to the series propagation of the surge and that a quantitative analysis cannot be based on the series propagation mode alone.

The peak interturn voltages in Figure 4 show clearly that maximum interturn voltage increases with decreasing surge front time. Thus the 5 p.u. 200ns test surge of the OCMA[5] standard, for example, will not ensure that interturn insulation can withstand a 5 p.u. surge of smaller front time. In fact, a surge of well below 5 p.u. can cause greater interturn stressing than the test surge, if the front time is short enough.

The ESI standard[4] when applied to a 13.8kV coil gives an interturn test voltage of 2.8kV r.m.s. or 3.96kV peak. To find the voltage which the OCMA test surge causes on this coil, Figure 3 can be used. The maximum interturn voltage for the 200ns surge is 25% of the applied surge. The applied surge is that which is produced at the surge generator. (The surge which actually appears at the winding terminal is greater than this due to a frequency dependent impedance mismatch effect.) In this case, the surge at the winding terminal was 157% of the original surge.

Therefore the 3 p.u. OCMA surge produces an interturn voltage of

$$13.8\text{kV} \times \sqrt{\frac{2}{3}} \times 3 \times \frac{25\%}{157\%} = 5.38\text{kV}$$

The 5 p.u. OCMA surge gives 8.97kV.

Thus it can be seen that the OCMA surge test stresses the interturn insulation much more severely than does the ESI test.

EFFECT OF INSULATION DIMENSIONS ON INTERTURN VOLTAGES

Three insulation levels were used to investigate the effect of the insulation dimensions. These were 3.3kV, 11.0kV and 13.8kV. In addition a fourth set of dimensions was used to show the effect of the interturn insulation dimensions alone. For this purpose the 11.0kV level was used but with 50% extra interturn insulation. The permittivity was kept constant throughout.

It was anticipated that the coils with thicker insulation would produce the higher p.u. interturn voltages, since the reduced interturn coupling would cause the series propagation mode to become more effective than the parallel mode. Figure 4 shows this to be the case. In particular, the curves relating to 11kV coils, with differing interturn insulations, show that the interturn voltage increases by 24.4% due solely to a 50% increase in interturn insulation thickness.

Variation in interturn insulation clearly causes variation in interturn stressing, therefore allowance should be made for the anticipated voltage distribution during the design process. In interturn insulation type tests, the test voltage is applied directly across a typical sample of interturn insulation, so no allowance is made for voltage distribution. Thus a coil which has a severely non-linear surge distribution can pass the type test and yet may not be adequately tested by the proof test surge.

EFFECT OF OTHER PARAMETERS ON INTERTURN VOLTAGE

Other coil parameters can be altered in the model in order to discover the manner in which they affect voltage distribution. It was found that fast fronted surges produce maximum interturn voltages which are substantially independent of the number of turns in the coil.[6] This result and the effect of coil shape on voltage distribution will be reported in detail in a future publication.

SURGE IMPEDANCE

Figure 5 shows the voltages to ground on each turn at the terminal junction of a 12 turn line end coil. The rise time of the surge as it left the switch was 50ns (0.05µs). The increase in voltage at the terminal of the coil is considerable. This increase in voltage is commonly thought of as being due to a mismatch of cable and winding surge impedances. In reality the effect is the net result of many internal reflections in the coil. However an effective surge impedance can be calculated using the impedance mismatch concept. The variation of surge impedance with surge front time is shown for 3.3kV, 11.0kV and 13.8kV coil in Figure 6.

Also included in Figure 6 is the surge impedance of an 11kV coil when subjected to the surge of irregular shape shown in Figure 7. This indicates that the shape of the surge, if different from the classical short rise time and long tail, modifies effective surge impedance. Consequently surge impedance alone is not a reliable indicator of overvoltage magnitudes as it is heavily dependent on frequency.

RECOMMENDATIONS AND CONCLUSIONS

It has been suggested in this contribution that the number and severity of surges which motor windings must endure has increased in recent years. Present methods of analysis of surge propagation through stator coils are inadequate and cannot be developed further.

A new general theory based on multiconductor transmission line theory and scatter matrices was briefly described. The further development of scatter matrices to include losses was also given, and a computer programme incorporating multiconductor transmission line theory and lossy scatter matrices was shown to give predictions of interturn voltages which reproduced the measured voltages with a high degree of accuracy.

The increase in interturn voltage with decreasing front time was expected and confirms the results of previous investigations. The non-linearity of the distribution also increases with decreasing rise time.

The larger percentage interturn voltage appearing on the higher voltage coils is clearly due to the decreased interturn coupling caused by the increased insulation thickness. Consequently interturn insulation thickness must be increased by a factor greater than that by which the voltage level is increased if the same safety margin is to be maintained.

While the OCMA test levels are a significant improvement on ESI 44-5, they may not be adequate where surges of very fast rise time exist. Type testing of interturn insulation takes no account of voltage distribution.

The surge impedance of windings has been shown to be dependent on both surge shape and rise time and is therefore of limited value as a machine parameter The surge impedances, calculated for surges with a smooth rise and long tail, show an increase in surge impedance magnitude with decreasing rise time.

The investigation into the effects of coil and surge parameters on voltage distribution has indicated various trends. However, the major benefit of the new method of analysis lies in its use as a design tool, which can be used to co-ordinate coil insulation to provide adequate factors of safety without overdesign.

ACKNOWLEDGEMENTS

The assistance of the Science and Engineering Research Council in funding Mr. McLeay for this work is gratefully acknowledged.

REFERENCES

1. Heller, B. and Veverka, A., 1966, "Surge phenomena in electrical machines", Iliffe, London.

2. Lammeraner, J. and Stafl, M., 1966, "Eddy currents", Iliffe, London.

3. Agrawal, A. K., Fowles, H. M., Scott, L. D. and Gurbaxani, S. H., August 1979, "Application of modal analysis to the transient response of multiconductor transmission lines with branches", IEEE Transactions on Electromagnetic Compatibility, Vol. EMC-21 No. 3, p.p. 256-262.

4. Electricity Supply Industry Standard 44-5, September 1978, Issue 2.

5. Oil Companies Materials Association, July 1981, Specification No. ELEC.1.

6. Wright, M. T. and McLeay, K., 1981, "Interturn voltage distribution due to fast transient switching of induction motors", IEEE Conference Paper PCI-81-14, Petroleum and Chemical Industry Conference.

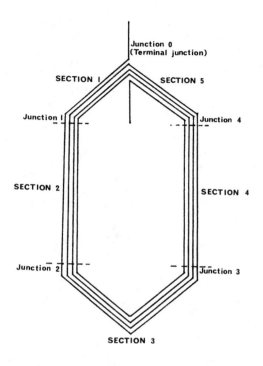

Figure 1   Sectionalised 4 turn coil

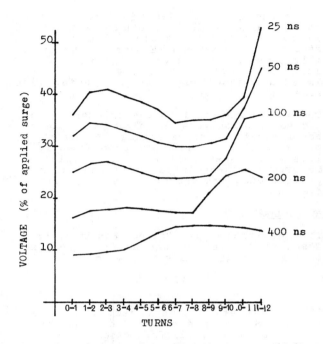

Figure 3   Interturn voltage distribution on a 13.8kV,
12 turn coil due to the various rise times
0-1 indicates the line end turn.

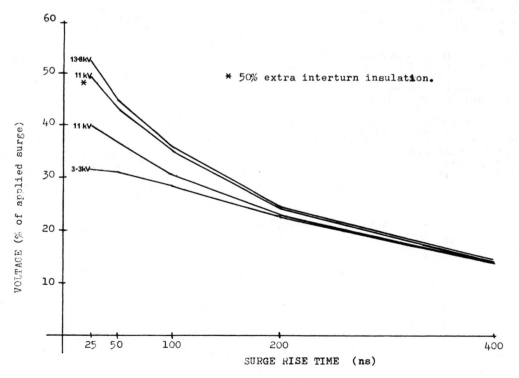

Figure 4   Maximum interturn voltage vs.   Surge rise time for various insulation levels.

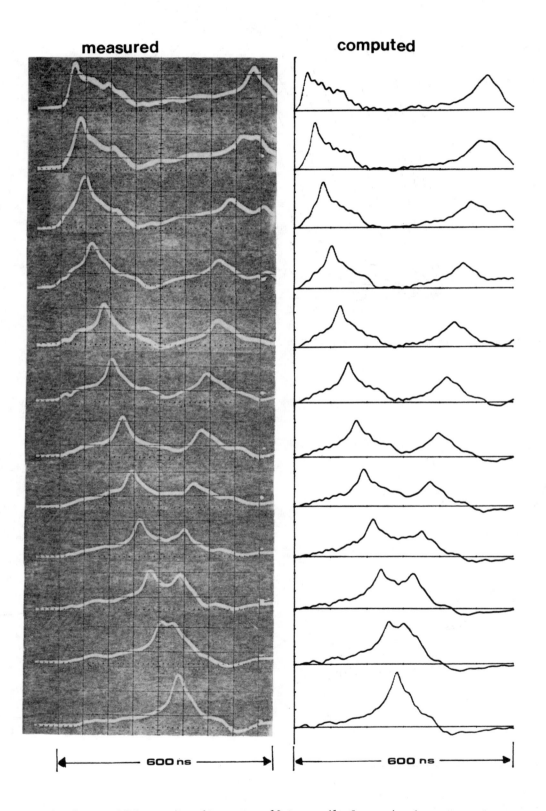

Figure 2 Measured and computed interturn voltages on a 12 turn coil. Successive interturn voltages on the line end coil.

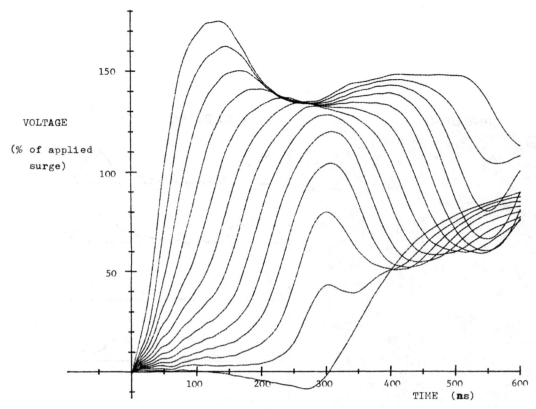

Figure 5   Turn to ground voltages vs. Time for 13.8kV, 12 turn coil (50 ns surge rise time)

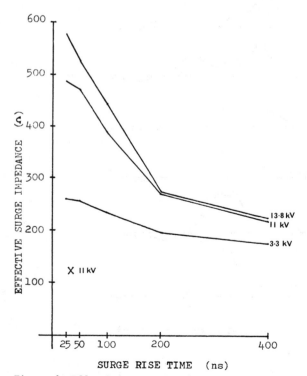

Figure 6   Effective surge impedance vs. surge rise time (various insulation levels)

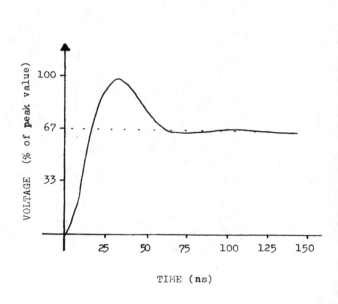

Figure 7   Irregular surge wave form

CONSIDERATIONS AFFECTING OPERATING COSTS OF ELECTRICAL MACHINES

T.A. Gallant and G.A. Thompson

Laurence, Scott & Electromotors Ltd., U.K.

INTRODUCTION

During the last decade it has become more apparent that energy resources are finite and therefore increasingly expensive. Most nations are now trying to rely less heavily upon oil by turning to coal or nuclear power, but it seems likely that the cost of energy in any form will continue to increase in the foreseeable future. One of the reasons for this is the fact that energy consumption increases with the standard of living in an industrialised society. Such a society will devote a significant proportion of its generated electricity to the powering of electric motors of all sizes and types. In the U.K. this figure is approximately 40%.

The relationship between the relative costs of purchasing and running electric motors is discussed in this paper.

In this country there has been a complacent attitude towards conservation of energy in all its forms. This is no less true of the users of electrical machinery than it is of domestic consumers. The reasons for this complacency are probably associated with an era of relatively cheap power costs which are now rapidly increasing. Figure 1 illustrates the trend of electricity costs in the U.K. for industrial users in pence/kWh for the last 30 years and shows that after a long period of relative stability, the cost since the early '70s has escalated rapidly.

Few people realize that an electric motor of any size, running continuously, could incur power charges which exceed the initial capital cost of the motor by a factor of about 20 times in the first year alone. In saying this we are not talking about an inefficient item but probably considering efficiencies in excess of 95% which are good when judged by many other standards. Whether they are good enough should be a matter for careful consideration at quotation or design stage.

All too often the first and perhaps only consideration is the initial cost of the machine. When these costs assume an unrealistic significance the automatic choice would appear to be a squirrel-cage single speed induction motor. Whilst it is true that such a machine might perform its duty in an efficient and reliable manner, a closer study of the site installation,could reveal that an initially more expensive variable speed drive would be cheaper in the long term.

Choice of Drive Motor

Having decided to give serious consideration to the problem of operating costs, the user must then investigate an apparently bewildering choice of drive motors some of which offer speed variation by various means. The majority of these are based on one of the following basic types of machine:

Squirrel-cage induction motor
Synchronous motor
Sliping induction motor
DC motor
N-S variable speed AC motor.

A more comprehensive list of drive motors is shown next to the flow chart (figure 5).

These are not placed in any particular order of merit and it is appreciated that there are other electrical or mechanical options currently available. The final choice must be made taking all relevant factors into consideration such as:-

a) Availability of suitable electrical supply
b) Working environment
c) Operating times
d) Standby requirements
e) Ease of maintenance and reliability.

In order to achieve the best economic solution it must be the users' ultimate responsibility to ensure that the correct type of drive motor is specified to the motor manufacturer with the appropriate emphasis on efficiency where this is considered necessary. The motor manufacturer must then put forward an offer which meets these requirements on a cost-effective basis and he may, at the same time, be able to suggest an alternative solution which is attractive and therefore worthy of further consideration.

The flow chart (see figure 5) is intended to assist a prospective purchaser of electric motors in making a correct choice. It must be stressed that this chart is simplified and will not cater for every conceivable alternative. The user would be wise to reconsider his options having performed the necessary calculations especially in borderline cases of running time etc.

It should prove most useful for fluid pumping and fan applications but will not necessarily cater for installations where variable speed could be required on purely practical grounds.

Assessment of Operating Costs

While the capital cost of drive equipment and their power costs are often compared on the basis of payback period i.e. the time required for the savings in power costs to equal the difference in initial cost of the drives, this form of assessment makes no allowance for interest on the money required to finance the installation. It is therefore necessary to consider some other means of comparison which will reflect the power charges associated with the drives over their anticipated operating life and this should be the money required to finance the power charges over this period. The comparison between drives would then be that of initial cost plus capitalised power cost of each drive.

The capitalised value can be obtained from the standard annuity calculation

$$P = \left[1 - \left(\frac{100}{100 + r} \right)^n \right] \frac{100a}{r}$$

where a = annual cost of power
       r = % interest rate
       n = number of years over which the power costs are to be capitalised.

The capitalised value of power costs, given above, takes into consideration interest rates and assumes that the annual power charges are the same for the anticipated life of the equipment.

Figure 2 shows the factors, for various interest rates and capitalisation periods, by which the annual power costs must be multiplied to give capitalised values.

As power costs are normally financed out of cash flow which can be assumed to inflate at the same rate as power charges, we consider that the capitalised power costs based on zero inflation give a more realistic evaluation. For this reason we have ignored inflation.

Likewise the capitalised value of a kW can be used as the basis for liquidated damages if this should be considered desirable within the terms of the contract. If the power charges are assumed to be 3 pence/kWh and the machine operates 6000 hours per year with interest rates say 10% per annum then the capitalised value of a kW over 25 years (making no allowance for inflation) would be £1,634.

While this figure can be used as a liquidated damage, it does also indicate to the motor manufacturer how much the initial cost of the machine can be increased to improve its performance such that the power required is reduced by 1 kW. It is clearly in the users' interests to take all benefits in operating costs into consideration and to give all necessary information for the manufacturer to make the most economic offer.

It is, of course, obvious that the greatest saving in power charges will be obtained in continuous processes which operate 24 hours/day and it is, therefore, important to choose the type of drive which will minimize power charges.

The choice may well be a variable speed drive with relatively high initial cost on the one hand, or a single speed induction motor with a relatively low initial cost on the other.

The Case for an Alternative to a Single Speed Machine

With a drive where variation in throughput is required, there are often various ways of achieving this objective. Taking the example of a fan where control of airflow is necessary, then one method is to simply throttle the air by means of a suitable damper. With a centrifugal pump drive variation in flow can likewise be achieved by the use of a valve. In both cases, due to the increased head or pressure losses across the restriction, together with the inherently lower pump or fan efficiency characteristic at this point, the input kW would be higher than would otherwise be necessary if a reduced speed was used instead. With a reduction in speed, to achieve the same throughput, there would normally be no head or pressure loss across the valve or damper and the inherent fan or pump characteristics would also be more efficient in this condition.

As a basis for comparing power costs, we have considered a pumping installation with a typical head/quantity curve as shown in figure 3 operating with on/off control to give the required average flow using a single speed induction motor alternatively a two speed induction motor.

The single-speed squirrel-cage induction motor is rated 645kW 985 rpm with the motor performance at pump load:-

Pump load	585 kW
Speed (rev/min)	985
Efficiency	95.2%
Power factor	0.88
Input kW	614.5
Input kVA	698

And the two-speed squirrel-cage induction motor is rated 645/327kW 985/740 rev/min with the following performance at the pump load conditions:-

Pump load	585 kW	297
Speed (rev/min)	985	740
Efficiency	95%	93%
Power factor	0.80	0.71
Input kW	615.8	319.4
Input kVA	770	450

The power charges have been considered based on a maximum demand charge night and day rate which is 2.86 pence per unit for all hours, except between 1 a.m. and 8 a.m., when the unit charge is 1.2 pence. An additional component based on maximum demand in each month is included at the following rates:-

	Supply capacity charge per month for any month	November and March	December, January and February	Any summer month
For each kVA of chargeable capacity	£0.18			
a) For each of the first 500kVA maximum demand		£1.52	£3.48	£0.5
b) For each kVA maximum demand above 500kVA		£1.41	£3.27	£0.48

To simplify the calculations of power charges, the average monthly maximum demand charge a) has been taken to be £1.42 and for b) £1.33. The calculations assume that the pumped flow is maintained at the various rates for 1 year and allow for maximum pumping rate for the 7 hours each night when the reduced unit charge is applicable. The single speed induction motor would, therefore, operate the required number of hours each day to give the required flow and the two-speed induction motor would operate 24 hours/day and so control the output by operating at low speed for the necessary time. The power required is therefore minimised in this way.

Six flow rates have been considered (735, 685, 580, 477, 388 and 240 litres/second) and the annual power cost for each drive has been based on the assumption that the equipment operates at each flow rate for $16\frac{2}{3}$% of the time.

The capital costs of the two drives being considered including control gear are:-

Single-speed, squirrel-cage induction motor £19,000.
Two-speed P.A.M. squirrel-cage induction motor £31,000.

Cost comparison of single-speed and two-speed squirrel-cage induction motors using on/off control of flow:-

	Single-speed	Two-speed
Annual power cost	£ 95,500	£ 89,900
Capitalised power cost	£867,000	£816,000
Capital cost	£ 19,000	£ 31,000
	£886,000	£847,000

The overall saving would therefore be £39,000 using a two-speed squirrel-cage induction motor.

If the power factor for the single-speed and two-speed squirrel-cage induction motors is corrected to 0.96, the maximum demand charge component of the power charges will be reduced and an additional cost for power factor correction capacitors incurred as follows:-

	Single-speed	Two-speed
Cost of power factor correction capacitor.	£ 900	£ 2,000
Reduction in annual power cost.	£6,300	£13,500

The affect of maximum demand on power costs can be significant and any reduction obtained either by improved power factor and/or reduction in peak kW load on the supply should be considered.

However, as many pumping installations and most fan drives are required to operate continuously, control of the drive output must be achieved either by throttling/damper control or by variable speed. The range of variable speed systems can broadly be divided into two categories, low and high loss systems most of which are indicated on the flow chart (see figure 5).

Two-speed P.A.M. squirrel-cage induction motors are increasingly being used for various applications where narrow speed ranges and falling torque characteristic drives are required. The comparisons shown in the preceding example illustrate the possible economic benefits which can be achieved by their use.

The P.A.M. method of connection gives speeds of 1480/980 rpm (4/6 pole) 980/740 rpm (6/8 pole) etc. In fact almost any required speed ratio can be achieved (with few exceptions) by a suitable choice of pole ratios. This machine possesses all the advantages of a squirrel-cage induction motor such as: simplicity, reliability, ease of maintenance, ruggedness and low initial cost.

The affect of choice of variable speed drive system is illustrated in the following comparison between an N-S variable speed AC motor and a slipring induction motor with rotor resistance control giving the required speed variation. The head/quantity curve for the pumping installation is shown on figure 4 and the relative motor performance figures used for the comparison are:-

Litres/second	735	685	580	477	388	240
Pump load kW	585	514	389	297	232	174
Speed rev/min	985	932	828	740	670	580

AC Variable Speed Motor						
Efficiency	93%	93%	92%	90.8%	89.8%	88.5%
Power factor	.92	.92	.88	.80	.75	.65
Input kW	629	553	423	327	258	197
Input kVA	684	601	480	409	344	302

Slipring Motor with Rotor Resistance						
Efficiency	94.7%	89.6%	79.4%	70.8%	64%	55%
Power factor	.88	.88	.87	.86	.84	.82
Input kW	618	574	490	420	362	316
Input kVA	702	652	563	488	432	386

The capital costs of the two drives including control gear are:

N-S variable speed AC motor £46,000
Slipring induction motor with rotor resistance £34,000

The annual power cost for each drive has been calculated on the assumption that they operate for the same length of time at each flow giving the following cost comparison:

Cost comparison of N-S variable speed AC motor and slipring induction motor with rotor resistance control

	N-S variable speed AC motor	Slipring motor with rotor Resistance Control
Annual power cost ...	£ 92,300	£103,800
Capitalised power cost	£838,000	£942,000
Capital cost	£ 46,000	£ 34,000
	£884,000	£976,000

The overall saving would therefore be £92,000 using an N-S variable speed AC motor.

High loss drives such as slipring induction motors with rotor resistance control, are dependent on increased losses to give wider speed variation and therefore efficiency is considerably reduced at relatively low speeds. It follows, therefore, that the slipring motor will give improved performance with reduced speed range. Figure 6 is a curve indicating the relative kilowatts loss for an N-S variable speed AC motor and a slipring induction motor with rotor resistance control, against speed.

The Case for High Efficiency

It will be apparent that, especially where long running times are likely, there can be a strong case for investing capital in a suitable drive motor of an initially more expensive type, such as a variable speed machine. There is often an equally strong argument, in such cases, for paying a premium for higher efficiency than is normally obtainable with a standard machine.

The motor manufacturer might well be asked why he does not design machines with the maximum efficiency in any event. In order to answer this question, it is necessary not only to quantify the typical losses in a machine but to understand manufacturing processes.

Designing a range of machines to cover all speeds, potential outputs and enclosures requires a significant degree of standardization of materials, components and manufacturing techniques. By doing this, the manufacturer is able to offer a machine which has a competitive selling price and a good performance.

Any improvement in efficiency will inevitably require the use of a larger quantity of possibly more expensive materials and could involve the use of a larger frame size. Although there might sometimes be a case for producing a parallel range of higher efficiency designs which would normally command a higher price, most manufacturers find it economic to adapt existing ranges in the specific cases where the appropriate calculations indicate that efficiency is of paramount importance.

The losses in a squirrel-cage induction motor can be summarised as follows:-

1. Windage and friction
2. Iron losses
3. Copper loss (I^2R) in the stator and rotor winding
4. "Stray" loss

Of these losses only items 2 and 3 are likely to be capable of showing a significant reduction since a well designed motor will already have an efficient cooling fan, possibly of the unidirectional trailing bladed type. Care will also have been taken to ensure that the "stray" losses are not excessive.

In order to illustrate the cost effectiveness of reducing the losses of a typical squirrel-cage induction motor by 20%, the increase in material costs (as a percentage of the motor selling price) has been tabulated against the cost/kilowatt loss, assuming a motor with an output of 500kW and an original efficiency of 95%.

Loss	Increased material cost (% motor price)	Reduction in total loss (%)	Cost/kW (% motor price)
Iron	2	7.6	1.0
Copper	1.5	12.4	0.46
Total	3.5	20	0.67

The reduction in iron loss in this example has been achieved only by the use of a more expensive low loss material without increasing the core diameter or length, whilst the copper loss has been reduced by increasing the stator and rotor copper section by approximately 20%. Although the reduction in iron loss will always be attainable (provided of course that high grade electrical sheet steel is not already employed), the reduction in copper losses may be inhibited by other design considerations. For the same flux level, an increase in copper sizes will usually increase the iron loss for example, but by an amount which is less than the improvement achieved by using a lower loss material.

These improvements therefore represent the maximum

which is likely to be expected without increasing the frame size and are usually very cost effective in most cases. Any further reduction in loss, however, will incur a more serious penalty of added material costs due, not only to the larger quantity of electrical sheet steel, but to the necessity of a larger frame to house the additional material, although it could still be cost effective when the capitalised value of a kilowatt is relatively high.

With any fixed or variable speed drive, it should be borne in mind that a non sinusoidal electrical supply could induce additional stray losses in the iron or windings, affecting actual efficiency and increasing operating temperatures. Although this is not normally a serious problem, it is worth bearing in mind, especially when contemplating the use of P.W.M. (pulse width modulation) or other invertor drives to vary the speed of an induction motor.

The inherent losses in any control equipment (static or otherwise) must also be allowed for when assessing operating costs.

CONCLUSIONS

Whilst many users have always taken running costs into consideration when selecting a suitable drive motor, this has, in the past, tended to apply mainly to major drives which are operating continuously.

It has been the aim of this paper to highlight the fact that a wider range of drives may be worthy of such consideration especially in view of the continual increase in energy prices. The figure of 1000 hours/annum operating time used in the flow chart was chosen deliberately to highlight this point and is indicative of the importance, which it is felt, should be attached to efficiency and running costs.

REFERENCES

1. Handbook of Electricity Supply Statistics 1981 (issued by the Electricity Council)

2. The Internal Purchasing Power of the Pound (Central Statistical Office)

3. Burch, R.H., Thompson, G.A. "Electrical variable speed drives for pumps", IEE Conference Publication No. 93, 1972, 69.

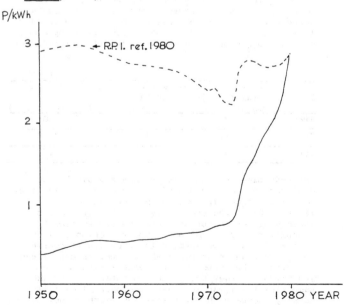

Figure 1 - Average Electricity Costs (pence/kilowatt-hour) for Industrial Users in the U.K. 1950-1980 ref.1 (Dotted line shows correction for retail price index (R.P.I.) referred to 1980) ref.2

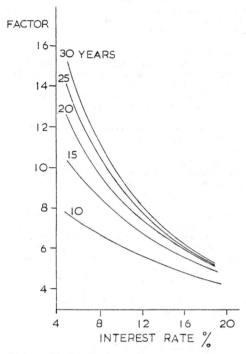

Figure 2 - Graph of multiplication factors for Annual Power Costs against Interest Rates for various Capitalization Periods.

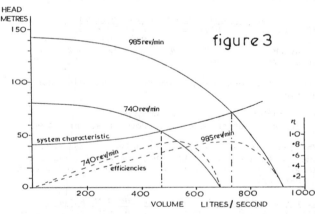

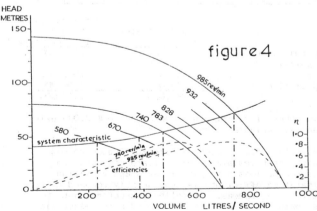

Figure 3 and 4 - Typical Head/Quantity Characteristics for a Pump Installation using various drive motors.

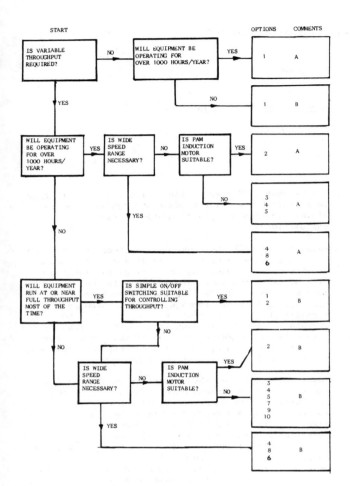

KEY TO FLOW CHART

OPTIONS

1. Single speed squirrel-cage induction motor
2. Two-speed (P.A.M.) squirrel-cage induction motor
3. N-S variable speed AC motor
4. Thyristor controlled DC motor
5. Slipring motor with static (Kramer) cascade
6. Synchronous motor with variable frequency supply
7. Slipring motor (rotor resistance control)
8. Induction motor with variable frequency supply
9. Two-speed squirrel-cage induction motor
   (single tapped winding)
10. Variable speed coupling using squirrel-cage
    induction motor

COMMENTS

A – with improved efficiency
B – cheapest suitable machine

Figure 5 – Flow Chart (and key)

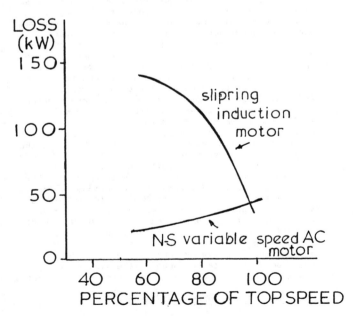

Figure 6 – Curves showing Power Loss (kW) against
speed for a slipring induction motor and an N-S
variable speed A.C. motor.

RECENT ADVANCES IN THE DESIGN OF CIRCULATOR MOTORS FOR ADVANCED GAS COOLED REACTORS

B. Jackson and J.P. Pestle   M.D. Wood

Laurence, Scott & Electromotors Ltd, UK   Cambridge University, UK

INTRODUCTION

The cooling medium in the advanced gas cooled nuclear reactor (AGR) is carbon dioxide at a pressure of approximately 40 atmospheres. The CO_2 circulators are driven by motors which with the exception of Dungeness B are all submerged in the cooling medium. The decision to employ a submerged motor was made because, in addition to the elimination of rotating high pressure gas seals, there is no need for any major openings in the reactor containment pressure vessel, which is important from the safety aspect. Cables for electrical supplies and instrumentation and pipes for cooling water and lubricating oil are taken through small easily sealed penetrations. The existing reactors at Heysham and Hartlepool employ vertical circulator motors whereas those at Hinkley B and Hunterston B have horizontal motors, of the type which are the subject of this paper.

At Hinkley B and Hunterston B each reactor is cooled by eight circulators which are mounted horizontally in eight radially spaced steel shutter tubes set in prestressed concrete at the base of the cylindrical reactor containment pressure vessel. The circulator impellers are driven at 2970 rpm by 11kV, 50 Hz, 2 pole squirrel cage induction motors and are in effect mounted directly off the drive end of these motors with control mechanisms mounted on the non drive end of the motors. The historical background, development, design and works testing of these motors is described by Schwarz (1). The motors have been operating satisfactorily since the early seventies. Figure 1 shows the major features of the circulator mounted in the shutter tube.

With the exception of vibration, only minor problems have been encountered in service at Hinkley B and Hunterston B. Wherever possible these problems have been reduced or eliminated by design changes in the circulator motors for the Heysham II and Torness AGR stations now under construction. Two prototype motors for these new stations have now been built and manufacture of the production motors has commenced.

SPECIFIC AGR DESIGN REQUIREMENTS

Environmental.

Operation of an electric motor in CO_2 at 40 atmospheres contaminated with both water vapour and lubricating oil gives rise to three different problems. Firstly, the high gas density (approximately 75kg/m^3) may cause relatively high windage losses. On conventional motors operating in air, windage losses of rotating parts excluding ventilating fans are usually insignificant. In this application these losses are in excess of 250 kW. This value is about 60% of the total mechanical and electrical losses even though all reasonable steps such as blocking off all gas passages through the rotor cage have been taken to minimise windage. A rotating assembly test rig (RAT Rig) consisting of a dummy rotor mounted in bearings and driven by a pony motor all enclosed in a pressure vessel, originally used for the Hinkley B/Hunterston B motor project, has been refurbished and updated to model the Heysham II/Torness motors. The rig has been used to establish the rotor windage and confirm the best stator slot geometry as suggested by design calculations.

Secondly, because the dense CO_2 is circulated through the motor and a water cooler to dissipate the motor electrical and windage losses, this gives rise to high pressure gradients around the motor which causes a problem in sealing the pressure fed bearings against oil leakage. This problem is magnified by the fact that the bearings have to operate satisfactorily down to atmosphere pressure at high rates of depressurisation and also over a wide range of operating speeds. The RAT rig has been used to test the bearings for these conditions.

Lastly the design of the electrical insulation system has to take into account absorption of gas by the insulation system at pressure and the effects of subsequent rapid depressurisation. Samples of insulation materials used in the motors and also energised coils have been investigated in two pressure vessels known as motorette test rigs. These enable accelerated ageing tests to be carried out under cyclic pressure and temperature conditions in CO_2 saturated with oil and water vapour.

Dual cooling media requirement.(Air/CO_2)

During normal operation the electrical and windage losses from the motor are dissipated by CO_2 at 40 atmospheres. The high gas density gives high Reynold's Numbers and hence good heat transfer from the surfaces of the machine, which is aided by the relatively high thermal capacity of the gas to give extremely effective cooling. However, during reactor commissioning, shutdown and certain abnormal operating conditions, the motor must also operate satisfactorily when running at full voltage in air at atmospheric pressure. At this pressure the load produced by the circulator impeller drops to about one sixtieth of the 5MW rated output, and therefore the stator and rotor copper losses are greatly reduced. Also the rotor windage losses are reduced to about 4 kW. However, the iron losses remain substantially unchanged and these have to be dissipated by air at atmospheric pressure which is a much less effective cooling medium. Therefore the heat dissipation surfaces in the motor and gas flows from the shaft mounted impeller have to be arranged to maintain winding temperatures within acceptable limits for the two different distributions of losses and for the two different cooling fluids. This is achieved by providing a ribbed stator frame which results in a large convection surface which is most effective at low gas density conditions when the bulk of the losses are in the stator back iron, whereas the gas flowing through the axial holes provided in the stator core and the airgap dissipate the majority of losses under high density conditions.

Mounting and secondary containment.

The motor is cantilever mounted in the shutter tube from its drive end endshield where it is held in position by twelve through-studs pretensioned to a total load of 900 tonnes, approximately 40 times the motor weight. This force is reacted by the non drive end endshield, thus imposing a large compressive force in the stator frame and both endshields. The high stud loading is necessary so that in the event of an accident causing loss of pressure from the shutter tube, the motor would act as a secondary containment device, behaving as a plug in the wall of the reactor containment pressure vessel. This initially high loading which is further increased during certain operating conditions calls for careful stress analysis of the frame and two endshields. The calculation is supplemented by testing all frame and endshield castings.

The method of mounting also gives rise to a potential vibration problem, which manifested itself in the Hinkley B/Hunterston B motors with serious consequences to the stator winding. Since the motor is mounted from its drive end endshield it tends to vibrate as a cantilever under the action of mechanical and electrical unbalance forces on the rotor and also due to aerodynamic forces acting on the circulator impeller. On the Hinkley B/ Hunterston B machines the resonant frequency of the circulator/shutter tube system for this mode of vibration was too close to the running speed leading to vibration levels higher than normal for this type of machine.

The vibration has contributed to accelerated ageing of the stator winding overhang system.

ADVANCES IN DESIGN TECHNIQUE

In the fifteen year interval since the motors for Hinkley B and Hunterston B were designed there have naturally been advances in almost all aspects of design. These advances have been applied to the motors for Heysham II and Torness. The three examples given below were chosen because each relates to the special problems associated with this project, although the latter two also have a general application.

Airgap windage loss.

The rotor core has bridged slots and a ground finish to minimise windage loss. The stator has set back slots to improve the gas flow/windage loss ratio through the airgap.

Fluid friction loss. The windage torque, M, of a rotating cylindrical surface is generally given in terms of a friction factor, c_f, defined by

$$c_f = M/\pi R^2 L \rho U^2 = 2\tau/U^2 \rho \dots\dots\dots(1)$$

where R is radius of cylinder
    L is length of cylinder
    ρ is density of fluid
    τ is shear stress in fluid
    U is peripheral velocity of cylinder

The motion of a fluid between two coaxial cylinders, one of which rotates, has been investigated by a number of workers, generally assuming smooth cylindrical surfaces. Because the roughness in the airgap of an electric motor is high and differs from stator to rotor due to the presence of stator slots, these investigations are of little use here. However, Hak (2) takes account of these features and his work is used as a design basis.

If the friction factor of the stator surface is taken as c_{fa} and that of the rotor surface as c_{fa}' then it can be shown that

$$c_f = \frac{1}{\left[\frac{1}{\sqrt{c_{fa}}} + \frac{1}{\sqrt{c_{fa}'}}\right]^2} \dots\dots\dots(2)$$

The relation between surface roughness, e and friction coefficient, c_f for circular pipes of diameter, D can be defined using Nikuradse's experimental data on turbulent flow in fully rough pipes as quoted by many sources including Streeter (3). This is

$$c_f = \frac{0.0625}{\left[\log_{10} \frac{3.72 D}{e}\right]^2} \dots\dots\dots(3)$$

Since the cross section of the air gap is an annulus, the hydraulic diameter which is twice the radial airgap, Y must be used. Thus for the stator surface with roughness, e

$$c_{fa} = \frac{0.0625}{\left[\log_{10} \frac{7.44 Y}{e}\right]^2} \dots\dots\dots(4)$$

and for the rotor surface with roughness, e'

$$c_{fa}' = \frac{0.0625}{\left[\log_{10} \frac{7.44 Y}{e'}\right]^2} \dots\dots\dots(5)$$

Substitution into (2) gives

$$c_f = \frac{0.0156}{\left[\log_{10} \frac{7.44}{\sqrt{ee''}}\right]^2} \dots\dots\dots(6)$$

Since the rotor has bridged slots the surface roughness is simply the machined surface finish. However, for the stator the roughness must be estimated from the depth and spacing of the set back slots. Aytekin and Berger's (4) experiments on turbulent flow in rectangular ducts having ribs normal to the direction of flow on one wall indicate a separated flow region in the lee of each rib with a re-attachment point 3.1 rib heights downstream of the rib. Therefore if the slot width were greater than 3.1 times the wedge set back, the roughness could be taken as equal to the wedge set back. However, this is not the case in this application, but the profile of the separated flow region suggests that the stator roughness can be approximated to one sixth of the slot width.

Thus the friction factor can be evaluated from equation (6) and the windage torque from equation (1) from which the power loss can be evaluated.

Kinetic loss. Power is also lost in the form of kinetic energy at exit from the airgap. This is given by $$P = V^2 Q \rho/2 \dots\dots\dots(7)$$

where Q is the flow of gas through the airgap, V is the mean tangential velocity of the gas leaving the airgap. It has been assumed that any residual tangential velocity carried over from the impeller is small enough to be ignored.

TABLE 1 - Comparison of calculated airgap windage loss for different stator/rotor with test results from RAT rig.

(Losses quoted as a percentage of airgap windage losses derived from testing of the chosen configuration.)

Stator/rotor configuration (Y is radial airgap)	Stator with slots set back 1.00Y Smooth rotor with N5 surface finish. (Chosen configuration)	Smooth stator with N8 surface finish. Smooth rotor with N8 surface finish.	Stator with slots set back 0.04 Y (flush wedge) Smooth rotor with N8 surface finish.	Stator with slots set back 1.00Y. Smooth rotor with N8 surface finish.	Stator with slots set back 0.04 Y (flush wedge).Smooth rotor with N5 surface finish.
Airgap windage loss derived from tests	100%	74%	129%	112%	82%
Calculated friction loss in airgap	91%	62%	108%	118%	84%
Calculated kinetic loss at exit from airgap	2.1%	16%	5.8%	2.7%	4.9%
Total calculated airgap windage loss	93%	78%	114%	121%	89%
Flow/windage loss ratio	100%	90%	50%	72%	70%

Comparison with test results. The RAT rig has been used to check the windage loss in the airgap for five different rotor/stator configurations. Although the windage in the airgap could not be directly measured, it was estimated by measuring the total output from the pony motor driving the rotor and subtracting bearing friction losses (known from tests at atmospheric pressure) and calculated windage losses arising from the cylindrical shaft surfaces, shaft and rotor faces, anti-reverse clutch, shaft mounted impeller and pony motor rotor. The results of these tests and a comparison with the airgap windage calculated by the method above are given in Table 1 which shows reasonable correlation between design and test.

Since a significant proportion of the motor loss is dissipated by gas flow through the airgap, it is obvious that an important factor in the overall thermal performance of the motor is the thermal capacity of the airgap coolant flow. Therefore a guide to the effectiveness of a particular air gap configuration is the ratio of airgap flow to airgap windage. This ratio is given in Table 1 which confirms that the 1.00Y set back slot stator design adopted on this motor, although incurring higher airgap windage losses than flush wedge designs, does improve the thermal performance of the motor.

Thermal Analysis.

Calculation Method. The total coolant flow through the motor has been established both by calculation and measurement on the prototypes running in air. The distribution of flow between the air gap and the axial ventilating holes through the stator back iron has been established by calculation. It has been assumed that Reynold's Number effects on flow are small so that the coolant flow and distribution when running in CO_2 at 40 atmospheres is essentially the same as that when running in air at atmospheric pressure. Tests in the RAT rig do not contradict this assumption.

The flow rates have been used to calculate the heat transfer coefficients from the various dissipating surfaces and best estimates of thermal conductivities of metallic parts have been made from published information. Due to its complex nature the conductivities of the stator winding insulation system have been measured on a simple test rig and also on complete coils.

The temperature rises in the motor have been calculated by creating a network of 233 nodes linked by conductances and then setting up finite difference equations to model the heat diffusion from each node as described by Roberts (5). Since radiation has not been incorporated in the thermal model, the finite difference equations are linear. Linear equations are frequently solved by matrix inversion techniques but in this case it has been found simpler to use an iterative process in which an initial estimate of the temperature at each node is made, which need not be very accurate. The estimated temperatures are then inserted in the finite difference equations to obtain a better approximation of temperature. The process is repeated until the solution converges, that is the temperatures from successive iterations do not change significantly. Use has been made of this calculation to ascertain the effect of flow distribution between the stator axial holes and airgap on winding temperatures and also to determine the most effective location of the stator holes. As a result the Heysham II/Torness motors have less cross sectional area of stator holes to promote more flow through the airgap than on Hinkley B/Hunterston B motors. In addition the positioning of the holes has been changed so that some holes have been placed close to the bottom of the stator slots as this proves the most effective location to removing heat from the stator teeth and windings without seriously impairing the flux paths through the core.

Comparison with test results. At the time of writing the prototype motors have not been run in CO_2 at pressure. Since the Hinkley B/Hunterston B motors were only fitted with sufficient thermocouples for monitoring in service, the best comparison of theory and practice that can be made is with one of the prototype motors running on no load at maximum voltage in air. This motor has additional thermocouples fitted in the stator winding, airgap and stator core. Figure 2 shows the measured and calculated temperatures for this running condition and in general indicates that the theoretical thermal model is slightly pessimistic. However, when the thermal model is applied to the loaded condition it indicates a maximum stator winding temperature of 106°C which is about 20°C lower than ETD temperatures recorded on the Hinkley B/Hunterston B motors on full load.

Vibration Analysis.

Calculation Method. The analysis is based on the method originally employed by Prohl (6) with extensions by Koenig (7). The application to an electric motor requires the introduction of an additional term due to the unbalanced magnetic pull. The analysis includes the effects of

a) mechanical unbalance which can be at any position

b) bearing stiffness and damping, including cross coupling terms

c) mass and stiffness of non rotating parts including stator frame, endshields, overhung stationary items and a portion of the shutter tube

d) unbalanced magnetic pull between rotor and stator

e) gyroscopic effects of rotor

f) shaft component masses and shaft stiffness.

The rotor is assumed to be made up of a number of weightless sections with masses concentrated at the ends of the sections. For each of these sections equations can be written down linking the four variables, shear force, bending moment, slope and deflection. Unbalanced magnetic pull is taken into account by adding a magnetic stiffness term to the shear force equation. The value of this term is the force due to magnetic unbalance when the rotor has unit radial displacement relative to the stator ignoring saturation effects.

Equations are also set up for the forces generated by the dynamic characteristics of the journal bearing oil film. These are simplified if it is assumed that the force displacement velocity relations are linear, which will be the case if the journal motion has small amplitudes. Similarly, equations of motion are set up for the masses and stiffnesses of the stationary parts.

The equations for the rotor sections together with the equations for the bearings form recurrence formulae by which a step by step calculation of the rotor can be carried out. The rotor ends are known to be free giving zero shear force and bending moment at these positions. The problem of determining the initial values of slope and deflection is overcome by successive application of the recurrence formulae allowing computation of these values.

Comparison with available data. At the time of writing no tests of the Heysham II/Torness motor flange mounted in the shutter tube have been carried out. However, the vibration response programme has been checked against standard results and against the available data from the Hinkley B/Hunterston B machines.

For the Heysham II/Torness design the length of the motor between bearing centres has been reduced and

the thickness of the unsupported portion of the shutter tube increased in order to raise the frequency of the troublesome resonance. The calculation indicates that these measures will increase the frequency of the resonance by 5 Hz and thereby reduce the amplitude of vibration at running speed by a factor of 4.

CONCLUSIONS

Recent advances in design techniques do not indicate a need for any radical alteration of the Hinkley B/Hunterston B design for the new motors. However, new techniques have led to better prediction of many aspects of the motor performance, particularly with respect to winding temperatures and vibration response.

ACKNOWLEDGEMENTS

The design of the Heysham II/Torness motors has been carried out in close collaboration with James Howden & Co., National Nuclear Corporation, Central Electricity Generating Board and South of Scotland Electricity Board, to whom sincere acknowledgements are due. The paper is published by kind permission of the directors of Laurence, Scott & Electromotors Limited.

REFERENCES

1. Schwarz, K.K., 1973, Proc. IEE, 120, 777-785.

2. Hak, J., 1956, Arch. f. Elektrotechn. 42, 257-272.

3. Streeter, V.L., 1966, "Fluid Mechanics", McGraw-Hill, New York.

4. Aytekin, A. & Berger, F.P., 1979, Nucl. Energy 18, 53-63.

5. Roberts, T.J., 1969, Proc. I.Mech.E., 184, Pt.3E, 70-84.

6. Prohl, M.A., 1944, J.App Mechanics, 12, Trans. ASME, 67, A - 142.

7. Koenig, E.C., 1961, J.App Mechanics, 28, Trans. ASME, 585-600.

22

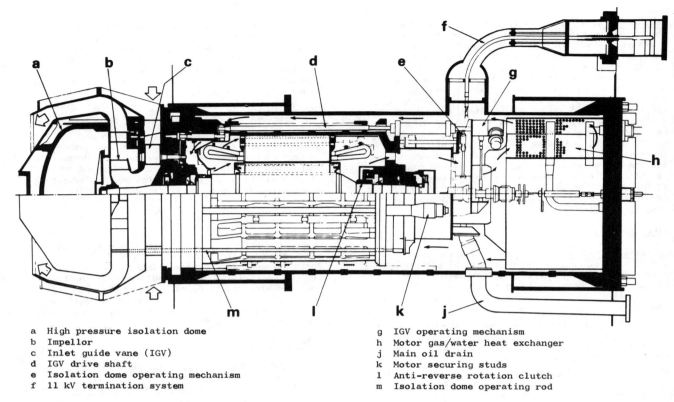

a High pressure isolation dome
b Impellor
c Inlet guide vane (IGV)
d IGV drive shaft
e Isolation dome operating mechanism
f 11 kV termination system

g IGV operating mechanism
h Motor gas/water heat exchanger
j Main oil drain
k Motor securing studs
l Anti-reverse rotation clutch
m Isolation dome operating rod

Figure 1 Diagram showing Hinkley B/Hunterston B circulator sectional arrangement.

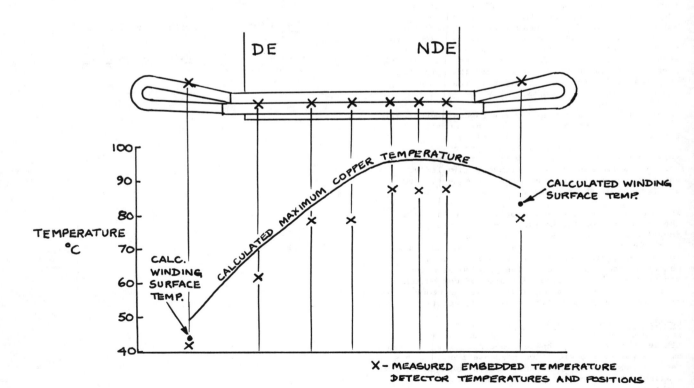

Figure 2 Comparison of calculated and measured temperatures on no load in atmospheric air

INSULATION OF HIGH VOLTAGE ROTATING MACHINES

J. E. Neal and A. G. Whitman

Jones Stroud Insulations, UK.

INTRODUCTION

During the last 25 years HV rotating machine stator coil insulation has been subject to continuous development, such that "Thermoplastic" type materials have now been replaced by "Thermosets".

This has led to significant material changes which, in turn have resulted in improved processing, reduced insulation levels and subsequently smaller, more efficient machines operating at higher levels of electrical, mechanical and thermal stress.

Whilst carrying out these changes machine reliability had to be maintained. As a result designers in the late 60's and early 70's were extremely cautious when modifying their well proven insulation levels and operating temperatures.

With the new materials having the capability of at least Class 155 thermal rating, this led to machines being designed with Class 155 materials but having only Class 130 temperature rises.

Stator coil wall thicknesses in all types of machines were slightly reduced but they were still based on the working electrical stress range of 1.77-2.0kV/mm.

With increasing material costs the necessity for designs which fully utilised the improved properties of the new materials, became essential. In addition process times had to be reduced and new methods of application explored.

Throughout the late 70's and into the 80's considerable development work has taken place with two basic processes becoming firmly established, namely 'Resin Rich' and 'Vacuum-Pressure-Impregnation' (VPI).

Simply, the Resin Rich process involves the application of materials which contain a high resin content and require no further resin addition. VPI involves the application of dry materials which are then subjected to a Vacuum-Pressure-Impregnation process using a synthetic resin.

Whilst both 'Resin Rich' and 'VPI' produce excellent machines they do have advantages and disadvantages. Therefore, the choice of which particular process to use is dependant on many factors, one of which being the initial capital expenditure.

Table I overleaf details these advantages and disadvantages but it must be again clearly stated that used correctly both systems produce excellent machines. How this is achieved depends on the manufacturers ingenuity and expertise in using to the full the properties and capabilities of modern day materials.

STATOR COIL MATERIALS

A wide range of materials are now available and therefore when designing an insulation system it is important that the parameters of each are fully understood. In an attempt to clarify this the basic stator coil materials, namely micapaper, synthetic resins and supporting materials are discussed.

Micapaper

In nature mica is one of the most widely distributed of all crystalline substances glistening in the surface of many granite and similar metamorphic rocks. Only two types of natural mica have found large scale useage in electrical insulation namely Muscovite and Phlogopite. Both of these occur in the extremely coarse grained granite types known as Pegmatite and these are found in the parts of the world where the process of cooling was very slow leading to the formation of large crystals sometimes a metre across.

The mica minerals are composed of complex hydrated aluminium silicates. In the case of Muscovite, potassium oxide forms a subsidiary constituent and variations in colour lead to two main classes e.g. Ruby and Green. Phlogopite micas also include potassium oxide but some of the aluminium is replaced by magnesium oxide, this can lead to dark and light coloured grades.

To use mica in modern manufacturing processes it must be available to close tolerances and at a competitive cost. This has been achieved by the manufacture of micapaper (a paper like material made wholly of mica with no synthetic bonding agent), Dubois and Bertsch (1). The reduction of the mica particles to the correct size is carried out by one of two processes
(a) Thermo-Chemical Process
(b) Mechanical Process

Both processes can be applied to Muscovite type micas but only the mechanical process can be used for Phlogopite which can withstand a much higher temperature, $900^{\circ}C$, before decomposition as compared with $600^{\circ}C$ for Muscovite.

The Thermo-Chemical Process consists of heating scrap Muscovite mica to $850^{\circ}C$ at which temperature the water of crystallisation is removed causing the material to expand. This enables a solution of sodium carbonate to penetrate into the crystalline structure of the materials such that the further introduction of sulphuric acid produces a violent reaction which breaks up the mica into very small flakes. After careful stringent washing to ensure the removal of all traces of chemicals, the resulting slurry is then fed onto a paper-making machine to produce a continuous sheet of micapaper.

The Mechanical Process is much simpler consisting as it does of bombarding the mica scrap with jets of high pressure water producing a slurry which is handled in the same manner as the product of the Thermo-Chemical Process.

TABLE I - Advantages/Disadvantages of Resin Rich and Vacuum-Pressure-Impregnation (VPI) Processes

Process	Resin Rich		Vacuum-Pressure-Impregnation	
	Advantages	Disadvantages	Advantages	Disadvantages
Plant	Low capital expenditure. Automated presses with computerised control now available.	Requires skilled operation.	Can be automated.	High capital expenditure, plant requires skilled operation and stringent chemical control of resin.
Coil Manufacture	No vacuum treatment required. All types of coils can be produced. New material can be introduced without plant modification. Flexible end windings can be designed for if required. Corona shields can be applied during processing and checked before winding. Any faults in processing usually restricted to one or two coils. Materials now available which are more tolerant during consolidation.	Each coil has to be processed on all types of machines requiring considerable skill. Materials need close control during manufacture and application.	All coils for a machine can be impregnated together, either in a stator frame or a separate jig. Materials more tolerant of processing.	High initial cost of resin to fill plant. TG and Hydro coils require individual consolidation after VPI processing. Any fault in processing could result in scrapping of a complete winding. Handling of 'dry' materials needs greater care. Flexible endwindings cannot be produced. Possibility of contamination of tank resin by incompatible tape resins with danger of exotherm and plant damage. Plant has to be continuously utilised for economic operation and to ensure resin shelf life not exceeded.
During Winding	Each coil can be fully tested (all machines) at BS test levels. Individual coil repairs can be easily made if found during winding or test.	Care to be taken during winding to prevent damaging coils. Coils have to be individually packed in slots. Blocking and bracing takes long process times. Further baking process needed to cure varnish treatments.	Motors can be dry wound with little damage to coils. Complete impregnation allows bracing to be simplified during winding. Possible tighter coils in slot to give better heat transfer.	Individual coils of completely impregnated machines cannot be tested thus complete impregnation cannot be checked. Also care to be taken to ensure corona shield not nullified by impregnating process. Difficult to repair manufacturing faults if found on test bed.
In Service	Repairs can be made and partial rewinds carried out at site.	Sealed windings need expertise to obtain with further varnish treatments essential.	Sealed windings of completely processed stators can be obtained without further varnish treatments.	Difficult to repair fully impregnated machines necessitating possible complete rewinds and removal to manufacturers works. Difficult to remove coils for rewind with possible core damage.

Properties. The different methods of manufacture produce micapapers which exhibit significant variations of some basic properties. These in turn can fundamentally affect the manufacture and application of micapaper based insulation materials.

Firstly, it is important to be able to eliminate the possibility of any contamination of the base micapaper, which in turn might adversely affect the behaviour of the impregnating resin being used either in the manufacture of a resin rich material or in the Vacuum-Pressure-Impregnation process. This is much easier to ensure when only de-mineralised water has been used as in the

Mechanical Process.

Secondly, the physical characteristics, size, shape and structure vary considerably and the implications of these must be considered in more detail.

In general, micapaper produced by the Thermo-Chemical Process consists of smaller particles than that produced by the Mechanical Process as is shown in the following histograms.

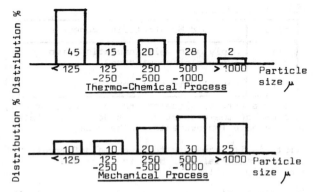

This basic difference in the spread of mica-particle size affects porosity, impregnation and the mechanical characteristics.

Impregnation/Porosity. To illustrate simply the impregnation/porosity characteristics a number of different micapaper/glass fabric based materials were hung in a heated quantity of (a) a typical VPI solventless impregnating resin and (b) a Resin Rich solution of resin/solvent. The solutions were coloured using a trace quantity of red dye and the distance travelled up the tape by the resins after a given time were recorded. The results are shown in Table II and clearly indicate the differences in micapapers produced by the two processes.

TABLE II

Micapaper Process	VPI Resin	Resin Rich Resin
Thermo-Chemical Muscovite	16mm	5mm
Mechanical Process Phlogopite	29mm	35mm
Mechanical Process Muscovite	33mm	36mm

Mechanical Characteristics. Studies by Shibayama and Kitagawa (2) have shown the effect of mica particle size on the mechanical reliability of the composite insulation when subject to mechanical and thermal ageing. The paper concludes that the most suitable micapaper structure is one where the particle size tends towards 500 microns as this gives the highest value of flexural strength at operating temperature and the highest number of cycles to failure at a given stress.

Further work, Futakawa et al (3) goes on to relate this to the insulation of actual high voltage stator coils, where the conclusion is reached that micapaper insulation systems which have the highest fatigue strength can be regarded as the best for high voltage stator windings.

Resin Systems

In the earlier insulation systems, naturally occurring resins were used. However the requirement for closer toleranced materials, together with consistency, has led to the development of a wide range of synthetic materials which can be tailor-made to give the optimum characteristics required by a particular application. Many different types of resin have been used but epoxies and polyester types predominate. These can be further sub-divided into those which are 'B' staged i.e. pre-catalysed and only require further processing by raising to a higher temperature to cause them to cure (Resin Rich)

and secondly those which require the addition of a further chemical during processing to complete the cure (VPI).

The first group includes such systems as the Epoxy Novolac group catalysed with Boron Triflouride Monoethylamine (BF$_3$400) or other similar catalysts. These lend themselves particularly well to the production of resin rich micapapers in view of their proven performance and in particular their long shelf life and excellent safe handling characteristics. Considerable knowledge has been accumulated in the use of these materials and a high degree of reliability can now be achieved. Parriss (4).

The contribution made by the resin to the final thermal rating of an insulation system is fundamental. Research carried out recently by modifying the standard formula has resulted in longer gel times and improved electrical/mechanical characteristics. Also evaluation to IEC 216-1 requirements has given this material a thermal rating of greater than 186^{0}C, Neal and Bertsch (5).

The second group involves resin systems for VPI and the ideal approach would be to apply a completely dry micapaper tape to the whole or part winding then VPI process with the chosen resin. Unfortunately such an approach would involve using micapaper tapes which were impossible to handle. A small amount of resin in these tapes is essential and in order to cure, this resin has to be entirely compatible with the VPI tank resin. In view of this, non-catalysed resins are preferable which then eliminate the chance of any "washed-out" catalyst triggering off a tank of expensive resin with disastrous consequences.

Here again accurate control is of paramount importance as any large variation in tape resin content may have considerable affect on the impregnation of the 'dry' insulated coil or winding.

Supporting Materials.

It has long been understood that glass reinforcing gives enhanced mechanical and thermal characteristics. This is especially true if care is taken to achieve a good 'wet-out' by a suitable treatment of the specially produced grades of cloth woven from "electric" quality glass yarn. A certain amount of size has to be incorporated to enable the glass cloth to be woven but experience has shown that if this is kept to 2.5% or less, excellent results are obtained.

A range of fabrics between 0.05-0.10mm thick are used with the actual weave construction being given as much attention as the thickness. The substance range is usually between 20-40gsm with tensile strengths of 12-20N/mm.

In the case of materials for VPI insulation systems the micapaper is sometimes protected by having a glass fabric on either side. In addition the glass acts as a wicking agent to improve impregnation, although greater efficiency can be obtained by replacing one of the glass fabrics by a thin polyester or glass paper.

Whilst products incorporating glass papers are considered to have better thermal classification these materials are very difficult to handle. Therefore polyester papers (0.05mm) which give more flexible and handleable products are in many cases preferred.

Glass cloths in this application are usually of a fine weave construction and at the lower end of the range i.e. 20-25 gsm.

In addition to glass fabric there has been an increasing use of polyester film either as an additional reinforcement or as the only backing material.

Film faced micapaper/glass products have found increasing acceptance where the introduction of the film has led to better performance because of its tougher nature both during machine taping and in subsequent coil forming operations.

The dielectric strength of the film materials, whilst initially high, could be reduced by the action of discharge erosion. This in turn can only be eliminated by ensuring an entirely void free insulation system.

STATOR COIL MANUFACTURE

Manufacturing a wide range of machines in turn requires a wide range of processes and expertise. Whilst in the past this may have been possible in one particular plant, with today's emphasis on quick throughput, tight designs/manufacturing limits, strict quality control and efficient use of the employed plant, this cannot always be achieved.

Particular plants are therefore designed to produce a specific range of machines but this is not always successful as the correct mix of machines is difficult to obtain. To illustrate this point the stator coil insulation systems for three typical AC machines are discussed. Namely:-
(a) 3.3kV   500 - 1000KW motor
(b) 13.2kV   80 - 120MW Hydro Generator
(c) 22kV   500 - 1000MW Turbo Generator

General

Stator coils are complicated in shape being in the main "Diamond" or "Half Coils" and as a result have demanded a high degree of manual labour. This has been due as much in the past to their design configuration as to the materials actually called for by the required insulation system.

All coils consist of conductors and turns with the insulation being divided simply into three categories namely:-
1. Conductor
2. Turn
3. Main Wall

3.3kV 500 - 1000KW

It is usual for such machines to have full diamond stator coils which consist of both conductors and turns and in the past the manufacturing schedule in Table III has been used.

TABLE III

Process	Old Manufacturing Schedule
(a)	Form bare copper or glass braid covered copper into a loop and pull to a diamond shape.
(b)	If bare copper, insulate conductors manually using two different materials for slot/endwinding if a rigid slot/flexible endwinding is required.
(c)	Insulate turns manually using two different materials (as b).
(d)	Consolidate conductor/turn stack slot portion.

continued

TABLE III CONTINUED

Process	Old Manufacturing Schedule
(e)	Apply main wall insulation (two types slot/endwinding).
(f)	Consolidate slot portion.

This is a very complicated schedule but by making full use of the properties of today's materials considerable improvements can be made.

First, is it necessary to have two different types of materials for both the slot and endwinding portions?

Secondly, is it necessary to apply separately the conductor and turn insulation?

If VPI is being used then as the complete stator is impregnated the machine winding will be rigid throughout. Resin Rich does allow the rigid slot/flexible endwinding system but can this be justified financially?

Conductor/Turn - Resin Rich. For efficient manufacture it is essential that the conductor/ turn insulation be one which then allows application by machine. To comply with this requirement a conductor/turn insulation material needs to be thin, have high dielectric and mechanical strength and be capable of being supplied in long, non-interleaved and accurately slit rolls.

To meet the above parameters polyester films of varying thicknesses (0.006-0.025mm) have been incorporated, giving a range of materials which are 'B' staged to give further resin flow. These materials are based on (50-120 gsm) Muscovite or Phlogopite micapapers, which are either sandwiched between a layer of glass fabric and polyester film or just carried on the polyester film alone.

Materials have a pressed thickness/layer of 0.07mm to 0.12mm with "flexible" and "rigid" when cured characteristics being available.

Based on the above a manufacturer can employ one material (possibly two widths to take care of the copper size) for all his conductor/turn requirements in diamond coil manufacture. This material being machine applied with the number of layers changing as per the voltage requirement.

Conductor/Turn - VPI. The same procedure and material type as detailed for Resin Rich can be utilised with the modifications to ensure that the resin system, if catalysed, is compatible with the tank resin. Preferably the tape resin should be uncatalysed as this eliminates tank instability.

Main Insulation - Resin Rich. The arguments for using one material throughout the coil can again be applied but in this instance the situation is not so clear cut.

If a consolidated slot portion is required and the endwinding insulation is to be applied after consolidation, then two different materials can be used. However can this be justified as material stocks will be increased and operators on the shop floor have to stop and change materials.

It is debatable whether it is essential to consolidate the slot portion on this type of machine as there are a large number of machines which are in service using the Unpressed System, Neal (6). The stator coil having been insulated throughout with a high bond resin rich glass backed micapaper (46% resin content). A system which, in the authors' opinion, is simple, needs no hot consolidation and gives a sealed Class 155 winding.

Voltage stresses of 2.3 to 2.6kV/mm can be employed with the correct number of layers to be applied being determined by dividing the consolidated material layer thickness into the designed wall thickness.

Main Insulation - VPI. With the VPI process one material, either glass fabric/micapaper or polyester paper/micapaper/glass fabric both based on 160 gsm micapaper, can be used.

As the resin contents in this type of tape are usually between 5-12% the tapes need more care in handling. However, by careful manufacture a 'dry' tape with little micapaper 'fly' can be successfully machine applied throughout the coil.

As a rough guide the number of layers to be applied is based on a material thickness of 0.15mm /layer and by taking the rated voltage e.g. 3.3kV and equating this to the number of layers, the figure of 7 layers to be applied is arrived at (3 x $\frac{1}{2}$ lap and 1 butt lap).

Considering therefore both Resin Rich and VPI processes a simplified manufacturing schedule could be as detailed in Table IV.

TABLE IV

Process	New Manufacturing Schedule
(a)	Machine apply conductor/turn insulation to bare copper.
(b)	Form loop.
(c)	Multi-press slot portion at loop stage.
(d)	Pull into diamond.
(e)	Machine apply main insulation throughout the coil.

13.2kV 80-120MW Hydro Generator

Stator coils for these machines are considerably larger (3 metres) and are of the diamond type and whether they are made as a full or a half coil is dependant on the manufacturers handling expertise. This type of machine is also designed to operate at slow speeds therefore the number of coils is considerable with a typical figure of 200+.

Coils can be multi or single turn/coil side. If a single turn/coil side construction is used then the coil is usually of the 'Roebel' construction in the slot portion to reduce losses.

The manufacturing schedule as detailed in Table III is again employed with the same considerations having to be taken into account e.g. is it necessary to have different slot/endwinding insulation? Can the insulation be machine applied?

With this type of machine, whether half or full coils, a rigid system throughout is now becoming more commonplace as the endwinding configuration allows for easier winding and repair.

Conductor/Turn - Resin Rich/VPI. Whichever type of design is employed the copper should be purchased covered. This covering can be either (a) synthetic resin coated glass braid or glass lapped or (b) resin rich glass backed micapaper.

Consolidation of the conductor/turn stack of this type of coil is essential in order to eliminate voids and provide a solid base on to which the main insulation can be applied.

Corona shields have been employed at the conductor/turn stack on this type of machine to reduce electrical discharges at the conductor/turn main insulation interface. Whilst this gives excellent loss tangent/voltage characteristics in the 'as made' condition it is essential that the bonding of the "shield" to the copper remains intact throughout the machine's life.

Main Insulation - Resin Rich. Efficient insulation application to this type of coil must be by machine and half coils lend themselves to machine taping more readily than full coils. The same material being taped throughout the coil length giving a rigid system when cured.

Glass backed micapaper materials based on 160 gsm micapaper Muscovite or Phlogopite are usually employed, but as many layers are applied, it is worth considering how these can be reduced to produce coils more economically.

First, the micapaper substance can be increased to give thicker material and micapapers of 250 and 365 gsm are now available. Whilst this improves the mica/glass ratio the application of substantially thicker materials 0.3 to 0.35mm can be more difficult.

A further solution has been to modify the glass backing fabric by using what is termed 'an open weave construction'. This has had two effects namely to reduce the initial cost of the material and also the number of layers applied. The use of an open weave glass allows easier compression, better resin flow and gives a more homogeneous structure. Neal (7).

Main Insulation - VPI. Stator half coils for this type of machine are first machine dry taped with a low resin content glass backed 160 gsm micapaper tape.

The taped coils, representing part of the winding, are then placed in a jig to ensure the shape is maintained during the impregnation process. After which the 'wet' coils have to be 'sized' in a press at 160°C, to establish full cure before winding.

High quality resins are essential for this type of winding to ensure low electrical loss at working temperature. Also the inclusion of polyester papers as backing materials have been found to increase the loss and are therefore not recommended.

22kV 500-1000MW Turbo Generators

Windings for this type of machine are internally water cooled with the stator being pressurised in Hydrogen.

Whilst being of the diamond type the coils, due to their size (approximately 12 metres in length) and weight, are always processed as half coils.

Conductor/Turn - Resin Rich/VPI. All coils are multi conductor, single turn/coil side and of the Roebel construction, incorporating hollow copper. This can be covered with synthetic resin coated glass braid or glass lap or machine taped with a 'B' stage resin rich glass backed micapaper tape.

The insulated conductors are first formed into the Roebel transposition and then laced together into the straight conductor stack. The straight conductor stack being next placed onto a former to shape into the half coil and have the end water boxes fitted.

The Roebel transposed conductor stack then has the transposition spaces filled with a micaceous putty and cured end to end to give a very accurate solid void free base ready for the application of the main insulation.

Half coils of this size require close processing control, to tight tolerances, in clean conditions, therefore the insulation material savings that can be made at this stage are small in relation to the overall cost.

Main Insulation - Resin Rich. The details given for hydrogenerator coil insulation hold true with the half coil being consolidated throughout.

Machine taping is again the most efficient and accurate method of application using 100 metre long non-interleaved rolls of resin rich glass backed (160-180 gsm) micapaper. Whilst Class 155 materials are employed, only their electrical/ mechanical properties are fully utilised due to the necessity of water cooling. Many layers of insulation are applied and therefore the thickest available micapaper should be used. Open weave glass backed tapes lending themselves to this type of coil giving savings of 10-20%.

Main Insulation - VPI. Machine taping is again essential to ensure accurate application at the correct tension for correct impregnation.

Extremely large autoclaves are necessary with the half coils being processed with similar materials as detailed in the Hydro section.

Correct processing is absolutely essential as several half coils are impregnated together and to recover them is a very costly exercise.

CONCLUSION

Class 155 HV machines operating with Class 155 temperature rises are now in service incorporating both modern materials and manufacturing techniques. However, continued insulation development is essential as Class 180 HV machines are being considered which will require even more sophisticated materials and methods of application.

REFERENCES

1. Dubois, A., and Bertsch, X., 1981, "New trends in micapaper" 15th EEIC pp 60-64.

2. Shibayama, K., and Kitagawa, T., 1977 "Mechanical Fatigue Strength of Micaceous Composite Insulation" EIC pp 179-182.

3. Futakawa, A., Hirabayashi, S., Tani, T. and Shibayama, K. 1977. "Mechanical Fatigue Characteristics of High Voltage Generator Insulation" EIC pp 209-214.

4. Parriss, W.H., 1971. "Material Requirements for Epoxy Novolak Bonded High Voltage Machine Insulation" GEC Journal of Science and Technology., Vol. 38 No. 4 pp 157-166.

5. Neal, J.E., and Bertsch, X., 1982. "Trends in Resin Rich and VPI Materials for H.V. Rotating Machines". BEAMA Insulation Conference.

6. Neal, J.E., 1978 "Unpressed Insulation for Class F Machines". Electrical Times.

7. Neal, J.E., 1979 "Modern Class 155 Resin Rich Insulation Systems for Hydroelectric Generators" National Colloquium on Insulation Systems for Hydrogenerators, Delhi, India. pp 1.1.1 - 1.1.13

THERMAL DEGRADATION OF INSULATION SYSTEMS FOR ROLLING STOCK MOTORS

T. Hakamada I. Kanoh

Hitachi Works of Hitachi, Ltd., Japan

INTRODUCTION

Insulation system of traction motors for rolling stock are getting higher thermal resistance in order to reduce their size and weight. Recently several kinds of resins, such as epoxy, polyimide, silicone .... have been used for these insulation systems. Some of these resins are applied in the form of vacuum pressure impregnation, others are in the pre-preg type according to their properties. In case of V.P.I., resins are required to be of solventless type, low viscosity and long pot life. To satisfy these requirement, Hitachi, Ltd. developed a resin named ISOX. This resin is a solventless type with good thermal resistance properties at 220°C or above. Using this resin, a new insulation system applicable to class H traction motors was developed.

Many models insulated with this system were utilized in various aging tests such as motorette test, heat cycle and vibration tests etc. Some of these were single stress, while others were multiple stress aging tests. From these evaluation tests, the relation between single stress and multiple stress aging tests became clear, and also it was shown that this insulation system was ranked at a thermal endurance at 220°C.

CLASS C SOLVENTLESS TYPE ISOX RESIN

Among members of a insulation system, impregnation resin is the most important factor as it affects coil's heat dissipation, mechanical property, dielectric strength, environmental resistivity to dust, water or chemical contamination. Materials such as polyimide, polyamideimide, silicone and polydiphenylether have been used conventionally. They, however, are unsuitable for impregnation resins because they are not of low viscosity and high flexibility. While epoxy resin is employed as a solventless type impregnation resin with relatively high thermal resistance, it can not withstand temperature exceeding 180°C.

Under the circumstances, a solventless impregnation resin replacing epoxy was sought. To fulfill this need, Hitachi Ltd. has developed a solventless type ISOX resin made chiefly of polyfunctional isocyanate and polyfunctional epoxide. Through the polymerization reaction, the resin forms isocyanurate rings with high thermal resistance and oxazolidone rings with high flexibility. This resin has a variety of excellent characteristics shown in TABLE 1. ISOX resin of liquid state features low viscosity at room temperature, easy impregnation, long pot life and repetitive use. Further-more, the glass transition temperature of cured ISOX is 285°C, tensile strength is no lower than 500 kg/cm^2 even at temperature as high as 230°C, tanδ at 220°C is only 0.3% showing no rise from room temperature. Figure 1 presents a result of a thermal endurance test conducted in accordance with IEC 216 concerning tensile strength and loss of mass. In Figure 1 tensile strength and loss of mass are unexpectedly on the same line. ISOX resin has class C thermal endurance with a temperature index no lower than 220°C.

TABLE 1-Various properties of heat-resistant solventless resins

Item		Type	ISOX resin (extra high heat resistant grade)	Heat resistant epoxy resin
Before curing	Appearance	——	Reddish brown, clear	Light yellow, clear
	Viscosity	25°C (P)	1.4	1,500
	Pot life	——	Usable repeatedly	Usable repeatedly
After curing	Glass transition temperature	(°C)	285	210
	Flexural properties at 25°C	Modulus (kg/cm^2)	3.3 x 10^4	3.2 x 10^4
		Distortion (%)	2.1	1.5
		Strength (kg/cm^2)	1000 (780 at 220°C)	920
	Tensile strength	230°C (kg/cm^2)	530	200 (at 200°C)
	tan δ	20°C (%)	0.2	0.5
		220°C (%)	0.3	2.0 (at 200°C)
	Volume resistivity	25°C (Ω cm)	5 x 10^{16}	5 x 10^{16}
		220°C (Ω cm)	3 x 10^{13}	2 x 10^{12} or below

CLASS C HIPACT INSULATION SYSTEM

Temperature Specifications of Traction Motors for Rolling Stock

Traction motors for rolling stock are designed and manufactured in conformity with the standerd specified by the International Electrotechnical Commission. IEC provides that the sum of temperature rise limit of winding and maximum ambient temperature be 220°C at the field windings and 200°C at the armature windings. These values are 40°C and 20°C higher than the allowable maximum temperature (180°C) for the insulation system respectively.

The ambient temperature does not necessarily reach 40°C on a long term basis and the load is considerably lower than the rated value on the average, so that it has been considered that an insulation life satisfactory under the ordinary operating conditions may be obtained.

However, to maintain higher reliability, the class H traction motor should preferably use an insulation system that endures temperatures up to 220°C at field windings and 200°C at armature windings.

The class C HIPACT insulation system developed by Hitachi, Ltd. is believed to meet this requirement.

Construction of Insulation System

Constructions of the insulation system for test models are shown in TABLE 2. Model No.1 was insulated with glass cloth backed recostituted mica and impregnated with solventless epoxy resin. Model No.2 was impregnated with ISOX resin instead of epoxy resin for Model No.1. Model No.3 was insulated with polyimide film backed reconstituted mica instead of glass mica in Model No.2.

All of these models were made being insulated with the above mentioned tape and glass tape for the outer surface, then assembled into a model core. Each model was impregnated with the assigned resin by vacuum pressure impregnation method and then cured. The appearance was shown in Figure 2. Model No.1 corresponds to a conventional insulation system for class F traction motors.

THERMAL DEGRADATION TEST

Traction motors for rolling stock are used under severe conditions; viz., they are subjected to thermal stress; mechanical stress caused by high speed and vibration due to bogie mounting; and environmental stress including water splash. Therefore various severe tests were performed on newly developed units to verify their reliability multilaterally.

TABLE 2-Insulation system of test model

Model No.	Construction of mica tape		Impregnation resin
	Backing	Mica	
1	Glass cloth	Reconstituted	Epoxy
2	Glass cloth	Reconstituted	ISOX
3	Polyimide film	Reconstituted	ISOX

All kinds of deterioration test such as heat aging, heat cycle, voltage endurance, vibration, water absorption, chemical resistance etc. have been done. From these tests, comparison between the methods described below are mainly discussed in this article. Figure 3 shows these thermal degradation test methods. Motorette, simplified motorette and heat aging are all sequential stress aging tests. The heat aging conditions are the same among these three methods and always three temperature conditions were applied to estimate a thermal endurance graph. A combined stress aging test shown in Figure 3 was also performed to compare the results with the above mentioned sequential stress aging tests.

TEST RESULTS

Electrical breakdown voltage of insulation system under thermal degradation is due to chemical kinetic theory as well known

$$\frac{dV}{dt} = kV \quad \dotfill (1)$$

where V = breakdown voltage (kV)
t = time (h)

This solulion is

$$\ln V = C - kt \quad \dotfill (2)$$

Arrhenius' velocity constant is given as

$$k = A\exp(-\frac{Q}{RT}) \quad \dotfill (3)$$

Therefore, a breakdown voltage V thermally aged at T(°K) for time t(h) becomes

$$\ln V = C - At\exp(-\frac{B}{T}) \quad \dotfill (4)$$

Since C is given as ln Vo when t=o, where Vo is the initial breakdown voltage

$$\ln \frac{V}{Vo} = -At\exp(-\frac{B}{T}) \quad \dotfill (5)$$

Accordingly, V/Vo in logarithmic scale is a primary function for time t.

Test Results of Model No.3

Figure 4 and 5 show the test results of the motorette method. Nondestructive insulation properties were measured after every one cycle described in Figure 3 (a) and also some of them were measured the breakdown voltage (V) at the end of every 5 cycles. The measured value were divided by the initial value (Vo) and plotted the value (V/Vo) as the vertical axis. Repeating such procedure for the aging temperature at 230°C, 250°C and 270°C, Figure 4 was obtained. When the thermal endurance is defined as 50% level of vertical axis, a time for V/Vo to reach the level is obtained for an assigned temperature respectively. Figure 5 is a temperature endurance graph which was drawn by using the relation between times and the temperatures. Therefore the temperature index of this insulation system is defined as 214°C.

Temperature-time curves for the test method of Figure 3 (b) and (c) were obtained through the same procedure. As clearly indicated in Figure 5, temperature index obtained through three aging methods are almost same value and the meaning which combined heat aging with vibration and/or moisture condition is almost meaningless for this insulation system.

Test Results of Model No.2

Model No.2 is only different in mica backing material of polyimide film from glass cloth of Model No.3. For this models, combined stress aging test was also conducted. The test results are shown in Figure 6, in which motorette and simplified moterette indicated almost same degradation rate at 270°C similar to the results of Model No.3 in Figure 5.

However the combined stress aging appears to be more severe than the sequential stress aging. (Aging condition of 230°C and 250°C on simplified motorette and combined stress aging test were abbreviated for Model No.2) And thermal endurance curve of Model No.2 obtain from the motorette was given as indicated on Figure 7. Temperature index of this insulation system is defined as 221°C.

Test Results of Model No.1

Model No.1 is only different in impregnation resin of epoxy from ISOX of Model No.2. Only motorette test had been done and the aging temperatures were 180°C, 200°C and 220°C, its temperature classification of class F or H. The temperature endurance curve is shown in Figure 7 comparing with that of Model No.2. This temperature index is 170°C.

CONSIDERATION

Concerning the three constructions of insulation system, various sequential stress aging test and a combined stress aging test were carried out.

One of the important results is that there is little difference among motorette, simplified motorette and just heat aging test. Non-destructive characteristics such as insulation resistance, tanδ, polarization index, partial discharge and so forth were measured, through which it was clear that these insulation systems were completely water tight and such insulation system has no effect of moisture in sequential stress aging test. To confirm this result, silicone pre-preg glass mica insulation system was compared with Model No.2. The results at 270°C aging are shown simultanuously in Figure 6. Silicone pre-preg insulation was far more infuluenced by moisture than ISOX V.P.I. insulation, the degradation rate is far larger and the effectiveness of combined stress aging was proved.

Next important result is that ISOX insulation system has excellent temperature index of 214°C and 221°C for Model No.3 and No.2 respectively. These index values are 44°C and 51°C higher than that of Model No.1 which have been applied for class F traction motors for a long time. Therefore this newly developed class C HIPACT insulation system is suitable for class H traction motors.

CONCLUSION

Combined stress aging test is useful to judge whether an insulation system is moisture proof or not.

For a high moisture resistant insulation, moisture absorption on the way of thermal aging test does not almost affect the life. Therefore a simple heat aging becomes convenient instead of what is called

motorette test which takes much time.

The insulation system impregnated with ISOX resin has a temperature index of 220°C and is suitable for class H traction motors.

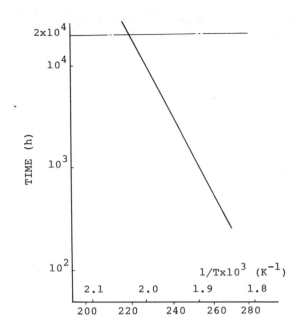

Figure 1 Thermal endurance of ISOX resin

Figure 2 Model for various thermal
deterioration test

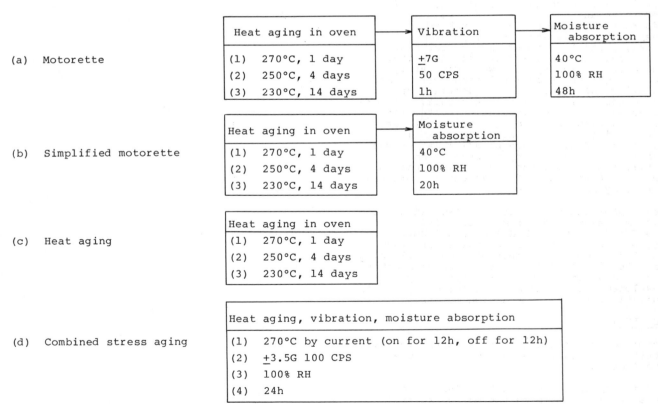

(a) Motorette

Heat aging in oven	Vibration	Moisture absorption
(1) 270°C, 1 day	±7G	40°C
(2) 250°C, 4 days	50 CPS	100% RH
(3) 230°C, 14 days	1h	48h

(b) Simplified motorette

Heat aging in oven	Moisture absorption
(1) 270°C, 1 day	40°C
(2) 250°C, 4 days	100% RH
(3) 230°C, 14 days	20h

(c) Heat aging

Heat aging in oven
(1) 270°C, 1 day
(2) 250°C, 4 days
(3) 230°C, 14 days

(d) Combined stress aging

Heat aging, vibration, moisture absorption
(1) 270°C by current (on for 12h, off for 12h)
(2) ±3.5G 100 CPS
(3) 100% RH
(4) 24h

Figure 3 One cycle of various thermal aging test

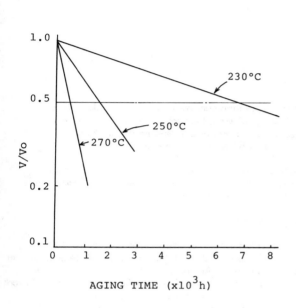

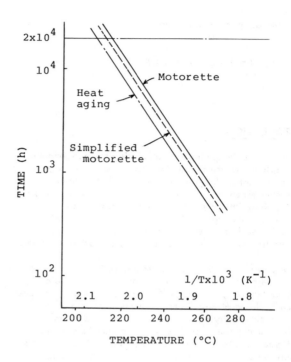

Figure 4 Degradation of breakdown voltage
under motorette test for Model No.3

Figure 5 Thermal endurance of Model No.3

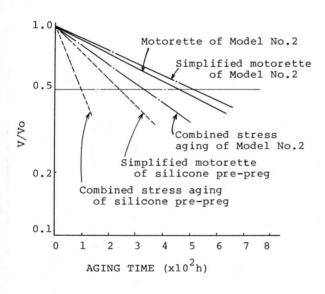

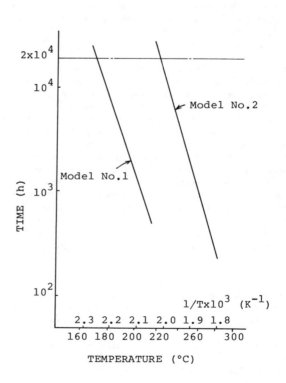

Figure 6 Degradation of breakdown voltage
at 270°C

Figure 7 Thermal endurance of Model No.2
and Model No.1

V.P.I. AND RESIN-RICH INSULATION SYSTEMS FOR HIGH-VOLTAGE INDUSTRIAL MACHINES - A COMPARISON

H.S. McNaughton and J. Nurse

GEC Large Machines Limited, UK

INTRODUCTION

The techniques available for calculating the performance of high voltage electrical machines have reached a stage where a complete set of design parameters, including thermal performance can be produced by computer in a few minutes. It is possible, therefore, for the engineer to select from several sets of computed data the optimum design for complying with the precise conditions for a particular application, or to meet a users specific operating requirements.

In the past, when design techniques were less refined, and more time consuming, the performance figures calculated, although normally acceptable, were not necessarily the best which could be attained. For example, because of the complexity of carrying out by hand a detailed thermal analysis of the conditions inside a machine the designer tended to work to conservative temperature rises. For this reason seldom did machines run at the maximum permitted value for the class of insulation used on the windings. The advent of computer-aided design techniques allows designers to select machine parameters which enable the windings to operate much closer to their full thermal capability than in the past.

In order that these precisely designed modern machines remain trouble-free throughout their service life, it is essential that the systems used for insulating the windings are designed to meet the stringent performance and operating conditions required by users of major items of electrical plant.

For many years all major electrical machine manufacturers have used insulation systems on their high-voltage windings based on micaceous materials bonded with synthetic resins. As is well-known, from the many technical papers[1,2,3,4] presented during the last 20 years, there are two basic systems which have grown up side-by-side based on thermosetting resins. These are known, by the somewhat misleading titles, as the resin-rich and the vacuum-pressure-impregnation (VPI) processes. In the UK until recently manufacturers have tended to place more emphasis on the resin-rich technique than those in Europe and America. However, with the advent of the more precise approach now being taken to overall machine design, and the need to utilise as efficiently as practicable all raw materials, it has become clear that, for many applications, there are significant advantages to be gained by adopting the global, or total, VPI process for stator windings.

The main purpose of this paper is to explain, as precisely as possible, the advantages of the two techniques from the point of view of the designer, manufacturer and ultimate user.

DESIGN REQUIREMENTS FOR INSULATION SYSTEMS

When in service stator windings are subjected to the combined effect of various stresses set up by the electrical, thermal and mechanical loadings. The levels of stress will depend on many factors, some of which are inherent in the machine design, whilst others depend on the duty cycle. For example the mechanical stresses imposed on a 12 pole, 3.3kV, a.c.

generator operating continuously 24 hours a day will be significantly different than for a 2 pole, 13.8kV, a.c. motor subjected to frequent direct-on-line (DOL) starts throughout its 8 hour per day operation.

In addition, depending upon the enclosure the operating environment may affect the overall performance and service life of the insulation system.

Electrical Stress

If one considers electrical stress, then this can lead to premature failure if the insulation thickness of the main ground wall is inadequate. Another, and probably more common problem area, is the level of the conductor/interturn insulation. This must have an intrinsic electric breakdown value many times greater than that required for normal continuous operation in order to withstand the high-voltages imposed between turns when the winding is subjected to fast-fronted switching surges. The ability of a winding to withstand these surges is dependent not only on the interturn insulation level, but also on the winding configuration. Low output high-voltage machines require many turns of small section copper. This can lead to a winding design where the physical separation between turns is a major factor in determining the high voltage surge withstand level of the coil. Figure 1 shows two examples of this condition. The first (a) is a single-section coil showing the critical flashover distance and the second (b) is a two-section coil with a top-to-bottom connection where the stress is even higher necessitating additional section insulation.

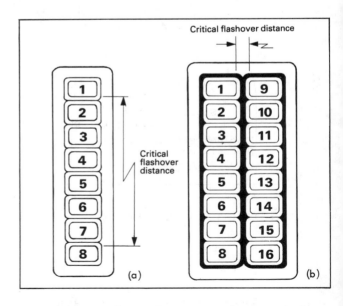

Figure 1 Stator coil design limitations for low output high-voltage machines.

TABLE A - Insulation withstand levels for various machine line voltages for standard resin rich and V.P.I. systems.

R.M.S. LINE VOLTAGE Un WINDING AND COIL DESIGN LEVELS.	3.3 (kV)	4.16 (kV)	6.6 (kV)	11.0 (kV)	13.8 (kV)
Winding withstand level when subjected to 1.2/50 μsecs. surges.	13.5	17	27	45	56
Winding withstand level when subjected to surges with wavefronts of 0.2 μsecs.	13.5	17	17	27	34
Coil withstand level - high frequency impulse across coil leads.	13.5	17	17	27	34

The recommended maximum surge withstand levels for standard industrial motors produced by GEC Large Machines are shown in Table A.

These levels are applicable to both resin-rich and VPI insulated windings, and comply with O.C.M.A.'s requirements for standard motors as laid down in their ELEC 1 specification. To comply with the five times peak of the phase voltage requirements for surges with wave-fronts of approximately 0.2 μ seconds as specified in the latter specification for 'Special Applications', then for machines with voltages over 4.16kV a higher level of interturn insulation is generally necessary.

Surges with faster wave-fronts and/or values in excess of these levels should be prevented from reaching the motor terminals by the fitting of correctly designed surge suppression devices. The latter must be fitted as close to the motor terminals as practicable.

Thermal Stresses

Thermal stresses from normal operating duty are allowed for at the design stage, but abnormal events, such as overloads and frequent short-circuit conditions can take the insulation temperature well beyond its maximum design value.

It is advisable, therefore, to protect machines against excessive thermal stresses by fitting suitable sensing devices that will either give warning or trip the machine off the line in an emergency.

Mechanical Stresses

Excessive mechanical stress can manifest itself in various ways, but the end result is nearly always the same - physical damage to the main dielectric, either in the slot or in the overhangs, resulting either in an interturn, ground wall or phase-to-phase failure. The breakdown can be initiated by vibration forces generated either within the machine or from some external source. A major cause of mechanical failures in the past was endwinding movement during DOL starting. This aspect of design has received close attention during the last decade, particularly in catering for motors with arduous duty cycles having many starts per day. Figures 2 and 3 show typical endwinding bracing techniques on a 13.8kV, 2 pole resin-rich insulated stator and a 6.6kV, 2 pole VPI global impregnated motor.

Figure 2 Endwinding of resin-rich stator.

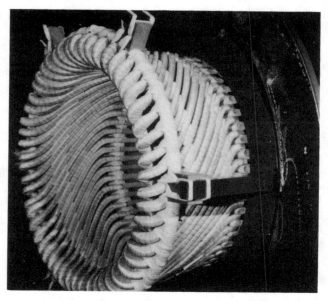

Figure 3 Endwinding of VPI stator.

Environmental Stresses

The final area of stress which is always of concern is that caused by environmental pollution which leads to contamination of the winding, with deposits ranging from conducting dust to corrosive acids. For the most severe environments the complete wound stator may require to be treated with a special varnish or resin coating instead of, or in addition to, the normal final treatment. Over a period of time in service endwindings and core portions of open ventilated machines can be exposed to large amounts of airborne dust and vapours. If the contaminants are removed by an approved method on a regular basis during programmed outages, then no harm is likely to come to the windings. If, however, the contamination is left to build up to a level such that it affects the surface properties of the winding, then the result can be a deterioration in the long-term performance of the machine. In some instances, for example in a textile factory where airborne fibres are prevelant, the contamination can build up to such proportions inside the machine that ventilation can be seriously impaired. This can lead to general overheating of the winding followed by premature failure.

RESIN-RICH AND VPI INSULATION SYSTEMS

Although the two alternative approaches to insulating machine windings have been in use for many years it may be useful to describe them briefly for those engineers who are not specialists on insulation systems.

The resin-rich system is in several aspects a logical development of the processes used in the past. Coils are wound first as flat loops using conductors insulated with either enamel and glass or a mica-based tape. After consolidating the slot portion under heat and pressure they are pulled-out into the well-known diamond shape. Thereafter, main ground insulation of glass or film backed, epoxide-resin-bonded micaceous tape are applied. During the manufacture of these tapes the epoxide resin has been partially cured to the 'B' stage condition. This makes the tape dry and flexible with handling characteristics that are suitable for hand or machine application. After application the slot portions are consolidated under heat and pressure to specified dimensions. This processing converts the flexible, partially cured resin in the tape into a solid, thermally stable material with excellent electrical, thermal and mechanical properties. The designation 'resin-rich' comes from the fact that the tapes contain an excess of resin over and above that required to produce adequate consolidation. During pressing this surplus resin is squeezed from the material so as to leave void-free main insulation. The insulation applied to the endwindings normally consists of either the same type of 'B' stage resin-rich tape or, alternatively, fully-cured, flexible tapes which are sufficiently resilient to allow the coils to be wound into the stator core without damage. Subsequently, after winding and connecting up into phase groups, endwinding bracing is carried out using cords and tapes. Where practicable, the completed stator is normally immersed in a solvented flexible varnish and stoved to cure all the partially cured resins in the winding.

In the classic VPI process coils and bars are insulated with micaceous tapes containing only the minimum of resin necessary to hold the basic mica and reinforced backing together. After insulating, coils and bars are placed in moulds, transferred to an autoclave and vacuum-dried to remove all air and moisture. Thereafter a low-viscosity, solventless epoxy or polyester resin is pumped into the autoclave to immerse the coils or bars. To assist full resin impregnation of all the interstices in the mica insulation dry air, under high-pressure, is applied in the autoclave.

After impregnation, coils and bars are cured by heat to thermoset the synthetic resin. By building in some permanently flexible tapings at the evolute portions of diamond-shaped coils it is possible to wind these fully-cured components into the stator core. Thereafter, the normal winding processes are completed. Although this basic VPI procedure is useful for manufacturing large coils or bars, especially those with single-turn windings for large hydro-generators, etc. a modified procedure has been developed for medium-sized stators. This is the global impregnation process. After insulating the coils with dry micaceous tapes they are wound into the stator core, connected up and braced using dry materials. The complete wound stator core is next placed in a large tank, vacuum-dried and then pressure-impregnated with solventless synthetic resin. Finally, the complete unit is stoved to thermoset all the resin which has impregnated the winding and associated bracing system. It is this latter process which makes the VPI process so attractive to the manufacturer of medium sized, high-voltage machines.

DEVELOPMENT TESTING OF INSULATION SYSTEMS

The ultimate test of any insulation system is extensive service in arduous environments. Although great care is taken to formulate laboratory test procedures which simulate real service conditions there is always the possibility that the artificial ageing of a particular property may be less, or greater, than expected. For this reason it is important to relate laboratory evaluations to systems with known service experience. This is not only so for the materials, or combinations of materials used, but also to confirm that the stress levels, clearances and various other parameters in the system are satisfactory.

Although there are many different tests used for checking the various aspects of an insulation system those associated with the long-term proving of the integrity of the interturn and main ground wall are especially relevant to high-voltage machines.

Interturn Insulation

For many years now, a considerable amount of attention has been paid to the long-term withstand capability of the interturn insulation of machines, especially motors. This topic is particularly relevant to machines which are subjected to frequent switching operations in service. There have been several technical papers[4, 5,] published recently suggesting that interturn failures have become more prevalent than in the past because of the increased use of vacuum devices. A more detailed examination of reported service problems tends to suggest that many switching devices produce fast-fronted surges, and that more likely reasons for the reported break-downs are either related to the design of the overall switch/cable/machine system, or that the motors had too low a design level of interturn insulation.

To assess the long-term ageing of conductor/interturn insulation, stator coil sections, insulated with several different materials, have been thermally aged at temperatures in the range $160°$ to $210°$ C. By including in the test programme thermal cycling, mechanical vibration and a controlled humid atmosphere typical service environments have been simulated. During the test a proof voltage was applied between adjacent turns. Figure 4 shows some of the results obtained on conductors insulated with polyester-enamel and glass-braid, glass-backed and polyester film backed resin-rich epoxide bonded micapaper.

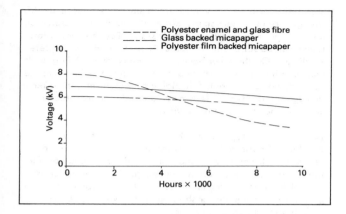

Figure 4 Change in dielectric strength of three types of interturn insulation when aged at 155° C.

It can be seen from the results that although the polyester-enamel and glass-covered conductors have a high initial dielectric withstand capability, the value gradually decreases when exposed to full Class 'F' temperatures for long periods of ageing. The polyester film-backed micapaper had a substantially better retention of electric strength than, perhaps, might have been expected. Two factors are particularly relevant to this result. The first is that the system, by its very nature, precludes all air from reaching the conductor-stack, and the second, that careful matching of the bonding resin and the polyester-film had been arranged so that during ageing no decomposition components were produced which interacted with each other to lower the overall thermal capability of the system. For completeness the results of ageing of polyester-enamel and glass at a lower temperature are shown on Figure 5.

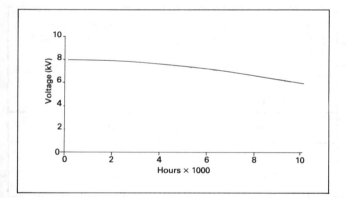

Figure 5 Change in dielectric strength of polyester enamel and glass insulated conductors when aged at 130° C.

The results indicate clearly why the use of this type of conductor on windings operating at no greater temperature than the maximum permitted for Class 'B' machines has been so successful for some 20 or 30 years.

Main Ground Insulation

Although the main reason in the past for electrical breakdowns of windings in service is caused by failure of the interturn insulation there is another factor which is of importance in

determining the overall life. This is the quality of the main ground-wall insulation. It is essential to ensure during the manufacture of all high-voltage stator coils and windings that no air-voids remain inside the main insulation after processing. If any voids are present, especially in the regions around the conductor-stack then discharging will take place inside all coils at, or near, the line end of the winding. This electrical erosion will cause deterioration of the bonding resin, followed by weakening of the mica platelets and any reinforcement tapes contained in the system. Once the damage has reached an advanced stage, then mechanical vibration of the conductors, or turns, inside the main ground wall will cause fretting and powdering of the insulating materials until eventually an interturn, or main-wall, breakdown will take place. To confirm that the quality of new coils and windings are satisfactory it is normal practice to check the quality of the dielectric using a Schering Bridge. This is the well-known loss-tangent test.

In order to confirm that an insulation system will give many years of trouble-free service it is necessary to carry out tests to establish how the loss-tangent values vary with ageing. Present day materials used in both resin-rich and VPI systems contain complex resin formulations. Although the processing techniques applied must be compatible with the materials used in the system it is important to appreciate that minor modifications made to one component, for example, to improve the handling characteristics of a mica tape, can lead to unexpected results in the long-term performance of the whole system.

To confirm the suitability of various systems it is usual to make cimplified coil-sections, such as the one shown on Figure 6, and submit them to thermal-ageing with voltage applied between the conductors and the external surface.

Figure 6 Restrained test bar.

By carrying out the test at higher than the normal maximum Class 'F' temperature, and at several times the standard 50 Hz supply frequency to accelerate the effect of discharging in the dielectric, data on performance can be obtained in months in the laboratory which is equivalent to several years in normal service. By carrying out such tests over a period of many years it is possible to compare the results obtained from proposed new systems with those obtained from older systems where the service life is already known.

The ideal system is one which shows very little, if any, change throughout a period of extended thermal-ageing as measured by loss-tangent readings. Minor changes are acceptable and certain systems, for example, those based on epoxide-novolak resins, have a characteristic shape as shown in Figure 7.

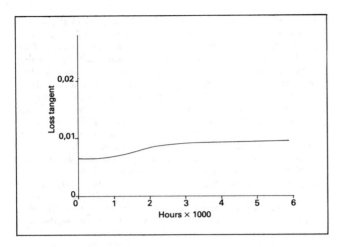

Figure 7   Minor change in loss tangent of epoxy novolak
based micapaper for H.V. ground insulation.

PRODUCTION AND TYPE TESTING

During the various stages of manufacture tests are carried out
on stator coils and windings to check the integrity of the fully
impregnated assembly. Vacuum-pressure-impregnated coils
must be treated in a different manner to those manufactured
using a resin-rich system because of the different resin content
in the insulation materials prior to impregnation.

The dielectric strength of resin-rich and individual VPI coils
cured in moulds is attained during the normal processing
schedule. After winding into the stator core and on

completion of the final varnish treatment the values of electric
strength are not significantly different from those measured on
the coils prior to insertion in their slots. For this reason test
levels can be set at similar values to those used for complete
windings. On the other hand, stator coils for the VPI global
impregnation process, which are 'dry' before winding into the
core, do not attain their full dielectric potential until after
impregnation. Hence, tests carried out during manufacture
must take account of this condition.

Table B shows a typical schedule of test levels for routine
checking of coils and windings for the two basic systems as
described. It can be seen that for an unimpregnated coil for
the VPI global impregnation process, the h.v. test value is
70% of the final impregnated test level. This value has
proved to be adequate for showing up any weaknesses on
coils insulated with this system.

Production testing of the interturn insulation of both resin-
rich and VPI coils is carried out by applying a high frequency
damped oscillatory surge across the coil leads. Test levels
used for stators up to 4.16 kV are the same for both systems.
For higher voltages the lower resin content of unimpregnated
VPI coils again limits the test levels which can be applied.

To demonstrate to specific users that both resin-rich and VPI
systems have adequate insulation withstand levels it is normal
practice today to carry out type tests on two stator coils
manufactured with the proposed insulation system. Typical
schedules of tests for the two systems are shown in Table C.
On resin-rich and individually VPI treated coils the procedure
is straight forward. On VPI coils for the global impregnation
process withstand tests on type test samples must be carried out
before and after treatment.

TABLE B - Routine test voltage levels for standard resin-rich and VPI coils and windings

Insulation system	Routine test		H.V. 50 Hz R.M.S. applied between coil leads and ground for 1 - min.	H.F. surge applied across coil leads. 5 impulses/coil
Global VPI	Coils Wedged and braced stator coils prior to connection	≤4.16 kV	1.5 Un	3 $\hat{U}$ph
		>4.16 kV	1.5 Un	2 $\hat{U}$ph
	Windings After impregnation. All voltages		2 Un + 1	—
Resin-Rich and individually treated V.P.I. coils	Coils Wedged and braced stator coils prior to connection. All voltages		2 Un + 1	3 $\hat{U}$ph
	Windings After impregnation. All voltages		2 Un + 1	—

$$\hat{U}ph = \frac{\sqrt{2}}{\sqrt{3}} \times \text{R.M.S. Line voltage (Un) in kV}$$

TABLE C - Type test voltage levels for resin-rich and VPI insulated coils.

Type test / Insulation system		H.V. 50 Hz R.M.S. applied between outside of coil and leads for 1 - min.		H.V. 50 Hz R.M.S. applied between contiguous turns for 1 - min.
		Slot portion	Endwinding	
Global VPI	Before impregnation	1.8 Un	1.5 Un	$\dfrac{Un}{3} + 1$
	After impregnation	1.5 (2 Un + 1)	2 Un	$1.5 \left(\dfrac{Un}{3}\right) + 1$
Resin rich and individually V.P.I. treated coils		1.5 (2 Un + 1)	2 Un	$1.5 \left(\dfrac{Un}{3}\right) + 1$

Un = R.M.S.   Line voltage in kV

In a similar way it is necessary to check that the quality of the main ground dielectric is satisfactory. On fully processed coils tests can be carried out to the procedure and limits specified in BS 4999 Part 61 without difficulty. For 'dry' unimpregnated coils loss tangent tests are only meaningful if carried out on individual phases of completed stators.

To demonstrate that the impregnation process is satisfactory, type tests can be carried out on coils mounted in model core assemblies which exactly duplicate the winding procedures used on the actual stator winding. On windings for machines with voltages higher than approximately 6kV, it is necessary to take into account the effect of the additional dielectric loss produced by the stress grading system normally applied to the straight portions of coils just beyond the ends of the slots.

ADVANTAGES AND DISADVANTAGES OF RESIN-RICH AND VPI SYSTEMS

Service experience with resin-rich and VPI techniques has shown that both systems are technically superior to the older thermoplastic materials. For the last two decades most major machine manufacturers in the UK have concentrated their attention on resin-rich systems. However, in the last few years the high cost of the labour intensive resin-rich processes and the need to produce windings which are universally capable of withstanding all types of environments has required manufacturers to reassess this position. For these reasons there has been a growing interest in the UK in the merits of VPI systems, especially for medium sized machines. To understand what this change means for machine designers, manufacturers and the ultimate user it is worthwhile to examine the advantages and disadvantages for each of these three disciplines.

From the insulation designers point of view, windings can be most usefully divided into two basic types - those with rigid consolidated slot portions and flexible taped endwindings, and those with rigid slot and endwinding portions. Most engineers tend to classify insulation systems into either resin-rich or VPI. This is not, however, the most useful way to distinguish them. There are, in practice, greater similarities between a resin-rich winding with consolidated slot and endwinding portions and a VPI winding, whether made as individual coils or as part of a global impregnation process, than with a resin-rich system with flexible overhangs.

To put the various aspects into perspective it is useful to examine the various electrical, thermal, mechanical and environmental characteristics in a little more detail.

The electric strength and intrinsic quality of the dielectric of both resin-rich and VPI systems are excellent. No problems should occur on any properly designed synthetic-resin winding due to deterioration of the basic dielectric by internal discharging. Similarly, the interturn and impulse withstand levels on both systems are readily made adequate for all normal service conditions. The long-term retention of properties are excellent as mentioned earlier under the section on Development.

From a thermal endurance stand-point both rigid and flexible systems can be made for full Class 'F' operation of stators with voltages up to at least 13.8kV. A major difference, however, between systems with rigid and flexible overhangs, which gives the former a significant advantage, is its much superior thermal conductivity. For this reason machines with consolidated endwindings, when correctly designed, will have significantly higher outputs than machines of the same size, but with flexible taped endwindings.

Mechanically, windings, based on rigid endwindings offer two advantages over those with flexible endwindings. Firstly, rigid systems normally have their insulation continuously applied to both the slot and endwinding portions. This practice enables the designer to use the minimum overall length of coil. Such an approach cannot be adopted for flexible taped endwindings because the system is discontinuous with scarf-joints at the ends of the slots where the endwinding and slot insulations merge together. The second major advantage of rigid endwinding systems is the inherent stiffness and consolidation of the overhangs which permits bracing to be carried out by inserting packing blocks wrapped with felt between adjacent endwinding arms. For resin-rich windings the felt is normally preimpregnated with B-stage epoxy resin. For VPI windings dry felt is used which picks up the required amount of liquid resin during the impregnation process. For windings with resilient overhangs the inherent flexibility does not permit packing and bracing to be carried out in such a simple manner. In the latter case, because of the greater flexibility it is necessary to insert blocks between endwinding arms and to hold them in place using several layers of tape or cord which encircle both the endwinding arms and the blocks.

Such a process has been well-proven by many years of service experience as adequate for even the most severe service duties. It is, however, expensive to carry out.

Environmental protection of windings against ingress of moisture, salt, cantamination etc. can be successfully achieved with most types of insulation system. However, in practice, sealing of all resin-rich windings is much more labour intensive, and hence more expensive than for VPI totally impregnated windings where the processing achieves the required finish without any difficulty.

From a manufacturing stand-point most resin-rich processes tend to be more labour intensive than those used on VPI windings. Although resin-rich windings with rigid overhangs do lend themselves to the use of automatic taping for main wall insulation, nevertheless the use of the same technique is more easily adapted to the manufacture of VPI coils. Substantial advantages for resin-rich windings are often claimed in that both interturn and slot portion loss-tangent measurements can be made on coils prior to winding. Although this claim is substantially true, it is practicable to interturn test individual coils for VPI windings at satisfactory withstand levels after inserting into the stator core, but before connecting up. The values achieved on coils after impregnation can be demonstrated by type-testing to have increased levels. Loss-tangent tests are normally carried out on all resin-rich coils before winding into the stator core. With a VPI winding such a test cannot be usefully carried out. Loss-tangent readings can only be made on the complete phase of a winding after impregnation. At this stage, due to the effects of dilution and any stress grading, only a global indication of the quality of the main dielectric is possible. A major reason for carrying out loss-tangent tests on resin-rich coils before winding is because each one is individually made and processed. Hence, the final quality is dependent on operator skill.

An advantage of a VPI process for the winding department is the greater ease with which the dry, unimpregnated coils can be wound into the stator core. With resin-rich coils great care must be taken to wind them tightly into their slots and to ensure that all wedges are tight. With a VPI process, stator coils insulated with soft, dry materials can be more easily wound to the same degree of tightness without risk of damage to the main insulation.

WINDING AND COIL REPLACEMENT

If a winding requires to be replaced or repaired, then certain factors need to be considered. Windings with rigid overhangs which suffer minor damage that does not require coil replacement can usually be repaired by conventional techniques and quickly returned to service. In situations where a drive is of prime importance, then it is possible to replace a coil side only, until such time that a replacement wound core can be interchanged. Users operating several machines of the same design often find it more convenient to hold a spare wound core assembly to minimise the turnround time in case of an emergency.

In the event of a problem with a machine having a flexible endwinding then, with care, a complete coil can be replaced by lifting a coil pitch after warming the machine to soften the varnish. It is advisable in this case to replace the complete coil pitch with new spare coils that can be held in storage for extended periods.

CONCLUSIONS

Windings manufactured using both resin-rich and VPI insulation systems meet the stringent requirements for high voltage machines for todays' environment where reliability is of paramount importance.

In the UK during the last two decades, systems based on resin-rich materials have predominated. However, in the past few years machine manufacturers have recognised the need to refine winding techniques, reduce overall costs and save energy. For these reasons they have had to re-examine all the insulation processes available to them. The technical and economic attractions of the VPI global impregnation process have been thoroughly investigated by GEC Large Machines and a decision has been taken to adopt it as the most logical system for insulating future standard ranges of industrial a.c. motors and generators. Although the initial cost of the required capital plant is high when compared with that needed for manufacturing resin-rich windings, the overall advantages for design, manufacture and technical performance fully justifies its installation.

REFERENCES

1. Laffoon, C.M., Hill, C.F., Moses, G.L., and Berberick, R.J., 1959, "A new high voltage insulation for turbine-generator stator windings", AIEE Transactions 70.

2. Blinne, K., Mader, O., and Peter, J., June 1961, "Orlitherm - A new high tension insulation", Bulletin Oerlikon No. 345.

3. Britsch, H., and Schuler, R., September 1967, "Micadur - Compact, fully impregnated stator insulation for high voltage machines", Brown Boveri Review, Vol.54, No.9.

4. Neal, J.E., 1972, "Development of high voltage insulation systems", GEC Journal of Science and Technology, Vol.39, No.1.

5. Adjaye, R.E., and Cornick, K.J., February 1979, "Distribution of switching surges in the line-end coils of cable connected motors", IEE Electric Power Applications, Vol.2, No.1.

6. Eriksson, A.J., November 1974, "Over voltage surges in industrial complexes", Symposium on H.V. Engineering in South Africa.

THE PROVISION OF DESIGN DATA FROM EXTENDED HEAT AGING TESTS

J. Heighes

Permali Limited, UK

INTRODUCTION

One of the important features in the evaluation of electrical insulation for rotating machines is to determine the maximum temperature it can safely withstand for the time the machine will be designed to operate, as organic based materials can be expected to deteriorate more rapidly at elevated temperatures. This temperature/time relation, permits the aging of insulating material to be accelerated by increasing the rate of deterioration at temperatures higher than the service temperature, from which the expected life at the service temperature may be determined by an extrapolation. This method of evaluation is described in IEC Publication 216 - Guide for the determination of thermal endurance properties of electrical insulating materials.

The method of test makes use of the general equation characteristic of thermal life, (reference 1), which is:-

$$\log t_f = \frac{Ea}{2.303 \ R.T.} + \log\left[\frac{g(P_f) - g(Po)}{A}\right]$$

where t_f = time for a property to change from an initial value Po to an end point P_f.

Ea = activation energy
R = universal gas constant
T = absolute temperature
g(P) = function of the observed property

Hence, it is expected that the graph of the logarithm of time (log t_f) against the reciprocal of the absolute temperature (1/T), will be a straight line with a slope proportional to the activation energy, (Ea). A limited extrapolation may be applied to this straight line to determine the time for the material to undergo that same property change at a lower temperature.

It has been shown, (reference 2), that the "ten degree doubling rule" used by insulation engineers for the simpler materials, cannot be used for the more complex glass reinforced polymerics. This is because, for different types of materials, the activation energy, (Ea) and hence the slope of the straight line, is different. For example, the phenolics tend to have a higher value of Ea and hence a steeper slope to the aging curve than the theoretical (10 degree) slope, and the epoxides give aging curves which are less steep than the theoretical slope.

Although useful data can be derived by the use of the IEC procedure, it is considered that the method is capable of extension, without deviating from the confinements of the specification, to provide data which is thought to be more meaningful to the designer of the insulation system of rotating machines. This paper is concerned with this extension of the test method.

THE SPECIFIED METHOD AND ITS LIMITATIONS

The method specified by IEC Publication 216 requires that samples be aged at a minimum of three temperatures at intervals of about 20°C and the end point, which may be a percentage of one of a number of electrical or mechanical properties, should be reached in not less than 500 hours at the lowest selected temperature. The number of hours taken to reach the selected end point, are each plotted against the reciprocal of the respective absolute temperatures, and the points must lie on a straight line for the extrapolation to be valid. A best fit will not do, as illustrated later. The extrapolation should not extend over more than 25°C. The basic method is illustrated in figure 1a and 1b from which it is seen that as an alternative to plotting the graph against the reciprocal of the absolute temperature, a conversion to the Celsius scale may be made, which results in a non-linear ordinate.

In this paper, the results obtained on glass reinforced electrical grade laminates are reported, as would be used for slot wedges and pole collars. For such applications, the designer is usually more interested in the mechanical properties of the material so that the property chosen to measure was the crossbreaking strength as specified in B.S. 2782 method 335A. The end point for any test temperature was taken as 50% of the initial crossbreaking strength when measured at room temperature, the initial strength being obtained after a 48 hour post cure at the lowest aging temperature as required by the specification. The aging ovens used were air circulating thermostatically controlled, the temperature distribution being checked by thermocouples. The samples were spread in a single layer on a wire mesh in the oven. The variation of temperature across the shelf was found to be 0.5°C and the variation due to thermostat control was found to be 1°C.

The need to meet the specified requirements is illustrated in figure 2 which gives the results for a glass mat reinforced polyester laminate. An aging temperature of 220°C was obviously too high for this material as the point does not lie on a straight line with the 200°C and 180°C points. A fourth point at a lower temperature confirms the 200°C and 180°C points as being valid. It will be seen that if data is required for this material at 140°C, the best fit curve for the points obtained at the three highest temperatures suggest a 50% strength retention after 100,000 hours (11.4 years), whereas the valid curve suggests that a 50% strength retention will be reached after 24,000 hours, (2.74 years). Hence it is essential that aging temperatures are not chosen which are too high for the material, or too high for the required extrapolation.

As written, the specification proposes that a comparison may be made of the performance of insulating materials or insulation systems by extrapolating the graph to 20,000 hours, the temperature index, which is about 2.25 years, a fraction of the expected operating life of many rotating machines. Also, the measurement of the change of the particular property has tended to be made at room temperature.

The results of tests made on a woven glass reinforced epoxide laminate, obtained in accordance with IEC Publication 216, are given in figure 3. The nominal aging temperatures were 240°C, 220°C and 200°C and the tests were made at room temperature. This results in a temperature index of 190 being quoted for this material (reference 3). Also in figure 3 are given comparable results for a high temperature phenolic laminate which allows a temperature index of 188 to be quoted. Hence a design engineer might justifiably come to the conclusion that he can use the two materials in identical circumstances when considering the thermal aging properties, if he is only offered the temperature index. However, the slopes of the two curves show this not to be so; the high temperature phenolic laminate has a very high temperature cability in the short term, quite suitable for use in a machine of Class C rating providing the life of the machine is not expected to be more than say 2 years. This is shown by the high temperatures for which the straight line relation exists. On the other hand, the epoxide laminate will apparently give very many years of satisfactory service in a Class F machine, much longer apparently than would the phenolic, as indicated by the relative slopes of the two straight lines.

In addition, the comparsion made at room temperature is only valid if a similar comparison may be made at the operating temperature and there is evidence that different materials will not exhibit the same percentage strength retention at elevated temperatures. Hence, it is concluded that to quote a temperature index to a designer is not going to be of much practical significance to him, particularly if the result is derived from room temperature testing.

THE EXTENDED TEST METHOD

In attempting to provide more useful data to the design engineer, the assumption has been made that his need is for information in terms of the life of the material at a predetermined temperature rather than, as suggested by the specification, a temperature index for a pre-determined time neither of which may bear any relation to either the operating temperature or the anticipated life of the machine. The alternative therefore is to extend the aging times so that the results may be safely extrapolated to normal working life and to test at the anticipated working temperature of the machine.

If then, it is required that the life of a material be determined if it is to be used at 155°C then the aging temperatures should be 180°C (155°C + 25°C), 200°C and 220°C, providing that the resulting points lie on a straight line. The test temperature should also be 155°C. The end point could be a precentage strength retention of the initial room temperature strength or of the initial strength at 155°C. The former is recommended as this will show up a material with poor strength retention at the higher temperatures.

As will be seen from figure 4, this may necessitate extending the aging time at the lowest temperature to the order of 20,000 hours but the advantage of these longer times is that results are provided which show that the woven glass reinforced epoxide would be expected to have 50% strength retention at 155°C after 9.5 years and the mat glass reinforced epoxide should have a 50% strength retention after 22.8 years. When tested at 180°C after aging at 180°C the mat glass reinforced epoxide still has a 50% strength retention after 11,400 hours (1.3 years) which shows that the material would be expected to give long service at 155°C even with occasional temperature rises up to 180°C, as in a railway locomotive motor, for example.

These times are, of course, relative to the total running time of the machine. Most rotating machines of the type expected to give 25 to 30 years service life are shut down at intervals for maintenance and may also run for periods well below maximum load and hence at a lower temperature. The indications are that temperature cycling will reduce the life of the insulation. When samples from a mat glass reinforced epoxide laminate were cooled to room temperature every 500 hours over a period of 5000 hours aging at 200°C, the reduction in strength was 10% more than for similar samples which were aged continuously for 5000 hours. However, it is suggested that the reduction could be considerably less if the insulation was cycled between 155°C and room temperature, compared with cooling from 200°C.

OTHER CONSIDERATIONS

Although cross breaking strength has been used to monitor the rate of aging, for laminate applications such as slot wedges and pole collars, change of compressive strength and change of thickness with aging are important.

The change in compressive strength of a woven glass epoxide laminate seems to be much less than the change in the crossbreaking strength over the same period. When tested at 155°C the compressive strength reduced from 265 MN/m² to 230 MN/m² after 6000 hours at 180°C, a strength retention of 87% compared with 50% strength retention of crossbreaking strength over the same aging period. These tests are also currently being made for a mat glass reinforced epoxide laminate.

For the materials evaluated, the epoxide based laminates appear to be much less likely to reduce in thickness than do the polyester based laminates. A mat glass reinforced polyester laminate, as used to derive figure 2, showed a 12% reduction in thickness on a 5mm thickness after 22,000 hours at 155°C and a high temperature polyester laminate, claimed by the manufacture to be Class H, gave a 34% reduction in thickness on a 3mm thickness after 6000 hours at 200°C. The comparative figures for a mat glass reinforced epoxide is 4.0% reduction in thickness when aged at 200°C, with no change of thickness measured when the material was aged at 155°C.

The reduction in thickness is not due entirely to surface oxydation. If it was, the thickness reduction would be expected to be independent of the thickness of the laminate. As can be seen from table 1, the thickness reduction for a mat glass reinforced epoxide laminate increases by a factor of 2 between a thickness of 3mm and one of 25mm, when aged at 180°C.

TABLE 1 - Effect of material thickness on thickness reduction during aging at 180°C.

Material Thickness mm	Thickness Reduction mm		
	2000 h	5000 h	8000 h
3	.04	.05	.07
5	.065	.07	.085
12.5	.07	.085	.10
25	.085	.10	.13

As an alternative to the measurement of cross breaking strength to monitor the rate of aging, the change of heat distortion point is attractive, (temperature of deflection to B.S. 2782, Method 121C). The temperature is determined at which a fixed deflection of the sample is reached due to a stress of 10% of the initial crossbreaking strength. This could indicate both the rate of aging and the suitability of a material for high temperature use. However, although the results are useful for comparative purposes, it is doubtful if they can be as readily applied to the design application as can the crossbreaking strength results, as the heat distortion temperature does not, of course indicate the maximum temperature at which it is safe to use the material, but shows the rate of change of stiffness of the material, with aging.

There is one aspect which the presentation of results in the form of percentage strength retention will mask. If we compare the aging curves from which the 180°C points were obtained for the same two materials (figure 5), it is seen that the woven glass reinforced material initially has twice the crossbreaking strength of the mat glass reinforced material. Hence the crossbreaking strength which is taken as the end point for the woven glass laminate, is twice as high as that for the mat glass laminate. However, it is interesting to note that if the same end point is used for both materials, that is 120 MN/m², this being the 50% strength of the mat glass laminate, the life of the two materials is almost the same (figure 4).

CONCLUSIONS

The use of IEC Procedure 216 allows for the derivation of data which is more applicable to design than the specification at first suggests.

Measurements made at room temperature on materials which are to be used at high temperature do not seem to be of much value and a 20,000 hour result is only of value for a machine with an anticipated running life of 2 to 3 years. The extension of the method to a test temperature of the same order as the temperature which the insulation will experience in the machine and to aging times which allow for an extrapolation, (not exceeding 25°C), to the same machine insulation temperature, may be made at a cost of little extra in man hours plus the cost of running aging ovens for 2 to 4 times as long.

The method still does not allow for the effect of temperature cycling and the results presented in this paper do not show the effect of adjacent materials in the machine insulation system. However, it is considered that the data so far obtained does indicate that glass reinforced epoxide laminates are suitable for use in Class F machines and probably in Class H machines, depending on the temperature reached by the insulation and the time for which it will be heated to that temperature. At least they appear to merit inclusion in the machine manufacturer's evaluation of insulation systems for use at these temperatures.

Glass reinforced polyester resin laminates are attractive to rotating machines applications because of lower price but caution is recommended where retention of thickness is critical.

REFERENCES

1. Krizanovsky, L., and Mentlik, V., 1978, The use of thermal analysis to predict the thermal life of organic electrical insulating materials. J. Thermal Analysis, 13 571-580.

2. Aggleton, M.J., and Heighes, J., 1982, An evaluation of the thermal aging of glass reinforced laminates. BEAMA Insulation Conference.

3. Heighes, J., 1978, Heat aging of electrical laminates. Reinforced Plastics Conference, 93-95.

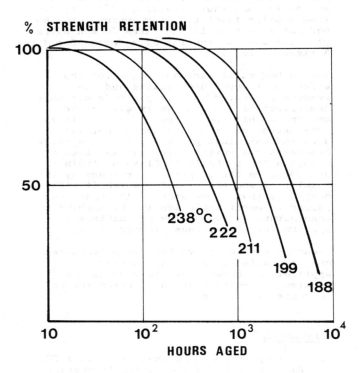

Figure 1a. Determination of the times at various temperatures to reach the end point of 50% strength retention.

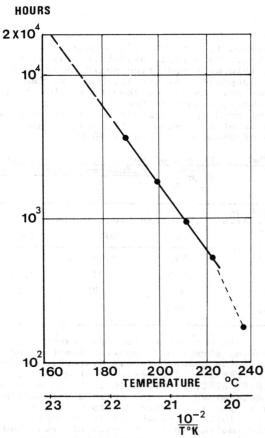

Figure 1b. The thermal endurance graph derived from figure 1a. Note the invalid point.

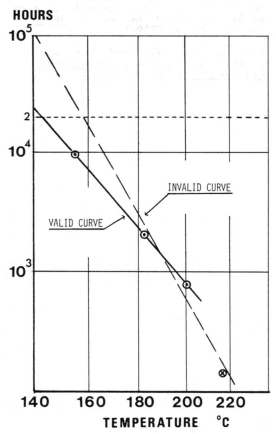

Figure 2. Illustration of the danger of using a point obtained at an aging temperature too high for the material.

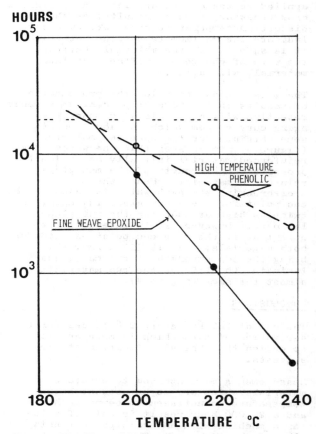

Figure 3. The effect of resin system on the slope of the thermal endurance graph. Laminates made with identical reinforcements.

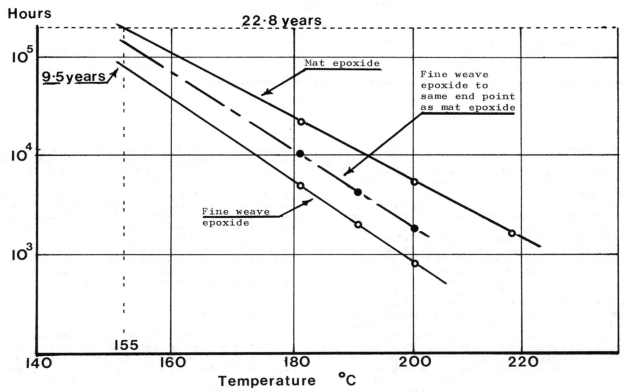

Figure 4. The expected life of glass reinforced epoxide laminates operating at 155°C. Also illustrated is a comparison using the same strength retention for both laminates. All tests made at 155°C.

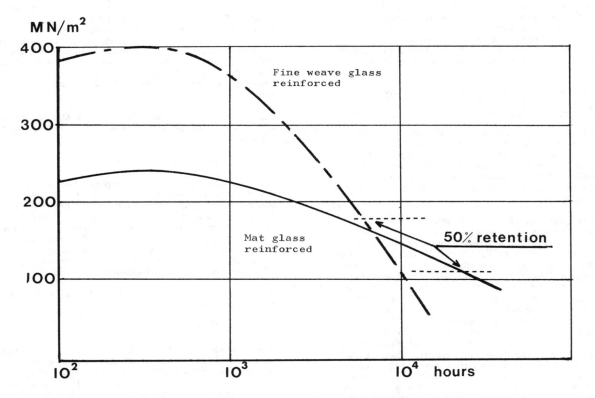

Figure 5. Comparison of crossbreaking strengths of fine weave and mat glass reinforced epoxide laminates tested at 155°C.

THE PREDICTION OF THE RESPONSE OF SPECIAL ELECTROMECHANICAL DRIVE SYSTEMS

J.R. Smith and A.F. Stronach   K. Goodman

University of Aberdeen, U.K.   Laurence Scott and Electromotors Ltd.

INTRODUCTION

Induction motors normally operate at speeds close to synchronism. In these cases simple mathematical models are generally sufficient for predicting their performance. However, in order to predict with sufficient accuracy the starting current, torque and the time to reach full speed for large motors, the simulation model must be capable of allowing for depressions in the supply voltage, include the facility to account for the variation of parameters due to saturation and speed changes, and be capable of representing the dominant modes of oscillation due to electromechanical interaction. In order that these non-linear variations are accounted for throughout a simulation, the basic two-axis induction motor model (1,2) must be modified to permit changes in parameter values as the solution requires, and external system initiated variations, such as supply voltage fluctuations, can only be included by dynamically representing the overall system or a representative section of the system. In much the same way a correct assessment of the electro-mechanical interaction requires the mechanical load to be represented including individual inertias, connecting shaft-stiffnesses and an adequate estimate of the various damping coefficients and the variation of these coefficients as a function of the amplitude of the cyclic torque variations.

The paper discusses these various factors which affect the simulation of the run-up and operational characteristics of large induction motors which are situated in practical schemes. The paper is illustrated by examples in which simulated results are directly compared to those available from test.

MODELLING REQUIREMENTS FOR SPECIALISED DRIVE

PERFORMANCE CALCULATIONS

The requirements for a successful simulation of an induction motor driven process or plant essentially depends on two main considerations. The first concerns the type of system to which the motor is connected and the second concerns the degree of mathematical representation for the induction motor driven system.

In considering the first of these factors the following points must be assessed. If the induction motor of interest is connected to a large power complex for which very little variation in voltage and frequency is expected subsequent to the motor starting or operating abnormally, then the inter-action of the system and the machine is such that a single motor simulation (3-7) may suffice in the assessment of the motors overall behaviour. If however, the motor is connected to a small isolated system (8-10) where for example, the run-up of a motor is accompanied by severe voltage fluctuations and frequency variations, it becomes essential to take account of the system in a representative manner in addition to the particular drive under consideration. The motor then becomes a component of the system; other components being associated with the generation system and control, the inter-connecting network and other drive types. It is to the second type of system that the present paper

relates. Details of the various modelling require-ments for a selection of typical system configurations is given in references (8,9,11-13) respectively.

The second factor concerning the effective simulation of an induction motor drive system relates to the modelling of the drive system itself. This may be considered in two parts. The first concerns the degree of mathematical representation considered necessary and the second concerns the driven mechanical system. The composite model (8,9) is formulated by taking account of the interaction between the electrical and mechanical sub-systems.

INDUCTION MOTOR MODELLING

The dynamic operation of the induction motor has been the object of detailed study for many years. The basic model used may be related to an elementary machine in which only the fundamental space harmonic of airgap magnetic field is considered and the assumptions made are clearly set out in the work of Stanley (1). For the purposes of the present paper it is required that the induction motor model must be capable of accurately simulating a direct on-line start condition and predicting behaviour in the for-ward speed region subsequent to various disturbing influences. In its most simple form the model is not sufficiently accurate to predict transient operation. However, by modifying the parameters to account for deep-bar effect and leakage flux path saturation good agreement between predicted and test characteristics may be obtained (5-10). In order to achieve a high level of simulation accuracy the basic model is modified in such a manner as to facilitate the variation of parameters, due to saturation and speed change effects, throughout the solution sequence.

The basic terminal equations (8) of the induction motor may be expressed in synchronously rotating axes as

$$p[i] = [L]^{-1}\{[v] - ([R] + \omega_r[G_1] + \omega_f[G_2])[i]\} - (1)$$

The explicit forms of the component matrices are given in references (8,14). The advantages in nominating a synchronously rotating frame of reference are mainly concerned in effecting a simplified and efficient computation. In this frame the need to transform between separate sets of axes, specified for individual machine types, is eliminated. In addition, in the steady state the vectors [V] and [i] of equation (1) are independent of time.

The torque produced by an induction motor is less than that computed from

$$T_e = [i]^t [G_1][i] \qquad\qquad --(2)$$

due to stray load loss. Stray loss is associated with parasitic torques that are produced in the machine owing to harmonic fields in the airgap. These harmonic fields are caused by the distribution of the stator and rotor windings in slots in the stator and rotor surfaces. In this paper it is assumed that the principal effects of these parasitic torques in the forward speed region are not present. However, an approximate estimation (12) of stray loss may be included by assuming that this loss varies approximately as the square of the current. In large motors this loss is about 0.1 - 1%. Nevertheless it should be included to avoid the possibility of over optimistic results being obtained.

Machine Parameter Variation

The terminal characteristics of induction motors are critically dependent on rotor resistance and the total leakage reactance. Rotor resistance varies due to the eddy currents which flow in the solid cage rotor conductors and the rotor leakage reactance is also varied by the interaction of the rotor-bar eddy currents, but in the case of the latter a more pronounced change is caused by the saturation of the iron associated with the leakage flux paths in the machine. Previous investigations (15) have considered this problem by considering a single rotor bar and its associated iron. However, in practice the saturation effect will differ with the position of the conductors and the simple approach very often gives an over estimation of the effect. Both a reduction in leakage reactance and an increase in rotor resistance gives rise to an increased steady-state starting torque. Approximate analytical and numerical methods (16) have been used quite successfully to study deep-bar effect in the dynamic state. The quasi-steady-state method usually favoured to represent the variation of these quantities is based on the steady-state values of resistance and reactance calculated for each speed within the range of interest. In the transient mode of operation the transient eddy currents are ignored. The fact that these pseudo steady-state techniques do give rise to satisfactory results, with an accuracy commensurate with that of the supplied data, should not mask the fact that these methods are essentially approximate in origin. An investigation (17) comparing the conventional method with an analysis based on the airgap and electromagnetic fields shows the difference in the variation of the rotor resistance and leakage reactance to be of the order of five percent at starting and virtually zero from half to full speed.

Equations in mechanical axes

The equations in the mechanical axes for various drive types take the general form (6-9)

$$p[\theta] = [A][\theta] + [B][u] \qquad --- (3)$$

The equations are formulated from the lumped inertias along the shafts and the corresponding shaft stiffnesses and damping coefficients. In general the stiffnesses are assumed to remain constant over the operating range except in the case of special couplings (7). In practice it has been found that mutual damping is dependent on the magnitude of the torque oscillations but the variation is usually small and generally ignored. The formulation of marine propeller drives is given in reference (9) and pump drives in reference (8).

SYSTEMS ANALYSED

To illustrate the accuracy of simulation for practical systems where attention is focussed on the performance of a particular induction motor drive two practical small systems are considered. The first concerns an induction motor driven variable pitch propeller drive (9) for which the starting performance on a limited supply is important. The second concerns a large induction motor driven water injection pump associated with an off-shore platform installation. Both examples involve the simulation of responses of a small self contained system. A diesel generation system is specified for the

marine application and a gas turbine generation system for the off-shore application. The system configuration for each test is given in Figures (1), (5) and (7). Principal data for each system are also provided.

Aspects of induction motor design for marine system

When considering the design of large motors for use in systems of limited generating capacity it is often desirable to specifically design the machine rather than use a standard design which may be less expensive to produce. The motor used in connection with the marine application were specifically designed to produce a pull-out torque of 2.3 pu and possess a good power factor. For standard machines in this size range a value of 1.8 pu for the pull-out torque would be more typical. The magnitude of the starting current is affected by the flux level, slot profile, number of slots and the winding configuration and the starting torque may be optimised by selecting specially shaped rotor bars to obtain the most advantages a.c. to d.c. resistance ratio. In addition larger frame sizes can increase efficiency albeit with a first cost penalty. It is essential with designs of this type to check the run-up curve at all speeds to ensure satisfactory operation especially with reduced voltage conditions. Rotor resistance may be required to be increased to give improved torque in the 70-90 percent speed region. Alternatively double cage rotors may be used.

SIMULATED AND SITE-TEST RESULTS

Marine system test 1 : Propulsion motor start

The system configuration for this test is shown in figure (1). The test is concerned with an emergency start condition i.e. the direct on-line starting of one 2240 kW motor on two diesel engine driven 4 MVA generators with a standing load on the auxiliary supply board of 0.92 MW. The transient responses of motor current from simulation and test are compared in Figures (2) and (3). Other system variables including motor torque, generator power and motor speed are given in Figures (4a - d).

Marine system test 2 : Motor start on high standing load

The system configuration for this test condition is shown in Figure (5). The test is concerned with the overall performance of the system subsequent to the run-up of the tenth and last motor in the system. The system is arranged to have a typical standing load representing 81 percent full load. Figure (6) illustrates the simulated results for the principal variables of interest.

Pump start

The system configuration for this test is shown in Figure (7). This test is concerned with the normal start of a 3.5 MW induction drive motor for a water injection pump. The supply consists of a single 14 MW gas turbine driven generator. The recorded test results for system voltage and motor current are shown in Figure (8) and the simulated results for these variables are shown in Figure (9). The simulated speed response for the motor is shown in Figure (10).

CONCLUSIONS

The results of the studies undertaken, which are to some extent validated by site-test results, serve to illustrate the need to include a representation of the system in addition to providing an induction motor formulation, capable of producing simulated responses of an accuracy commensurate with the tolerances in supplied data. This is clearly shown in the marine system tests where the system supply voltage and frequency are seen to vary appreciably. Both simulations associated with this system configuration are affected by the turbo-charged engine response. The first represents a start condition from a low standing load and the second from a high standing load. The effect of the turbo-charger improving the transient response (9) of the engine will be restricted in both cases leading to a small extension to the run-up time of the motors. In the assessment of an induction drive responses or the interacting responses of several induction machines many planned operating conditions may be catered for if a rigorous representation of the system is formulated. Although a general form of analysis based on traditional methods may be used, the degree of representation for the drives should be such that all aspects of the modelling of the electrical and mechanical system should be enhanced to include the complete shaft dynamics, including gear boxes and clutch mechanisms, together with a systematic simulation of the switching and protection representation.

REFERENCES

1. Stanley, H.C.: 'An analysis of the induction motor', AIEE. Trans., Vol. 57, 1938, pp 751-755.

2. Krause, P.C., and Thomas, C.M.: 'Simulation of symmetrical induction machinery', IEEE Trans., Vol. PAS-84, No. 11, 1965, pp 1038-1053.

3. Smith, I.R. and Sriheran, S.: 'Transient performance of the induction motor', Proc. IEE, Vol. 113 (7), 1966, pp 1173-1182.

4. Slater, R.P., Wood, W.S., Flynn, F.P. and Simpson, R.: 'Digital computation of induction motor transient torque patterns', Proc. IEE, Vol. 113 (5), 1966, pp 819-822.

5. Smith, J.R., Penman, J. and Abd-Allah, H.: 'The simulation of the transient response of singly excited electrical machines', Int. J. Comp. in Elect. Engg., Vol. 3 (3), 1977, pp 271-279.

6. Middlemiss, J.J.: 'Current pulsation of induction motor driving a reciprocating compressor', Proc. IEE, Vol. 121 (11), 1974, pp 1399-1403.

7. Binns, K.J., Smith, J.R., Buckley, G.W. and Lewis, M.: 'Pre-determination of current and torque requirements of an induction motor driven steel-bar rolling-mill', Proc. IEE, Vol. 124 (11), 1977, pp 1019-1025.

8. Smith, J.R., Rogers, G.J., and Buckley, G.W.: 'Application of induction motor simulation models to power station auxiliary drives', IEEE Trans., Vol. PAS-98, No. 5, 1979, pp 1824-1831.

9. Smith, J.R., Stronach, A.F., Tsao, T. and Goodman, K.A.: 'Prediction of the transient response of marine systems incorporating induction motor propulsion drives', Proc. IEE, Vol. 127, Pt. B (5), 1980. pp 308-316.

10. Lloyd, M.R., Smith, J.R., and Buckley: 'The prediction of the torque and current requirements for large induction motor drives', IEE Conf. Pub. No. (170), 1978, pp 81-90.

11. Ho Henberg, M.S.: 'Simplified stability analysis of a distribution system in a chemical plant with induction motors', Proc. IEE, Vol. 122 (4), 1925, pp 421-427.

12. Kalsi, S.S., Stephen, D.D. and Adkins, O.: 'Calculation of system fault currents due to induction motors', Proc. IEE, Vol. 118 (1), 1971, pp 201-214.

13. Sriharam, S.: 'Digital simulation of a group of induction motors', Proc. IEE., Vol. 122 (12), 1975, pp 1399-1401.

14. Rogers, G.J.: 'Linearised analysis of induction motor transients', Proc. IEE, Vol. 112 (10), 1965, pp 1917-1926.

15. Agawal, P.D. and Alger, P.L.: 'Saturation factors for leakage reactance of induction motors', IEEE Trans. 1961, pp 1037-1042.

16. Jones, P.E. Mullineux, N., Reed, J.R., and Stoll, R.L.: 'Solid rectangular and 'T' shaped conductors in semi-closed slots', J. Eng. Math., Vol. 3 (2), 1969, pp 123-135.

17. Rogers, G.J. and Benaragama, D.S.: 'An induction motor model with deep-bar effect and leakage inductance saturation', Archiu fur Elektrotechnik, Vol. 60, 1978, pp 193-201.

18. Smith, J.R., Abd-Allah, H.M. and Jones, K.M.: 'Prediction of torsional oscillations in turbo-generator units connected to series compensated transmission systems', Proc. IEE, Vol. 126 (5), 1979, pp 411-420.

PRINCIPAL SYMBOLS AND PLANT DETAILS
Marine System

D	diesel engine 3.53 MW rated, 4.1 MW max., 1000 rpm
G	generators, 4MVA, 6p
M_9, M_{10}	pump motors 2.23 KW, 1480 rpm
M_1, M_2, M_7, M_8	main propulsion motors, 2.24 MW, 1480 rpm
$M_3 - M_6$	thruster motors 1.49 MW, 990 rpm
GB	gearbox
C	pneumatic clutch, max torque 3 x f.L. torque
P	pump
T_1, T_2	transformers 6.6 KV/415V 2.25 MVA, Dy 11 .
$M_{S1} - M_{S11}$	auxiliary drive motors

Platform System

T	gas turbine, 14.2 MW; 6500 rpm
GB	gearbox
G	generator, 18 MVA; 1800 rpm; 60 Hz
M	water injection pump motor, 3.6 MW; 3600 rpm
P	water injection pump

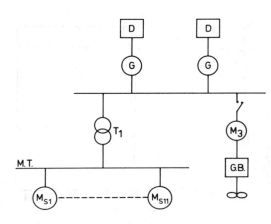

Fig. 1

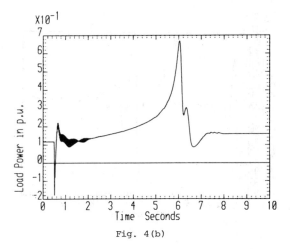

Fig. 4(b)

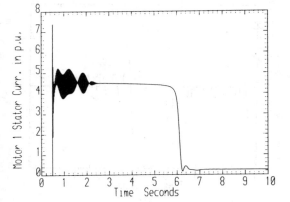

Fig. 2

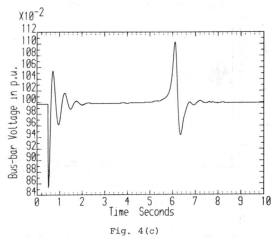

Fig. 4(c)

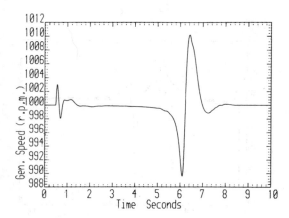

Horizontal scale 1 sec/division
Vertical scale 2.66 current/division
Fig. 3

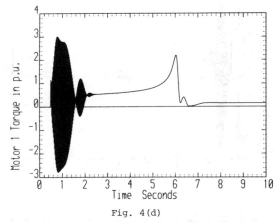

Fig. 4(d)

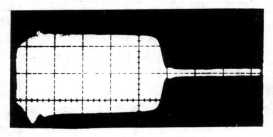

Fig. 4(a)

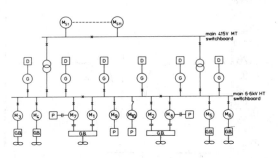

Full Marine System Representation
Fig. 5

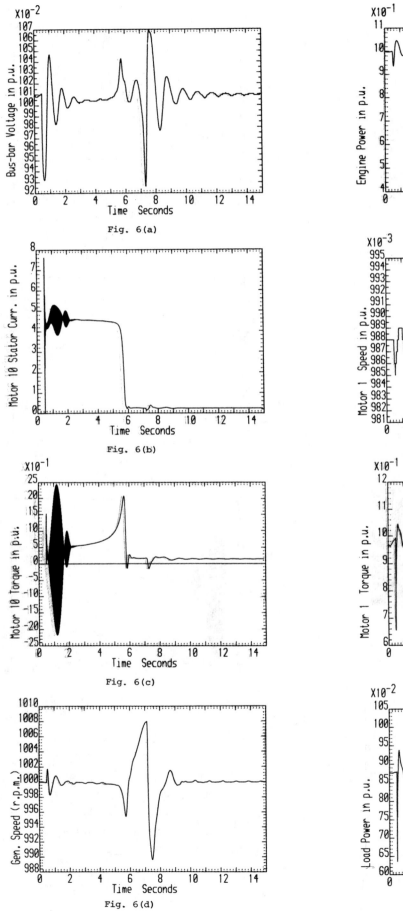

Fig. 6(a)

Fig. 6(b)

Fig. 6(c)

Fig. 6(d)

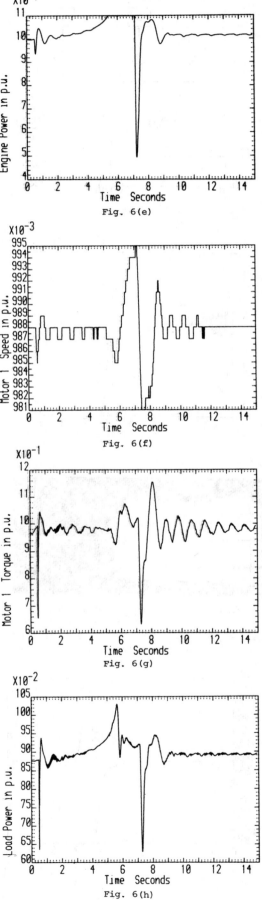

Fig. 6(e)

Fig. 6(f)

Fig. 6(g)

Fig. 6(h)

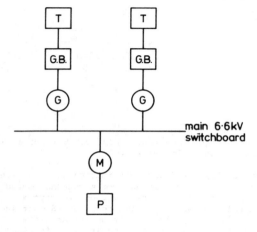

Fig. 7

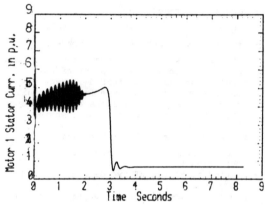

Fig. 9(a)

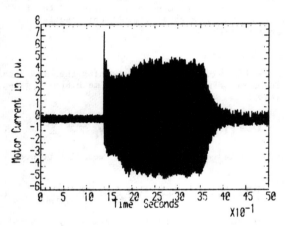

Fig. 8(a)

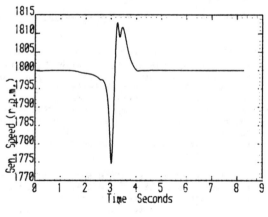

Fig. 9(b)

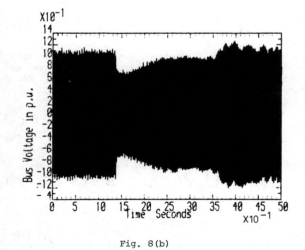

Fig. 8(b)

Fig. 10

TRANSIENT PERFORMANCE OF INDUCTION MOTORS IN ELECTROMECHANICAL SYSTEMS

M.R. Lloyd

Laurence, Scott and Electromotors Limited, U.K.

LIST OF PRINCIPAL SYMBOLS

R_1 - stator winding phase resistance

R_{21} - total rotor winding referred resistance (no saturation and no deep bar effects)

R_{2s} - total rotor winding referred resistance (saturation and deep bar effect included at stall)

R_{22} - rotor winding referred resistance of effective second cage for sub-transient calculation

W_1 - supply angular velocity = $2\pi f$

X_m - magnetising reactance

X_1 - stator leakage reactance (unsaturated)

X_{1s} - stator leakage reactance (saturated)

X_{21} - total rotor winding referred leakage reactance (no saturation and no deep bar effects)

X_{2s} - total rotor winding referred leakage reactance (saturation and deep bar effects at stall)

X_{22} - rotor winding referred leakage reactance of effective second cage for sub-transient calculation

g_m - rotor rotational voltage coefficients

g_r - frame of reference rotational voltage coefficients

Θ_1, Θ_2 - angular positions of two degree of freedom system

J_1, J_2 - moments of inertia of two degree of freedom system

C - combined torsional damping coefficient of coupling and shafts

K - combined torsional stiffness of coupling and shafts

W_r - rotor angular velocity

W_f - frame of reference angular velocity

INTRODUCTION

The transient performance of electrical machines has received increasing attention over the last few years. This is primarily due to the application of digital computers to large and sophisticated models of electromechanical systems (Humpage et al (1)). The increasing power and solution speeds of modern digital computers reduces the need to make simplifying assumptions in the electrical machine model (Kalsi and Adkin (2), Rogers (3)).

The induction motor model requires special attention due to the complex parameter variation caused by the non-linear effects of leakage flux path saturation and deep bar effects in the rotor circuits. Correct assessment of these non-linearities requires the calculation of leakage reactances and resistances to be constantly modified by rotor speed and conductor current (Smith et al (4)). These parameters are then used in a step by step solution of the system equations to evaluate transient torques and currents during various system disturbances (Lloyd (5)).

With the increasing system short circuit levels currently being installed, larger induction motor units are being considered. For these increasing unit powers the fault contribution of induction motors becomes more important and the correct prediction of the machine performance under these conditions is required

for the design of suitable short circuit protection in the system (Kalsi et al (6)).

Traditionally the fault contribution of induction motors has been calculated from a constant speed evaluation of the machine equations to give a transient reactance and time constant (Slater and Wood (7)). Using the full transient analysis of the machine the fault contribution is found to also exhibit a sub-transient reactance. The traditional constant speed analysis is refined to give these two reactances. A comparison is then given of the two calculated values against actual test results on a large induction motor.

SOLUTION METHOD

The familiar matrix equation governing the electrical performance of rotating electrical machines is given by (Lloyd and Smith (8)):-

$$v = ir + lpi + ig_mw_r + ig_rw_f \qquad (1)$$

with suitable re-arrangement this equation becomes:-

$$pi = l^{-1}v - l^{-1}(r + g_mw_r + g_rw_f)i \qquad (2)$$

Once the current matrix has been solved by integrating equation (2) the electrical air gap torque is calculated from:-

$$t_e = ig_mi^t \qquad (3)$$

However a particular electromechanical system cannot be uniquely represented by equations (1) - (3) unless the mechanical features are correctly modelled. For example a two-degree of freedom system will require the following additional equations:-

$$t_e = j_1p^2\theta_1 + k(\theta_1 - \theta_2) + cp(\theta_1 - \theta_2) \qquad (4)$$

$$k(\theta_1 - \theta_2) = j_2p^2\theta_2 - cp(\theta_1 - \theta_2) + t_L \qquad (5)$$

In the same manner as for the electrical circuits all non-linearities such as gearbox backlash and non-linear shaft and coupling stiffnesses must be included to correctly predict the system performance (Bishop and Mayer (9)).

The system equations (1) - (5) are arranged in single order differential equation form and then solved by an integration technique such as the Runge-Kutta or Predictor-Corrector method (Buckley et al (10)).

COMPUTER PROGRAMME

The solution of the differential equations governing the electrical machine performance are exceedingly complex and several techniques are used to simplify them. If the three phase equations are retained for the electrical machine there are mutual flux linkage terms that are functions of position and time. The inversion and multiplication of matrices containing such complex variable values is very time consuming if computer subroutines and packages are used. The additional problem of parameter variations in the equations further complicates the solution technique.

The transformation to a d-q axis model simplifies the electrical machine equations sufficiently to enable longhand inversion and multiplication of the machine matrices prior to use in the integration routines. The elimination of computer subroutines to perform these operations gives a considerable saving in computer storage and running times as well as simplifying the inclusion of parameter variation. Additionally the choice of a frame of reference relevant to the particular problem reduces the need for very small step lengths in the integration routine (typically 5 milliseconds is sufficient for fault calculation if a synchronously rotating frame is used).

By using d-q axis transformations and a suitable speed for the frame of reference the majority of balanced operating conditions can be considered. However if unbalanced fault conditions require evaluation it is more convenient to work directly in phase variables and tolerate the increased computing times for these particular problems.

INDUCTION MOTOR PARAMETER VARIATION (Smith and Hamill (11)).

The current in the stator windings of an induction motor during transient conditions, such as starting, reswitching and fault conditions is much greater than the normal rated current. Because of this the iron associated with the stator and rotor leakage flux paths becomes saturated and the effective leakage reactance is reduced. Also in many machines, particularly those with deep rotor bars (normally in excess of 25 mm for copper), the eddy currents induced by the slot leakage flux at power frequencies are significant and these also reduce the leakage reactance and at the same time, increase the effective rotor resistance. A reduction in leakage reactance gives rise to increased values of transient currents and torques while an increase in rotor resistance will increase torque values while reducing the time constants of the transient phenomenon. Hence clearly the accuracy with which predictions can be made is based on the correct assessment of the machine parameter variation during the transient period.

The Representation of Deep Bar Effects (Jones et al (12), Silvester (13)).

There are two distinct methods of representing this phenomenon. The first is quasi-static in which the steady state values of resistance and reactance are calculated for a particular speed that occurs during the transient period. This is achieved by using either analytical solutions which exist for certain common bar shapes or ladder network approximations when the rotor bar geometry is too complex to permit a reasonable analytical solution. In both cases the transient eddy currents are ignored. To overcome this problem a second method is to include extra circuital equations which represent coupled coils. The parameters of the coils can be calculated from a modal analysis of the rotor bar. If the slot geometry is complex the eddy modes can be calculated by using a discretised field solution.

In very large motors the rotor bars are usually rectangular and the resistance, self and mutual inductance between the coils representing the eddy current effects and the main rotor circuit can be easily derived. Test results have confirmed that four

eddy-current modes are sufficient for use in a transient model of a large machine with a deep rectangular bar, although for other geometries more modes may be necessary to account for the peripheral field variation.

The Representation of Leakage Inductance Saturation (Agarwal and Alger (14), Swann and Solomon (15)).

Several authors have analysed this problem by considering a single isolated slot and its associated iron. It is generally accepted that the tooth lips are the first part of the iron circuit to saturate. This is not necessarily the case as other parts of the iron circuit can saturate, depending on the shape of the magnetic circuit. Since the principle of superposition can no longer be accurately applied to a saturated magnetic path, the calculation of separate saturated leakage reactances will give some errors. The method used in these simulations is related to a general geometry and evaluates the saturation of an area carrying several flux components, some of which may be limited by saturation elsewhere in the machine magnetic circuit. All the fluxes are then added vectorily to obtain the total flux.

The accuracy with which saturation can be assessed is related to the modelling of the B-H characteristics of the core lamination material. This should also allow for permeability variation that can occur with large diameter segmental stator cores.

THREE PHASE FAULT CONTRIBUTION OF AN INDUCTION MOTOR

D-Q Model Solution

When the terminals of an induction motor are shorted there is a flow of electrical energy towards the fault at the expense of the rotor kinetic energy. The accurate calculation of this fault contribution is required for the rating of circuit breakers, cables and ancillary equipment. The magnitude of the initial fault current peak is a function of the machine design parameters, the loading of the machine and the location of the fault. Figure 1 shows the calculated asymmetrical current magnitudes for a three phase fault at the motor terminals of a 4000 kW 4 pole unloaded induction motor.

Close examination of the fault current waveform reveals a transient and sub-transient period of differing time constants and peak values as given in Figure 2. This result would appear to be contrary to the theory of synchronous machines where the presence of a sub-transient and a transient reactance is due to two rotor windings i.e. a field winding and a damping winding. A squirrel cage machine has only one winding but still exhibits a sub-transient reactance. The reason for this is the presence of rotor deep-bar effect and the saturation of leakage flux paths. The effect of these non-linearities is to produce an effective second cage which produces the sub-transient phenomenon.

Constant Speed Solution (Lyon (16)).

When the speed of the machine is assumed constant during the period of the fault condition then the machine equations can be linearised and solved directly.

If the impedance of the actual squirrel cage is represented by $Z_{21} = R_{21} + jX_{21}$ under the conditons of no saturation and no deep bar effect; a second parallel impedance, $Z_{22} = R_{22} + jX_{22}$, can be calculated such that the combined impedance of Z_{21} and Z_{22} gives the stall impedance of the rotor, $Z_{2s} = R_{2s} + jX_{2s}$. Z_{22} then represents an effective cage that allows for the saturation and deep bar effects at stall. A further refinement is to allow for saturation around the stator slots by considering the saturated stator leakage reactance.

The transient and sub-transient reactances and time constants for "double-cage" induction motors are of course related to the two physical cages.

$$\text{If} \quad Y = \frac{R_{2s}}{X_{2s}^2 + R_{2s}^2} - \frac{R_{21}}{X_{21}^2 + R_{21}^2} \qquad (6)$$

$$Z = \frac{X_{2s}}{X_{2s}^2 + R_{2s}^2} - \frac{X_{21}}{X_{21}^2 + R_{21}^2} \qquad (7)$$

$$\text{then} \quad R_{22} = \frac{Y}{Z^2 + Y^2} \quad \text{and} \quad X_{22} = \frac{Z}{Z^2 + Y^2} \qquad (8),(9)$$

and the transient and sub-transient reactances become

$$X' = X_1 + \frac{X_{21} X_m}{X_{21} + X_m} \qquad (10)$$

$$X'' = X_{1s} + \frac{X_m X_{21} X_{22}}{X_m X_{21} + X_{21} X_{22} + X_m X_{22}} \qquad (11)$$

These reactances are shown in operational impedance form $(X(jsw))$ in Figure 3.

The relevant time constants are calculated from:-

$$T_a = \frac{X''}{W_1 R_1} \quad \text{secs} \qquad (12)$$

$$T' = \frac{1}{W_1 R_{21}} \left[\frac{X_m X_1}{X_m + X_1} + X_{21} \right] \quad \text{secs} \qquad (13)$$

$$T'' = \frac{1}{W_1 R_{22}} \left[\frac{X_m X_{1s} X_{21}}{X_m X_{21} + X_{1s} X_{21} + X_m X_{1s}} + X_{22} \right] \quad \text{secs} \qquad (14)$$

These time constants and reactances can then be used to calculate the peak asymmetrical currents occurring under three phase fault conditions using the design parameters from the motor equivalent circuit values.

$$\hat{I}_{asm} = 1.41 \left[\left(\frac{1}{X''} - \frac{1}{X'} \right) e^{-\frac{1}{2t''f}} + \frac{1}{X'} e^{-\frac{1}{2t'f}} + \frac{1}{X''} e^{-\frac{1}{2t_af}} \right] \qquad (15)$$

For the calculation of unsymmetrical fault conditions similar equations can be derived involving zero, negative and positive sequence impedances (Lloyd (17)).

RESULTS

A 4000 kW 4 pole unloaded induction motor was disconnected from the supply and subsequently shorted across its terminals. This involves running the motor at an overvoltage prior to disconnection and then timing the circuit breaker closure to coincide with the motor terminal voltage equalling the normal internal airgap voltage. This sequence in fact requires initiation of the closure of one circuit breaker (to produce the fault) before the opening of

the other (to isolate from the supply). The magnitude of the resulting current in each phase was recorded on an oscillogram. The process was repeated numerous times to obtain peak asymmetrical currents in each phase in turn. A representative oscillogram is shown in Figure 4. From these traces values of the transient and sub-transient reactances and time constants were calculated. These are compared to the values calculated from the full dynamic model and the constant speed solution in Table 1.

The results confirm that the speed of the motor remains nearly constant during the first few cycles of the fault but thereafter begins to decrease giving shorter transient and armature time constants than calculated by the constant speed calculation.

TABLE 1 - Short Circuit Values for 4000 kW, 4 Pole Induction Motor.

Value	Constant Speed Model	D-Q Model	Test Result
X' pu	0.268	0.248	0.257
X'' pu	0.174	0.167	0.160
T' secs	0.17	0.12	0.10
T'' secs	0.014	0.015	0.013
T_a secs	0.048	0.052	0.048
$\hat{I}_{asy}$ pu	13.0	13.8	13.7
Speed Change rpm/sec	0	146	150

CONCLUSIONS

An initial assessment of the fault contribution of an induction motor can be made using manufacturers data in the formula described in this paper. If the decay of the fault current is required beyond the first few cycles then a full dynamic solution will give more reliable answers. These conclusions are supported by test results on an unloaded industrial induction machine.

REFERENCES

1. Humpage, W.D., Durrani, T.E., and Carvalno, V.F., 1969, "Dynamic-response analysis of inter-connected synchronous-asynchronous machine groups", Proc. IEE, 116, 2015-2027.

2. Kalsi, S.S., and Adkin, B., 1971, "Transient stability of power systems containing both synchronous and induction machines", Proc. IEE, 118, 1467.

3. Rogers, G.J., 1965, "Linearised analysis of induction motor transients", Proc. IEE, 112, 1917-1926.

4. Smith, J.R., Penman, J., and Abd-Allah, H., 1977, "The simulation of the transient response of singly excited electrical machines", Int. Journ. of Comp. in Elec.Eng., 3, 271-279.

5. Lloyd, M.R., 1978, "Transient and oscillatory torques in Rotating Electric Machines", LSE Eng. Bulletin, 14, 17-21.

6. Kalsi, S.S., et al, 1971, "Calculation of system fault currents due to induction motors", Proc. IEE, 118, 201-215.

7. Slater, R.D., and Wood, W.S., 1967, "Constant speed solutions applied to the evaluation of

induction motor transient torque peaks", Proc. IEE, 114, 1429-1435.

8. Lloyd, M.R., and Smith, J.R., November 1978, "The prediction of the torque and current requirements for large induction motor drives", IEE colloquium on the design and maintenance of large industrial drives.

9. Bishop, and Mayer, October 1976, "A case for the high fidelity analysis of non-linear electro-mechanical system dynamics", IEEE Conference, Chicago, Paper No. 20A, 544-551.

10. Buckley, G.W., et al, 1978, "Application of induction motor simulation models to power system and industrial applications", 13th UPE Conference, Heriot-Watt Univ.

11. Smith, I.R., and Hamill, B., 1973, "Effect of parameter variations on induction motor transients", Proc. IEE, 120, 1489-1492.

12. Jones, D.E., et al, 1969, "Solid rectangular and T-shaped conductors in semi-closed slots", Journ. of Engrg. Maths, 3, 123-135.

13. Silvester, P., 1968, "Dynamic resistance and inductance of slot embedded conductors", IEEE Trans. PAS-87, 250-256.

14. Agarwal, P.D., and Alger, P.L., 1961, "Saturation factors for leakage reactance of induction motors", IEEE Trans. 1037-1042.

15. Swann S.A., and Solomon, W., 1963, "Effective resistance and reactance of a rectangular conductor placed in a semi-closed slot", Proc. IEE, 110.

16. Lyon, W.V., 1954, "Transient analysis of alternating current machinery", Wiley.

17. Lloyd, M.R., January 1981, "Dynamic starting performance of synchronous motors", IEE colloquium on Performance of Electromechanical Systems:- Prediction, Simulation, Experience."

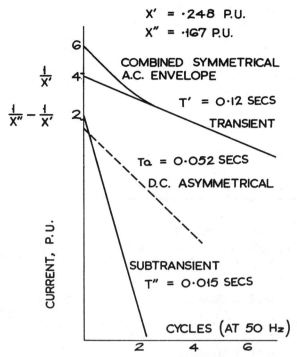

$X' = \cdot248$ P.U.

$X'' = \cdot167$ P.U.

COMBINED SYMMETRICAL A.C. ENVELOPE

$T' = 0\cdot12$ SECS

TRANSIENT

$T_a = 0\cdot052$ SECS

D.C. ASYMMETRICAL

SUBTRANSIENT

$T'' = 0\cdot015$ SECS

CYCLES (AT 50 Hz)

FIGURE 2 : TYPICAL TRANSIENT AND SUBTRANSIENT REACTANCES AND ASSOCIATED TIME CONSTANTS

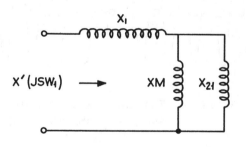

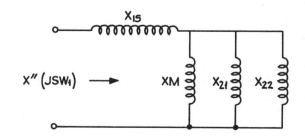

FIGURE 3 : EQUIVALENT CIRCUITS FOR TRANSIENT AND SUBTRANSIENT REACTANCES

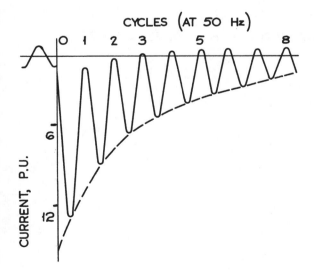

FIGURE 1 : TYPICAL ASYMMETRICAL PHASE CURRENT FOLLOWING A 3 PHASE FAULT ON AN INDUCTION MOTOR

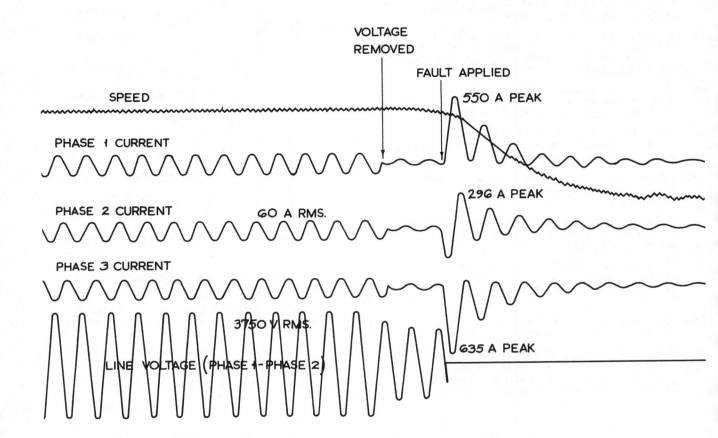

FIGURE 4 : TYPICAL OSCILLOGRAM OF PHASE CURRENT FOLLOWING 3 PHASE
FAULT ON AN INDUCTION MOTOR

ELECTROMECHANICAL PROBLEMS OF LINEAR INDUCTION MOTORS WITH ANISOTROPIC SECONDARY PART

L. Szentirmai - F. Tóth

Technical University for Heavy Industry, Miskolc, Hungary

INTRODUCTION

In recent years interest has been focussed on the application of linear induction motors to transportation, control and storage systems. As a consequence variable special devices are required for differing applications and the no-load speed should be determined in accordance with the system parameters concerned.

Linear induction motors (l.i.m) can be classified into 3 categories according to their speed such as low-speed - up to 3 m/s - mean speed - ranging between 3 and 15 m/s - and finally high-speed motors - up to approximately 150 m/s speed. The lowspeed l.i.m is employed mainly in automatically operated processes and robot - techniques, the mean speed machines could be advantageous for internal transport, forwarding and conveyor systems employed in industry as well as for city transport. The high-speed motors should be preferred in fast transportation systems e.g. for long distance inter-city operations.

It is well known that the efficiency of linear motors is far lower than that for rotating machines', although the principle of operation does not differ in a significant way (1). This low efficiency stops the wide-spread employment of l.i.m particularly at the present time when great efforts are made to reduce energy-consumption all over the world.

First of all it is worth mentioning the effect of the air-gap which is far wider here than in the traditional rotating machine. Owing to the longer air-gap, the excitation current of l.i.m is higher, and the power factor will be decreased. In addition to low efficiency, the other disadvantage of l.i.m is low power-factor, thus the utilization factor of l.i.m will be less for the condition when the volume and ventilation plus cooling relations are equal to a rotating machine.

However, the efficiency and power factor of a l.i.m provided with non-ferromagnetic secondary part can be increased by reducing the relative air-gap. The basis of a new configuration, illustrated in Figure la, is that there are gaps milled into the non-ferromagnetic secondary part and these gaps are filled with favourable ferromagnetic material. In this way the secondary part loses its isotropic character and at the same time the computation of motor parameters becomes more difficult.

This paper deals with the computation of the electromechanical problems of such a l.i.m. To simplify computation the real l.i.m presented in Figure la should be substituted by an ideal mathematical model.

MATHEMATICAL MODEL

To create the mathematical model of l.i.m (Fig. lb) a few simplifications should be introduced as follows:
a) The air-gap has a constant value and the effect of the primary winding is taken into consideration by Carter-factor k_C:

$$\delta' = k_C \delta \tag{1}$$

b) The primary part has infinite length and width, then its magnetic permeability $\mu_{Fe} = \infty$ and electric conductivity

$$\sigma_{Fe} = 0.$$

c) The primary winding can be considered as a very thin layer, and thus the current carried in it can be determined by peripheral current (2):

$$\vec{K}_1 = K_{1m} e^{i(\omega t - ax)} , \tag{2}$$

where τ is the pole pitch of the primary part, ω is the angular frequency of mains and $a = \pi/\tau$. The amplitude of peripheral current is:

$$K_{1m} = \frac{\sqrt{2} \, m_1 \, \omega \, \xi_1}{p\tau} I_1 \tag{3}$$

where m_1 is the number of phases, p is the number of poles and ξ_1 is the winding factor. The direction of primary current in the z-direction.

d) The secondary part is moving in the x-direction with velocity $\underline{v}$ i.e. $v = v_o(1 - s)$ and $v_o = 2\tau f$

where $\underline{s}$ denotes the slip.

e) The secondary part provided with the anisotropic configuration can be substituted by a particular model which can be considered an isotropic part regarding electrical machine computational methods (3) and it has the following features:

σ electric conductivity can be obtained from the formula of

$$\sigma_{mean} = \sigma_{Al} \frac{\Delta}{t} \tag{4}$$

where Δ is the distance between two gaps provided with aluminium within modulus $\underline{t}$ as shown in Fig. la.

Magnetic permeability in the x-direction is given by:

$$\mu_x = \frac{t}{\dfrac{t - \Delta}{\mu_{Fe}} + \dfrac{\Delta}{\mu_o}} \tag{5}$$

and magnetic permeability in the y-direction is given by:

$$\mu_y = \frac{\mu_{Fe}(t-\Delta) + \mu_o \Delta}{t} \tag{6}$$

f) It should also be noted that x, y, z coordinates are attached to the primary part.

g) The width of the secondary part has a finite value, thus a correction factor should be introduced for computation according to (4) as follows:

$$K_s = 1 - \frac{th\left(\dfrac{\pi b}{\tau}\right)}{(1 + th\frac{\pi b}{\tau} \, th\frac{(\ell - b)}{\tau})\frac{\pi b}{\tau}} \tag{7}$$

where 2ℓ is the width of the secondary part and $2b$ is the width of the primary part.

MAGNETIC FIELD OF PRIMARY AND SECONDARY PARTS

The magnetic field of the air-gap and the secondary part can be computed by the employment of Maxwell's equations. They can be simplified by the introduction of vector-potential $\overline{A}$ as follows that,

For the air-gap it is evident:

$$\frac{\partial^2 \overline{A}_\delta}{\partial x^2} + \frac{\partial^2 \overline{A}_\delta}{\partial y^2} = 0 \tag{8}$$

and for the secondary part we obtain:

$$\frac{1}{\mu y}\frac{\partial^2 \overline{A}_2}{\partial x^2} + \frac{1}{\mu x}\frac{\partial^2 \overline{A}_2}{\partial y^2} + i\sigma_{mean}\overline{A}_2\, \omega +$$

$$+ \sigma_{mean}\, v\, \frac{A_2}{x} \tag{9}$$

where $\overline{A} = A_m e^{-iax}$.

After differentiation of equations (8) and (9) twice for x then re-arranging them we obtain:

$$\frac{\partial^2 \overline{A}_\delta}{\partial y^2} = a^2\, \overline{A}_\delta \tag{10}$$

and

$$\frac{\partial^2 \overline{A}_2}{\partial y^2} = \beta^2\, \overline{A}_2 \tag{11}$$

where $\beta = \sqrt{\dfrac{\mu x}{\mu y}\, a^2 + i\, \mu x\, \omega\, s\, \sigma_{mean}}$

The form of solution of equations (10) and (11) may be expressed as:

$$A_\delta = D_1 e^{(ay)} + D_2 e^{(-ay)} \tag{12}$$

$$A_2 = R_1 e^{(\beta y)} + R_2 e^{(-\beta y)} \tag{13}$$

where the constants D_1, D_2, R_1 and R_2 may be calculated from the determination of limiting conditions as follows:

1) at the primary part and air-gap junction:

$$\frac{\overline{B}_{1x}}{\mu_{Fe}} - \frac{\overline{B}_{\delta x}}{\mu_o} = \overline{K}_1 \tag{14}$$

2) in the central line of the secondary part:

$$\overline{B}_{2y} = 0 \quad \text{and} \quad \overline{B}_{2x} = 0 \tag{15}$$

3) at the secondary part and the air-gap junction:

$$\overline{B}_{\delta y} = \overline{B}_{2y} \tag{16}$$

$$\frac{\overline{B}_{\delta x}}{\mu_o} = \frac{\overline{B}_{2x}}{\mu_x} \tag{17}$$

from which we obtain:

$$D_1 = R_e^{-ac}(ch(\beta c) + \frac{\mu_o}{\mu_x}\, \frac{\beta}{a}\, sh(\beta c)\,) \tag{18}$$

$$D_2 = R_e^{ac}(sh(\beta c) - \frac{\mu_o}{\mu_x}\, \frac{\beta}{a}\, sh(\beta c)\,) \tag{19}$$

$$R = -\frac{K_{1m}}{N} \quad : \quad R_1 = R_2 = R \tag{20}$$

where

$$N = \frac{a}{\mu_o}\, ch(\beta c)\, sh(a\delta) + \frac{\beta}{\mu_x}\, sh(\beta c)\, ch(a\delta) \tag{21}$$

After substituting the constants, the following formulas can be obtained for the values of vector-potential:

$$\vec{A}_\delta = -\frac{K_{1m}}{N}\, (ch(\beta c)\, ch\, a(y-c) + \frac{\mu_o}{\mu_x}\, \frac{\beta}{a}\, sh(\beta c)$$

$$sh\, a(y-c)\,)\, e^{i(\omega t - ax)} \tag{22}$$

$$A_2 = -\frac{K_{1m}}{N}\, (ch(\beta y))\, e^{i(\omega t - ax)} \tag{23}$$

We are now in the position to ascertain the values of vector-potential, therefore the characteristic parameters of l.i.m such as air-gap power, tractive force, losses, etc., can be determined in an accurate way.

AIR-GAP POWER, TRACTIVE FORCE AND EFFICIENCY

The power per unit surface flowing through the air-gap into the secondary part can be determined by the employment of Poynting-vector:

$$\overline{S}_\delta = -\frac{1}{2}\, (\overline{E}_{\delta zm}\, \overline{H}^*_{\delta xm}) \tag{24}$$

where

$$\overline{H}_{\delta x} = \frac{1}{\mu_o}\, \frac{\partial \overline{A}_\delta}{\partial y}\bigg|_{y=c+\delta}$$

$$\overline{E}_{\delta z} = -\frac{\partial \overline{A}_\delta}{\partial t}\bigg|_{y=c+\delta}$$

The tractive force per unit surface or in other words the tractive force density of the secondary part is:

$$f_x = -\frac{1}{2}\, Re\left\{\, \overline{i}_{2m}\, B^*_{2ym}\,\right\} \tag{25}$$

The magnetic induction and current density in the secondary part can be expressed also with vector-potential:

$$\overline{B}_{2y} = -\frac{\partial \overline{A}_2}{\partial x} = -ia\, \frac{\overline{K}_1}{N}\, ch(\beta y)$$

$$\overline{i}_2 = -i\sigma_{mean}\, \omega s\, \overline{A}_2 = i\sigma_{mean}\, \omega s\, \frac{\overline{K}_1}{N}\, ch(\beta y)$$

After substituting these two latest formulas into equation (25) the tractive force density will be:

$$f_x = \frac{1}{2}\, Re\left\{\, a\sigma_{mean}\, \omega s\, \frac{K^2_{1m}}{NN^*}\, ch(\beta y)\, ch(\beta^* y)\,\right\} \tag{26}$$

Tractive force per unit surface can be given as:

$$F_x = f_x \int_o^c dy$$

Mechanical power per unit surface can be obtained from:

$$P_M = F_x\, v \tag{27}$$

The effective power per unit surface into the secondary part across the air-gap can be obtained from:

$$P_2 = Re\left\{\, S_\delta\,\right\} \tag{28}$$

The objective of this paper is to make a comparison between the parameters of two l.i.m both having the same primary but two quite different, anisotropic and isotropic secondary parts.

If we suppose that the current-input of the primary is constant i.e. K_1 has a constant value and if on the other hand the power-input of the primary part is neglected, then the efficiency and power factor may be considered to be comparative figures and they can be expressed by the following formulas:

$$\eta = \frac{P_M}{P_2} \qquad (29)$$

$$\cos \rho = \frac{P_2}{S_\delta} \qquad (30)$$

COMPUTATION AND LABORATORY FINDINGS

The results of computations are given in Figures 2, 3 and 4 and obtained from equations (24) - (30). Synchronous speed in Figure 2 is $v_o = 3$ m/s while in Figure 3:6 and in Figure 4: $v_o = 9$ m/s.

The results given in Figures 2-4 are referred to that case where the weights of aluminium conductor in an anisotropic part is equal to an anisotropic secondary part's weight. Thus, it is supposed that $\Delta = t/2$ for both parts and the thickness of isotropic secondary part is c = 2 mm, and further the thickness of the anisotropic secondary part is c = 4 mm and the air-gap is δ = 5 mm.

The results seen in the figures show that the characteristics of a l.i.m provided with anisotropic secondary part (dashed line) gives a better result at each computed speed than the motor with the isotropic secondary part (full line).

The computation results have been verified by laboratory measurements performed with a model made in Bulgaria. The basic parameters of the model were as follows:
rated voltage 380 V, pole-pitch 0.0378 m, number of poles 8, width 0.1 m, width of secondary part 0.2 m, thickness of secondary part 0.002 m. Aluminium material used for the isotropic part and aluminium plus iron were employed for the anisotropic secondary part, in the latter configuration Δ = 0.01 m, and t = 0.02 m. The air-gap between primary and secondary part was 0.003 mm.

The results taken by both computation and laboratory measurement at slip s = 1 are presented in Table 1.

REFERENCES

1. Laithwaite, E.R.: Induction machines for special purposes. Chemical Publishing Co Im., New-York, 1966. 337 page.

2. Poloujadoff, M.: The Theory of Linear Induction Machinery, Oxford, 1980. 276 page.

3. Mischin, E.: Theory of the Squirrel-cage Induction Machine Derived Directly from Maxwell's Field Equation. The Quarterly Journal of Mechanics and Applied Mathematics 1954. vol. VII. Part 4, page 472-487.

4. Bolton, H.: Transverse Edge Effect in Sheet-rotor Induction Motors. Proc. IEE, vol. 116, No.5, MAY 1969, 725-731 page.

TABLE 1 - Comparative figures for two l.i.m having isotropic and anisotropic secondary part

		L.I.M with Isotropic secondary part			L.I.M with Anisotropic secondary part	
		From catalogue	Computed	Measured	Computed	Measured
δ	mm	3	3	3	3	3
c	mm	2	2	2	2	2
s		1	1	1	1	1
I	A	5	5.15	5.25	4.19	4.63
F	N	140	172	172	150	124
P	kW	1.4	1.36	1.39	1.04	1.1
U	V	380	380	395	380	395
Q	kVAr	*	3.1	3.3	2.56	2.97
S	kVA	*	3.39	3.59	2.76	3.17

* Not given

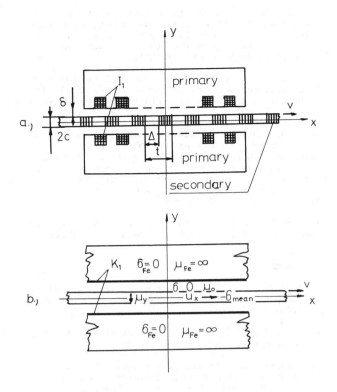

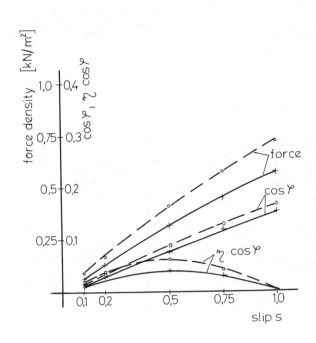

Fig.1 a) Basic principle of a linear
          induction motor provided with
          anisotropic secondary part
       b) Mathematical model for a linear
          induction motor with anisotropic
          secondary part

Fig.2) Characteristics based on computation
        results at speed 3 m/s

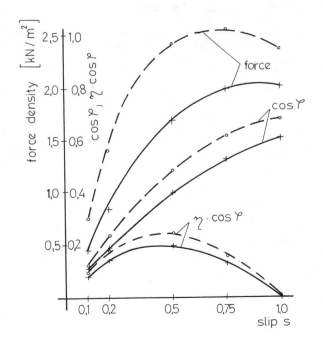

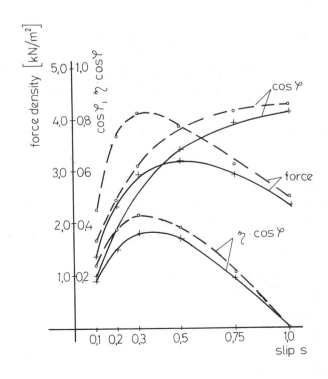

Fig. 3) Characteristics based on computation
         results at speed 6 m/s

Fig. 4) Characteristics based on computation
         results at speed 9 m/s

THE INFLUENCE OF UNBALANCED MAGNETIC PULL ON THE CRITICAL SPEED OF FLEXIBLE SHAFT INDUCTION MACHINES

M. T. Wright, D. S. M. Gould and J. J. Middlemiss

Parsons Peebles Motors and Generators, U.K.

INTRODUCTION

An accurate assessment of critical speed is necessary to avoid the possibility of vibration and damage under operating conditions. Rigid shaft machines are usually designed so that the first critical speed occurs some 30% above running speed. Flexible shaft machines, running between first and second critical speeds, are usually designed to run some 30 to 40% above first critical speed.

The critical speeds of an induction motor are determined by:

a. Mass and stiffness distribution in the rotor

b. Bearing oil film stiffness

c. Bearing support structure dynamics

d. Unbalanced magnetic pull

Much work has been done over the last decade on methods of modelling the complex interactive dynamics of rotors, oil films and support structures, in order that critical speeds can be determined to an acceptable degree of accuracy.

Over the same period of time, the demand for large two-pole induction motors has increased. This has led to a dramatic increase in the use of motors running between first and second critical speeds. Without using oversized shaft diameters and, hence, larger, non-optimum, frame sizes, it is not possible to build rigid shaft two-pole induction motors with ratings in excess of about 3000kW. (It is normally advantageous to commence flexible shaft construction well below 3000kW. In Europe most manufacturers make the change at about 2000kW, depending on the cooling system employed for the machine.)

Early experience in the development of such machines indicated an anomaly in the calculation of critical speed: calculated values of critical speed were consistently lower than those measured on test. It was found that calculated and measured speeds correlated well for the unexcited condition, i.e. where the machine is allowed to run down through the critical speed with no voltage on the stator winding. The introduction of unbalanced magnetic pull (UMP) to cater for the influence of rotor/stator eccentricity was therefore considered to be the source of error.

THE EFFECT OF UMP

Most methods of calculating UMP, in use, are based on similar theories and give similar results.[1]

The usual starting point is to consider the Maxwell stress distribution between two uniformly-magnetised eccentric cylinders (the stator and rotor airgap surfaces) and then to evaluate the resulting nett force along the plane of interest. Corrections are then introduced for the influence of saturation, rotor damping currents and parallel paths in stator windings.[4] These methods, although simple, are known to give adequate results for multi-pole machines but anomalous results for two-pole machines. The two-pole machine has been suspected to be a special case.

Only a few authors eg [3] have attempted to account for the influence of pole number on UMP. The effects and causes of UMP have received much attention in the literature (e.g. 1, 2, 3). This paper is concerned with UMP arising from offset in the axis of the stator bore and rotor (see Figure 1) which gives rise to both stationary and rotational forms of UMP.

The rotational form of UMP contains a spectrum of Maxwell stress waves, the dominant component of which rotates in the positive sequence at rotor speed and is amplitude modulated at twice slip frequency. The nature of this component is similar to mechanical unbalance and, as such, does not influence the critical speed, but does influence the severity of vibration when the rotor runs through critical speed.

The stationary form of UMP gives rise to a force, the position of which is fixed relative to the stator, which alters the effective shaft stiffness and, hence, the critical speed.

Although many analyses of stationary UMP have been given which suggest a variety of relationships between mean UMP and airgap eccentricity, it is generally agreed, and has been demonstrated by Binns and Dye (2), that, up to about 10% eccentricity, the force is proportional to the ratio of eccentricity and mean airgap.

i.e. $F \propto \Delta/g$

This linear relationship allows the definition of an equivalent negative mechanical stiffness (F/Δ) which can be combined with the shaft system stiffness to determine critical speed.

An approximate measure of the influence of this negative stiffness is given by

$$\frac{\omega_\Delta}{\omega_s} = \frac{K_{ump}}{2.K_s}$$

i.e. the per unit shift in critical speed is roughly one half the ratio of "UMP stiffness" to shaft system stiffness.

Due to the variation in oil film stiffness and damping coefficients between the horizontal and vertical planes, and differences in structural stiffness referred to these planes, the horizontal and vertical vibration spectra reach their peaks at different running speeds.

This discrimination between horizontal and vertical critical speeds can be of the order of several hundred rev/min, with peak vibration in the vertical plane occurring at the higher running speed. This has been shown clearly during factory tests.

METHOD OF CALCULATING UMP

The modification to existing methods of calculation, proposed in this paper, is concerned wholly with the geometrical influences of different pole numbers. The beneficial influences of saturation, parallel circuits and squirrel cage damping may be introduced, in the usual manner, as corrections to the basic calculation.

It is assumed that:

a. Airgap mmf is sinusoidally distributed

b. Airgap flux density is inversely proportional to the sum of the airgap lengths traversed by a line of that constant flux density

c. UMP is directly proportional to eccentricity.

The Maxwell stress at any angular position, 'α' is

$$\sigma_\alpha = \frac{B_\alpha^2}{2\mu_0} \qquad (1)$$

Since the stress is proportional to B_α^2, the assumed sinusoidal flux-density distribution is usually replaced by an effective rms flux-density inversely proportional to the airgap at angle 'α'

i.e. $$B_{\alpha rms} = B_{rms} \cdot g/g_\alpha \qquad (2)$$

where B_{rms} and g relate to the concentric condition and

$$g_\alpha = g - \Delta \cos\alpha \qquad (3)$$

This procedure is, however, only valid for machines with large pole numbers, where the adjacent north and south pole airgaps traversed by a single line of flux are approximately equal. For a machine with a low pole number, the adjacent north and south pole airgaps traversed by a flux line may vary significantly. This is particularly apparent for the case of main interest, the two-pole machine.

For the general case, therefore, the term 'g_α' in equation 2 must be replaced by an "effective airgap",'$g_{\alpha e}$' which is the mean of the airgap length traversed by a line of flux at angle and the airgap length traversed by the same line of flux in the adjacent pole pitch.

Where the stator mmf is sinusoidally distributed, the airgap flux density at angle α is then given by

$$B_\alpha = B_m \cdot g/g_{\alpha e} \cdot \sin p\alpha \qquad (4)$$

where B_m is the peak flux density for the concentric condition.

By combining (1) and (3) we have for the vertical UMP acting on the displaced rotor of Figure 1:

$$F = \frac{B_m^2 g^2}{\mu_0} \int_0^\pi \frac{\cos\alpha \cdot \sin^2 p\alpha \cdot d\alpha}{g_{\alpha e}^2}, \qquad (5)$$

where $g_{\alpha e}$ is determined independently for each circumferential section of the stator considered in building up the integral for 0 to π

The analysis shows that the two-pole machine has a maximum UMP where the field axis is aligned as shown in Figure 2a (M = M sin pα) and zero UMP where the field is as shown in Figure 2b (M = M cos pα). The resulting twice line frequency variation has an amplitude equal to the mean UMP and is given by one half the maximum UMP.

i.e. $$F(2 \text{ pole}) = \frac{1}{4} \cdot \frac{\pi D \ell}{4\mu_0} \cdot B_m^2 \cdot \frac{\Delta}{g} \qquad (6)$$

This result gives a value of static UMP the quarter of that given by the classical, "infinite pole number solution".

In general, for any pole number,

$$F = Q \cdot \frac{\pi D \ell}{4\mu_0} B_m^2 \frac{\Delta}{g} \qquad (7)$$

where the values of Q (the pole number correction), calculated for various pole numbers is given in the table below.

poles	2	4	6	8
Q	0.25	0.712	0.86	0.896

As expected, as the number of stator poles becomes large, the value of Q approaches unity and the solution approximates to the "infinite pole number" solution. This is due to the fact that, as the number of poles becomes large, the airgap lengths for adjacent north and south pole flux lines become nearly equal.

TEST RESULTS FOR CRITICAL SPEED MEASUREMENTS ON TWO-POLE MACHINES

The analysis given in the previous section suggests that the static UMP of a two-pole machine is only a quarter of that predicted by classical methods.

A series of tests were conducted on a flexible shaft 3.3kV 50 Hz 2-pole motor to substantiate the theory.

The rotor was deliberately unbalanced and run at discrete speeds over a range known to cover that of the shaft criticals. With full supply volts, the first set of readings were taken at normal running speed. Vibration levels at the bearings were recorded in both the vertical and horizontal planes together with the phase angles. The supply frequency was then dropped and the rotor run at the first step change in speed, the supply voltage being adjusted to maintain constant UMP. A second set of readings were then taken and the procedure repeated throughout the speed range. The maximum recorded vibration levels coupled with a 180° phase change denoted the critical speeds associated with full UMP.

To ascertain the change in critical speed associated with a marked reduction in UMP, the exercise was repeated with the supply voltage dropped to 1000V at normal running speed, the lowest practicable for the test. Again, the maximum recorded vibration levels coupled with a 180° phase change denoted the critical speeds associated with the reduced UMP.

The unexcited critical speeds were determined from run-down plots and corresponded closely to the calculated figures.

Figure 3 is a graph of the calculated reduction in critical speed against "hard over" UMP for the rotor system under consideration. Using the classical method of calculation, the "hard over" UMP is 52,000N, but the analysis suggests that the true figure is only 13,000N. The corresponding figures for the reduction in shaft critical speeds being 250 r.p.m. and 50 r.p.m.

From the test results, it was apparent that the influence of full UMP had relatively little effect in lowering the critical speeds. The measured figures indicated that UMP lowered both critical speeds by less than 50 r.p.m. thus indicating that the revised method for calculating UMP for 2-pole motors gives realistic results in practice.

CONCLUSIONS

This contribution has given a single practical method of taking account of the influence of pole number on UMP. In particular, it has provided an explanation for the anomalous behaviour of the two pole machine and has demonstrated the relatively minor influence of UMP on shaft critical speed.

REFERENCES

1. Von-Kaehne, P., 1963, "Unbalanced magnetic pull in rotating electric machines". ERA report Z/T142.

2. Binns, K. J., Dye, M. 1973, "Identification of principal factors causing unbalanced magnetic pull in cage induction machines", Proc. IEE, V120, No. 3, p.p. 349-354.

3. Covo, A., 1954, "Unbalanced magnetic pull in induction motors with eccentric rotors", Trans.Am.Inst.Elec.Eng., 73, Pt. IIIB, p.p. 1421-1425.

4. Robinson, R. C., 1948, "The calculation of unbalanced magnetic pull in synchronous and induction motors", Trans.Am.Inst.Elec.Eng., 62, p.p. 620-624.

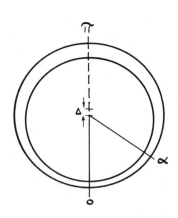

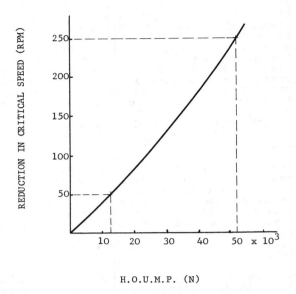

Figure 1   Angular reference position for vertically displaced rotor

Figure 3   Calculated effect of various values of "hard over" U.M.P. for the rotor system under test

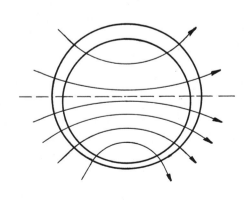

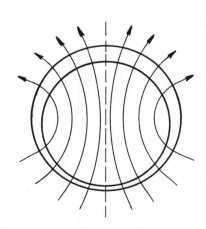

(a)   Maximum pull

(b)   Zero pull

Figure 2   Two pole field positions for maximum and minimum pulls

UNBALANCED MAGNETIC PULL IN THREE PHASE TWO POLE INDUCTION MOTORS WITH ECCENTRIC ROTOR

R.Belmans, W.Geysen, H.Jordan, A.Vandenput

University of Leuven, Belgium

INTRODUCTION.

Many authors already analysed the constant magnetic pull in induction motors with eccentric rotor (e.g. Freise and Jordan (1), Jaenicke and Jordan (2), Frohne (3), Binns and Dye (4), Covo (5)). Kovacs (6), Jordan et al (7) and Früchtenicht et al (8) also indicate the presence of a vibrational component. An eccentric rotor position also gives rise to homopolar fluxes as indicated by Emde (9), Jordan and Taegen (10) and Schroeder and Seinsch (11). In (6), Kovacs analysed the relationship between the homopolar flux and the vibrational component of the magnetic pull in a two-pole machine having a dynamically eccentric rotor.

In this paper we try to analyse the relationship between the homopolar flux and the unbalanced magnetic pull in a physically clear way. In order to limit the mathematical efforts and to gain more physical insight, the following idealizing suppositions are made:
1. both rotor and stator surfaces are perfect cylinders, the axis of the rotor is parallel to the axis of the stator bore;
2. the effects of slotting are neglected,
3. the permeability of the iron paths is infinite,
4. the rotor does not possess a squirrel cage; the air-gap magnetic field is therefore not damped by axial rotor currents.
5. the effects of the magnetomotive force harmonics are neglected.

Although at first sight these suppositions may be considered to be quite restricting, some useful and new results can be drawn from this analysis.

CALCULATION OF THE RADIAL FLUX DENSITY DISTRIBUTION.

In order to calculate the radial flux density distribution in the machine air-gap, we use Ampère's law in a plane perpendicular to the machine shaft (fig.1):

$$\frac{db_A{}^\delta(\mathbf{x},t)}{dx} = \mu_o R a_m(\mathbf{x},t) \qquad (1)$$

with $a_m(x,t)$ the distribution function of the magnetomotive potential drop over the arc x. As mentioned above, we only consider the basic harmonic of this distribution function. Hence for a two-pole machine:

$$a_m(\mathbf{x},t) = -A_m \sin(x-\omega t-\phi_m) \qquad (2)$$

Integrating eq.(1) yields:

$$b_A(\mathbf{x},t)\,\delta(\mathbf{x},t) = \mu_o\left[A_m R\cos(x-\omega t-\phi_m)+v(0,t)\right] \qquad (3)$$

with v(o,t) an unknown integration constant.

If the rotor is eccentrically positioned with respect to the stator bore, the air-gap width as a function of the arc x and the time t is (fig.2):

$$\delta(x,t) = \delta_m\left[1-\epsilon\cos(x-\omega_\epsilon t-\phi_\epsilon)\right] \qquad (4)$$

with the relative eccentricity:

$$\epsilon = \frac{e}{\delta_m} = \frac{e}{R-r} \qquad (5)$$

and the pulsation:

$$\omega_\epsilon = \begin{cases} 0 & \text{(static eccentricity)} \\ (1-s)\,\omega & \text{(dynamic eccentricity)} \end{cases} \qquad (6)$$

Eq.(6) is valid if $\delta_m << R$ [ref.(3)].

The air-gap permeance varies inversely as the air-gap width:

$$\Lambda(x,t) = \frac{1}{\delta(x,t)} = \sum_{\lambda=o}^{\infty}\Lambda_\lambda\cos\left[\lambda(x-\omega_\epsilon t-\phi_\epsilon)\right] \qquad (7)$$

The Fourier coefficients Λ_λ are [(see ref. (7)]:

$$\Lambda_\lambda = \begin{cases} \dfrac{1}{\delta_m}\dfrac{1}{\sqrt{1-\epsilon^2}} & (\lambda = 0) \\[3mm] \dfrac{2}{\delta_m}\left(\dfrac{1-\sqrt{1-\epsilon^2}}{\epsilon}\right)^\lambda\dfrac{1}{\sqrt{1-\epsilon^2}} & (\lambda > 0) \end{cases} \qquad (8)$$

Substituting eq.(7) into eq.(3) yields the radial flux density distribution:

$$b_A(x,t)=\mu_o\Lambda(x,t)\left[A_m R\cos(x-\omega t-\phi_m)+v(0,t)\right] \qquad (9)$$

A first relationship between the homopolar flux Φ_h and the integration constant v(o,t) is found by integrating the radial flux density distribution function over the rotor surface:

$$\Phi_h = \int_0^{2\pi} b_A(x,t)Rl\,dx =$$

$$\mu_o\left\{A_m R\frac{\Lambda_1}{2}\cos\left[(\omega-\omega_\epsilon)t+(\phi_m-\phi_\epsilon)\right]+\Lambda_o v(0,t)\right\}2\pi Rl$$

$$(10)$$

In order to obtain a second relationship, we apply Ampère's law in a plane containing the machine shaft (fig.3),(ref.(10)):

$$\frac{b_A(x,t)\delta(x,t)}{\mu_o} + \frac{B_{s_o}(t)\Delta_o}{\mu_o} + \sum_{n=1}^{\infty}\frac{B_{s_\nu}\Delta_\nu\cos(\nu x-\omega_\nu t-\phi_\nu)}{\mu_o}$$

$$= \theta_o(t)+\sum_{n=1}^{\infty}\hat{\theta}_n(t)\cos(nx-\omega_n t-\phi_n) \qquad (11)$$

As we are searching for a second relationship between ϕ_h and $v(o,t)$, we are merely interested in the angle-independent terms of eq. (11). Using eqn.(3) and (11) yields:

$$v(0,t) + \frac{B_{s_o}(t)\Delta_o}{\mu_o} = \theta_o(t) \qquad (12)$$

$\theta_o(t)$ is the ring current encircling the machine shaft.

The homopolar flux must have zero divergence, therefore:

$$B_{s_o}(t) = \frac{\phi_h}{2A_s} \qquad (13)$$

The factor 2 indicates the splitting up of the homopolar flux into two identical parts.

We now consider an extreme case. As the rotor of the motor has no bars, no current will flow in the short-circuit ring[$\theta_o(t)\equiv 0$] if it is interrupted ($R_R = \infty$). The quantities related to this situation are denoted with the index ∞. Combining eqn. (10), (12) and (13) yields:

$$\phi_{h\infty} = \frac{\mu_o A_m R\Lambda_1 \pi R1}{1+\frac{\Lambda_o \pi R1\Delta_o}{A_s}} \cos\left[(\omega-\omega_\epsilon)t+(\phi_m-\phi_\epsilon)\right]$$

$$= \phi_{h\infty}\cos\left[(\omega-\omega_\epsilon)t+(\phi_m-\phi_\epsilon)\right] \qquad (14)$$

$$v_\infty(0,t) = \frac{A_m R\Lambda_1 \frac{\pi R1\Lambda_o}{2A_s}}{1+\frac{\Lambda_o \pi R1 \Delta_o}{A_s}} \cos\left[(\omega-\omega_\epsilon)t+(\phi_m-\phi_\epsilon)\right] \qquad (15)$$

We conclude that due to the normal, axial currents in the stator winding and the non-uniform air-gap, a homopolar flux is generated. While the short-circuit ring is interrupted, this homopolar flux is not damped by a ring current.

In general however, there will be a current in the short-circuit ring damping the homopolar flux. The missing relationship between $\theta_o(t), v(o,t)$ and ϕ_h can be derived from the voltage differential equation of the short-circuit ring. The total flux, linked by it is:

$$\phi_h = \phi_{h\infty} + 2L_R\theta_o(t) \qquad (16)$$

with L_R the inductance of the ring, which is calculated below. The factor 2 again arises from the division of the homopolar flux. Using complex quantities, the voltage differential equation of the short-circuit ring is:

$$R_R\underline{\theta}_o(t) + \frac{1}{2}\frac{d\Phi_h}{dt} = 0 \qquad (17)$$

or using eq.(16):

$$R_R\underline{\theta}_o(t) + L_R\frac{d\underline{\theta}_o}{dt} = -\frac{1}{2}\frac{d\Phi_{h\infty}}{dt} \qquad (18)$$

The solution of this equation is:

$$\underline{\theta}_o(t) = -\hat{\underline{\theta}}_o e^{j\left[(\omega-\omega_\epsilon)t+\phi_\theta\right]} \qquad (19)$$

with

$$\phi_\theta = \phi_m-\phi_\epsilon-\text{arctg}(-\alpha_R) \qquad (20)$$

$$\hat{\theta}_o = \frac{\phi_{h\infty}}{2L_R\sqrt{1+\alpha_R^2}} \qquad (21)$$

wherein

$$\alpha_R = \frac{R_R}{(\omega-\omega_\epsilon)L_R} \qquad (22)$$

The pulsation of the homopolar flux $(\omega-\omega_\epsilon)$ is either the supply pulsation (static eccentricity) or the slip pulsation (dynamic eccentricity).

In order not to lose the physical insight into the problem, we will limit the further discussion to two important extreme cases: $\alpha_R = 0$ and $\alpha_R = \infty$.

Fully damped homopolar flux ($\alpha_R = 0$).

The homopolar flux is fully damped if either the short-circuit ring has an extremely low resistance ($R_R \to 0$) or the pulsation of the homopolar flux is very high [$(\omega-\omega_\epsilon) \to \infty$]. In both cases α_R tends to zero. All quantities related to this situation are denoted with the index 0.

If the homopolar flux at t=0 is zero, eq.(17) yields:

$$\phi_{h_0} = 0 \qquad (23)$$

Hence, using eq.(10):

$$v_o(0,t) = -A_m R\frac{\Lambda 1}{2\Lambda_o}\cos\left[(\omega-\omega_\epsilon)t+(\phi_m-\phi_\epsilon)\right] \qquad (24)$$

Combining eqn.(14), (16) and (24), we find:

$$L_R = \frac{1}{\frac{1}{\Lambda_o\pi R1\Lambda_o} + \frac{\Delta_o}{\mu_o A_s}} \qquad (25)$$

Eq.(25) is the definition of the inductance of a circuit, i.e. the inductance is the reciprocal of the total magnetic resistance encountered by the flux linked by this circuit.

We conclude that the homopolar flux is zero if α_R tends to zero. Nevertheless the integration constant is not zero [ref.(7)] but is given by eq.(24).

The radial component of the magnetic flux density in the machine air-gap is [eqn.(9) and (24)] :

$$b_{A_o}(X,t) = \mu_o \Lambda(X,t) A_m R \left\{ \cos(x - \omega t - \phi_m) \right.$$

$$\left. - \frac{\Lambda_1}{2\Lambda_o} \cos\left[(\omega - \omega_\varepsilon)t + (\phi_m - \phi_\varepsilon)\right] \right\} \quad (26)$$

Undamped homopolar flux ($\alpha_R = \infty$).
If either the short-circuit ring is interrupted ($R_R = \infty$) or the pulsation of the homopolar flux is extremely low [($\omega - \omega_\varepsilon) = 0$], no current will flow in the ring damping the homopolar flux. The homopolar flux and the integration constant are given by eq.(14), resp.(15).

As can be seen from these equations, Φ_{h_∞} and $v_\infty(0,t)$ depend upon the ratio V of the magnetic resistance at the front ends of the machine and the mean value of the air-gap magnetic resistance:

$$V = \frac{\Delta_o}{\mu_o A_S} \mu_o \pi R1 \Lambda_o \quad (27)$$

$$= \frac{\text{magnetic resistance at the front ends}}{\text{magnetic resistance of the air-gap}}$$

Combining eqn.(9), (15) and (27) leads to the equation of the radial air-gap flux density distribution:

$$b_{A_\infty}(X,t) = \mu_o \Lambda(X,t) A_m R \left\{ \cos(x - \omega t - \phi_m) \right.$$

$$\left. - \frac{\Lambda_1}{2\Lambda_o} \frac{V}{V+1} \cos\left[(\omega - \omega_\varepsilon)t + (\phi_m - \phi_\varepsilon)\right] \right\} \quad (28)$$

If the magnetic resistance at the machine front ends tends to infinity ($V \to \infty$), the homopolar flux vanishes, as can be derived from eq. (14) and the air-gap flux density is given by eq. (26) ($\alpha_R = 0$). This result is physically evident: in both cases, no homopolar flux passes the machine front ends.

If the magnetic resistance at the frond ends is zero (V=0), the integration constant vanishes [eq.(15)]. The homopolar flux then reaches a maximum value [eq.(14)] and the air-gap flux density becomes [eq.(28)]:

$$b_A(X,t) = \mu_o \Lambda(x,t) A_m R \cos(x - \omega t - \phi_m) \quad (29)$$

CALCULATION OF THE UNBALANCED MAGNETIC PULL.

The unbalanced magnetic pull is given by the differentiation of the total magnetic energy in the machine:

$$F = \frac{\partial W_m}{\partial e} = \frac{1}{\delta_m} \frac{\partial W_m}{\partial \varepsilon} \quad (30)$$

The total magnetic energy in the machine consists of the magnetic energy in the air-gap W_{mA} and the magnetic energy at the front ends W_{ms}; both parts depend on the relative eccentricity and the magnetic resistance ratio V. Hence:

$$F = \frac{\partial W_{mA}}{\delta_m \partial \varepsilon} + \frac{\partial W_{ms}}{\delta_m \partial \varepsilon} \quad (31)$$

The air-gap magnetic energy equals:

$$W_{mA} = \int_0^{2\pi} \frac{b_A^2(X,t)}{2\mu_o} \delta(x,t) R1 \, dx \quad (32)$$

while the magnetic energy due to the field in the machine front ends is given by:

$$W_{ms} = \frac{B_{So}^2}{2\mu_o} 2\Delta_o A_S \quad (33)$$

If $\alpha_R = \infty$ the combination of eq.(32) with eq. (28) and of eq.(33) with eqn.(13) and (14) yields the total magnetic energy:

$$W_{m_\infty} = (A_m R)^2 \frac{R1 \pi \mu_o}{2\delta_m} \frac{1}{\sqrt{1-\varepsilon^2}} \left\{ 1 - \left(\frac{1-\sqrt{1-\varepsilon^2}}{\varepsilon}\right) \frac{V}{V+1} \right.$$

$$\left. + \frac{1}{V+1}\left(\frac{1-\sqrt{1-\varepsilon^2}}{\varepsilon}\right)^2 \cos\left[2(\omega - \omega_\varepsilon)t + 2(\phi_m - \phi_\varepsilon)\right] \right\} \quad (34)$$

As we can see, the magnetic energy contains a constant and a vibrational term. The unbalanced pull can therefore be written as:

$$F = F_c + \hat{F} \cos\left[2(\omega - \omega_\varepsilon)t + 2(\phi_m - \phi_\varepsilon)\right] \quad (35)$$

The pulsation of the vibrational component is either the double supply frequency (static eccentricity) or the double slip frequency (dynamic eccentricity).

An elementary differentiation of eq.(34) yields the expressions of the constant pull and the amplitude of the vibrational component:

$$F_{c_\infty} = (A_m R)^2 \frac{R1 \pi \mu_o}{2\delta_m^2} \frac{\varepsilon}{(1-\varepsilon^2)^{3/2}} \left\{ 1 - \left(\frac{1-\sqrt{1-\varepsilon^2}}{\varepsilon}\right)^2 \right.$$

$$\left. \frac{V}{V+1}\left[\frac{V+2}{V+1} + \frac{2}{\varepsilon^2}\sqrt{1-\varepsilon^2}\right] \right\} = (A_m R)^2 \frac{R1 \pi \mu_o}{2\delta_m^2} f_c \quad (36)$$

$$\hat{F}_{\infty} = (A_m R)^2 \frac{R1\,\pi\mu_o}{2\delta_m^2} \frac{\varepsilon}{(1-\varepsilon^2)^{3/2}} \left(\frac{1-\sqrt{1-\varepsilon^2}}{\varepsilon}\right)^2 \tag{37}$$

$$\frac{1}{V+1}\left\{\frac{1}{V+1}+\frac{2}{\varepsilon^2}\sqrt{1-\varepsilon^2}\right\} = (A_m R)^2 \frac{R1\,\pi\mu_o}{2\delta_m^2}\,\hat{f}$$

In fig.4 the relative constant magnetic pull f_c is plotted versus the relative eccentricity ε for various values of the magnetic resistance ratio V. We can conclude that the linear relationship between the pull and the eccentricity only holds for small values of ε. The values obtained in ref.(7), are valid if V=0. If due to the magnetic resistance at the front ends no homopolar flux can be established in the machine, the constant pull is practically halved in comparison with the values obtained for V=0.

In fig.5 the relative amplitude of the vibrational component of the magnetic pull $\hat{f}$ is plotted versus for the same values of V. Again the amplitude considerably decreases as the magnetic resistance ratio increases. If the magnetic resistance tends to infinity, the vibrational pull vanishes.

The results for α_R =0 are the same as these for α_R = ∞ and V= ∞ as in both cases, no homopolar flux passes the machine front ends. Substituting V= ∞ in eqn.(36) and (37) yields:

$$F_{c_o} = (A_m R)^2 \frac{R1\,\pi\mu_o}{2\delta_m^2} \frac{\varepsilon}{(1-\varepsilon^2)^{3/2}}$$

$$\left\{1-\left(\frac{1-\sqrt{1-\varepsilon^2}}{\varepsilon}\right)^2\left(1+\frac{2}{\varepsilon^2}\sqrt{1-\varepsilon^2}\right)\right\} \tag{38}$$

$$\hat{F}_o = 0 \tag{39}$$

The eccentric position of the rotor of an induction machine not only causes a radial pull, but also a small pulsating torque. The differentiation of the magnetic energy with respect to the angular position ($\omega_\varepsilon t + \phi_\varepsilon$) of the rotor eccentricity yields:

$$T = \frac{\partial W_m}{\partial(\omega_\varepsilon t + \phi_\varepsilon)} = (A_m R)^2 \frac{\pi R1\,\mu_o}{2} \frac{1}{\sqrt{1-\varepsilon^2}}$$

$$\left(\frac{1-\sqrt{1-\varepsilon^2}}{\varepsilon}\right)^2\left(\frac{1}{V+1}\right)\sin\left[2(\omega-\omega_\varepsilon)t+2(\phi_m-\phi_\varepsilon)\right]$$

$$= (A_m R)^2 \frac{\pi R1\,\mu_o}{2}\,T' \tag{40}$$

The pulsation of this torque is also either the double supply pulsation (static eccentricity) or the double slip pulsation (dynamic eccentricity).

In fig.6 the relative amplitude T' is plotted versus ε for various values of the ratio V. This torque is very small in comparison with the rated torque of the machine and vanishes if the homopolar flux is zero.

CONCLUSION.

Although a lot of idealizing suppositions are made one very important conclusion can be drawn from this analysis: if a homopolar flux due to the eccentricity of the rotor of the motor is established, the unbalanced magnetic pull will contain a vibrational component and a small pulsating torque, both having either the double slip frequency if the rotor is dynamically eccentric or the double supply frequency for a statically eccentric machine rotor. The measures taken to eliminate homopolar fluxes as non- magnetic end shields or non-magnetic rings between the bearings and the end shields, also avoid the appearance of a vibrational pull and a pulsating torque. By these measures the constant pull is practically halved.

REFERENCES.

1. Freise,W., and Jordan,H., E.T.Z.-A, 83, 229-303.
2. Jaenicke,P., and Jordan,H., Siemens Forsch. und Entwick.,5, 249-256.
3. Frohne,H., Arch. für Elektrotechnik, 51, 300-308.
4. Binns, K.J., and Dye, M., Proc.I.E.E., 120, 349-354.
5. Covo,A., Trans. A.I.E.E., 1954, 1421-1425.
6. Kovacs,K.P., I.E.E.E.-P.A.S., 1977, 1105-1108.
7. Jordan,H., Schroeder R.D., and Seinsch, H.O., Arch. für Elektrotechnik, 63, 117-124.
8. Früchtenicht,J., Schroeder,R.D., and Seinsch,H.O., E.T.Z.-Archiv,3, 389-396.
9. Emde,F., Elektro. und Maschinenbau, 40, 577-560.
10. Jordan,H. and Taegen,F., ETZ-A, 85, 865-867.
11. Schroeder,R.D. and Seinsch,H.O., ETZ-Archiv, 3, 7-12.

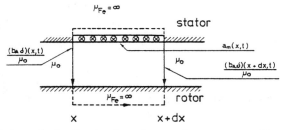

Figure 1 Ampère's law in a plane perpendicular to the machine shaft.

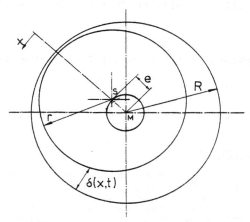

Figure 2 Air-gap of a motor with an eccentric
rotor.

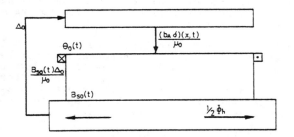

Figure 3 Ampère's law in a plane containing
the machine shaft.

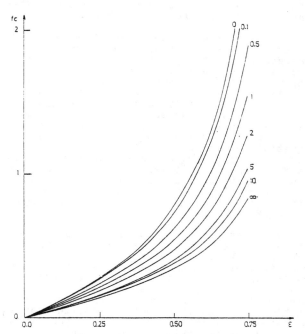

Figure 4 Relative constant magnetic pull versus the relative eccentricity ε. Parameter: magnetic resistance ratio V.

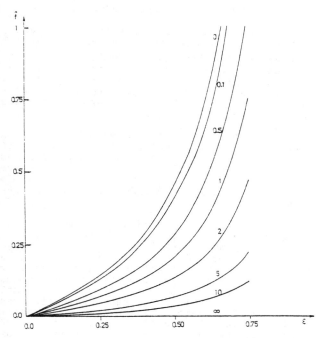

Figure 5 Relative amplitude of the magnetic
pull versus the relative eccentrici-
ty ε. Parameter: magnetic resistance
ratio V.

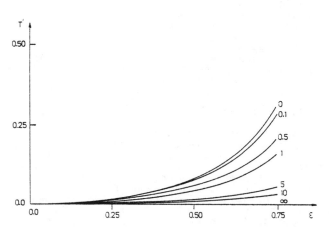

Figure 6 Relative amplitude of the pulsating
torque versus the relative eccentri-
city ε. Parameter: magnetic resistance ratio V.

THE INTERFACE BETWEEN FINITE ELEMENT METHODS AND MACHINE DESIGN

M.Tarkanyi, E.M.Freeman. P.P.Silvester and D.A.Lowther

G.E.C. Large Machines Ltd., ICST, McGill University, McGill University

INTRODUCTION

There has been a rapid development in the use of finite element solution techniques over the past decade. The falling cost of computer power has meant that problems of ever increasing size may now be solved. Two major problems remain. The cost of entering data, and of evaluating the results, can be one or two orders of magnitude higher than the cost of 'solving' the problem.

To a great extent, these problems are now eased by the ready availability of inexpensive interactive graphics on small dedicated computers. It is now possible to input finite elements models. of high complexity, with very little effort in a very short time. Typically, models may be input in 1 to 2 hours, instead of one to two weeks. as previously. The same computer can be employed to solve the resulting set of equations, in relatively short solution times. A post-processor may then be used to extract any quantities, or information, required. It is obviously imperative that any such facility should be easy to learn and use; in short, it should be very user friendly.

However, it has to be borne in mind that the field solution is only the first step in the design process. The machines design engineer has to guarantee a certain level of machine performance. He needs to calculate voltages, excitations, losses, time constants, etc. The use of finite elements. or any other method. is therefore only of use insofar as it assists him in obtaining that information. Standard design methods are quite adequate for the majority of cases where loadings are not excessive. However, where the rating is being pushed beyond the normal limits, it is necessary to carefully re-examine the whole design process. It is now possible to solve many of the 2D field problems which arise. It only remains to integrate the techniques into the design process.
This paper describes some the factors influencing the choice of a suitable system for use in an industrial environment, and the some of the problems which might arise in implementing and using it.

FIELD PROBLEMS IN MACHINES

The literature is rich in papers on the use of numerical methods for the solution of the sort of field problems which occur in electrical machines. Many of these papers have originated in university environments, where the emphasis has often been, not unreasonably, on obtaining a higher degree, rather than the production of bugproof, 'friendly', software. In addition, the work often relies heavily on access to very large, expensive, computing facilities. The result is, sadly, that a great number of the latest developments cannot be readily transferred to an industrial environment.

There are many examples of field problems which occur in machine design, electromagnetic, thermal and, of course mechanical. For the purposes of this paper the emphasis here is mainly on the first two. Frequently such problems are treated away from the main design office. What is required is an integrated in-house system, which greatly reduces the cost and time involved, and in addition gives the designer full control and flexibilty needed to reach an optimum solution.

While all real problems are 3-D, their solution, now and in the forseeable future, is often costly and impracticable for day-to-day use in the design office. Every effort should be made to reduce such problems to 2-D through the use of reliable approximations based on engineering experience.

CHOICE. INTRODUCTION AND LIAISON

The first step taken was to decide to buy in software, rather than write it in-house. With this in mind, the next step was to choose the software and hardware. The main considerations affecting the choice were these:
1. The whole system had to be operable by the engineers in the design office.
2. It had to be easy to learn and operate.
3. It had to be relatively inexpensive.
4. It had to be possible to easily extend both the software and the hardware.

The introduction was done in two stages. Firstly, an engineer with an analytical background familiarised himself with the system. Second, after installation, the design engineers were given the opportunity of solving their real problems, initially under guidance. This learning period was found to be, on average, two days.

The liaison with the software house is a vitally important factor, for the success of the project. Inevitably there are problems which require attention by the software designers, but more positively, there is the feedback of suggestions for enhancing future versions of the system.

At GEC Rugby it was decided to purchase a commercially available finite element package, and its attendant DEC based hardware. Some 20 months experience of this system has now been gained mainly in solving non-linear magnetostatic problems. but it has also been used to solve certain thermal problems. With the original version it was possible to assemble finite element models with up to 1000 nodes; define up to 27 problems, having different combinations of material properties and excitations; solve those 27 problems; and then post-process them using a 512*512 eight colour graphics system. It is now possible to program the post-processor, so that once a sequence of commands has been input, the whole sequence can be repeated indefinitely, thus reducing, yet again, the engineering effort required. In addition means are provided for the input of magnetisation characteristics, both soft and hard. One very powerful feature is the provision of file managers, so that at any stage, it is possible to switch to, or from, other computer systems, eg you might have your own solver on another machine. This flexibility makes the whole package extremely versatile. It is described fully in the references.

PRACTICAL ASPECTS

There are numerous difficulties which can arise when first applying finite element techniques to rotating machine problems. It is frequently necessary to compromise, while maintaining an acceptable level of accuracy. The following points, some of which are obvious, might serve as a useful guide.

1. Model planning, Before building the model, careful thought should be given to all the alternative geometries, excitations and materials, to be studied. By suitable labelling, certain regions can easily be changed from iron to air without having to define a new model.

Some simplifying decisions have to be made to ignore unimportant details such as the insulation between iron and copper, in most of the electromagnetic studies. This obviously does not apply to thermal problems. It is at this stage that high field strength regions should be anticipated and finely discretised accordingly. A special study has shown that a crude discretisation in the air-gap and tooth tip region, can lead to overestimation of the gap mmf. This is mainly due to oversimplification of the tooth fringing field.

2. Representation of thin layers, such as unwanted gaps at joins, insulation in thermal problems, etc. In order to avoid discretisation of a large number of elements, having bad aspect ratios, it is often possible, with care, to arbitrarily increase the thickness and the permeability, in proportion. This need not affect the field in the regions of interest. This is only permissible where the flux lines are mainly perpendicular to the thin layer.

In more complicated cases, such as gaps around T-heads and spiders, the region might have to be studied separately, and a B-H curve obtained for the resultant composite region.

3. Theoretically, slotted regions can frequently be modelled as homogeneous, anisotropic regions. However, since the present package does not yet accommodate anisotropy, some other form of modelling must be found. In a tooth/slot region, where the flux lines are mainly radial, an equivalent magnetisation curve may be defined, where:

B-equivalent = B*(t-s)/t + MUO*H*(s/t)

and   B-equivalent = equivalent density
                          over slot pitch

        B = real density in the tooth

        s = slot width; t= slot pitch

If the slots are parallel, a good approximation can be obtained by using 't' at 1/3 of the slot depth from the narrowest end of the tooth. The above approximation can only be used where the main point of interest is not in the slotted region.

4. Adjustment of axial length. The various parts of the machine have to be referred to a common reference length, since this assumption is inherent in any 2-D flux plot. The equivalent magnetisation curve is simply:

B-equivalent = B * (iron length/
                      reference length)

This adjustment ensures that the mmf along the region is exact. but the B values have to be rescaled. The most convenient choice of reference length is the axial length of the air-gap modified for ducts and fringing. This avoids having dummy air permeabilities different from unity.

5. Boundaries. Many problems in the r-theta plane have readily identifiable boundaries of flux lines or symmetry lines. Where this is difficult to achieve, within a pole-pitch, because of a non-integral slot/pole value, it is possible to replace the actual slotting with an equivalent slotting. This is done by keeping the iron/air ratio unaltered to maintain the tooth density at a realistic value. This is permissible only if the subsequent change in slot/gap ratio is negligible.

6. Equivalent excitation. Equivalent slotting leads naturally to the idea of equivalent excitation. For example, for an a.c. machine the analysis need only be conducted for the fundamental current loading.

7. Leakage in a direction normal to the plane of interest can be allowed for by artificially increasing the permeability of the 2-D leakage path. This has to be done carefully, but experience has shown that it can be very successful.

8. Checking of results. A visual inspection of a simple flux plot, can be an invaluable indicator of the correctness of material and excitation settings. Another obvious method is to check the mmf/(integral H dl) ratio. If the highly saturated regions are not properly discretised, this ratio can be far from unity. A plot of H along a critical path of high saturation, or small gaps, can be highly revealing. Flux density distribution curves can be useful in showing if field concentrations appear where expected. Their absence could be due again to poor discretisation. Care should always be taken to ensure that contour paths lie in a definite region, rather than on a boundary, where ambiguities arise. It is also useful to be able to check material properties and excitation levels.

APPLICATION EXAMPLES

To illustrate some of the points mentioned above, and to show the types of problem which may now be easily tackled, examples are given below. The emphasis is on the problem and the assumptions and approximations made, rather than on the results obtained.

1. Field distribution in the interpolar space of d.c. traction machines for commutation analysis.

For this problem the objectives are:

(a) To establish that the compole is not saturated when all excitations are applied simultaneously. For this a full pole pitch model is required, as in Fig. 1. If unsaturated, then much time and effort may be saved, because a half pole pitch model may be used. Fig. 2., and linear superposition is possible when determining all quadrature axis ampere turns.

(b) To find the field distribution for each individual excitation, namely, armature, compensating winding, interpole winding and main field winding. At least 20 points are required.

(c) To find the mmf distribution across the interpole front and back gaps, for a number of gap combinations. This has to be evaluated for each component of quadrature axis excitation.

The overall objective of the investigation is to obtain sufficient information to construct field distribution curves, for any combinations of gaps and ampere turns.

The first model corresponds to a pole pitch, because the field is asymmetrical about the compole centreline due to the main field excitation. Since only the mean value of the field density is required on the armature surface, it is possible to replace the individual armature slots by a current layer. The armature diameter, D, is accordingly reduced by making use of the Carter coefficient.

D-model = D - 2*(Carter coeff. - 1)*(air-gap)

The model is shown in Figure 1. The change of gap materials is accommodated by defining separate regions which are later given material attributes as required, these may be noted at the end of the interpole.

The peripheral density of the discretisation is determined by the need for 20 points equally spaced between the edge of the main pole and the compole centre line. The radial density of elements has to be high in the compole air-gaps. It has been found that at least four element layers are necessary, for acceptable accuracy in the mmf calculation.

Firstly, all excitations are applied, and the flux density levels in the compole are determined. If below the saturation value, then a greatly simplified model, Fig. 2., can be used. The iron is assumed to be infinitely permeable, and the main pole air-gap is modelled by a current element at the tip of the pole. This current is set equal to the sum of the armature currents and compensating winding currents, taking the signs into account.

The required quantities are easily obtained from the post-processor. These are for unit excitation currents. The actual field values are then determined by superposition and scaling. The curves in Fig. 2. show the normal flux density variation on the rotor surface between the compole centre line and the edge of the main pole, for unit compole current, and two air-gaps.

In a typical commutation study, four gap combinations and three types of quadrature axis excitation are required. This might have to be done for several different geometries. Commonly, this could mean 50 to 60 separate solutions to be studied. This highlights the importance of a good flexible post-processor, which can be easily programmed to extract any desired set of quantities. This is easily done with the system described in this paper.

2. Open circuit excitation and pole flux leakage in synchronous machines.

The objectives here were to allow for pole leakage, and to calculate the open circuit curve. Use is made here of some of the techniques listed above. The stator slots per pole were non-integral. These were therefore replaced by an equivalent integral number of slots, so that a single pole could be studied. Earlier studies had shown that at least four layers of elements were necessary in the air-gap, in order to obtain accurate field values. The magnetisation curves were scaled, as indicated above, to the axial length. The leakage flux from the ends of the poles was modelled by increasing the permeability of the interpolar air regions, these may be noted in Fig. 3. This might seem rather unreasonable at first sight, but the results obtained appear to be very good, and so this method appears to be pragmatically justified.

To study the effect of on-load conditions, the same basic model may be used. The stator currents are replaced by an equivalent sinusoidal current loading. This is established by means of vector diagrams and load data. The recent paper by Turner and Macdonald describes a refined method for tackling this problem.

3. Thermal Problems.

The package can also be used to examine temperature distributions and heat flow in machines. The analysis to show how this is done will not be described here, only the results of one study are given. Fig.4. shows part of the outline of a field winding. Fig.5. shows a set of isothermal lines, the single point indicates the location of the hot-spot.

CONCLUSIONS

The system described is in regular daily use in a design/development environment. There are now versions which can accommodate 4000 nodes or more, and within a short time it will be possible to deal with axisymmetric, permanent magnet and eddy current problems. The new version of the post-processor will be much more powerful and flexible. It will have characteristics similar to the RUTHLESS post-processor referred to below.

Finally, it should be emphasised that the sytem is only as good as the engineers using it. To obtain the maximum advantage from it, the users must have a good, sound understanding of the basic engineeering principles which underly this subject.

ACKNOWLEDGMENTS

The authors are most grateful to Mr. K.F.Raby of GEC Large Machines. Rugby, for his help and encouragement in the preparation of this paper.

REFERENCES

1.   Raby, K.F., 'On getting the right answer', Chairman's Address. SET Division, Proc.IEE. (Jan. 1982).

2.   Silvester, P.P., Lowther, D.A. and Freeman. E.M., 'Finite element mesh generation using a small computer with interactive raster graphics', ICEM. Athens (Sept.1980).

3.   Silvester, P.P., Lowther, D.A. and Freeman, E.M., 'An interactive graphics post-processor for electromagnetic field problems', MICAD 80, Paris (Sept.1980).

4.   Silvester, P.P., Lowther, D.A., Freeman, E.M. and Csendes, Z.J., 'The preprocessing. solution and postprocessing of finite element electromagnetic field problems using a small dedicated computer with raster graphics', Eng.Soft.Conf., Imperial College. London, (May 1981).

5.   Csendes. Z.J., Freeman. E.M., Lowther, D.A. and Silvester, P.P., 'Interactive computer graphics in magnetic field analysis and electric machine design', IEEE Winter Power Meeting (Feb.1981). PAS, 1981. 6, pp2862-69.

6.   Turner, P.J., and Macdonald. D.C., 'Finite element prediction of steady state operation of a turbine generator using conductivity matrices', IEEE Trans. on Magnetics, MAG-17, No.6. Nov. 1981. pp3262-3264.

7.   Lowther. D.A., Silvester, P.P., Freeman, E.M., Rea. K., Trowbridge. C.W., Newman. M. and Simkin. J., 'RUTHLESS - a general purpose finite element post-processor', Compumag. Chicago (September 1981).

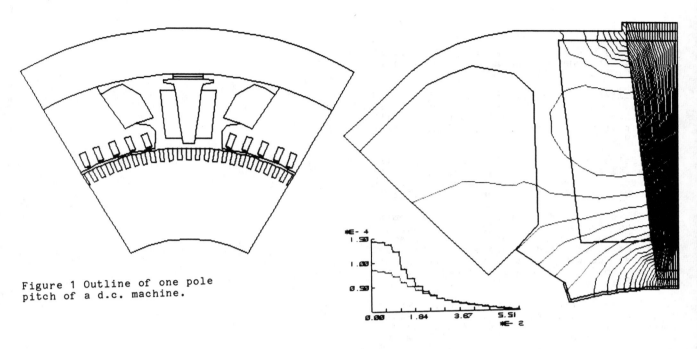

Figure 1 Outline of one pole
pitch of a d.c. machine.

Figure 2 Half pole pitch model showing
leakage flux and two plots of radial
flux density at the armature surface.

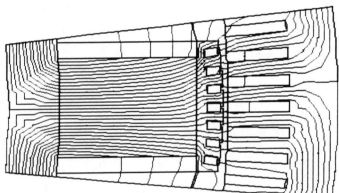

Figure 3 One pole pitch of a salient
pole synchronous machine showing a
field plot and the dummy interpolar
air regions.

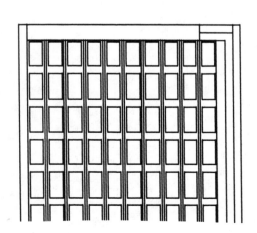

Figure 4 Outline of part of a field winding
for a thermal study.

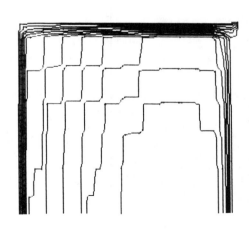

Figure 5 The solution to the thermal
problem showing isothermal lines.
The single point indicates the hotspot.

THE INFLUENCE OF THE TYPE OF DRIVE ON THE DESIGN OF LARGE D.C. MOTORS

J.W. Pratt

GEC Large Machines Limited, Rugby, U.K.

1.0 INTRODUCTION

D.C. Motors with armature diameters greater than about 0.7 m are normally designed to suit particular applications. The influence of performance requirements and site conditions on the design of these large motors will be considered with examples of three types of drive. Firstly, however, a brief review will be made of the effects of drive requirements in general on the size and proportions of large d.c. motors.

2.0 GENERAL RELATIONSHIPS

2.1 Armature Dimensions

Three important performance limitations for an armature of diameter D and core length L are illustrated in Figs. 1, 2 and 3. It has been assumed, for the purposes of the curves, that armature frequency determines the choice of radial depth of the armature conductor.

Fig. 1 shows the maximum continuous power output P per unit armature diameter. This limit is based on maintaining the average voltage between adjacent commutator segments below a level to ensure freedom from flashover under normal conditions. It depends on the type of armature winding, and for a duplex lap winding the limit may theoretically be double that for the more commonly used simple lap winding. The limit is also influenced by the permissible temperature rise for the armature.

The relationship between the maximum for the product $\hat{P}.s$ and armature frequency is shown in Fig. 2. Here $\hat{P}$ represents the peak power at top speed and s is the speed range (ratio top speed n:base speed N) by field weakening. This is a commutation limit and the form of the curve has been obtained using a simplified reactance voltage formula. Since $\hat{P}.s$ is the limit, the speed range, s, can in many cases, be increased at the design stage if $\hat{P}$ is reduced.

Fig. 3 illustrates the variation in maximum continuous base speed torque per unit armature volume with armature frequency. This limitation is determined largely by the permissible temperature rise of the armature. Some of the factors which determine the permissible motor temperature are:

(a) Limitations imposed by customers' specifications.

(b) Class of insulation.

(c) Ambient temperature at site.

(d) Altitude at site.

For an armature design, therefore, there is a minimum diameter (Fig. 1)and a corresponding minimum core length (Fig. 3). The diameter may be increased to improve commutation performance (Fig. 2), or to reduce the overall length, but the top speed must be limited if high centrifugal forces are to be avoided.

2.2 Field System Dimensions

Restrictions imposed on the outside dimensions of the motor can influence the choice of armature diameter and the space available for the main field. In the past, control systems frequently necessitated several windings on the main poles and thus dictated the space required. This is no longer the case and the modern trend is towards poles of much reduced radial height, and hence larger diameter armatures for given outside dimensions.

In addition it is now usual for large d.c. motors to have laminated magnet frames so that they can respond quickly to changes in armature or field currents, and thus commutate satisfactorily under high speed control and thyristor supply conditions. The magnet frame laminations are supported by a fabricated steel structure which can further increase the overall radial dimensions of the machines, and special mechanical design features may be necessary to meet specific dimensional restrictions.

3.0 EXAMPLES OF DRIVES

The relationship between performance requirements, site conditions and the design of machines will be considered using three heavy industrial drives as examples.

3.1 Primary Mill Twin Drive

An example of the layout of a twin drive for a reversing primary mill is shown in Fig. 4. The two motors are connected to the mill rolls through a flexibly jointed shaft system that allows the gap between the rolls to be varied and also allows the distance between the motor axes to be greater than that between the roll axes. There is a mechanical limit to the angle between the spindles, and it is therefore necessary to limit the distance between the motor axes to avoid the use of very long spindles and subsequent increased foundation and building costs. This is the main reason for the staggered mounting arrangement with a jack shaft passing above (or, in some cases, below) the forward motor. For the same reason it is necessary for the radial dimensions of the armature, field system, magnet frame supporting structure and the jack shaft all to be at minimum values. Minimum armature inertia is also important for these machines, which reverse rapidly every few seconds in normal operation. On the other hand the mechanical design must not be weakened. The motors must withstand severe mechanical forces resulting from the rapid acceleration, roll slipping, shock loadings and torsional oscillations associated with a primary mill rolling, perhaps, 20 tonne steel ingots.

However, the small armature diameter requirement can cause problems with high ratios of P/D (Fig. 1), and it also tends to produce long armature cores which have inherently difficult commutation characteristics. Primary mill drives have high ratios of peak to nominal torque, typically 2.5, and operate under conditions of rapidly changing load. Commutation at peak load can therefore be a critical factor in their design. P/D can be increased by increasing the specific electric loading of the armature, and commutation can be improved by reducing the radial depth of the armature slots. In such cases the problem then becomes one of temperature rise. The analytical methods now available to optimize heat transfer are of great assistance in overcoming this problem.

Considerable design effort may be needed to produce motors within the specified power and diameter limitations, but, even so, sometimes it may not be possible to obtain the power required using a single armature, and a more expensive tandem arrangement of two armatures may have to be used instead. It is worth noting at this point that failure to take full advantage of the thermal capabilities of the insulation system may have a detrimental effect on other important aspects of the design (.e.g commutation at peak load), and produce an unbalanced design.

3.2 Direct-Coupled Winder Motor

Few of the restrictions imposed on a twin drive apply to a direct-coupled winder motor. Usually there is no dimensional restriction on the diameter of the winder motor, and the inertia of the armature is small compared with that of the drum, ropes and vehicles. The exception is in mines over approximately 2000 m deep where it is necessary to have underground winders to operate to the deeper levels. In these cases the armature must be designed within the dimensions of the mine shaft with a clearance, on occasions, of as little as 50 mm, and all contributions to its dimensions then need to be considered in detail. The magnet frame presents less of a problem because it can normally be split into two parts.

Freedom of choice of armature diameter may result in large diameters and short core lengths, particularly for those armatures that are overhung from the winder drum as shown in Fig. 5. For this arrangement, with an armature of perhaps 30 tonnes, the designer tries to obtain a short distance from the drum bearing to the centre of gravity of the armature in order to ease the bending stresses in the drum shaft.

Shorter cores, combined with no speed range by field weakening, tend to make commutation for winder motors easier than for most types of mill motors. Conventional guides to commutation, such as reactance voltage, become of less value in assessing maximum ratings. In some instances, commutation is not limited by sparking at the segments leaving the brush, but by segments entering under the brush. This form of sparking can be influenced, not only by the electromagnetic design of the motor, but also by the choice of brush holder and brush grade and by the peak brush current density which may be maintained for about one minute in every five to ten minutes. The heating of the brush face under these severe overload conditions aggravates commutation difficulties.

Normally, a direct-coupled winder motor can be designed to operate up to the thermal limit of the insulation system without difficulty. This makes it all the more important to ensure a uniform temperature distribution in the armature winding. It is worth noting that the different constructional requirements of winder and mill motors, such as the use of heavier armature endwinding banding for the mill motors, may necessitate different internal ventilation arrangements.

3.3 Strip Mill Motor

Modern strip mills require high-power machines operating at high speeds. Typical ratings are 4500 kW, 150/380 r/min for the finishing stand of a hot strip mill and 2500 kW, 200/450 r/min for a tandem cold mill motor. In addition there may be dimensional limitations imposed by the mill stand layout and, in the case of cold mills, armature inertia may be restricted by the need to minimize acceleration time. The result is that these machines are among the most difficult d.c. machines to design.

The machine frequency at top speed is high in comparison with the primary mill or winder motor, and it is necessary to use a shallow armature conductor or, alternatively, to sub-divide a deeper conductor to limit eddy current losses. The total conductor depth is, in any case, normally limited to help commutation. Consequently the permissible P/D figure may be low (Fig. 1) and the designer may be forced towards increasing diameters. On the other hand, space restrictions, peripheral speed limitations and inertia requirements favour reducing the armature diameter. The optimum design will balance all the factors, and may have average volts between commutator segments, reactance voltage, armature and commutator peripheral speeds all approaching their limits. With this type of drive, therefore, careful specification of the requirements by the customer is particularly important.

4.0 DEVELOPMENTS

Class F insulation is now commonly used for large d.c. machines, but some customers request the lower Class B temperature rises to allow a thermal margin. There is, however, an increasing awareness on the part of machine users that there can be considerable gains, as mentioned earlier, in taking advantage of the full temperature capabilities of the insulation system. Complete Class H insulation systems, which allow machines to operate at higher temperatures, have been available for many years but their use in large d.c. motors is not widespread. On the other hand one disadvantage of operating motors, particularly low-speed motors, at high temperatures is a reduction in efficiency. Most d.c. motors could, in fact, be designed for higher efficiency by increasing the quantity of copper they contain and increasing their sizes, but the initial cost would also increase and initial cost is normally treated as the more important consideration.

Competition has encouraged manufacturers not only to reduce their costs, but also to pursue technical developments aimed at improving the performance of d.c. motors.

Greater attention has been paid to the calculation of losses and to the detailed analysis of heat flow using ventilation and thermal networks. Similarly sophisticated methods are now available for the computation of electromagnetic fields using finite element techniques and for the prediction of commutation performance. These techniques, backed by experimental verifications, are enabling designers to meet increasingly stringent drive requirements more effectively.

ACKNOWLEDGMENT

The author wishes to thank GEC Large Machines Limited for permission to publish this paper.

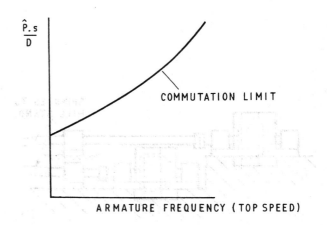

Figure 2   Limit of the product (peak power at top speed)X(speed range by field weakening) per unit armature diameter.

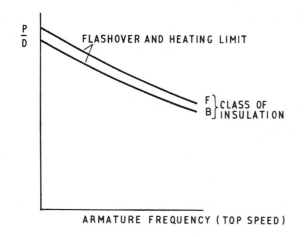

Figure 1   Limit of the power output per unit armature diameter.

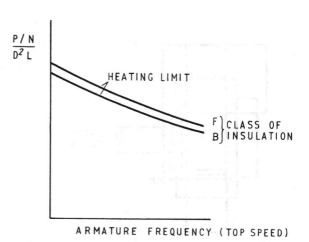

D - ARMATURE DIAMETER
L - CORE LENGTH

Figure 3   Limit of the base speed torque per unit D^2L.

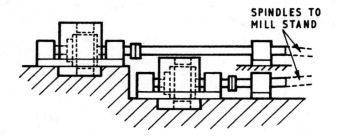

Figure 4   Twin drive motors for primary mill.

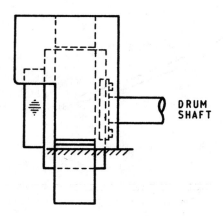

Figure 5   Overhung mine winder motor.

THE DESIGN TRIANGLE

A. Tulleth

Parsons Peebles Acoustics, NEI Peebles Ltd., UK

INTRODUCTION

Many papers have been written on aspects of the measurement and control of noise and vibration from rotating electrical machines, the dynamic mechanical responses of stators and shaft/rotor/bearing systems, the effects of electrical load on noise level, bearing instability and prediction of noise levels from design data. Relatively few authors, however, have discussed the problems facing the designer of machines with low noise and vibration levels or the difficult design compromises which may have to made to achieve these levels bearing in mind that the cost of applying noise and vibration reduction measures may be a critical factor. Modern machines are smaller and lighter than their predecessors and are more likely to be of unit construction so factors which, in the past, were relatively unimportant may assume a greater significance. The design engineer must take into account the effects of changes in construction techniques on the noise and vibration characteristics of machines so that the mathematical model can be adapted to reflect current forms of construction.

This paper, which is concerned with the general philosophy of reducing noise and vibration levels, lists the main sources of noise and vibration, discusses the methods and options of noise and vibration control open to the design engineer, and describes the "design triangle" approach to control of noise and vibration in rotating electrical machines.

Advances in data acquisition, presentation, storage and retrieval techniques permitted by the use of microcomputers are described and the effects of possible developments in noise and vibration control and machine structure materials are examined.

Although much of the comment which is made applies to all types of electrical machine the emphasis of this paper is directed mainly toward induction machines.

THE DESIGN TRIANGLE

Much useful information on aspects of the dynamic responses of rotating electrical machines can be extracted from the literature but data of more immediate value can be accumulated from contractually agreed tests or diagnostic measurements in the machine manufacturer's factory. If the results of these measurements differ markedly from calculated values then clearly either the design mathematical model was wrong, the machine was tested under the wrong conditions or the data applied to the mathematical model was incorrect. It may be difficult, at a later date, to determine which of the three possibilities applies since machines will be held on a test bed for the minimum time required to demonstrate compliance with specified limits and it is unusual to have a complete time record of all of the important parameters.

The "design triangle" approach, with its emphasis on close mixing of the following three ingredients, is essential if noise and vibration levels are to be reduced on a successful and consistent basis:-

a)   the mathematical model of the machine.

b)   the dynamic response of the machine.

c)   the dynamic characteristics of the construction materials.

These three features form the design triangle. Each is important because it affects, and is affected by, the other two.

Mathematical Model

From the noise and vibration point of view the most interesting part of the machine is the stator core. Its dynamic reponse to the magnetic forces generated in the airgap has been the subject of many papers including (Brauer (1), Alger (2), Erdelyi (5), Tsivitse (8) and Ellison and Moore (13)). Methods of calculation of the natural frequencies and modes of vibration of the stator have been described in many other papers ((1), (2), Ellison and Yang (14) and more recently, Girgis and Verma (6))

Analyses of the stator as a continuous mechanical system have used fewer simplifying assumptions as the computing power available to process the equations has increased. Little experimental evidence appears to be have been published relating the stator natural frequencies and vibration modes calculated using the published equations with values measured on medium or large industrial machines. Different analytical methods appear to have given results of varying degrees of accuracy (14) since some of the mathematical models only fitted only one type of construction.

The other main parts of the machine whose mathematical models must be good are the shaft/rotor/bearing system with the bearing supports and the baseplate which supports the magnetic circuit and the rotating assembly. Eshlemann (7) discussed at length the response of rotor systems and gave many references, Rieger (12) discussed the dynamics of flexible rotors in bearings and Marsh (15) discussed the stability of journal bearings. The mechanical design of machine baseplates is becoming more important as unit construction techniques are developed.

The rotor/shaft/bearing system mathematical models have been treated in the same manner as the stator core because the shaft and rotor have normally been described in terms of lumped masses and not as continuous systems. Although this is changing, the validity of new mathematical models will have to be tested if the results obtained from them are to be believed.

It is clear that a good mathematical model is essential and that if the model doesn't fit then calculated and measured stator or shaft natural frequencies may differ dramatically. Manufacturers, who must produce machines with low noise and vibration levels, have little option but to test the validity of their own mathematical models by making systematic, detailed measurements on whole machines and subassemblies.

The Dynamic Response of the Machine

The response of the complete machine can only be adequately checked in a test area equipped with the appropriate power supplies and loading facilities. Comparison of its performance at rated load and speed with specified upper limits of noise and vibration (BS4999 Part 51 (17) and BS4999 Part 50 (16) contain typical test codes) will show whether or not it is acceptable to the purchaser. If the specified upper limits are exceeded the reason for this must be ascertained by making diagnostic measurements and comparing the results of these measurements with the acoustic design of the machine.

Noise and vibration can be measured using accelerometers, eddy-current proximity probes, velocity transducers, strain gauges and microphones. The signals which these produce can be analysed, displayed and recorded using narrow-band spectrum analysers, plotters and analogue or digital storage devices. Before making measurements it is customary to check airgap dimensions, shaft/enclosure clearances, bolt tensions, oil levels, winding connections and the other mechanical settings which must be correct if the machine is to function in the intended manner.

Using the instruments the whole audible spectrum, or any selected portion of the spectrum can be examined and the frequency and amplitude of discrete components can be measured and recorded. These can then be compared with the predicted values. If a prominent peak in the spectrum has been the cause of rejection and it is revealed to have been predicted the the source of the problem is clear. If the peak cannot be traced to a known source then the instrumentation must be used to locate the source. This may involve making noise and vibration measurements over a range of supply frequencies and voltages and varying such parameters as bearing oil pressure and cooling air velocity and to monitor magnetic circuit, air and oil temperatures. The large volume of data accumulated may, in the case of an extended exercise, become embarrassing, particularly if a solution to the problem proves elusive but the data recorded will, almost invariably, contain the clues which lead to the source.

The information obtained, whether or not it points directly to the source, must be disseminated quickly in an easily digested form.

Dynamic Characteristics of Materials

Calculated stator or shaft natural frequencies will be incorrect if the mathematical model is not good, if the values of the dynamic properties of the materials used or the values of bearing pedestal or oil film stiffness are wrong.

Values of the dynamic properties of materials are usually available from the manufacturer but it is wise to remeasure them in the laboratory under conditions which approximate as closely as is possible to those encountered in the machine to ensure that they are correct and that non-linearities, if they exist, are identified.

Sometimes it is difficult to tell whether the machine mathematical model, or the input data, is wrong so it is essential, after the properties of the materials have been remeasured, to make vibration measurements on samples, cut to a simple shape whose mathematical model is known and mounted under known conditions. After it has been demonstrated that calculated and measured natural frequencies agree to an acceptable accuracy measurements should be made to determine the response of stator cores and shaft/rotor/bearing assemblies using the materials, to evaluate the mathematical model.

NOISE AND VIBRATION SOURCES

There are three main types of noise and vibration excitation:-

Magnetic Excitation

The frequencies and modes of the magnetic force waves which are generated in the airgap of a rotating electrical machine have been discussed in the literature ((1), (2), (4), (8), (9)). These force waves will only cause high noise or vibration levels if they coincide with or closely approach, in frequency and mode, natural frequencies of the stator.

Asymmetries in the magnetic circuit can contribute to pulsating noise (10) which normally is not harmful to the machine but is, subjectively, disturbing.

Unbalanced magnetic pull, caused by magnetic or mechanical asymmetry, can cause strong forces to be applied between the rotor and stator.

Magnetically excited noise and vibration can be reduced in amplitude by reducing the amplitude of the magnetic forces or by ensuring that the forcing frequencies are not close to structure natural frequencies.

Mechanical Excitation

There are noise and vibration sources in a machine which are unaffected by changes in the airgap flux density and whose amplitude and frequency are functions of the machine speed only. These sources include cooling fans, ball and roller bearings, sleeve bearings and mechanical unbalance in the rotor circuit. Forces produced by these sources may be sufficiently small in amplitude to cause noise only or, if they coincide with the natural frequencies of structural components, to cause high noise and vibration levels.

Mechanically excited noise and vibration usually indicates damage, poor dynamic balance, operation in an unstable mode or operation close to a natural frequency of vibration.

The forces causing mechanically excited vibration can be reduced by improving dynamic balance or by modifying the mechanical response. Fan noise can be reduced by changing the number of blades or staggering them to avoid interactions with stationary obstacles.

Rieger (12) has discussed at length the unbalance response of flexible rotors in bearings including the effects of non-rigid bearing supports.

Aerodynamic Excitation

Broad-band and discrete-frequency noise is generated by the cooling air as it passes through the machine. Broad-band noise is caused by turbulent air passing over machine surfaces and between the rotor and stator. Pure tone excitation of the stator core may be caused by air impinging on the stator teeth and cooling slots. High-velocity air passing supports may cause vortex shedding and fan blades passing stationary obstacles may generate pure tones. Coverwork may be buffeted by the airflow and contribute to the noise and vibration spectrum.

Measures should be taken at the design stage to ensure that coverwork is stiffened and damped so that it doesn't "drum". Aerodynamically excited noise can be reduced by using the smallest acceptable fan, by ensuring that the air circuit is streamlined as much as possible and that projections on the surface of the rotor and stator are minimised.

Increase in Noise Level With Load

The components of noise or vibration most likely to increase in amplitude with load are those which are electromagnetically excited and associated with the mmf slot harmonics. Since many industrial machines normally operate at full load, factory tests should, ideally, be made with the machine operating at this condition. It may be impossible to test large machines on load in the factory.

Brozek (9) analyses the sources and discusses their relative importance when applied to high-speed polyphase induction motors.

NOISE AND VIBRATION REDUCTION MEASURES

Generation of magnetically and aerodynamically excited pure tone noise may be minimised by careful design and by using proven "standard" designs. Where it is necessary to achieve lower noise levels then acoustic treatment can be applied to the enclosure of the machine, attenuators can be fitted to air inlets and outlets and vibration damping materials can be applied to sheet metalwork. In an extreme case a free-standing acoustic enclosure can be fitted over the machine.

Vibration can be reduced by careful design of shaft/rotor/bearing systems, the use of resilient mounts to isolate coverwork from the rest of the machine and, most importantly, fine dynamic balancing.

Add-on noise and reduction measures such as those described above should be specified when the machine is designed so that valuable time is not wasted during the test program.

INFLUENCE OF MICROCOMPUTING TECHNIQUES

The time taken to acquire sufficient test data may delay location of the source of excessive machine noise or vibration. The microcomputer, in conjunction with the new generation of real-time spectrum analysers, offers the facility to collect and store detailed test data, from any type of transducer with an electrical output, in the factory and at site in a very short time. Vibration spectra can be compared directly to determine the effect of modifications to the machine or changes in test conditions. Floppy disks provide a convenient medium for storage and retrieval of data in digital form.

One-third or full octave analyses of the noise at many positions round a machine may be required to demonstrate compliance with standards (17) and large quantities of data may have to be tabulated for inclusion in test reports. The microcomputer offers an inexpensive, portable, flexible means of collecting, processing, comparing and tabulating test data. Corrections for the effect of background can be made with ease and calculated values can be compared with specified upper limits.

Vibration spectra from the shaft or bearings of a machine can be stored, discrete components in them identified in amplitude and frequency and potential sources located. It is even possible, with existing technology, for the microcomputer to analyse a spectrum and, on the basis of its findings, suggest remedial action.

Many modern instruments have digital output ports which enable them to be connected and controlled by microcomputers so fully automated diagnostic systems may be available soon. The computer would have to be programmed to seek answers to a series of standard questions and, on the basis of the answers it received, to suggest possible sources.

DEVELOPMENT OF MATERIALS

High-level noise and vibration are caused by:-

a) Coincidence of magnetic force waves and stator natural frequencies of vibration.

b) Excitation of shaft critical speeds by unbalance forces and magnetic and mechanical asymmetries.

c) Unstable operation of, or damage to, bearings.

d) Complex interactions between mechanical and electromagnetic systems.

e) Aerodynamic excitation of mechanical components or production of siren tones.

f) Mechanical resonance of coverwork.

g) Noisy ventilation fans.

Some of these phenomena can be treated quite simply by modifying mechanical components but others, because they require the development of complex computer programs and a great deal of practical "know-how", are not so easily treated.

The problem of interaction between forces and stator natural frequencies could be virtually eliminated if a highly damped core material, with the appropriate magnetic characteristics was developed. The amplification associated with mechanical resonance would disappear along with much of the time-consuming and difficult noise prediction.

The use of a highly damped alloy for rotating machine shafts is an attractive possibility because, once more, the problems associated with mechanical resonance would be eliminated. The author has investigated the use of such alloys but the results, for materials currently available, were not encouraging because damping factor decreased as temperature increased.

Problems associated with vibration of coverwork can be easily overcome by making the machine enclosure from composite panels having, on their inner surface, a layer of high-density sound absorbing material which also provides vibration damping. This sort of material is already available but machine enclosures may have to be modified to simplify use of the material.

CONCLUSION

As long as the upper limits of noise and vibration from rotating electrical machines continue to be reduced there will be a need for an approach such as the design triangle to ensure that manufactured machines can meet these limits.

ACKNOWLEDGEMENT

The author wishes to thank the Directors of NEI Peebles Ltd. for giving their permission for this paper to be published.

REFERENCES

1. Brauer, J.R., 1976,
    "Magnetic Noise of Induction Motors",
    IEEE Trans. Pow. App. Syst., PAS-95,
    66-73.

2. Alger, P.L., 1954,
    "The Magnetic Noise of Polyphase
    Induction Motors", Trans AIEE, 118-125.

3. Eis, R.O., 1975,
    "Electric Motor Vibration - Cause,
    Prevention and Cure.", IEEE Trans. Ind.
    Appl.", 1A-11, No. 3, 267-275.

4. Sperling, P-G., 1970,
    "Experience in the prediction of
    Electromagnetically Generated Machine
    Noise",
    Siemens Review, XXXVII, 192-197.

5. Erdelyi, E., 1955,
    "Predetermination of Sound Pressure
    Levels of Magnetic Noise of Polyphase
    Induction Motors", Trans. AIEE, Paper
    No. 55-726, 1-27.

6. Girgis, R.S., and Verma, S.P., 1981,
    "Method for accurate determination of
    resonant frequencies and vibration
    behaviour of stators of electrical
    machines", IEE Proc., 128 Pt. B, 1-32.

7. Eshlemann, R.L.,
    "Flexible Rotor-bearing system dynamics.
    1 - Critical Speeds and Response of
    Flexible Rotor Systems", ASME, 1-49.

8. Tsivitse, P.J. and Weihsmann, P.R.,
    1971, "Polyphase Induction Motor Noise",
    IEEE Trans. Ind. & Gen. Appl., IGA-7,
    339-358.

9. Brozek, R.J., 1973,
    "No-load to Full-load Airborne Noise
    Level Change on High-speed Polyphase
    Induction Motors", IEEE Trans. Ind.
    Appl., IA-9, 180-200.

10. Summers, E.W., 1955,
    "Vibration in 2-pole induction motors
    related to slip frequency", AIEE Trans
    (Power App Syst), 74, 69-72.

11. Muller, R, 1964,
    "The problem of noise in rotating
    electrical machinery", A.C.E.C. Rev.,
    No. 1, 10-25.

12. Rieger, N.F.,
    "Flexible Rotor-Bearing System Dynamics.
    III. Unbalance Response and Balancing
    of Flexible Rotors in Bearings", ASME,
    1-29.

13. Ellison, A.J., and Moore, C.J.,
    1968, "Acoustic Noise and Vibration of
    Rotating Electrical Machines", Proc.
    IEE, 115, 1633-1640.

14. Ellison, A,J,, and Yang, S.J., 1971,
    "Natural frequencies of stators of small
    electric machines", Proc IEE, 118,
    185-190.

15. BS4999 : Part 50 : 1978,
    "Specification for General Requirements
    for Rotating Electrical Machines. Part
    50. Mechanical performance - vibration."

16. BS4999 : Part 51 : 1973,
    "Specification for General Requirements
    for Rotating Electrical Machines. Part
    51. Noise Levels"

Figure 1 A modern, acoustically-treated, unit-construction machine

Figure 2 Measurement of the critical frequencies of a shaft in its bearings.

Figure 3 A two-channel frequency analyser being set up with a microcomputer and interactive digital plotter for vibration spectrum recordings

RESONANT FREQUENCIES AND VIBRATION BEHAVIOUR OF STATORS OF ELECTRICAL MACHINES

S.P. Verma

Department of Electrical Engineering, University of Saskatchewan, Saskatoon, Sask., Canada S7N 0W0

INTRODUCTION

Modern electrical machine design trends, following increasing economic pressures, are towards the adoption of lighter and cheaper construction of machines for given outputs. This means full utilization of active materials and increased magnetic and current loadings. As a result, the electrical machine has become very much noisier than before. The magnetic forces acting on the stator and rotor of an electrical machine may produce excessive vibrations and noise, especially when the frequencies of the exciting forces are equal to, or near, the natural frequencies of the members of the machine concerned. The vibrations and, consequently, the noise level produced by an electrical machine can, therefore, be reduced to a large extent by modifying the dimensions of the parts of the machine in such a way that their mechanical response to the exciting forces is diminished. The determination of resonant frequencies and vibration characteristics of the main components of an electrical machine is, thus, of much importance in relation to the reduction of the noise, which is itself of increasing importance due to international concern these days [1,2].

Several authors [3,4,5] have given methods of calculating electromagnetic noise of electrical machines by considering only the vibrations of the stator-core, which is subjected to the electromagnetic forces. The stator-core has been invariably treated as a thin-shell in most of the analyses available in the literature. However, the ratio of the thickness of the stator-core to its mean radius may well exceed the value of 0.2 in the case of special low-noise machines, machines of small capacities, 2-pole medium-size and several other types of machines. Hence, the assumption of a thin-shell may lead to considerable error in the results.

Stators of electrical machines are, in general, much more complicated than a single ring. An outer frame is usually provided to support the stator-core. In the modern construction of the electrical machines, the thickness of the frame is generally kept small. In very recent investigations, it has been observed that the frame can play a very important role in the problem of noise production in electrical machines. The consideration of the effects of frame is, therefore, very important in the investigations related to the problem of noise in electrical machines.

An accurate determination of resonant frequencies and natural response of stators is essential for the reduction of the electromagnetic acoustic noise in electrical machines. Several investigators have developed analyses for this purpose. A close review of these analyses would reveal the following:

i.   The stator-core was treated as a thin ring in several analyses. Such an approximation can be erroneous especially for stators with thick cores [6].

ii. Analyses are confined to only the lowest resonant frequency of a mode. Such a confinement can be partially attributed to the fact that investigators have considered the lowest frequency as the only significant resonant frequency with respect to vibration problems in electrical machines. Although this may be true for small machines, it is certainly not the case with large machines where several resonant frequencies for each mode of vibration may lie within the critical frequency range of noise production.

iii. Only plane vibrations of stators, involving radial and tangential components of displacement, were taken into account in the analyses. In fact, stators are subjected not only to radial and tangential vibrations but also to axial vibration.

iv. Authors invariably assumed uniform distribution of amplitudes of vibration along the machine-length. This, however, may not be the case in the presence of skewing or in machines of considerable length.

In general, the stator of electrical machines is subjected to axial, torsional and radial vibrations. All these vibrations can be excited simultaneously during the machine operation. For this and the reasons mentioned before, an analysis of a general nature based on three-dimensional considerations is required for the determination of the various natural frequencies.

In references [7] and [8] an analysis based on three-dimensional considerations was developed. In the analysis, both stator-core and frame were treated rigorously while teeth and windings were considered as additional masses. It is well-known that teeth and windings have a large effect on the values of resonant frequencies of stators. Therefore, an accurate simulation of teeth and windings is essential. In addition, the previous analysis is limited to only special modes along the machine-length. In actual practice, the longitudinal modes are actually a combination of these special modes. In the previous approach where equations of motion were derived by satisfying equilibrium and compatibility conditions, the complex boundary conditions in presence of teeth and windings along with free end conditions of the stator pose considerable difficulties. Therefore, one has to resort to an approach based on the "energy method" in which one avoids the simulation of such boundary conditions while considering teeth and windings rigorously [9]. The energy-method also permits accurate simulation of the actual modes of vibration along the machine- length.

In this paper, a brief description of an analytical method based on the three-dimensional theory of elasticity and using the energy-method is presented. Complete details of the analytical method are given in reference [10].

In order to verify the validity of the analysis, extensive experimental investigations were carried out on several models which represent stators of small, medium and large electrical machines. The models were so chosen that each model serves a specific purpose in the course of the investigations. The usual practice of investigating only a single model or models representing machines of nearly the same power capacity is generally inadequate for the

Purpose of studying such a complex problem of vibrations and noise as encountered in electrical machines.

Another important objective of the experimental investigations which were conducted in the course of the study presented in this paper was to explore the actual contribution of teeth, windings, frame and laminations towards values of resonant frequencies and vibration behaviour of stators at resonance. Important as it is, sufficient information in this connection is not available in the published literature. A close review of the published work would reveal the following:

i. There is an obvious controversy between investigators concerning the dynamics of teeth and windings. While some considered teeth and windings as additional masses [11], others treated them as cantilevers with enhanced lateral vibrations at the tooth-resonances [5] and the rest did not account for such resonances at all. According to Ref. [5], teeth and windings contribute significantly to values of resonant frequencies of stators.

ii. Some investigators realized the important role which the frame plays in the natural response of stators while others suggested to leave the frame entirely out of the calculations for its slight contribution.

iii. Investigators invariably treated the laminated stator-core as solid with isotropic properties. The extent of approximation involved in such an assumption has never been assessed. In fact, treating the actual laminated structure of stators rigorously or even by introducing equivalent material constants, similar to those derived by White [12] for thin laminated cylinders, would lead to very complicated analyses which may not be even needed.

In view of the above, the results of the experimental study presented here should provide an insight for proper incorporation of effects of teeth, windings, etc. for accurate determination of values of resonant frequencies. The paper consists mainly of two parts. the first part is devoted to the derivation and the experimental verification of the analysis while the second part deals with the experimental study of resonant frequencies and natural response of stators as affected by teeth, windings, frame and laminations.

PART I: ANALYSIS AND EXPERIMENTAL VERIFICATION

Stator Under Consideration

The stator under consideration is of the encased type, where the thick stator-core with teeth and windings is encased by a thin frame provided with cooling ribs as shown in Fig. 1. Stators of encased construction, which are increasingly used these days for machines of small and medium power capacities, are also quite suitable for the initiation of a rigorous analysis for the determination of resonant frequencies and natural response of stators.

Method of Analysis

The well-known energy method [9] is used for the derivation of the frequency equation of the stator under consideration. By using this method, one avoids the difficult problem of satisfying the boundary conditions all along the junctions between the various components of the stator. The only assumptions made in the analysis are those related to the homogeneity and linearity of the materials involved, the free body motion of the stator and neglecting the effects of terminal box, side caps,

feet, etc. These assumptions have been found appropriate by several investigators.

Derivation of the Frequency Equation

According to the three-dimensional theory of elasticity, the kinetic and potential energies of a cylindrical shell of length "L" and inner and outer radii "r_i" and "r_o", respectively, can be obtained in the form:

$$K.E. = \frac{\rho}{z} \int_{z=0}^{z=L} \int_{\theta=0}^{\theta=2\pi} \int_{r=r_i}^{r=r_o} [(\frac{\partial u}{\partial t})^2 + (\frac{\partial v}{\partial t})^2$$

$$+ (\frac{\partial w}{\partial t})^2] \, r \, dr \, d\theta \, dz \qquad (1)$$

and

$$P.E. = \frac{1}{2} \int_{z=0}^{z=L} \int_{\theta=0}^{\theta=2\pi} \int_{r=r_i}^{r=r_o} [\sigma_r \varepsilon_r + \sigma_\theta \varepsilon_\theta + \sigma_z \varepsilon_z + \tau_{r\theta} \gamma_{r\theta}$$

$$+ \tau_{rz} \gamma_{rz} + \tau_{\theta z} \gamma_{\theta z}] r \, dr \, d\theta \, dz \qquad (2)$$

Equations (1) and (2) can be used to determine the energy components of both the stator-yoke and the frame-shell by direct substitution of the proper parameters.

Energy components in teeth, windings and cooling ribs can be obtained by treating these parts as discrete beam-type elements attached to the body of the stator. Considering the realistic relative dimensions of these elements in electrical machines, it is sufficient to use the following approximate expressions of kinetic and potential energies of a cantilever:

$$K.E. = \frac{\rho}{2} A \int_{z=0}^{z=L} [(\frac{\partial u_b}{\partial t} + r_c \frac{\partial^2 w_b}{\partial z \partial t})^2 + (\frac{\partial v_b}{\partial t} + r_c \frac{\partial^2 w_b}{r_b \partial \theta \partial t})^2$$

$$+ (\frac{\partial w_b}{\partial t})^2 + R_{c\theta}^2 (\frac{\partial^2 w_b}{\partial z \partial t})^2 + R_{cp}^2 (\frac{\partial^2 w_b}{r_b \partial \theta \partial t})^2] \, dz \qquad (3)$$

and

$$P.E. = \frac{1}{2} \{EA \int_{z=0}^{z=L} [(\frac{\partial u_b}{\partial z})^2 + 2r_c \frac{\partial u_b}{\partial z} \frac{\partial^2 w_b}{\partial z^2}$$

$$+ R_{s\theta}^2 (\frac{\partial^2 w_b}{\partial z^2})^2] \, dz + GJ \int_{z=0}^{z=L} (\frac{\partial^2 w_b}{r_b \partial z \partial \theta})^2 \, dz\} \qquad (4)$$

Using the ordinary Ritz' method, the components of displacement are approximated by the following finite double-power series:

$$u = \sum_{i=1}^{M} \sum_{j=1}^{N} \sum_{k=0}^{\infty} (a_{ijk} \cos k\theta + b_{ijk} \sin k\theta) \, z^{i-1} r^j$$

$$v = \sum_{i=1}^{M} \sum_{j=1}^{N} \sum_{k=0}^{\infty} (c_{ijk} \cos k\theta + d_{ijk} \sin k\theta) \, z^{i-1} r^j$$

$$w = \sum_{i=1}^{M} \sum_{j=1}^{N} \sum_{k=0}^{\infty} (e_{ijk} \cos k\theta + f_{ijk} \sin k\theta) \, z^{i-1} r^j \qquad (5)$$

where, a_{ijk}, b_{ijk}, etc. are coefficients of the expansion which will also serve as the generalized coordinates of the system. M and N are two integers and determine the size of the mathematical model which represents the vibrating system. These two integers would, eventually, determine the accuracy of calculations.

In deciding upon the form of displacement distribution given above, several considerations, related to the stator construction and nature of vibrations of stators, have been taken into account. The extent to which the estimated distribution of displacement agrees with the actual distribution will be judged only after values of resonant frequencies predicted by the analysis are compared with measured values.

Having assumed the mode-shape functions for the displacements u, v and w, the total kinetic and potential energies of the stator can be readily obtained in terms of the generalized coordinates of the system before they are introduced into the well-known Lagrange's equation for conservative systems. This leads to a set of homogeneous equations. The coefficient matrix of these equations yields the frequency equation of the stator. The frequency equation can be easily expressed in terms of dimensionless quantities so that it may be applicable to stators of small as well as medium and large-sized machines. A complete description of this analytical method is given in reference [13].

Vibration Behaviour of Stators at Resonance

In the course of the theoretical investigations on the nature of the vibrations associated with resonant frequencies of stators, it has been found from the analysis that:

1) Circumferential mode-shapes of stators of encased construction are pure sinusoids with no coupling between modes of different orders. Consequently, a simpler form of mode-shape distribution, rather than the general form given in equation (5), may be sufficient.
2) In the presence of even a minor asymmetry in the construction of a stator, the stator exhibits dual resonances at each of its resonances. While the two resonances will differ by only a few cycles on the frequency scale, the identical circumferential mode-shapes associated with the two resonances will be a quarter of a wavelength phase displaced.
3) Stators have two sets of resonant frequencies associated with two types of modes along the stator length. One group of the resonant frequencies is associated with symmetric radial and tangential vibrations but anti-symmetric axial vibrations, while the other group is associated with anti-symmetric radial and tangential vibrations but symmetric axial vibrations.
4) All three components of displacement are associated with every resonant frequency [8]. Whereas first order resonant frequencies are associated with predominant radial vibrations, second and third order resonant frequencies are associated with predominant axial and predominant tangential vibrations, respectively. Accordingly, a purely electromagnetic radial, tangential or axial force having an exciting frequency equal to, or near, any of the resonant frequencies of the stator may give rise to significant responses not only in its own direction but also in the other two directions.
5) Vibrations associated with the zero mode are either coupled radial and axial or pure torsional depending on the order of the resonant frequency.
6) Vibrations associated with resonant frequencies of short stators, where amplitudes of vibration are almost equal along the stator length, are either plane vibrations involving coupled radial and tangential components of displacement or pure axial vibrations. The plane vibrations are again

decoupled into pure radial and pure torsional in the case of the zero circumferential mode.

Experimental Verification of the Analysis

Nine models were experimented in the course of the present studies. Each individual model was designed with a view to serve a specific purpose. Seven of the nine models were made primarily for the purpose of examining the validity of the analysis. This group of models has an increasing degree of complexity in construction such that each model examines the validity of a particular aspect of the analysis. Experiments were also conducted on a model made of real laminations of the stator of a medium-sized induction machine and on a real stator of a 7.5 hp induction motor. Details of the various models are presented in reference [13].

For each model, values of all possible resonant frequencies of the model as well as amplitudes and mode-shapes (circumferential and longitudinal) of the associated vibrations were measured. The measured frequency response of a toothed model is given in Fig. 2 for illustration. In Fig. 2, resonance peaks which belong to the actual resonance spectrum of the model are identified by the corresponding values of resonant frequency, the order of the frequency, and the associated circumferential mode of vibration. The remaining peaks are identified as parasitic resonances which are either tooth-resonances or dual resonances marked by "D".

Comparisons made between the experimental and the analytical results show that the analysis delivers reasonable accuracy for the calculation of both the first and the third order resonant frequencies of stators [14]. Also, the single trigonometric function assumed in the analysis for displacement distribution along stator circumference is found to be valid. Unlike the general frequency equation, a frequency equation derived on the basis of the assumption of equal amplitudes of vibration along the machine length is found to deliver results with substantial errors.

In the course of the experimental investigations, third order resonant frequencies as predicted by the analysis have been traced, which proves the actual existence of resonant frequencies other than the lowest resonant frequency for each mode of vibration. These higher resonances may well lie within the critical frequency range of noise production, especially in the case of large machines.

In the course of the search process for second order resonant frequencies as predicted by the analysis, it was difficult to establish a correlation between values of this group of frequencies and values of measured axial resonances. It is believed that the point excitation is incapable of exciting the actual axial resonances in a model.

The experimental results have also proved the validity of the assumption of the analysis that amplitudes of vibration are not equal along machine length and that resonant frequencies of stators may be associated with a symmetric or antisymmetric longitudinal mode of vibration. Two other important phenomena predicted by the analysis were also supported by the experimental results. These are the phenomenon of dual resonance and the phenomenon of coupling between various components of displacement. These phenomena are of practical significance. The experimental results have also proved that the theoretically predicted relation of "inverse proportionality" between values of resonant frequencies and stator diameter is true. Such a relation would mean that in the case of large machines, a greater number of resonant frequencies may lie within the critical frequency range of noise production. Consequently, a higher possibility of coincidence between exciting frequencies and resonant frequencies is created which could eventually lead to noisier machines.

PART 2: CONTRIBUTION OF TEETH, WINDINGS, FRAME AND LAMINATIONS TO RESONANT FREQUENCIES AND VIBRATION BEHAVIOUR OF STATORS AT RESONANCE

Measurements on five experimental models were used for the purpose of this study. To investigate the effect of teeth, for example, measured values of resonant frequencies and amplitudes of vibration of a slotted model which coincides with the stator laminations of a 150 hp induction motor were compared with those of a smooth model which coicides with the yoke of the stator. A similar procedure was used to conduct the other parts of the study. Detailed investigations are presented in reference [5].

Important findings of this study are:

1) Windings impose considerable restriction on lateral movements of teeth to such an extent that the combined effect of teeth and windings on values of resonant frequencies approaches a mass-effect. This is demonstrated in Table 1; where resonant frequencies of a smooth model are compared with those of a corresponding model with teeth & windings. As shown in Table 1, the tooth

& winding factor, which is calculated on the basis of the ratio between frequencies of models with and without teeth and windings, almost coincides with the combined mass-effect of teeth and windings calculated as:

$$\sqrt{\frac{\text{Mass of Yoke alone}}{\text{Mass of Yoke + teeth + windings}}} = \sqrt{\frac{12.3}{19.7}} = 0.79$$

2) Frames in the encased construction have slight effect on values of resonant frequencies, and therefore, can be ignored in the calculations as a first approximation.
3) The laminated structure of stators can be adequately treated as solid in the calculation of resonant frequencies. This conclusion is based on the results reported in Table 2.
4) Teeth cause an appreciable increase in amplitudes of vibration due to their own lateral vibrations especially at frequencies lying in the region of tooth resonance. On the other hand, windings and laminations suppress vibrations of stators to a large extent while frames cause only slight damping of vibrations.
5) Teeth, windings, and frame have a slight effect on material damping of stators. On the contrary, material damping in presence of laminations is significantly greater than that of solid structures expecially at lower flexural circumferential modes.

TABLE 1 - Measured values of resonant frequencies for the study of the combined effect of teeth and windings.

Mode	First Order Resonant Frequencies			Third Order Resonant Frequencies		
n	Model V (yoke alone)	Model VI (with teeth & windings)	Tooth & Winding Factor	Model V (yoke alone)	Model VI (with teeth & windings)	Tooth & Winding Factor
0	—	—	—	3831	3011	0.79
1	—	—	—	5367	4392	0.82
2	599	515	0.86	8440	7026	0.83
3	1652	1357	0.82	11897	10008	0.84
4	3067	2420	0.79	16720	*	—
5	4687	3720	0.79	**	*	—
6	6542	5023	0.77	**	*	—

* Frequencies could not be traced ** Frequencies were not measured, being > 20 kHz

TABLE 2 - Measured values of resonant frequencies of models III and VIII for the study of effect of laminations.

Mode	First Order Resonant Frequencies			Third Order Resonant Frequencies		
n	Model III slotted solid	Model VIII slotted laminated	Difference in %	Model III slotted solid	Model VIII slotted laminated	Difference in %
0	—	—	—	3290	3312	+0.7
1	—	—	—	4476	4497	+0.5
2	510	537	+5.3	5124	4899	-4.4
3	1358	1387	+2.1	5219	4967	-4.8
4	2411	2495	+3.5	5409	5228	-3.3
5	3444	3538	+2.7	5757	5388	-6.4
6	4122	4246	+3.0	6679	6765	+1.3
7	4327	4461	+3.1	8023	8048	+0.3

A direct application of the findings of this study is in the derivation of proper expressions for the effects of teeth, windings, frame, and laminations on resonant frequencies of stators. The incorporation of such expressions in analyses for accurate determination of values of resonant frequencies of stators is very important in relation to the problem of electromagnetic acoustic noise in electrical machines.

Further investigations were carried out on the laminated stator structure of a 4-pole 125 h.p. induction motor. This stator is shown in Fig. 3. Efforts are directed to develop simplified methods to determine resonant frequencies with the required degree of accuracy.

SYMBOLS

A	Cross-sectional area
E	Modulus of elasticity
G	Shear modulus of elasticity
J	Torsional constant
$R_{c\theta}$	Radius of gyration of area about centroidal axis parallel to coordinate θ
R_{cp}	Polar radius of gyration of area about centroidal axis
$R_{s\theta}$	Radius of gyration of area about an axi parallel to coordinate θ at the supporting structure
r, θ, z	Cylindrical coordinates
u, v, w	Axial, tangential and radial components of displacement
u_b, v_b, w_b	Components of displacement at the base
r_b	Radius of curvature of the base
r_c	Distance between the centroid and the base
r_i, r_o	Inner and outer radii
ρ	Material density
μ	Poisson's ratio
$\sigma_r, \sigma_\theta, \sigma_z$	Components of normal stresses
$\varepsilon_r, \varepsilon_\theta, \varepsilon_z$	Components of normal strains
$\tau_{r\theta}, \tau_{rz}, \tau_{\theta z}$	Components of shear stresses
$\gamma_{r\theta}, \gamma_{rz}, \tau_{\theta z}$	Components of shear strains

ACKNOWLEDGEMENT

The financial support from the Natural Sciences and Engineering Research Council of Canada and the University of Saskatchewan for this research work is gratefully acknowledged.

REFERENCES

1. Davies, R.J., "Noise from electrical machines – the community and the worker", Proc. I.E.E., Vol. 117, No. 1, January 1970, p. 126.
2. Shapiro, H. and Fallon, W.H., "Low-noise motor design", Elect. Mfg., May 1960, 65, pp. 265-269.
3. Putz, W., "On the magnetic noise of salient-pole synchronous machines" (in German), Zeitschrift für Elektrotechnik, 1948, pp. 53-59.
4. Jordan, H. and Frohne, H. "Determination of resonance frequencies of stators of polyphase motors" (in German), Lärmbekämpfung N., 1957, 1, pp. 137-140.
5. Frohne, H., "On the main Parameters which determine the Noise-Level of Asynchronous Machines" (in German), Doctoral Thesis, Technical University of Hannover, W. Germany, 1959.
6. Ellison, A. and Yang, S., "Natural Frequencies of Stators of Small Electric Machines", Proc. I.E.E., Vol. 118, No. 1, January 1971, pp. 185-190.
7. Verma, S.P. and Girgis, R.S., "Resonance Frequencies of Electrical Machine Stators having Encased Construction, Part I: Derivation of the General Frequency Equation", IEEE Trans., Vol. PAS-92, No. 5, September/October 1973, pp. 1577-1585.
8. Verma, S.P. and Girgis, R.S., "Resonance Frequencies of Electrical Machine Stators Having Encased Construction, Part II: Numerical Results and Experimental Verification", IEEE Trans., PAS-92, No. 5, September/October 1973, pp. 1586-1593.
9. Anderson, R.A., "Fundamentals of Vibrations", The Macmillan Company, New York, 1967, Chapter II.
10. Girgis, R.S. and Verma, S.P., "Method for accurate determination of resonant frequencies and vibration behaviour of stators of electrical machines", IEE-Proceedings (England), Paper No. 1011B, Power App. Section, Vol. 128, Pt. B, No. 1, January 1981, pp. 1-11.
11. Erdelyi, E., "Predetermination of the Sound-Pressure Levels of the Magnetic Noise in Medium-Induction Motors", Ph.D. Thesis, University of Michigan, 1955.
12. White, J.C., "The Flexural Vibrations of Thin Laminated Cylinders", Journal of Engineering of Industry, ASME Trans., November 1961, pp. 397-402.
13. Verma, S.P. and Girgis, R.S., "Experimental verification of resonant frequencies and vibration behaviour of stators of electrical machines; Part 1 – Models, experimental procedure and apparatus", IEE-Proceedings (England), Paper No. 1012B, Power App. Section, Vol. 128, Pt. B, No. 1, January 1981, pp. 12-21.
14. Verma, S.P. and Girgis, R.S., "Experimental verification of resonant frequencies and vibration behaviour of stators of electrical machines; Part 2 – Experimental investigations and results", IEE-Proceedings (England), Paper No. 1013B, Power App. Section, Vol. 128, Pt. B, No. 1, January 1981, pp. 22-32.
15. Girgis, R.S. and Verma, S.P., "Resonant frequencies and vibration behaviour of stators of electrical machines as affected by teeth, windings, frame and laminations", IEEE Trans., Vol. PAS-98, 1979, pp. 1446-1455.

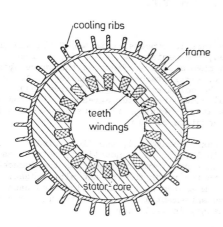

Figure 1   Cross-section of the stator under consideration

Figure 3   Laminated stator structure of a 4-pole
125 h.p. induction motor (core alone)

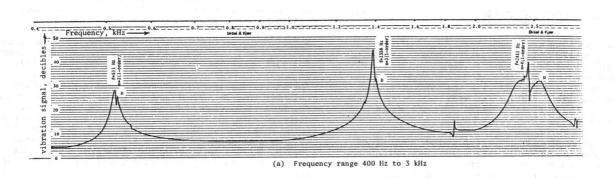

(a)   Frequency range 400 Hz to 3 kHz

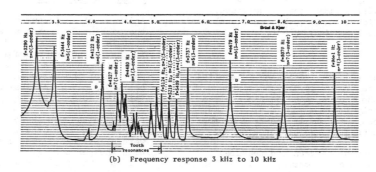

(b)   Frequency response 3 kHz to 10 kHz

Figure 2   Measured resonance spectrum of Model III (solid slotted-ring with teeth alone)

ELECTROMAGNETIC SIMULATION OF THE FLUX DECAY TEST FOR DETERMINING TURBINE-GENERATOR PARAMETERS

P.J. Turner   and   D.C. Macdonald

formerly: Imperial College, London.   Department of Electrical Engineering,
now: Stafford Laboratory,   Imperial College,
            G.E.C. Power Engineering Ltd.,   London, SW7 2BT, U.K.
            P.O. Box 30, Stafford, ST17 4LN, U.K.

INTRODUCTION

The finite-element method has been used for some
12 years for solving electromagnetic field problems (1).
Most of the published work has been devoted to steady-
state conditions, but similar methods have been used
to solve transient problems. Here a transient
2-dimensional analysis is used to simulate the
turbine-generator flux decay test (2), in which the
machine is excited via the stator from the supply network. The supply is suddenly removed, and the
subsequent decay of stator voltage and field current
is observed. Calculation is made for a 500 MW
generator for which there are test results measured by
the C.E.G.B. Flux density and eddy current plots provide insight into the action of the machine. Machine
reactances and time constants from test and calculated
performance compare well. The effect of saturation
and eddy currents in individual parts of the rotor is
investigated, and the significance of each is assessed.

METHOD

The transient electromagnetic field within a cross-
section of a turbine-generator can be described by:

$$\frac{\partial}{\partial x}\left\{ \nu\, \frac{\partial A}{\partial x} \right\} + \frac{\partial}{\partial y}\left\{ \nu\, \frac{\partial A}{\partial y} \right\} = -J + \sigma\left\{ \frac{\partial A}{\partial t} \right\} \ \ldots\ldots\ldots (1)$$

In numerical terms, this is approximated by magnetic
vector potential, A, and current, I, at nodes between
first-order elements by:

$$\left[S \right]\left\{ A \right\} = \left[I \right] - \left[\Delta\sigma \right]\left\{ \frac{\partial A}{\partial t} \right\} \qquad \ldots\ldots\ldots (2)$$

Numerical equations are formulated by the nodal
method (3), rather than by the variational approach,
but the difference is slight. An iterative
Newton-Raphson technique is used to converge the iron
permeability in each element and the current at each
node to a consistent solution at each time step, as was
done previously for field decrement (4) and sudden
short-circuit tests (5).

The conductivity matrix $\left[\Delta\sigma \right]$ ensures that the induced
currents arising from $\partial A/\partial t$ values are represented in
the solution, and at each iteration the set of
simultaneous equations, (2) above, is solved using
Jennings' modified Gaussian-elimination Scheme (6).
An initial time-step may take 7 iterations, but,
subsequently, with sufficiently short time-steps,
3 iterations may suffice to reduce the fractional rms
error in potentials to less than 10^{-7} (7).

FLUX DECAY TEST

In the flux decay test (2), the generator is excited
from the stator, and the rotor is driven at synchronous speed with the flux aligned on the desired
axis. The stator supply is suddenly disconnected,
and the subsequent decay of flux is observed by the
rotational voltage induced in the stator winding.

Fig. 1 shows good agreement between the measured
points and the calculated decay curve, (a), for the
d-axis with the field coupled to a discharge resistor
of about twice the field winding resistance.

When the test is repeated with the field winding short-
circuited, the resistance of the field circuit is
found to have a strong effect on the curve obtained.
Initially, a resistance corresponding to $120^{\circ}C$ was
used in the calculation (Fig. 1, Curve (b)).
Curve (c) shows the better agreement with the measured
points that was obtained with the more realistic light-
load temperature of $60^{\circ}C$.

In the q-axis decay test, the field winding has no
current in it, and the conductivity matrix has only
leading diagonal terms representing the induced
current in the rotor forging and slot wedges. Fig. 1
shows the measured points and calculated decay curve,
(d). The agreement is good, but the measured values
have a larger initial drop.

The reason for this discrepancy was initially thought
to be that the discretisation was too coarse at the
rotor surface, and the study was repeated with 997,
instead of 500, nodes for half a pole-pitch. This
allowed the depth of surface elements to be reduced by
a factor of 5. Fig. 2 shows that this only brought
the calculated curve a little nearer the measured one.

The remaining discrepancy is thought to arise because
the bulk of the eddy currents flow initially in the
pole surfaces, as shown in Fig. 3. In the calculations, the poles have been taken as solid steel, but
in the real rotor stiffness-equalisation gashes occur
at intervals, increasing the resistance to eddy
currents near the surface. Modern designs commonly
have pole-face wedges, and this difficulty in calculation has been removed.

Rotor body effects: No tests were made with the field
circuit open, but calculations made for a d-axis decay
for this condition are shown in Fig. 1 as Curve (e).

Initially, the q-axis flux decays more rapidly. The
eddy current plots show that current quickly penetrates
the slotted portion of the rotor during the d-axis,
compared with the relatively slow penetration into the
rotor poles during the q-axis test. However, the ultimate rate of decay of flux on the q-axis is slower than
that on the d-axis because the large rotor-pole area
is available to carry eddy currents which link most of
the q-axis flux.

PARAMETER DETERMINATION

An argument in favour of flux-decay tests has been that
the machine is tested at a flux level comparable with
that in operating conditions. The initial flux level
is that of normal operation, but the extraction of any
long time-constant from a decay curve will use the
portion of the curve where the flux level has fallen
below 0.3 p.u., and the eddy currents have progressed
into the rotor body.

A calculation was therefore made to find out if the
decrease in flux density and change in permeabilities
were significant. The d-axis decay was re-calculated
with the permeabilities held constant at their initial
values. The difference brought about by fixing permeabilities was very small, and is reflected in slight
changes in parameters shown in Table 1. The change in
the field current was negligible.

It is difficult to understand how the difference in degree of saturation can cause so little change in performance, and more work is required to see whether this is generally true for other machines. The complicated behaviour of the rotor core and poles is demonstrated by the flux pattern during the q-axis decay in Fig. 4. The flux density in the core has remained at virtually the initial value, but, instead of flowing into the stator, has gone into a leakage path across the surface of the poles, and the flux density there has become approximately twice that in the core.

Table 1 shows parameters from the two-time-constant fit obtained when exponentials are fitted to the decay curves along the machine axes. The differences between simulation and test values are small, indicating that computations done at the design stage could make tests unnecessary. They would also be cheaper.

Effect of different rotor circuits: Calculations have been made to show the relative importance of the rotor damping circuits by obtaining d-axis flux decays with different parts of the rotor conducting. Results are shown in Table 2.

One or more exponentials are used:

$$V = A e^{-t/T_1} + B e^{-t/T_2}$$

The decay curve of some circuits acting alone, such as the field winding, the rotor wedges and rotor teeth, can be fitted very well by a single exponential curve. The permeabilities of all elements were kept at their initial values, and the inability to fit the decay curve with an exponential must arise from diffusion of flux and eddy currents within the region being considered. When the rotor poles or core are considered conducting, a variety of exponentials may be used to represent the decay, but each is only a good fit over a limited range. Two bad fits are shown for each.

Although the wedges and teeth are large conductors, they are compact when compared with the rotor body and the poles, and diffusion effects are comparatively small. When the field winding, wedges and teeth are considered together, the resulting long time constant is virtually the sum of their individual values. The fast time constants become smaller in the presence of the field winding, as it confines initial changes in flux into leakage paths across the tops of the rotor slots.

The whole of the rotor without the field winding produces a problematical fit: it is poor with two time constants, and a variety of combinations is possible, 2.7-6.5s being accompanied by 0.7-1.3s. If the rotor body effects are considered alone, and for long enough, the best exponential fit has one time constant even longer than that arising from the field circuit. A sensible first approach to modelling the d-axis might be to sum the time constants of the winding, wedges and teeth (7.36s) and allow the pole and rotor body to account for the remainder (1.58s). A more thoughtful combination could result in an equivalent circuit similar to those used for many years, and more recently extended to have several damping circuit branches. The advantage of this approach would be that the relation between rotor components and circuit elements would be known, and the behaviour in other conditions would be better modelled.

CONCLUSIONS

D- and q-axis flux decay tests have been simulated successfully by transient finite-element analysis. The principal shortcoming was in the q-axis, the high initial resistance of the rotor pole surface resulting from the presence of rotor-stiffness-equalisation gashes not being represented. In the absence of a field winding, the behaviour of each rotor axis is similar, the difference being understandable in terms of the shape of the rotor cross-section.

TABLE 1: Machine parameters derived from the flux decay test, and from calculation: p.u. reactance and s

Source	X_d	X_d'	X_d''	T_{do}'	T_{do}''	X_q	X_q'	X_q''	T_{qo}'	T_{qo}''
Test	2.59	0.483	0.312	9.5	2.5	2.16	1.4	0.6	2.9	0.6
Calculation (a)	2.39	0.441	0.275	8.27	2.7	1.97	1.16	0.66	2.96	0.8
Calculation (b)	2.39	0.530	0.321	8.95	2.7					

Calculation (a) is with permeabilities correctly up-dated at each step.
Calculation (b) is with permeabilities kept constant at initial values.

TABLE 2: D-axis flux decay: initial voltage 22 kV
Permeabilities of elements held constant: field winding resistance corresponds to 60°C

Part of rotor considered conducting	Voltage t = 0+	X_1 (p.u.)	Exponential fit				Comments
			A	T_1	B	T_2	
All and the field winding	20,241	0.1913	17,124	8.95	1,920	2.7	
Field winding only	18,951	0.3317	18,951	6.209			Perfect fit
Wedges only	20,186	0.1974	20,012	0.0803			Good fit
Teeth only	20,222	0.1934	18,032	1.0737			Reasonable fit
Pole only	12,180	1.0683	948 / 4,985	2.0 / 0.1			Very poor fit
Core only	17,786	0.4584	4,000 / 7,000	2.7 / 1.0			Very poor fit
Wedges and field winding	20,186	0.1974	18,975	6.285	981	0.0045	
Teeth and field winding	20,222	0.1934	19,020	7.209	1,000	0.01	
Wedges, teeth and field winding	20,222	0.1934	19,040	7.285	920	0.02	
Wedges, teeth, core and poles	20,261		11,500 / 3,224	2.7 / 6.5	7,500 / 15,000	0.7 / 1.3	Poor fit: $T_1 \simeq$ 2.0-7.0s

Surprisingly, the use of initial permeabilities throughout a decay curve calculation produced virtually no change in the performance. The action of the different rotor circuits on the d-axis flux have been defined. The rotor poles and body are not well-fitted by exponential curves.

The method has been shown to be useful in modelling realistic and hypothetical test conditions. It is hoped to continue similar studies, to show which parameters determined here, and in other calculations, are relevant to particular machine operating conditions.

ACKNOWLEDGMENTS

Thanks are due to the C.E.G.B. for test results, to G.E.C. Power Engineering Ltd. and S.E.R.C. for a CASE studentship, to Professor E.M. Freeman for use of MAGMESH, and to S.E.R.C. for other computing facilities. The help and guidance of many colleagues are gratefully acknowledged.

REFERENCES

1. Silvester, P., and Chari, M.V.K., 1970, I.E.E.E. Trans. PAS, 89, 1642-1649.

2. Shackshaft, G., and Poray, A.T., 1977, Proc. I.E.E., 124, 1170-1178.

3. Hannalla, A.Y., and Macdonald, D.C., 1975, I.E.E.E. Trans. on Magnetics, 11, 1544-1546.

4. — 1976, Proc. I.E.E., 123, 863-898.

5. — 1980, Proc. I.E.E.(c), 127, 213-220.

6. Jennings, A., 1966, Computer J., 9, 281-285.

7. Turner, P.J., and Macdonald, D.C., 1982, Paper 82WM 101-4, to be published in I.E.E.E. Trans. PAS.

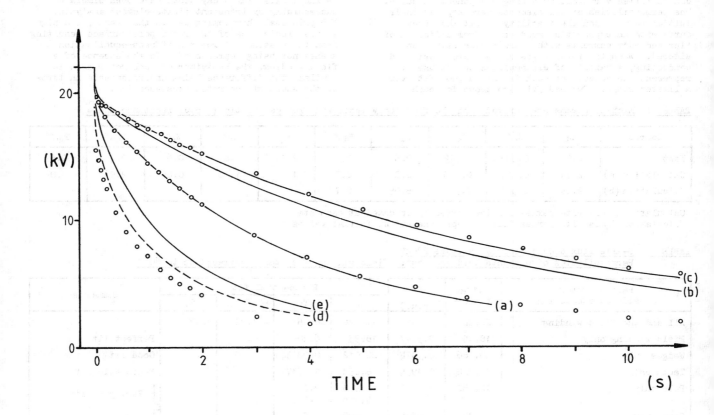

Fig. 1: Flux decay curves computed with 500 nodes and measured points:
    (a) d-axis with discharge resistor in the field circuit
    (b) d-axis with short-circuited field winding at 120°C
    (c) d-axis with short-circuited field winding at 60°C
    (d) q-axis decay
    (e) d-axis decay with the field open

    o o o Points measured by the C.E.G.B.
        corresponding to Curves (a), (c) and (d)

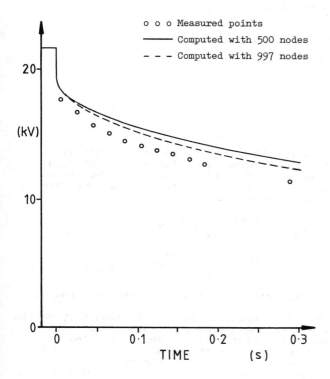

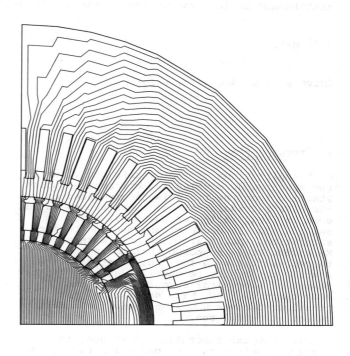

Fig. 2: Q-axis decay curves with more nodes.

Fig. 4: Q-axis flux 0.3074s after the start of a
flux decay calculated with 997 nodes.

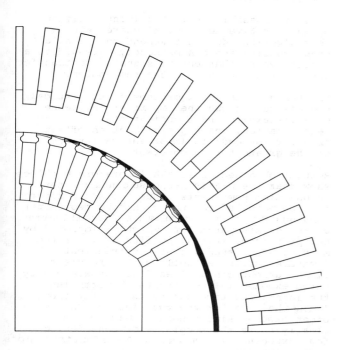

Fig. 3: Eddy current contours in the rotor
2.0×10^{-4}s after the start of a q-axis
decay.

MEASUREMENT OF THE DYNAMIC PARAMETERS OF SYNCHRONOUS MACHINES

J.C. Maun

University of Brussels, Belgium

1. INTRODUCTION

Most applications of the dynamic behaviour of the synchronous machine are currently studied starting from the two axis theory based on the PARK's transformation. This theory builds upon an idealization of the synchronous machine. The fundamental assumptions concern saturation, space harmonics and leakage. Moreover, it is supposed that the rotor can be represented by a few equivalent circuits. A solid rotor must be modelled as an infinite number of electrical circuits where the eddy currents flow. With saturation, the behaviour becomes non-linear and the modelling is not strictly true.

We see that the theoretical developments involve a set of assumptions which have been criticized by some authors. Nevertheless, we think that local studies of flux and currents are not necessary for most of the present modelling applications.

Results given by the simulations will be really accurate only if we dispose of a complete model as well as of a set of adequate parameters. Now we must point out that the test methods have but little evolved. The main criticisms for the standard test methods are :
1- The treatment is manual and graphic.
2- The theoretical developments leading to the relations giving the parameters are based on analytical solutions. This implies
   - a lot of simplifying assumptions ;
   - the impossibility to consider models with enough electrical circuits.
3- The treatment of these tests does not use all of the experimental signals and, sometimes it does not consider all the available data.
4- It is not uncommon to have a discrepancy between a simulation using the derived parameters and experimental results, particulary for the dynamic behaviour seen from the field circuit access.

Therefore, four classical methods have been developed with the same approach :
1- The use of a numerical data acquisition.
2- A complete automatisation of the treatment based on the use of a mini-computer.
3- The derivation of the response parameters by an optimal numerical identification.
4- The use of all the data and of all the available signals for a simultaneous identification taking the common parameters into account.
5- The developments of new methods to derive the parameters based on the complete analytical expressions and on the provided sensibility of the parameters.

2. THE STATOR DECREMENT TEST AT STANDSTILL

It is well-known that the transient current is constituted by a sum of decaying exponentials. The rotor position allows to excite both the q- or the d-axis circuits. For the d-axis, it is fundamental to note that we dispose of a measure at the stator as well as at the rotor. The currents are given, for the d-axis, by

$$i_d(t) = \sum_{i=1}^{nd+2} I_{di} \, e^{-t/T_{di}} \qquad \sum_i I_{di} = I_{do}$$

$$i_f(t) = \sum_{i=1}^{nd+2} I_{fi} \, e^{-t/T_{di}} \qquad \sum_i I_{fi} = 0$$

The transfer functions have the same poles.

The first problem consists in indentifying the amplitudes and time constants. A numerical automatisation of the graphic semi-log plot method increases the treatment swiftness and excludes a good deal of the operator subjectivity. But the derivation of the components is carried out step by step and does not lead to a global optimum of the signal identification. It is better to use a static optimalisation algorithm like the Proni-Householder method based on a constant step sampling and on a non-linear transformation of the time constants. The identification is then very accurate, but the algorithm complexity limits strongly the number of samples that it is possible to handle in a mini-computer.

Another possibility is the identification by an iterative mean least square method. This algorithm does not depend on a constant step sampling and can be easely extended to a simultaneous treatment of signals the transfer functions of which have the same poles.

The tests of those algorithms on theoretical signals have shown the important influence of a mistake in the transient start determination, and especially of an offset error. This leads to important variations on the greatest time constant.

Results obtained on 14 kVA laboratory machines show that the q-axis response contains three exponential components. Thus the solid rotor must be modelled for the q-axis by two damper windings. But it is principally the identification of the d-axis parameters which is improved by our procedure. Indeed, we find out, for the machine under study, that the transient armature current as well as the transient field current can be identified separately by three exponential components. Nevertheless, the identified time constants are far from being the same for the two signals. On the other hand, a simultaneous identification clearly shows the necessity of considering four exponential components. The identifications then prove more stable and accurate.

These results allow to calculate the resistances and the inductances of d- and q-axis equivalent circuits. The d-axis model contains two damper windings with two mutual leakage inductances between the rotor circuits.

3. THE SUDDEN THREE-PHASE SHORT CIRCUIT TEST

The treatment of this test by the envelopes method in a semi-log plot is derived from the well-known classical analytical expressions of the short-circuit currents displaying the transient and subtransient reactances and time constants. Those equations are based on a lot of simplifying assumptions. Indeed the correct expressions can be written, for a model with two damper windings on the whole

$$
\begin{aligned}
i_a(t) = \; & I_{ao}\cos(\omega_r t + \alpha_o + \varepsilon_o) \\
& + I_{a1}\cos(\omega_r t + \alpha_o + \varepsilon_1)e^{-t/T_{c1}} \\
& + I_{a2}\cos(\omega_r t + \alpha_o + \varepsilon_2)e^{-t/T_{c2}} \\
& + I_{a3}\cos(\omega_r t + \alpha_o + \varepsilon_3)e^{-t/T_{c3}} \\
& + I_{a4}\cos[(\omega_r - \omega_c)t + \alpha_o + \varepsilon_4]e^{-t/T_{c4}} \\
& + I_{a5}\cos[(\omega_r + \omega_c)t + \alpha_o + \varepsilon_5]e^{-t/T_{c4}}
\end{aligned}
$$

$$
\begin{aligned}
i_f(t) = \; & I_{fo} + I_{f1}\,e^{-t/T_{c1}} \\
& + I_{f2}\,e^{-t/T_{c2}} \\
& + I_{f3}\,e^{-t/T_{c3}} \\
& + I_{f4}\cos(\omega_c t + \varepsilon_f)e^{-t/T_{c4}}
\end{aligned}
$$

The use of these complete expressions is essential for an identification, not only of the envelopes, but of all the available data, which was the only means to improve basically the treatment of this test.

A detailed study of the influence of every classical assumption constitutes a serious criticism of the accuracy of the standard test treatment. It shows effects neglected by the classical treatment like the influence of the q-axis circuits on the 2 ω and subtransient components, as well as a difference in phase between the alternating components.

For the identification of these complete expressions, it is necessary to take a great care of the preliminary data conditioning. Indeed, the theory and the deduced algorithms require a strictly constant rotation speed. Therefore, we have transformed the time scale in a fictitious one linked to the rotor position that it is necessary to measure.

The transient response parameters, amplitudes, phases and time constants are identified by a mean least square method. Nevertheless, this identification can be greatly improved by a simultaneous treatment of several signals, for example the three phase currents or a phase and the field current.

Indeed, it appears that the amplitude and the phase of the aperiodic component, as well as the forced pulsation can not be accurately identified by only one phase current. In the same way, the identification of the subtransient components is nearly impossible on the field current because those components are blinded by the alternate term. On the other hand, a measure of the forced pulsation is easy with this signal. A simultaneous treatment of the three phase currents greatly improves the identification of the aperiodic term and consequently of the 2 ω component.

But it is specially a simultaneous treatment of a phase and the field current that offers the best reliability of all the parameters given by this test.

This method has been tested on laboratory machines. Results obtained show clearly the necessity to take into account the complete analytical expressions. Indeed, we point out that this procedure is the only way accurate enough to derive a model which can simulate correctly the three phase current as well as the field current.

From the identification results of the short-circuit currents, the derivation of the internal parameters leads to a difficult problem. Theoretically, it is possible to deduce a set of parameters for both the axis. But the influence of the q-axis circuits is too small with this test to have a satisfactory accuracy by this way. An original method has then been developed which consists in taking this influence into account under the form of corrections to derive the parameters of the common denominator of the transfer functions, namely the d- and q-axis short-circuit time constants. In spite of certain approximation in the treatment of the q-axis values, we obtain this way a greatly improved accuracy in the derivation of all the parameters.

4. THE STANDSTILL FREQUENCY RESPONSE TEST

An important development of this test took place during the last years. This test leads to a measurement of the harmonic impedances

$$
\begin{aligned}
v_d/i_d &= Z_d(j\omega) = R_a + j\omega L_d(j\omega) \\
v_q/i_q &= Z_q(j\omega) = R_a + j\omega L_q(j\omega)
\end{aligned}
$$

Unfortunately, there is a difficult problem of measurement accuracy for the d-axis, because the dynamic behaviour of the harmonic inductance is blinded by the armature resistance. The synchronous reactance and the transient time constants will be derived with a poor accuracy by this test. The use of the field current can resolve this problem. Indeed, the transmittance between the armature and the field current is given by

$$
i_f/i_d = T(j\omega) = j\omega G_f(j\omega)
$$

The armature resistance does not step in this expression and an accurate identification will be possible at low frequency.

The frequency response identification is achieved by a classical iterative algorithm which minimizes the square sum of the absolute distances between the measurement and the theoretical vectors. This algorithm has been improved to respond to the specific needs of this test. It allows a simultaneous treatment of the harmonic responses of two signals of which the transfer function poles are the same, like $Z_d(j\omega)$ and $T(j\omega)$.

The test results show that the identification can be done simultaneously on the two d-axis measures with a two damper windings model. We point out that the treatment of only the harmonic impedance, although it identifies the response accurately, leads to a model with one damper winding. The values of the synchronous reactance and of the time constants are then very different from the ones given by other tests or by the simultaneous treatment. This proves the necessity to take this transmittance into account for the treatment of the d-axis response. Moreover, it must be noted that, for the two axis, the algorithm puts a pole and a zero out of the studied frequency band although it was already very large - .04 Hz to 60 Hz. This phenomenon shows the limits of the two axis theory for the description of the dynamic behaviour of machines with solid rotor. For the higher frequencies under study, the phase of the impedances do not reach 90 degrees accurately. The impedance behaviour matches with theoretical conclusions it is possible to draw from a study of the flux into the rotor. The q-axis is more affected because we do not dispose in this case of a second measurement increasing the sensibility of the identification at low frequency, as for the d-axis.

5. ON-LINE FREQUENCY RESPONSE TEST

In this small signal test, the system "synchronous machine" must be considered as a system with two inputs, the field voltage and the mechanical torque, and two outputs, the stator voltage and the load angle - or the speed. The system can be completely characterized by the four transmittances between the inputs and the outputs

$$\Delta U/\Delta V_f = |G_{uf}|\underline{/\phi_{uf}}$$
$$\Delta U/\Delta T_m = |G_{ut}|\underline{/\phi_{ut}}$$
$$\Delta \delta/\Delta V_f = |G_{\delta f}|\underline{/\phi_{\delta f}}$$
$$\Delta \delta/\Delta T_m = |G_{\delta t}|\underline{/\phi_{\delta t}}$$

The theoretical study of these harmonic responses can be done by a linearization of the equations of the dynamic behaviour round a steady-state point. It is possible to calculate the dominant poles and zeros making simplifying assumptions. A detailed study of the numerical values of the equations terms shows that this method leads to important errors. It is better to calculate the values of the theoretical harmonic responses without any assumptions. These values are then identified to derive the dominant poles and zeros in the useful frequency band, between 0.2 Hz and 10 Hz. We point out that the dominant poles, one real and two complex conjugate ones, are the same for the four transmittances. Moreover, the poles and the zeros vary considerably with the working point.

The measurement of these transmittances is somewhat difficult because the inputs have a small amplitude and the machine is rotating. However, the measurement procedure gives accurate values, but into a narrow frequency band. The frequency band it is possible to study is convenient to identify the dominant poles and zeros, but it does not allow an accurate derivation of the internal parameters like the damper windings parameters. This method is not adequate to solve this problem. On the other hand, it gives information of fundamental importance for study and design voltage and speed controllers.

Figures 5 and 6 show two examples of results. The differences between the theoretical and experimental results can be explained by phenomenon neglected in the theoretical study, especially the saturation. Nevertheless, we must point out inaccuracy in the determination of the zeros placed in the higher frequencies under study because the gain of the transmittances decreases rapidly in this zone.

6. CONCLUSION

Although the developed treatments and algorithms lead to a more complete and reliable set of parameters, this improvement has not required a prohibitive increase of the test complexity. Moreover, the use of a standard computer system leads to an efficient test automatization. Thus, it is now possible to obtain fast the complete test results on site. The great care taken in this study of efficient identification algorithms, of the treatment of all the data and particularly of all the available signals leads to the derivation of a more reliable set of dynamic parameters. These tests show yet the limits of the two axis theory, which explain the variations between the parameters deduced from each developed test.

It also appears that none of these tests can be considered better than the others. The simplest tests, especially when the machine is at standstill, allow do deduce the parameters corresponding to the most complete models. But the synchronous machine is then placed in conditions far from a normal operating point. The sudden short-circuit test and especially the on-line frequency response test set the machine in more normal conditions. This excludes some risks of errors but the tests are more difficult to treat and thus the model complexity which it is possible to use is more limited.

Finally, it must be pointed out that the methods developed in this study are adapted to treat the responses of the great turbo-generators. Our tests are being done on laboratory machines because it is easier to study on these the limits of the various methods. Moreover, the poles and the zeros of the transfer functions are closer for these small machines and they constitute an ideal test for the measurement and identification methods before applying them to great synchronous machines.

7. REFERENCES

1. Adkins, B., Harley, R.G., 1975, "The general theory of alternating current machines", Chapman and Hall, London, England.

2. Canay, I.M., 1969, "Causes of discrepancies on calculation of rotor quantities and exact equivalent diagrams of the synchronous machine", IEEE Trans., PAS-88, 1114-1120.

3. Manchur, G. et al., 1972, "Generator models established by frequency response tests on a 555 MVA machine", IEEE Trans., PAS-91, 8 p.

4. Barret, P., Roquefort, Y.M., 1973, "Calculation and measurement of frequency response of large turbogenerators in the presence of small disturbances", IEEE Trans., PAS-92, 1348-1357.

5. Watson, W., Manchur, G., 1974, "Synchronous machine operational impedances from low voltage measurements at the stator terminals", IEEE Trans., PAS-93, 777-784.

6. Shackshaft, G., 1974, "New approach to the determination of synchronous machine parameters from tests", Proc.IEE, 121-11, 1385-1392.

7. Takeda, Y., Adkins, B., 1974, "Determination of synchronous machine parameters allowing for unequal mutual inductances", Proc.IEE, 121-12, 1501-1505.

8. Marxsen, A.L., Morsztyn, K., 1977, "Analysis of synchronous machine transient tests using a minicomputer", Proc. IEE, 124-4, 377-380.

9. Shackshaft, G., 1977, "Implementation of a new approach to the determination of synchronous machine parameters from tests", Proc. IEE, 124-12, 1170-1178.

10. Umans, S.D., Wilson, G.L., Mallick, J.A., 1978, "Modelling of solid rotor turbo-generators. Part 1 & 2", IEEE Trans., PAS-97, 269-291.

11. de Mello, F.P., Hannett, L.H., 1981, "Validation of synchronous machine models and derivation of model parameters from tests", IEEE Trans., PAD-100, 662-672.

12. Diggle, R., Dineley, J.L., 1981, "Generatorworks testing-Sudden-short-circuit or standstill variable-frequency-response method", Proc. IEE, 128-4, 177-182.

13. Hallingstad, O., 1980, "Estimation of synchronous machine parameters", Modelling, Identification and Control, I-1, 1-15.

TABLE 1 - Comparison of results obtained on a 14 kVA salient poles machine

	Three-phase short-circuit	Stator decrement	Frequency response
X_d	1.103	1.071	1.080
X_d'	.226	.264	.256
X_d''	.169	.229	.219
X_d'''	——	.194	.201
T_{do}'	522.7	444.8	470.4
T_{do}''	15.86	57.1	56.5
T_{do}'''	——	6.40	3.27
T_d'	107.3	109.5	111.6
T_d''	11.85	49.5	48.4
T_d'''	——	5.42	3.00
T_{kd1}	10.95	63.7	64.2
T_{kd2}	——	4.21	2.59
X_q	.650	.657	.630
X_q''	.491	.516	——
X_q'''	——	.403	.310
T_{qo}''	44.6	43.8	——
T_{qo}'''	——	4.82	6.26
T_q''	33.7	35.5	——
T_q'''	——	3.79	3.00

Reactances in p.u.
Time constants in ms

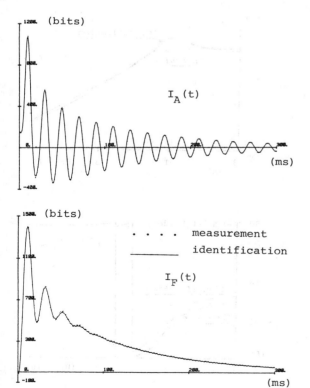

Figure 1 Sudden three-phase short-circuit on a 14 kVA synchronous machine

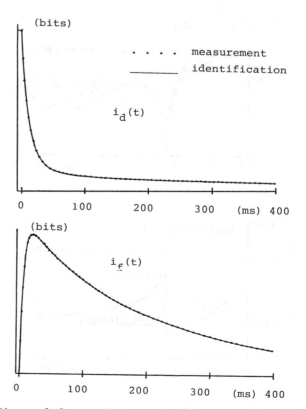

Figure 2 d-axis decrement test at standstill on a 14 kVA synchronous machine

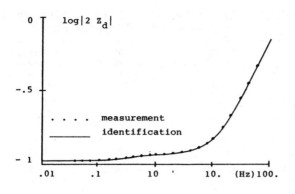

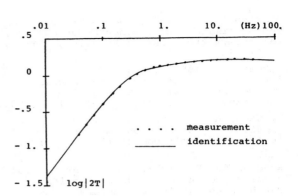

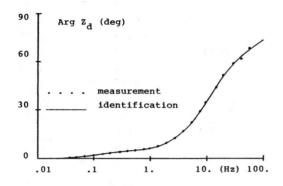

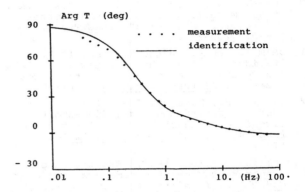

Figure 3 Standstill frequency response test :
d-axis operational impedance

Figure 4 Standstill frequency response test :
transmittance between i_d and i_f

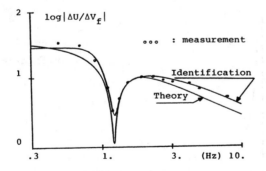

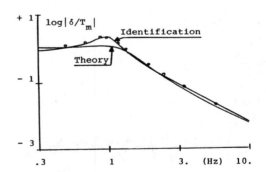

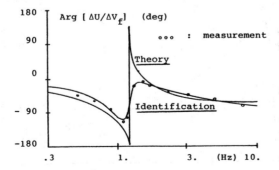

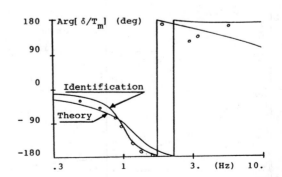

Figure 5 On-line frequency response test :
transmittance between U and V_f

Figure 6 On-line frequency response test :
transmittance between δ and T_m

GENERATOR PARAMETER PREDICTION FROM COMPUTER SIMULATION OF THE STANDSTILL VARIABLE-FREQUENCY INJECTION TEST

A.B.J. Reece, G.K.M. Khan and M.J. Chant

Stafford Laboratory, G.E.C. Power Engineering Ltd.,
P.O. Box 30, Stafford ST17 4LN, U.K.

INTRODUCTION

Designers of synchronous generators are increasingly being pressed to provide a whole range of generator parameters for machine-on-system studies. The normal machine model has a field winding and one damper coil on the direct-axis of the rotor, and a single damper coil on the quadrature-axis. This is an appropriate model for the laminated-pole machine with a damper winding, but, as will be shown later, solid-pole turbine-generators need a larger number of effective coils to represent skin effect in the rotor.

Whatever the order of the model, how can the parameters be obtained? The widely-used "instantaneous short-circuit test" starts with the machine on open-circuit, and therefore flux is established on the direct-axis, so that direct-axis parameters only are obtained. Also, unless digital recording and processing are used, short time constant components are very subject to error. Shackshaft and Poray (1) have proposed the "stator-excited flux decay test", in which the machine is run synchronously, with excitation from the system only, and the relative position of the stator mmf and the rotor direct-axis controlled by the turbine input. The machine is then disconnected from the system, and the voltage decay recorded. Analysis leads to several values of reactance and associated open-circuit time constants, depending on the number of exponentials identified in the decay curve.

The stator-excited flux decay test is a valuable test because, in addition to giving parameters on any axis, the flux values during the test are comparable with those during normal machine operation. However, it can only be carried out at site, and requires special arrangements there, so that opportunities for testing are few. The "stator direct-current decay test", in which the rotor is stationary and direct current, typically of several hundred amperes, is injected into the stator winding to set up flux on the required axis is more convenient, and can be carried out in the manufacturer's works. The stator winding is shorted, the supply removed, and the stator current decay analysed for exponential components. The method has been advocated by Gosbell, of the University of Sydney, and investigated by Tremblay (2).

A test which is now receiving a good deal of attention is the "standstill variable-frequency injection test", in which relatively small currents, of selected frequencies, are injected in turn into the stator winding to obtain operational impedances for the two axes, and also a relationship expressing the stator:field-winding coupling. Reactances, time constants, and the stator:field transfer function can be obtained by fitting polynomials corresponding to the selected number of rotor circuits. If required, the leakage reactances and resistances of these circuits can also be derived. The test can be criticised because contact resistance effects in the damper circuits will be more severe at standstill than when running at normal speed, flux levels are low, and there is an implicit assumption in the analysis that superposition can be applied. However, it does enable models of the required order to be obtained for both direct- and quadrature-axes. It also suggests a way in which parameters might be calculated, for the test can be simulated by digital modelling, using the finite-element method. This paper will refer briefly to parameter determination by curve-fitting to test data for a 350 MW generator, and go on to describe computer simulation of the test. The validity of the method is examined by comparison of calculated and test characteristics and derived parameters for the 350 MW generator.

THE OPERATIONAL IMPEDANCES

The governing machine equations are (Adkins and Harley (3)):

$$U_d = s\psi_d + \omega\psi_q + R_a i_d$$

$$U_q = -\omega\psi_d + s\psi_q + R_a i_q$$

where:

$$\psi_d = L_d(s) i_d + G(s) U_f$$

$$\psi_q = L_q(s) i_q$$

$L_d(s)$, $L_q(s)$ are the axis operational impedances, and $G(s)$ is the field flux to field voltage transfer function.

With sinusoidally-varying currents, $s = j\omega$ and $L_d(s)$, $L_q(s)$ and $sG(s)$ are functions of frequency.

The object of both test and calculation is to determine $L_d(s)$, $L_q(s)$ and $G(s)$ by first deriving the frequency responses, and then fitting functions of the desired form to these responses. $L_d(s)$ and $L_q(s)$ are the stator impedances for a stationary rotor, with current injected into the stator to set up excitation on the relevant axis. It can be shown that $sG(s)$ is the ratio of current (referred to the stator) induced in the field winding to the stator current acting on the direct-axis.

CURVE-FITTING

The functions $L_d(s)$, $L_q(s)$ and $sG(s)$ can be written:

$$L_d(s) = L_d \frac{(1 + sT_d')(1 + sT_d'') \dots}{(1 + sT_{do}')(1 + sT_{do}'') \dots}$$

$$L_q(s) = L_q \frac{(1 + sT_q')(1 + sT_q'') \dots}{(1 + sT_{qo}')(1 + sT_{qo}'') \dots}$$

$$sG(s) = \frac{sG(1 + sT_1) \dots}{(1 + sT_{do}')(1 + sT_{do}'') \dots}$$

where the number of terms in numerator and denominator depends on the order of model (i.e. the number of rotor circuits) required.

A curve-fitting program has been written to minimise the sum of the squares of the errors in the real and imaginary components. The program uses Powell's Minimisation Technique, and incorporates Harwell Sub-routines VA05A and MB11A. Convergence is reliable and speedy. In the case of the direct-axis, $L_d(s)$ and $sG(s)$ are fitted simultaneously, since the denominators are the same. The use of "mutual" data, along with "self" data, reduces the degree of arbitrariness in determination of circuits to represent the rotor, and hence brings about a closer identification with physical components.

Test values of $L_d(s)$, $L_q(s)$ and $sG(s)$ for a 350 MW 2-pole generator are shown in Figs. 1, 2 and 3 respectively. Curve fits are also shown, 2- and 3-rotor circuits being used for $L_d(s)$ and $sG(s)$, and 1- and 2-rotor circuits for $L_q(s)$. The comparisons suggest that the normal use of two circuits is adequate for the direct-axis, and that two circuits, as compared with the usual one, are desirable for the quadrature-axis.

The very low frequency values of $L_d(s)$ and $L_q(s)$ are effectively synchronous reactance values, and they are about 10% lower than the values obtained from works tests and conventional calculations. The difference is a consequence of the low excitation level in the tests, which causes operation on the initial permeability part of the steel magnetisation curves: the value derived from the usual works tests corresponds to no ampere consumption on the iron parts of the magnetic circuit.

SELECTION OF PERMEABILITY FOR CALCULATIONS

As a means of obtaining machine transient parameters, the frequency response approach is sometimes criticised because tests are with low currents, usually in the absence of bias fields, and, in any case, the method assumes the system is linear and superposition applies. The situation in the machine in service is indeed complex: induced fields in the rotor will be roughly at right angles to the main flux pattern, and may be small or large, depending on whether the machine is experiencing small perturbations or large transient disturbances caused by a fault. Fortunately, in large modern generators, much of the induced current in the rotor flows in non-magnetic wedges, damper strips and the field winding, so that saturation effects are probably not dominant in the transient mode (the effect on initial load angle is, of course, important).

Experience has shown that quite good correlation between calculated and test frequency responses can be obtained by using a single value of 100 for the relative permeability of the rotor iron. Some formal justification for this is provided by Minnich (4), who measured incremental permeabilities of rotor steel for small excursions of magnetisation parallel to a wide range of bias flux densities. He included the case of zero bias, and found an incremental permeability of 113 and a differential permeability of 134. The value of 100 has been used in the calculations described below.

CALCULATION OF FREQUENCY-RESPONSE CHARACTERISTICS

If end effects are negligible, or sufficiently small to be taken into account by a simple adjustment factor on resistivity, the flux distribution set up by a sinusoidally-varying stator mmf can be obtained by solving the following 2-dimensional equation for the complex vector magnetic potential, A:-

$$\frac{1}{\mu}\left\{\frac{\partial^2 A}{\partial x^2} + \frac{\partial^2 A}{\partial y^2}\right\} = j\,\omega\,\sigma\,A + \frac{j\,\omega\,\sigma}{n}\sum_{1}^{n} A_n - J$$

$$(1) \qquad (2) \qquad (3)$$

where: (1) relates to components in which induced currents are dependent on local flux linkages

(2) relates to the field winding in which induced current density is uniform across the coil cross-section, and dependent on the mean flux linkage with the winding

(3) relates to the source (in this case, stator) current density, in areas where $\sigma = 0$

This can be solved by the finite-element method, which involves dividing the area into triangles in each of which the magnetic flux density is constant. Very

fine discretisation is needed in steel, where the depth of penetration at 1 kHz is only about 1 mm. When calculating impedance-frequency characteristics for the direct- and quadrature-axes, symmetry means that only a half pole-pitch need be considered. In view of the low excitations, it is reasonable to make the stator iron infinitely-permeable: it can then be excluded from consideration, and computation costs are kept down. As discussed earlier, a relative permeability of 100 is used for the rotor iron.

Fig. 4 shows the discretisation used for the 350 MW generator, which had aluminium alloy wedges in the pole-face and winding slots. Stator ampere-turns are set up in turn on the direct- and quadrature-axes, and set to pulsate at the selected frequency. The fundamental of the flux wave at the stator surface leads to the complex inductance of the active region at the stator bore. The slot and end-winding components of stator leakage reactance must be added to give the terminal inductance. The rotor:stator transfer function (equal to referred field current:stator current) is simply derived from the calculated field-winding current.

RESULTS

Figs. 5, 6 and 7 compare the calculated and test values for $L_d(s)$, $L_q(s)$ and $sG(s)$ respectively. In these calculations, the resistances of current paths through the retaining ring, including contact resistance, have been represented by a resistivity factor of 3, a value based on approximate analysis. Agreement in both modulus and phase is good for $L_d(s)$, where the presence of the closed field tends to dominate the situation. Though the shapes of the calculated and test curves for $L_q(s)$ are similar, there is a displacement of the S-bend, and the errors exceed those previously found for generators with stainless steel wedges, and typified by Fig. 8. It seems likely that the errors result from the approximate treatment of end impedances, including contact resistance, which will be proportionately more important for a low resistivity wedge material. The $sG(s)$ comparison also shows a "shift" between the calculated and test curves, probably for similar reasons, though in this case the approximate treatment of the end turns of the field winding will be an additional factor, particularly at low frequencies. These complicating factors are being investigated, using 3-dimensional calculation methods.

Table 1 compares the derived reactances and time constants obtained from the calculations and tests. The normal model has two rotor coils on the direct-axis and one rotor coil on the quadrature-axis: the higher order model has an additional rotor coil on each axis. In the case of the normal model, for a single damper circuit on the quadrature-axis, the associated reactance has been described as x_q', so allowing the 2-circuit case of the higher order model to have a second reactance, described as x_q''. This practice differs from the normal for the single-coil case, which, because of its association with a damper, rather than a field, coil, is commonly referred to as x_q''.

The calculated reactances for the normal model agree moderately well with test values, but there are substantial errors in the time constants. The reactances of the higher order model agree very well, but again, the calculated time constants are substantially higher: the longest time constants are about 50% greater, and the shortest more than three times the test values. These results support the belief that too small an allowance has been made for additional sources of resistance in the rotor current paths.

TABLE 1: Comparison of Calculated and Test Parameters

Para-meter	Normal model		Higher order model	
	Calc.	Test	Calc.	Test
x_d	1.942	1.867	1.942	1.866
$x_d{}'$	0.311	0.283	0.283	0.284
$x_d{}''$	0.247	0.170	0.245	0.218
$x_d{}'''$			0.225	0.206
x_q	1.842	1.748	1.898	1.836
$x_q{}'$	0.301	0.314	1.190	1.003
$x_q{}''$			0.275	0.261
$T_d{}'$	1.441	0.915	1.453	0.918
$T_d{}''$	0.007	0.003	0.015	0.005
$T_d{}'''$			0.005	0.001
$T_{do}{}'$	8.989	6.028	8.980	6.019
$T_{do}{}''$	0.008	0.005	0.018	0.006
$T_{do}{}'''$			0.006	0.001
$T_q{}'$	0.220	0.124	1.933	1.031
$T_q{}''$			0.133	0.044
$T_{qo}{}'$	1.344	0.69	3.083	1.887
$T_{qo}{}''$			0.578	0.170

Reactances are p.u.: time constants are in seconds.

CONCLUSIONS

Whilst the standstill variable frequency injection test has still to be shown to give parameters suitable for use in the various types of power system transient studies, it is a convenient way of obtaining data for the two axes, and for evaluating the effect of design changes.

A logical method of predicting parameters is essential, and the computer simulation of the frequency response test described in the paper is relatively straight-forward and cheap to carry out. The calculations for the 350 MW generator with aluminium alloy wedges show the main features of the test results are predicted quite well, though discrepancies are greater than experienced for generators with higher resistivity wedges. The errors are probably associated with end-effects, and will be investigated further.

It is concluded that the computer simulation procedure described is a valuable aid to the design engineer.

ACKNOWLEDGMENTS

The authors acknowledge the contribution of colleagues in G.E.C. Turbine Generators Ltd. in the measurement work, and are grateful to G.E.C. Power Engineering Ltd. for permission to publish.

REFERENCES

1. Shackshaft, G., and Poray, A.T., 1977, "Implementation of new approach to determination of synchronous-machine parameters from tests", Proc. I.E.E., 124, No. 12, 1170-1178.

2. Tremblay, J.P., 1972, "Determination of the parameters of a synchronous microgenerator using a static direct current method", M.Sc. Thesis, University of London.

3. Adkins, B., and Harley, R.G., 1975, "The General Theory of Alternating Current Machines", Chapman & Hall, London.

4. Minnich, S.H., 1981, "Incremental permeabilities for transient analysis of large turbine generators by the finite-element method", J. Appl. Phys. (USA), 52, No. 3, Pt. 2, 2428-30.

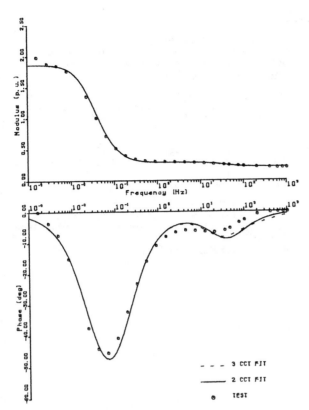

Fig. 1:   350 MW turbine-generator:
Test $L_d(s)$ with 2- and 3-circuit fits.

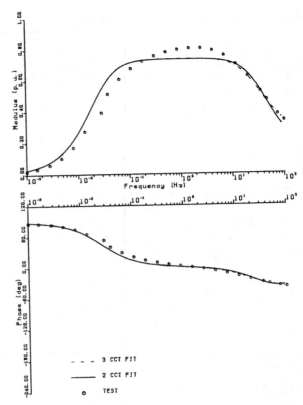

Fig. 3:   350 MW turbine-generator:
Test $sG(s)$ with 2- and 3-circuit fits.

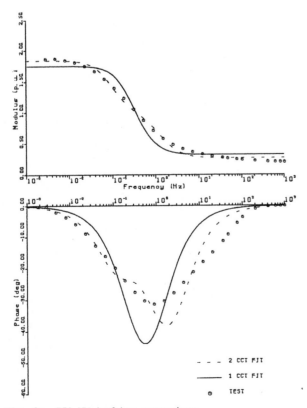

Fig. 2:   350 MW turbine-generator:
Test $L_q(s)$ with 1- and 2-circuit fits.

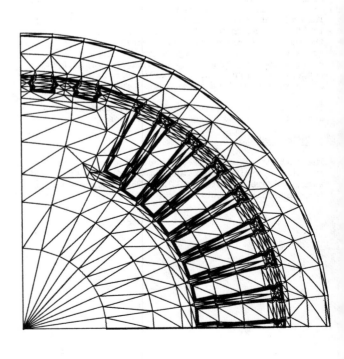

Fig. 4:   350 MW turbine-generator:
Finite-element discretisation of gap and
rotor.

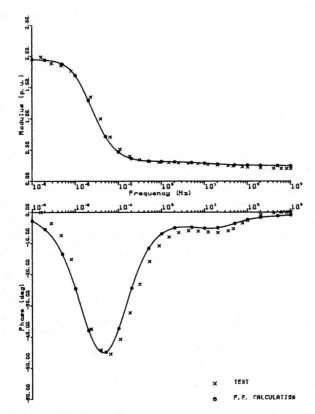

Fig. 5: 350 MW turbine-generator:
Comparison of calculated and test $L_d(s)$.

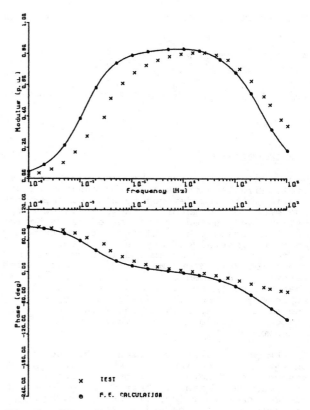

Fig. 7: 350 MW turbine-generator:
Comparison of calculated and test $sG(s)$.

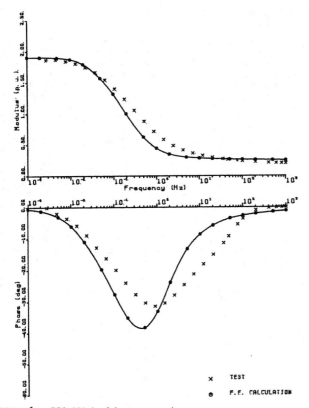

Fig. 6: 350 MW turbine-generator:
Comparison of calculated and test $L_q(s)$.

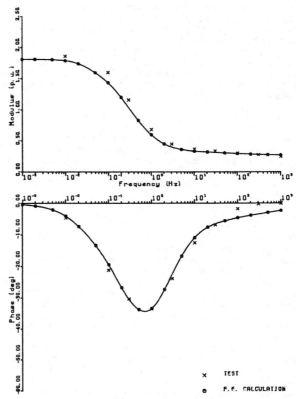

Fig. 8: 660 MW turbine-generator with stainless
steel wedges:
Comparison of calculated and test $L_q(s)$.

THE EFFECTS OF SUPPLY TIME HARMONICS ON THE TORQUE-SPEED CURVES OF SQUIRREL CAGE INDUCTION MOTORS

A.A.D.F.P. Gomes and C.F. Landy

University of the Witwatersrand, Johannesburg, Republic of South Africa

INTRODUCTION

Recent developments in the power electronics field have lead to an ever increasing use of static switching devices to control the torque and speed of ac motors. Invariably the output voltage and current waveforms of these devices contain numerous harmonics and these harmonics have detrimental effects on the motor performance. The order and magnitude of these harmonics depend on the design as well as the nature of the load being supplied. For a 3-phase circuit the harmonics that exist are typically of order -5,+7,-11,+13 etc where the sign indicates the phase rotation of the respective harmonic relative to that of the fundamental.

In the past, extensive research has been done on squirrel cage induction motors in order to assess the effects that these harmonics have on their performance. This work has covered areas such as machine efficiency, stability and generation of parasitic torques. It has been shown[2][3][4][5] that supply time harmonics give rise to an increase in the copper and iron losses, to pulsating shaft-torques and to a small reduction of the steady-state torque produced by the motor. It is, however, usual to ignore the detrimental effects that supply time-harmonics have on the average steady-state torque of the motor as they are normally assumed to be very small. Murphy[9] has estimated the average torque produced in a 2 Hp motor by the 5th supply time-harmonic having a magnitude of 20% of that of the fundamental. In this calculation he assumes a threefold increase in rotor resistance due to skin effect at the harmonic frequency and the torque was found to be only 0,125% of the fundamental torque. In addition, it is argued that the average torques due to the positive-sequence harmonic motor currents tend to cancel the average torques due to the negative-sequence harmonic currents and the overall effect is a slight reduction (less than 1,0%) in the steady-state torque[9].

Based on these two arguments most researchers[2][3][9] ignore the effects of the supply time-harmonic on the average torque of the motor. As will be shown later, this is not always the case and cognisance must be taken of the fact that the negative-sequence harmonic motor currents can be much larger than the positive-sequence harmonic currents, depending on the type of device and associated modulation policy (eg current source inverter, voltage source inverter, etc). A widely used modulation policy for use in pulse width modulated inverters is that described by Müller[8] and it can give rise to very large values of harmonic currents being present in the motor. In addition to the fact that the negative- and positive-sequence harmonic motor currents are not necessarily equal, the characteristics of the squirrel cage itself must be taken into account. This is so because in many machines the normal fundamental braking torque is far larger than

the motoring torque due to excessive deep bar effects, space-harmonic effects and possible double cage effects. However the braking region of operation for negative-sequence time-harmonics (-5,-11,etc) coincides with the motoring region of the positive-sequence time-harmonics (+7,+13 etc). Therefore it is possible that the average torques produced by the negative-sequence time-harmonics can be far larger than those produced by the positive-sequence time-harmonics and, hence, effective cancellation will not occur.

Further in some machines large space-harmonic torque dips are present, particularly in the braking region. As the braking region of the negative-sequence time-harmonics coincides with the normal motoring region any large space-harmonic torques of the negative-sequence time harmonic currents must give rise to additional torque dips in the motoring region.

This paper describes a method of assessing the effects produced on the normal torque-speed curve of a motor due to the presence of time-harmonic currents in the stator winding and their associated space-harmonic fields being present in the airgap.

SPACE HARMONIC FIELDS PRODUCED IN AN INDUCTION MOTOR.

The windings of both stator and rotor are housed in slots. Consequently the current carrying conductors are not uniformly distributed around the stator and rotor surfaces but are grouped in slots. This results in a mmf produced by the windings when excited with a sinusoidally time varying voltage, being a stepped rather than a smooth sinusoid. This waveform can be described in terms of a fundamental and a series of harmonics. These harmonics will be designated space-harmonics and depend solely on the construction of the machine and the layout of the windings. As shown by Alger and others[1][6] these fields can influence the torque-speed characteristics of the machine.

The mmf produced by either a narrow (60°) phase or broad (120°) phase spread winding can be expressed in terms of the following equation

$$f_{ph} = \sum_{q_1} \frac{2 \, i_c \, N_1}{\pi \, q_1} Keq_1 \, Kmq_1 \cos q_1 \theta_1 \quad \text{----(1)}$$

where q_1 = the harmonic order based on a fundamental of the complete machine

N_1 = the turns in series in the machine

i_c = the current per conductor

Keq_1 = the coil pitch factor

Kmq_1 = the winding distribution factor

θ_1 = angular position on stator in mechanical measure ie. measured on the basis that the complete machine constitutes 2π radians

If the current in the conductors varies sinusoidally with time then it can be shown[6] that the mmf produced per phase contains a series of pulsating waves. These waves can be represented in terms of two travelling waves moving in opposite directions. The other phases of the winding will also produce similar fields and the total field produced is the sum of the contributions in all phases. The total mmf produced by a 3-phase stator winding carrying 3-phase currents can be described in terms of the mechanical measure as

$$f_1 = \sum_{q_1} \frac{3\sqrt{2}\ I_1\ N_1}{\pi\ q_1}\ Kwq_1\ \sin(\omega t - q\theta_1) \quad\text{------ (2)}$$

where I_1 = the RMS current per phase
ω = the supply angular frequency

The space-harmonics that occur are given by

$$q_1 = 3\ K_5\ p + p \quad\text{------ (3)}$$

where K_5 = any +ve or -ve even integer including zero when considering a narrow phase spread winding.

p = number of pole-pairs in the machine.

These harmonics which are present in the mmf field produced by the stator appear as rotating waves moving relative to the stator and rotor. Each of these mmf harmonics gives rise to a flux density wave in the airgap of the machine which will travel with the same speed and in the same direction as that of the harmonic mmf wave. The fields will induce emf's in the rotor winding, the magnitude of which will depend on the rotor winding pitch and distribution factor. The resultant currents that flow in the rotor winding will be determined by the impedance of the rotor circuit at the frequencies of the induced emf's due to the respective stator harmonic waves. The rotor winding will now produce a series of harmonic mmf's due to the currents induced by the stator fields. Each current in the rotor winding, due to its respective stator field, will produce its fundamental and associated series of harmonic mmf's. These rotor mmf's for a squirrel cage rotor with Q_2 bars are defined by

$$f_2 = \sum_{r_2} \frac{\sqrt{2}\ I_{rq}\ Q_2}{2\pi\ r_2\ p}\ Kwr_2\ \cos(s_q\omega t - \emptyset_{rq_1} - r_2\theta_2)$$

$$\text{------ (4)}$$

where I_{rq} = the RMS current per bar
r_2 = harmonic order of rotor harmonic mmf based on a fundamental of the complete machine
Kwr_2 = winding factor for r_2 harmonic field (usually = 1 except if rotor bars are skewed)
$\emptyset_{rq_1}$ = rotor circuit phase angle at the frequency resulting from q_1 harmonic inducing field
θ_2 = angular position in mechanical measure

The rotor space-harmonics that exist, are given by

$$r_2 = Q_2\ K_6 + p_1 \quad\text{------ (5)}$$

where K_6 is any positive or negative integer including zero. These rotor harmonics will

also move relative to the rotor and stator.

Equations (3) and (5) define the harmonic fields that exist in a squirrel cage induction motor as a result of the stepped nature of the mmf wave. A table of harmonic content can be drawn up using these two equations. Such a table is shown in Table 1 for a 24 slot stator/36 slot rotor 4 pole squirrel cage motor. In this case the complete machine is taken as fundamental wavelength and all values of K_5 greater than $|\pm 8|$ and K_6 greater than $|\pm 2|$ have been ignored. This is so because the mmf harmonic magnitudes are inversely proportional to the harmonic order, so all higher harmonics are negligible.

As shown[16], a flux density wave produced by the stator winding and a mmf wave produced by the rotor winding can interact to produce some average torque if and only if the following three conditions are satisfied:

(i) the waves must have the same number of poles;
(ii) the waves must standstill with respect to one another;
(iii) A space displacement must exist between them.

Table 1 shows that there are cases where stator and rotor fields have the same order. There are three such groups. The group $K_6 = 0$, ie. $q_1 = r_2$ gives rise to the normal asynchronous torques present in induction motors, the magnitude of which are given by:

$$Tq_1 = \frac{3\ q_1}{2\pi\ p\ N_s}\ \frac{Ephr\ Irq_1}{s_{q1}}\ \cos\emptyset rq_1 \quad\text{------ (6)}$$

where N_s = synchronous speed in rps
$Ephr$ = emf induced in rotor due to stator harmonic
Irq_1 = resultant rotor current

There are other occasions when $r_2 = q_{1b}$ (ie. when the rotor harmonic r_2 initiated by some stator harmonic q_{1a} has the same order as another stator harmonic q_{1b}) and when this occurs severe cogging torques result. These are clearly seen in the torque-speed curve of this machine shown in Figure 2(a).

The third condition that may occur is $r_2 = q_{1b}$. This does not happen in this machine but when it does, it is known to give rise to synchronous torques at speeds defined by the number of poles of the harmonics and their speeds[6].

The relative magnitudes of the asynchronous harmonic torques present in a machine depend on the stator/rotor slot combination, the number of pole-pairs in the machine and the winding configurations. This is so because the harmonic differential leakage reactance is dependent on these factors. As shown by others[16] any reduction of the rotor harmonic leakage reactance of a particular $r_2 (= q_1)$ harmonic bar current. This leads to an increase in any asynchronous or synchronous torques due to that harmonic current and these effects are thus compounded.

SPACE-HARMONIC FIELDS DUE TO SUPPLY TIME-HARMONICS.

When time-harmonics are present in the supply a similar type of analysis can be used to establish the nature of the space-harmonic fields existing in the airgap of a machine. Clearly each supply time-harmonic will give rise to a family of of space-harmonics having the same orders as those defined by equations (3) and (5), and shown in Table 1 for the case of a 4 pole 24 slot stator/36 slot rotor squirrel cage motor. The stator and rotor space-harmonics will interact and produce torques as previously described.

If one now considers any two space harmonic fields with the same number of poles, one produced by the stator winding and the other by the rotor winding, due to two different supply time-harmonics, their speeds of rotation will be different as these are functions of the supply frequency. Consequently they do not standstill with respect to one another and no average torque is produced. However, they will give rise to pulsating torques. Consequently the overall average torque developed by the machine is equal to the algebraic sum of all the average torques that result from the interaction of the space harmonic fields of each respective supply time-harmonic. The pulsating torques are superimposed on the total average torque.

THEORETICAL TORQUE-SPEED PREDICTIONS - EQUIVALENT MODEL

The assessment of the table of harmonic content for the experimental motor (4 pole 24 slot stator/36 slot rotor), Table 1, in conjunction with the measured torque-speed curve at reduced voltage using a 50 Hz sinusoidal supply, figure 2, shows that the space-harmonics of concern are the principal phase-belt and the primary slot harmonics. Clearly then any equivalent circuit used to predict the performance of this motor must of necessity take account of these space-harmonics. The equivalent circuit used is as shown in figure 1 and it follows along similar lines to those described by Landy[6]. All the secondary quantities are referred to the primary using the principle of mmf balance as the basis for equivalence. Therefore the secondary resistances (R21,R25,etc.) appear as slip dependent values whereas in the actual machine it is the secondary emf's and secondary leakage reactances that vary with slip. The reactances X21,X25,X211 and X213 are the leakage reactances of the secondary and are reactances at the supply frequency. The magnitudes of these reactances will vary with the speed as well as the supply frequency owing to deep bar and surface eddy current effects. The slot permeance harmonics are a result of the fundamental mmf acting on the slotted airgap boundary and consequently their magnetising reactances, shunted by their secondary circuit impedances, must appear within the magnetising branch of the fundamental. The slot mmf harmonic effects are a consequence of the total primary current and therefore their circuits must appear in the total primary current path.

A computer program was developed to calculate the magnitude of the different resistances and magnetising and leakage reactances in terms of the rotor speed as well as the supply frequency. Having established these values the currents through the paths of the equivalent model are then calculated and from these the harmonic asynchronous torques are computed using equation (6).

The q_1 space harmonic torque is positive if the rotor speed is smaller than the synchronous speed of the q_1 space-harmonic, n_{sq1} negative if the rotor speed is greater than n_{sq1} and zero if the rotor speed is equal to n_{sq1}. The overall torque developed by the

motor is equal to the algebraic sum of all space-harmonic torques. This model can thus be used to predict the torque-speed curve of the motor for different supply time-harmonics, the total torque being the sum.

The validity of the model was established by predicting the torque-speed curve produced by a pure 50 Hz supply and then comparing this with the torque-speed curve actually measured as shown in figure 2(a).

EXPERIMENTAL SET-UP

The machine used is a 7,5 kW inverted squirrel cage induction motor. The main exciting winding is housed in 24 slots on the rotating member. The squirrel cage is constructed from solid copper bars and two brass endrings which bolt onto the bars. This winding is housed in 36 slots. The secondary core housing the squirrel cage is located into a supporting inner frame which is attached to the fixed outer main frame via three spring-steel plates. The inner frame can then rotate relative to the outer frame against the action of the spring-steel plates. Such movement is produced by the reaction torque of the secondary/core assembly and this actual movement is detected by a position transducer. Since the reaction torque is balanced by the spring action of the spring-steel supporting plates, the output of the position transducer can be calibrated in terms of the torque. The rotating member is coupled to a flywheel which greatly increases the system rotational inertia. This increased inertia ensures that the motor accelerates and decelerates slowly during run-up while motoring, and slow-down while braking. The time constants of the motor electrical circuits are thus very considerably shorter than those of the mechanical system and therefore the machine currents and magnetic fields can be assumed to be steady-state for all speeds. This enables the steady-state torque-speed curve to be measured by merely running the motor at full speed in one direction then plugging it and allowing it to decelerate to zero and accelerate to full speed in the opposite direction. The speed is measured by means of a dc tachometer attached to the flywheel.

An auxiliary impulse commutated McMurray inverter was used. This type of inverter has good characteristics for this application. It has good inherent voltage regulation as well as the ability to handle wide variations in load current, power factor and frequency. Its ability to continue operating after the sudden increase in load from no load to full load is of great importance especially for the case of on-line starting of squirrel cage induction motors.

The pulse width modulated signal is obtained by superimposing a constant magnitude sinusoidal signal at the fundamental frequency (ie. the modulating signal) with a variable amplitude triangular signal at a higher frequency (ie. the carrier signal). The resultant modulated signal consists of a train of constant amplitude pulses the widths of which are defined by the points of intersection of the sinusoidal and triangular signals. A pulse width modulated signal of this type is usually defined in terms of three parameters, namely, the frequency ratio between the two signals, the ratio of their peak values and the phase displacement between their zeros. Müller[8] discusses the effects that these parameters have on the harmonic content of the output line voltage of a 3-phase inverter.

In the inverter used in this work, the control circuitry was designed such that these three parameters could be varied independently, thus providing a means of controlling the magnitudes as well as the relative frequencies of the harmonics of the output voltage waveform of the inverter.

EXPERIMENTAL AND PREDICTED TORQUE-SPEED CURVES FOR THE MOTOR SUPPLIED FROM THE INVERTER

The effects of the supply time-harmonics on the average torque-speed curve can be predicted by determining the torque-speed curves produced by each supply time-harmonic and then adding them up algebraically. This implies that magnetic saturation has been neglected.

The experimental motor was supplied from the inverter employing a modulation that stresses the 5th supply time-harmonic and reduces the 7th supply time-harmonic, as shown in the frequency spectrum of the output line voltage of the inverter figure 3. Under these conditions the magnitude of the 5th supply time-harmonic is 100% of that of the fundamental. One would then expect the effects of this supply time-harmonic on the average torque of the motor to be much larger than those of the 7th supply time-harmonic.

Using the computer program and the values from the frequency spectrum of the output line voltage of the inverter, the torque-speed curves for the fundamental, 5th and 7th supply time-harmonics were predicted as shown in figure 4. The higher harmonics were ignored as their torque contributions were small. The overall torque was then obtained by adding these 3 curves, keeping in mind that the torque-speed curve for the 5th supply time-harmonic must be reversed. Figure 5 shows the resultant curve obtained together with that measured experimentally.

It is clearly seen from these curves that the average torque produced by the 5th supply time-harmonic is large and consequently the effects of the space-harmonics of this supply time-harmonic are very visible. The 11th space-harmonic of the 5th supply time-harmonic produces a dip at a speed of 681 rpm reducing the fundamental pullout torque by 6%, and the 5th space-harmonic of this supply time-harmonic produces a dip centered at 1 500 rpm. However, due to the shape of these asynchronous torques, the 5th space-harmonic torque of the 5th supply time-harmonic does not reduce the fundamental average torque as much as it would have had this 5th space-harmonic been negligibly small.

Further tests were done on a conventional 380V star connected, 1,5 kW dumbell squirrel cage motor. The torque-speed curve obtained with a sinusoidal supply was compared with that obtained when the motor was supplied from the inverter with an output line voltage frequency spectrum identical to that shown in figure 3. As it can be seen from figure 6 there is a remarkable reduction of the overall torque produced by the motor. This is mainly due to the fact that the rotor circuit resistance for the 5th supply time-harmonic currents is much higher than that for the fundamental currents. The reason is that the high frequency currents tend to flow on the

high resistance portion of the cage whereas the low frequency currents flow on the low resistance portion of the cage. These results clearly illustrate the added effects due to the cage characteristics.

CONCLUSIONS

The results show that, although not all the inverter-motor systems suffer from the problems mentioned, caution must be exercised when choosing a modulation policy for a particular motor. The points to guard against are, firstly, the effects of the cage characteristics giving an overall reduction in average motoring torque and, secondly, the effects of possible large space-harmonic torques being present in the braking region of the fundamental torque-speed curve. This latter aspect is particularly relevant in 2 pole machines which all exhibit large 5th space-harmonic fields[7].

Further the assessment techniques described are relatively simple and have been shown to be reliable.

ACKNOWLEDGEMENTS

The authors wish to express their thanks to the University of the Witwatersrand and the Council for Scientific and Industiral Research (CSIR) for the laboratory facilities made available to them and for the financial support provided during this investigation.

REFERENCES

1. Alger, P L, "Induction Machines", 2nd edition, (Gordon and Breach, 1970).

2. Beck, C D, and Chandler, E F, "Motor drive inverter ratings", IEEE Transactions, IGA-4, 1968, p589.

3. Chalmers, B J and Sarkar, B R, "Induction-motor losses due to nonsinusoidal supply waveforms", Proc.IEE, vol 115, 1968, p1777.

4. De Buck, F G G, "Losses and parasitic torques in electric motors subjected to PWM waveforms", IEEE Transactions, Vol. IA-15, No 1, 1979, p47.

5. Klingshirn, E A and Jordan, H E, "Polyphase induction motor performance and losses on nonsinusoidal voltage source", IEEE Transactions, vol PAS-87, No 3, 1968, p624.

6. Landy, C F, "An investigation of an induction motor with view to leakage effects and developed torque", Phd thesis, 1979, University of the Witwatersrand.

7. Landy, C F, "A technique for assessing space-harmonic effects in squirrel cage induction motors", Trans. SAIEE, vol 73 part 1, 1982.

8. Müller, E and Rickie, F, "Undershoot Control Techniques and their influence on inverter output voltage", Brown Boveri, Rev 1-73, p35.

9. Murphy, J M D, "Thyristor Control of AC motors", 1st edition (Pergamon Press, 1973).

K_s	$q_1\downarrow$	$K_6\rightarrow$ −2	−1	O	+1	+2
		$r_2 = 36 K_6 + q_1$				
−8	−46	−118	−82	−46	−10	−26
−6	−34	−106	−70	−34	+2	+38
−4	−22	−94	−58	−22	+14	+50
−2	−10	−82	−46	−10	+26	+62
O	+2	−70	−34	+2	+38	+74
+2	+14	−58	−22	+14	+50	+86
+4	+26	−46	−10	+26	+62	+98
+6	+38	−34	−2	+38	+74	+110
+8	+50	−22	+14	+50	+86	+122

<u>Table 1</u> – Table of harmonic content for 3 phase, 4 pole squirrel cage induction motor, 24 slot stator/ 36 slot rotor.

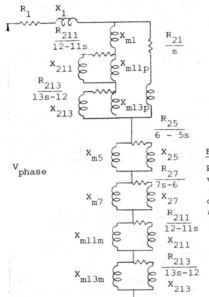

<u>Figure 1</u>

Per phase equivalent circuit (steady-state) of exp. motor as per Landy[6]

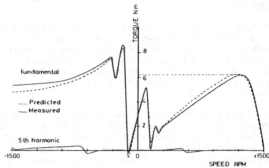

<u>Figure 3</u> Frequency spectrum of the output line voltage of inverter. Vert. scale 16 V/div, hor. scale 50 Hz/div.

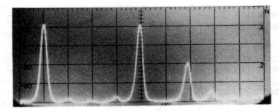

<u>Figure 4</u> Predicted torque-speed curves for fundamental voltage of 64 V and 5th harmonic voltage of 64 V. Torque-speed curve for 7th harmonic voltage of 32 V is not shown as it is too small.

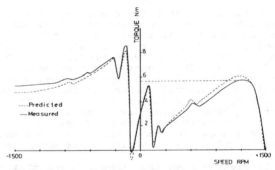

<u>Figure 5</u> Predicted and measured torque-speed curves for the motor when supplied with inverter as per fig. 3.

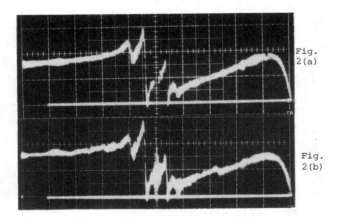

Fig. 2(a)

Fig. 2(b)

<u>Figure 2</u> Measured reduced voltage torque speed curves of exp. motor (Hor. scale 300 rpm per div, ± 1500 rpm, Vert. scales 3.37 Nm/div).
(a) Normal sinusoidal supply 64V
(b) Inverter supply, as per fig. 3.

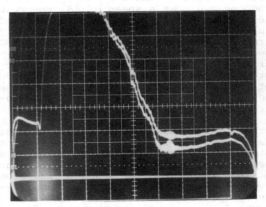

<u>Figure 6</u> Torque-speed curves for dumbell squirrel cage motor with 50 Hz sinusoidal supply at reduced voltage of 64 V and with inverter supply as per fig. 3.

THE DESIGN OF TRIAC-CONTROLLED PSC INDUCTION MOTORS FOR VARIABLE-SPEED FAN DRIVES

S.K. Al-Lami, T.S. Birch and D. Howe

University of Sheffield, U.K.

INTRODUCTION

Permanent-split-capacitor (PSC) motors are well suited for small fan-drive applications in, for example, air-conditioning systems. Furthermore, speed control over a wide range can often be achieved simply and cheaply by triac-phase control of the voltage applied to the motor. However, a feature of this method of control is that as the speed is reduced the rotor and main winding currents, and the associated copper losses, rise to a maximum at a slip of about 1/3. This then presents a heating problem since there will, at the same time, be a loss of motor cooling from the integral cast rotor fan normally used in these machines. Since the maximum current can be limited by increasing the rotor resistance, high resistance rotors are usually employed on motors intended for triac control. However, this design change alone would generally be unacceptable since it leads to a reduction in output at rated voltage. PSC motors intended for variable voltage operation therefore require a different balance of design parameters from that for single-speed motors.

In general, economic considerations will restrict the freedom of the designer to vary many of the principal design factors. As a result a number of novel design changes for voltage-controlled fan drives (1,2), which by enhancing the increase in rotor resistance with slip are effective in reducing low-speed losses without reducing full-load speed, have not found general application. Thus, in this paper, it has been assumed that changes to the lamination geometry would be too costly an exercise and the only quantities which are considered as practical design variables are the stack length, the number and gauge of the main and auxiliary winding turns, the auxiliary circuit capacitance and the rotor end-ring section. Other commercial and production procedures may well influence the overall design procedure adopted by a particular manufacturer. However, by highlighting those aspects of the design to which the variable-speed performance is most sensitive, and by presenting an approach by which the performance of given designs can be evaluated, we hope to give guidance and background information which will be helpful in establishing a design procedure.

Designing PSC motors to a specification is notoriously difficult even within the practical restrictions outlined above. At best one can neglect 2nd-order effects, such as core losses, space-harmonics and saturation, at the initial design stage and apply fundamental and/or semi-empirical analyses. However, since these secondary effects play such an important part in determining the overall performance and temperature rise of the motor, the success or failure of a design can only be judged by subsequently re-calculating the performance from the design data with the effects included. The process of evolving a design to satisfy a complete performance specification is, therefore, one of repeated design and analysis, for which a reliable method of calculating the performance and temperature rise is essential.

APPLICATION AND DESIGN SPECIFICATION

In addition to the quantities which are usually specified for a single-speed application, the form of the torque/speed characteristic of the fan must be specified since this will determine the variation of losses with speed in a voltage-controlled motor. The usual duty requirement will be for about a 175% pull-out torque, to allow an adequate margin for possible undervoltage and overload, a 50% minimum starting torque, to assure starting against the friction torque of belt drives, and a full-load slip <0.08, for maximum air-movement at rated voltage. Typically a two-to-one speed range would be required by varying the voltage applied to the main winding only, the auxiliary winding remaining on full-voltage. This is preferred to voltage control on both windings since the total losses and the level of pulsating torques, and hence the tendency to overheat and to generate acoustic noise, are lower.

The motor will normally have Class B insulation, which restricts the average temperature rise to about 80°C above a 40°C ambient. To achieve the highest full-speed rating within this thermal limit the designer would aim to produce a motor having a drooping loss/speed characteristic. Further, for satisfactory drive stability the motor and load torque/speed characteristics should have a stable intersection over the specified speed range, and the speed/voltage characteristic should be more or less linear.

DESIGN PROCEDURE

Of the different types of split-phase induction motor the PSC motor is the most difficult to design since the designer has to meet both the minimum starting torque requirement and the full-load torque at a specified speed using only one configuration of the windings. Nevertheless, design methods based on the work of Veinott and Trickey (3,4) are quite convenient for motors intended for single-speed operation, particularly when the starting torque requirement is relatively low as in this application. However, even when the designer is limited to varying only the winding details and stack length there can be a marked variation in the balance of these quantities which meet the design requirement, and the ultimate choice will be determined by commercial and production considerations.

The same methods can also be used to arrive at a design for triac-controlled PSC motors, although the balance of the design quantities now has to be tailored to overcoming the inherent problem of overheating, in addition to achieving the specified starting, pull-out, and full-load torques. The method of performance calculation must obviously differ however, so as to account for the very significant effects of time-harmonic currents introduced by a phase-controlled triac. Another essential requirement is the evaluation of temperature rise since this may limit the rating of the motor. It also affects the winding resistances in the equivalent circuit from which the performance is calculated. In this investigation an empirical formula (5) was used to calculate the cooling characteristic from the shape (outside diameter and length) of the motor. The formula was verified by temperature measurements taken on the main, auxiliary and rotor windings of a number of motors. These did not differ by more than 10°C from the figure predicted from total losses. However, larger temperature differences may well occur in designs giving a greater imbalance between the loss densities in the two windings. To determine the temperature rise at a particular speed an iterative procedure was used. From an estimate of the likely temperature of the windings their resistance is calculated and the total copper, iron and parasitic losses evaluated. The temperature rise is then calculated from the empirical formula and if this differs from the estimated value by more than, say 2°C, the procedure is repeated.

In this paper the design approach is illustrated for the case of 4-pole, 220V, 50Hz motors of 250W nominal full-load rating.

Single-Speed Motor

The basis of most design methods for PSC motors is firstly to determine the stack length and the main winding design to give a proportion of the ultimate pull-out torque required, and secondly to design the auxiliary winding and to select its capacitor to give nearly balanced two-phase performance at full-load. As well as fulfilling the performance specification outlined earlier, a successful design needs to have an acceptable slot fullness (typically 65% max.), winding current density, pulsating torque and temperature rise. Therefore, from trial values of stack length, maximum flux density and wire sizes, a design is evolved by working through a design/analysis cycle until all conditions are satisfied. Usually the analysis would be based on the chain equivalent circuit (6), whose parameters can be evaluated from the design data, allowing for the effects of core saturation, distortion of the magnetic field due to skew and space harmonics, and temperature.

Fig.1 shows the performance characteristics of an acceptable design in a lamination of 140mm outside diameter and 40.6mm stack length, with the B_{60} gap density limited to 0.7T. The temperature rise at full-load is only 45°C. A smaller diameter lamination could well lead to a temperature limited design because of the poorer cooling characteristic. It will be seen that the motor can produce some 2/3 of the required pull-out torque when operating on the main winding alone, a typical figure on which to base the main design. The component loss curves show how the relative proportions of the losses change with speed, the largest components at the lower end of the speed range being the

main and rotor winding copper losses.

Variable-Speed Motor

In order to establish whether a design can meet the extended specification for voltage-controlled motors its performance on triac-phase control must be predicted. The simplest and most direct method of doing this is by state-variable analysis (7), using the off-time of the triac as the independent variable. Unfortunately the introduction of time-harmonic voltages now precludes the direct inclusion of space harmonic and saturation effects in the analysis and also the calculation of iron losses and surface losses at the stator and rotor teeth. However, these can be taken into account by using parameters in the state-variable model predicted under sinusoidal voltage control together with the corresponding iron and surface losses. These are determined, over the speed range, from the intersection of the fan characteristic with the motor torque/speed curves for different voltages. Fortunately most of the parameters are not particularly sensitive to voltage. The iron and surface losses normally account for a significant component of the total loss only around full-speed, when the off-time of the triac is small anyway. The magnetising reactance is sensitive to voltage and speed but again its main effect on performance is between full-load and no-load when the triac is in full conduction.

Fig.1 shows the predicted variable-speed performance of the single-speed motor designed earlier. It will be seen that predictions based on sinusoidal voltage control are woefully inadequate for indicating its performance on triac control. As the firing angle is increased the level of distortion in the current waveforms increases, particularly in the main and rotor windings. The time-harmonic currents then add significantly to the power loss in the motor and its subsequent temperature rise, so much so as to render the motor unsuitable for triac control. A further effect is the increased level of the twice-supply frequency torque component, which results from running away from the speed at which the phases are balanced, and additional harmonic pulsating torques are also produced.

Within the design constraints the required improvement in variable-speed performance can only be achieved by carefully modifying the balance of all the parameters. An obvious parameter to increase, however, is the rotor resistance since, as has already been pointed out, this leads to a reduction in losses, albeit at the expense of the high-speed performance. Some increase in rotor resistance can be obtained by using thinner section end-rings on the rotor bars, although a practical limit is imposed by interbar losses. An increase in the axial length of the motor can also be used thereby improving cooling at the same time. In this design example, the end-ring section was reduced to 1/2 of that of the single-speed motor, and the axial length was increased by 5mm, giving an increase in rotor resistance of 65%. After incorporating these design changes and proceeding to the most effective design, by the same approach that was used for the single-speed motor, the maximum temperature rise was reduced by some 20°C. However, despite this marked improvement, the motor still overheated on triac phase-control.

A further way of reducing copper losses in both the stator and rotor windings in the troublesome region around 2/3 of full-load speed is to design the auxiliary winding and its capacitor to give balanced operation at a lower speed than is normally selected for single-speed motors. By doing this the backward field losses will be reduced at the lower end of the speed range, and indeed eliminated at the speed selected to give balanced conditions. Of course this change now gives increased backward field losses at the higher speeds. Fig.2 shows the phasor diagram at balance, where V_M is the estimated main winding voltage (under sinusoidal voltage control) at the proposed balance speed. This design strategy requires the usual equations (4) for calculating the auxiliary/main winding turns ratio K and the capacitive reactance X_C for single-speed motors to be re-written in terms of the winding voltages V_M and V_A. Neglecting the capacitor resistance, the equations become

$$K = \frac{V_A B - K_a r_{1m} I_m^2}{V_M A - r_{1m} I_m^2}$$

and

$$X_C = \frac{V_A K - KK_a B r_{1m} + K^2 B r_{1m}}{A}$$

where K_a = Main/Aux.conductor area ratio

A,B = real and imag.components of main winding current at the proposed balance speed and applied voltage.

Because the speed/voltage characteristic is usually non-linear, being initially less sensitive to voltage changes, a value of main winding voltage of about 1/2 rated supply voltage was assumed to correspond to the required balance speed of about 2/3 synchronous speed. Fig.3 shows the performance characteristics of a successful variable-speed design embodying this additional design change.

It will be seen that the motor fulfils the starting and pull-out torque requirements, although the full-load speed, and hence output power, is slightly lower than for the single-speed design. The motor still exhibits a rising loss/speed characteristic on triac control despite now having a drooping characteristic on variac control. The increase in losses as the speed is reduced is, however, much less than for the single-speed motor on voltage-control, and with its improved cooling characteristic gives an acceptable temperature rise. Within the restrictions imposed on the design, and without modifying the controller to reduce the time-harmonic content of the applied voltage (8), it does not seem possible to obtain a loss characteristic which falls with speed. The rotor winding still accounts for the largest proportion of losses, but the loss inbalance in the main and auxiliary windings over the speed range is reduced substantially, assisted in part by having the auxiliary winding just one wire gauge higher than that of the main winding. The fall off in auxiliary winding losses as the speed is reduced then offsets to a greater extent the increase in losses in the main and rotor windings with speed reduction and increasing current distortion. Large amplitude pulsating torques, having a twice-supply frequency fundamental component, can be produced under triac phase-control. Fig.3 shows the instantaneous torque together with the harmonic spectra at a speed of 850 rpm. The harmonic torque pulsations can add significantly to noise, and mechanical vibration and in this respect the performance characteristics will need to be judged with regard to the application. It will be seen that by aiming for electrical balance at about 1000 rpm the twice-supply frequency torque pulsation at that speed is now lower than that at the full-load speed. Since control is not exercised by the triac until the firing angle exceeds the power factor angle the speed is initially insensitive to the firing angle. Beyond this however the speed changes fairly linearly with firing angle.

CONCLUSIONS

The paper has shown that the performance of PSC motors on triac phase-control is very different to that on variac-control. Whilst the rotor resistance is the most critical design parameter, regard to other features, such as motor shape (diameter/length), to improve the loss dissipation capability, and the electrical balance of the windings, to reduce backward field losses at the lower speeds, will assist in working towards a successful design. The usual method of designing the auxiliary winding circuit of single-speed motors has been modified to allow for nearly balanced operation at the lower end of the speed range.

Although the paper has concentrated on accounting for the presence of time-harmonics in the motor there is likely to be considerable scope for modifying the controller, to reduce the harmonic content (8), and the cooling arrangements, to have, for example, air-over motor from the fan load.

ACKNOWLEDGEMENTS

The authors acknowledge the help and cooperation of GEC Small Machines Ltd.

REFERENCES

1. Alger, P.L., Mester, R.L. and Yoon, R.G., 1964, IEEE, PAS, 93(2), 989-997.

2. Chalmers, B.J., and Hamdi, E.S., 1981, IEE 2nd Int. Conf. "Small and Special Machines" London, 16-18.

3. Veinott, C.G. 1959 : "Theory and Design of Small Induction Motors", McGraw-Hill.

4. Trickey, P.H. 1932, AIEE Trans., 57, 780-785.

5. Private Communication, GEC Small Machines Ltd., England.

6. Sims, C.R., 1974 : Ph.D Thesis, University of Sheffield, England.

7. Novotny, D.W., and Fath, A.F., 1968, IEEE. PAS 87(2), 597-603.

8. Williamson, S., Pearson, D., and Rugege, A.M., 1981, Proc. IEE, 128(B), 201-206.

112

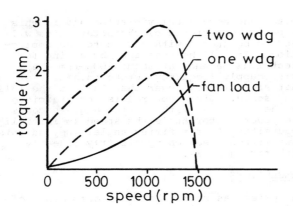

Design Details

Turns Distribution: Main : 54-80-83,SWG24
                     Aux : 60-124-60(½x120)
                                      SWG26

No.of slots: Stator = 36
             Rotor = 44

Max. slot fullness = 45%
B₆₀ gap density = 0.7T
Aux. Wdg. Cap. = 8.8μF
Cap. voltage : NL = 400
               FL = 351
Motor temp. at NL = 72°C

(a) Rated Voltage

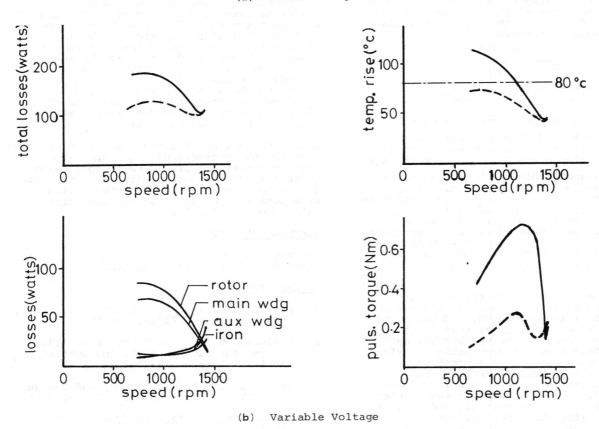

(b) Variable Voltage

FIG.1. Performance curves of 'single-speed' motor

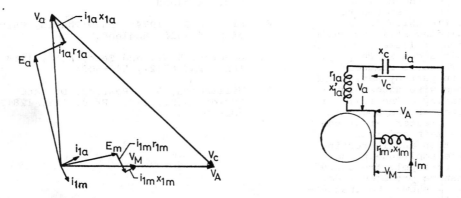

FIG.2. Phasor diagram for voltage-controlled motor at balanced operating condition.

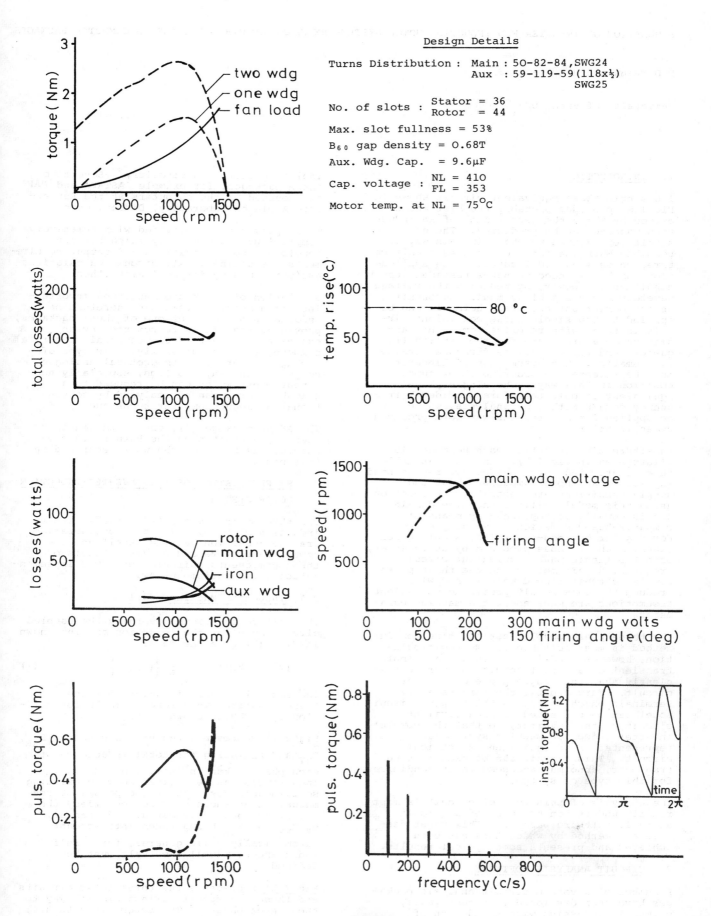

FIG.3. Performance curves of 'variable-speed' motor.

SIMULATION OF INVERTER FED INDUCTION MOTOR SYSTEMS BY MEANS OF CIRCUIT ANALYSIS COMPUTER PACKAGES

P D Evans and H A Al-Obaidi

University of Bath, UK

1. INTRODUCTION

The single phase equivalent circuit shown in Fig 1(a) provides probably the best known method by which the performance of an induction machine can be predicted. The use of a single representative phase in this way is possible when the machine receives a balanced three phase sinusoidal supply. Its application can be extended to non-sinusoidal supply conditions, however, by reducing the voltage waveforms to a set of harmonic components, using Fourier series. Each harmonic can be applied to the single phase equivalent circuit in turn (with reactive components and slip value appropriate for the applied frequency) and the overall performance obtained by summation. The assumption of linearity must be accepted in order to allow superposition in this way. The single phase equivalent circuit therefore provides a frequency domain method of analysis, which can be applied for any regular waveform produced by an inverter.

An alternative induction machine model is illustrated in Fig 1(b). In this case all three stator and rotor phases are represented explicitly and no assumptions about the supply conditions are necessary. A solution using this model utilises the time domain, and is usually accomplished by means of a computer-based numerical time step method. For regular but non-sinusoidal supply conditions, such as those produced by an inverter, both the single phase equivalent circuit frequency domain method and the three phase coupled circuit time domain method will produce the same result providing equivalent assumptions are made about the machine parameters.

The three phase coupled circuit time domain method is most suitable for system simulation, however, and in particular can handle transient or abnormal conditions more conveniently than the single phase equivalent circuit. Furthermore, the three stator terminals which appear in the coupled circuit model can be connected to an equivalent circuit of the inverter, so that the complete inverter-induction machine system can be represented as an equivalent electrical circuit. This circuit can be used to study transient, abnormal and some fault conditions for this type of system.

The analysis of this type of circuit is most readily undertaken by means of a circuit analysis software package. This paper describes a method by which this has been achieved and presents some typical results.

2. CIRCUIT ANALYSIS SOFTWARE

A number of advanced circuit analysis packages have been developed in recent years, primarily to assist with the design of increasingly complex electronic circuits,

including microchip circuitry. Several of these packages, for example 'ASTAP' and 'NAP' are mounted on the computers at the Rutherford Appleton Laboratory, Didcot, Oxon.

These packages are provided with relatively simple input languages by which circuit topology, input conditions and output requirements are defined. All circuit calculations are performed by internal algorithms.

Simulation of the above-mentioned inverter-induction motor systems can therefore be undertaken by means of one of these packages, providing that it is represented by an equivalent circuit of conventional electrical components. More generally, this type of package amounts to a theoretical analogue computer, and any problems, especially non-linear ones, which can be reduced to a suitable form, can be analysed by conventional analogue computer techniques.

The ASTAP package (1), one of the earlier ones to be mounted on the Rutherford computers, was used for the work described in this paper.

3. REPRESENTATION OF THE INVERTER-INDUCTION MOTOR SYSTEM

The three main components of the inverter-induction motor system under consideration are the induction machine itself and the power transistors and diodes. Models of these components suitable for ASTAP implementation are described below.

3.1 Induction Machine Model

The voltage equations governing the coupled circuit model of the induction machine shown in Fig 1(b) take the form:

$$[v] = [R][i] + \frac{d}{dt}\left\{[L][i]\right\} \qquad \ldots (1)$$

The equivalent circuit which represents these equations in a form suitable for solution by ASTAP is shown in Fig 2.

Fig 2(a) represents the stator circuit, L_{RR}, L_{YY} and L_{BB} being the total inductance of each phase taken in isolation. Mutual inductances can be defined between existing self inductances. For three phases, three mutual inductances must be specified, the reciprocal nature of mutual inductances, eg M_{RY} and M_{YR} being taken into account automatically. (In general, for m self inductances, $m(m-1)/2$ mutuals must be defined.)

Fig 2(b) represents the three rotor circuits and these are specified in a similar way to the stator phases. The rotor circuits are, however, shown as three isolated circuits, and the condition that the sum of the rotor currents is zero may be imposed by means of an additional circuit, shown in Fig 2(c).

Fig 2(c). The three dependent current sources in this current, denoted by J_1, J_2 and J_3 are equal to the three rotor currents I_1, I_2 and I_3 respectively. The resistance R_J is set to a high value, typically $1M\Omega$, thereby ensuring the sum of the currents is effectively zero.

Fig 2(d) provides for the mutual coupling between the stator and rotor circuits.

For example, the dependent voltage source E_R in Fig 2(a) represents the coupling terms between the red stator phase and the three rotor phases, m = 1, 2 and 3:

$$E_R = \frac{d}{dt} \sum_{m=1}^{3} M_{Rm} i_m \qquad \ldots (2)$$

This equation expands mathematically in the form:

$$E_R = \sum_{m=1}^{3} M_{Rm} \frac{di_m}{dt} + \sum_{m=1}^{3} i_m \frac{dM_{Rm}}{dt} \quad \ldots (3)$$

The time varying inductance component of equation 3 cannot be handled by ASTAP, and this equation must be reduced to the general form:

$$E_R = \sum L_x \frac{d}{dt} (J_x) \qquad \ldots (4)$$

The required result is achieved by using circuits of the form shown in Fig 2(d), where $L_x = 1$ and $J_x = \sum_{m=1}^{3} M_{Rm} i_m$. E_R, the dependent voltage source, is then equal to the voltage across L_x. The coupling between the stator and rotor circuits is therefore achieved by means of dependent voltage sources E_R, E_Y, E_B, E_1, E_2, and E_3, each of which is produced by the method described above.

Fig 3 contains typical theoretical and experimental results for an induction machine, under both motoring and generating conditions, when driven from a six step inverter. The experimental results were obtained by driving the induction machine from a power transistor inverter, supplied from a 108V d.c. source and providing a 50Hz quasi-square output. The theoretical results were derived for the induction machine models alone, supply conditions being provided by appropriate ideal voltage sources. All induction machine parameters were calculated from machine dimensions and winding details (2). Three identical sets of theoretical results were obtained by three separate methods using the same basic data and assumptions. The methods were:

- the single phase equivalent circuit, using superposition of voltage harmonic sets;
- a numerical time-step method with the coupled circuit model of Fig 1(b);
- an ASTAP solution using the equivalent circuit of Fig 2.

These results indicate that the proposed induction machine model using the ASTAP circuit analysis package is correct.

3.2 Device Models

The internal behaviour of power diodes and transistors under switching conditions is extremely complex, and is difficult to predict accurately by any method. For the present purposes, therefore, relatively simple electrical equivalent circuit models were used.

The diode model, illustrated in Fig 4(a) is based on the ideal diode equation, which is modified by the emission coefficient, η. Some additional components were also included in the model:

- R_B represents the bulk resistance of the diode. This is a series resistance component which affects the forward voltage drop of the diode at high current levels. This value was obtained experimentally.

- R_S provides for the reverse leakage current of the device.

- C_D is the sum of the diffusion and transitional capacitances and was estimated theoretically by a recommended method (3).

The Ebers-Moll method was used as the electrical equivalent circuit for the power transistors. This is one of the standard equivalent circuits for transistors operating under non-linear conditions. The equivalent circuit, which is illustrated in Fig 4(b), can be seen to incorporate two back-to-back diode models plus dependent current sources. The parameters for this equivalent circuit were obtained experimentally by making measurements (3) at the three terminals of the devices.

The power transistors used for the experimental work were monolithic Darlington devices (Toshiba 2SD646) but they were treated as single devices for the equivalent electrical circuit.

As explained, the semiconductor device models were necessarily very approximate. However, they were sufficient, as far as the induction machine was concerned, to provide a reasonable representation of the inverter. However, they would not be suitable for such considerations as transistor switching losses, and parasitic inverter components such as stray inductance were not included in the model.

4. ABNORMAL SYSTEM BEHAVIOUR

By use of the models for induction machine, power transistors and diodes described in the previous section an equivalent circuit model of a three phase inverter, Fig 5(a), and the induction motor can be represented in the ASTAP package. System simulation under prescribed conditions can then be undertaken.

The results of one example are presented in Fig 6. This case examines the behaviour of the inverter and induction motor if one leg of the inverter becomes inoperative. The precise situation simulated is defined by the switching sequence in Fig 5(b). The inverter has been operating under steady state quasi-square conditions when at time t_f, when T_4 switches OFF, neither T_1 nor T_4 come on again at their prescribed times, ie the active devices in the leg become inoperative, although their two complementary diodes are still connected in the circuit. The predicted behaviour of the circuit is shown in Fig 6. Of particular interest are:

(i) The motor torque, which changes from being substantially constant to a pulsating torque as the induction machine is driven in a single phase mode by the remaining two operational legs of the bridge. The results presented are for a constant rotational speed, which can be assumed to apply immediately after the fault but the dynamics of the mechanical system can also be incorporated by conventional analogue computer techniques.

(ii) The device currents in the operational legs increase significantly. The peak transistor current rising from 47 Amps under normal conditions to 69A - ie an increase of almost 50% within two cycles of the fault. This type of information can assist in device selection and in the formulation of protection schemes.

It can also be seen that diodes 1 and 4 in the inoperative leg carry short bursts of current of about 10A peak. The currents in diodes 3 and 6 also fall to low levels, but diodes 2 and 5 carry currents which increase in the same way as the transistor currents.

5. CONCLUSIONS

Circuit analysis software packages are now well developed and provide access to sophisticated computing facilities by means of simple input codes.

Although primarily designed for electronic circuit analysis, it has been shown that they can be applied to power electronic - electrical machine systems. An example for a power transistor inverter-induction machine system has been demonstrated.

This facility provides a method of simulating system operation not only under steady state conditions - for which other methods exist - but also under transient, fault and abnormal conditions. It therefore provides a powerful method for investigating theoretically the interaction of power conditioning units and the electrical machines.

Further development of this technique has also been explored. Such features as the individual rotor conductors in a squirrel cage, skin effect in these conductors, nonlinear magnetic circuit conditions and system dynamics can all be included.

6. REFERENCES

1) Advanced Statistical Analysis Program (ASTAP), IBM Program Number 5796PBH.

2) Al-Obaidi, H.A.: "The Analysis of Inverter Fed Induction Machine Systems", thesis to be submitted for the degree of PhD, University of Bath, 1982.

3) Bowers, J. and Sedore, S.: "Sceptre: A Computer Program for Circuit Systems Analysis", Prentice-Hall, 1971.

7. ACKNOWLEDGEMENTS

The authors would like to thank Professor J F Eastham of Bath University for his help and encouragement, to Mr Peter Dewar of the Rutherford Appleton Laboratories for his support with ASTAP, and to SERC for provision of computing resources.

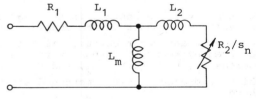

(a) Single phase equivalent circuit

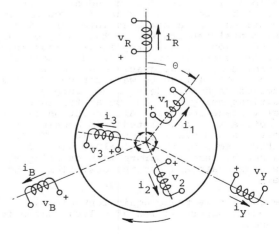

(b) Three phase coupled circuit model

Fig 1   Circuit Models for Induction Machines

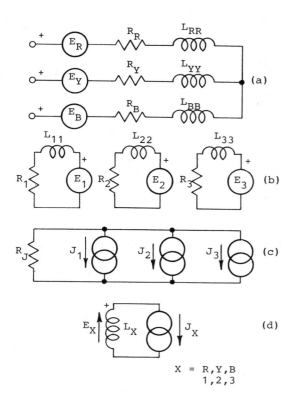

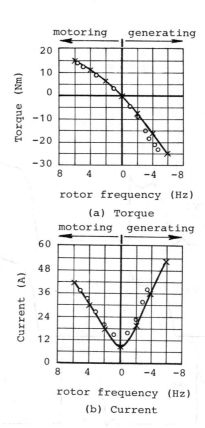

(a) Torque

(b) Current

Fig 2   'ASTAP' Model of Induction Machine

Fig 3   Induction Machine Results

o   measurements
x   predictions

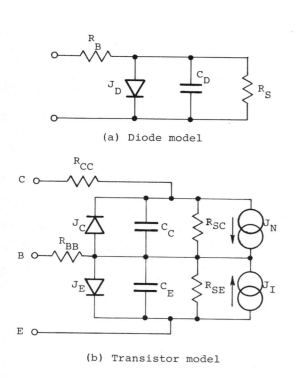

(a) Diode model

(b) Transistor model

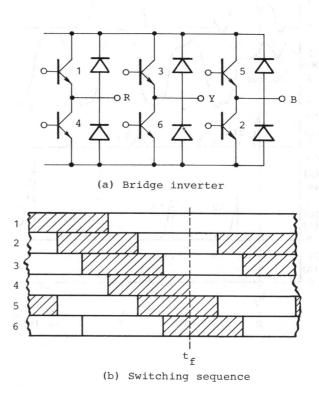

(a) Bridge inverter

(b) Switching sequence

Fig 4   Circuit Models for Power Semiconductor Devices

Fig 5   Bridge Inverter and Fault Switching
Sequence

118

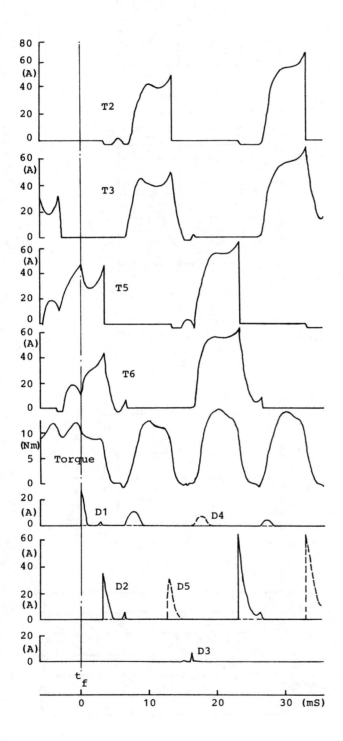

<u>Fig 6</u>   Inverter-Motor Fault Simulation

ELECTROMAGNETIC DETECTION OF DAMAGED REGIONS IN LAMINATED IRON CORES

J. Sutton and B.F. Chapman

Central Electricity Research Laboratories, C.E.G.B., U.K.

INTRODUCTION

Stator cores of turbogenerators and other electrical machines are built up of thin steel laminations which are each coated with a thin layer of electrical insulation to prevent the magnetic flux rotating around the core inducing eddy currents between laminations. In many generators the laminations are electrically connected together through building bars at the back of the core so that if the insulation is defective near the stator bore, then a conducting path is formed through which currents are induced by the rotating flux. The heating from the induced currents is highest at the contacts between the laminations where both the current density and resistance are high and these damaged regions can become hot in service. Such "hot spots" can also occur in generators in which the laminations are electrically insulated from the stator frame. In this case the electrical circuit is completed through defective interlamination insulation near the core back.

Hot spots may develop during operation due to the ingress of foreign bodies into the bore or to the deterioration of interlamination insulation. Damage may also occur during assembly or maintenance of the generator. If allowed to persist, hot spots can damage the insulation on the adjacent conductor bars and even grow to damage extensively the core itself. Hence hot spots should be detected and if possible repaired during routine generator overhauls.

Stator cores are usually tested for hot spots by removing the rotor and installing a ring flux winding to produce a circumferential flux around the core. To induce about 80% of the rated flux density in a 500 MW stator requires a 3 MVA supply to be connected to a 15 turn winding of 300 A, 11 kV cable wound through the bore and around the outside of the casing.

The best test method is to use an infra-red camera mounted on a remotely-controlled trolley to scan along and around the bore surface measuring the temperatures at the tips of the stator teeth. Any damage on the teeth tips produces obvious surface hot spots, but careful measurements are needed to detect more insidious damage below the teeth tips which may take about an hour to yield a measurable temperature rise at the surface.

A new test system known as El CID - Electromagnetic Core Imperfection Detector - has been developed at CERL. The test also requires a ring flux winding but needs only a 13 Ampere 240 V supply even for a large (660 MW) generator. The winding gives only a few percent of the normal operating flux and the resulting electric field along the core ($\sim$5 V m^{-1}) induces small currents to flow through any damaged areas of the core. The heating from these currents is insignificant but the currents can be detected and measured electromagnetically.

THEORY OF FAULT CURRENT DETECTION

The theory of measurement of fault currents is based on Ampères law. Considering any closed loop of integration, the line integral of magnetic field around a current flowing along an iron surface is equal to the current, I, i.e.:-

$$I = \oint H.d\ell = \int_{AIR} H.d\ell + \int_{IRON} H.d\ell$$

Long faults. For a long fault current path, where the fields are dominated by the current flowing along the iron surface, $H_{IRON} = H_{AIR}/\mu_x$ where μ_x is the relative permeability of the iron ($\sim$2,000) and so $I \simeq \int_{AIR} H.d\ell$.

For alternating magnetic fields the line integral between two points (difference in magnetic scalar potential) can be measured with a Chattock [1] magnetic potentiometer. It consists of a long thin solenoid wound on a flexible insulating former with a double layer of fine wire. The r.m.s. output voltage of the coil is:-

$$V = \mu_o \omega nA \int H.d\ell \qquad \ldots\ldots(1)$$

where the line integral is along the coil between its two ends, n and A are the number of turns per metre and cross-sectional area of the winding and ω is the angular frequency of the r.m.s. field H. The output is independent of the length of the coil and the path taken by it. Hence when the two ends are placed on an iron surface to bridge a current flowing along it, the output voltage is a measure of the current.

Short faults. The treatment above ignores the fields produced in the iron by the radial currents in the plane of the laminations to and from the back of the core. The total axial current through a fault is formed by radial currents flowing through pairs of laminations; one such current path is depicted in Fig.1. In reality the currents through the laminations are not concentrated line currents as depicted by AB and CD in Fig. 1, but this case is considered since it enables us to evaluate an upper limit for the reduction in $\int_{AIR} H.d\ell$ due to radial currents in the iron.

Referring to Fig. 1 we consider a path of integration abcda. The line integral of magnetic field measured in air is:-

$$\int_d^a H.d\ell = I - \int_a^b H.d\ell - \int_c^d H.d\ell - \int_b^c H.d\ell \quad (2)$$

The integrals $\int_a^b H.d\ell$ and $\int_c^d H.d\ell$ are both negligible since the contribution from the surface current BC is very small, while the components due to the currents along AB and CD parallel to the lines of integration, are zero. It remains to evaluate $\int_b^c H.d\ell$ which is affected by the laminated structure of the core.

Because of the small air gaps between laminations the effective permeability of the core is anisotropic. Following Jacobs et al (2) the core is regarded as a homogeneous anisotropic material with the actual relative permeability, μ_x, in the plane of the laminations and a lower value, μ_y, transverse to the laminations. This value is given by

$$\mu_y = \frac{\mu_x}{1 + \gamma(\mu_x - 1)} \simeq \frac{1}{\gamma} \text{ for } \mu_x \gg 1 \ldots (3)$$

where γ is the fraction not occupied by the iron. For typical values of $\mu_x = 2000$ and $\gamma = 0.05$, $\mu_y = 19.8$.

To evaluate $\int H.d\ell$ between two points in the iron, we use the magnetic scalar potential function ψ defined by $\Delta\psi = H$. Since $\nabla.B = 0$ and $B_x = \mu_0\mu_x H_x$ and $B_y = \mu_0\mu_y H_y$, the potential around a current flowing along the z axis satisfies the equation

$$\mu_x \frac{\partial^2 \psi}{\partial x^2} + \mu_y \frac{\partial^2 \psi}{\partial y^2} = 0.$$

Using the transformation $x' = x/\sqrt{\mu_x}$ and $y' = y/\sqrt{\mu_y}$ we obtain the solution

$$\psi = \frac{I}{2\pi}\alpha' \text{ where } \tan\alpha' = \beta\frac{x}{y} \text{ where } \beta = \left(\frac{\mu_y}{\mu_x}\right)^{\frac{1}{2}}.$$

From the above solution we evaluate $\psi_b - \psi_c = \int_b^c H.d\ell$ between points $b(-x_1,y_1)$ and $c(x_1,y_1)$ in Fig. 1 due to the opposing currents along AB and CD at $x = 0$ and $y = \pm y_2$ and, using equation (2), obtain the line integral in air:-

$$\int_d^a H.d\ell = I\left[1 - \frac{1}{\pi}\left(\tan^{-1}\frac{\beta x_1}{y_2+y_1}+\tan^{-1}\frac{\beta x_1}{y_2-y_1}\right)\right] \ldots (4)$$

In practice two sizes of Chattock potentiometer are used with spans $(2x_1)$ of approximately 100 mm and 10 mm compared to a typical fault length $(2y_2)$ of 10 mm. From equations (4) we calculate that the maximum response (at $y_1 = 0$) measured with the large coil is expected to indicate 50% of the actual current while the small coil should measure 94%. If the permeability were isotropic the method would be much less useful since the measured values would be only 6% and 50% of the actual current.

Although the above treatment illustrates the principle of measurement, the situation is more complicated in practice because the current varies along the length of the fault and spreads out in the planes of the laminations and because of the effect of the stator teeth.

Effect of Excitation Winding

For the El CID test the Chattock potentiometer is normally used to measure differences in magnetic potential between adjacent teeth.

Even in the absence of any core damage there is a large potential between them due to the current through the excitation winding along the axis of the bore. The excitation current, I_W, needed to produce the electric field for the test (typically 5 V m^{-1}) varies considerably between stators but is typically 50 Ampere-turns. Since the permeability is fairly constant around the stator, the m.m.f. from the winding is distributed almost uniformly around the bore with most of it being developed across the conductor slots. Hence the m.m.f. between adjacent teeth, not carrying fault currents, is simply I_W/N where N is the number of teeth, typically 50. Hence the m.m.f. between adjacent teeth due to the winding is typically $\sim$1A. This m.m.f. is much larger than that from a small, but possibly significant, fault current.

Discrimination against the I_W signal is achieved using a phase sensitive detector to measure the component of magnetic potential in phase quadrature with the excitation current. Representing the excitation current by $i_W = \sqrt{2} I_W \sin\omega t$ it is found that the fault current through the damaged region is:-

$$i_F = \sqrt{2}\frac{\ell_f}{\ell_c}V_w\left(\frac{R_F\cos\omega t + \omega L_F\sin\omega t}{R_F^2 + \omega^2 L_F^2}\right)\ldots(5)$$

where R_F, L_F and ℓ_f are the resistance, inductance and length of the fault circuit respectively, ℓ_c is the length of the core and V_w is the peak voltage of a single turn excitation winding around the core. This equation shows that if the fault current is low ($R_F \gg \omega L_F$) it is almost in phase quadrature with the winding current and therefore readily measured.

A battery operated signal processor has been developed for use inside the stator bore. The unit contains a high gain (up to 10^5) amplifier and phase sensitive detector. The phase of the excitation current is derived from a large (100 mm) diameter coil in the bore. Since the phase sensitive detector has good (better than 99%) discrimination against signals in phase with the reference, its output voltage is virtually independent of any voltage induced in the Chattock potentiometer by the excitation current.

OPERATING El CID

The excitation winding around the stator (typically 6 turns of 15 A cable) is connected to a 3 kVA mains supply to generate the ring flux and establish an electric field of $\sim$5 V m^{-1} along the bore.

To test a complete core, the sensing head is scanned along adjacent conductor slots in the bore (Fig. 2). The span of the Chattock potentiometer within the head is adjusted until it just bridges between the farthest corners of adjacent teeth. The processed signal from the sensing head is fed to an XY plotter which also records the output from a distance transducer giving the position of the sensing head along the bore. As the sensing head is scanned back and forth along adjacent conductor slots around the bore, a series of lines, one for each slot (pair of teeth), is recorded. It usually takes two operators less than a total of eight hours to complete a test on a large generator.

INTERPRETING THE TRACES; PROS AND CONS

If a core is in perfect condition the measured responses are all virtually straight lines; the approximate amplitude of any fault current and position of the damage can be read from deviations beyond specified limits on the graphs.

The m.m.f. measured between two teeth with the large Chattock potentiometer is less than the actual fault current for two reasons,both associated with the limited axial extent of typical fault currents. The first, discussed previously, is that there can be significant magnetic fields in the iron (equation (4)). The second is that the diameter of the Chattock potentiometer (6.5 mm) is comparable to the length of a typical damaged area and so the average m.m.f. measured across the diameter is less than peak current at the centre of the fault.

To explore the effects of short faults, techniques were developed for measuring the absolute magnetic potentials at the teeth tips and for temporarily applying faults to a stack of core from a 500 MW generator. To facilitate comparison of three different faults the measured teeth tip potentials were normalized by dividing by the peak magnetic potential differences measured across the shorting building bar at the core back. Fig. 3 shows schematically the normalized peak magnetic potentials for three faults A, B and C each 10 mm long at different radial positions on tooth 14. All three faults give the same potential on the neighbouring teeth (13,15), but these are only about 40% of the potential adjacent to the fault. The normalized potential changes from +0.5 to -0.5 directly across fault A in the centre of tooth 14 as expected and it is not significantly attenuated for fault B, only 10 mm below the tooth tip. The tooth tip potential however, is reduced to 0.25 when the fault lies 150 mm below the tooth tip (20 mm above the slot bottom, position C). Fig. 4 shows the Eℓ CID responses measured with the standard sensing head for the three faults A, B and C normalized so that each corresponds to the same fault current. The amplitudes and directions of the magnetic potential differences in Fig. 4 are readily interpreted with reference to the corresponding absolute potentials in Fig. 3. The responses are significant only if the damage lies within, or just outside, the span of the Chattock potentiometer; in the latter case the response is negative (Fig. 4B). Tooth tip damage (Fig. 4A), giving identical responses on adjacent scans, is readily distinguished from deep-seated damage (Fig. 4C). All three types of response have been found during tests on complete stators and the operators could tell correctly where the damage was. The responses demonstrate an important advantage of the Eℓ CID test over the thermal method since the Eℓ CID response to damage at the bottom of a slot is nearly as large as that resulting from damage at a tooth tip.

Once damage has been detected on a tooth tip from the recordings (or by other means) its exact position and fault current amplitude can be measured using the miniature Chattock potentiometer spanning directly across the fault. This method has proved very useful in monitoring the progress of the grinding and etching operations used to repair core damage since the excitation winding is unobtrusive

and the response is instantaneous.

The ease of installing and powering the excitation winding is an important attraction of Eℓ CID, and some 60 tests have been made in the last four years. The system is patented by the CEGB and is now commercially available.

In both the thermal and the Eℓ CID tests it is possible that some damage may go undetected because neither test fully simulates the magnetic, thermal and mechanical conditions in an operating generator. These factors could influence electrical contacts between laminations at the back of the core. The thermal test may give better simulation since the core vibrates and expands thermally during the test.

The thermal test might itself exacerbate core damage, especially if deep-seated,since the core is not cooled during testing as it is in operation. There is no possibility of the Eℓ CID test causing core damage and no difficulty in making a complete survey on a severely damaged core.

ACKNOWLEDGEMENT

The work was carried out at the Central Electricity Research Laboratories and is published by permission of the Central Electricity Generating Board.

REFERENCES

1. Chattock, A.P., 1887, Phil.Mag., 24, 94

2. Jacobs, D.A.H., Minors, R.H., Myerscough, C.J., Rollason, M.L.J. and Steel, J.G., 1977, Calculation of losses in the end region of turbogenerators, Proc.IEE, Vol.124, No.4, pp.356-362.

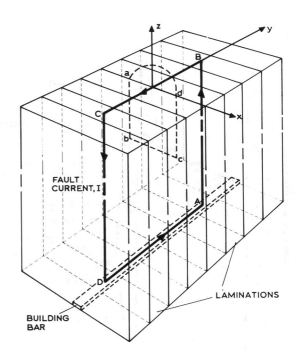

Figure 1 Section of laminated core showing fault current circuit ABCD and an integration path abcd.

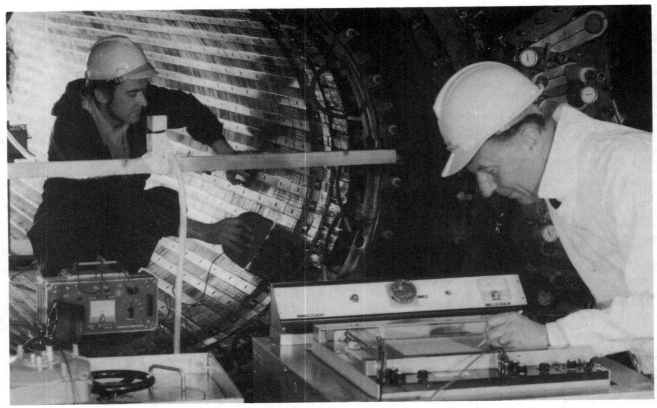

Figure 2 Eℓ CID test being carried out on a 500 MW stator.

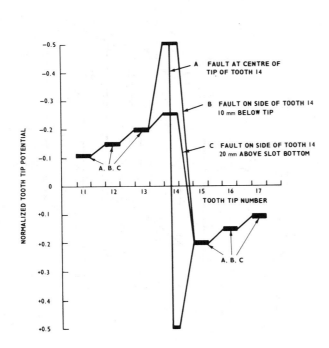

Figure 3 Schematic of normalized peak magnetic potentials for three faults A, B and C each 10 mm long on tooth 14.

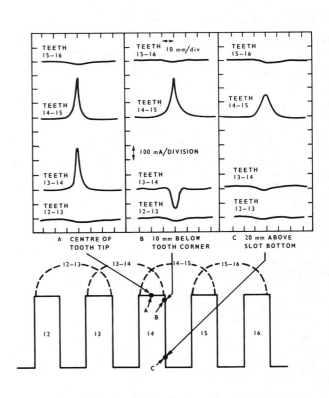

Figure 4 Responses measured along neighbouring teeth for three faults each 10 mm long and carrying the same current.

PREVENTION OF CATASTROPHIC FAILURE OF LARGE GENERATORS BY EARLY DETECTION OF OVERHEATING

I. LODGE

North Eastern Region Scientific Services Dept.

Central Electricity Generating Board

INTRODUCTION

The last fifteen years has seen the introduction of large generators with ratings of 500MW and above. These machines have been subject to a variety of catastrophic faults only rarely encountered on smaller units. Most serious of these have been core faults involving the melting of large quantities of stator iron with consequent damage to the stator winding and, in some cases, the rotor.

When core faults began to occur regularly in 1969, there were no methods by which they could be reliably detected until the molten iron burned through the winding insulation and the stator earth fault protection operated. On some occasions, generators have had to be manually tripped following internal explosions or other obvious signs of a major failure.

At the time, only the thermocouples installed in the core by the manufacturer could indicate overheating was taking place. The number of core thermocouples is limited by practical considerations so that the volume covered is a small percentage of the total. Moreover, it has been the practice to fit thermocouples to only one end of a stator core. Of eleven core faults on 500 and 660MW generators in the U.K., only one occurred near enough to a thermocouple for the overheating to be detected.

The number of core faults led to the initiation of extensive research work in the CEGB aimed at determining their cause and methods of detecting them in their early stages.

Recently, there have been a series of faults involving overheating of stator winding conductors. Here again, the faults have remained undetected by standard generator instrumentation until major damage has taken place.

Serious faults on large generators have not been confined to the CEGB. In 1970, the first instrument designed specifically to give early warning of overheating in a generator was developed in the USA. This was known as the Core Monitor.

The device is however, capable of detecting overheating anywhere in the generator, so long as insulation material is involved.

Work has been carried out in North Eastern Region Scientific Services Department of the CEGB over the past few years to evaluate the CM and its usefulness as a generator protective device.

THE EARLY DETECTION OF OVERHEATING IN GENERATORS

The many electrical insulating materials used in large generators are essentially similar. They consist of organic polymers, either natural, such as bitumen, or, more commonly, symthetic epoxy resins.

Materials such as glass fibre or mica are included to improve mechanical or electrical properties.

When organic insulation is heated, it begins to chemically decompose. Some of the decomposition products are released into the generator hydrogen. Methods of detecting overheating in generators are generally based on instruments or techniques sensitive to the thermal degradation products of insulation.

Analysis of Generator Hydrogen

When insulating materials are heated, organic gases such as ethane, ethylene etc are given off into the generator hydrogen. The earliest method used for the attempted detection of overheating was to take stator hydrogen samples at regular intervals and analyse them for organic impurities using gas chromatography.

The method suffers from several disadvantages. The majority of generators have an existing concentration or organic impurities in the hydrogen. These are the same materials as produced by heating insulation and their concentration varies continuously due to hydrogen drier cycling and make-up. The increase in concentration due to a developing fault would not be detected until large quantities of insulation were heated to high temperatures.

The response time of the system is poor and the detection of rapidly developing overheating is unlikely unless continuous samples are taken. Automatic sampling systems with limited analysis capability have been developed but have not proved suitable for operational service.

Attempts to use gas analysis to determine the source of known generator overheating have been unsuccessful. Only the detection of acetylene, not normally present in generator hydrogen, provides any useful information, being indictive of undesirable electrical activity or extremely high temperatures.

Production of Particles

Insulating materials heated to over 180°C begin to breakdown chemically and give off vapour. The vapour forms a supersaturated layer above the surface where it is rapidly cooled by the generator hydrogen. Spontaneous condensation takes place under such circumstances, small droplets containing a few molecules being formed (Davis and Rideal 1961).

These droplets will grow by further condensation on their surfaces and will become stable if their free energy falls with increasing radius. The total free energy ΔG available to vapourise a droplet is given by:-

$$\Delta G = \frac{1}{\nu} \{\frac{4}{3} \pi a^3\} \{\mu_\ell - \mu_\nu\} + 4\pi a^2 \gamma_o$$

Where ν is molecular volume of liquid
   a is droplet radius
   $\mu\ell$ and $\mu\nu$ are chemical potentials of liquid and vapour
   γ_o is surface tension of bulk liquid

At temperatures below the liquid boiling point, $\mu\ell < \mu\nu$ so that the first term is negative. Once a critical value of radius has been exceeded therefore, ΔG will start to fall and the droplet will be stable. Lack of physical data for the breakdown products of the

insulation materials used in generators precludes
calculation of actual values of critical radius.

As the droplets grow and become stable, they will be
carried away in the hydrogen stream. The size to
which individual droplets ultimately grow will depend
on the time they remain in the supersaturated vapour
above the insulation surface. This time will vary
depending on the position in the vapour cloud where
the droplet initially forms. The aerosol carried away
by the hydrogen stream will therefore contain droplets of many different sizes.

Heating insulation in a generator should thus give
rise to an increasing concentration of small droplets.
i.e. an aerosol. Once droplet formation ceases, due
either to the cause of the heating being removed or
the complete pyrolysis of the insulation involved,
the concentration will start to fall due to a
combination of evaporation, coagulation and plating
out. The lack of data on the aerosol material and
the absence of accurate theory makes the investigation
of droplet loss difficult, but observations during
site tests show that the concentration falls to
below the detectable level within about 15 minutes.

Under normal circumstances, therefore, an aerosol
will not be present in generator hydrogen and its
existence will generally indicate that organic
material is being heated.

A device capable of continuously monitoring generator
hydrogen for aerosols will therefore serve to give
warning of overheating.

Detection of Aerosols in Generator Hydrogen

The aerosol produced by overheating insulation can
be detected by a suitable ion chamber. Simple
devices of this type are widely used as smoke
detectors for fire alarm systems. An ion chamber
specifically designed for generator hydrogen monitoring is shown in Fig 1. The device is connected
across the generator cooling fan so that a constant
through-flow of hydrogen is maintained.

The first section of the ion chamber is lined with a
weak α- emitter. Cloth impregnated with thorium
oxide, as used in the manufacture of gas mantles, is
normally used. The hydrogen is ionised by α-
bombardment and then passes into the electrode system.
A potential gradient is maintained across the gas
path by applying a fixed voltage to the centre
polarising electrode. With a sufficiently high
polarising voltage, all ions of the appropriate sign
will be deflected to the collector.

The ions collected cause a small current (typically
10^{-12} to 10^{-11} A) to flow in an external circuit
connected between the collector electrode and the
chamber wall. This current can be measured using
an electrometer amplifier.

When small aerosol droplets enter the ion chamber,
ions will become attached to them. Ions of opposite
charge will recombine on the droplets and so be lost.
Several ions of the same sign may also become attached
to a droplet, the actual number depending on the
droplet radius. After a certain time, the ion-droplet
mixture attains equilibrium (Rich, Pollack and
Metnieks 1962). It can be shown theoretically that
the number of charges on a single particule will rise
from one for radii below 0.05 μm (Keefe, Nolan and
Rich 1959). to over 10 for a radius of 10μm .

The droplets are too heavy to be deflected to the
collector electrode and the associated charges are
therefore carried out of the ion chamber. The chamber
output current will thus be reduced when an aerosol
is present in the hydrogen. For maximum sensitivity,
the ion-droplet mixture must remain in the ionising
section until equilibrium is achieved. This fixes

the maximum hydrogen flow rate through a chamber with
given volume and α-source activity. A typical ion
chamber has a time to equilibrium of about six seconds
(Skala, 1966).

When pure hydrogen is flowing through the GCM ion
chamber, two processes take place continuously. Ions
are produced by collision between α-particles and
hydrogen molecules and these ions then begin to
recombine. Under conditions of fixed pressure and
flow, the difference in production and recombination
rates gives rise to a steady concentration of free
ions in the hydrogen entering the electrode section.

If all the free ions of one polarity are driven to the
collector electrode, then the current flow in the
external amplifier circuit will be given by

$$\text{Io} = \text{Qe}. \sqrt{\frac{q}{\alpha}} \quad \text{(Skala 1974)}$$

Where Q is hydrogen flow rate
   e is charge on election
   q is ion production rate
   α is ion recombination rate

α and e are known constants, so that q may be obtained
by direct measure of Q and Io.

Theorectical analysis shows that when droplets enter
the ion chamber, the fall in output current ΔI is
given by

$$\frac{\Delta I}{\text{Io}} = \frac{k}{\sqrt{q}}$$

Where k is a constant dependent on droplet size and
concentration. For a given k, the value of the above
expression may be used as an expression of CM
senstivity S. For two CM's having sensitivities
S_1 and S_2, the relative sensitivity S_R is given by

$$S_R = \frac{S_1}{S_2} = \sqrt{\frac{q_2}{q_1}} = \frac{I_{o2}}{I_{o1}} \frac{Q_1}{Q_2}$$

Measuring Io for two CM's at known gas flows enables
their relative sensitivities to be predicted.

GENERATOR CORE MONITOR SITE TESTS

Small scale laboratory tests can never be
truly representative of the conditions inside a
large generator. It is not practical to duplicate
the effects of rapid cooling of particles in a high
gas flow rate and their dilution in a large, well
mixed volume of hydrogen.

Particulation is essentially a surface phemonena.
For a given material at a fixed temperature above
200°C, the total number of particles given off will
be proportional to the surface area. Heating known
areas of insulation to fixed temperature inside a
generator on which a CM is installed will allow
that CM to be calibrated in terms of area and
temperature so long as sufficient particles are
produced to affect the monitor output.

Arrangements were therefore made to install
Insulation samples with heaters in the gas space
of a large generator.

Heating solid insulation in a hydrogen stream so
that the exposed surface has an even temperature is
difficult. The majority of pyrolysers were therefore
designed to heat a thin coating of varnish. Two
materials were used - a bituminous varnish as used on
core plate and a general-purpose electrical varnish.
The second varnish is sprayed onto the bore and
endwindings of finished stators by UK manufacturers.
It is therefore likely to be one of the first

materials in the hydrogen stream to particulate when overheating takes place in either the core or the stator winding.

The varnishes were applied by brush to brass-cased cartridge heaters with the terminal ends mounted in die-cast boxes. The exposed surface of each heater was 110 cm^2 and pyrolysers having one, two and three heaters were produced. A thermocouple was attached to the mid point of each heater.

The pyrolysers were installed inside the generator stator casing at the inlets to two of the hydrogen coolers. An ageing period of just over a year was allowed before tests were carried out.

A standard commercial core monitor was installed on the generator for the tests, together with equipment which gave a continuous read-out of the total gaseous organic impurity level in the stator hydrogen.

Pyrolyers were heated in two ways: heating rapidly to 220°C (just over first particulation temperature), and heating rapidly to over 500°C (maximum particulation temperature). A range of sample areas for each varnish was heated enabling CM reponse to be calibrated in terms of sample area for maximum and minimum particulation temperatures.

The results of the tests are summarised in Fig 2. As predicted, the reduction in CM output is linearly related to the sample area for any one material and heating mode. For a given sample area, the output reduction is much larger at the higher temperature corresponding to maximum particulation rate.

It is interesting to compare the results obtained with those published by General Electric (Carson, Barton and Echeveria, 1970). Strips of core plate coated in epoxy paint were mounted in a large generator stator and heated by passing a high current through them for about one minute. The temperature achieved is not given but would have exceeded 500°C as the varnish was charred. The GE results are reproduced in Fig 2 . The greater CM response for a given area is most likely a result of the rapid heating rate of about 500°C/min compared to the 100°C/min achieved during our tests.

At no time during the test was there a significant change in the hydrogen organic impurity level.

OIL MIST

It has been found that oil leaking into a generator stator via the rotor shaft hydrogen seals can form a mist of small droplets which are then carried in the gas stream.

Oil mist will be detected by a CM in exactly the same way as the products of overheated insulation. If a generator is operated with oil mist being produced, then the presence of this mist will cause CM alarms, interfering with the detection of any particulates from insulation.

There are three viable basic methods by which an oil mist may be produced in a generator. These may occur singly or in any combination.

Mechanical Production of Oil Mist

There are several conceivable ways in which oil may be atomised mechanically. One mechanism would involve leakage through the hydrogen seals forming a thin film of oil on the rotor shaft. This could be thrown off, at a step change in diameter for instance, to form small droplets.

If it is assumed that an oil film on a spinning shaft is maintained by surface tension and subject only to hoop stress, then the maximum film thickness t is

given by:-

$$t = \frac{2\gamma}{\ell (100\pi r)^2} \text{ } \mu m$$

where: γ is the surface tension of oil (.03N m^{-1})
 ℓ is the density of oil (900 kg m^{-3})
 r is the shaft radius

For $r = 0.25$ m, $5 = 0.01$ μm. Rotor shaft radii generally lie between these limits. If it is assumed that any droplets produced by the oil film breaking up have maximum diameters equal to its thickness, then the radius of these droplets would be between 0.0015 and 0.005μm. It can be shown theorectically that droplets in this size range would not be detected by a CM. In practice, it is probable the surface roughness of the shaft would prevent the formation of such thin films.

Direct leakage from the seal face in the form of a fine jet of oil could lead to the generation of a mist. Experiments have shown, however, that it is extremely difficult to produce a fine mist in this manner unless a specially designed atomiser is used. (Carson et al, 1977). It is therefore considered unlikely that on oil mist could be formed by direct leakage. A third possibility is oil leakage reaching the rotor fan, where impact with the rotating blades could cause a mist to be generated. If adequate quantities of oil are to reach the fan, there would have to be major leakage at the seals or a large ingress of oil due to operational error. General Electric quote only one instance of mechanically produced oil mist being detected by a CM. This followed an accident on the works test bed when a large quantity of oil entered the stator casing (Carson et al, 1977). It is desirable that a CM should detect such an occurrence, since oil in large quantities is known to damage generator insulation and accelerate wear in glass fibre components subject to abrasion.

No evidence of mechanically produced oil mist has so far been found on any CEGB generator fitted with a CM. It can therefore be said with some certainty that a mechanically produced oil mist is unlikely to occur in a generator under correct operational conditions.

Thermal Production of Oil Mist

Laboratory experiments have been carried out which showed that a mist detectable by a CM could be produced by either heating a pool of oil or by allowing oil droplets to fall onto a hot surface. The oil vapourises rapidly to form a supersaturated vapour above the heated surface. Spontaneous condensation takes place under these conditions and small droplets are formed. The droplets will grow to a size dependent on the time for which they remain in the supersaturated vapour. This time will vary and so a polydisperse aerosol will be produced. The gas flow rate over the oil surface will also affect the removal rate of droplets and hence will control their diameters. Heating generator insulating materials produces particles by a similar mechanism, although it is thought that depolymerisation may take place before evaporation.

It was shown experimentally that less than 0.1 ml of oil dropped onto a surface at 250°C in a vessel with a 1 1.s^{-1} throughflow of hydrogen caused the output of a GCM to fall almost to zero within a few seconds, recovery taking up to an hour. Operation of the CM test filter caused the monitor to rise to clean gas level, proving that oil mist was being produced.

A pool of oil was heated at 50°C per minute in a hydrogen stream which was then passed to a CM. Particulation began at 120°C, thereafter increasing rapidly with temperature. The above temperature is the minimum at which particulation takes place. An increase in hydrogen flow across the oil surface will cause vapour to be removed at a greater rate. A higher temperature (i..e evaporation rate) will therefore be needed to produce a supersaturated vapour enabling the formation of droplets. It has been shown that particulation temperature is linearly related to hydrogen velocity (Carson et al, 1977) and can vary between 124 and 160°C)

Electrical Protection of Oil Mist

Arcing and/or sparking is known to take place in generators when circulating currents in the stator structure flow through areas of high or chaning contact resistance. Examples have been seen on the building bar key blocks of   generators and on the core backs of   generators.

It has been found in the laboratory that if an arc is initiated through a thin film of oil, then an oil mist detectable by a CM is formed.

The exact method by which an oil mist is formed electrically is unknown. It is suspected that the main cause is the heat generated by the arc producing evaporation in the same manner as direct heating. During laboratory experiments, the spoon holding the oil film through which the arc was struck became very hot (certainly over 100°C)

The Significance of Oil Mist

The presence of mechanically produced oil mist serves only to indicate that a large quantity of oil has entered the generator. No information regarding the condition of the generator is provided, other than the possibility of a problem with the hydrogen seals.

Thermally produced oil mist indicates that some part or parts of the generator are operating in excess of 120°C. In areas of the generator where there are high hydrogen flow velocities, the temperature will be correspondingly higher. Such temperatures exceed the maximum allowed in the generator specification and therefore indicate the presence of a potential fault. An oil mist produced electrically also shows that there is a problem in the generator.

When it is suspected that oil mist is being detected by a CM, collection and chemical analysis of the droplets can be used to provide definite identification. Whilst it is not possible to reliably differentiate between particles from insulating materials using existing analysis techniques, oil mist produced by any of the methods considered can be readily identified. A thermally or electrically produced oil mist is a definite indication of overheating or arcing in the generator and possibly serves as an early warning of a developing fault. The presence of oil mist must therefore not be ignored and a CM installation must not be modified so that it is no longer capable of detecting oil mist.

CORE MONITOR SITE EXPERIENCE

Core monitors have been in use in the USA for 10 years and for about half this time in the CEGB. CM's are now installed on all single-shaft 500 and 660 MW generators in N.E. Region.

These eleven CM's have proved reliable, many instruments having operated for over three years without faults. The only failures reported have been a panel meter with collapsed movement bearings and a broken lead on an electrometer amplifier feedback resistor both failures were probably due to vibration.

Alarms on CM Site Installations

There have been a number of occasions when CM's installed on operational generators in North Eastern Region indicated an alarm condition. These are considered individually below. No GCM false alarms have been recorded.

660 MW Generator 'A'. CM's were installed on this machine after discovery of a core hot spot during a flux test. The CM's, installed one at each end of the generator, were fitted for research purposes as the temperature of the hot spot could be monitored continuously. Transient CM alarms (Fig 3) were recorded with increasing frequency over a period of several weeks until a catastrophic core fault developed away from the known hot spot. Both CM's alarmed approximately five minutes before molten iron from the fault burned through the stator winding insulation and the earth fault protection tripped the generator - Fig 4.

Identical simultaneous indications were always given by both monitors, indicating that significant mixing between the gas circuits as each end of the generator takes place. Only one CM is therefore needed on a two fan generator.

660 MW Generator 'B'. Following the experience on Generator 'A' CM's were installed on Generator 'B' to gain operating experience on what was thought to be a fault-free machine. Transient alarms similar to these seen on 'A' were recorded but with a much higher frequency. It was found that if the machine was operated at steady load and reactive output, the frequency of alarms could be minimised.

Chemical analysis of the aerosol detected by the CM's and collected on filters showed it to be thermally produced oil mist. When the machine was removed from service and inspected, it was found that the stator was liberally coated with oil which had caused significant damage to the endwinding structure.

There was clear evidence that oil had been heated by currents flowing between the stator casing and the core frame via a poorly insulated clamp plate.

500 MW Generator. The CM installed on this generator gave indications of slowly developing overheating. Transient changes in output were first seen, followed by a steady fall over approximately 90 minutes - Fig 5

The unit was manually tripped after extensive checks on the CM which included use of the test filter and substituting a current source for the ion chamber.

When the generator was inspected, it was found that two stator bars had been overheated due to blockage of a cooling water hose.

THE USE OF CM's ON OPERATIONAL GENERATORS

Normal Operation

The normal CM output current with no particles present in the hydrogen is dependent only on the gas flow rate and pressure. The actual magnitude of the current has no effect on sensitivity to particles and is hence of little importance.

A high gas flow rate is desirable as it minimises response time to any particles formed in the generator and should also reduce any tendency for condensation to take place in the ion chamber. In most practical situations, it will be possible to obtain the manufacturer's recommended flow of about 130mls^{-1}.

The actual CM output voltage is then dictated by the electrometer amplifier gain setting. A "clean gas" output of 80% full scale is used. This allows the level to rise due to small variations in hydrogen pressure or drift in the electronics without exceeding the maximum.

Interpretation of Reductions in CM Output

When particles are present in the generator hydrogen, the CM output will fall. The actual reduction will depend on the size distribution and number concentration of the particles. In a practical situation, both these quantities will be unknown since they cannot be measured using existing techniques. It is therefore of little use to relate a fall in output on a CM installed on an operational generator to theorectical predictions of particle concentration.

Experiments have indicated that changes in CM output caused by particles from overheated insulation may be related to surface areas and temperatures. It is however, not possible to state for instance, that a certain area of insulation heated to $200^{\circ}C$ is acceptable, particularly when a smaller area at $500^{\circ}C$ will give the same CM response. Any overheating must be considered dangerous and therefore the CM should ideally be operated so that the slightest fall in output is acted upon.

It is not possible to realise the ideal situation in practice. The ion chamber is inherently noisy and the CM output fluctuates by $\pm 5\%$. Additional smoothing would adversley affect the response time of the monitor. Small changes in output can also take place due to ambient temperature effects on the electronics etc. Consideration of these, together with the need for an adequate safety margin to avoid false alarms, dictates that no action should be taken until the CM output falls below 50% full scale. Adopting this alarm level implies that the monitor will be sensitive to areas of overheated insulation between 100 and 700 cm^2 depending on temperature.

The damage likely to have taken place by the time a CM alarm is produced will depend on the type of fault involved. The two most common types of serious fault are considered.

Core Faults. Experience with core faults suggests that overheating is initiated just below the bottom of the stator winding slots. There is unlikely to be significant movement of hydrogen between laminations and any particles formed there will not be carried into the main gas spaces. The quantity of interlaminar insulation exposed at the slot surfaces is very small and unlikely to produce a particle concentration detectable by the CM. It has been shown that high temperatures at the slot bottom only result in slight increases at the bore surface. The area of varnish overheated in the gas vents will be very small during the early stages of a core fault and will therefore remain undetected.

Once the overheating develops to the stage where the adjacent stator conductor insulation becoms heated, a large amount of particulating material is involved. Even if zero gas flow between the stator winding and slot side is assumed, the pressure rise due to vapourisation of insulation will cause vapour to be ejected into the air gap and condense to particles. It is not possible to accurately predict when a sufficient quantity of insulation would be overheated so as to generate a CM alarm. The data in Fig. 2 shows that a maximum area of 700 cm^2 would be needed if the overheated insulation were exposed to the stator hydrogen. If this is increased by a factor of two to allow for the confining effects of the slot, the resultant 1400 cm^2 represents only a short length of conductor bar - say 20 cm of one side of a typical bar. Core faults detected at such an early stage should still be easily detected by high voltage flux test and are often repairable if prompt action is taken. Such repairs can reduce outage times significantly if spare stators are not available and have proved reliable on past occasions. Prompt removal of the generator from service will also minimise the changes of secondary damage to the stator winding and rotor.

Stator Winding Cooling Fault

Stator winding faults initiated by overheated conductor bars are another source of major outages. In such cases, a large proportion or even the whole of at least one bar is affected, often due to restricted cooling water flow. Assuming a heat transfer coefficient of $100 \text{ Wm}^{-2}\text{K}^{-1}$ from the bar outer surface to the hydrogen and thermal conductivities of $0.1 \text{ Wm}^{-1}\text{K}^{-1}$ for epoxy-mica insulation and $0.3 \text{ Wm}^{-1}\text{K}^{-1}$ for bitumen-mica, copper temperatures of $626^{\circ}C$ and $1480^{\circ}C$, grossly exceeding the melting temperature of $1050^{\circ}C$, would be required to produce surface temperatures of $200^{\circ}C$. These estimates are based on equilibrium conditions; in a practical condition the copper temperature would rise over about 30 minutes with the insulation surface temperature lagging behind. The temperatures achieved when particulation started at the outer surface would therefore be higher than the above figures.

The heat transfer coefficient used above is for a stator bar in an unrestricted hydrogen stream such as in the endwinding area. Heat transfer to the core in the slot portion will be much lower and there will be a much lower differential between copper and surface temperatures in this region. The pressure rise due to evaporation in the confines of the slot will force vapour and particles into the air gap hydrogen stream. An incident on a 500 MW generator involving loss of cooling water to two stator bars showed that sufficient particulation took place to give a CM alarm without the need for copper temperatures to exceed the melting point by 50%. Large quantities of bitumen had been ejected from the ends of the worst affected bar and it is probable that particles from this source were responsible for the CM alarm. The high pressures generated inside an overheated bar may also cause vapour to be forced to the surface and there form particles.

It can therefore be said with some certainty that an overheated stator bar will give rise to a CM alarm before insulation breakdown takes place with the possibility of consequential core damage.

The rotor winding is directly cooled by hydrogen and hence the CM will detect any overheating in this area.

Action Following a CM Alarm

When a CM alarm is recorded, action must be taken to reduce the overheating and consequent damage. A course of action has been determined which is based on the experience gained during the evaluation of CM's.

The first action following a CM alarm must always be to verify that the reduction in output is due to particles in the hydrogen rather than an instrument fault. In the case of a genuine alarm, inserting the test filter will restore the output to "clean gas" level within 10-15 seconds. Alarm units have been developed which carry out the verification process automatically and their use is essential to avoid the possibility of operator error.

Once an alarm is ver ified, action must be taken immediately to prevent further development of the fault. The location of the overheating will be unknown and hence corrective action must cover all possibilities. Some faults, particularly those affecting the stator core, develop quickly and thus there will be no time to try a range of potential corrections.

A significant reduction in load is the optimum corrective action to cater for the majority of serious faults. A load reduction causes the stator current to be reduced thus reducing winding temperature. Core axial flux is reduced cutting one cause of overheating in an area of the core most susceptible to failure. The rotor current and voltage are also reduced which should reduce any overheating in this area.

The initial load reduction should be the maximum achievable without tripping coal mills. This allows a quick return to full load if the CM alarm is successfully cleared. Such a load reduction, from 660 to 400MW was found to clear monitor alarms on generator 'B' above. If the CM alarm persists after a load reduction then further reductions of similar size must be made. The time delay between successive load reductions depends on the recovery rate of the CM once particulation ceases. One minute will normally be sufficient time for an increase in monitor output to be apparent if a load reduction has had the desired effect.

The unit must be tripped if the alarm is still present at zero load.

Should one or more load reductions be successful in clearing the alarm, then an attempt may be made to restore generation.

The fault may have stabilised or even burned itself out without causing major damage. If further CM alarms result from a load increase, then an operating point just below the alarm point must be determined by experiment. The decision on whatever to continue operation at reduced load must then be made on economic grounds.

Particle samples should be taken during the initial alarm, preferably by an automatic unit controlled from CM. The analysis techniques currently available are of insufficient sensitivity to detect particles from overheating insulation. CM alarms can also be caused by oil mist, however, and this can be readily identified.

Basically, oil mist is usually produced thermally and therefore indicates undesireable heating. If oil mist is identified as the cause of CM alarms and a decision is made not to take the generator out of service for inspection, then increased risk of failure must be accepted. In such a case, a second CM with heated ion chamber, which does not react to oil mist, may be installed while the problem is investigated. The second monitor will only alarm when insulation is overheated should the fault develop further.

The courses of action detailed above are summarised in the flow chart of Fig 6.

Location of Overheating

The CM has been shown to be capable of detecting small areas of overheated insulation inside a generator. The monitor does not provide any information as to the actual material involved. Existing chemical analysis techniques are much less sensitive than the CM to insulation degradation products and can only be relied on to detect oil mist. Even if the required sensitivity were achieved, the similar chemical makeup of most generator insulating materials could well make differentiating between them difficult. (Barton et al, 1981).

In the absence of adequate analysis techniques, there is no indication of which area of the generator is overheating. The CM is so sensitive that the damage may be too minor, depending on its location in the generator, to be detected by inspection or available tests if rapid corrective action is taken following an alarm. Localised overheating in a conductor bar due to subconductor insulation breakdown, for instance, may well give rise to CM alarm but will be extremely difficult to locate using existing test techniques. Correlation between CM alarms and the incidence of radio frequency currents in the generator neutral may be of assistance in such a case (Emergy et al 1979).

There is thus a need for a method of reliably locating the source of overheating. The most promising soluation to this problem is to coat the generator surfaces with a range of materials giving off chemically different particles at the particulation temperature of the underlying insulation. The materials could alternatively be incorporated in the insulation. Materials of this type, known as tagging compounds, contain microcapsules which rupture at $200^{\circ}C$ and are now used in the USA (Barton et al 1981).

The microcapsules contain one of eight compounds which particulate readily. The particles are sufficiently different chemically to ensure reliable analysis using gas chromatrography.

The use of such materials requires urgent investigation so that a reliable system of locating the overheating detected by a CM can be developed.

Cost Effectiveness of CMs

Two clearly definable strategies can be employed when considering the installation of generator condition monitors. Firstly, only generators considered to be most at risk can be fitted with CM's. The assessment of risk of failure is extremely difficult unless there is clear evidence of a type fault on a particular design. Existing monitoring systems such as thermocouples cannot guarantee that overheating will be detected - indeed detection of overheating by such means is exceptional. Assessing risk of failure from operating history is also unreliable.

In the absence of a reliable risk assessment technique, then, the second strategy - the installation of CM's on all large generators - must be considered. The CM is demonstrably the only device capable of continuously monitoring a generator and detecting overheating at an early stage.

The potential savings make the cost of fitting CMs insignificant. The cost of a complete CM system including automatic sampler and alarm units is approximately £10,000 and represents less than one day's lost generation on 500MW fossil fired unit.

Accurate assessment of potential savings resulting from widespread use of CMs is difficult. Long outages following major faults have often been avoided by the fitting of replacement stators. These were either designated spares or units intended for other, un-completed stations. Taking the worst case of no available spare, if a core fault were to remain undetected then a complete stator rebuild could be necessary, taking over a year.

If a CM were installed and detected the fault in its early stages so that only limited damage took place, then a repair could be possible. This could be carried out in about 100 days resulting in a saving of 128 GWD.

A detailed study of generator faults in the USA over the eight years to 1977 has been carried out by the Electrical Power Research Institute (Emery et al 1979).

The total loss of generation due to generator faults was 4706 GWD. Of this, 43% was due to stator winding faults, 15% to core faults and 5% to rotor winding faults. It is estimated that the total saving if CMs had been used on all generators, and prompt action had been taken after a verified alarm, would have been 893 GWD - 19% of the total loss. This represents the highest potential saving obtainable with any of the available generator monitoring systems. The lost generation due to core faults alone could be reduced by 68%.

The ERPI survey also shows that the risk of failure rises rapidly with generator rating. Generators with ratings over 600MW averaged three times the forced outage time of 500MW machines and ten times that of units under 300MW. The greatest potential savings due to the use of CMs are therefore likely to be on the largest and most efficient generators where replacement costs are highest.

CONCLUSIONS

All insulating materials used in generators produce an aerosol of small particles when heated to over about 180°C. The maximum rate of production occurs between 300 and 500°C. Actual temperatures for initial and maximum particulation depend on the rate of heating.

The CM is the only monitoring device available which is capable of detecting overheating anywhere in a generator before it develops into a major fault.

The CM is capable of detecting an area of between 100 and 700 cm² of overheated insulation depending on the temperature and material.

Oil leaking into a generator stator through the hydrogen seals can be converted into a fine mist by mechanical, thermal or electrical means.

Mechanically produced oil mist in generators is virtually unknown and its presence considered unlikely under operational conditions.

Thermally and electrically produced oil mists in a generator are indicative of problems which may lead to failure.

Oil mist will be detected by a CM in the same way as particulates produced by overheated insulation.

Rapid corrective action following a verified CM alarm can significantly redude fault damage. Installation of CM's on all large generators can be expected to contribute to a sizeable reduction in forced outage time.

The CM only detects overheating; it provides no indication of the location. Techniques which can give this information are urgently needed.

ACKNOWLEDGEMENTS

This work was carried out by the North Eastern Region Scientific Services Department and is published by permission of the Director General of the North Eastern Region of the Central Electricity Generating Board.

REFERENCES
1. Barton, S.C., Carson, C.G., Gill, R.S., Ligan, W.V. and Webb, J.L. (1981) Implementation of Pyrolysate Analysis of Materials Employing Tagging Compounds to Locate an Overheated Area in a Generator, IEEE PES Summer Meeting, July.

2. Carson, C.C, Barton, S.C. and Echeveria, F.S. (1970). Immediate Working of Local Overheating in Electrical Machines by the Detection of Pyrolysis Products. IEEE Summer Power Meeting 71 TP 154 PWR.

3. Davies, C.N. (1966) Aerosol Science. Academic Press, London.

4. Davies, J.T. and Rideal, E.K. (1961) Interfacial Phenomena, Academic Press, London.

5. Emery, F.T. Haley, P.H. Brandt, G.B. and Gottliels, M. (1979) On-Line Monitoring and Diagnostic Systems for Generators. EPRI Report NP-902.

6. Grobel, L.P. and Carson, C.C. (1969) Overheating Detector for Gas Cooled Electrical Machines. U.S. Patent 342 7880.

7. Keefe, D., Nolan, P.J. and Rich, T.A. (1959) Charge Equilibrium in Aerosols according to the Bolzman Law. Proc. R.I.A. 60A.

8. Lui, Y.H. Whitby, K.T. and Yu, H.S. (1966) A Condensation Aerosol Generator for Producing Manodisperse Aerosols in the Size Range 0.036 to 1.3 J. de Res. Atmos. 2.

9. Megaw, W.J. and Wiffen, R.D. (1963) Measurement of the Diffusion Coefficient of Homogeneous and Other Nuclei. J de Res. Atmos.1.

10. Skala, G.F. (1966) The Ion Chamber Detector as a Monitor of Thermally Produced Particulates. J. de Res. Atmos April/Sept.

11. Skala, G.F. (1974) The Generator Condition Monitor and its Application to the Hydrogen Cooled Generator. 41st Int. Conf. of Doble Clients.

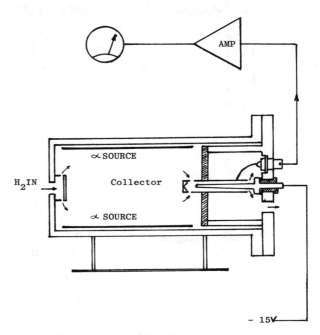

Figure 1   Ion Chamber

130

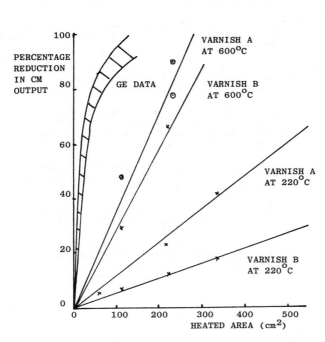

Figure 2   Results of C.M. Site Tests

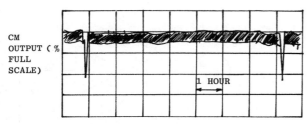

Figure 3   C.M. Transient Alarms

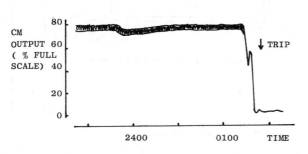

Figure 4   CM Response to Core fault

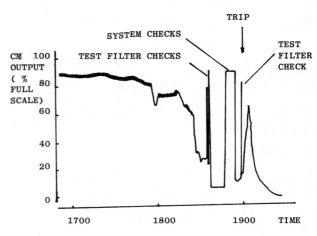

Figure 5   CM Response to Overheated Stator
Conductor Bar

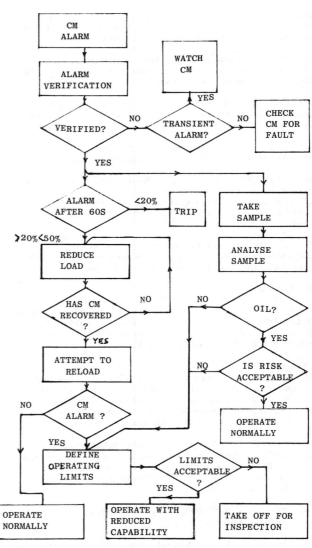

Figure 6   CM Alarm Procedure

CONDITION MONITORING OF TURBOGENERATORS

J.W. Wood, M.J. Ryan   P. Gallagher   D. Gunton

NEI-Parsons Ltd.   IRD Ltd.   NEI-Electronics Ltd.
                                        (RP Automation)

INTRODUCTION

The principle of a condition monitor was described over a decade ago, Skala (1). Such instruments have been widely used on turbogenerators in the USA but in the UK they have been, perhaps quite rightly, the subject of prolonged R & D investigations. Basically the condition monitor is a sensitive smoke detector. Overheating within a machine produces both gases and particles and the condition monitor responds essentially only to the latter. However, the response is in the form of a meter indication which depends on the amount, position, and heating rate of the insulation affected, and not every indication is indicative of impending failure of a machine. In addition there are sources of spurious indication, eg oil leaks. Consequently if the instrument is to be useful it must be used within an operating procedure and have additional analytical equipment attached to it to form a condition monitoring system, the results of which should guide operational decisions.

The principle of a condition monitor has been described, and operating procedures discussed previously, Wood et al (2). One problem in developing an overheating detection system has been the link between a condition monitor and the additional diagnostic equipment. This has been solved in a recently developed condition monitor which has a facility for the manual or automatic insertion of filters to collect particles when an indication occurs. The logic controlling the automatic insertion and the reasons for choosing it are described.

Both gas, Kelley et al (3) ,and particle collection, Wood et al (2,4), and Ryan (5), have been made the basis of analytical techniques intended to determine the cause of a condition monitor indication. Gas analysis has been favoured in the USA while the author's company have used UV fluorescence, Wood et al (4), and Ryan (5), and IR absorption spectroscopy to identify the source of material collected on filters inserted in the gas stream either permanently or when a condition monitor alarm occurs. The design of a prototype fluorescence detector is described, and results from this and an IR spectrometer are discussed.

Sacrificial coatings, Ryan (5), Hogg et al (6), and Pietsch et al (7), may improve the location of the source of overheating. Research is being undertaken in collaboration with Brighton Polytechnic who are making a fundamental study of the micro-encapsulation of materials which can be selected to release particles or gases into the coolant gas at desired temperatures. The advantages of such techniques and the work being undertaken in the author's research laboratory on sacrificial coatings containing fluorescent materials are discussed.

CONDITION MONITOR

Design details and results obtained from condition monitors in laboratory and site experiments have been described previously, Wood et al (2). The monitor described operates on a differential principle, Fig. 1, to reduce sensitivity to gas pressure and flow variations; the downstream chamber does not receive any particles, these being removed by the filter μF_1.

The gas circuit, Fig. 1, includes filters which can be inserted in a pre-selected sequence set by various switches on the instrument front panel. This facility greatly increases the usefulness of the instrument for condition monitoring purposes. The sequence control incorporates the following features:

Auto Test (Alarm Verification)

Upon receiving an alarm signal from the monitor gas is diverted through the test filter μF_2 which removes all particles from the gas. If, after a pre-determined time, the monitor does not return to its quiescent state the alarm must have been false and a monitor fault indication is given. Normally insertion of the filter restores quiescent conditions and removes the alarm signal thereby automatically removing filter μF_2 and restoring the alarm signal. If, however, the signal is not restored after removal of the filter then the alarm, although genuine, must have been transient and a transient indication is given. The restoration of the alarm produces an alarm valid indication.

The auto test function is optional, if selected alarm verification will precede one of two timing sequences described below.

Delay Timing and Sample Sequence

A variable delay period may be set before or after a variable sample filter insertion period. Both periods are set by respective front panel thumbwheel switches. Choosing delay before sampling ensures that the alarm condition must be sustained for a pre-determined period before filter sampling. Transient indications will therefore be ignored.

Delay after sampling ensures immediate sampling and vetos sampling for subsequent monitor responses within the delay period.

A maximum of four samples may be taken sequentially. Indication is given of the stage reached in the sequence and after the fourth sample the unit must be reset. The control is achieved by a dedicated microprocessor which facilitates any substantial changes which experience may indicate as desirable, and the interfacing with remote control points.

Filters obtained when an alarm is recorded

are available for examination and analysis by the techniques described below.

UV FLUORESCENCE SPECTROSCOPY

The Fluorescence Detector

The UV fluorescence detector was specially developed for the analysis of particles collected from the coolant gas stream, since no suitable instruments were commercially available to fulfil requirements. The main advantage foreseen for the instrument was the speed with which analyses could be made.

In the prototype instrument, Ryan (5), the collected material is irradiated with monochromatic (365nm) UV light and the emission fluorescence is projected via an optical filter arrangement onto the photocathode of a photomultiplier, Fig. 2. Seven band pass filters covering the visible spectrum are housed in a disc which can be rotated in front of the photomultiplier to resolve the emission spectrum.

Experimental Procedure

Laboratory procedure

Eight insulating materials, Table 1, were examined in experiments to determine the response of the fluorescence detector to material collected on filters following overheating. The materials were individually heated in hydrogen at a pressure of 3 bar and of purity better than 99.5%. Each sample was heated at a controlled rate of 4°C/min to a maximum temperature of 500°C. The overheated particles were collected over four temperature ranges within the 500°C range. Three samples of each material were examined to obtain representative results.

The filter used to collect the particles is a 2.5cm diameter diaphragm filter with a 0.2 µm pore size. An uncontaminated filter fluoresces giving a deep purple colour. This background spectrum was subtracted from the spectral response obtained for the contaminated filter to give the actual emission spectrum of the contamination.

Site procedure

Condition monitors similar to the one previously described which included the facility for the insertion of filters were connected up to a 500 MW generator on site. Insulating materials, Table 1, were deliberately overheated within the hydrogen gas

Table 1 - Materials Examined in Laboratory (A) and Site (B) Experiments.

No.	Description	A	B
1	Asphalt based stoving varnish	*	
2	Asphalt based stoving varnish with inorganic filler	*	*
3	Asphalt based mica bonding varnish	*	*
4	Epoxy resin 1	*	
5	Alkyd ester varnish	*	*
6	Epoxy resin 2	*	
7	Epoxy resin 3	*	
8	Aromatic polyamide paper	*	
9	Compressed cellulose fibre		*
10	Graphite coated compressed cellulose fibre		*

stream of the generator. The pyrolysis particles produced were collected on filters and then analysed using the UV fluorescence detector to attempt to identify the overheated insulation.

Results

Typical examples of the results obtained are shown in Figs. 3 and 4. The differences between the spectra obtained for the material collected on a filter when the asphalt based stoving varnish was overheated can be attributed to the type and amount of particles generated at a given temperature. Thermogravimetric analysis (TGA) of the material shows it to have two principal thermal decomposition reactions (in which there is rapid weight loss) in hydrogen over the temperature ranges 280°C to 395°C and 395°C to 490°C.

Materials 4, 6 and 7, Table 1, are all epoxy resins and the IR results from them are discussed in the next section. Space has limited the inclusion of UV fluorescence spectra but those for the epoxy resins are distinctly different and examples will be shown when the paper is presented.

The fluorescence spectra obtained, however, do depend on the temperature and rate of heating and this complicates the interpretation of results.

One experimental finding is that the materials obtained from several different original materials at relatively low temperatures, about 200°C, fluoresce over a similar frequency range.

IR SPECTROSCOPY

The fluorescence detector will produce a result almost immediately a filter is available. To obtain an IR spectrogram the material on a filter must be prepared by incorporating it into a potassium bromide (KBr) disc. Technique is critical in the manufacture of the disc. Moisture and excess solvent can affect the final spectrum to such an extent, if not controlled, that comparisons are impossible. Preparation of the disc (grinding) itself is also very important.

IR spectra of three epoxy resins, 1 (material 4, Table 1), 2 (6), 3 (7), are shown in Fig. 5. The materials analysed were prepared during the laboratory investigations described previously, and the particles were collected over the whole of the temperature range examined rather than over four temperature ranges as for the fluorescent detector samples.

Normally identification of materials by IR spectroscopy depends upon comparison with standard spectra for either standard materials or specific commercial compounds. In the present investigation these standard spectra have been prepared from the materials shown in Table 1 under known conditions. It is to be anticipated that these spectra will depend upon the temperature range and temperature rate of rise to which the materials are subjected, but it is anticipated that changes will only be minor, and data is in the process of being obtained. The procedure adopted to recognise materials is complicated because bonds which are specific to one type of compound are few. It is best therefore to adopt a process of elimination, for example if the 1225 cm^{-1} band were absent then the substance could not be a compound such as an epoxy resin because this contains an aromatic ether group.

Table 2 gives a guide to the main absorption peaks found in the compounds listed in Table 1. Specifically the differences, eg between epoxy resins 1, 2, and 3, Fig. 5, would be established as follows:

Structural: The aromatic content of epoxy resin 3 is much greater than that of epoxy resin 1 which in turn is greater than epoxy resin 2; compare bands at 2800 to 3000 cm^{-1} and also 1600, 1500 and the region 600-850 cm^{-1} These differences may be accounted for by the different types of hardener and accelerator used.

Functional groups: The relative epoxy content produces differences in band intensity, i.e. the intensity of bands at 3400, 1225, and 815 cm^{-1}, compared with a C-H band, e.g. 1600 cm^{-1}. This might also result from differences in the type of hardener and accelerator used.

SACRIFICIAL COATINGS

The experiments described in the previous sections were undertaken with insulating materials, largely in the form of coatings, unmodified by the addition of other materials. It has been proposed that the use of sacrificial coatings either in the form of directly applied coatings containing additives or microcapsules containing additives might simplify identification of the source of overheating. Also, since the additive might be arranged to pass into the gas stream at a relatively low temperature, this technique could give prior warning of substantial overheating. It might certainly

be advantageous to code say six areas of a generator using such techniques, and consequently research investigations were instituted in collaboration with Brighton Polytechnic, who undertook a fundamental investigation into the use of microcapsules. However, in parallel with this investigation the authors began to examine the possibility of including fluorescent pigments either into the insulating resins used directly or as sacrificial coatings. Although the experiments are only at an initial stage it has been possible to demonstrate that such materials do effect the fluorescence observed, i.e. that they do pass over with particles when the insulation is overheated. Fig. 6 illustrates this.

SUMMARY AND CONCLUSIONS

The basis for a condition monitoring system has been described. While this type of system will probably be adopted for hydrogen cooled turbogenerators initially it could be used equally as well for air cooled machines and motors. Interpretation of a condition monitor instrument indication has been shown to be a possibility using combined UV fluorescence and IR spectroscopy techniques; a new condition monitor incorporates automatically insertable filters to obtain samples for analysis. Though at the moment UV fluorescence spectroscopy and IR spectroscopy are essentially laboratory techniques, it may be sufficient to retain them as such provided a cost effective strategy is worked out regarding operation of a machine which is producing indications of overheating. At the moment operational experience is very limited and it is regarded as unlikely that a complete failure could be averted in all instances by acting on a sustained condition monitor alarm. The objective should perhaps be surveillance and investigation of any transient indications together with adoption of a procedure such as that outlined in the previous paper, Wood et al (2) for operation, to safeguard against an incipient failure.

REFERENCES

1. Skala, G.F., May 9-13, 1966, 6th Conf. on Condensation Nuclei, Albany, N.Y..

2. Wood, J.W., Ryder, D.M., Ryan, M.J., and Gunton, D., 1980, Canadian Elec. Assocn. Symp. Paper.

3. Kelley, J.K., Auld, J.W., Herter, V.J., Hutchinson, K.A., and Rugenstein, W.A., 1976, IEEE PAS, 95, 3.

4. Wood, J.W., Ryder, D.M., and Gallagher, P.L., 1978, IEEE Paper F78 660-0.

5. Ryan, M.J., 1982, BEAMA Conf. Paper.

6. Hogg, W.K., Ryder, D.M., and Wood, J.W., 1981, IEEE CEIDP Paper

7. Pietsch, H.E., Fort, E.M., Phillips, D.C., and Smith, J.D.B., 1977, IEEE PAS, 96,5.

ACKNOWLEDGEMENTS

The authors would like to thank NEI-Parsons Ltd., IRD Ltd., and NEI-Electronics (R P Automation) Ltd., for permission to publish this paper and CEGB for supporting parts of the work.

Table 2 - Material Main Absorption Wave Numbers

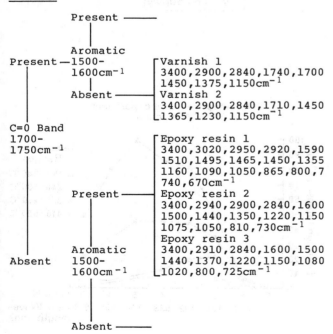

```
                    Present ─────

                    Aromatic
                    1500-        ┌Varnish 1
Present ──1600cm⁻¹  │            │3400,2900,2840,1740,1700
          │         │            │1450,1375,1150cm⁻¹
          │         Absent ──────┤Varnish 2
          │                      │3400,2900,2840,1710,1450
          │                      └1365,1230,1150cm⁻¹
C=O Band
1700-                            ┌Epoxy resin 1
1750cm⁻¹                         │3400,3020,2950,2920,1590
          │                      │1510,1495,1465,1450,1355
          │                      │1160,1090,1050,865,800,7
          │                      │740,670cm⁻¹
          │         Present ─────┤Epoxy resin 2
          │                      │3400,2940,2900,2840,1600
          │                      │1500,1440,1350,1220,1150
          │                      │1075,1050,810,730cm⁻¹
          │         Aromatic     │Epoxy resin 3
Absent    1500-                  │3400,2910,2840,1600,1500
          1600cm⁻¹               │1440,1370,1220,1150,1080
                                 └1020,800,725cm⁻¹

                    Absent ─────
```

Varnish 1 - Material 1, Table 1
Varnish 2 - Material 3, Table 1

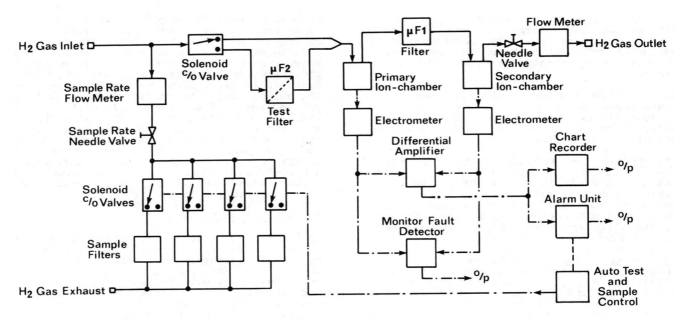

Figure 1 Schematic diagram of condition monitor and sampler.

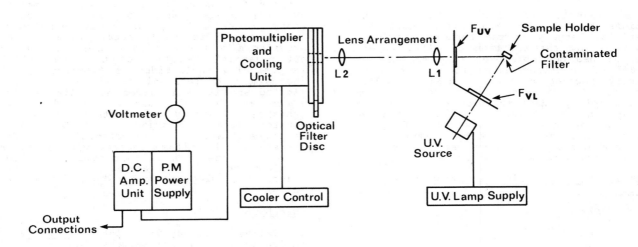

Figure 2 Schematic diagram of Fluorescence detector

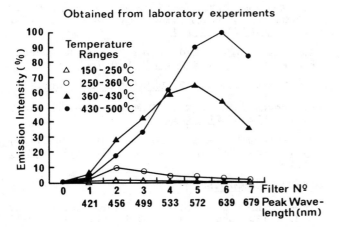

Figure 3 Fluorescence spectra of overheated asphalt based stoving varnish.

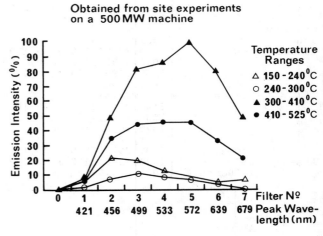

Figure 4 Fluorescence spectra of overheated asphalt based stoving varnish.

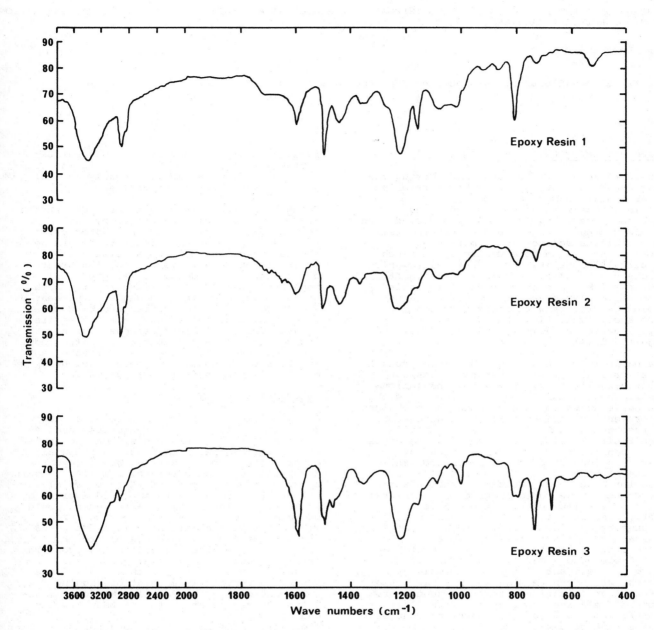

Figure 5 I.R. Spectra of three overheated epoxy resin materials.

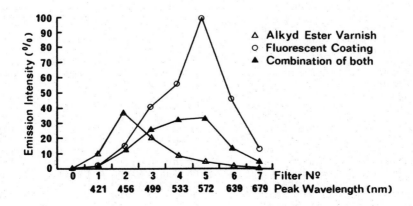

Figure 6 Fluorescence spectra of overheated doped alkyd ester varnish

A MEANS OF IDENTIFYING AND LOCATING THERMAL, THERMOMECHANICAL DEGRADATION OF ELECTRICAL INSULATION WITHIN ELECTRICAL MACHINES

W.K. Hogg and D.M. Ryder

Electrical and Electronic Engineering Department, Brighton Polytechnic, U.K.

INTRODUCTION/RECENT DEVELOPMENTS

Considerable effort has been made during the past decade to develop instruments referred to as Condition Monitors (C.M.) in order to obtain an early warning of overheating problems, resulting in insulation degradation, within hydrogen cooled turbine-generators. The condition monitor is primarily an advancement of the Core Monitors, although in certain countries and industrial organisations the original name is retained. At present, C.M's are commercially available from particular manufacturers of hydrogen-cooled generators with in-service and laboratory evaluations being made, Wood et al,(1) Barton et al,(2), Ryder et al(3) and Hogg et al.(4)

The basic function of the C.M. is to produce an electrical response when particles/gas/materials emitted by overheated insulation pass through a sensitive ion chamber. Within the USA considerable success has been claimed in preventing serious failure of generators by responding to C.M. alarms. However, electricity suppliers are generally cautious in responding to C.M. signals which may result in load shedding or desynchronisation of the machine. This is particularly the case for base load (nuclear) stations where increased outage costs incurred from the use of less efficient plant can prove very costly even in the relatively short term. At present on site a C.M. alarm does not indicate to the operator the cause for the alarm (with confidence), nor its location within the generator. If the cause of the alarm can be identified as a thermal type process which can be related to a particular material and location within the generator, then the relative importance of the alarm can probably be assessed. These procedures can be time consuming and often interpretation of results difficult and inconclusive. Within the USA, both laboratory and in-service experiments have been made for several years using 'tagging compounds', which are usually a composite with epoxy resin paint. Over a few years success has been claimed, using tagging compounds which, when overheated, produce discrete gas chromatograms, at selected temperatures, from compounds giving warning of thermal problems within the generator.(2) Very recently, however, limitations have developed due to a type of ageing of tagging compounds above 100 ^{o}C, also great emphasis has been placed on automatic gas sampling at the time of a CM alarm inherently due to the relatively rapid dispersion of injected gas. A 'new approach' is being considered to overcome the problems of premature ageing of tagging materials, using encapsulated compounds; no details were given.(2) This encapsulation of coded compounds is not a new innovation within the UK, as difficulties with coding/tagging paints were carefully evaluated and consequently a parallel course of development was pursued. A brief description of initial data on encapsulation coding was provided early in 1981 and reported later that year.(4)

Commercial UK condition monitors (CM) currently use Ultra-Violet Spectroscopy (UV) techniques, in particular the characteristic fluorescence emission spectra to determine the nature of the particles of material collected on PTFE filters. The fundamental operation of this detector has previously been published and a detailed report on the CM and tagging/coding compounds is presented from industry at this conference by Wood et al.(5) Discussions of the relative merits of available analytical methods, which include Gas Chromatography (GC), Infra-red Spectroscopy (IR), Thin-layer Chromatography and UV Spectroscopy, have been previously critically assessed.(1),(2),(3),(4).

ENCAPSULATED CODING MATERIALS

Early warning of thermal/thermomechanical degradation of insulation materials used in hydrogen-cooled generators within encapsulated materials has been under fundamental and experimental development for several years. Encapsulated coded saturated solutions within epoxy paints were considered to be an alternative arrangement, with improved ageing protection. The physical arrangement could be advantageous in certain critical areas within the generator, which includes parts of the stator core, windings and rotor, particularly at the higher temperatures. This parallel coding development perhaps has already been justified in the light of the few years service assessment of tagging compounds within the USA.(1) No doubt since all materials deteriorate, certain tagging/coding compounds will have differing ageing properties affecting their long term efficiency. In some respects there is an analogy with high-voltage circuit breakers which may be in service for 10 years or more without operation, but must operate when a certain fault condition occurs.

Micro-capsules containing saturated solutions can be produced between 100-500 μ diameter with wall thickness from 10-100 μ. The number of these capsules/unit area and the temperature at which they burst can be varied. Temperature ranges being studied using gelatine capsules are 80-130 ^{o}C and 120-220 ^{o}C. On bursting the saturated solutions produce solid sub-micro particles of selected materials. This paper gives details of the more fundamental considerations of coding techniques which are part of an industrial collaboration project. The industrial application part of this project is outside the scope of this paper.

PRACTICAL USE OF CM/OPERATIONAL PROCEDURES

Considering the existing knowledge of the

complex chemical interactions caused by thermal degradation of polymeric materials, with possibly other material degradation mechanisms interacting, it has been a substantial achievement both using GC and UV techniques that condition monitors are in service. There should be a clear division between the CM and tagging/coded techniques.

(i) Condition Monitors detect and produce an alarm signal resulting from gas or particles directly from materials normally used in the generator construction. Consequently materials with certain functions in the design are deteriorating and analytical techniques then are used to determine the material producing the alarm. The location of the emission within the generator is not known, hence whether the process is critical in terms of serious failure is difficult to interpret, however if the process continues and becomes more severe, then the material detected could be from a critical region and some indication that action from the operator is necessary. In these conditions a response (minimum) time of 15 minutes is possibly the time available.

(ii) Coding/tagging techniques have been developed to use the same CM to give an early alarm of overheating which can be located and, if the condition continues/ accelerates, it is under consideration before a temperature is reached in which particles/gas from the insulation detected as in (i) are reached.

The difficulty with any monitoring device is the physical interpretation of their signals. The overall system should preferably be capable of identifying the overheated material at the location within the machine. False alarms, incurring high outage costs, should not approach savings in repairs, although this is a 'very grey' area involved with the availability of generating capacity, base load stations, industrialised countries and developing nations. Figure 1 shows a typical operational procedure.

EXPERIMENTAL PROGRAMME

Collaborating with an industrial organisation manufacturing condition monitors operating on material fluorescence characteristics, the choice of using solid relatively inert sub-micro particles from a saturated solution was attractive. There is also a wide choice of materials which produce easily identified (sharp/peculiar) emission spectra. Although the volume of gas evolved from a selected material when a micro-capsule bursts would be greater than the volume of sub-micron particles, gases defuse quickly and re-combine more readily, which is generally accepted. There is also the possibility that the techniques developed could be used with large induction motors in industries where short-term stoppages are very expensive, i.e. oil industry. Gases released would have oxidation and water interaction before being analysed, selected sub-micron material particles would be generally less susceptable. Other advantages are that the density can be increased to match a detection of monitoring instruments, the collected particles would be relatively few and finally, a narrow band, robust, high sensitivity spectrum analyser with computer comparison automat-ically triggered, could be produced relatively cheaply.

The experimental programme has the following objectives :

(1) To select 5-15 materials in saturated solution encapsulated (initial encapsulation material gelatine) which, when combined with epoxy paints, will burst at specific temper-atures depending on the physical capsule arrangement previously defined, over a temperature range of 80-220 $^{\circ}$C.

(2) To determine the quality control in terms of bursting temperature and the effect of thermal ageing of the system.

(3) To experimentally determine the effects of rate of temperature rise dT/dt on the bursting temperature before and after thermal ageing.

(4) With various H_2 flow rates/volume, what particle densities can be detected.

(5) To consider the interaction of coded particles with other degradation products over an equivalent 20 year lifetime which may reduce sensitivity.

(6) Although the ingress of oil can be elim-inated from the alarm system as it is easily detected, disassociation of the oil into light elements has been recorded and certain of these can, when overheated, combine with products from insulation, which may give valuable location data.

The above is obviously a long-term compre-hensive fundamental investigation. Within this paper only a limited amount of inform-ation can be given, although when presented, other findings will be reported.

Figure 2 shows a schematic arrangement of the experimental arrangements from the pressur-ised hydrogen test cell and simulated heated encapsulated coded saturated solution, to the final analyser, computer/storage display and recorder.

SIGNIFICANT EXPERIMENTAL RESULTS

Emission spectra for coded materials

Figure 3 shows typical fluorescence spectra of four coding compounds from bursting capsules in epoxy paint adhered to 2 cm square samples of mica.

Capsule size ranged from 100-500 μ, temper-ature range 100-200 $^{\circ}$C. Rate of linear rise in temperature 20 $^{\circ}$C/min.

Figure 3 also shows, for comparison, how emission spectra from overheated core plate insulation varies within the temperature range 200-500 $^{\circ}$C. The characteristics are similar and cover a relatively wide wave-length which would make identification diff-icult to interpret.

Thermal ageing and rate of temperature rise

Using the same physical arrangement as previously described, the bursting temper-atures are tabulated in terms of rate of temperature rise, before and after periods of thermal ageing. The results given are those using 20 or more experiments for each set of test results. Capsule bursting characteristics are almost independent of the saturated solutions. When thermally aged,

TABLE 1

Test No.	dT/dt, °C/min	Thermally aged at 90°C in air. N.P. for 100 hrs or 240 hrs	Initial bursting temperature with spread in results °C
X_{1a}	10	No	120-150
X_{2a}	15	No	120-155
X_{3a}	25	No	130-160
X_{4a}	40	No	130-160
X_{1b}	10	Yes	130-145
X_{2b}	15	Yes	130-145
X_{3b}	25	Yes	140-150
X_{4b}	40	Yes	140-150
Y_{1a}	10	No	160-200
Y_{2a}	15	No	160-205
Y_{3a}	25	No	165-200
Y_{4a}	40	No	165-205
Y_{1b}	10	Yes	170-180
Y_{2b}	15	Yes	175-185
Y_{3b}	25	Yes	170-180
Y_{4b}	40	Yes	175-180

both mica and metallic sheets were used, with no apparent discrimination.

It will be noted for the two batches of samples that the initial bursting temperature is not greatly dependent on the rate of temperature rise. There is a considerable spread in the initial bursting temperature range of both batches X and Y. Batch X was designed to burst at approximately 100 °C, whereas the spread in the initial bursting temperature is between 120 °C and 160 °C, (these are the extremes). It is worth noting that thermally ageing at 90 °C for 100 or 240 hours increases the initial bursting temperature by not more than 10 °C, but considerably reduced the spread to approximately 10°C. Batch Y was designed to burst at 140 °C and generally gave a similar result, therefore quality control techniques need to be more stringent. Although not shown, after a few hundred hours at 60 °C the same effect was observed. Consequently this may not be thermal ageing but a post curing process. Longer term thermal ageing and thermomechanical ageing is being presently studied and should be completed for presentation later.

Figure 4 shows an aged film on a metallic sheet after 240 hours at 90 °C. Comparison of this with an unaged film showed no topographical changes even at high SEM magnification. Figure 5 shows the capsules within the paint, and Figure 6 and Figure 7 high magnification of capsules which burst at 200 °C, dT/dt 40 °C/min; these photographs are typical examples.

Certain other objectives previously given, particularly the density of sub-micron particles related to H_2 flow rate/volume in terms of detector sensitivity, are being studied; findings are as yet incomplete. The present results obtained from the complete programme is outside the restrictions of this conference paper. More detailed results will be available and presented at the conference.

ACKNOWLEDGEMENTS

The authors wish to thank Brighton Polytechnic for providing research facilities. NEI Parsons are acknowledged for their continued general support and for specific items of equipment. NEI Automation Ltd., are also thanked for the extensive use of their commercial Condition Monitor.

REFERENCES

1. Wood, J.W., Ryder, D.M., Ryan, M.J. and Gunton, D. 1980, Int. Conf. Canadian Electrical Association, Generator Insulation.

2. Barton, S.C., Carson, C.C., Gill, R.S., Ligon, W.V. and Webb, J.L., 1981, IEEE Trans, PAS 100, 4983-4989.

3. Ryder, D.M., Wood, J.W. and Gallagher, P.L., 1979, IEEE Trans, PAS 98, 333-336.

4. Hogg, W.K., Ryder, D.M. and Wood, J.W., 1981, IEEE Int.Conf. CEIDP.

5. Wood, J.W., Ryan, M.J., Gallagher, P.L. and Gunton, D., 1982 IEE Int. Conference Electrical Machines.

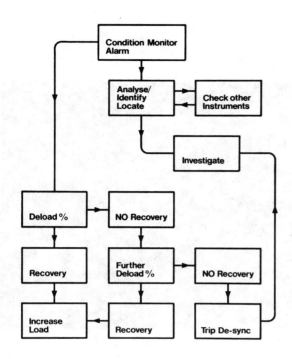

Figure 1.   Flow Diagram - typical
            operational procedure.

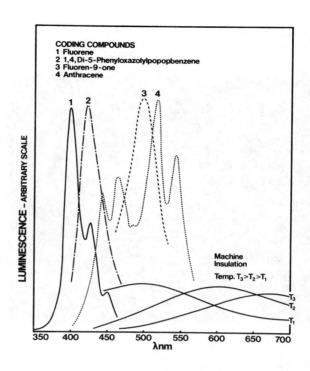

Figure 3.   UV Fluorescence Spectra.   Four
coding compounds compared with emission
spectra from overhead core plate particles.

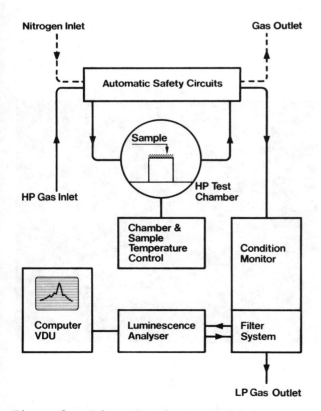

Figure 2.   Schematic of experimental
            arrangement.

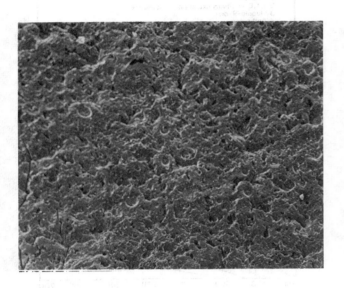

500 μ

Figure 4. Surface of coding film on metallic sheet. Thermal ageing 240 hours at 90 °C.

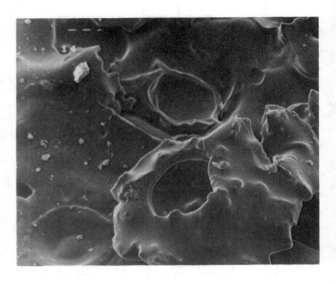

100 μ

Figure 6. Burst capsules emitting sub-micron particles. Temperature 200 °C, dT/dt 40 °C/min.

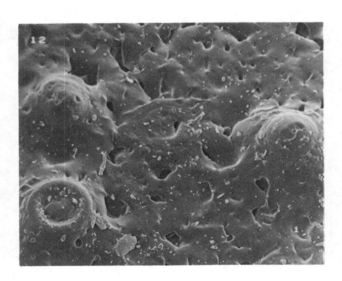

120 μ

Figure 5. Magnification of Figure 4 showing encapsulated solutions within an epoxy paint.

50 μ

Figure 7. Burst single capsule. Magnification of part of Figure 6. Temperature 200 °C, dT/dt 40 °C/min.

PERFORMANCE OF THYRISTOR-CONTROLLED UNIVERSAL MOTORS

F.I. Ahmed   I.A.M. Abdel-Halim and M.Z. El-Sherif

Cairo University, Egypt   Zagazig University, Egypt

Abstract

The paper presents a method for predicting the transient and steady-state performance of thyristor-controlled universal motors. The transient and steady-state performance were evaluated for a controlled d.c. supply and controlled a.c. supply. The effect of the triggering angle on the performance was also investigated. Transient components of torque and current are obtained. Experimental results obtained for a laboratory motor showed close agreement with theoretical results.

1. Introduction

Universal motors have many applications. They are usually used with many appliances such as drills, food mixers, sewing machines etc. Another application of the universal motor is in domestic washing machines[1], with the speed controlled using a triac to obtain suitable speeds for the washing and spin-drying periods. The performance of the controlled motor has not recieved much attention especially its transient performance. The purpose of this paper is, therefore, to investigate the motor transient and steady-state performance when it is fed a solid-state controlled d.c. supply or a controlled a.c. supply.

2. Basis of analysis

The universal motor can be supplied from either a d.c. controlled supply or an a.c. controlled supply.

2.1. D.C. Controlled supply

With a full-wave controlled d.c. supply, Fig. (1), applied to the motor with a triggering angle α, there will be two modes of operation. The first mode is during the conduction period of TH1 and D1 or TH2 and D2. The second mode is the freewheeling period when TH1 and D2 or TH2 and D1 are conducting.

For the first mode the differential equation describing the performance of the motor is

$$\sqrt{2}\,V\,\sin(\omega t + \alpha) = [R + LD + M\dot{\theta}]\,i$$
$$\text{or } Di = \frac{1}{L}\left[\sqrt{2}V\,\sin(\omega t + \alpha) - Ri - M\dot{\theta}\,i\right] \quad ..(1)$$

For the second mode the electrical equation is obtained as

$$0 = [R + LD + \dot{\theta}M]\,i$$
$$\text{or } Di = -\frac{1}{L}[R + M\dot{\theta}]\,i \quad \ldots\ldots\ldots\ldots (2)$$

The developed torque is obtained from

$$T = Mi^2 \quad \ldots\ldots\ldots\ldots\ldots (3)$$

The mechanical equation of the motor is given by

$$D\dot{\theta} = \frac{T - T_L(\dot{\theta})}{J} \quad \ldots\ldots\ldots (4)$$

2.1.1 Transient performance

The transient current following connecting the motor to a controlled d.c. supply is obtained by solving eqn. (1) numerically for the period

$$\frac{n\pi}{\omega} < t < \frac{(1+n)\pi - \alpha}{\omega}$$

where n is an integer has the value zero for the first half cycle, 1 for the second half cycle etc.. The values of current and speed obtained at the end of the conducting period are taken as the initial values for sloving eqn. (2) numerically to obtain the current throughout the freewheeling period. The torque is obtained at each step of the solution for both the conducting or the freewheeling periods by using eqn.(3). The variation of speed is taken into account by numerically integrating eqn.(4).

2.1.2. Current and torque components

The current and torque components for any operating speed by analytical solution of eqn.(1) to obtain the current and by using eqn.(3) to obtain the torque. The speed is assumed to remain constant. For the conducting period the current is obtained as

$$i = I_m\,\sin(\omega t + \alpha - \phi) + [i_o - I_m\,\sin(\alpha - \phi)]\cdot$$
$$\exp(-t/\tau)\,..(5)$$

where
$$I_m = \sqrt{2}V / \sqrt{(R+\dot{\theta}M)^2+(\omega L)^2} \quad \text{and} \quad \tau = \frac{L}{R+\dot{\theta}M}$$
i_0 is the value of current at the beginning of the conducting period. The torque for the conducting period is thus obtained as,
$$T = \frac{1}{2} M I_m^2 - \frac{1}{2} M I_m^2 \cos (2\omega t+2\alpha-2\phi) +$$
$$M[i_0 - I_m \sin(\alpha-\phi)]^2 \exp(-2t/\tau)$$
$$+ 2MI_m[i_0-I_m \sin(\alpha-\phi)] \sin(\omega t+\alpha-\phi)\cdot$$
$$\exp(-t/\tau) \qquad \dots\dots (6)$$

Thus throughout the conducting period the current has a sinusoidal component with supply frequency and exponentially decaying component whose initial value depends on the value of current at the beginning of the conducting period. The torque has four components a constant component, a sinusoidal component with double supply frequency, an exponentially decaying component with time constant of $\tau/2$ and a sinusoidal and exponentially decaying component with a time constant of τ.

For the freewheeling period the current will be
$$i_f = i_{fo} \exp\left[\left(\frac{(n+1)\pi-\alpha}{\omega} - t\right)/\tau\right] \dots (7)$$
where i_{fo} is the initial value of current for the freewheeling period. The torque during the freewheeling period will thus be given by
$$T_f = M i_{fo}^2 \exp\left[-2\left(t-\frac{(n+1)\pi-\alpha}{\omega}\right)/\tau\right] \quad (8)$$

2.2 A.C. Controlled supply

With full-wave controlled a.c. supply, Fig. (2), the two modes of operation will be either one thyristor is conducting or both of the two thyristors are not conducting. In this case eqns.(1), (3) and (4) are also applicable and numerical solution is used to obtain current and torque characteristics. Eqn. (1) is numerically integrated and speed variation is taken into account at each step of the solution by numerically inegrating eqn. (4). The torque at each step is obtained from eqn. (3).

2.2.1 Current and torque components

For constant speed the current expression for the positive half cycle will be
$$i = I_m[\sin(\omega t+\alpha-\phi)- \sin(\alpha-\phi)\exp(-t/\tau)]$$
$$\dots\dots (9)$$
this expression is valid until ωt is equal to the extinction angle and the current reaches zero value. The expression of the torque is thus obtained as
$$T = \frac{1}{2} MI_m^2 - \frac{1}{2} MI_m^2 \cos(2\omega t+2\alpha-2\phi) +$$
$$+ MI_m^2 \sin^2(\alpha-\phi)\exp(-2t/\tau)$$
$$- 2 I_m^2 M \sin(\alpha-\phi)\sin(\omega t+\alpha-\phi)\exp(-t/\tau) \quad (10)$$

3. Results
3.1 d.c. controlled supply

The steady-state and transient performance of a small universal motor were computed using the approach of analysis presented. Experimental results for the steady-state and transient current were also obtained and compared with theoretical results. In Fig.(3) the comparison for the steady-state current are shown and in Fig.(4) the results for the transient current are shown. From these figures, for the steady-state, a good agreement is obtained between the experimental and theoretical results. The computed transient and steady-state torque are also shown in Figs.(5) and (6) respectively. The current and torque components are also computed for the first few half cycles following starting of the motor. The current components are shown in Fig.(7) and the torque components are shown in Fig.(8) from which it is clear that the torque is composed of a constant component, a sinusoidal component with a frequency doulbe the supply frequency, exponentially decaying component with a time constant of $\tau/2$ and a sinusoidal and exponentially decaying component with a time constant of τ. During the freewheeling period the torque has only an exponentially decaying component.

3.2 a.c. controlled supply

The experimental and computed results of the steady-state current wave form were obtained and compared as shown in Fig.(9). From which good agreement is noticed. Computed results of transient current following starting of the motor was obtained and shown in Fig.(10). Also computed results of steady-state and transient torque are shown in Figs. (11) and (12). Torque components are also shown in Fig. (13). The components have the same nature as that of the d.c. condition.

4. Conclusions

A method for analysis of universal motors when derived from a d.c. or a.c. controlled source is presented. The steady-state as well as the transient performance in either case was obtained. Also torque components shows that the torque has four components during the conducting period for both the d.c. or a.c. operation and one component during the freewheeling period for the d.c. operation. Experimental results obtained validate the approach presented.

5. References

Pessina, G., Raffaldi, R. and Zimaglia, C. "Universal Motor: Some problems concerning the design in order to obtain good commutation conditions, reliability and high efficiency" Proc. of International Conference on Elec. Machines, September, 1980, Athens, pp. 445-451.

List of Symbols

V = r.m.s. supply voltage
R = total resistance
L = total inductance
M = mutual inductance
$\dot{\theta}$ = speed
i = instantaneous current
T = instantaneous torque
J = moment of inertia
T_L = load torque
D = operator d/dt
ϕ = phase angle

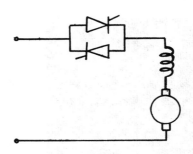

Fig. (2) Full-wave controlled a.c. supply

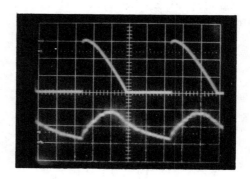

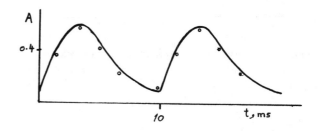

Fig. (3) Steady-state current with controlled d.c. supply
(α = 90° , $\dot{\theta}$ = 601 rad/sec)
_____ computed   o o o experimental

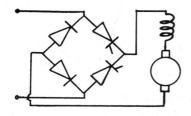

Fig. (1) Full-wave controlled d.c. supply

144

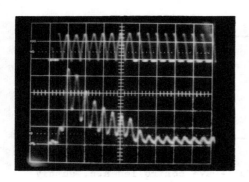

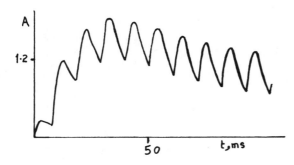

Fig. (4) Transient current following
starting with controlled d.c.
supply (α = 90°)

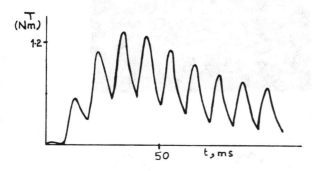

Fig. (5) Computed transient torque with
controlled d.c. supply (α = 90°)

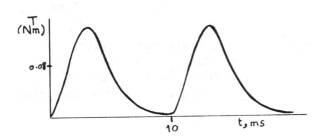

Fig. (6) Steady-state torque with
controlled d.c. supply (α = 90°)

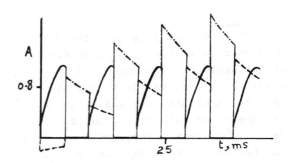

Fig. (7) Current components following
starting with controlled d.c.
supply (α = 90°)

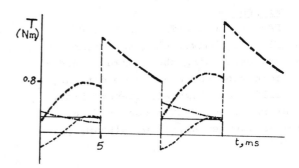

Fig. (8) Torque components following
starting with controlled d.c.
supply (α = 90°)

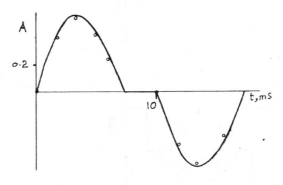

Fig. (9) Steady-state current with
controlled a.c. supply
(α = 90° , $\dot{\theta}$ = 539 rad/sec)

——— computed   o o o experimental

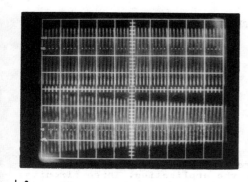

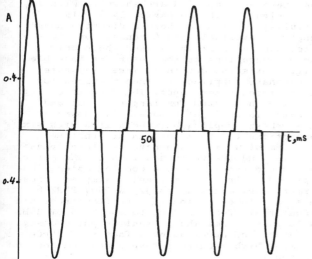

Fig. (10) Transient current following
starting with controlled a.c.
supply (α= 90°).

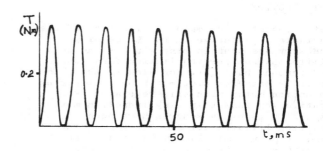

Fig. (12) Transient torque with
controlled a.c. supply. (α = 90°)

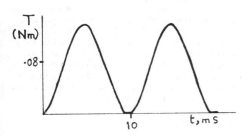

Fig. (11) Steady-state torque with
controlled a.c. supply
(α = 90° , $\dot{\theta}$ = 539 rad/sec)

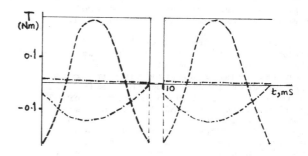

Fig. (13) Torque components with
controlled a.c. supply
(α= 90° , $\dot{\theta}$ = 0).

CYCLO-CONVERTER FED INDUCTION MOTOR DRIVES FOR MINING APPLICATIONS

D.S. Weddle and R.G. Rodwell

R.P. Automation, NEI Electronics Ltd., Gateshead, U.K.

SUMMARY

Cyclo converter induction motor drives are finding increasing application in the mining industry. There are a number of reasons for this and these will be explained together with features of the electrical design, construction and maintenance, and fault finding techniques particularly for underground equipments installed in hazardous areas.

INTRODUCTION

Until recently the major application of the variable speed drive in the U.K.mining industry has been in mine winders and to a limited extent for ventilation fans, and underground haulages. For winders the prime mover is either a d.c. motor or a slip ring induction motor with slip regulator. For ventilation fans slip ring induction motors with slip recovery schemes have been occasionally applied. Some haulages have used slip ring machines with liquid slip regulators or fixed stepped resistors.

For haulages the slip regulator is a crude control and has had to be used in conjunction with the haulage braking system to obtain smooth take up of slack rope and smooth acceleration. A true variable speed drive allows good control of speed to take up slack rope, smooth acceleration and retardation at defined rates, and where loads have to be lowered down long gradients the re-generated power provides significant reduction in energy costs. Application of radio control to the variable speed drive allows the speed of the haulage to be controlled by a driver travelling with the load.

In many UK collieries the coal face is a considerable distance from the bottom of the mine shaft and consequently there is substantial loss of working time in transporting workers to and from the coal face. There is also a problem in moving material and equipment to the coal face. Haulages may have a length of up to 6-10km and demand a motor of 375KW or greater underground, while for surface mounted drift haulages, motors of 750KW or more may be necessary.

For surface installations a cyclo converter fed induction motor drive competes with a thyristor converter fed d.c. machine while underground a cage induction motor has no peer particularly in a hazardous area where explosive atmospheres add to the problems of the dirty environment.

CYCLOCONVERTER

Power Circuits

The theory of the cycloconverter has been known for many years and is well documented (Pelly (1)). A considerable number of circuits are possible depending on the constraints of the application. Three circuits that have been applied are shown in Figs 1a, b, c. Figs 1a, 1b are basically 6 pulse circuits; 1a is used where a direct 3 phase supply is available and 6 connections to the motor can be made; 1b is used where only three connections to the motor are feasible (e.g.on existing machine). Three separate three-phase supplies are then required for the cycloconverter input. The circuit of Fig 1c has been adopted for larger drives and operates in a 12 pulse mode. Six separate three phase supplies have been used with six connections to the motor. An alternative arrangement would be to have two three phase supplies and twelve connections to the motor. This would result in more complex motor windings and control scheme, but a simpler transformer. Equipments up to 375KW 900V 24HZ 6 pulse are in operation in both flameproof and 'industrial' forms and up to 800KW 1800V 24HZ in 12 pulse form. The present 12 pulse design is capable of uprating by a factor of three by using higher current thyristors and forced air cooling.

The thyristors used are conventional converter types subject to the same rating constraints as for converters for d.c. motor drives, and are protected against overcurrent by high speed fuses. The fuses are used as a last resort; instantaneous overcurrent detect-ion inhibits all firing pulses and a time lagged overcurrent trip protects against sustained overcurrent.

Where a single 1100 volt 3phase supply is available the three phases of the cyclo converter are supplied directly through line reactors to provide some decoupling and dv/dt protection in conjunction with conventional R-C snubber circuits. In the flameproof version bulk overvoltage and dv/dt protection is now provided by capacitors connected across the supply lines and the snubber circuits provide a small amount of auxiliary protection. This assists in reducing the heat dissipated within the enclosure.

Firing Pulses and Controls

The thyristors have gate pulses applied throughout the required conduction period to prevent serious interference from the commutation of the other phases of the converter and intermittent conduction in the event of discontinuous current conditions at light load or due to voltages impressed on one phase of the motor due to transformer action from the other phases. The firing pulse units are optically coupled to the controls and hence electrically isolated from them. An auxiliary transformer provides power for the active gate pulse circuits. Reliable detection of zero current to allow safe changeover from positive output current to negative current is essential, and at frequencies approaching

25HZ minimum possible changeover time is required otherwise reduction of output occurs. The voltage across the thyristors in the cycloconverter bridges are monitored to determine if current is present. When the thyristor anode/cathode voltage is low, the thyristor is assumed to be on, and changeover is inhibited; when the voltage is high the thyristors are off. The voltage detector is also optically isolated from the control circuits.

The firing pulses for each phase are generated with reference to the 50HZ supply and controlled by the input signal from the three phase waveform generator. The amplitude and frequency of the signal is determined by the desired speed of the motor and the load on the shaft. The pulses are gated to positive or negative bridges according to the demanded polarity of the current but subject to permissive changeover from the thyristor voltage detectors.

The three voltage reference waveforms are generated digitally to achieve the required degree of symmetry, both between the three phases and between successive half cycles.The control strategy aims for a linear relationship between the maximum output voltage at any particular frequency and the output frequency (linear V/f characteristic). At very low frequency the output voltage has to be increased to overcome the predominant resistive component of motor impedance. At loads below half rated torque the output voltage is reduced below that predicted from a linear v/f characteristic. This has the effect of increasing the slip/torque ratio and improves the control stability.

Most systems are provided with simple controls in which the output frequency and hence motor speed is set by a signal from a potentiometer operated by the drivers control lever. The drive is thus essentially open loop as far as speed is concerned, but because of the close speed regulation of the induction motor (typically 9 rev/min at rated torque for a four pole machine) additional speed control loops are not normally required. The drives are fitted with a slip limit control which compares demanded speed with actual speed (from a tacho-generator). When the difference (or slip) exceeds a preset level the cyclo converter output frequency is reduced. The slip limit is analogous to current limit in the d.c. motor control. Closed loop speed controls are applied in some instances to obtain better control of motor speed.

Performance

Good control of speed is obtained with simple control schemes up to 1.5 or 2.0 p.u. torque, however because of the small speed regulation the system is somewhat stiff under shock loading conditions and some softening is required to reduce the current levels in these circumstances. Acceleration to and deceleration from rated speed in times as short as 4 seconds against rated torque are easily achieved. The drive is inherently regenerative so that transition from motoring to overhauling loads and vice versa requires no action from the driver.

Efficiency of cycloconverter and motor exceeds 90% from 0.5 to 1.25 p.u. torque at speeds over 500 rev/min for a 4 pole 25HZ machine. Fig 3. In common with many variable voltage variable speed drives power factor is not particularly good and only exceeds 0.7 at 1.0 p.u. torque near top speed. The major bonus of this type of drive in the present applications occurs when lowering heavy loads down long inclines where there is a considerable energy recovery. In one instance recovery of the full capital cost within two years is anticipated due to energy recovery.

Motor Design

In common with other means of converting from AC to DC, AC to AC or DC to AC, the cycloconverter introduces harmonics into the motor supply voltage and a small degree of discontinuity to the resulting motor current waveform. This is due to the need to switch, at zero current, from the converter bridge producing positive current to the bridge producing negative current (and also from negative to positive bridge).

The voltage harmonics are harmonics of the cyclo supply frequency and their main effect is to increase the copper loss of the cage rotor winding. To minimise this loss, the effective rotor reactance is kept as high as possible while the effective rotor resistance is made as low as possible. In practice this usually means that the motor is designed with a high reactance rotor slot, consistent with meeting the motor pull-out torque requirements. The rotor bar is always selected to have a low AC/DC resistance ratio. However, even when these steps are taken, and in particular with a 6 pulse cycloconverter, where the harmonic voltage amplitudes are larger, the motor may require derating to allow for the additional harmonic losses.

Efficiency and thermal rating of the motor make it desirable to reduce to a minimum the rotor copper loss due to currents at the fundamental cyclo output frequency. However, speed control loop design is made easier if the slip at rated torque is increased from the value that results from an optimum motor design. A compromise between motor design, and application requirements has therefore to be made.

Mechanical effects result from the discontinuities in the motor current waveform which produce an air gap torque oscillation. The fifth and seventh harmonics in the current waveform produce harmonic fields, both of which interact with the fundamental field to produce a torque oscillation at six times motor supply frequency. This torque oscillation affects both the shaft system and the stator supporting structure through to the holding down bolts. To minimise machine vibration the stator frame must be torsionally stiff and care must be taken to avoid any serious mechanical resonances.

Construction

The construction of the cycloconverter drive depends on the application and environment. The two basic modes of construction are a more or less standard industrial type and a flameproof type for use in hazardous and sometimes fairly severe environments.

Industrial equipment. In the industrial equipment the drive would be constructed as a three bay cubicle and follows a pattern not uncommon in a.c. or d.c. drives. The first bay contains the incoming gland box, isolator, vacuum contactor, line fuses for thyristors, surge suppression components and input voltage /current/power measurement. The second bay contains the thyristors mounted on heatsinks, dv/dt protection components and output gland box. Within this bay the heatsink/thyristor arrangement is typical in that the thyristor is bolted directly to the aluminium heatsink which then acts as one busbar of the system.

Six thyristors are mounted within a frame which constitutes an easily unplugged output module. Six such modules make up the standard 6 pulse, three phase, 6 wire output unit. This arrangement is primarily intended for natural cooling but may be forced cooled if desired. The third and final bay houses the control modules, relays, test and monitor equipment, fault indicators, power supplies etc.,

Occasionally a drive in this format may be allowed in a safe area underground. The equipment remains very similar but may if required be made of heavier gauge metal and totally dust proofed with filters. Any prohibited materials (which may not be transported bare underground as spares) are replaced with more appropriate types. Within this described format a drive may be rated up to 750KW (plus overload capability). Above this level twelve pulse systems become predominant and the constructional details are as for a large d.c. drive converter, i.e. a suite of cubicles comprising a double bay unit at one end housing control and relay functions. Converter cubicles are added as necessary by output power requirements.

Flameproof Equipment. When hazardous area applications are considered the constructional requirements are much more stringent. Equipment must be flameproof (FLP) (i.e. able to withstand an internal explosion without igniting external gases) or intrinsically safe (I.S.) (i.e. not give rise to sparks with sufficient energy to ignite the surrounding gases), or a combination of both. Special consideration must be given to the following requirements :-

1) Failure to safety under any fault conditions.

2) Because of point 1 the performance of the materials and the construction during fault conditions must be carefully laid down and tested, e.g. insulating materials which may be subject to arcing must not give out a gas which will cause a higher explosion pressure than that for which the equipment is certified.

3) The normal power semiconductor firing circuits must be safely integrated with other mining equipment especially I.S. circuits, where creepage distance requirements are very large.

4) Sensitive electronic circuits and high voltage semi-conductors must be protected from the sometimes harsh mining environment.

5) The equipment must be as small as possible to help in transportation and siting.

6) The equipment must allow ease of maintenance and fast repair of breakdowns.

Unless they infringe one or more of the above requirements as many components as possible are utilised in both industrial and flameproof equipment. This helps to reduce both manufacturing costs and customer spares holdings.

Fig 4 illustrates the basic flameproof unit. Control cards, monitor functions and relay systems are incorporated in the rear of the door. Access to the control system is therefore readily available as soon as the door is opened. The thyristor firing units with h.v./l.v. optical isolators are mounted on the roof of the case. On the rear wall can be seen the internal part of the thyristor stacks and dv/dt protection circuits. Line fuses and reactors are mounted on the base with surge suppression circuits and input C.T's mounted on the left hand wall. Finally, the right hand wall mounts the power supplies unit.

On the external left hand wall are the input /output connectors. One 300A adaptor provides the main 1100V supply. Two 300A adaptors carry the six wire supply to the motor. One 50A connector is used for the auxiliary 550V supply whilst two multi-pin connectors carry the control input/output functions.

Interface with other equipment. The cyclo-converter will have to interface with backup switchgear, haulage monitoring systems, radio control systems and possibly remote control/ safety systems. These may have I.S. or non I.S. interfaces and quite possibly require analogue/digital signals differing from those in the cycloconverter. Conversion of all such signals takes place in a small separate auxiliary unit to which all external system signals are routed.

It would be easy to underestimate the problems of combining sophisticated power semiconductor control equipment with a flameproof case. Two of the more obvious problems should be mentioned.

With this type of control complexity it would have been preferable to make the control system I.S. However, the best technical position for the I.S./FLP interface would then have been at the thyristor firing units themselves, i.e. 36 I.S./FLP channels all of which must have no significant delay in propagation or rise time of signals. In the latter case rise times should be considerably better than one microsecond. Commercially available optical isolators tend to be compromises between voltage withstand, speed of response and noise immunity. An optical isolator of suitable characteristics is found to have much smaller creepage and clearance distances than required for an FLP/I.S. barrier. Indeed, values of one quarter that required, seem to be the order of the day. To re-encapsulate and remount standard devices can be hideously expensive in terms of cost and space.

Cooling. Despite these latter comments optical cables now available will allow these difficulties to be overcome. A more fundamental problem is the inherent losses from the thyristors themselves. In a 375KW drive this can amount to over 4KW and in a flameproof unit these losses are generated in a case with a confined volume of less than one cubic metre. Quite obviously this heat must be removed but the standard techniques of thyristor cooling (described for the industrial unit) are not acceptable. A solution is to insert a thermally conducting, electrically insulating barrier between the thyristor and the case wall. Heatsinks (of acceptable material) mounted externally on the case wall will conduct much of this heat away. Whilst this provides a workable solution in practical terms, in economic terms it is far from optimum. The thyristor junction to air thermal resistance may be five or six times greater than a value easily attainable in an industrial unit. This means utilisation of the thyristor is perhaps only 20% of its capability in other applications.

A better technical solution is water cooling
but the problems of pressure reduction, water
quality and, perhaps greatest of all, waste
water removal in a mine make this method un-
popular.

Fig 5 shows the first 375KW unit which was
commissioned during August 1980. In the fore-
ground right is the small Interface Unit for
signal marshalling and processing. Next to it
is the Cycloconverter, and then the two backup switchgear units which also provide
haulage monitoring and supplies. These two
units are now generally combined into one
case. At the very end is a standard mining
transformer. The roadway runs away to the
left with the haulage engine to the right of
the Cycloconverter and Interface units.

Commissioning

In the initial commissioning of cycloconverters three prime problems appeared.
Firstly as with most power semiconductor
equipment correct main/auxiliary phasing is
essential. This is normally checked with an
oscilloscope which obviously cannot be used
in flameproof installations. Secondly, transducer inputs (e.g. tachogenerator feedback)
tended not to be stable enough because of a
combination of load fluctuations and mounting
arrangement. Lastly, the load itself was
sometimes dynamically underestimated.

For the first two points the creation of
passive test equipment, very tight drawing
specifications between companies and modified
mounting/adjusting methods cured such problems.
The last point however is more difficult as a
load such as a rope haulage comprises perhaps
the classical weight and spring case, but with
a spring perhaps 8km long. The type of roadway,
rope friction losses, rope tension and rope
tensioning method all make an apparently
simple load produce some interesting transients. Again rectification was not normally a
major problem as in many cases the cycloconverter's ability to react to external
load fluctuations proved sufficient. Even so
on an FLP system the adjustments that were
required took time.

Commissioning of industrial units generally
presented similar problems but, in a more
normal environment, were much less difficult
to cure.

Fault Finding

Both industrial and flameproof units can be
equipped with the same fault finding methods.
However because fault finding in the flameproof unit is much more difficult this will
be described in more detail.

The front of the unit has four windows
through which can be seen retained fault
indication and presence (or of course absence)
and quality of all firing pulses. These, with
basic metering and fault finding tables,
formed the fault location mechanism.

Recently a sixteen channel digital voltmeter
(operated from outside the unit) has been
added. This combined with control signal
level tables for defined conditions and the
previously mentioned fault and pulse
monitoring form a good 'pyramid' type fault
locating structure. This allows the normal
system of modular replacement for fault
correction within hazardous areas.

REFERENCE

1. Pelly B.R., 1970, Thyristor Phase -
    Controlled Converters and Cycloconverters
    Wiley Interscience.

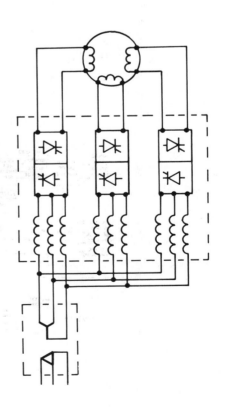

Fig 1a. 6 pulse cycloconverter
6 wire output

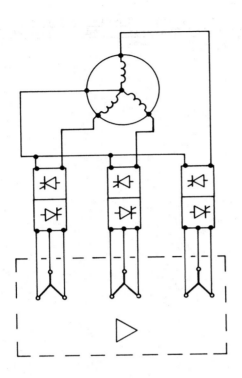

Fig 1b. 6 pulse cycloconverter
4 wire output

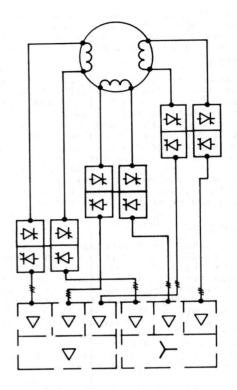

Fig 1c. 12 pulse cycloconverter
6 wire output

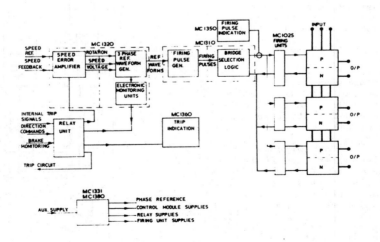

Fig 2. Control System Schematic

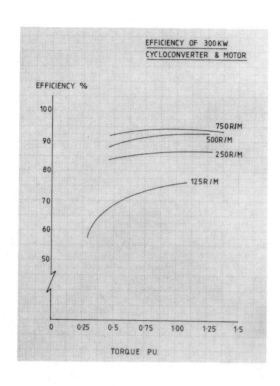

Fig 3. Efficiency of cycloconverter
and motor

Fig 4. Front view, flameproof
cycloconverter

Fig 5. Flameproof cycloconverter
installation

VARIABLE SPEED CONVERTER DRIVES FOR POWER STATION AUXILIARIES

B. Barker

CEGB, Generation Development and Construction Division

1. INTRODUCTION

With an increased emphasis now being placed on energy saving methods coupled with the need to reduce overall costs and increase productivity it is not altogether surprising that increasing attention has been given to improved means of providing variable speed for power station auxiliary drives.

The recent rapid development of a.c. variable speed drives has now reached a stage where the overall performance and reliability will result in an increasing application of such drives for controlling and varying flow or speed.

2. AVAILABLE A.C. CONVERTER DRIVES

Four basic types of drive are available

- Force commutated converter/cage induction motor drive
- Machine commutated converter/synchronous motor drive
- Static slip energy recovery converter system/ wound rotor slip-ring induction motor drive
- Cyclo-converter/cage induction motor drive

The fundamental difference between cyclo-converter and converter drives is the absence of a d.c. link. The cyclo-converter is a frequency changer with maximum output frequency limited to approximately 30% to 40% input frequency in order to maintain an acceptable waveform. It is ideal for applications involving frequent starting and stopping but alternative forms of converter are preferable for high power continuous running drives eg, fans, pumps etc.

Slip energy recovery systems with static converters and slip-ring induction motors have been used, particularly on the Continent for boiler feed pump drives. A major disadvantage is the brushgear associated with the slip-ring motor which adversely affects reliability and increases maintenance. The use of cage induction motors up to the limit of forced commutation (about 1.5MW) and brushless synchronous motors above this level, (up to about 20MW) avoids these problems.

The three basic types of converters in use for a.c. drives are

- voltage source
- current source
- pulse-width-modulated (PWM)

All three types inject harmonics into the power supply system, the amount of which is significantly affected by the type of arrangement used for the rectifier. This arrangement also significantly affects the power factor. The harmonic levels must not have an adverse effect on the system or other connected plant and must be taken into account in the design of the associated driving motor.

The voltage source converter can be used with standard design low leakage reactance motors. It can also be used to modify existing constant speed drives to variable speed without a change of cage induction motor. This converter type imposes low dynamic voltage stresses on the motor but has a generally poorer power factor than the current source system although the efficiencies are similar.

The current source converter is rugged in terms of withstanding effects of local short circuits, has a relatively simple basic circuit and can readily provide re-generation facilities. A current source converter has to be matched closely to a relatively high leakage reactance motor and the machine/converter compatibility needs to recognise the relatively high voltage stress and transient spikes in the converter output.

The pulse width modulated type of converter requires to be matched to the motor design which needs to be based on a relatively high leakage reactance and in addition needs to be able to accommodate regular high transient voltage pulses. Overall the system is more complex than the other two types of force commutated converter.

Machine commutated converters with synchronous machine drives are well established and their previous uses include starting schemes for large hydro-generators, gas turbine sets and synchronous compensators. They have additional merits when used with brushless excitation arrangements on the motor.

3. ADVANTAGES

In general, the advantages offered by these types of variable speed converter drive can be summarised as follows:-

- High efficiency which is maintained at reduced powers and speeds.

- High speed range (10 to 1 readily achievable) with speed accuracy (1%).

- Starting current is low (i.e. 1 to 1.5 x full load current compared with 4 to 4.5 x FLC on cage induction motor) with possible cost savings on power system and less arduous starting conditions on motor.

- Regenerative braking can be provided if necessary.

- Converter equipment can be continuously monitored. Low repair or component replacement times are possible.

- Reduced space required local to driven equipment compared to cage induction motor with a fluid coupling.

- Maximum speed is not limited by power system supply frequency e.g. speeds greater than 3000 rev/min on 50Hz supply are possible.

4. FUNCTIONAL REQUIREMENTS

The basic functional requirements for power station converter drives is given below:-

Continuous operation - 106% to 90% rated voltage. 96% to 102% rated frequency.

Ambient conditions - normally 0°C to 40°. relative humidity 95%.

Starting conditions - 80% voltage.

Transient conditions - 75% V at 50Hz for 5 mins. without injurious heating.
- motors to recover in event of system disturbance causing loss of volts for up to 0.2 secs. followed by sudden restoration initially to 60% V for 3 secs. followed by sudden restoration to 80% and ultimate recovery to normal.

Reliability - High value of Mean Time Between Failure (MTBF) required.
- For automatic standby a high reliability of response to start demands required.

Harmonics - Voltage distortion ≯ 7% with individual harmonic components ≯ IEC 146-2 Fig. 2.

Thyristors - IEC 146 and 146-2
- Load conditions as Duty Class II of IEC 146 Table IV. Thyristor case temperatures ≯ 70°C. Thyristors to be arranged on a MODULAR basis. Adequate MONITORING facilities for all major functions to be provided.

Converter Components - Generally to BS 9000. Capacitors containing non bio-degradable toxic fluids not to be used.

Power Transformers and Chokes - Dry naturally air cooled type.

Motors - ESI 44-3 and 44-3 BS5000 Part 40.

Seismic Vibration - Qualification required for Nuclear plant.

5. COST COMPARISON - BOILER FEED PUMP DRIVE

The speed of converter fed motors is not restricted by the power supply frequency, consequently a wide choice of speeds, including speeds above 3000 rev/min is available thus permitting greater optimisation of the overall pump drive system.

For example, feed pumps in the range 8 to 20MW with speeds up to 5000 rev/min could be directly driven by a converter brushless 2 pole synchronous motor. For pump speeds greater than this, eg 8000 rev/min pumps which have been used in CEGB power stations, a speed increasing gearbox would be necessary with a 2 or 4 pole motor.

Cost comparisons with alternative types of drive need to take into account any differences in running costs. In the case of cage induction motor/fluid coupling drives the slip losses in the fluid coupling can be significant, particularly at reduced loads. There are therefore potential cost savings with converter fed synchronous motor drives.

Other factors which need to be quantified and taken into account are as follows:-

- differences in pump costs (eg 5000 rev/min v 8000 rev/min pump)

- any additional savings from converter fed motors because of reduced start-up kVA allowing reduced requirements on the auxiliary supply system components or possible savings on the driven plant (eg lower transient torques on gearboxes).

- any change in plant layout and space requirements.

- efficiency at reduced loads.

- savings in hydraulic system control equipment.

- differences in maintenance costs.

- differences in reliability.

6. DISCUSSION

Variable speed drives using AC motors capable of a 10 to 1 speed range can now be considered as contenders for a wide range of power station auxiliary drives where variable flow or speed is required. The two basic drive systems are forced commutated converter with cage induction motor for use to around 1.5MW and machine commutated converter with brushless type synchronous motor for use up to around 20MW.

Both types of converter fed drive could be used to replace existing drives (eg AC commutator motors, fixed speed drives etc) without necessitating extra space for the drive motor.

The advantages of converter fed AC motor drives are further enhanced if prolonged operation at part load is needed, where the better efficiency of the converter fed drive over other forms of drive provides additional savings in operating costs.

A recent application for variable frequency converter equipment is the motor driven gas circulators on AGR reactors. The 5MW submerged CO_2 cage induction motors are supplied at reduced powers and speeds to provide a low speed barring facility and to meet other operating and emergency requirements. A high reliability is required. The output of each converter equipment is approximately 500 kVA.

7. ACKNOWLEDGEMENTS

This paper is presented by permission of the Central Electricity Generating Board.

THE ANALYSIS AND COMPUTATION OF A 3-PHASE CYCLOCONVERTER/INDUCTION MOTOR DRIVE HAVING ISOLATED OUTPUT PHASES

J.E. Brown, P. Vas and R. Thornton

University of Newcastle upon Tyne, U.K.

INTRODUCTION

The objective of this paper is to describe an analytical method of obtaining the periodic transient solution of the performance equations of a 3-phase cage induction motor supplied by a six-pulse non-circulating-current cycloconverter, the latter having isolated output phases and the motor operating at an assumed constant speed. Furthermore, to compare results obtained from the analytical solution with those obtained by a complete step-by-step solution of the machine equations and with those obtained by direct experiment.

It is a feature of the well-known arrangement under consideration that the three phases of the motor are isolated from each other and each is connected separately to a separate output phase of the cycloconverter. It follows that the sum of the stator phase currents of the motor is not constrained to be zero and it will only be zero at those instants when the sum of the phase voltages is zero. In general the instantaneous phase voltages do not sum to zero and consequently they have "instantaneous zero-sequence components" (1), related to but not identical to the zero-sequence components of steady-state symmetrical component theory.

The need to take account of the zero-sequence components has been recognised by Jacovides (2), (3) in his very different approach to the analysis of the drive considered here. His treatment of this aspect of the problem is deliberately approximate and a similar approximation will be adopted here, that of assuming that the zero-sequence reactance is equal to the stator leakage reactance. In the first of his two papers (2) Jacovides suggests that the "assumption is usually unimportant since there are no zero-sequence currents in a squirrel cage rotor". This represents a misunderstanding of the problem which he corrects in the second paper (3) where he draws attention to a paper by one of the present authors and Butler (4) from which it can be deduced that proper accounting for the zero-sequence system would demand that the effects of the third space harmonics of the stator m.m.f. be taken into consideration. It is these effects that are neglected in the assumption and the consequences will be discussed later, but it may be stated now that for the case considered here the calculated current waveforms are very satisfactory, whereas the calculated torque waveforms are less so.

The authors wish to draw attention to two other features of the analysis presented in the present paper. Firstly an expression is given for the fabricated output voltage of the cycloconverter which they would submit is more general and more convenient for its purpose than those given in one of the standard works on the cycloconverter (5). Secondly the internal voltage equations of the induction motor are expressed in terms of the first time-derivatives of the flux linkages, rather than that function of the currents. Consequently they can be expressed in the required state variable form, with flux linkage as the state variable, without the complication of inverting an inductance matrix to obtain the system matrix (6),(7). Furthermore the flux linkages are continuous and therefore more satisfactory for the purposes of digital computation than the currents which are, of course, discontinuous.

THE OUTPUT VOLTAGES OF THE CYCLOCONVERTER

The fabricated output voltage of phase A of the cycloconverter can be expressed in the following form

$$u_A(t) = KS_{1A} \left\{ \cos\alpha_{1A} - \sum_{i=1}^{\infty} \right. \tag{1}$$

$$\left\{ \left[\sin([6i-1]\alpha_{1A})/(6i-1) - \sin([6i+1]\alpha_{1A})/(6i+1) \right] \sin 6i\omega_1 t \right.$$

$$\left. + \left[\cos([6i-1]\alpha_{1A})/(6i-1) - \cos([6i+1]\alpha_{1A})/(6i+1) \right] \cos 6i\omega_1 t \right\} \right\}$$

where

$\omega_1 = 2\pi f_1$ and f_1 is the fundamental input frequency.

$K = 6V/2\pi$ and V is the line-to-line input voltage.

S_{1A} is a switching function of value ± 1 specifying which bridge (positive or negative) is conducting. The instants at which this function changes state are determined by the "load displacement angle", $\emptyset_O$, (5) being the phase angle of the load at the fundamental output frequency. The function S_{1A} is illustrated in Fig. 1 in which $\emptyset_O = -40^O$.

α_{1A} is a general firing angle depending on the firing strategy to be adopted. The strategy employed in the calculations which follow was one using linear timing waves and sinusoidal modulating waves. Thus α_{1A} takes the form $\alpha_{1A} = (1-r \sin \omega_O t) \pi/2$ where r is the modulation depth $\omega_O = 2\pi f_O$ and f_O is the fundamental output frequency. The function α_{1A} is illustrated in Fig. 2.

The voltages $u_B(t)$, $u_C(t)$, the switching functions S_{1B}, S_{1C} and the firing angles α_{1B}, α_{1C} are similar in form to the corresponding functions for phase A but mutually phase displaced by an angle $2\pi/3$ relative to fundamental frequency scale. Examples of fabricated voltages are given later in Fig. 3.

THE INTERNAL VOLTAGE EQUATIONS OF THE MOTOR

The equations of the motor are derived from

the standard form

$$\underline{u} = \underline{\underline{R}}\,\underline{i} + p\,(\underline{\underline{L}}\,\underline{i}) \qquad (2)$$

where

$\underline{u} = [u_{SA}, u_{SB}, u_{SC}, u_{ra}, u_{rb}, u_{rc}]^T$ is the voltage column vector and u_{ra}, u_{rb}, u_{rc}, the rotor voltages, are zero,

$\underline{i}$ is the corresponding current column vector,

$\underline{\underline{R}}$ is the resistance matrix, and

$\underline{L}$ is the inductance matrix.

The coefficients of the $\underline{L}$ matrix contain terms which are functions of speed but if constant speed is assumed and saturation is neglected the equations can be transformed into stationary orthogonal and zero-sequence axes with constant coefficients by the application of the normal ABCabc→ODQodq transformation. The stator voltages u_{SA}, u_{SB}, u_{SC} are equal to the cycloconverter output voltages u_A, u_B, u_C, provided that the current flow is continuous. These voltages must be specified from Eqn.(1) and subjected to the same transformation.

The transformed equations are

$$u_{SD} = R_S\, i_{SD} + \frac{d\Psi_{SD}}{dt} \qquad (3)$$

$$u_{SQ} = R_S\, i_{SQ} + \frac{d\Psi_{SQ}}{dt} \qquad (4)$$

$$u_{rd} = R_r\, i_{rd} + \frac{d\Psi_{rd}}{dt} + \omega_r \Psi_{rq} \qquad (5)$$

$$u_{rq} = R_r\, i_{rq} + \frac{d\Psi_{rq}}{dt} - \omega_r \Psi_{rd} \qquad (6)$$

$$u_{SO} = R_S\, i_{SO} + \frac{d\Psi_{SO}}{dt} \qquad (7)$$

$$u_{ro} = R_r\, i_{ro} + \frac{d\Psi_{ro}}{dt} \qquad (8)$$

Eqns. (3)-(6) are one form of Park's equations. Eqns. (7) and (8) are the instantaneous zero-sequence terms essential for the case under consideration where the motor currents and voltages are not constrained to be zero. If it is assumed that the effects of the triplen space harmonics of the mmf produced by the stator zero-sequence currents can be neglected then the flux linkage Ψ_{SO} is a leakage flux linking the stator only. It follows that this flux can induce no voltage in the rotor and consequently no rotor current will flow and there will be no rotor flux linkage Ψ_{ro}. Thus Eqn. (8) can be eliminated.

These equations can be expressed in state variable form, with the flux linkages as state variables, as follows

$$\underline{\dot{x}} = \underline{\underline{A}}\,\underline{x} + \underline{\underline{B}}\,\underline{u} \qquad (9)$$

where, the state variable column vector

$$x = [\Psi_{SD}, \Psi_{SQ}, \Psi_{rd}, \Psi_{rq}, \Psi_{SO}]^T, \qquad (10)$$

the system matrix (7)

$$\underline{\underline{A}} = \begin{bmatrix} -\dfrac{1}{T'_S} & 0 & \dfrac{k_r}{T'_S} & 0 & 0 \\[2ex] 0 & -\dfrac{1}{T'_S} & 0 & \dfrac{k_r}{T'_S} & 0 \\[2ex] \dfrac{k_S}{T'_r} & 0 & -\dfrac{1}{T'_r} & -\omega_r & 0 \\[2ex] 0 & \dfrac{k_S}{T'_r} & \omega_r & -\dfrac{1}{T'_r} & 0 \\[2ex] 0 & 0 & 0 & 0 & -\dfrac{1}{T'_{SO}} \end{bmatrix} \qquad (11)$$

where

T'_S is the stator transient time constant

T'_r is the rotor transient time constant

$k_S = L_m/L_S$

$k_r = L_m/L_r$

T'_{SO} is the stator zero-sequence time constant,

the control matrix

$$\underline{\underline{B}} = \begin{bmatrix} 1 & 0 & 0 & 0 & 0 \\ 0 & 1 & 0 & 0 & 0 \\ 0 & 0 & 0 & 0 & 0 \\ 0 & 0 & 0 & 0 & 0 \\ 0 & 0 & 0 & 0 & 1 \end{bmatrix} \qquad (12)$$

and the forcing column vector

$$\underline{u} = [u_{SD}, u_{SQ}, u_{rd}, u_{rq}, u_{SO}]^T \qquad (13)$$

Eqn. (9) is the equation to be solved.

The procedure described above may be compared with that in an earlier paper by Chattapadhyay and Rao (8) where no general expression is given for the fabricated voltages and where the zero-sequence equations were not required. Furthermore, by taking the currents which are discontinuous as state variables complications were introduced there which do not arise when, as here, the fluxes are so taken.

SOLUTION OF THE STATE VARIABLE EQUATION

The state variable equation, Eqn. (9), can be solved numerically by any of several numerical methods. However, because constant speed conditions have been assumed the coefficients in the transformed equations are constants and therefore an analytical solution can be obtained. In general this solution takes the form

$$\underline{x}\,(KT) = e^{\underline{\underline{A}}T}\,\underline{x}\big[(K-1)T\big] - \big[\underline{\underline{I}} - e^{\underline{\underline{A}}T}\big]\,\underline{\underline{A}}^{-1}\underline{\underline{B}}\,\underline{u}\big[(K-1)T\big]$$

$$(14)$$

where

T is the incremental time step during which u(t) is assumed to be constant,

K is an integer,

$\underline{I}$ is a unit matrix.

This equation can be used to yield numerical values by direct computation for any instant of time, once the initial condition $\underline{x}(0)$ has been obtained, by using the repetitive nature of the waveforms.

COMPUTED AND EXPERIMENTAL RESULTS

Results have been computed for a machine having the following parameters.

$R_S = 0.806\Omega$, $R_f = 0.759\Omega$, $L_S = L_r = 0.12$ H

$L_m = 0.112$ H, pole pairs = 2, slip = 0.09, $\phi_o = -40°$

and for the following conditions

supply voltage = 243V, supply frequency = 50Hz,

fundamental output frequency = 16.67Hz, modulation depth = 0.4

time step = 0.1 ms, total time = 100ms.

Fig. 3 shows the cycloconverter output voltages computed from Eqn. (1) and Fig. 4 shows the corresponding currents computed from the analytical solution.

Figs. 5 and 6 show the corresponding results computed from a complete step-by-step solution of the machine equations expressed in an ABCdqo reference frame, where again for the reasons discussed above there can be no zero-sequence reactions in the rotor. Each stator phase voltage is obtained from the appropriate form of Eqn. (1) so long as the phase is conducting, but when the equation for a particular phase would lead to current of incorrect polarity the terminal voltage is calculated as the induced e.m.f. in that phase, and the current is constrained to be zero. In this way all eight possible operating modes of the cycloconverter are taken into consideration rather than only the three-phase mode as is the case with the analytical solution.

A comparison of the two sets of results shows that the voltages and currents are in close agreement except for the small discrepancies to be expected in the regions where the currents are discontinuous. Typical experimental voltage and current waveforms for the conditions specified are shown in Figs. 7 and 8 and a careful examination of these will show that they agree well with the calculated results.

Figs. 9 and 10 show the torques calculated by the two methods. A comparison of the two torque waveforms shows that they are very similar in form, but the mean values differ being 95 Nm for the analytical solution and 84 Nm for the step-by-step solution, over the period considered. The measured value was 85 Nm, but it should not be concluded that the step-by-step solution gives the "correct" value of torque. The effect of the third space harmonics of flux on the torque is greater than on the currents and voltages and until these are taken into account it would be premature to consider the accuracy of the torque calculations. Suffice it to say that the mean values are approximately correct.

CONCLUSIONS

It has been shown that the periodic transient solution of the performance equations of a 3-phase induction motor supplied by a six-pulse non-circulating-current cycloconverter and operating at constant speed can be obtained by an analytical method. The analytical solution gives results in close agreement with those obtained by the more complicated step-by-step method, particularly when the regions of current discontinuity are small as in the example chosen here.

A general expression has been given for the fabricated voltage waveform of the cycloconverter which allows any firing strategy to be incorporated, and avoids the use of approximations for the switching function based on Fourier analysis. The latter cannot give correct results at the switching points whereas the method used here gives an accurate representation of conditions at these points.

In the future the analytical solution will be extended to include the regions of current discontinuity by modifying the state variables to take account of the asymmetries then occurring. A more complete treatment of the general asymmetry arising from the presence of instantaneous zero-sequence voltages will be developed by taking into account the effects of the triplen harmonics in the magnetic field produced by the stator currents. Finally there are several modes of induction motor operation for which it is important to include the effects of main flux path saturation, as is illustrated in another paper before this Conference (9). A little consideration will show that this is particularly true for low frequency operation of the cycloconverter/induction motor drive and the authors will be attempting to modify the analysis presented in the present paper to take account of that presented in Ref. (9).

REFERENCES

(1) Lyon, W.V., "Transient Analysis of A.C. Machinery. An Application of the Method of Symmetrical Components", Chapman and Hall, 1954.

(2) Jacovides, L.J., "Analysis of a cyclo-converter-induction motor drive system allowing for stator current discontinuities", IEEE Trans. Industry Applications, V.IA-9, No. 6, pp206-215, 1973.

(3) Jacovides, L.J., "Analysis of Induction Motor Drives with a Nonsinusoidal Supply Voltage using Fourier Analysis", IEEE Trans. Industry Applications, V.IA-9, No. 6, pp741-747, 1973.

(4) Brown, J.E., and Butler, O.I., "The Zero-Sequence Parameters and Performance of Three-Phase Induction Motors," Proc. IEE, Monograph No. 92, 1954.

(5) Pelly, B.R., "Thyristor Phase-Controlled Converters and Cycloconverters", New York: Wiley 1971.

(6)   Racz, I., "Thyristorized Electrical
      Machine Drives", Power Engineering
      Conference, Budapest, 1970.

(7)   Vas, P., "Generalized Transient Analysis
      of Induction Motors", Archiv Fur
      Electrotechnik, 1978.

(8)   Chattapadhyay, A.K., and Rao, T.J.,
      "State-Variable Steady State Analysis of a
      Phase-Controlled Cycloconverter - Induction
      Motor Drive", IEEE Trans. Industrial
      Applications, V.IA-15, No. 3, p311, 1979.

(9)   Brown, J.E. and Vas, P., "The phenomenon
      of intersaturation in the transient
      operation of induction motors arising from
      saturation of the main flux path", Proc.
      IEE Conf. on Electrical Machines - Design
      and Applications, July 1982.

ACKNOWLEDGMENTS

The authors wish to acknowledge financial
support from the Science and Engineering
Research Council and the close co-operation
of Mr. A. Oram, Mr. R. Thorburn and Mr. P.
McLaughlin of Reyrolle Parsons Automation.

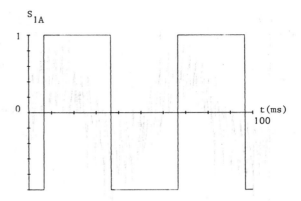

Fig. 1   Bridge Control Signal S_{1A}

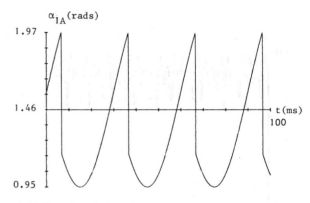

Fig. 2   Firing Angle α_{1A}

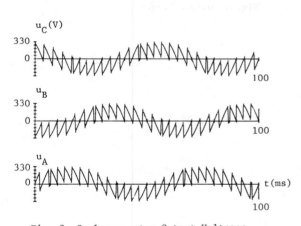

Fig. 3   Cycloconverter Output Voltages

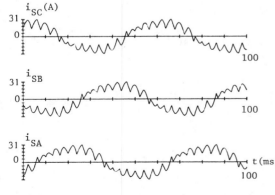

Fig. 4   Motor Phase Currents

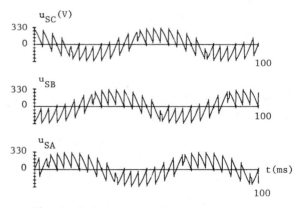

Fig. 5   Cycloconverter Output Voltages

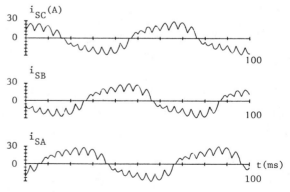

Fig. 6   Motor Phase Currents

158

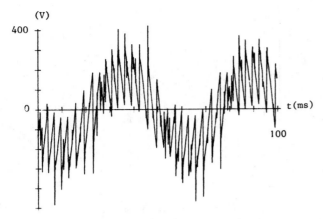

Fig. 7 Cycloconverter Output Voltage

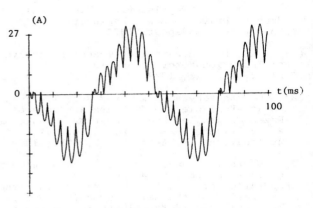

Fig. 8 Motor Phase Current

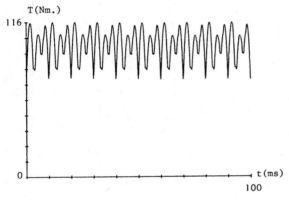

Fig 9 Output Torque

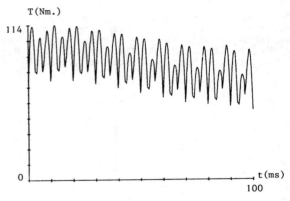

Fig. 10 Output Torque

AN EXPERIMENTAL STUDY OF FLOW AND HEAT TRANSFER IN GENERATOR ROTOR COOLING DUCTS

P.L. Stephenson

Central Electricity Research Laboratories, Kelvin Avenue, Leatherhead, Surrey

NOMENCLATURE

c_p	specific heat at constant pressure
C_T	overall loss coefficient (eqn. 1)
d	test section diameter
G_{rr}	rotational Grashof number ($H\Omega^2\beta\tau d^4/\nu^2$)
H	radius of rotation
h	heat transfer coefficient
J	rotational Reynolds number ($\Omega d^2/\nu$)
k	thermal conductivity
N_u	Nusselt number (hd/k)
P_r	Prandtl number ($c_p\mu/k$)
R_e	axial Reynolds number (Wd/ν)
S_w	swirl number ($H\Omega/W$)
W	axial velocity
ΔP	overall pressure drop
β	bulk expansivity
μ	dynamic viscosity
ν	kinematic viscosity
ρ	density
τ	axial air temperature gradient
Ω	rotational speed (radians)

INTRODUCTION

The rotor windings of large turbogenerators are normally cooled by passing hydrogen through the hollow copper conductors. To obtain basic information about the flow and heat transfer characteristics of such cooling ducts, a rig has been constructed to study flow and heat transfer in a duct rotating about a parallel axis. The rig uses air rather than hydrogen but is designed to operate at values of the governing non-dimensional parameters that are similar to those occurring in actual generators. This paper reports some of the results that have been obtained with the first test section. This was circular in cross section, despite the fact that most rotor cooling ducts are rectangular, because it was thought best to study the simple circular geometry first. The results for higher flowrates are considered here, as these are more relevant to actual generators; measurements at lower flowrates will be reported elsewhere.

PREVIOUS WORK

Experimental studies of heat transfer for turbulent flow in a circular duct rotating about a parallel axis are reported in references (1)-(7); mass transfer analogue measurements are also reported in (3) and (7). These studies show that the heat transfer is increased by rotation, but to a lesser extent than in laminar flow. Several studies have also suggested that the effect of rotation is more pronounced in developing than in fully developed flow. An approximate analytical solution for high rotation rates has been reported by Nakayama (8), and a numerical solution by Majumdar et al. (9). General surveys of the likely effects of rotation are given in references (10) and (11).

BRIEF DESCRIPTION OF RIG

The rig consists of a hollow rotor that contains a test section up to 1.5 m long at a radius of rotation of 0.48 m. This is rotated by an electric motor with variable speed drive via a belt at speeds up to 2200 rpm. Air is supplied via a flow meter and a coupling to one end of the shaft, passes along the hollow shaft through one of the main bearings and then via a radial passage to the test section itself. The air is exhausted axially at the end of the test section (Fig. 1). Temperatures are measured by thermocouples and the signals are transmitted to a separate instrument pod. Here they are amplified, multiplexed and transmitted via instrument sliprings. The rig has various safety checks built into its control systems and is operated manually. A PDP 11/40 computer is used to log all the readings and for subsequent off-line data analysis.

The present test section consists of a thick walled aluminium tube, internal radius 9.53 mm, external radius 14.29 mm. A number of thermocouples are fitted to the test section and their leads are brought out via grooves in its outer surface. Round the outside of the test section are wrapped two layers of insulation tape, an electrical heater, two further layers of insulation and then a layer of resin insulation out to a radius of 31.06 mm. Three thermocouples are fitted to the outside of this insulation and are used to derive the radial heat loss. The whole test section then fits into an annulus containing further thermal insulation. The inlet air temperature is measured by a single thermocouple. Four thermocouples plus two mixing vanes are provided at the test section outlet, and the air outlet temperature is taken as the average of the two measured values at the second (downstream) mixing vane. The only pressure measurement made at present is the overall pressure drop between a point upstream of the air coupling and ambient conditions.

DATA ANALYSIS

Local Nusselt numbers were calculated using a method similar to that of references (5), (6) and (12). A polynominal expression (usually tenth order) was fitted to the measured wall temperatures, and readings more than about 1°C from this curve were rejected. This rejection of certain readings was necessary as some thermocouples worked reliably only at lower rotational speeds. From this polynominal expression, the axial variation of air temperature and heat input to the air were calculated. To do this, the axial heat loss was calculated from the tube dimensions, and the radial loss from preliminary experiments with zero air flowrate. The local values of Nusselt number were then found. The measured air outlet temperature was not used in this procedure. Instead, it was used to provide a check on the overall heat balance, errors in which were always less than 4%.

The axial variation of Nusselt number was displayed graphically by computer, to enable the portion of the duct where the heat transfer was fully-developed to be estimated.

The pressure rise due to rotation was allowed for in calculating the overall pressure loss coefficient, which was defined as follows:

$$C_T = \frac{2\Delta P + \rho H^2 \Omega^2}{\rho W^2} \qquad \ldots (1)$$

RESULTS

Apart from the heat loss calibrations at zero flowrate mentioned earlier, the first measurements were for the test section stationary and with air flow. The fully developed Nusselt number was measured at three Reynolds numbers between 22,000 and 33,000, and was found to agree to within 7-11% with values from the correlation (13)

$$N_u = 0.023 \ R_e^{0.8} \ P_r^{1/3} \qquad \ldots (2)$$

This level of agreement was regarded as satisfactory.

Measurements were then made at nominal flow rates of 6.7 and 10 g/s (Reynolds numbers of 22,000 and 33,000), rotational speeds between 280 and 2200 rpm, and with the heat input adjusted to give maximum wall temperatures of either 90 or 130°C. This gave values of S_w up to 4.6, and values of G_{rr} between 1.6×10^3 and 6.8×10^5.

Typical axial variations of local Nusselt number, deduced from these measurements, are shown in Fig. 2. These results are for a nominal R_e of 33,000 and a maximum wall temperature of 130°C. Qualitatively similar results were obtained for all the conditions mentioned above.

The values of mean and fully developed Nusselt numbers for all the tests are shown in Figs. 3 and 4. They are plotted against S_w; for a constant R_e that is equivalent to plotting against rotational speed. There was no systematic variation between the values of N_u for the two different wall temperatures; both sets results are included in Figs. 3 and 4.

As the only pressure loss measurement was for overall pressure drop, the measurements apply only to the present rig and therefore are not reported in detail. The overall pressure loss coefficient, C_T, increased slowly with increasing rotational speeds but the increases were only small, namely 10% or less. There was no systematic variation between the measurements for the two different maximum wall temperatures, and between these results and additional measurements with no heat input to the test section.

DISCUSSION

The present results show that rotation has only a fairly small (up to 20%) effect on either mean or fully-developed values of Nusselt number, for the conditions studied here. The effects of rotation are greater near inlet than in fully developed flow. The Nusselt numbers increase at first with increasing rotational speed but then either reach a steady value or even decrease slightly. Also, the Nusselt numbers do not vary systematically with heat input. These findings are qualitatively in agreement with results of Morris and Woods (6). However, there are two important differences. Firstly, there is no indication in (6) of the Nusselt number ever decreasing with increasing rotational speed. Secondly, the present measurements imply a smaller variation of heat transfer wtih rotation. Morris and Woods correlated their results for mean Nusselt number in the inlet region with an expression

$$N_u = 0.0089 \ R_e^{0.78} \ J^{0.25}$$

The present measurements of mean Nusselt number were correlated in the same way, using a nonlinear least squares procedure, solely for the purpose of comparing with the above expression. The correlation derived from the present measurements was

$$N_{um} = 0.039 \ R_e^{0.72} \ J^{0.05} ,$$

with a maximum error of 6%.

There are a number of reasons why the present measurements show a much smaller variation with J (and therefore with rotation) than those of ref. (6). Firstly, the data of ref. (6) were for the inlet region, where rotation effects are greatest, while the present data are for the whole test section. Secondly, the earlier data were for lower R_e (up to 20,000) than the present results, and rotation effects are likely to be more pronounced at lower R_e values. Thirdly, the earlier data were for lower values of J (up to 1200) compared with the present work (J values up to 4300) and the Nusselt number appears to vary more rapidly with J for lower J values.

Sakamoto and Fukui (3) obtained heat transfer measurements for fully developed flow in a rotating parallel duct for both laminar and turbulent flow. They found that the effect of rotation for turbulent flow with R_e above 10^4 was so small that they studied in detail only the results for lower R_e. This is qualitatively in agreement with the present findings that rotational effects are small for $R_e = 2 \times 10^4$ or 3×10^4.

There are two main mechanisms that occur in rotating pipe flow and cause the increases in heat transfer (see refs. 1-8). The first is the interaction between density differences and centripetal acceleration, and therefore depends on the temperature differences and thus the heat input. The second is the effect of the inlet conditions, which are determined by the flow in the rotating radial inlet tube and test section inlet chamber, and are related to the Coriolis acceleration. The present measurements show a greater change in heat transfer near inlet than in fully-developed flow. Also, the measured Nusselt numbers and pressure loss coefficients do not vary systematically with maximum test section temperature and therefore with heat input. These two facts suggest that the predominate mechanism is the effect of rotation on inlet conditions to the test section.

As the increase in pressure drop with rotation is likely to give higher than expected rotor winding temperatures, it clearly warrants further study. Therefore a second test section is being built and commissioned at present, and this will enable the static pressure drop along the test section itself to be measured. It will also be possible to make heat transfer measurements, as with the first test section.

The present work suggests that rotational effects are small (generally less than 20%) for the conditions occurring in the rotors of large generators. However, two points must be made. Firstly, rotational effects on heat transfer are significant in developing flow, and therefore need to be considered in cooling systems with comparatively short axial ducts, such as subslot plus axial duct systems. Secondly, although rotation improves heat transfer and therefore gives lower winding temperatures, it also increases the pressure drop. The consequent drop in coolant flowrate may then give an increase in winding temperatures that outweighs the reduction due to improved heat transfer. This point has been demonstrated experimentally by Morris and Dias (5).

CONCLUSIONS

An experimental facility has been successfully built and commissioned to measure the effects of rotation on turbulent heat transfer in a duct rotating about a parallel axis, for flow conditions found in the rotor winding ducts of large generators. Measurements obtained on the first test section have shown that rotation increases heat transfer coefficients by up to 20%, and the overall pressure loss coefficient by up to 10%, for Reynolds numbers between 22,000 and 33,000 and rotational parameters appropriate to large generator rotors. The effects of rotation on heat transfer are greatest in developing flow, and therefore are more important in cooling systems with short axial flow paths. The effects of rotation on pressure drop are important, as they can lead to lower than expected flowrates and therefore higher than expected winding temperatures. A second test section is therefore being commissioned that will enable detailed static pressure drop measurements to be made.

ACKNOWLEDGEMENTS

The help and assistance of Mr F.H. Gawman in conducting the experiments described here is gratefully acknowledged. The work was carried out at the Central Electricity Research Laboratories and is published by permission of the Central Electricity Generating Board.

REFERENCES

1. Humphreys, J.F., Morris, W.D. and Barrow, H., 1967, Convection heat transfer in the entry region of a tube which revolves about an axis parallel to itself, Int. J. Heat and Mass Transfer, 10, 333.

2. Le Feuvre, R.F., 1968, Heat transfer in rotor cooling ducts, Thermodynamics and Fluid Mechanics Convention, I. Mech. E., London.

3. Sakamoto, M. and Fukui, S., 1970, Convective heat transfer of a rotating tube revolving about an axis parallel to itself, Fourth International Heat Transfer Confs., vol. III, paper FC7.2, Paris-Versailles.

4. Woods, J.L., 1976, Heat transfer and flow resistance in a rotating duct system, D. Phil. Thesis, Sussex Univ.

5. Morris, W.D. and Dias, F.M., 1976, Experimental observations on the thermal performance of a rotating coolant circuit with reference to the design of electrical machine rotors, Proc. I. Mech. E., 190, 561.

6. Morris, W.D. and Woods, J.L., 1978, Heat transfer in the entrance region of tubes that rotate about a parallel axis, J. Mech. Sci., 20, 319.

7. Mori, Y., 1973, Forced convection heat transfer in a straight pipe in a centrifugal field III, Central Electricity Generating Board translation CE 7440 (1973).

8. Nakayama, W., 1968, Forced convection heat transfer in a straight pipe rotating about a parallel axis, Int. J. Heat Mass Transfer, 11, 1185.

9. Majumdar, A.K., Morris, W.D., Skiadaressis, D. and Spalding, D.B., 1976, Heat transfer in rotating ducts, Imperial College Heat Transfer Section report HTS/76/5.

10. Petukhov, B.S. and Polyakov, A.F., 1977, Heat transfer and resistance in rotating pipes (survey), Power Engng., 15, 104.

11. Morris, W.D., 1977, Flow and heat transfer in rotating coolant channels, AGARD Conf. preprint No. 229, 50th meeting of AGARD Propulsion and Energetics Panel, Ankara, Turkey.

12. Lau, S.C., Sparrow, E.M. and Ramsey, J.W., 1981, Effect of plenum length and diameter on turbulent heat transfer in a downstream tube and on plenum-related pressure losses, J. Heat Transfer, 103, 415.

13. Knudsen, J.F. and Katz, D.L., 1958, Fluid Dynamics and Heat Transfer, McGraw-Hill, New York.

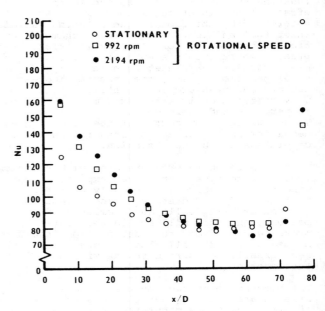

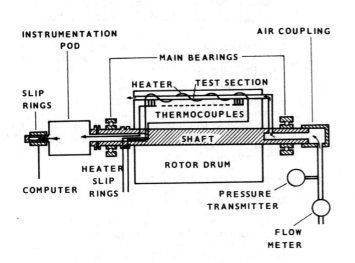

FIG. 1 GENERAL ARRANGEMENT OF RIG

FIG. 2 AXIAL VARIATION OF LOCAL
NUSSELT NUMBER

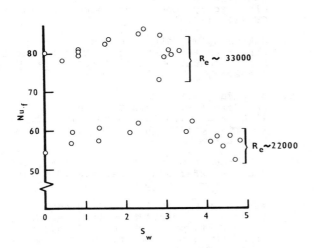

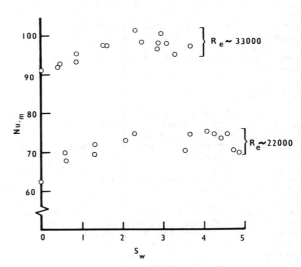

FIG. 3 VARIATION OF FULLY-DEVELOPED
NUSSELT NUMBER WITH SWIRL NUMBER

FIG. 4 VARIATION OF MEAN NUSSELT
NUMBER WITH SWIRL NUMBER

MEASUREMENTS OF CORE ENDREGION LOSSES AND CALCULATIONS OF CORE TEMPERATURES FOR A 500 MW TURBOGENERATOR

J.A. Lapworth and I.R. Funnell

C.E.G.B., Central Electricity Research Laboratories, UK.

SYMBOLS

a   rate of change of core temperature before change in heat generation

b   rate of change of core temperature after change in heat generation

C   core laminate thermal capacity per unit volume

T   true core temperature

T_o true core temperature when heat generation changes

T'   measured core temperature

T_o' measured core temperature when heat generation changes

t   time after change in core heat generation

W   core heat generation per unit volume

W_a core heat generation before change in load condition

W_b core heat generation after change in load condition

δ load angle of machine

ρ core laminate density

τ temperature sensor time constant

c,d,e   parameters used in equations

INTRODUCTION

The increases in turbogenerator specific ratings over the past 30 years which have enabled unit ratings to be increased from 60 MW to 660 MW and 1300 MW have greatly increased machine leakage fields. This has meant that machine design has had to be increasingly refined in order to manage the effects of these fields. In the stator core, for instance, endregion axial leakage fluxes generate eddy currents in the plane of the core laminations, so the machine designer has to limit these fields and provide sufficient cooling for the endregion heating. It has also been shown (e.g. Jackson (1)) that axial and radial leakage fluxes play an important part in the development of core faults, and there has been some interest in the circulating currents that are generated in the machine framework by radial leakage fields.

Recently there have been significant advances in the calculation of turbogenerator endregion fields (e.g. Jacobs et al. (2)) and in the understanding of the effects of machine parameters such as load angle, rotor current and stator voltage (e.g. Singleton et al. (3)). Unfortunately there has always been a shortage of experimental data with which theoretical predictions could be compared.

The work described here was undertaken as part of an investigation into how well core endregion heating and temperatures can be predicted from first principles. One of the objectives of the work described in this paper was to measure core endregion losses for a machine using the rate of change of temperature method (e.g. Gilbert (4), Ball and Lorch (5)) to provide experimental data to help validate methods of calculating magnetic fields and losses in machines. A second objective was to derive a means of modelling the cooling of the stator core of a machine. Calculated core temperatures, predicted from either calculated or measured losses, could then be compared with measured temperatures.

The measurements were made on a 500 MW machine for which a large amount of data on the effects of load conditions on core temperatures was already available. The stator had been particularly well instrumented with thermocouples, and had the further advantage that the endregion design was relatively simple, so that interpretation of measurements would be straightforward.

MEASUREMENT OF CORE ENDREGION LOSSES

The measurement of heat generation rates by the rate of change of temperature method depends on the fact that after a sudden change in heat generation the initial change in the rate of change of temperature at any point is dependent only on the change in heat generation and the thermal capacity of the material. Eventually, the rate changes as heat begins to diffuse into neighbouring areas having different heat generations.

Ideally, temperature sensors with fast responses are required to be able to measure accurately the initial rate of change of temperature. Certainly, for regions of high conductivity which are intensively cooled, such as the flux screen or clamping plate, fast sensors are essential. However, for stator core regions, which have very much longer cooling time constants, it is possible to obtain useful results with the standard thermocouples fitted (which have time constants of the order of 30 secs), especially when there is no rapid variation of losses locally.

The core temperature, T, at a point in a structure after a sudden change in local heat generation is shown in fig. 1 and can be expressed as

$$T = T_o + b t + c t^2 \qquad \ldots(1)$$

The rate of change of temperature immediately afterwards, b, is related to that immediately before, a, by

$$b - a = (W_b - W_a)/\rho.C \qquad \ldots(2)$$

The temperature, T', as measured by a sensor with a finite response time, τ, is also shown in fig. 1 and is given by

$$T' = T_o' + a\tau + b(t - \tau) + c(t^2 - 2\tau t + 2\tau^2)$$

$$+ ((b - a).\tau - 2 c.\tau^2) \exp(-t/\tau) \qquad \ldots (3)$$

Provided the sensor time constant is somewhat shorter than the initial linear period, the initial rate of change of temperature and the sensor time constant can be determined from the measured sensor response using curve fitting techniques.

MEASUREMENT RESULTS

The measurements reported in this work were obtained using an analogue signal multiplexer and a digital voltmeter controlled by a small microcomputer. The computer was programmed to continuously monitor load conditions while the generator was on load, recording load conditions and core temperatures every 30 seconds in a temporary store containing the last 10 sets of measurements. Whenever a criterion for a sudden change in load condition was met the computer caused load conditions and core temperatures to be recorded with intervals of 3 seconds between each set of readings, for a period of about 15 minutes. In this way measurements could be made automatically without interference to the normal operation of the generator.

Measurements have been made when the machine came off load during routine unloading sequences, giving core losses for low load/open circuit conditions, and also after sudden changes in load condition produced whenever the generator transformer tap changer was operated, when the variation in core losses with load conditions can be obtained. The transient temperature change after the rotor field was tripped during an unloading sequence is shown in fig. 2 for a core tooth thermocouple position. The thermocouple time constants estimated from such responses ranged up to 50 seconds. For the core tooth positions these measurements give averaged values of core loss densities about the measurement positions.

Core endregion losses are greatest at high loads and leading power factors, so it is important that experimental data is available for a full load leading power factor condition. Unfortunately, no measurements were made for trips from high loads, so core losses for a full load leading power factor condition had to be derived by extrapolation from the low load values using the measured changes in losses with load angle. The change in load angle for a tap change from 63 to -5 MVar at 478 MW is shown in fig. 3 and the corresponding transient temperature change for a core tooth thermocouple is shown in fig. 4. The variation of measured core loss changes with change in load angle, δ, is shown in fig. 5 for a core tooth position. The simplest correlation describing the variation of core loss, W, with load condition (e.g. Minors (6)) is

$$W = d - e \cos \delta \qquad \ldots (4)$$

From the slope of plots such as fig. 5 a value for the coefficient e was derived for each measurement position, and the expression used to extrapolate measured core losses from low load to a full load leading condition. As an independent check on this method measured core temperature rises above cold gas temperature were plotted against cosine of load angle, giving results as shown in fig. 6. If the variation of core loss density with load angle does not change significantly locally, a similar correlation to (4) for core temperature rise should apply. Both extrapolation methods gave very similar results.

More complicated correlations involving rotor current and stator voltage as well as load angle were tried, but no better fit could be obtained to the experimental data. The fact that no significant rotor current dependence was apparent for this machine is thought to be due to its rather low magnetic loading.

CALCULATION OF CORE TEMPERATURES

The cooling of the stator core was modelled using the computer program ANDUIN (Stephenson (7)) developed at CERL to solve problems involving heat conduction through a structure with heat transfer to coolant flowing through ducts in the structure. A lumped parameter representation is used, the structure being subdivided into elements, and the heat transfer equations being incorporated into a matrix equation relating the temperatures of the elements to the heat generated within them.

A fully three dimensional representation of the basic symmetry unit of the machine was used. Part of the cylindrical mesh used is shown in fig. 7. The main features of the cooling that had to be incorporated were the anisotropic core thermal conductivity, the arrangement of radial and axial cooling ducts with mixing of the coolant flows where appropriate, heat transfer from core surface to coolant gas, and coolant gas temperature rises. All were explicitly represented. A large mesh of 3438 nodes was required, resulting in a problem size of 1.1 M bytes of computer storage. Fortunately, data input for the calculations is minimised by automatic mesh generation.

A comparison of calculated temperatures using measured core losses with measured temperatures for a core tooth position is shown in fig. 8 for the full load leading power factor condition. There is reasonable agreement at the end of the main core section and in the two adjacent core packets. The most important factor in determining the core temperatures for this particular core design was found to be the local core losses. The differences between calculated and measured temperatures further into the main core section is therefore attributed mainly to the measurements underestimating true values of core losses in this region.

SUMMARY

In the calculation of core temperatures for a machine from design data, the step involving the most uncertainty is the calculation of core endregion fields and losses, and more work is required to validate the calculation methods.

A fully three dimensional calculation of the cooling of a turbogenerator is possible using existing computer programs, the accuracy of the representation being dependent on the maximum size of program that can be handled on the computer.

A lot of information about core endregion losses in machines can be obtained using

standard thermocouples, although a large
volume of data has to be collected and fairly
sophisticated computer based processing used.
Novel means of obtaining information about
the variation of core losses with load condition, from data recorded during the normal
operating regime, have been described.

The CEGB has machines coming into service
which have been specially instrumented for
studying endregion fields, and the work described in this paper will continue to help
assess the computer programs which have been
developed for the electromagnetic and thermal
modelling of machines.

ACKNOWLEDGEMENTS

The authors would like to acknowledge the
help of the staff of the CEGB South Eastern
Scientific Services Division, in particular
Mr D. Ward, in obtaining the measurements
described in this work.

REFERENCES

1. Jackson, R.J., 1978, "Interlamination
    voltages in large turbogenerators", Proc.
    IEE, 125, 1232-1238

2. Jacobs, D.A.H., Minors, R.H., Myerscough,
    C.J., Rollason, M.L.J. and Steel, J.G.,
    1977, "Calculation of losses in the end
    region of turbogenerators", Proc. IEE,
    124, 356-362

3. Singleton, R.C.C., Marshall, P. and
    Steel, J.G., 1981, "Axial magnetic flux
    in synchronous machines: the effect of
    operating conditions", IEEE Trans., PAS-100,
    1226-1233

4. Gilbert, A.J., 1961, "A method of
    measuring loss distribution in electrical
    machines", Proc. IEE, 108, 239-244

5. Ball, D.A. and Lorch, H.O., 1965, "An
    improved thermometric method of measuring
    local power dissipation", J. Sci. Instr.,
    42, 90-93

6. Minors, R.H., 1974, "Core endregion
    heating in turbogenerators: the import-
    ance of load angle", CEGB report
    RD/L/N 172/74

7. Stephenson, P.L., 1979, "ANDUIN - A
    general program for solving non-linear
    heat conduction and convection problems,
    Part II: Users guide", CEGB report
    RD/L/P 2/79

The CEGB reports (6) and (7) are obtainable
from the Librarian, CERL.

The work described in this paper was carried
out at the Central Electricity Research
Laboratories, and is published by permission
of the Central Electricity Generating Board.

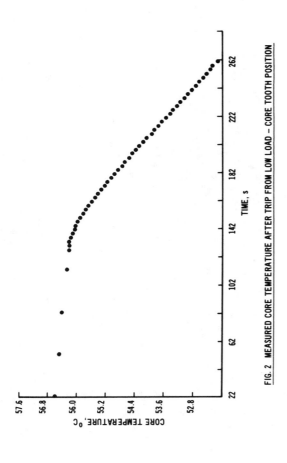

FIG. 1 CORE TEMPERATURE MEASURED AFTER CHANGE IN HEAT GENERATION — THE EFFECT OF SENSOR TIME CONSTANT

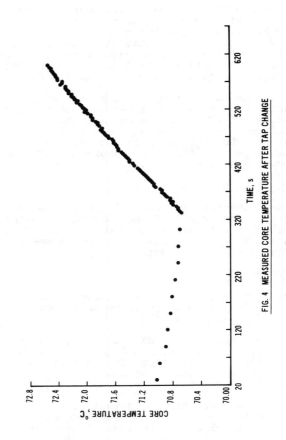

FIG. 2 MEASURED CORE TEMPERATURE AFTER TRIP FROM LOW LOAD — CORE TOOTH POSITION

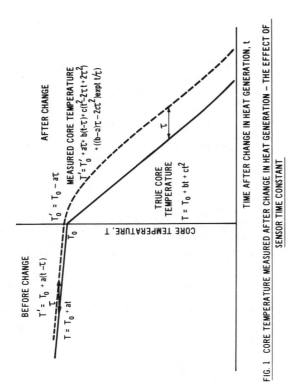

FIG. 3 CHANGE IN LOAD ANGLE FOR A TAP CHANGE

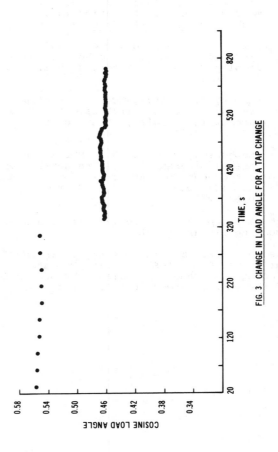

FIG. 4 MEASURED CORE TEMPERATURE AFTER TAP CHANGE

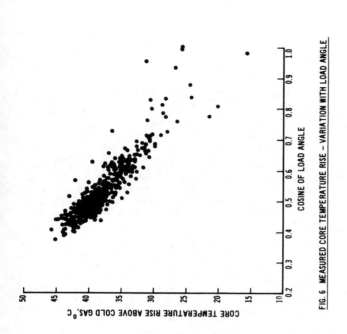

FIG. 6   MEASURED CORE TEMPERATURE RISE – VARIATION WITH LOAD ANGLE

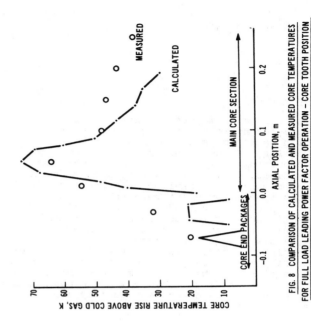

FIG. 8   COMPARISON OF CALCULATED AND MEASURED CORE TEMPERATURES
FOR FULL LOAD LEADING POWER FACTOR OPERATION – CORE TOOTH POSITION

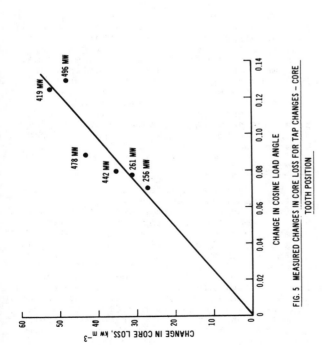

FIG. 5   MEASURED CHANGES IN CORE LOSS FOR TAP CHANGES – CORE
TOOTH POSITION

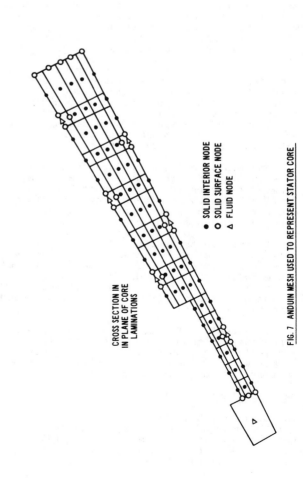

FIG. 7   ANDUIN MESH USED TO REPRESENT STATOR CORE

U.K'S FIRST DIRECT-WATER-COOLED PUMPED STORAGE GENERATOR-MOTOR

G.K. Ridley

GEC Large Machines Ltd.

INTRODUCTION

The U.K. home market has not hitherto demanded hydro-electric generators of the high rating necessitating direct-water cooling. Without the opportunity of demonstrating the ability to produce such machines, it is difficult to break into the world market for capital electrical goods of this type. Pumped-storage schemes are not as dependent upon natural hydraulic conditions for the determination of maximum machine ratings as are straight hydro projects. Individual machines may therefore be highly rated, in which case direct- water cooling may be essential or at least very advantageous. Nevertheless the high output Dinorwic machines (reference 1) did not need to be direct-water-cooled and they are not so in the interests of simplicity.

There are, however, other considerations than merely heat dissipation, as is well known (reference 2). Direct-water-cooling reduces machine size, which may significantly reduce underground excavation; so often a feature of hydro-electric schemes, not only from the consideration of hydraulic but also environmental conditions. Direct-water-cooling may also reduce losses and this is important when there is a high capitalisation value. There were good reasons, therefore, for the North of Scotland Hydro Electric Board giving careful consideration to water-cooled machines for future Pumped Storage schemes, even though individual machine ratings may not demand these measures. It is desirable to gain experience of the special conditions appertaining to such machines before embarking on a large project.

GEC and NSHEB found, therefore, a mutual interest in replacing one of the existing Generator-Motors in the Cruachan Power Station by a new machine having both stator and rotor direct-water-cooled. The machine concerned had a synchronous speed of 600 r.p.m., and at the time of its manufacture in the early 1960's few large salient-pole machines in the world operated at so high a speed. Unfortunately, critical speed calculation methods were less sophisticated than those available today and the machine ran closer to its critical speed than is desirable.

It is evident that there is a need for a U.K. capability to manufacture the largest hydro-electric machines. This first U.K. direct-water-cooled hydro-electric machine is therefore of national significance.

BASIC DESIGN

The basic layout, shown in figure 1, is of well known conventional top bracket form for vertical machines. The two main parallel beams of the thrust bearing bracket are mounted on machined facings at the top of the stator frame through which the total bearing load is transmitted to the stator soleplates. Side arms are secured to the stator frame. Use of water-cooling has permitted a reduction in stator core length from 2.286 metres to 1.345 metres. Hence the guide bearing centres are brought closer together which raises the critical speed to a value safely above normal running speed, and indeed above the maximum overspeed which the set may experience. The reduction in length of the machine is vividly illustrated by figure 2.

Since the machine under consideration was a replacement, abnormal limitations were placed upon the design. Primarily the new machine had to fit the same space diametrally as its predecessor(reference figure 3.) Only a small increase (3.7%) in the stator bore was possible, therefore. Moreover, the reduction in rotor inertia had to be limited to an inertia constant (H) of not less than 3.5. The original H value was 5. Also, there should be no significant change in reactance values. All these factors meant that the full potential of direct-water-cooling could not be exploited although the Output Coefficient is increased by 58%. Furthermore, whilst the technology of direct-water-cooling the stator winding was accepted by NSHEB as well known and well tried within GEC, there was less confidence regarding direct-water cooling of the rotor winding. It was specified, therefore, that air cooling of the rotor should be possible as a last resort if water-cooling proved unsuccessful. The design will permit the field coils to be changed to include only solid copper turns. This would allow adequate air cooling. In fact, any change might be avoided provided full advantage was taken of the Class F insulation materials. Notwithstanding this cautious design approach, GEC has demonstrated very successfully, by the use of a rig, all the essential features required of a water-cooled rotor.

SPECIAL FEATURES

The major saving in losses in a direct-water cooled machine is achieved through the minimisation of the windage friction loss. A certain amount of cooling air is needed, however, to remove the pole face heating loss. This air inevitably absorbs heat from other parts also which must be assessed when determining the required air quantity. The natural fanning action of the salient poles is not an advantage. Since there are no air ducts formed in the stator core, the air path must be axial rather than radial as is the normal arrangement in an air-cooled machine. Measures taken to reduce the rotor windage loss to a minimum include the smoothing of the interpolar space and the ends of the rotor(reference figure 3,) together with the extension of the stator slot wedges to the bore surface to make that as smooth as possible also.

It would have been possible to utilise some of the necessary cooling air to remove heat from the ends of the stator core. Experience by others has shown that especial care is required with regard to core end cooling. The decision was taken that a more positive effect would be achieved by using water as the cooling medium. Provision of this feature, however, necessitated considerable development work. A major problem was the prevention of buckling of the backing plate to which the cooling tubes were to be brazed. Initially it was expected that the end lamination of the stator core would be used as this backing plate but finally a relatively thick stainless steel material had to be used.

Whilst the stator winding cooling water provides a major heat sink, this is not the sole means provided for dissipating all the remaining stator core loss. A substantial part is conducted away through copper cooling tubes inserted into U-shaped notches in the back of the core. These tubes are held by spring steel clips in order to maximise heat transfer between the tubes and the laminations. As this machine is the first of a type, twice as many such cooling tubes are provided as are theoretically necessary. Operation is possible using either all or half the tubes.

STATOR WINDING

Water-cooled stator windings have been applied successfully for many years in large turbo-generators. Metropolitan-Vickers, a constituent company of today's GEC, was in the van of such development and today GEC Turbine Generators Ltd. is one of the world's leading manufacturers of water-cooled-turbo-generators. Undoubtedly GEC possesses much expertise in the basic relevant technology. The water-cooled feature expected to give fewest problems, therefore, is that relevant to the stator winding. Nevertheless, there are significant differences in the application of such technology to hydro-electric machines.

One significant factor is the work site for the assembly of the stator winding into the core. Hydro-electric machines being of low speed compared to turbo-generators are of larger diameter, although shorter in core length. It is not possible, therefore, to transport large hydro-electric machine stators in one piece. Inevitably there must be some assembly in the field, even if some of the winding could be wound into sections of the core in the factory. In the case of a water-cooled machine, for which the number of stator slots is relatively fewer than for a comparable air-cooled machine (there was over 40% reduction in the particular case of the Cruachan machine), any factory assembly is scarcely worthwhile since so great a proportion of the winding cannot be assembled. Apart from that it is highly desirable, in the case of large pumped-storage generator-motors, subjected to many operational mode changes, that the stator core should be assembled as a continuous spiral and this can only be achieved in the power station, for reasons indicated already.

The consequence of site erection, at least for Cruachan, was that use of the stator core as a jig for shaping prototype bars of the winding was not possible. Correct shaping was most important due to limited flexibility

of the bar-to-bar connections and also of the endwinding insulation which is consolidated. The bar-to-bar connections were designed to carry both the electric current and the cooling water and although there is complete freedom in two degrees of movement there is virtually none in the third. This means that the stand-pipes extending from the corresponding top and bottom bar end water-boxes have to be as parallel as possible. Some difficulty was experienced in achieving this for bars manufactured before they could be tried in the core. A further disadvantage of using the end connections for both electrical and hydraulic purposes is that the current carrying section is reduced considerably. Although the extra heat can be dissipated readily enough by the water, the increase in electrical loss is not negligible, even though the length of the connectors is relatively short.

The technique for making the several brazed joints involved in each of these connectors was found to be not so well established as expected. A survey of other manufacturer's practice showed no absolute concensus and within our own organisation, over the development period of this first water-cooled hydro-electric machine, there was a certain amount of new thinking. To a degree, therefore, we developed our own technique and teething problems were encountered arising largely from inadequacies in the special operator training needed for this highly skilled work. The appropriate test criterion for soundness of joints appeared initially to be less stringent than in turbo-generator practice. Hydro-electric machines operate in air at atmospheric pressure rather than in hydrogen at a greater pressure than that of the water. The requirement, therefore, is to prevent water leaking out instead of hydrogen leaking in. However, when leak problems arose at site, it was decided that nothing less than a gas test would adequately demonstrate soundness of these joints.

ROTOR WINDING

Although transference of cooling water into and out of the stator winding is by the well tried form of teflon hoses, a new development was needed for the rotor field winding. This depends on carbon seals which are, however, of standard type and, as mentioned earlier, were very successfully demonstrated in a test rig. The water-box developed permits the intake of water at the top of the shaft system from whence it flows through a tube within the hollow centre of the shaft down to the underside of the generator-motor rotor (reference figure 4) to be fed through a flexible portion to a distribution system for all 10 poles connected hydraulically in parallel. At each pole, the cooling water is connected to three turns of the field winding containing a water passage at their inner periphery. These three turns of each field coil are themselves hydraulically in parallel. After a single pass round the coil, the water returns to an exit collection system leading back into the centre of the shaft system and thence through the water-box back into the stationary pipework.

WATER TREATMENT PLANT

Hydro-electric machines have intrinsically a greater number of stator slots than corresponding turbo-generators. It has usually been assumed, therefore, that it would be necessary to put a number of hydro-electric machine stator bars in series hydraulically in order to keep the number of water circuits to manageable proportions e.g. reference 3. The Cruachan machine, however, has only 99 slots and it was decided, in the interests of simplicity, to use a one-pass water system, with the water flowing through the winding from bottom to top.

Provision of the necessary low conductivity cooling water for the winding is less readily achieved in hydro stations than in thermal stations. In a hydro-station although the treated water system may be charged first with imported condensate, the purity of the water has to be maintained solely by the water treatment plant. Although treatment facilities are provided in thermal stations, make-up water or new charges of the system are readily obtainable from the condensate system. The water treatment plant for Cruachan was designed as a modular unit, mounted for convenience of transport on two baseplates. It comprises the elements shown in figure 5. The entire system is of stainless steel or bronze. Level switches in the treated water tank and raw-water tank control the intake of make-up water. A conductivity sensor in the main circuit controls the bleed of water into the by-pass loop for treatment as necessary. To minimise the ingress of oxygen, both water tanks are provided with a blanket of nitrogen over their water surfaces. These are interconnected to balance the pressure in the system. Less concern for oxygen content arises in the case of thermal stations because the make-up supply is condensate.

A question arose in the design of the Cruachan treated-water system as to the need for the field cooling circuit to be included. As the field voltage is low, using treated water is not essential. It was decided, however, that it would be good practice to use low conductivity water for all water circuits in intimate contact with electrical circuits. The only consequence is that the drain from the rotor water-box may necessitate a greater compensation for loss than otherwise. To ensure positive flow of either make-up water or water bled from the main circuit the treatment through the by-pass loop, a booster pump is included in that part of the circuit.

THERMAL DESIGN

Whilst the electro-magnetic design was relatively standard, the thermal design required special consideration. A thermal network was set up to make a detailed investigation into the expected heat distribution. This is different form turbo-generators since the hydro-electric machine does not operate in an atmosphere of hydrogen. From this study it was found that only 5 of the 36 strands per stator bar need by hollow to carry the required flow of cooling water. Also determined by this means was the size of cooling tubes located at the back of the core and the heat balance relative to the special core end cooling and transference of heat to the air at both the bore and outer periphery of the core.

A special problem in the design of the cooling water system for the water-cooled hydro-electric machine operating in air, as compared to a turbo-generator filled with hydrogen, is that of controlling the external surface temperature of winding components so as to avoid condensation. It is of particular concern in relation to the teflon hoses between the stator bars at high voltage and the water bus or manifold at earth potential. This is especially so at the bottom of the machine where the cooled air emerges from the air coolers. The protection system adopted involves a humidity sensor fitted in the incoming air stream which transmits a signal to a control valve in the raw cooling water inlet to the treated water coolers. The degree of cooling of the treated water is thus controlled whilst full flow through the windings is maintained. It is important to keep water flowing through the teflon tubes as otherwise the resistive leakage current down the column of static water in the tubes would quickly cause it to boil. The basic criterion for determining the length of such tubes is that the column of water should not boil within less than 1 minute with no flow. The length used for the Cruachan machine is appreciably in excess of that basic requirement.

The multiplicity of variable factors likely to produce condensation on the teflon tubes creates too great a complexity to permit a complete definition of the system settings prior to operation of the machine. It will be necessary to tune the system during the commissioning tests.

TESTING

Commissioning a machine of this type, which has been built without pre-erection and testing in the factory, is a major task. GEC has had good experience of this in several other hydro-electric schemes (as reported in reference 4), although these did not involve direct-water-cooled machines. The test programme for this machine comprises three basic sections. First there are those tests which ensure that the design concept is materialised during manufacture and erection. These are essentially quality control tests. Then there are the tests made on the completed machine to check its general serviceability. Finally, tests are required to prove the performance of the machine in terms of efficiency, temperature limits and a general ability to perform the required duty.

The performance tests are of most interest. Included with them are measurements to provide experimental data on this first U.K. manufactured direct-water-cooled generator-motor. NSHEB readily agreed with the importance of gleaning maximum information, but requested facilities for the repetition of the measurements involved throughout the machine's life with minimum interruption to normal operation. With this policy in view, a permanent test cubicle is provided to which are brought connections from a considerable number of thermocouples distributed throughout the stator core by which the heat distribution can be assessed. Included also are thermocouples by which the loss in the ends of the stator core may be determined from the rate of rise of temperature immediately after applying excitation. This is of special interest because it is hoped to determine the efficacy of measures taken to reduce the end loss. In general, the stator teeth have two 3mm wide slits to a radial depth equal to the stator slots and to an axial depth of 50mm at each end of the core. Calculations predict that these slits will significantly reduce the extra loss generated in these core end portions by stray axial flux. Over a small portion of the core, and at one end only, the slits in the teeth have been omitted in order to give a comparison of the loss with and without the slits.

It is important, also, to determine how much heat is dissipated by the several cooling circuits. This is done calorimetrically and involves high accuracy measurement of water flow and temperature rise. For the latter there are fitted resistance type temperature detectors in the cooling water inlet and outlet pipework of each heat absorption circuit, connected so as to indicate temperature rise. They are brought out to a suitable indicator in the permanent test cubicle. For occasions requiring the highest accuracy, the RTD connections are made to a special test instrument. The thermocouples provided in the stator core and the air circuit, on the other hand, need always to be extended from their termination in multi-pin type connectors to suitable test instrumentation which is set up for the occasion.

In order to measure cooling water flow without interruption of machine operation there are provided extra valves and pipework whereby the water can be diverted from its normal path to high accuracy measuring devices. For raw water circuits the measured water goes to waste. Such measurement is considered best carried out by a calibrated measuring tank technique. For treated water circuits, however, not only is it highly desirable to conserve the low conductivity water but it is not permissible to expose such circuits to the atmosphere. In this case, therefore, the treated water is by-passed through high accuracy flow meters, which need be fitted only when required.

Despite the desirability of the policy of facilities for continuous monitoring of all test results without preventing normal use of the generator-motor, it is not practicable to carry this through entirely. This applies particularly to the measurement of stator winding copper temperature and that of the surface of the endwinding insulation. Interest is increasingly being centred on the heat transfer achieved through stator winding insulation and there is a trend for customers' specifications to call for a guarantee of temperature rise limits as measured on the copper rather than only by the traditional method of ETD's buried in the separator between bar or coil sides in the slot. Research into the thermal conductivity properties of insulation, in order to increase machine specific ratings, has been carried out by manufacturers for a long time. Consequently the desirability of making such measurements in the field is fully accepted in the case of machines not previously erected and tested. Nevertheless this calls for considerable precautions which preclude the possibility of normal operation at the time or even of retaining the connections to the test probes. This means that the thermocouples attached under the insulation to the copper of the stator bar strands have to be terminated normally in a socket on the endwinding. For test purposes and under strictly controlled conditions, these connections can be extended to instrumentation located in insulated booths. Similarly, monitoring of thermocouples attached to the surface of the endwindings is only permissible by using protected instrumentation under special test conditions.

In addition to other tests to establish parameters and performance which are normally of interest such as Open and Short Circuit excitation characteristics, reactances and time constants, full load losses and noise level, it is important to investigate the efficacy of the measures taken to reduce rotor windage friction loss.

Further special features of testing a water-cooled machine arise when proving the soundness of the stator winding insulation. In order to obtain a realistic measurement of insulation resistance (IR), the winding side of the water connections must be insulated adequately from ground, as shown by Hummer and Zwicknagel (5). Consequently, the treated water ring mains at either end of the stator are insulated and have insulated flanges. For normal operation, the ring mains are solidly earthed and this is removed only for the IR measurement. When a high voltage pressure test is applied, it is essential that there is a flow of water.

CONCLUSION

Site erection of the first U.K. manufactured direct-water-cooled generator-motor is now well advanced, despite some inevitable teething troubles as described above. It is hoped to report the results of the site tests at the Conference.

Finally, I wish to thank the Directors of GEC Large machines Ltd. and the North of Scotland Hydro-Electric Board for permission to present this paper.

REFERENCES

1. Ridley, G.K. & Maltby, D.J., October 1978, GEC Journal for Industry, 'Dinorwic Generator-Motor Units', 132-139.

2. Meyer, E., April/May 1968. The Brown Boveri Review. 'Maximum power rating of high-speed synchronous machines for hydro power stations', 201-207.

3. Neidhofer, G., January 1970. Brown Boveri Review. 'Roebel bar windings for large synchronous machines', 4-14.

4. Ridley, G.K., November/December 1966. A.E.I. Engineering, 'Site testing of large hydro-electric A.C. synchronous machines, 286-196.

5. Hummer, A & Zwicknagel W., Marz 1979, ÖZE, Jg32, Heft 3, 'Isolationsmessungen und-prüfungen bei Wasserkraftgeneratoren mit direkt wassergekühlten Wicklungen', 221-225.

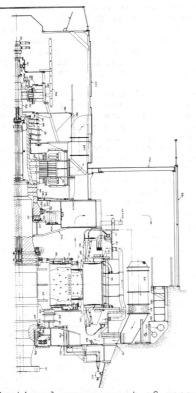

Figure 1 Sectional arrangement of generator-
motor and auxiliary machines.

Figure 2 Old and new rotors.

Figure 3 Rotor being lowered into stator

Figure 4 Underside of rotor

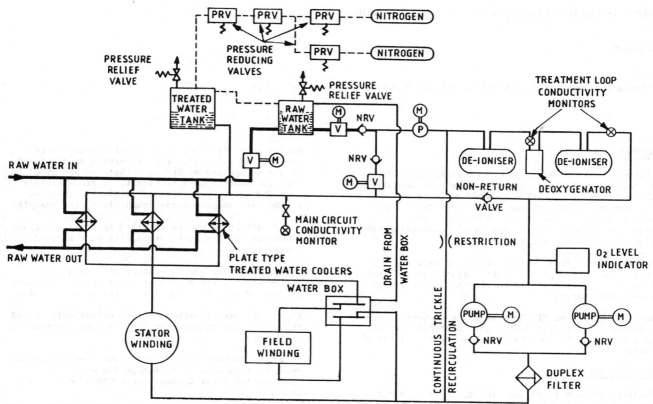

Figure 5 Simplified schematic diagram of treated cooling water circuit

PROSPECTS FOR SLOTLESS DC MOTORS IN RAILWAY PROPULSION

E. Spooner

British Railways Board, R & D Div, Railway Technical Centre, Derby, U.K.

SUMMARY

Slotless armature windings are proposed for use in dc railway motors as a means of improving commutation. The reactance emf which is a rough measure of commutation quality is smaller by a factor of about 3 in a slotless armature than in an equivalent conventional one. Other aspects of commutation are also better in the slotless motor.

The absence of teeth makes for a comparatively saturation-free magnetic characteristic which results in a natural torque-speed curve with improved high speed performance.

An experimental 90 HP slotless motor is nearing completion and five 340 HP motors destined for use on a main line locomotive are in the early stages of construction.

INTRODUCTION

Traction systems based upon the d.c. series motor are compact, reliable and cost effective. Their main operational drawback is the requirement for regular inspection and maintenance of the commutator and brushgear. Systems based on brushless motors are unlikely to be economically competetive for general applications unless the cost of the associated power electronic equipment can be reduced by a factor of two or more. D.C. traction motors are therefore likely to remain popular with users.

For the designer of a dc traction motor the over-riding consideration is to achieve satisfactory commutation over the full operating range of speed and current. Satisfactory commutation implies (a) that little or no sparking occurs at the brushes during normal operation, (b) that even when severe overloads are applied (to perhaps twice the continuously rated current), sparking is not excessive and (c) that transient loads or sudden load changes do not result in flashover. Just as vital as the electrical aspects of commutation are the mechanical aspects; loss of contact between brush and commutator due to shock or vibration and mechanical instability of the commutator structure at speed are common causes of sparking and flashover.

The concept of slotless armature windings illustrated in Fig. 1 is put forward as a means of more easily achieving good commutation in terms of reduced sparking under normal or overload conditions and of improved resistance to flashover under transient conditions. The paper gives a brief comparison between the commutation conditions in conventional and slotless armature windings. This is followed by a consideration of their differing performance and thermal characteristics. An outline is given of planned development work at the British Railways Board Research and Development Division to realise practical forms of the slotless d.c. traction motor.

Before about 1910 many electrical machines were constructed using slotless or surface windings and it was recognised at the time that the use of slots made commutation more difficult. Various factors made the adoption of slotted windings attractive at the time despite worse commutation, for example:

(i) The coils can be retained against radial and tangential forces much more easily in a slotted armature.

(ii) The coils are in contact with iron over a larger area in slots so that the thermal resistance is reduced and the winding temperature is reduced.

(iii) The use of carbon brushes effectively solved the problem of commutation for the specific ratings of the day.

(iv) Slotless windings would have been secured by means of a banding of ferromagnetic wire and consequently their commutation would have been less than ideal.

Interest is again being shown in slotless windings for other forms of electrical machine such as turbogenerators (1) and present day circumstances favour a return to slotless windings in traction motors because:

(i) Modern insulation materials employing reinforced synthetic resins are much stronger than the "natural" materials previously employed so that the mechanical support provided by slots and teeth is not essential.

(ii) Much thinner coverings are needed with modern insulation and much higher temperatures can be tolerated so that the thermal advantage of the slotted armature is not so important.

(iii) Despite the availability of a wide variety of brush grades and the use of split brushes, commutation has returned as the dominant problem area with modern high-speed, highly-rated motors.

(iv) It is no longer necessary to use ferromagnetic wire for securing the coils of a slotless armature. Non-magnetic wire has been available for several decades and glass fibre is now the most commonly used material for banding the end windings of slotted machines.

A programme of slotless motor development carried out in the Soviet Union during the 1970s has been reported (2,3,4) by Bocharov and others. Two locomotives have been in operation with traction motors of 1000 HP continuous rating converted to slotless form. The results of this work appear to be encouraging.

COMMUTATION

The theory of Lamme (5) is commonly employed at the design stage for assessing the severity of the electromagnetic conditions for commutation. The reactance emf which is taken as the measure of the severity of these conditions is induced by the passage of the armature conductors through the quasi-static magnetic field within the commutation zone of the machine. In interpole machines the commutation zone contains the following identifiable components of the flux:

(i) End winding leakage flux.

(ii) Slot leakage flux.

(iii) Band leakage flux (if magnetic banding wire is used).

(iv) Interpolar space leakage flux - absent if the full number of full-length interpoles are fitted.

In a modern traction motor end winding leakage flux accounts for $\frac{1}{4}$ to $\frac{1}{3}$ and the slot leakage flux for the remainder of the total commutation zone field and in turn for the reactance emf. Eliminating slots therefore can be expected to give a reduction in reactance emf by a factor of up to 3 or 4 and to give a corresponding improvement in commutation. Fig. 2 compares the reactance emf calculated for a 1000 HP 4 pole traction motor currently used in British electric locomotives with the predicted reactance emf in a slotless motor design using the same frame and field system.

The true situation is probably better than this. In interpole machines, it is not the reactance emf itself which causes sparking but the degree of mismatching between the reactance emf and the emf induced by the field of the interpole. Varying saturation of the interpole prevents accurate matching over the wide range of armature current. The arranging of groups of conductors together into slots gives rise to differences in reactance emf between coils so that complete matching becomes impossible. The shortage or excess of interpole-induced emf must be complemented by the emf due to the coil resistance and the brush-commutator contact. A mismatch of up to about 2 V could be accepted before sparking becomes intolerable. In typical traction motor designs this corresponds to an average reactance emf of about 7 V. If a slotless winding is employed, the lower interpole flux required should alleviate the interpole saturation problem to some extent, and the more uniform arrangement of conductors should reduce the differences in reactance emf between coils so that a greater average could be accepted.

The phenomenon of flashover is highly complex and can be caused in several ways. A particularly important cause in traction motors is mechanical shock and vibration resulting in temporary loss of brush contact. A slotless armature has features which suggest that this event should be less likely to give rise to a flashover. Hellmund (6) has analysed the sequence of events following the loss of contact as follows:

(i) As contact is lost, an arc is drawn between the brush and the commutator bars which were formerly in contact and between adjacent bars.

(ii) The arc current decays at a rate determined by the arc voltage, the coil induced emf and the coil inductance.

(iii) The rotation of the armature carries the coils connected to the arcing bars toward the main poles where emf is induced.

(iv) If the emf induced by the fields near the edges of the main poles becomes sufficient to sustain the arc before the arc has naturally extinguished then a flashover from brush to brush is likely to follow.

Such flashovers can be avoided if there is ample space between the edge of the commutation zone and the edge of the main pole and if the coils have a low inductance so that arcs are extinguished rapidly. Clearly the slotless winding gives a marked improvement by way of reduced coil inductance. In addition the commutation zone will generally be narrower because short-pitch windings offer no advantage in a slotless winding. The effect of the reduction in the width of the commutation zone is partly offset by increased width of the fringe field of the main pole in the larger gap needed to house a slotless winding.

PERFORMANCE

A typical uncompensated locomotive motor of around 1000 HP rating has an airgap of about 10 mm at the centre of the main pole and about 20 mm at the edge. The magnetic characteristic of this motor is given in Fig. 3 which separates the component due to the iron parts of the magnetic circuit but excluding the armature teeth. A slotless version of this motor would possess the magnetic characteristic obtained in Fig. 3 by adding the mmf requirements of the iron to those of the enlarged airgap used in the slotless motor (17 mm). The slotless motor clearly needs more field mmf to drive a given flux across its larger gap except at very high fields where the absence of teeth to saturate just about offsets the difference in airgap. If the numbers of armature and field winding turns are the same, we should expect the torque and speed for a given high current to be similar. For lower currents, the slotless motor will give higher speed and lower torque. The curves of tractive effort against speed for the two motor types are given in Fig. 4 for identical numbers of field and armature turns and for the same supply voltage and regulation impedance. The difference in current drawn at the higher speeds is responsible for the different shapes of the curves of reactance emf given in Fig. 2.

The improvement at high speeds shown in Fig. 4 results simply from the lower flux density for a given current in the series field winding. This can be achieved in slotted motors by the normal process of field weakening using divert resistors. However the scope for such improvement is restricted by the inability of slotted motors to commutate high currents at high speed. With the slotless motor this restriction will not apply and the possibility exists of achieving further improvements over that given in Fig. 4 by means of field weakening. Thermal considerations and wheel-rail adhesion limits are the factors which will determine the ultimate capability of a slotless motor rather than commutation.

LOSSES

Eliminating the armature teeth immediately eliminates about half the armature iron loss. It also widens the permissible range of magnetic steels since the remaining iron operates at flux densities well below saturation. A low-loss grade of steel can therefore be used and a further reduction in iron loss by a factor of 2 or so will be achieved.

Pole-face loss caused by the high frequency pulsations in field at the main and interpole surfaces as the armature teeth pass is totally eliminated.

Placing the armature conductors in the airgap subjects them to eddy current losses induced by the main field in addition to those normally induced by leakage fields. To keep this loss to an acceptably low level it is necessary to use conductors built from strands less than about 1.5 mm wide in the tangential direction. The pitch of the conductors in most traction motors employing simple lap windings with single turn coils is around 2.5 mm. The conductors should therefore be split into two parallel strands and to avoid currents circulating between strands a transposition is required at the rear knuckle of the coil. Despite the subdivision and transposition, the eddy current loss can be serious and offsets the gain in iron and pole face losses.

The strands have to be arranged with their long side in the radial direction. This means that the strands present a wide face to the tangential leakage fields and the resulting eddy current loss can be substantial.

Taken together, the calculated losses for the slotless version of the 1000 HP mentioned above are comparable with the slotted motor over most of the speed range. The difference appears to favour the slotless version slightly at the higher speeds but is not significant.

THERMAL CONSIDERATIONS

Using standard methods, a steady-state thermal network with 22 nodes has been developed to model the slotless motor. Operating temperatures are found to be somewhat lower than in a slotted motor working at the same current. Typically an average winding temperature of 150°C would be expected in place of 160. The principal reason for this conclusion appears to be that the entire armature surface is used for heat transfer to the cooling air, whereas in a slotted motor, the tops of the slot wedges are ineffective. This difference in thermal resistance gives an effective increase in continuous rating of about 5%.

If the recent practice of using glass-fibre banding is followed however the extra thermal resistance which is imposed over the whole armature surface - not just at the ends as in a slotted motor - causes the continuous rating to be about 10% less than for the slotted motor. The expense of using a non-magnetic steel banding is amply justified therefore.

DEVELOPMENT PLANS

An experimental slotless motor is currently (end of 1981) nearing completion and will be undergoing laboratory tests during the first half of 1982. This machine uses the frame etc. of a 90 HP motor used in electrical multiple unit trains. An early objective is to compare the results of black band commutation tests of this machine and an unmodified motor of the same original type. Of particular importance will be overspeed and vibration tests to examine the structural integrity of the armature. The armature core and the arrangement of coils are illustrated in Fig. 5.

Work has started to convert 5 motors of 340 HP continuous rating. Two will be tested initially in the laboratory and subsequently designated as spares for the other three which it is intended will be fitted to one bogie of a Class 45/1 2500 HP main-line diesel-electric locomotive. A valuable feature of this particular motor is that the characteristics of the motor are hardly changed by the conversion to a slotless armature so that the three slotted motors will share load correctly with the three slotless ones and useful comparative trials can be conducted under service conditions.

CONCLUSIONS

Present day circumstances favour a return to the slotless construction of traction motor armatures.

The commutation of slotless machines is expected to be no longer the dominant factor restricting the design and operation.

Adopting slotless construction also permits higher powers to be attained at high speeds.

Provided that non-magnetic steel is used for the banding some increase in continuously rated current should be possible.

ACKNOWLEDGEMENTS

The author wishes to thank the Director of Research, British Railways Board for permission to publish this paper.

The author wishes also to acknowledge the benefit gained from numerous discussions with colleagues and friends in the Department of Mechanical and Electrical Engineering, British Railways Board, at the Derby Locomotive Works of British Rail Engineering Ltd and at Wilson Ford Ltd of Nottingham.

REFERENCES

1. Spooner, E., 1973, "Fully Slotless Turbogenerators", Proc. IEE 120 (12) pp 1507-1518.

2. Bocharov, V.I., 1972, "A Traction Motor with a Slotless Armature", Elektricheskaya; Teplovoznaya, Tyaga (6) 17-18 (in Russian) - Translation available from British Lending Library.

3. Bocharov, V.I., Sedov, V.I., and Kraizman, B.N., 1977, "No Load Losses in D.C. Traction Motors", Elektrotekhnika, 48, no 2, pp 10-13, (in Russian), Translation in Soviet Electrical Engineering (U.S.A.), 1977, Vol 48, no 2, pp 17-20.

4. Bocharov, V.I., and Sedov, V.I., 1976, "Evaluating the Thermal Loading of a Slotless Traction Motor Armature", Elektrotekhnika, 47, no 12, pp 30-32, (in Russian) Translation in Soviet Electrical Engineering (USA), 1976, Vol 47, no 12, pp 53-56.

5. Lamme, B.G., 1911, "A Theory of Commutation and its Application to Interpole Machines", Proc. AIEE 1911 pp 2049-2094.

6. Hellmund, R.E., 1935, "Flashing in Railway Motors Caused by Brush Jumping", AIEE Trans. 1935 54 p 1178-1185.

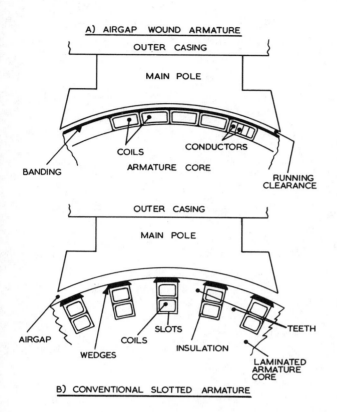

Figure 1 - Transverse cross sections of slotless and slotted motors in active position.

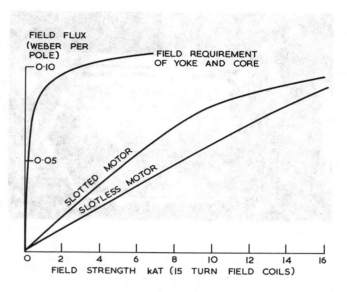

Figure 3 - No-load magnetic characteristics of typical slotless and slotted 1000 HP motors.

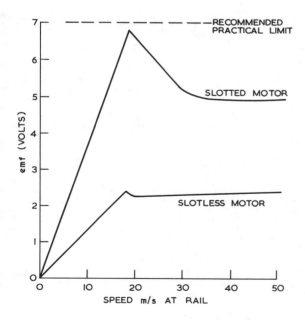

Figure 2 - Reactance emf with typical slotless and slotted 1000 HP 4 pole motors.

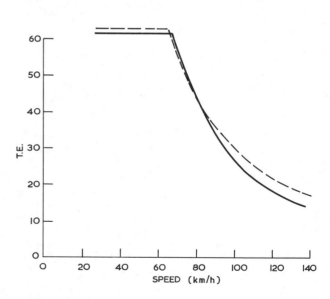

Figure 4 - Tractive effort per motor VS vehicle speed for typical slotless and slotted 1000 HP motors.

Figure 5 - Armature core and coils of 90 HP
        experimental slotless motor.

A 500 kW EDDY-CURRENT DYNAMOMETER

B.J. Chalmers   S.F. Ward and A.A. Pride

UMIST, UK   Froude Engineering Ltd., UK

INTRODUCTION

A 500 kW eddy-current dynamometer has been developed, which is the latest and largest machine in a new product range (1) primarily for use in the testing of automotive engines and associated components. The dynamometers are dry-gap, homopolar, disc-type, induction machines, arranged as shown in Figure 1. A pulsation of unidirectional flux is produced by rotation of a simple toothed steel rotor and causes power to be dissipated as induced eddy-current losses in a pair of stationary iron lossplates. Heat is removed by water flowing in internal circumferential channels formed in the face of each lossplate remote from the air gap.

The loading of this range of machines is very high by electrical machine standards. Thus, the peak air-gap flux density reaches about $1 \cdot 5$T and electric loading in the loss members is of the order of 150 A/mm on mean active diameter at base speed. The design figure for maximum loss density is 100 W/cm^2 based on active lossplate surface area, which is several times greater than that in a modern turbine generator. The air spaces between rotor and stator are ventilated by rotor action which maintains the rotor surfaces below 100°C, despite their small separation from the lossplates which attain steady-state surface temperatures of up to 250°C.

DESIGN CONSIDERATIONS

The design analysis procedure used in the development has been reported (1) and uses the proportionalities at maximum torque T_m and the speed at which it occurs N_m :-

$$T_m \propto \frac{DL_p F^2}{g_e} \qquad \ldots\ldots\ldots\ldots (1)$$

$$N_m \propto \rho \frac{p^2 g_e^2}{D^3 k_e F} \qquad \ldots\ldots\ldots\ldots (2)$$

Corrections are made for the variation of pulsation amplitude which occurs when the ratio pulsation wavelength/air gap is changed. Symbols used here are D = effective diameter, L = effective length, p = number of rotor teeth, F = pulsating m.m.f. per pole, g_e = effective air gap, ρ = lossplate resistivity at operating temperature, k_e = end-effect factor.

A primary aim was to achieve a steeply-rising torque/speed curve and adequate maximum torque, with low cost and rotor inertia. After initial selection of leading dimensions the influence of p was considered. The main effects of increasing p are :-

(1) Increases of T_m and N_m
(2) Decreased pulsation flux per pole and depth of penetration δ; the required lossplate thickness d is then reduced.

(3) Reduction of d increases the dissipation capacity, for a specified maximum temperature rise.
(4) k_e is increased, owing to the reduced pole pitch, and reduces N_m.
(5) With sufficiently high p, the torque may exceed that required. Air-gap length may then be increased and/or excitation decreased. Flux densities and unbalanced axial force are then reduced, and reduced rotor thickness and inertia may be considered.

On the other hand, with low p, δ is increased and may exceed d. There is then an associated loss of performance (1). For large machines, substantial benefits are to be gained by optimising p. Figure 2 compares computed torque/speed characteristics for p = 9 and p = 18, with 4 A excitation and ρ adjusted for temperature at each operating point. It is seen that p = 18 is advantageous at speeds down to as low as 310 rev/min. p = 9 has inadequate maximum torque margin and just fails to attain rated power at base speed (see Table 1).

TESTED PERFORMANCE

The tested 500 kW machine had $0 \cdot 602$ m rotor diameter and 1200 excitation coil turns. Figure 2 gives some measured torque/speed points for both p = 18 and p = 9 with 4 A excitation, compared with the computed predictions and with the required performance envelope.

An overall comparison of the new dynamometer and the largest machine in the older range of wet-gap drum-type construction is given in Table 1.

AXIAL LOAD PROBLEMS

Disc machines are prone to suffer from unbalanced axial forces. The symmetrical twin-coil excitation system shown in Figure 1 was adopted to minimise these problems, whilst achieving a saving in overall size compared with a single-coil system. Even so, a number of mechanical design changes were necessary during the development of the 500 kW machine, including :-

(i)   design of adequate rotor thickness to prevent bending of the teeth.
(ii) shaft material changed from a magnetic steel to stainless steel; this allowed a homogeneous hub to be used and reduced asymmetries of flux distribution near the inside diameter of the lossplates.
(iii) modification of rotor hub arrangement, to incorporate a larger spigot diameter and more fixing screws.
(iv) modification of the fixing of lossplates, to reduce distortion caused by high thermal stresses.

TABLE 1 - Comparison of old and new designs

	Old Design	New Design
Maximum power, kW	373	500
Base speed for maximum power, rev/min	1380	1900
Maximum speed, rev/min	3500	4500
Maximum torque, Nm	2590	2500
Inertia, kgm^2	4·86	2·25
Weight, kg	2083	1626
Relative cost	1·0	1·035
Relative power/cost	1·0	1·31
Relative torque/weight	1·0	1·24

APPLICATIONS

The characteristics of high torque at low speed and low parasitic loss at high speed make the range of dynamometers suitable for testing a wide range of prime movers. Extensive field trials, endurance tests and operating experience have led to rapid industrial acceptance, the user list currently totalling over 200 machines. Large-scale industrial applications are associated with automatic handling and testing of engines. The thyristor-control of dynamometer excitation is frequently operated under computer control, as in an installation where up to 40 200 kW engines are tested per day. Other applications include research and development departments of manufacturers of engines and associated equipment, fuel and oil test laboratories and vehicle chassis dynamometers.

The 500 kW machine is for use in applications requiring particularly high torque at low speeds. These include a wide range of transmission testing requirements and testing of diesel engines for buses and trucks.

An advantage of the closed-circuit water-cooling system is the adaptability to recovery of energy. The outlet water at 70-90°C may be used for many purposes, such as pre-heating of boiler feed water. An example within the test bed is the heating of bulk supplies of oil and water for automatic filling of engines prior to test, thus reducing their warm-up time on the test bed.

Illustrations of machine construction and applications will be included in the presentation, together with further results of a current programme of tests.

REFERENCES

1. Chalmers, B.J. and Dukes, B.J., 1980, Proc. IEE, 127, B, pp.20-28.

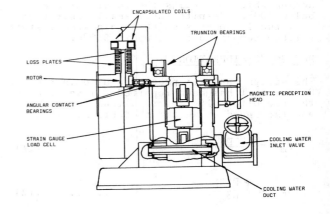

Figure 1.   Cross-section of dynamometer.

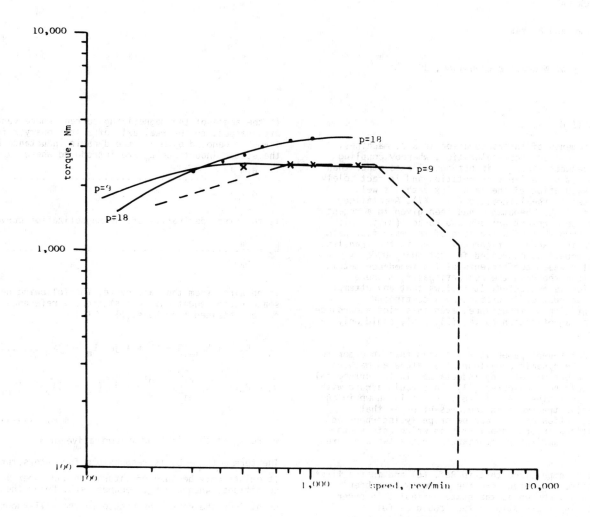

Figure 2.   Torque/speed characteristics with 4A excitation.
            Computed curves.
            Test points : ●p = 18, x p = 9
            ---------- = required performance envelope.

THE PHENOMENON OF INTERSATURATION IN THE TRANSIENT OPERATION OF INDUCTION MOTORS ARISING FROM SATURATION OF THE MAIN FLUX PATH

J.E. Brown and P. Vas

University of Newcastle upon Tyne, UK

INTRODUCTION

The phenomenon of intersaturation in a.c. machines, sometimes called cross-saturation, whereby coupling occurs between windings in orthogonal axes other than as a result of saliency or rotation and in fact solely due to saturation of the main flux path, is well documented in the literature (1) - (7). A detailed analysis of the phenomenon has been given in a recent paper by the present writers and Kovacs (8) in which it was shown that if saturation of the main flux path is taken into account rigorously then in the transient voltage equations expressed in stationary DQdq axis form all sixteen coefficients of the impedance matrix differ from those in the conventional form where saturation is neglected. It follows that any attempt to take account of saturation by a continuous representation of inductance, even in strict accordance with the magnetization curve, (9), (10), could only be in error.

In another recent paper it was stated that in order to predict the dynamic behaviour of a saturated machine two different magnetizing inductances in two orthogonal axes should be considered (11). This would accord with the analysis given in Ref. (8), but it is shown in an alternative treatment in the present paper that intersaturation effects can be properly incorporated in equations in orthogonal axes in which both stator inductances and rotor inductances in the two axes are equal.

It must be emphasized that in Ref. (8) and in the first alternative presented here the currents have been deliberately chosen as the state variables in order that the intersaturation effect could be fully explained mathematically in equations of a general form enabling the errors in alternative treatments to be demonstrated. However the present paper goes on to show that if flux linkages are taken as state variables saturation can be fully taken into account, including the effects of intersaturation, without revealing the nature of the latter.

GENERALISED SPACE-VECTOR EQUATIONS INCORPORATING THE EFFECTS OF MAIN FLUX PATH SATURATION

It was shown in Ref. (8) that the stator and rotor space vector (12) voltage differential equations in a general reference frame rotating at an arbitrary speed ω_a will take the following form in which no restriction is made for saturation of the main flux path

$$\bar{u}'_S = R_S \bar{i}'_S + L_{S1}\frac{d\bar{i}'_S}{dt} + \frac{d\bar{\psi}'_m}{dt} + j\omega_a(L_{S1}\bar{i}'_S + \bar{\psi}'_m) \quad \dots\dots\dots\dots\dots (1)$$

$$\bar{u}'_r = R_r \bar{i}'_r + L_{r1}\frac{d\bar{i}'_r}{dt} + \frac{d\bar{\psi}'_m}{dt} + j(\omega_a - \omega_r)(L_{r1}\bar{i}'_r + \psi'_m) \dots (2)$$

where R_S, L_{S1} and R_r, L_{r1} are the stator and rotor resistances and leakage inductances respectively, $\bar{u}'_S$, $\bar{u}'_r$, $\bar{i}'_S$, $\bar{i}'_r$, $\bar{\psi}'_S$, $\bar{\psi}'_r$ are the stator and rotor voltage, current and flux space vectors in the arbitrary reference frame, and ω_r is the speed of the rotor. $\bar{\psi}'_m$ is the space vector of the magnetizing flux and

$$\bar{\psi}'_m = L_m \bar{i}'_m = L_m(\bar{i}'_S + \bar{i}'_r). \quad \dots\dots\dots\dots\dots\dots (3)$$

If the angle of the magnetizing current space vector with respect to the real axis of a stationary reference frame is denoted by μ and the dynamic inductance L and the static inductance L_m are introduced where

$$L = \frac{d|\bar{\psi}_m|}{d|\bar{i}_m|} \dots\dots\dots\dots\dots\dots\dots\dots\dots\dots\dots (4a)$$

is the first derivative of the magnetization curve and

$$L_m = \frac{\bar{\psi}_m}{\bar{i}_m} \dots\dots\dots\dots\dots\dots\dots\dots\dots\dots\dots\dots\dots (4b)$$

is obtained from the same curve, the following new space vector equations in a stationary reference frame can be obtained from Eqns. (1) - (3)

$$\bar{u}_S = R_S\bar{i}_S + L_{S1}\frac{d\bar{i}_S}{dt} + L\frac{d\bar{i}_m}{dt} + j\omega_\mu(L_m - L)\bar{i}_m \quad \dots\dots\dots (5)$$

$$\bar{u}_r = R_r\bar{i}_r + L_{r1}\frac{d\bar{i}_r}{dt} + L\frac{d\bar{i}_m}{dt} + j\omega_\mu(L_m - L)\bar{i}_m - j\omega_r(L_{r1}\bar{i}_r + L_m\bar{i}_m) \quad \dots\dots\dots (6)$$

where ω_μ is the first time derivative of μ.

The term $\omega_\mu(L_m - L)$ is responsible for intersaturation. It exists only because of saturation and under linear conditions, when $L = L_m$, becomes zero. Under these conditions the equations reduce to the well-known form.

THE NEW GENERAL TWO-AXIS EQUATIONS

If equations (5) and (6) are resolved into their real and imaginary parts and if for simplicity a cylindrical rotor machine is assumed the following matrix equation is obtained

$$\dots\dots (7)$$

$$
\begin{vmatrix} u_{SD} \\ u_{SQ} \\ u_{rd} \\ u_{rq} \end{vmatrix}
=
\begin{vmatrix}
R_S+(L_{S1}+L)p & -\omega_\mu(L_m-L) & Lp & -\omega_\mu(L_m-L) \\
\omega_\mu(L_m-L) & R_S+(L_{S1}+L)p & \omega_\mu(L_m-L) & Lp \\
Lp & \omega_r L_m - \omega_\mu(L_m-L) & R_r+(L_{r1}+L)p & \omega_r L_r - \omega_\mu(L_m-L) \\
-\omega_r L_m + \omega_\mu(L_m-L) & Lp & -\omega_r L_r + \omega_\mu(L_m-L) & R_r+(L_{r1}+L)p
\end{vmatrix}
$$

where $L_r = L_{r1} + L_m$.

Equation (7) is a complete alternative to equation (13) of Ref. (8) and it will be shown below that it has advantages over the latter.

In equation (7) both L and L_m are continuously changing with $\bar{i}_m$ because of saturation and consequently all sixteen terms of the impedance matrix are affected. Coupling is created between stator SD and SQ axes, between rotor rd and rq axes and between stator and rotor SD and rq, and SQ and rd axes, by the term $\omega_\mu(L_m - L)$.

In the absence of saturation this term becomes zero, the cross-coupling due to saturation disappears and equation (7) reduces to the normal form of the DQdq equations, (e.g. Equation (A 10) of Ref. (8)). It is evident that it cannot be correct to seek to take account of main flux path saturation by simply representing the magnetizing inductance as an appropriate continuous function of the magnetizing current in the normal equations.

It is worth noting that the self inductances in the stator SD and SQ axes are both equal to $L_{S1} + L$, and those in the rotor rd and rq axes are both equal to $L_{r1} + L$. Therefore, as pointed out above, it is not essential to have different inductances in orthogonal axes in order to take account of saturation.

Finally it can also be shown that at the instants when the position of the magnetizing current space vector is in one or other of the two axes there is no coupling due to intersaturation. Physically this arises because magnetizing current only flows in that axis along which the magnetizing space vector is directed. As a consequence it is possible to devise special reference frames in which the $\omega_\mu(L_m - L)$ intersaturation term is eliminated, but a discussion of these special reference frames will be deferred until another occasion.

The non-linear voltage differential equations, equation (7), can be solved by well-known numerical techniques using a digital computer. For this purpose the equations are rearranged into the following state variable form,

$$\dot{\underline{x}} = \underline{\underline{A}} \, \underline{x} + \underline{\underline{B}} \, \underline{u} \quad ....(8)$$

where

$$\underline{x} = \begin{bmatrix} i_{SD}, & i_{SQ}, & i_{rd}, & i_{rq} \end{bmatrix}^T \quad ....(8a)$$

is the column vector of state variables

$$\underline{u} = \begin{bmatrix} u_{SD}, & u_{SQ}, & u_{rd}, & u_{rq} \end{bmatrix}^T \quad ....(8b)$$

is the column vector of voltages

$$\underline{\underline{A}} = -\underline{\underline{L}}'^{-1}\underline{\underline{R}}' \quad ....(8c)$$

is the state matrix

$$\underline{\underline{B}} = \underline{\underline{L}}'^{-1} \quad ....(8d)$$

is the control matrix.

$\underline{\underline{L}}'$ and $\underline{\underline{R}}'$ can be obtained directly from equation (7) and for instance

$$\underline{\underline{L}}' = \begin{bmatrix} L_{S1} + L & 0 & L & 0 \\ 0 & L_{S1} + L & 0 & L \\ L & 0 & L_{r1} + L & 0 \\ 0 & L & 0 & L_{r1} + L \end{bmatrix} \quad ....(8e)$$

This is a very much simpler form than that given in equation(21d) of Ref. (8) in which all sixteen terms are non-zero, and it leads to a considerable reduction in computing time.

AN ALTERNATIVE APPROACH UTILIZING FLUX-LINKAGES AS STATE VARIABLES

As an alternative to the above the following simpler equations in the stationary reference frame can be derived from equations (4) and (5) if the flux-linkages are taken as state variables.

$$\frac{d\psi_{SD}}{dt} = u_{SD} - \frac{1}{T_{S1}} (\psi_{SD} - |\overline{\psi}_m|) + \omega_\mu\psi_{SQ} \quad ....(9)$$

$$\frac{d\psi_{SQ}}{dt} = u_{SQ} - \frac{\psi_{SQ}}{T_{S1}} - \omega_\mu\psi_{SD} \quad ....(10)$$

$$\frac{d\psi_{rd}}{dt} = u_{rd} - \frac{1}{T_{r1}} (\psi_{rd} - |\overline{\psi}_m|) + (\omega_\mu - \omega_r)\psi_{rq} \quad .....(11)$$

$$\frac{d\psi_{rq}}{dt} = u_{rq} - \frac{\psi_{rq}}{T_{r1}} - (\omega_\mu - \omega_r)\psi_{rd} \quad ....(12)$$

where T_{S1} and T_{r1} are stator and rotor leakage time constants, respectively, and $|\psi_m|$ is the absolute value of the magnetizing flux space vector. It is evident from equations (9) - (12) that although a stationary reference frame is used there is coupling between the stator axes because of the ω_μ terms and additional coupling between the rotor axes because of these terms.

Although it is clear that the cross-coupling is associated with ω_μ the specific intersaturation factor $\omega_\mu(L_m - L)$ is not revealed. However its effect is taken into account quantitively when equations (9) - (12) are used in computation. For this purpose only the static inductance L_m needs to be known, as the dynamic inductance L is not required.

THE APPLICATION OF THE NEWLY DEVELOPED EQUATIONS

The newly developed equations, Eqn. (8) or Eqns. (9) - (12), to-gether with the equation of motion completely describe the transient behaviour of cylindrical-rotor a.c. machines when saturation of the main flux path is to be taken into account. They give results which agree exactly with those given by the equations in Ref. (8), but they are simpler and require less computing time than the latter.

The equations have been developed to meet the need to calculate the performance of an induction motor in a new method of braking where high levels of saturation are encountered and where two or three separate stages of braking may exist (13). For the calculation of the second and third stages accurate calculation of the earlier stage(s) is essential. The results of this work will be presented elsewhere.

In the present paper the results of calculations of the familiar transient starting performance of an induction motor at various levels of saturation by conventional methods and by the equations given above will be considered in order to highlight the effect of taking saturation into account by the methods described here.

The calculations were performed for a 3-phase laboratory machine having the magnetizing curve shown in Fig. 1 and the following parameters

$R_S = 1.86\Omega$, $R_r = 2.12\Omega$,

$L_{S1} = 0.011$ H, $L_{r1} = 0.006$ H,

$J = 0.0625$ kg.m^2,

$U_1 = 240$ V, $U_2 = 360$ V

Fig. 2 shows the curves of L_m and L the static and dynamic inductances, respectively, derived from Fig.1., as functions of the magnitude of the magnetizing current space vector. It can be seen that for low values of the latter $L = L_m$ and there is no intersaturation effect. However for high levels of saturation the difference between the two curves is very great and the intersaturation effects may be expected to be significant.

It should be emphasized that in deriving the inductance functions from the magnetization curve by the fitting of successive curves care must be taken to ensure that both the fitting curves and their first derivatives match at the beginning and end points of the successive intervals.

Figs. 3 and 4 show the torque developed by the machine during run-up for voltages U_1 and U_2 giving different levels of saturation and Fig. 5 shows the corresponding currents. Curves A are calculated using the conventional equations, curves B are calculated by the methods given here, and curves C are calculated using the conventional equations but seeking to take account of saturation by the use of the true continuous representation of the L_m function.

Curves A and B of Fig. 3 show very little difference as is to be expected. Curves A and B of Figs. 4 and 5 show significant differences particularly in the torque peaks, but the most significant result is that shown by curve C in Fig. 4. Assuming curve B in the figure to be 'correct' it appears that the method on which curve C is based gives a very incorrect calculation of the torque particularly in that it underestimates the torque peaks. In general curves B are much closer to curves A than to curves C.

These results are typical of others which have been obtained for the braking mode for which experimental verification will be presented later. They serve, without experimental verification, to illustrate the main point the authors wish to make, namely that saturation and intersaturation effects are significant, as is generally accepted, and that they can and should be taken into account in calculations by the methods described here which satisfy the demands of mathematical rigour.

CONCLUSIONS

A new set of generalised equations have been developed, with currents deliberately chosen as state variables, which describe the transient performance of an induction motor with saturation taken into account. They reveal the nature of the intersaturation phenomenon.

An alternative set of equations has also been developed, with flux-linkages as state variables which take saturation into account without revealing the nature of this phenomenon.

Calculations based on the two sets of equations are identical. Calculations based on conventional equations but with the magnetizing inductance represented by the proper continuous function of the magnetizing current give very different results. When these results are compared with those obtained by ignoring saturation it emerges that it would be better to so ignore it than to attempt to take it into account by the deceptively attractive approximation used in these calculations and adopted elsewhere.

Finally the authors would point out that because of the generality of its form the theory is capable of much further development and in particular will be applied to the case of the salient-pole machine.

REFERENCES

1. Adkins, B., Harley, R.G; "The general theory of alternating current machines. Application to practical problems". Chapman and Hall, London 1975.

2. White, D.C., Woodson, H.H.; "Electromechanical energy conversion". Wiley and Sons, 1959.

3. Slemon, G.R.; "Equivalent circuits for transformers and machines including non-linear effects". Proc. IEE. V. 100, pp 129-143, 1953.

4. Slemon, G.R; "Equivalent curcuits for single-phase motors". AIEE Transactions, V. 74, pp 1335-1343, 1956.

5. Shackshaft, G; "Data requirements", Symposium on Power System Dynamics, U.M.I.S.T., Manchester, 1973.

6. Shackshaft, G., Henser, P.B.; "Model of generator saturation for use in power system studies". Proc. IEE, V. 126, pp 259-263.

7. Demerdash, N.A., Hamilton, H.B.; "A simplified approach to the determination of saturated reactances of large turbogenerators under load". Trans. IEEE, PAS 95, pp 560-569, 1976.

8. Brown, J.E., Kovacs, K.P., Vas, P.; "A method of including the effects of main flux path saturation in the generalised equations of a.c. machines". IEEE, PES. Winter Meeting, Feb. 1982. Paper WM 239-2 to be published in IEEE Trans. PAS.

9. Smith, J.R., Rogers, G.J., Buckley, G.W.; "Application of induction motor simulation models to power station auxiliary pump drives". IEEE Trans. PAS. 98, pp 1824-1831, 1979.

10. Harashima, F., Haneyoshi, T., Inaba, H.; "Operating performance of inverter-fed induction motors considering magnetic saturation". IEEE PAS, pp 586-591, 1980.

11. Melkebeck, J.A.A.; "Some effects of the magnetising field saturation in induction machines". 16th UPEC University of Sheffield, April 1981.

12. Kovacs, K.P., Racz, I.; "Transiente Vorgange in Wechselstrommaschinen". Akademia Kiado, Budapest 1954.

13. Brown, J.E., Gamble, C.R., Norman, F.; "The rapid braking of induction motors utilizing capacitor-self-excitation techniques". 16th UPEC.

ACKNOWLEDGEMENT

The authors would like to acknowledge financial assistance from the Science and Engineering Research Council.

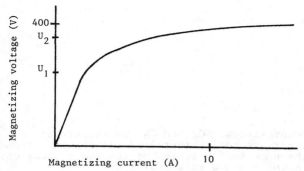

Fig. 1 Magnetization curve

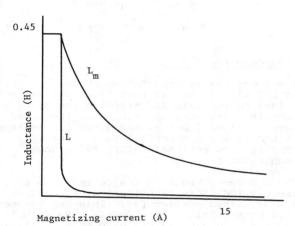

Fig. 2   Static and dynamic inductances

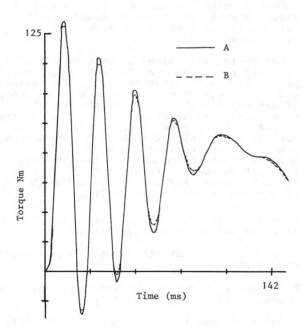

Fig. 3 Torque variation of an induction motor on
run-up for a voltage U_1

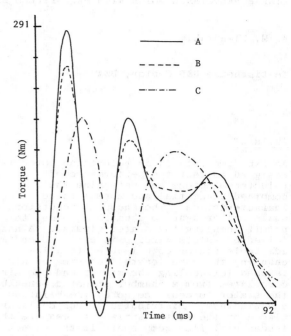

Fig. 4   Torque variation of an induction motor on
run-up for a voltage U_2

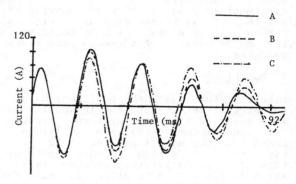

Fig. 5 Current variation of an induction motor
on run-up for a voltage U_2

LINEAR RELUCTANCE MOTOR WITH HALF-FILLED END-SLOTS STATOR WINDING

A. M. El-Antably

Westinghouse R&D Center, USA

ABSTRACT

An experimental linear reluctance motor is designed to test the performance of reluctance motors and determine their combined tangential and normal force characteristics. The ends of the stator coils are brought to a patching panel to permit changing the stator winding. A half-filled end-slots winding is utilized and an adaptable stator core is used to allow changing the core length. Compressed air is used for cooling the stator and the air circulates from a chamber situated beneath the stator to cool the core, the main and end windings. Distributed search coils are placed on the stator surface to measure the fundamental flux components in the direct- and quadrature-axis positions. Search coils are also used to measure the core flux. The stator is equipped with a platform which has piezoelectric force transducers capable of measuring forces in 3-orthogonal directions. Numerical solution of the field equations for the LRM in the direct- and quadrature-axis positions is used to predict the flux density, tangential and normal forces. Good agreement is reported between experimental and theoretical values of flux density and forces. It is shown that LRMs could be used for the propulsion of advanced land-transport vehicles.

INTRODUCTION

Linear synchronous machines (LSMs) have recently attracted interest in applications with advanced transport systems. Linear reluctance motors (LRMs) are similar to LSMs, but they do not have dc field excitation. LRMs have the advantage over LSMs of having relatively cheaper tracks which consists of a reaction rail made from mild steel. LRMs are proposed to provide propulsion and lift force to magnetically suspended vehicles for advanced urban transport systems.

This paper will describe an experimental LRM which was used to test the characteristics of LRMs. A procedure for the design of LRMs for transport applications is outlined and some predicted values are validated by experimental results.

Theoretical Model

A semi-analytical solution to the airgap field equations of an LRM having a segmental-rotor was used, it was described earlier (1). The segmental rotor was represented by a continuous iron surface with a periodic magnetic potential distribution. A closed form solution for the airgap field in the direct (D) and quadrature (Q)-axis positions is provided. The machine is represented by an equivalent circuit shown in Figure 1, where R_s and X_ℓ is the stator resistance and leakage reactance per phase,

respectively. C_d and C_q are the airgap reactance coefficients and are obtained from the numerical solution of the field equations in the D and Q axis positions.

The resistance R and reactance X are given by

$$R = \frac{1}{2} X_m (C_d - C_q) \sin 2\delta \qquad (1)$$

$$X = X_m (C_d \cos^2\delta + C_q \sin^2\delta) \qquad (2)$$

Procedure for the LRM Design

The Romag (2) transportation system has used an LRM with a notched rail (i.e. salient pole rotor) to levitate and propel a low speed vehicle. However, no details of the motor were provided. Boldea and Nasar (3) designed an LRM having a segmental rotor, but they used the conventional rotary reluctance machine theory.

The LRM described here was designed to be incoporated in an existing test rig, which was described earlier (4). This has imposed some constraints on its design. Nevertheless these design constraints have been partially offset by designing an LRM with an adaptable core and windings. The design procedure is as follows,

1-Determine the specifications (nominal airgap length, motor rated thrust, motor rated vertical force and maximum terminal line voltage).

2-Choose initial values of pole pitch, slot to tooth ratio, number of slots per phase, number of turns per coil, slot details and rotor segment specifications. The design of the rotor segments was done using the numerical field solution. The basis for the choice of the optimum segment shape is the consideration that as much iron as possible should be removed from the back of the segment in order to maximize the quadrature-axis intersegmental reluctance, subject to the constraint that local saturation should be avoided in the D-axis position.

3-Obtain approximate values of C_d and C_q from the curves given in reference (1).

4-calculate the LRM steady-state performance and weight.

5-If needed, readjust the turns per coil for maximum stator current density.

6-Check optimum LRM performance and weight.

7-The numerical field solutions is subsequently used to obtain more accurate values of C_d and C_q for calculating the performance.

Table 1 shows the details of the designed LRM. It should be noted that this is not an optimum design, as the design was constrained due to the fact that the LRM should drive an existing test facility. The optimum design of LRMs for transport applications will be discussed in a later publication. A double-layer lap half-filled end slot winding described by Oberretl (7) was used. The extended winding, also described by Oberretl, was utilized and results will be shown elsewhere. An adaptable core was employed by butting sections to the main 4-pole section core as shown in Figure 3. Ooi (5) have shown that the motor length must be an integral multiple of the pole pitch to avoid vertical force pulsations and this has been observed in this LRM. Figures 2, 3, and 4 show the details of this motor, search coils on the stator surface are similar to those designed by Caldentey (6). Figures 2 and 5 show the cooling air cycle.

Experimental Results

Figures 6, 7, and 8 show good agreement between measured and predicted flux densities and forces.

CONCLUSIONS

The procedure for designing the LRM for transport applications has been outlined. It is possible to design an LRM to provide some of the lift force and adequate propulsion to a magnetically suspended vehicle for advanced transport systems.

ACKNOWLEDGMENTS

This work has been done at Sussex University (in England) and the author is grateful to Dr. J. D. Edwards, Dr. G. Williams and Mr. R. Doe. This project was funded by the Science Research Council of England.

REFERENCES

1. Edwards, J. D. and El-Antably, A. M., "Segmental-rotor linear reluctance motors with large airgaps", Proc. IEE, 1978, 125, (3), pp. 209-214.

2. Ross, J.A., "ROMAG transportation system", Proc. IEE, 1973, 61, pp. 617-620.

3. Nasar, S. A. and Boldea, I, "Thrust and normal forces in a segmented-secondary linear reluctance motor", ibid, 1975, 122, (9), pp. 922-924.

4. Lindon, P., et al, "Closed-loop control of LRMs for traction applications", IEE Electrical Variable-Speed Drives Conference Publication No. 179, pp. 191-194.

5. Ooi, B. T., "Homopolar linear synchronous motor dynamic equivalents", IEEE Trans., 1977, Vol. MAG-13, No. 5, pp. 1424-1426.

6. Caldentey, E. L., "Measurement of load-angle of LRMs", D. Phil. Thesis, Sussex University (U.K.), 1977.

7. Oberretl, K., "Linear motors with s special double-layer windings", IEE Conference publication No. 120, 1974, pp. 15-21.

Table 1 LRM Design Sheet

Pole pitch	152.4mm
No. of poles	6
Slots p.p.p.p.	2
No. of slots	42
Tooth width	8.0 mm
Slot width	17.4 mm
Slot depth	66.5 mm
Core length	1074.8 mm
Core depth	73.5 mm
Core width	152.4 mm
Airgap length	12.5 mm
Airgap flux density	0.294 T
Segments speed	5 m/s
Normal force (at $\delta = 0$)	2.170 KN
Tractive force (at $\delta = 45°$)	314 N
Current loading	73 kA/m

Parameters

C_d	0.93
C_q	.54
X_c	3.35 Ω/phase

Winding

Double layer, compact, half-filled end slots, series star

Total turns/coil	48
Conductor material	Copper
Conductor area	6.125 mm^2
Coil-span/coil-pitch ratio	1:1
Length of mean turn	838.2 mm
R_S (stator resistance)	0.36 Ω/phase

For transport systems a speed of 20 m/s is appropriate, and the prediced performance is given as follows:

Frequency	65.6 Hz
Speed	20 m/s
X_c	13.4 Ω/phase
Goodness factor	37.3
Leakage inductance	6.4 Ω/phase
Efficiency (at $\delta = 45°$)	0.88 p.u.
Power factor (at $\delta = 45°$)	0.182 p.u.
Line voltage	927.7 V
Line current	28.28 A
Input	45.4 KVA
Total losses	1.58 KW
Output power	6.28 KW

LRMs have high efficiency and a low power factor and effective ways of improving the power factor has been found and will be reported later. The weight of this LRM has not been optimized as it was stationary in the test facility while the segmental track was moving, for experimental convenience.

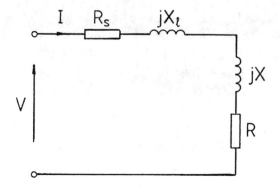

Figure 1 Equivalent circuit for LRM

Figure 2 A photo of the LRM showing the coils, the end-connections panel and the cooling system

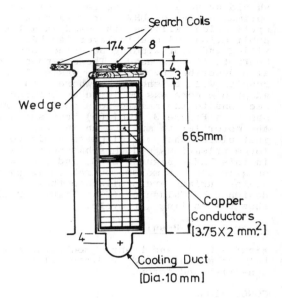

Figure 4 Slot details of the LRM stator

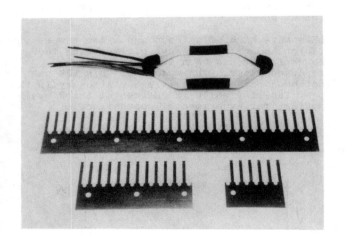

Figure 3 A stator coil and core laminations

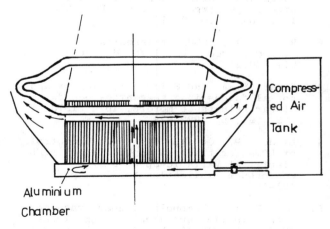

Figure 5 Cooling air scheme for the LRM stator

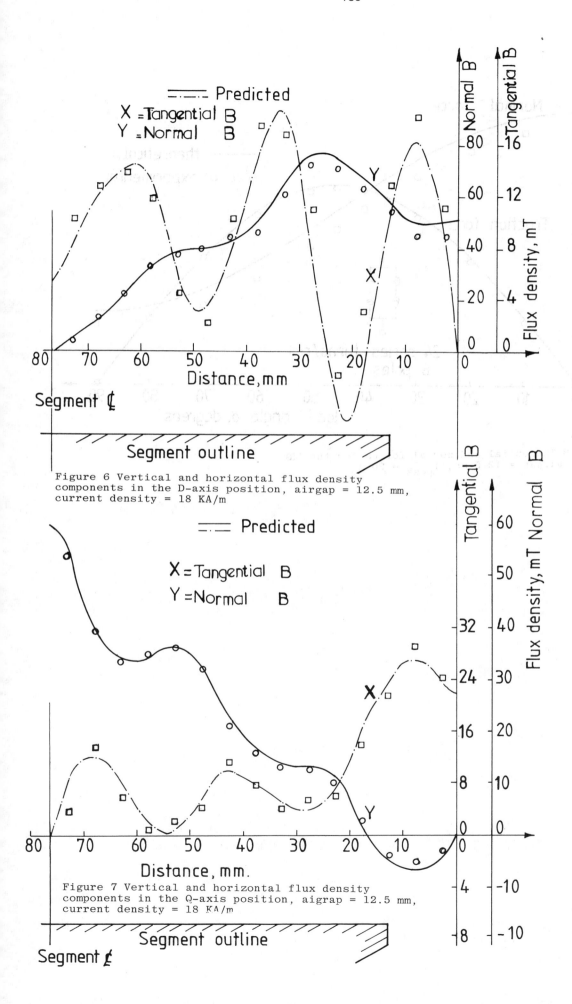

Figure 6 Vertical and horizontal flux density components in the D-axis position, airgap = 12.5 mm, current density = 18 KA/m

Figure 7 Vertical and horizontal flux density components in the Q-axis position, aigrap = 12.5 mm, current density = 18 KA/m

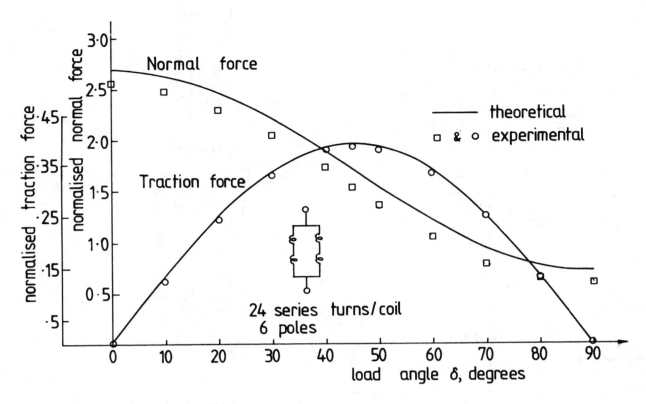

Figure 8 Tangential and normal forces for the LRM
stator, airgap = 12.5 mm, I_{peak} = 20 A

AN IMPROVED RELUCTANCE MOTOR

P.J. Lawrenson   M.H. Nagrial

University of Leeds, UK   Faculty of Eng'g, Univ. of Garyounis, Benghazi, Libya

INTRODUCTION

The flux guided reluctance motors are modern class of reluctance motors. They are attaractive due to their one-piece lamination and ease of construction. The earlier attempts to exploit flux guided designs (including single and multi-flux guides per pole) did not result in improved performance (Kostko(1), Honsinger(2), Fong and Htsui(3)). The earlier designs did not employ optimum dimensions for flux guides. The availability of modern high speed digital computers had been the main reason to employ numerical optimization techniques for prediction of optimum designs (Nagrial & Lawrenson(4)). The optimum design is predicted using a 3 h.p induction motor as a base machine. As the induction and reluctance motors have similar stators the reluctance motor rotor is optimized, fabricated and tested as no improvement is to be gained by optimizing stator due to temperature rise consideration. The aim of this article is to present the experimental performance obtained from the optimized design. It has been found that based on synchronous performance, the reluctance motor could be rated equal to induction motor. The increased output had been around 30% more than the best available earlier reluctance motors. The new design had improved pull-in performance and did not exhibit any instability when operated with variable frequency supply.

DESIGN OPTIMIZATION

A general optimization problem can be defined as follows:-
Find $X = (x_1, x_2, \ldots \ldots x_n)$
such that $/F(X)/$ is an optimum and $g_i(x) \geqslant 0$

for $i=1,2,\ldots\ldots m$ where x is a set of independent variables and $g_i(x)$ is a set of constraints, and $/F(X)/$ is termed as objective function. The Powell method is conjunction with SUMT technique (4) is employed to predict the optimum design for flux guided reluctance motor. The objective function is formulated with a view to achieve maximum output from a given frame size while meeting other performance requirements, formulated as constraints. Though a number of objective functions can be formulated but the following has been used in the present study.

$$F(X) = \frac{-\text{Full load output}}{10^3} - P\sum_{i=1}^{m}\frac{1}{g_i(x)} \qquad (1)$$

where P is the penalty parameter whose value is decreased after successive optimization. Apart from the performance requirements to be constrained, the independent design variables (design dimensions) are also constrained to have upper and lower bounds. The design variables are expresed as logs of design dimensions. It serves two purposes; firstly the variables are automatically scaled to a narrow range which increases convergence rate and secondly the design dimensions are indirectly constrained to have positive values. It has been found that no significant improvement in performance could be achieved in small frame sizes when stator dimensions are also optimized, though it is likely to achieve higher output in the case of bigger machines. Table:1 shows the performance obtained when both stator and rotor dimensions and rotor only are optimized. Employing 6 variables (stator+rotor) has not resulted in any significant improvement in output though it has substantially increased computing time which is evident from the number of function evaluations.

TABLE 1:-Optimum output with number of variables.

No.of Variables	Output(Kw)	No. of function Evaluations
2 (Rotor)	2.479	48
3 (Rotor)	2.4814	52
6 (Stator+Rotor)	2.5192	294

Moreover, employing multi-flux guides (1 flux guide per pole) may not be attractive from mechanical considerations and the improvement in output may not be justifiable due to increased manufacturing cost for small machines. Table 2 shows the maximum performance achieved for 1,2 and 3 flux guides per pole respectively.There is negligible increase in output power.

TABLE 2:-Optimum output with increasing flux guides

Flux guides/Pole	Output(Kw)	No.of Function Evaluations
1	2.479	48
2	2.531	168
3	2.533	258

Therefore, the stator dimensions are kept fixed and the rotor with one flux guide per pole is assumed. It has been found that channel depth behond a certain value (40 x air gap length) has no significant influence on the output of reluctance motor and even the channel depth does not affect the position of optimum and T. Similarly a smaller air gap length would be beneficial electromagnetically, the air gap length is limited by mechanical considerations.Hence, the channel depth and air gap length are taken as fixed, the later equal to induction motor air gap length. In earlier approaches (1,2,3), the iron bridges at the end of flux guides have been assumed to be highly saturated and hence to behave as non-magnetic space. It has been shown elsewhere (Nagrial (5)) that though the iron bridges are highly saturated but this does not mean that it carries negligible flux. An experimental method accounting for the effects of iron bridges has been given in the form of a factor termed as bridge correction factor (F_b). This factor has been employed to modify flux guide permeance factor (W/T). The optimum design is also sensitive to iron losses. The iron losses in reluctance motor does not remain constant but varies with load. They could be 150-200% of the no load losses. It is important to have a reliable iron loss figure available and in present approach it was obtained by actual tests on reluctance machines. A standard modern induction motor is selected as a base machine for design and comparison purposes. The existing motor rotor laminations including slotting has been used to reduce cost and time involved in building the rotor. It may be worth mentioning that optimum configuration always result in a symmetrical design as opposed to asymmetrical design proposed in reference (3). The design program is capable of taking asymmetry into account but to simplify the process and reduce number of variables, a symmetrical design is assumed. Fig.1 shows the cross-section of optimum reluctance motor rotor as predicted using optimization technique. The important design parameters for the optimum design are given below:

Channel width/pole pitch γ = 0.306
Flux guide span/pole pitch α = 0.75
air gap length g=0.012"
Flux guide thickness T=0.25"
Channel depth = 40 x air gap length

The rotor slots and channels are filled with copper and flux guides are without any conducting material.

PERFORMANCE CHARACTERISTICS

Synchronous Performance

Fig.2 shows the synchronous characteristics for the optimum reluctance motor compared with a modern commercial reluctance motor.The full load output is equal to full load induction motor output. The reluctance motor rating is taken as 2/3 of the pull-out power and it is operated at full load for about 5 hours to check the temperature rise. The temperature rise is about 40°C in one hour and remains the same for another 4 hours. The same temperature rise is obtained for equivalent induction motor. This confirms the approach adopted for rating of reluctance motors. It may be mentioned that the iron losses in the reluctance motors are usually higher than induction motors at full load and it is likely that reluctance motors may be rated higher than induction motors if the iron losses can be reduced,as there are no rotor copper losses due to synchronous nature of operation.

Pull-in Performance

In most applications, the reluctance motors are required not only to have higher output while running at synchronous speed but should be able to synchronize higher inertia loads at full load.If it is so then the motor may be derated on the basis of pull-in performance. Fig.3 shows the pull-in characteristics for optimum machine. It is found that the new reluctance motor is capable of synchronising 5 times rotor inertia at full load. The present rotor is of a high inertia because of stainless steel end plates and long shaft. A commercial, die cast rotor manufactured to the same design would have lower inertia and hence better pull-in performance. Fig.3 also shows the pull-in characteristics for a modern commercial reluctance motor .

Stability

The modern reluctance motors are often operated in variable-speed applications and supplied from variable frequency sources. It is well known that the reluctance motor exhibit instability for a band of frequencies. The instability may be quantitavely defined and easily measured by a curve in V/f, f plane. The normal operation requires constant V/f, to keep constant flux per pole, with some adjustments at lower frequencies, and thus either the instability curve must be non-existant or it should be well below the rated V/f of the machine. It has been shown by Lawrenson and Bowes (6) that higher inertias may increase the tendency to instability.The optimum rotor did not exhibit any instability even at low V/f values and higher inertias. Though a rotor with non-optimum channel width (γ =0.25) and optimum flux guide (α =0.75) did exhibit instability but that was also well below the rated V/f as shown in fig.4 Table 3 shows the comparison of new optimum rotor compared with existing other designs of reluctance motors(Cruickshank e.al.(1),(3)). This comparison has been drawn on the basis of existing literature (3,7). It can be seen that full load power is much higher in the case of new optimum design.The basis of comparison of pull-in power is likely to be significantly pessimistic for the new machine (due to use of copper bars,stainless steel end plates etc). The other designs are beleived to be die-cast aluminium and having low rotor inertias.

TABLE 3: Comparison of New Optimum Design with other Best Designs.

	Fong	A.L.A.	New Optimum Design
Reluctance Motor / Induction Motor	0.8125	0.75	1.0
p.f. (F.L.)	0.70	0.70	0.68
(F.L.)	76.0	68.0	80.5
Pull-in Power+ / Induction Motor	0.8125	0.75	1.08
Stability	*	*	Stable

+Pull-in results are given for connected inertia = 4.5 x rotor inertia and full load
*Proper results not available

CONCLUSIONS

It has been shown in the present paper, that by employing mathematical optimization techniques, a much improved reluctance motor of flux guided type has been predicted. A prototype design is fabricated based on theoretical predictions.The experimental performance for the optimum reluctance motor are given and it is shown that the new motor had superior overall performance compared with best available designs.Based on synchronous output, the new motor is rated equal to induction motor in the same frame size. It is an improvement of around 30% over existing reluctance motors. The experimental results are in conformity with theoretical predictions. It can be concluded that the same design approach can be employed for larger h.p. reluctance motors.

ACKNOWLEDGEMENTS

The authors would like to thank University of Leeds for experimental and computational facilities. M.H.N. would also like to acknowledge

the facilities provided by Garyounis University.

REFERENCES

1. Kostko,J.K. 1923 J.Am.I.E.E.,42, pp. 1162-
   1168
2. Honsinger,V.B. 1971,IEEE Trans,PAS-90,pp
   298-304
3. Fong,W and J.S.C. Htsui 1970,Proc.IEE,
   117(3),pp 545-551
4. Nagrial,M.H. and P.J. Lawrenson 1979,
   Electric Machines & Electromechanics,
   3 pp.315-324
5. Nagrial,M.H. 1974 "Synthesis of reluctance
   motors for optimum transient performance"
   Ph.D. Thesis, University of Leeds,U.K.
6. Lawrenson,P.J. and S.R. Bowes 1971,Proc IEE
   118(2),pp 356-369
7. Cruickshank,A.J.O. et.al. 1971,Proc IEE
   118(7), pp. 887-894

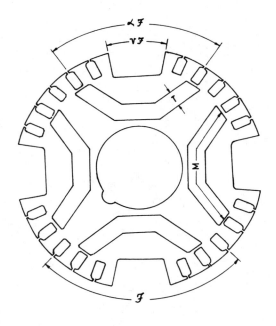

Fig.1 New optimum reluctance motor rotor

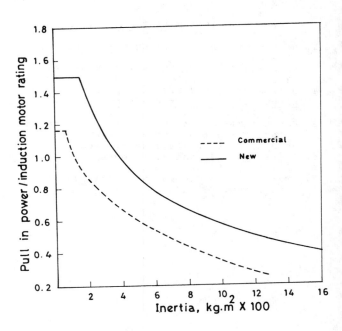

Fig.3 Pull-in characteristics of optimum design
       compared and modern commercial reluctance
       motor

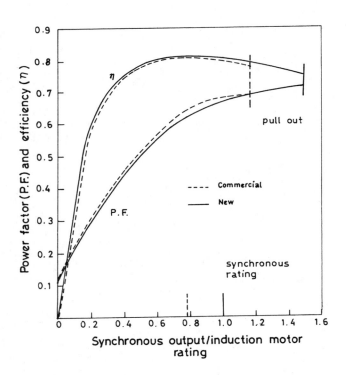

Fig.2 Synchronous performance of optimum
       design compared with a modern reluc-
       tance motor.

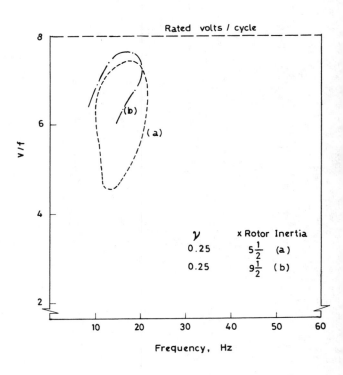

Fig.4 Variable frequency stability of a non-
       optimum design (γ=0.25, α=0.75(optimum))

CALCULATING VIBRATION AND STRESSES OF LARGE ELECTRICAL MACHINE STATOR END-WINDINGS, FOR BOTH STEADY LOAD AND TRANSIENT CONDITIONS

S Potter and G D Thomas

CEGB Central Electricity Research Laboratories, Leatherhead, Surrey, UK

INTRODUCTION

The stator end-windings of large generators during full load operation, and of large motors during the large current transient at start-up, experience very high oscillatory electromagnetic forces. During the last decade or more with increases in machine ratings, designs of stator end-winding support structures have developed rapidly to minimise problems caused by the resulting vibration. Large machines are required to operate for 20 to 30 years and consequently a wide variety of machines, in various stages of modification, are in operation at any one time. To investigate problems and to assess new designs or the effects of proposed modifications would be an almost impossible task experimentally, considering costs, time available and the usual urgency in obtaining results. The need to have theoretical methods available to assess such situations is therefore widely recognized. Development of theoretical methods for calculating natural frequencies, normal modes of vibration and forced vibration and stresses of stator end-windings started at CERL over 10 years ago. The theoretical techniques are incorporated in a suite of computer programs. The programs have been used widely within the CEGB; most of our large generators have been analysed for full load operation and a recent application has been to the vibration of a large motor at start-up. The programs are also available, on request, for use by manufacturers either on CEGB computers or on their own computers.

The electromagnetic forces for given operating conditions are calculated by idealising the conductors as a number of current-carrying filaments as described by Lawrenson (1). The structural idealisation is obtained using the finite element displacement method (eg Zienkiewicz (2)). Calculated responses take the form of displacement levels and stresses. Both are important since relative motion between conductors and supports may cause fretting of insulation, whilst excessive stresses may fatigue copper sub-conductors or insulation. The calculated natural frequencies of vibration allow the likelihood of resonant responses to be assessed and resonant amplitudes calculated for given damping levels.

This paper gives an outline of the theoretical methods used and also presents calculated results for full load operation of a 500 MW generator, and for the start-up of a 3000 hp 11kV motor.

THEORETICAL METHODS

Electromagnetic Forces

The complex curved geometry of involute end-windings requires the use of a numerical approach to determine their electromagnetic forces. The programs use the method due to Lawrenson (1), which idealises the finite thickness, curved conductors by a number of infinitesimally thin, straight, current-carrying filaments. The stator end-windings at the non-connection end usually consist of an array of identical conductor bars, so an idealisation is only specified for a single conductor. The coordinates of the end-points of each filament are specified in cylindrical (r, θ, z) axes, where z lies along the machine axis outwards from the stator. Fig.1 shows a typical filament idealisation of a conductor projected onto the (r, z) plane. The Biot-Savart Law gives the magnetic field at the centre of each filament due to all the conductors; the contribution to the field from the rotor end-windings is also included and image methods account for the rotor shaft and stator end permeability. The force per unit length on each filament is given by the vector product $\underline{I} \times \underline{B}$.

The conductors are grouped into a number of phase groups each group carrying a different phase current. For example, a 2-pole machine has 6 phase groups carrying phases A, -C, B, -A, C, -B respectively, so that neighbouring groups differ in phase by 60°. Three of these phases are simply the other three connected in reverse. For a 2-pole machine, the forces on the first three phase groups are identical on corresponding conductors of the other half of the end-winding. This symmetry reduces the computation required. The program can also be applied to more complex stator windings such as multipole 'fractional slot' types.

Forces for steady load. During steady load, each phase group has the same current amplitude; for stator current frequency w, the force on the ith filament of the nth phase group is approximately of the form

$$F_n^i = F_{ST}^i + F_C^i \cos (2wt - 2(n-1)\phi) + F_S^i \sin (2wt - 2(n-1)\phi) \qquad \ldots (1)$$

where ϕ is the phase difference between the current in neighbouring groups. The approximation is due to spatial harmonics in the rotor magnetic field. The rotor harmonics produce small end-winding forces at higher integer multiples of the stator current frequency. To obtain the static, cosine and sine Fourier coefficients in equation (1) we require F_n^2 for 3 adjacent phase groups to obtain 3 equations in the 3 unknowns. F_1^i, F_2^i and F_3^i are calculated for all values of i, corresponding to an instantaneous set of phase currents which are normally taken to be $I_A = I_O$, $I_{-C} = \frac{1}{2}I_O$, $I_B = -\frac{1}{2}I_O$, $I_{-A} = -I_O$, $I_C = -\frac{1}{2}I_O$, $I_{-B} = \frac{1}{2}I_O$, where I_O is the current amplitude. The vibration during steady load is produced by the time-varying part of the forces only, producing vibration at 100Hz for 50Hz stator current.

Forces for transient stator current. We must consider the total force since even a static force applied suddenly produces vibration at structural natural frequencies. For motor starts and fault conditions producing 'balanced' phase currents (ie, their sum is always zero), the instantaneous forces are given at time t by

$$F_n^i(t) = \left[I_M(t)/I_g \right]^2 \left[F_{ST}^i + F_C^i \cos 2(\theta(t) - (n-1)\phi) + F_S^i \sin 2(\theta(t) - (n-1)\phi) \right] \qquad \ldots (2)$$

where $\tan \theta(t) = \dfrac{I_B(t) - I_C(t)}{\sqrt{3}\, I_A(t)}$ ....(3)

and $I_M(t) = \left| \dfrac{I_A(t)}{\cos \theta(t)} \right| = \left| I_A(t) \sqrt{1 + \tan^2 \theta(t)} \right|$ ....(4)

This follows from the representation of balanced phase currents in the form $I_A(t) = I_M(t)\cos\theta(t)$, $I_B(t) = I_M(t) \cos(\theta(t) - 120^\circ)$, and $I_C(t) = I_M(t)\cos(\theta(t) - 240^\circ)$, which are analogous to those producing the forces defined by equation (1) viz $I_A(t) = I_o\cos wt$, $I_B(t) = I_o\cos(wt - 120^\circ)$, $I_C(t) = I_o\cos(wt - 240^\circ)$. Care must be taken to determine the correct quadrant for $\theta(t)$, since x is multi-valued for a given value of $\tan x$.

Unbalanced phase currents can occur due to a single phase short-circuit or unbalanced motor start and equations (2) - (4) do not apply. The force on the ith filaments in the 3 groups of conductors carrying phase A(and -A), B(and -B) and C(and -C) current must be expressed in the form

$$\begin{bmatrix} F_A^i \\ F_B^i \\ F_C^i \end{bmatrix} = \begin{bmatrix} f_A^i & 0 & 0 & f_{AB}^i & 0 & f_{AC}^i \\ 0 & f_B^i & 0 & f_{BA}^i & f_{BC}^i & 0 \\ 0 & 0 & f_C^i & 0 & f_{CB}^i & f_{CA}^i \end{bmatrix} \begin{bmatrix} I_A^2 \\ I_B^2 \\ I_C^2 \\ I_A I_B \\ I_B I_C \\ I_A I_C \end{bmatrix}$$ ....(5)

f_A^i is the force per unit length on the ith filament in the 'A' group of conductors for $I_A = -I_{-A} = 1$ and $I_B = -I_{-B} = I_C = -I_{-C} = 0$, and similarly for f_B^i and f_C^i with appropriate permutations of the values of current. f_{AB}^i is the force per unit length on the ith filament of the 'A' conductors from all the 'B' conductors for $I_A = -I_{-A} = 1$, $I_B = -I_{-B} = 1$, $I_C = -I_{-C} = 0$, with similar permutations for the other subscripted matrix elements.
  By symmetry,

$$f_A^i = f_B^i = f_C^i$$ ....(6)

$$f_{AB}^i = f_{BC}^i = f_{CA}^i$$ ....(7)

and $f_{BA}^i = f_{CB}^i = f_{AC}^i$ ....(8)

(NB $f_{AB}^i \neq f_{BA}^i$)

We need only calculate f_A^i, f_{AB}^i and f_{BA}^i therefore. Setting $I_A = -I_A = 1$ and the other phase currents to zero gives f_A^i for all i. f_{AB}^i and f_{BA}^i are obtained by setting $I_A = -I_{-A} = I_B = -I_{-B} = 1$ and $I_C = -I_{-C} = 0$, to obtain forces denoted by f_{AAB}^i and f_{BBA}^i, which are forces on filaments in phases 'A' and 'B' respectively due to unit current in both 'A' and 'B' conductors. Thus,

$$f_{AB}^i = f_{AAB}^i - f_A^i$$ ....(9)

and $f_{BA}^i = f_{BBA}^i - f_B^i = f_{BBA}^i - f_A^i$ ....(10)

For steady load or balanced transient current, therefore, a single run of the force program is required, whereas for unbalanced transient currents, two runs of the force program are required.

Finite element models

Conductors. Finite element methods (2) are used widely in the dynamic analysis of structures. Thomas and Wilson (3) have reported the CERL application of straight Timoshenko beam finite elements to curved end-winding conductors and Thomas et al (4) presented a review and theory of these elements. 'Element A' of ref. 4 is used to represent the conductors.

The beam element mesh is chosen to coincide with the filament mesh used in the force calculations. Thus, fig.1 also represents the beam element idealisation of a conductor bar. The conductor bars are assumed to be rigidly fixed at the core end, although other boundary conditions could be represented if required. The data required are the bending stiffnesses of the conductor bar (EI) in its two principal bending planes, torsional stiffness (GJ) and mass per unit length. The conductors are not homogeneous; therefore, the effective values of EI and GJ are best determined by experiment. The most reliable experiment is to measure the free-free natural frequencies of a straight length of conductor, or a formed end-winding conductor. Free-free conditions eliminate uncertainty about clamping conditions; frequencies for straight samples can be compared with analytical formulae and for curved samples iterative use of finite element calculations will determine the stiffnesses. Table 1 lists the natural frequencies calculated using the CERL programs and their percentage difference from corresponding measured natural frequencies, for a large generator end-winding conductor rigidly clamped at the core end. The results are for separate halves without the inter-layer electrical connector.

TABLE 1. Calculated natural frequencies of inner and outer layer halves of a large generator end-winding conductor with percentage difference from measured natural frequencies.

inner layer (nearer rotor)		outer layer	
calc (Hz)	% difference	calc (Hz)	% difference
6.02	0.8	5.42	12.9
8.02	25.1	7.28	3.3
30.31	4.5	27.25	5.7
50.91	2.5	44.43	5.8
58.88	3.9	56.31	5.3
99.67	7.3	94.20	1.1
139.5	10.3	125.12	12.7
187.46	11.3	174.50	8.7
235.9	9.4	202.34	11.4
329.82	1.3	296.97	2.4

There is good agreement between the calculated and measured natural frequencies, with most calculated frequencies being within 10% of the measured values, and also between the measured and calculated mode shapes. The homogeneous beam element model certainly provides a satisfactory representation of the dynamics of the conductors for vibration frequencies up to 300 Hz.

Complete end-winding structure including supports

Most stator end-windings, at the non-connection end, consist of a number of identical, coupled substructures arranged symmetrically about the axis of the machine. Such structures are termed 'rotationally periodic' or 'cyclically symmetric'. A method of analysing this type of structure exactly considering only a single substructure was developed at CERL. Thomas (5) presented the theory for free and forced harmonic vibration and Fricker and Potter considered transient forced vibration (6).

The displacements of the structure are expressed as the sum of a finite number of spatial Fourier harmonics. Each Fourier harmonic has a different spatial phase difference between neighbouring substructures, given by

$$\phi = \frac{2\pi n}{N} \qquad \dots (11)$$

where the independent values of n are given by n = 0, 1, 2 ... N/2 for even N and n = 0, 1, 2 ... (N-1)/2 for odd N.

For a mode of free vibration, n is the number of circumferential wavelengths eg, an ovalling mode has n = 2; a torsional mode n = 0, etc. For forced vibration, symmetry in the electromagnetic forces results in some of the spatial Fourier harmonics being zero. During steady load, a 2-pole stator end-winding with 6 phase groups has force distributions on neighbouring phase groups identical in amplitude but differing in phase by 120°. Thus the forces and hence vibration 'rotate' around the winding. Thomas [5] showed that the Fourier components, or 'rotating components' as he called them, contributing to the response under these conditions correspond to

$$n = L + M(p-1) \quad \text{for} \quad p = 1, 2 \dots N/M \quad \dots (12)$$

where L = no. of groups of neighbouring substructures with forces at corresponding positions in each group identical in both amplitude and phase; M = no. of groups of neighbouring substructures with forces at corresponding positions in each group identical in amplitude; and N = no. of identical substructures. A 2-pole stator with 6 phase groups has L = 2 (ie, two halves) and M = 6 (ie the phase groups).

Often, some component of the support structure will have a different periodicity to the conductor bars; eg, a support beam may be fitted at every 3rd slot position. By idealising these beams by one at every slot but with $\frac{1}{3}$ the actual mass and stiffness, the size of the finite element model would be reduced to represent one complete conductor with its periodic part of the idealised support structure. The response of a 2-pole end-winding with 42 slots would contain seven spatial Fourier harmonics defined by

$$n = 2, 8, 14, 20, 26, 32 \text{ and } 38 \qquad \dots (13)$$

Each Fourier harmonic has a separate equation of motion obtained by applying 'complex constraints' of the form

$$u'' = u'e^{i\phi} \qquad \dots (14)$$

between corresponding displacements on the two boundaries of the substructure, where ϕ is given by equation (11). For steady load, the harmonic part of the forces for a single phase group are expressed as a sum of spatial Fourier harmonics, each corresponding to a particular value of n. The solutions to the N/M forced responses are summed to give the actual response of each substructure.

The transient problem is treated by calculating the instantaneous forces at a large number of small time intervals. If there are L groups of substructures such that the instantaneous forces on substructures 1, 2, 3 ... N/L are identical on corresponding substructures in the group (N/L) + 1, (N/L) + 2, ... 2N/L and similarly for all L groups, then the independent Fourier harmonics excited by the forces (6) correspond to

$$n = Lp \quad \text{where } p = 0, 1, 2 \dots N/2L \text{ for N/L even}$$
$$\text{and } p = 0, 1, 2 \dots (N/L-1)/2 \text{ for N/L odd}$$
$$\dots (15)$$

A 2-pole stator has L = 2, so, for example, a 42-slot machine would have excited spatial harmonics for values of n given by

$$n = 0, 2, 4 \dots 20 \qquad \dots (16)$$

Full details of the substructure finite element models are given in refs. [5] and [6].

Conductor bar stresses. The internal structural forces are calculated from the beam finite element stiffness matrices and the calculated displacements. The homogeneous beam elements take the material properties of copper. The axial stress component determines the likelihood of fatigue of copper subconductors or cracking of insulation. This stress has contributions from bending in both weak and stiff bending planes and from the axial tension/compression, so the stresses will differ at each of the four corners of the conductor cross-section at a given position along the conductor. The stresses are determined as the four possible sign permutations of the expression

$$S_{1,2,3,4} = F/A_e \pm M_1 B/I_1 \pm M_2 A/I_2 \qquad \dots (17)$$

where F = axial force, A_e = effective cross-section area = $A_C + (E_I/E_C)A_I$ (A_C = copper cross-sectional area, A_I = insulation cross-sectional area, E_C = copper Young's modulus, E_I = insulation Young's modulus); M_1 and M_2 are the bending moments in the weak and stiff bending planes respectively; I_1 and I_2 are the second moments of area for bending in the weak and stiff bending planes (such that multiplication by E_C gives measured EI properties of the conductor bar), and A and B are the distances of the copper corners from the neutral planes for stiff and weak plane bending respectively.

APPLICATIONS

Steady load response of 500 MW generator

Fig. 2 shows the substructure finite element model representing a typical 500 MW generator end-winding. Elements between C and D, E and F, and H and I represent brackets, beams and ring beams of the support structure. Dashed lines denote 'lumped stiffnesses' representing the stiffness of packing and insulation between conductors and supports or between neighbouring conductors. Elements parallel to the θ (circumferential) axis join corresponding nodes (i.e. with the same r and z coordinates) on the two substructure boundaries. The element between J and K, for example, represents a circumferential support ring beam. All other elements are drawn in projection on the r-z plane. The inner and outer halves of each conductor are wound in opposite directions to meet at G, so each half conductor crosses, and hence is coupled through packing to, a number of conductors in the other layer. For example, in fig. 2, the nodes labelled L and N have a spatial position corresponding to node M, but in the 9th substructure. The complex constraint applied between corresponding degrees of freedom at nodes such as L and M is

$$u_L = u_M e^{im\phi} \qquad \dots (18)$$

where ϕ is given by equation (11) and m is the number of rotations of the substructure through $2\pi/N$ radians about the axis of the machine, required to move node M to the original position of node L (m=+8 in this case). The values of m are marked in fig. 2 by each node for which degrees of freedom are eliminated by complex constraints. Clamped boundary conditions are imposed at A and B; the constraints at C depend on the support structure design. The contribution to stator end-winding vibration from imposed motion of the stator core can be calculated approximately by applying the rotating oval deformation of the stator core as a boundary condition at A, B and C.

The analysis of a design usually consists of the calculation of its natural frequencies and mode shapes and the response to the electromagnetic forces at 100 Hz and at any natural frequencies close to 100 Hz. Table 2 lists calculated and measured n=2 and n=4 natural frequencies for the 500 MW end-winding, which are those predominantly excited. The n=4 modes are equivalent to those for n=N-4=38 (see equation (13) for the excited n-values). The end-winding is a modern design with epoxy-mica insulation and a typical stiff support structure. The measurements were variable speed tests but the limited speed range covered only allowed resonances in the range 86 - 101 Hz to be found. Results are available for two machines of the same type, denoted by a and b.

TABLE 2. Natural frequencies of a 500 MW stator end-winding (Hz).

	Calculated			Measured	
n	k=1	k=0.3	k=0.2	m/c (a)	m/c (b)
2	100.3	84.0	78.0	96	86
4	107.3	92.4	86.9		92
2	145.6	114.7	100.9		
4	166.5	134.2	122.4		
2	198.2	136.0	122.1		
2	216.5	159.5	143.2		
4	279.6	178.1	154.5		
2	280.7	180.8	155.3		

The k=1 results are for a manufacturer's measured values of inter-conductor and conductor to support structure packing stiffness and conductor insulation stiffness (normal to its surface). The k=0.3 and k=0.2 results are for uniform reductions in these inter-connection stiffnesses by factors of 0.3 and 0.2 respectively. The natural frequencies are clearly sensitive to the packing stiffness; therefore, noticeable differences between the natural frequencies of machines of the same type may be expected. Relaxation of packing stiffness in service would cause the natural frequencies to fall. The limited number of measured natural frequencies are within the range of calculated frequencies; in particular, the first two k=0.3 frequencies are in good agreement with those measured on machine b.

Table 3 lists the calculated vibration amplitudes at the nodes marked P and Q along the involute in fig.2, together with amplitudes measured near these positions on machines a and b during the first two weeks of operation. The measurements quoted are the average of three sets from corresponding points in three phase groups at the non-connection end. The results are for full load operation; the calculations ignored imposed motion from the stator core.

TABLE 3. Vibration amplitudes μm (0-pk).

		Calculated			Measured	
		k=1	k=0.3	k=0.2	m/c (a)	m/c (b)
P	r	15	22	28		
	θ	8	19	31	R 18	16
	z	3	5	11		
Q	r	15	22	26	T 20	18
	θ	7	18	32		
	z	4	5	13	A 13	16

The forcing frequencies used for the k=1, k=0.3, and k=0.2 cases were 100 Hz, 100 Hz and 100.9 Hz; therefore, for k=1, the first n=2 mode is excited at resonance, and for k=0.2, the second n=2 mode is excited at resonance. A resonant response is controlled by the structural damping, commonly quantified by a 'Q-factor'.

Tests suggest Q-factors of about 100, 40 and 7 for the conductor bars, support beams and packing respectively. The damping is inversely proportional to the Q-factor. These damping levels were used in the calculations. Modal Q-factors for an assembled end-winding are normally about 10-15 for the important lower modes.

The calculated and measured results can only be compared directly for circumferential motion (θ or T). The R and A axes are inclined at 30 degrees (winding cone semi-angle) to the r and z axes, with R normal to the cone surface. The measurements are in best agreement with the k=0.3 calculations; this is consistent with the good agreement of measured and calculated end-winding natural frequencies for k=0.3. Table 4 presents the maximum calculated cyclic copper stress amplitudes for each case.

TABLE 4. Calculated cyclic stress amplitude in copper. $MN\ m^{-2}$

k=1	k=0.3	k=0.2	unsupported
2.88	3.97	4.93	15.0

The stress amplitudes for the values of k considered are very low, as the fatigue limit for copper is about 55 MN m^{-2}. These results all give the maximum stress at either node R or S, corresponding to vibration amplitudes of the end-connectors (G) of about 50μm 0-pk for k=1 and 150μm 0-pk for k=0.2. Measured amplitudes at G are generally about 80μm 0-pk. The maximum cyclic stress calculated for a conductor bar completely unsupported except for clamped conditions at points A and B is 15.0 MN m^{-2} (at point B), corresponding to vibration at G of about 170 μm 0-pk but higher levels of about 300 μm along the involutes.

Vibration monitoring has shown isolated cases of increased vibration in the θ-direction on individual end-connectors. Calculations suggest as a cause loosening of packing, or locally defective packing, over part of the involute near region F, producing a detuning of natural frequencies causing an individual conductor to resonate at 100Hz. The maximum calculated resonant stress in a loose conductor for 500μm 0-pk amplitude is 36 MN m^{-2}, still considerably below the fatique limit. A resonance may show up by a rapid rise in vibration over a few days; in one case the vibration fell again rapidly, suggesting more slackening, causing detuning of the natural frequency to below 100Hz.

The calculated results are very encouraging for the long-term integrity of the end-windings, a conclusion supported by the reliable performance of such machines to date.

Response of 3000hp, 11kV motor end-windings at start-up.

The end-winding transient vibration and stresses at start-up of a 3000hp, 11kV motor have been calculated using the programs. The stator has 36 slots with the 36 end-winding conductors arranged in six phase groups of six conductors. The electromagnetic forces were calculated for the balanced start-up currents of 4.5 per unit (ie 4.5 x steady-load current). The phase currents contain dc off-sets at start-up, so the transient forces include a component at 50 Hz in addition to 100Hz and steady components. The response was calculated for the first four cycles of start current ie, 80ms. The transient forces were calculated at 200 equal time-steps of 0.4 ms using equations (2)-(4). This time-step gives a smooth representation of the transient forces since the 100Hz time period is divided into 25 steps. The sub-structure idealisation included one conductor , so N = 36. Since L=2 for a 2-pole stator, from equation (15) we find the excited spatial Fourier harmonics to be those for n = 0,2,4, ... 18. Table 5 lists the lowest three calculated natural frequencies for various assumed conditions of the support structure, for n = 0 and 2.

TABLE 5 Calculated motor end-winding natural frequencies (Hz)

n	fully supported	support ring uncoupled		Single unsupported conductor
	Packing blocks rigidly bonded to insulation		free slipping of packing blocks over insulation	
0	165.9	99.8	41.9	21.1
	196.3	148.1	142.5	70.7
	228.7	179.7	175.1	103.7
2	195.3	124.4	48.6	
	195.3	166.6	156.6	
	251.1	204.5	181.0	

The lowest calculated natural frequencies vary between 165.9Hz for a support structure in a fully effective condition to 21.1Hz for an unsupported conductor, so there is clearly the possibility of a conductor undergoing resonant vibration if relaxation of the supports occurs. The dc off-sets in the stator current decay rapidly and for most of the start-up period the current swings symmetrically positive and negative with approximately constant amplitude. Under these conditions the n = 0 component of the forces is approximately constant, so we need only consider resonant responses of n = 2 and higher order modes. Fig 3(a) shows the graphical program output for the θ-direction response about half-way along the inner involute, taking the model for the support structure in fully effective condition. The results are for the 6th conductor of the 1st phase group. The uni-directional, 50Hz,and 100Hz contributions to the response are apparent. Fig 3(b) shows the modulus of the corresponding axial stress at the core end on the inner half conductor, where the maximum calculated stress occurs. The peak deflection of nearly 200μm and peak stress of 26 MNm^{-2} are very low for instantaneous levels. At a resonance, it can be shown that for the level of damping assumed (Q = 15), the resonant component of the response will reach about 81% of its final amplitude after 8 cycles of vibration (80 ms). This allows the results at resonance to be interpreted. Calculations at resonance for relaxed supports indicate that response amplitudes of greater than 1 mm could occur with associated cyclic stress amplitudes throughout the start-up of greater than the fatigue limit of copper. Calculations for an unsupported conductor indicate large amplitudes of a few mm but fairly low cyclic stresses, so very loose conductors would probably suffer fretting wear to insulation at support positions, rather than fatigue. It is clear that stiff support structures can reduce start-up vibration and stresses to acceptable levels. However, to maintain low responses over a long service life may require the use of a thin layer of flexible material between supports and insulation, or encapsulation of supports and insulation, to prevent fretting damage to the insulation. Preliminary measurements of start-up vibration amplitude on this motor showed peak levels of about 700μm, which are within the range of calculated values for various assumed support conditions.

The calculated copper stress can be used to calculate the axial strain on the surface of the insulation, assuming a linear variation of strain through the conductor cross-section. This assumption appears to be supported by recent work by Futakawa et al (7) and calculated insulation strains can be compared with mechanical strength data of insulation (see eg Futakawa et al (8), (9)) to assess the risk of failure.

CONCLUSIONS

1. A suite of computer programs has been applied to detailed calculations of generator and motor stator end-winding vibration and stresses under both steady load and transient conditions. The programs use the finite element displacement method,and the Lawrenson method to determine the electromagnetic forces. The results are in good agreement with measurements for both natural frequency and response calculations.

2. The calculations are sufficiently accurate to perform design assessments. The programs aid evaluation of vibration problems, such as a resonant response, and therefore informed decisions can be taken as to whether an examination can await the next routine inspection.

3. The computer programs can be made available for potential users outside the CEGB.

ACKNOWLEDGEMENTS

The authors would like to acknowledge the work of D.L.Thomas, who pioneered end-winding vibration calculations in the CEGB, and also the work of various colleagues whose measured and calculated results are quoted.

REFERENCES

1. Lawrenson, P.J., 1965, Proc. IEE, 112(6),1144-1158.

2. Zienkiewicz, O.C., "The Finite Element Method in Engineering Science", McGraw-Hill.

3. Thomas, D.L., and Wilson, R.R., 1973, J. of Sound and Vibration, 26(1), 155-158.

4. Thomas, D.L., Wilson, J.M., and Wilson, R.R., 1973, J. of Sound and Vibration, 31(3), 315-330.

5. Thomas, D.L., 1979, Int. J. for Numerical Methods in Engineering, 14, 81-102.

6. Fricker, A.J., and Potter, S., 1981, Int. J. for Numerical Methods in Engineering, 17, 957-974.

7. Futakawa, A., Yamasaki, S., and Kawakami, T., 1981, IEEE Trans. on Electr. Insul., EI-16(4), 360-370.

8. Futakawa, A., Hirabayashi, S., Tani, T., and Shibayama, K., 1978, IEEE Trans. on Electr. Insul., EI-13(6), 395-401.

9. Futakawa, A., and Yamasaki, S., 1981, IEEE Trans. on Electr. Insul., EI-16(1), 31-39.

This work was carried out at the Central Electricity Research Laboratories and is published by permission of the Central Electricity Generating Board.

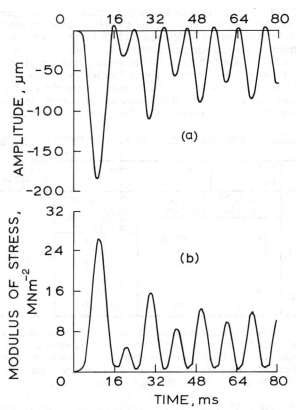

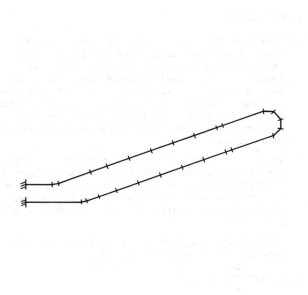

Figure 1 Straight filament idealisation of an
end-winding conductor

Figure 3 Calculated transient vibration and stress of
3000hp motor end-winding conductor at start-up

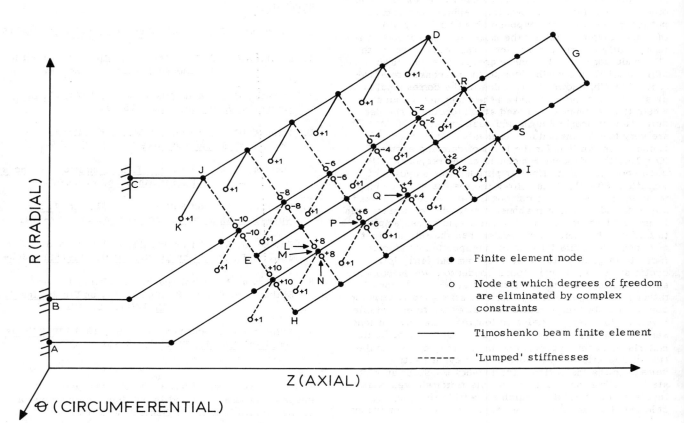

Figure 2 Typical finite element mesh of a large generator end-winding

MEASURING FLUX AND INTERLAMINAR VOLTAGE IN TURBINE GENERATOR END REGIONS

R. Platt, L.C. Kerr and A.F. Anderson

NEI Parsons Ltd., UK

INTRODUCTION

In the end regions of large turbine driven generators, extraneous fluxes, which may be insignificant in small machines, cause appreciable eddy currents and interlaminar voltages which, in turn, influence loss and temperature patterns within the machine. Therefore before the designer can predict the likely effect of any particular change in design parameters upon performance, he must first appreciate how changes in operating conditions or machine geometry affect the flux distribution. Whilst this paper describes flux and interlaminar voltage measurements only, it should be seen as covering only part of a much broader spectrum of theoretical and experimental work aimed at furthering the understanding of large machines and improving them.

Finite element analysis (Phemister (1)) is widely used to model two dimensional electromagnetic fields, but three dimensional calculations can be expensive, especially when saturation is taken into account. Modelling three dimensional fields under transient conditions as yet demands too much computer power to be applicable for large scale problems. Hence the importance of experimental measurement on machines.

GENERAL APPROACH TO INSTRUMENTATION

Flux densities and interlaminar voltages have been measured in detail in the end regions (Fig. 1(a)) and in other parts of generator stators up to 800 MW rating. As changes in flux in one place tend to produce effects elsewhere, it is inadvisable to confine search coils to only the areas thought to be of immediate interest. For instance, coils may sometimes be included to measure leakage flux at the back of core and in the core frame ribs; parts often neglected, but which experience shows contribute to the machine iron losses (Abolins and Rieger (2)).

In addition to the investigations on production machines, a test rig comprising the two ends of a full size 660 MW generator has been built to aid the future designs of large machines. Almost nineteen hundred sensors of various types were installed, some in positions not acceptable in production machines.

Groups of sensors and their leads must be designed to give a high signal to noise ratio and avoid disturbing the local environment in a way that will alter the quantity being measured. They must be robust enough to withstand service conditions, fail safe, and be installed into the machine without disrupting the manufacturing programme.

A significant part of the cost of instrumentation lies in the support arrangements to accurately locate and orient the sensors, their lead runs and terminal connections, rather than in the sensors themselves. Documentation which specifies the characteristics of each sensor, their spacial positions in relation to a known frame of reference and their terminal connections, is essential. Without it no data capture and handling system can function and no meaningful analyses made.

FLUX MEASUREMENTS WITH SEARCH COILS

Search coils are the most robust, convenient and cheapest transducers to obtain complete information about alternating fluxes. Their principle of operation is expressed by:

$$e = -(AN) \frac{dB}{dt} \quad \cdots \cdots \cdots (1)$$

where e (volts) is the instantaneous value of emf induced across the terminals of a coil of N turns of average area A (m^2) embracing flux of density B (tesla). The coil constant (AN) fixes its sensitivity for a given rate of change of flux density.

Search coils range from single turns of wire wound around a packet of laminations to determine the flux distribution in the core, to those of a few thousand turns wound on formers to measure the flux entering iron from air gaps. Coil constants are chosen to give a high signal to noise ratio. An upper limit is imposed on coil constants by dimensional restrictions and by the minimum size of wire used to wind the coil (in practice 52 swg, i.e. 0.02 mm dia.).

Construction of Search Coils

Coils of various sizes and sensitivities are required and techniques have been developed to wind and terminate them from fine wires. In some locations, only simple coil formers are necessary, whilst other locations demand a specific design. All coils however have either circular or rectangular sections and examples are illustrated in Fig. 2.

A typical cylindrical coil (Fig. 2(a)) used in the end region and on the back of core has several thousand turns of 48 swg enamel insulated copper wire wound on a nylon former: the coil with its terminal pins is encapsulated in epoxy putty. Sensitivities of the order of 90 V(rms) T^{-1} peak value of sinusoidal flux at 50 Hz are obtained. In places such as the end winding region, groups of three cylindrical coils are mounted mutually at right angles to measure the flux density in all three planes. Special cylindrical coils to measure axial flux density in the core have formers without flanges and comprise 5000 turns of 52 swg wire encapsulated in epoxy resin (Fig. 2(b)).

Small rectangular section coils are used to measure radial and axial flux densities particularly in the air gap regions (Figs. 2(c) and (d)). These are wound with 46 or 48 swg wire over epoxy glass formers to obtain appropriate sensitivities. Coils to measure flux densities in two planes using only one former arrangement (Fig. 2(e)) are used in some locations.

To measure flux over a relatively large area, such as that leaking radially from the back of core, coils of only a few turns of 30 swg wire are used. These are wound in a single layer into recesses in a rectangular 'picture frame' former (Fig.2(f)).

Calibration and phasing of search coils

The coil constants (AN) of large single layer coils are accurately calculated from the coil dimensions and the number of turns. However the constants of small multi-layer coils cannot be determined in this manner since their effective area is not accurately known and they must therefore be calibrated.

To determine the area-turns of these coils, both the unknown coil and a standard cylindrical coil of known area-turns, wound with a single layer of wire, are placed with their axes coincident inside a solenoid of considerably larger dimensions. A virtually uniform field is embraced by the coils. Both coils are connected to a potentiometer and a sensitive null detector, and calibrations are made with sinusoidal currents of 50 Hz supplying the solenoid. From the resistance on each side of the null point on the potentiometer and the area-turns of the standard coil, the area-turns of the coil undergoing calibration is calculated. This technique makes the calibration independent of variations in the supply to the solenoid, and it fixes the terminal polarity (phase) of the unknown coil. This phasing enables coils to be installed according to a convention for defined directions of flux.

Search Coil Installation

An investigation into one or more regions of a generator may require the installation of between a few and several hundred coils of different types in locations as typified in Fig. 1(a). In regions where high gradients of flux density are expected such as in the air gap near the core ends, a number of coils are installed within close proximity to one another.

The installation must comply with stringent specifications so that it does not affect the performance or reliability of the machine. Care is therefore taken in the design of the coil assemblies, the choice of materials used, the techniques adopted to secure the assemblies to the stator and the lead runs. Other precautionary measures include the use of end winding models to check the integrity of coil arrangements under high voltage stresses as exist during over voltage tests, the establishment of voltage breakdown levels of leads and insulating conduits, the temperature capabilities of the components and gas flow considerations. The final installation must be robust enough to withstand production procedures and service operating conditions.

A typical installation of individual coils behind the back of core is shown in Fig. 1(b). Where possible, groups of coils and their leads are attached or encapsulated into pre-assembled units to reduce installation time within the manufacturing programme. Examples of this are an assembly of coils for attaching to special stator slot wedges to measure axial and radial flux densities in the air gap (Fig. 1(c)), and also a comprehensive arrangement of coils for installing on the back of core (Fig. 1(d)). Cylindical coils to measure axial flux within the core are bonded with their leads into recesses in 2.4 mm thick rubberised asbestos segments normally used to accommodate the core supervisory thermocouples (Fig. 1(e)). This forms a robust unit ready for installation during core building.

Connections are made to the search coils using pairs of fine multi-strand PTFE insulated wire. These pairs are tightly twisted to avoid flux loops. The leads are run in the stator via suitable conduits to hermetic connectors on the outer casing.

LAMINATION VOLTAGE PROBES

The main flux in a 500 MW generator stator induces a voltage of less than 50 mV between axially adjacent segmental core laminations. Near the core ends however, the interlaminar voltages are greater due to the effects of axial flux perpendicular to the plane of the laminations, and also the radial flux leaking from the back of core (Jackson (3)).

To obtain a measure of these voltages and also to improve the understanding of core behaviour, lamination probes have been installed on the back of the core of a 500 MW generator. These probes have enabled interlaminar voltages within groups of laminations near the core end to be measured under various load conditions. The voltage between a lamination in each group and the adjacent keybar was also measured. This enabled the potential of each lamination in a group to be determined with respect to the keybar.

To install the lamination probes, a hand held laser microwelder was used to attach fine gold plated molybdenum wires of approximately 0.1 mm diameter to the edges of adjacent individual core laminations. These are themselves only 0.35 mm thick excluding insulation. The microwelder employs an accurate optical system developed from a laser opthalmascope. The weld melt was established as being less than the thickness of the coreplate to avoid creating interlaminar short circuits. Fine wires laser welded to laminations on the tooth of a model generator are shown as an example inset in Fig. 3(a).

Laser welding was only the first stage in a comprehensive and quite lengthy installation operation of the type already described. Each group of fine wires was joined to a more substantial measurement lead containing individually twisted pairs of multi-strand PTFE insulated wire using a connector assembly attached with adhesive to the back of core. On one twisted pair, the voltage between the first lamination in a group and the adjacent keybar was measured. On the other pairs, the interlaminar voltages were measured (Fig. 3(a)).

MEASUREMENTS AND DATA HANDLING

Continuing developments in measuring

instruments and computers are eliminating many tedious procedures and have reduced to an entirely different order the time taken for measurements, their storage and presentation. Search coil and potential probe voltages usually have complex waveforms and they can be analysed in two ways. In one, the magnitude and phase of each harmonic of the wave is stored and the wave can be reconstituted on a computer; in the other, the wave is recorded using either analogue or digital techniques. Each method has advantages in certain situations and both are used.

For example, the magnitudes and phase angles of the components of repetitive search coil voltages are measured up to the 15th harmonic with a specially designed complex wave analyser which may be used manually or with a computer controlled data logging system. The phase reference signal used for the analyser is synchronous with the wave undergoing measurement and is derived from a source such as the line voltage. A subsequent version of the complex waveform analyser has been described by Locke (4). For non-repetitive voltage waveforms, such as those obtained from some voltage probes, a transient recorder has proved suitable. This instrument records 1000 consecutive samples over a selected time period (minimum 0.1 ms), each sample being stored as an 8 bit digital number. Thus complete cycles or selected portions of the waveform can be recorded and transferred to paper tape or micro-computer disc for subsequent analysis.

During any test programme large amounts of data are collected and preferably these are systematically stored in a computer data base for subsequent analysis. This enables characteristics particular to a machine design to be ascertained and comparisons to be made between machines. Efficient management of the data base is therefore essential.

SOME SELECTED RESULTS

The following examples of measurements taken on generators are a very small selection from data collected over several years.

Calculations indicated that were the rotor pole lengths to be less than that of the stator core, the axial flux at the core ends would be reduced. In consequence, losses and temperatures would also be reduced. To verify this prediction a 200 MW stator was tested with both a normal length rotor and a rotor with its poles shortened by an air gap length at each end. The axial flux densities measured in the stator teeth (Fig. 4) were considerably reduced with a shortened pole length at normal open circuit voltage. As a similar trend was obtained on load, rotors since then have been advantageously shortened.

The radial leakage flux densities behind the back of core in a 500 MW 60 Hz generator on open circuit are shown in Fig. 5(a). Picture frame search coils used for these measurements were located only on the main section of core between the end and central radially ventilated regions. Flux densities are highest in regions close to the radial vents, probably because the ventilated regions have less iron. In general the radial leakage flux rises sharply above 16 kV.

A sudden short circuit test on this generator from 50% of normal voltage on open circuit induced voltages in the coils at positions 1 and 7 as shown in Fig. 5(b). Near the central ventilated region the flux voltage collapses, whilst near the core end it rises to approximately fifty times its steady state value before decaying to a value greater than its pre-fault level. These waves illustrate the balance of rotor and stator magnetising forces in the air gap and their imbalance in the end region under transient conditions: they also show that leakage fluxes under transient conditions also involve part of the iron circuit as well as the end winding region. This illustrates the importance of considering the transient leakage fluxes in a machine as well as the steady state flux. The results are similar to those already reported by Anderson (5) for small a.c. series motors under start-up conditions.

To obtain the flux distribution within the core of the model generator described previously, single turn coils were wound around core sections utilising the axial and radial vents. These coils would not be acceptable on a production machine. Whilst the total flux in the back of core on open circuit is sinusoidal, the local fluxes are distorted as shown in Fig. 6 due to the reluctances of their various paths.

An example of an interlaminar voltage waveform measured under load conditions on a 500 MW generator is shown in Fig. 3(b). The waveform contains sharp peaks and varies in a random manner between two states of different amplitude. Positive and negative peaks appear and disappear independently. The magnitude of the interlaminar voltage (approximately 2.5 V peak) is of a different order to that arising from the main flux in the machine acting on its own. The investigation into this subject continues.

CONCLUSIONS

Flux and interlaminar voltage measurements in turbine generator end regions have made significant contributions to the development of larger machines. The measurements have provided information of immediate use to the designer and have complemented theoretical calculations. They have also shown phenomena which sometimes has not been entirely anticipated such as that obtained under transient conditions.

The design of the sensors, their accuracy of location, their support assemblies and the measurement procedures and data handling all require considerable attention to detail to ensure that reliable and sensible results are obtained relevant to the investigation.

ACKNOWLEDGEMENTS

The authors thank NEI Parsons Ltd. for permission to publish this paper and CEGB, Ontario Hydro of Canada, ETSA and SECWA of Australia for their collaboration with the experimental work. The authors also acknowledge the contributions to these investigations made over many years by their colleagues, in particular the late A.F. Craddock, J.A. Denham, B.F Ewles, B. Johnson, P.V. Rao, P.A. Sowler and A. Walton.

REFERENCES

1. Phemister, T.G., 1977 "Magnetic field calculation by Fourier analysis within finite elements", (presented at International Symposium on Innovative Analysis in Applied Science, Versailles). In course of publication in International Journal of Numerical Methods in Engineering.

2. Abolins, A., and Rieger, F., 1975, "Test results of the world's largest four pole generators with water cooled stator and rotor windings", IEEE Trans., PAS-94, 1103-1110.

3. Jackson, R.J., 1978, "Interlamination voltages in large turbogenerators", Proc. IEE, 125, 1232-1238, also discussion on this paper, 1980, Proc. IEE, 127, Pt.C, 114-120.

4. Locke, D.H., 1979 "A power frequency waveform analyser to measure harmonic magnitude and phase", Conference on Electronic Test and Measuring Instrumentation (IEE), Testmex, 9-12.

5. Anderson, A.F., Bedford, T., and Craddock, A.F., 1981 "Transient leakage flux in small universal motors", Proc. IEE, 128, Pt. B, No. 5, 253-254.

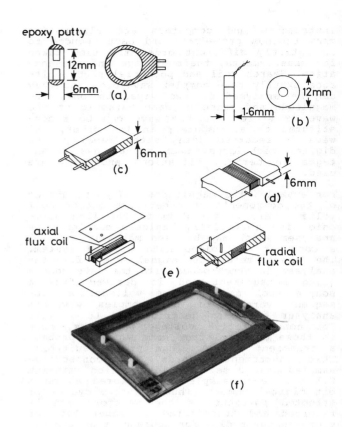

Figure 2 Examples of search coils

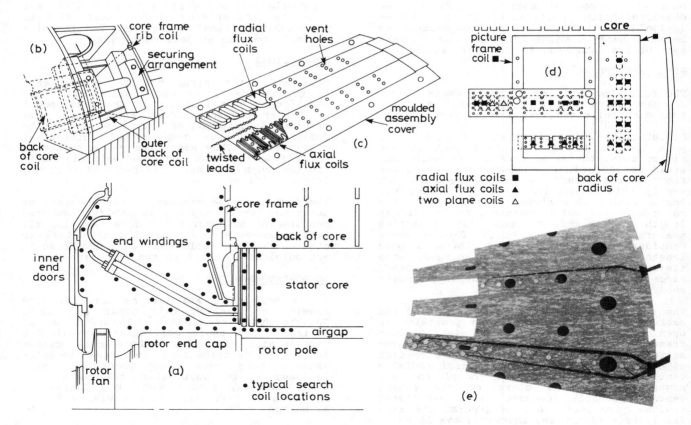

Figure 1 Sectional view of the end region of a generator, typical search coil locations and examples of assemblies

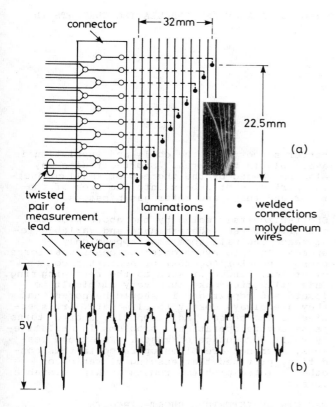

Figure 3 Connections of lamination voltage probes and an example of a 50 Hz interlaminar voltage wave

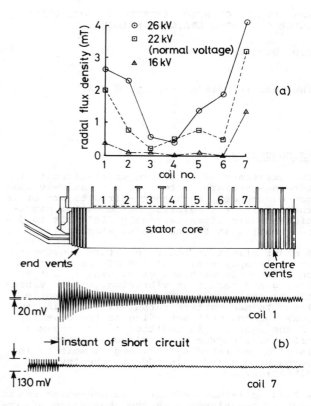

Figure 5 Flux density behind back of core on open circuit and search coil voltages during a sudden short circuit test

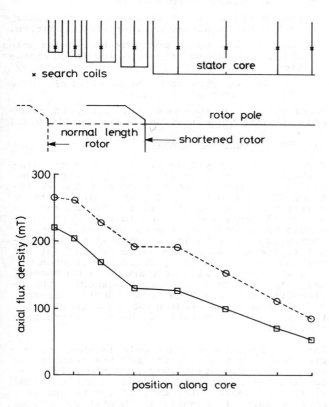

Figure 4 Axial flux density in stator teeth at normal open circuit voltage with normal and shortened rotor lengths

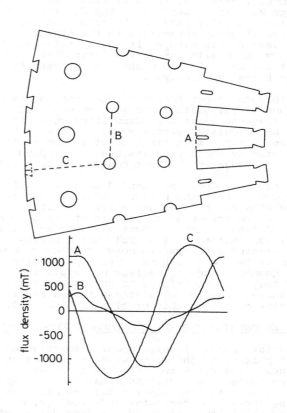

Figure 6 Radial and circumferential flux waves in a core section of a full scale model generator on open circuit

THE EFFECTS OF ROTOR INTERTURN SHORT-CIRCUITS ON VOLTAGE IMBALANCE AND CIRCULATING CURRENTS IN LARGE GENERATOR STATOR WINDINGS

G.W. Buckley

The Detroit Edison Company, U.S.A.

INTRODUCTION

The existence of interturn short-circuits in turbine-generator rotors is a relatively common occurence. Such short-circuits are often the result of insulation or conductor migration and are often extremely difficult to detect during an inspection at standstill.

A major effect of rotor interturn short-circuits is assymetric heating of the rotor which, on a two-pole machine, gives rise to rotor bowing and resultant vibration. These vibration levels may or may not be sufficiently large to necessitate output limits being imposed on the unit depending on the severity of the shorts. In addition to the thermal effects, a degree of unbalanced magnetic pull is also generated by the unequal mmfs acting on each pole and this adds to the level of vibration.

A less well-known effect, but one which can be equally troublesome, is the phenomenon of circulating currents in the stator winding. On two pole machines, because of the connection of the stator winding, only harmonic currents can flow. On four pole machines however, sub-harmonic, harmonic, and ultrasubharmonic currents may flow depending on the distribution of the short-circuits in the rotor and the method of group connection in the stator. Machines fitted with split phase differential relays can easily detect this circulating current and may trip the machine or prevent it from being synchronized.

The present paper describes the problem and a method of calculation whereby the magnitude and frequencies of the circulating currents can be calculated approximately. It will be shown that the magnetization of all poles is affected by short-circuits and not simply that of poles adjacent to that containing shorts.

The present paper is intended to give a brief introduction to the problems usually associated with rotor interturn short-circuits, with special reference being made to stator winding circulating currents. Most of the discussion will concentrate on four pole units because circulating currents are more troublesome here than on two pole machines. Four pole units are commonly used in nuclear power plants, and they are, therefore, of considerable importance. Sample calculations for an actual machine exibiting this problem are included.

CAUSES AND LOCATION OF INTERTURN SHORT-CIRCUITS

Interturn short-circuits occur primarily in that portion of the rotor winding located underneath the rotor retaining ring and are most often caused (on operational machines) by migration of the turn insulation, thermal ratcheting (creep) of the rotor end-windings, loosening of end-turn blocking, or degradation of the retaining ring insulating liner. Short-circuits also occur in the slotted portion of the rotor, but these are less common because

better support for the coils and insulation is available in that area. Short-circuits may also be caused by the ingress of small conducting particles or debris into the area of the rotor end turns and rotor gas passages.

Short-circuits created by the above problems are often of an indeterminate and variable resistance and will sometimes appear only at speeds close to synchronism as centifugal forces press conductor together or against a common electrical conductor such as the retaining ring. This will often make them very difficult to locate and repair and it should be noted that they are always costly to eliminate, irrespective of the cause. Additionally, shorted turns cause severe operational problems in a relatively small percentage of cases. For these reasons, machines are often operated in this condition, provided that ensuing vibration or other related problems remain within tolerable levels.

EFFECTS OF INTERTURN SHORT-CIRCUITS

There are three major detrimental effects of rotor interturn short-circuits, but the severity of the effects depends very much on the extent of the shorts and also upon their distribution. These effects are:-

1. Assymetrical rotor heating, which can cause mechanical imbalance and increased vibration.

2. Unbalanced magnetic pull from successive poles which can also contribute to increased vibration.

3. Circulating currents in the parallel circuits of each stator phase winding.

Other conditions such as shaft, bearing bracket and end-plate magnetization are also possible.(1)

Assymmetrical Rotor Heating

When a short circuit occurs on a pole the distribution of I^2R loss in that pole changes, the degree of change being dependent on the resistance of the short. If the short (or contact) resistance is high, very little of the turn current is bypassed and the loss in the turn is almost unchanged. As the contact resistance decreases, the loss in the short increases until it reaches a maximum value of 1/4 that of the unshorted turn loss, which occurs when the turn and short resistances are equal (and hence half of the turn current is bypassed). Short-circuits therefore lead to a reduction in the overall loss in the winding and, consequentially, the average temperature of the pole containing the short.

Thermal expansion of this pole is therefore restricted to a small degree and the rotor tends to bow in a direction away from the pole containing the short. This leads to a condition similar to shaft whirl and, if the number of shorted turns is significant (say three or more), severe vibration can result at even moderate loads. The greatest reduction in temperature and consequent thermal unbalance is with a solid contact of zero resistance (1) because the loss in both the turn and contact is zero. The classic symptoms are increasing vibration with increasing field current. Usually a small vibration component due to unbalanced magnetic pull appears immediately as the field current is increased from one value to another and a larger component, due to rotor bowing, grows progressively as the pole temperature gradually adjusts to the new loss distribution. A further possible cause of sudden changes in vibration level is shorts that occur under the influence of conductors expanding thermally due to load current and suddenly making contact. Excellent information on this topic is given by Rosenberg in a number of valuable papers. (1-3)

Unbalanced Magnetic Pull

Four pole generators have also been known to exhibit unbalance due to short-circuits. (2) Although their larger diameters make them stiffer and hence more resistance to lateral vibration, unbalanced magnetic pull across the airgap tends to offset this advantage. In cases where the number of shorted turns is more than one, this additional component of force can be quite significant. A simple calculation for a four pole machine with a 25 degree (mechanical) pole span, 6 meter core length, 1.5 meter diameter rotor, 75 mm airgap, 5000 A full load field current, with a single, zero resistance short-circuit in the slot adjacent to the pole head, shows that the unbalanced magnetic pull (UMP) is equal to about 4700 Newtons (or about 1060 lbf) at full load. This particular machine has five turns in this slot and it is quite common for complete coils to be short-circuited on such a machine. If this were the case, the UMP would increase to 23,500 Newtons (5300 lbf), quite significant. These calculations though do not allow for equalizing currents in the stator.

Since the maximum flux density on the pole containing the short is reduced, the UMP is directed away from the pole. This is in the same direction as the force due to rotor bowing. In general, when a number of separate shorts are present on different poles, the UMP may worsen, or it may get better, depending on which poles are affected. On a two pole machine, shorts on both poles will always improve UMP over the single short case and may also improve assymmetrical heating. On a four pole machine, shorts on consecutive poles will generally worsen UMP while shorts on alternate poles will reduce it.

The effect of a particular short on UMP is worst for a turn wound in the slot adjacent to the pole head and is least for a turn in the slot farthest from the pole head. This is because the peak demagnetizing effect of a short is largest for a turn of smallest effective pitch, i.e., one close to the pole head. Mechanical considerations also enter into the picture though because the UMP generated by a short in the slot farthest from the pole head on a two pole machine is very close to zero, whereas the UMP for the same case on a four pole unit is still significant. However, saturation of the stator core and teeth also plays a part in determining the precise overall effect.

The presence of parallel circuits in the stator winding tends to reduce UMP because equalizing currents can flow to offset the unbalanced airgap fluxes.(4) The use of equalizing connections can aid greatly in this regard but they generally require an alternate pole group connection which is usually not possible in 4 pole machines having fractional slot windings. UMP due to static eccentricity is almost non-existent in two pole machines because the two airgaps are in series magnetically and the effective pole areas are more or less equal. This may not be true if a rotor short-circuit causes the UMP because the effective pole widths can be modified, as will be shown later.

Stator Winding Circulating Currents

A further problem which can be generated by rotor interturn short-circuits is the phenomenon of stator winding circulating currents. This is not normally a problem on two pole machines since only harmonic currents can flow. However, on machines with four or more poles, subharmonic and ultrasubharmonic currents can flow. The amount and frequencies of current flowing is intimately dependent on the number of poles, the type of stator winding connection used and also upon other related factors such as airgap size and harmonic winding factors. The present paper is intended to concentrate on this problem as it relates specifically to four pole machines with fractional slot windings, although much of the discussion is general in nature.

Circulating currents flow between the parallel circuits in a phase winding and create additional heating over and above that which the stator winding may be designed to endure. The maximum number of parallel circuits possible in a machine with an integral slot winding is equal to the number of poles, and with a fractional slot winding, is equal to the number of repeatable groups in a phase. Ordinarily, the emf induced in each of these circuits is equal in magnitude and phase and, therefore, no circulating currents will flow between the circuits in the phase winding. However, if for some reason, a different amount of flux links one or more of these circuits, then a different voltage is generated and circulating currents can flow. This imbalance of flux is initially created by different peak flux densities on successive poles but can be aggravated by the method of group connection used on the stator. In turn, the group connection possible is restricted when a fractional slot winding is used, especially on machines with small numbers of poles.

CALCULATION OF VOLTAGE IMBALANCE

In this section we will describe a simple method of calculating the voltage imbalance and circulating current in a four pole machine employing a fractional slot winding. The method will be applied to predicting the circulating current in a small example machine with a number of shorted turns. With small amounts of development, the method can also be used to predict UMP and circulating currents in machines employing other types of group connection.

MMF Distribution of Shorted Turns

In a machine operating normally, the spacial distribution of rotor mmf is very nearly trapezoidal when the minor discontinuities introduced by slotting are ignored. The effect of short-circuits in the rotor is to produce a local loss of mmf, thereby reducing the peak and average values of mmf over the pole(s) containing the short-circuits.

This loss of mmf due to the shorted turns can be represented in an analytical model in several ways. However, perhaps the most easy way to think of them is as a demagnetizing mmf distribution acting against that of the main field on the particular pole or poles containing the short-circuits, see Fig. 1. We then only need to think of the elemental problem introduced by the short circuits rather than the full problem, which would be the normal condition minus the small discontinuities in mmf introduced by the short-circuits. This implies that the problem is a linear one where the principle of super-position can be applied, although we know this not to be exactly the case. Saturation exists in the main flux paths of the generator, thereby introducing a non-linearity. However, the loss of mmf tends to make the problem more linear rather than less linear so we will presume at this time that this is a valid assumtion. By making these assumptions we can obtain an idea of how severe the circulating currents might be with only modest amounts of computation.

Calculation of emf

Fig. 1 shows the mmf distribution of one or more short-circuits in the slot adjacent to the pole head on a four pole generator. The shape of this waveform is dependent on the effective pitch of the short-circuited turn(s) and also upon the amount of current bypassed, I_{fs}. Although the waveform for short-circuit(s) in a single slot has been shown here, in general, short-circuits may exist on more than one pole, so the spacial mmf function will be neither even nor odd and will contain both even and odd harmonics. We can represent this waveform as a Fourier Series of the form

$$F_{ng} = \left\{ A_O + \sum_{n=1}^{\infty} (A_n Cos(\frac{n\pi x_r}{P_O \tau}) + B_n Sin(\frac{n\pi x_r}{P_O \tau})) \right\} \quad ...(1)$$

Where A_O is always zero and the coefficients A_n and B_n are to be determined later. Equation (1) is written in terms of rotor coordinates, x_r, which are related to the stator coordinates by the equation

$$x_s = x_r \pm vt \quad ...(2)$$

where v is the linear velocity at the stator surface, the sign being determined by the direction of rotation. Substitution of (2) into (1) gives

$$F_{ng} = \left\{ \sum_{n=1}^{\infty} \left[A_n(Cos(n\pi x_s/P_O\tau) Cos(n\omega_m t) \right.\right.$$

$$-Sin(n\pi x_s/P_O\tau) Sin(n\omega_m t)) + B_n(Sin(n\pi x_s/P_O\tau)$$

$$\left.\left. Cos(n\omega_m t) + Cos(n\pi x_s/P_O\tau) Sin(n\omega_m t)) \right] \quad ...(3) \right.$$

Suppose we define new mmf's F_d and F_q as

$F_d = A_n Cos(n\pi x_s/P_O\tau) + B_n Sin(n\pi x_s/P_O\tau)$ and

$F_q = -A_n Sin(n\pi x_s/P_O\tau) + B_n Cos(n\pi x_s/P_O\tau) \quad ...(4)$

this gives

$$F_{ng} = \sum_{n=1}^{\infty} F_d Cos(n\omega_m t) + F_q Sin(n\omega_m t) \quad ...(5)$$

where ω_m is the angular velocity of the rotor and $(\pi x_s/P_O\tau) = \theta_r$ the angle subtended at the rotor center in moving a linear distance x_s from an arbitrary position on the stator surface. The corresponding airgap flux density is

$$B_{ng} = \frac{\mu_O}{K_c g} \left\{ \sum_{n=1}^{\infty} (F_d Cos(n\omega_m t) + F_q Sin(n\omega_m t)) \right\} \quad ...(6)$$

where K_c is a gap extension factor to allow for slotting (5,6) and g is the gap width. The flux linking a single coil on the stator is

$$\Phi = \int \overline{B}.d\overline{A} \text{ where } d\overline{A}=RLd\theta_r=(RL\pi/P_O\tau)dx_s \quad ...(7)$$

Hence the flux linking the first coil in the group is

$$\Phi = \int_{-\lambda\pi/2P_O}^{\lambda\pi/2P_O} \sum_{n=1}^{\infty} \frac{RL\mu_O}{K_c g}(F_d Cos(n\omega_m t) + F_q Sin(n\omega_m t))d\theta_r \quad ...(8)$$

$$\Phi = \sum_{n=1}^{\infty} \frac{RL\mu_O}{K_c g} \left\{ Sin(n\pi\lambda/2P_O)(2A_n/nCos(n\omega_m t) \right.$$

$$\left. +2B_n/nSin(n\omega_m t)) \right\} \quad ...(9)$$

and the corresponding induced emf = $-N_c d\Phi/dt$

$$e_c = \sum_{n=1}^{\infty} \frac{N_c DL\mu_O \omega_m}{K_c g} \left\{ (A_n Sin(n\omega_m t) \right.$$

$$\left. -B_n Cos(n\omega_m t)) Sin(\frac{n\pi\lambda}{2P_O}) \right\} \quad ...(10)$$

The term $Sin(\frac{n\pi\lambda}{2P_O})$ in equation (9) is the effective pitch factor for the coil and N_c is the number of turns in each coil (usually $N_c=1$).

Summation of Coil emfs

The machine to be considered has a 3 phase, 4 pole fractional slot winding in 90 slots. Before we can calculate the voltage induced in each half phase, we need to know the positions of each coil with respect to the airgap field.

In a fractional slot winding, the number of slots/pole/phase can be represented by (7),

$$q = \frac{N}{\beta} = \gamma = \frac{b}{\beta} = (\frac{15}{2}) = 7 + \frac{1}{2} \quad ...(11)$$

Hence in our case, N = 15, β= 2, γ = 7, b = 1 and there are $2P_O/\beta$ = 2 recurrent groups in each phase. Thus the winding is limited to 2 parallel circuits per phase and this is utilized in our example machine. Each phase within the recurrent group has β- b (= 1) groups with γ (=7) single coils and "b" (=1) coil groups with γ + 1(=8) single coils.

A primary attraction of fractional slot windings is that they behave as a winding with a large number of slots/pole/phase because successive pole-phase groups within the recurrent group creep in the magnetic field. This has the effect of giving very high distribution factors. However, in our case, the fundamental has only two poles (equivalent to a 30 Hz subharmonic when viewed from the stator) and the winding behaves a little differently. We can compute the effective distribution factor for this fundamental in the same manner as for a conventional integral slot winding except that separate distribution factors apply to each pole phase group (one of 7 and one of 8 coils) within the recurrent group of N (15) coils. It is simply given by

$$K_{dnk} = \frac{Sin(nN_k\alpha/2)}{N_k Sin(n\alpha/2)} \quad ...(12)$$

Where α = angle between slots $(2\pi/90)$ and N_k is the number of coils in the pole-phase group considered. For the fundamental, these equal 0.9903 and 0.9873 for the 7 and 8 coil pole-phase groups respectively. Even though considered separately, these give identical group voltages for the second harmonic (60 Hz) as they would if the distribution factor were computed in the normal manner for a fractional slot winding. The group emf is then, simply given by

$$e_{gkn} = N_k K_{dnk} e_{cn} \quad ...(13)$$

where N_k is the number of series connected coils in the Kth group.

Calculation of Voltage Imbalance

To calculate the voltage available to drive current through the parallel winding paths, we simply sum the voltages induced in each group cyclically around the phase winding. Remembering that a consecutive pole connection is used (fractional slotting here precludes the use of an alternate pole connection) and that the magnetic axes of each pole-phase group differ by 90 mechanical degrees, the voltage imbalance is given by

$$e_{un} = N_1 K_{dn1} e_{cn} \underline{/0} \;-N_2 K_{dn2} e_{cn} \underline{/-n\pi/2}$$

$$-N_1 K_{dn1} e_{cn} \underline{/-n\pi} \;+N_2 K_{dn2} e_{cn} \underline{/-3n\pi/2} \quad \ldots (14)$$

or in full

$$e_u = \frac{N_c DL \mu_o \omega_m}{K_{cg}} \sum_{n=1}^{\infty} Sin\left(\frac{n\pi\lambda}{2P_o}\right)\Big\{ N_1 K_{dn1}\big[A_n Sin(n\omega_m t)$$

$$-Sin(n(\omega_m t-\pi))\big\} -B_n(Cos(n\omega_m t)-Cos(n(\omega_m t-\pi)))\big]$$

$$+N_2 K_{dn2}\big[A_n(Sin(n(\omega_m t-3\pi/2))-Sin(n(\omega_m t-\pi/2)))$$

$$-B_n(Cos(n(\omega_m t-3\pi/2))-Cos(n(\omega_m t-\pi/2))\big]\quad \ldots(15)$$

which simplifies to

$$e_u = N_c DL \mu_o \omega_m \sum_{n=1}^{\infty} Sin\left(\frac{n\pi\lambda}{2P_o}\right)\Big\{ N_1 K_{dn1}(1-Cosn\pi),$$

$$(A_n Sin(n\omega_m t)-B_n Cos(n\omega_m t))+N_2 K_{dn2}(Sin(n\pi/2)$$

$$-Sin(3n\pi/2))(A_n Sin(n\omega_m t)+B_n Cos(n\omega_m t))\Big\}\quad \ldots(16)$$

Substitution of n = 2 into eqn (16) shows that the 2nd harmonic (60 Hz) emf acting around the loop is zero, which is as expected. Moreover, all even harmonics are absent from the circulating current, as are all harmonics having the number 6 as a factor. These latter harmonics give rise to what are commonly known as triplen harmonic currents in the stator. However, the winding does allow subharmonics (notably 30 Hz) and ultrasubharmonics (90 Hz, 150 Hz, 210 Hz, ect.) to flow. These can cause troublesome heating if not detected and it is probably advisable to fit a split-phase differential protective relaying system to machines which use a consecutive pole group connection on the stator and which have more than one circuit per phase. This leads to a more expensive machine because it requires nine bushings as opposed to the normal six. External costs may also increase because of a more complex isolated phase bus arrangement and a larger number of current transformers.

Evaluation of Fourier Coefficients A_n and B_n

The Fourier coefficients A_n and B_n in eqn (1) are obviously determined by the shape of the shorted turn mmf waveform. In turn, this mmf wave is determined by the number and distribution of shorted turns. If a four or more pole machine is considered, and shorts on more than one pole are present, both A_n and B_n have finite values. If shorts exist on only one pole or a two pole machine is being considered, B_n is zero.

For space reasons, an extensive discussion of this subject is not possible, so we will restrict considerations to shorts of zero resistance on one pole only. If the notation of Fig. 1c is used, the coefficients A_n and B_n become

$$A_n= \sum_M \frac{2}{n\pi} I_{fsm} Sin\left(\frac{n\alpha_m\pi}{4P_o\tau}\right) \text{ and } B_n=0 \quad \ldots(17)$$

where I_{fsm} are the ampere-turns bypassed in the mth rotor slot and $\alpha_m/2P_o\tau$ is the fractional pitch of the rotor coil containing the shorts. Using the data shown in Table 1, the values of

A_n for a completely shorted coil in the slot adjacent to the pole head (m = 1) at full load are given in Fig. 2. It will be noted that quite high values (-ve and +ve) exist for a wide range of values of n. Fourier coefficients for other combinations of short circuits can be computed as necessary.

Effects of Armature Reaction

Because the voltage imbalance drives current through the windings, a reaction field is induced which limits the flow of current. For currents flowing completely through the winding, the reactance representing the effects of armature reaction is the direct-axis magnetizing reactance, X_{md}. In our case a somewhat different reactance applies and we need to calculate what this reactance is. Using the basic definition of inductance as the ratio of stator flux linkages to field current, we can calculate the effective harmonic magnetizing inductance by integrating eqn (16) with respect to time, dividing the result by the bypassed field current, I_{fs}, and multiplying it by the harmonic angular frequency, $n\omega_m$.

The flux linkages in the stator take the form

$$\Phi = \sum_{n=1}^{\infty} (\Phi_{dn} Cos(n\omega_m t)+ \Phi_{qn} Sin(n\omega_m t)) \quad \ldots(18)$$

the Sin $n\omega_m t$ and Cos $n\omega_m t$ arising because of rotation of the rotor. Following the previously described procedure gives the result

$$X_{sfn}=\frac{2DL\mu_o\omega_m N_c}{K_{cg}} Sin\left(\frac{n\pi\lambda}{2P_o}\right)\Big\{ A_n((1-Cosn\pi)N_1 K_{dn1}$$

$$+(Sin(\frac{n\pi}{2})-Sin(\frac{3n\pi}{2}))N_2 K_{dn2} Cosn\omega_m t+B_n(Sin(n\pi/2)$$

$$-Sin(3n\pi/2))N_2 K_{dn2}-(1-Cosn\pi)(N_1 K_{dn1})Sin(n\omega_m t)\Big\}$$

$$\ldots(19)$$

or

$$X_{sfn} = X_{sdn} Cosn\omega_m t + X_{sqn} Sin\, n\omega_m t \quad \ldots(20)$$

where X_{sqn} is a pseudo-quadrature-axis reactance.

A curve showing the variation of X_{sfn} with n for the values of A_n given in Fig. 2 is shown in Fig. 3. As can be seen, the harmonic magnetizing reactances fall very rapidly with increasing harmonic order. After the first few harmonics, the leakage reactance is the primary component of the impedance limiting the flow of harmonic current. Corresponding values of e_{un} are given in Fig. 4.

Circulating Current

In calculating the circulating current it is assumed that the normal slot leakage reactance is the same for the circulating current as it is for the load current flowing through the winding. This would be so, provided that the circulating currents do not change the phase of currents normally seen in each slot.

We have calculated the magnetizing reactance in the previous section and, to determine the total impedance in the circuit, we simply need to add to this the armature leakage reactance, corrected for the appropriate frequency and the number of circuits in the machine. The armature resistance can also be corrected for frequency changes if desired. For a two circuit machine

$$i_{cn} = e_{un}/(4R_{an}+j(X_{sdn}+2nX_{al})) \quad \ldots(21)$$

where X_{al} is the armature leakage reactance at n = 2 when viewed from the machine terminals. Using the values of e_{un} given in Fig. 4, with $X_{al} = -.13$ pu at n = 2, $i_{cl} = 173.3$ amps (0.054 pu), quite significant.

EFFECTS OF SHORTS ON POLE MAGNETIZATION

By referring to Fig. 1, we can see that the short-circuit partially demagnetizes pole 2 in the same diagram. Similarly, the shorted turn mmf also acts against the normal direction of magnetization of poles 1 and 3. However, this same mmf strengthens the magnetization of pole 4. Because Gauss' theorem holds, all poles have the same total flux emanating from or flowing into them. Thus, because the flux densities are different, the effective pole widths must change from the values seen in the unshorted condition. The poles still may be considered to span 180 degrees magnetically but this is no longer 90 or 180 mechanical degrees.

In practice, the above condition is limited because the return path for the flux (induced by the negative part of Fig. 1(c)) is quite long so there is still a tendency for the two poles adjacent to that containing the short to be affected most.

CONCLUSIONS

Rotor shorted turns can cause troublesome circulating currents, the magnitudes and frequencies of which are fixed by the stator group connection, the number of poles, the extent and location of rotor shorts, the airgap size, and harmonic winding factors. Lower order harmonics (≤ 7) are most troublesome and above this, other harmonic currents can be neglected. Depending on the cause, it may be advisable to fit split phase differential relays to some four pole machines with consecutive pole stator group connections. This scheme can be used to trip the machine if necessary.

ACKNOWLEDGEMENTS

The author is indebted to Mr. L. G. Gifford and Mr. J. R. Mather of the Detroit Edison Company for many valuable discussions and information related to this topic.

REFERENCES

1. Rosenberg, L. T., 1955, *AIEE Trans*, 38-41

2. Rosenberg, L. T., 1978, *IEEE Summer Meeting* Paper A78, 4587-8

3. Rosenberg, L. T., 1971, *Allis Chalmers Eng. Rev.*, *36*, 17-21

4. Siskind, C. S., 1954, Alternating Current Armature Windings, McGraw-Hill, 187-193

5. Binns, K. J., 1964, *Proc IEE*, *111*, 1847-1858

6. Carter, F. W., 1926, *J. Inst. Elect. Engr*, *359*, 1115-39

7. Liwshitz, M. M., 1943, *AIEE Trans*, 664-666

TABLE 1 - Machine Data for Sample Calculation

D	L	ω_m	g (mm)	K_c	I_f(F.L)
1.46m	5.5m	188.5	55	1.1	714

I_f(N.L)	V_{rated}	I_{rated}
350	14400	3210

P	$\text{Cos}\phi$	X_d(60)	X_{al}	R_f(75°C)
60MW	0.75	1.24pu	0.13pu	0.262Ω

λ	P_o	Slots	Parallels
19/22.5	2	90	2

R_a (75°C)	St. Conn	Slots(rotor)	α_m
0.00352Ω	Y	40	0.317m

Rot. Turns/Pole	Turns Shorted	N_c
85	17	1

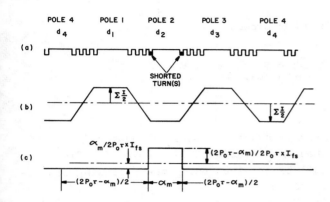

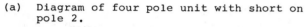

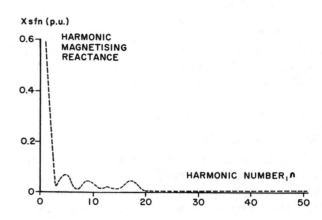

(a) Diagram of four pole unit with short on pole 2.

(b) Normal (simplified) rotor mmf distribution.

(c) Shorted turn mmf distribution.

<u>NB</u> Values of X_{sfn} in above figure are for odd values of n only. Data as Table 1.

Figure 1 MMF Distributions

Figure 3 Variation of magnetizing reactance, X_{sfn}, with Harmonic Number, n.

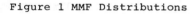

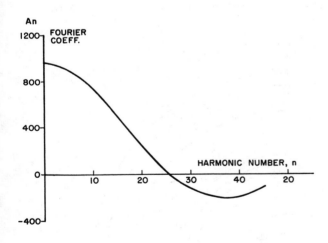

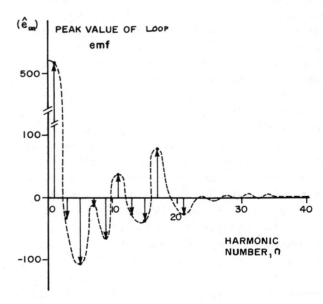

<u>NB</u> Above coefficient applies to a short in 1st slot for machine data given in Table 1.

<u>NB</u> Above values of $\hat{e}_{un}$ apply only to machine data in Table 1.

Figure 2 Variation of Fourier Coefficient, A_n, with Harmonic Number, n.

Figure 4 Variation of loop emf, e_{un}, with Harmonic Number, n.

NONLINEAR MAGNETIC FIELD ANALYSIS OF A PERMANENT-MAGNET D.C. TACHOGENERATOR BY THE FINITE ELEMENT METHOD

D. Stoia   M.M. Radulescu

Department of Electrical Engineering   Rolling-Stock Mechanical Enterprise
University of Brasov, Romania   Cluj-Napoca, Romania

1.   INTRODUCTION

The accurate determination of two-dimensional magnetic field distribution in electrical machines is an essential problem for the design and performance prediction of such machines. Classical analytical and analog solutions to this problem are possible only for idealized cases of gross simplifying assumptions concerning geometries, material properties and boundary conditions. Complex geometries, media interfaces and material nonlinearities are generally not suitable for traditional approaches and, therefore, require the use of numerical methods.

With the advent of modern digital computers, numerical methods have become practical in engineering design. The finite element method has emerged during the past decade as a useful numerical method for magnetic field analysis of electrical machines. The method is based on formulating the magnetic field equations in variational terms and extremizing the associated energy functional by a set of trial functions approximating the solution. It is especially effective for field computation in small electrical machines in which it is not possible to measure the magnetic field values precisely.

This paper describes the application of the finite element method for solution of nonlinear permanent-magnet field problems in two-dimensions using vector potential formulation. The numerical method is applied to the analysis of the magnetic field distribution in a strontium-ferrite permanent-magnet d.c. tachogenerator at no load condition. The corresponding air-gap flux density waveforms are also shown. Inhomogeneity and B-H curve nonlinearity of magnetic materials are taken into account.

2.   NONLINEAR VARIATIONAL STATEMENT OF THE MAGNETIC FIELD PROBLEM INVOLVING PERMANENT MAGNETS

The variational field model of a per-

manent-magnet d.c. tachogenerator, which quadrant cross-section is shown in Figure 1, will be obtained using the following assumptions :

(a) The electromagnetic field quantities are independent of the z-coordinate measured along the air gap.

(b) Only axially directed components of the magnetic vector potential, $\bar{A} = \bar{u}_z A_z(x,y) = \bar{u}_z A(x,y)$ and of the current density, $\bar{J} = \bar{u}_z J_z = \bar{u}_z J$, exist.

(c) The iron parts are isotropic and the B-H characteristics are single-valued.

(d) The magnetic field outside the machine being assumed negligible, the external contour of the stator is treated as a line of zero vector potential.

(e) At no load conditions, the pole axis is also a line of zero vector potential.

The above assumptions are quite common in electrical machine analysis. They limit the problem to two dimensions and the field

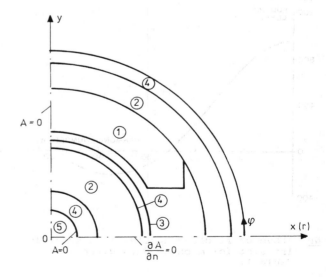

Fig.
Figure 1. Quadrant cross-section of the permanent-magnet d.c. tachogenerator (scale 2 : 1).

region to a quarter part of the machine cross-section. The latter consists of a permanent-magnet stator zone 1, two iron zones 2 representing internal and external stator yokes, a thin non-magnetic cup-type rotor zone 3 and four sub-regions 4, i.e. air-gap and non-magnetic zones, all with free space reluctivity ($\nu_o = (1/4\pi)\ 10^7$ m/H) and a shaft zone 5.

From the Hamilton's principle applied to macroscopic magnetostatics, the nonlinear variational field model [2] involves the extremization, in suitable boundary conditions, of the action integral :

$$F = \int_R [\,(\int_0^B \bar{H}\,d\bar{B}) - \bar{J}\bar{A}]\,dR\ ,\qquad (1)$$

wherein the integrand is the Lagrangian of the nonlinear magnetic field, defined as a difference between cinetic coenergy and potential energy terms. For the field region of figure 1, by assuming a given permanent magnetization $\bar{M}_p = \bar{B}_r$ ($\bar{B}_r$ is the remanent magnetic flux density) and a field-dependent reluctivity $\nu = \nu(B)$, the constitutive field equation takes the forms :

$$\bar{H} = \nu(B)\ (\bar{B} - \bar{B}_r)\ ,\qquad (2)$$

in the permanent-magnet stator zone ;

$$\bar{H} = \nu(B)\ \bar{B}\ ,\qquad (3)$$

in iron sub-regions and

$$\bar{H} = \nu_o\ \bar{B}\ ,\qquad (4)$$

in zones containing non-magnetic materials. Therefore, the solution of the two-dimensional magnetic field problem with boundary conditions specified in Figure 1 is obtained by finding a field function which extremizes the value of the general nonlinear energy functional :

$$F = \int_R [\,(\int_0^B \nu(B)(\bar{B} - \bar{B}_r)\ d\bar{B}) - JA]\,dxdy.\ (5)$$

Homogenous Neumann condition and continuity conditions at material interfaces are implicitly satisfied by the functional extremization process.

3. FINITE ELEMENT SOLUTION OF THE PERMANENT-MAGNET FIELD PROBLEM

First-order triangular finite elements of unrestricted geometry, topology and containing material inhomogeneities are used for discretizing the field region as shown in

Figure 2. The meshes of this hexa-triangular grid enclose elemental regions of constant reluctivity, current density and flux density. 630 triangles and 352 nodes are used to represent the quadrant of the examined permanent-magnet d.c. tachogenerator. The discretization is drawn semi-automatically on the basis of the geometrical input data.

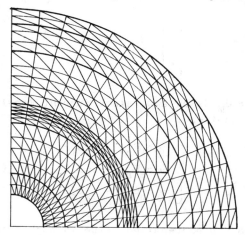

Figure 2. Discretization of the field region by first-order triangular elements.

Inside an elemental triangle the field function (i.e. magnetic vector potential z - component $A(x,y)$ is linearly interpolated from the three vertex values :

$$A(x,y) = \frac{1}{2\Delta} \sum_{k=l,m,n} (a_k + b_k x + c_k y)A_k,\ (6)$$

where Δ is the triangle area, the index k ranges over the triangle vertices l,m,n and a_k, b_k, c_k are given by $a_l = x_m y_n - x_n y_m$, $b_l = y_m - y_n$, $c_l = x_n - x_m$, and so on.

Differentiating (6), one obtains the value of magnetic flux density inside each triangle :

$$B = \frac{1}{2\Delta}\ [(b_l A_l + b_m A_m + b_n A_n)^2 +$$
$$+ (c_l A_l + c_m A_m + c_n A_n)^2\,]^{1/2}\quad (7)$$

Equation (5) is adapted to suit the finite element structure and represented as a summations over the elemental regions. Functional extremization is achieved by setting the first derivative of (5) to zero with respect to each of the nodal values of potential function.

After considerable algebra [2] one obtains a suitable discrete representation of (5) for only one triangle :

$$\frac{1}{4\Delta}\begin{bmatrix} \nu_x\, b_l^2 + \nu_y\, c_l^2 & \nu_x\, b_l b_m + \nu_y c_l c_m & \nu_x b_l b_n + \nu_y c_l c_n \\ & \nu_x\, b_m^2 + \nu_y c_m^2 & \nu_x b_m b_n + \nu_y c_m c_n \\ \text{symetric} & & \nu_x b_n^2 + \nu_y c_n^2 \end{bmatrix} \begin{Bmatrix} A_l \\ A_m \\ A_n \end{Bmatrix}$$

$$= \frac{(J + J_M)\,\Delta}{3} \begin{Bmatrix} 1 \\ 1 \\ 1 \end{Bmatrix} \qquad (8)$$

where J_M is an equivalent current density representing :

$$J_M = \frac{3}{2\Delta} \begin{Bmatrix} \nu_y c_l B_{rx} - \nu_x b_l B_{ry} \\ \nu_y c_m B_{rx} - \nu_x b_m B_{ry} \\ \nu_y c_m B_{rx} - \nu_x b_n B_{ry} \end{Bmatrix} \qquad (9)$$

J_M is a predetermined value in each triangle of the permanent-magnet zone, where J is not present.

When expressions similar to (8) are written for each and every triangle of the discretization grid and the corresponding terms added, a single matrix equation is obtained for the entire field region, in the form :

$$[M]\ \{A\} = \{S\} , \qquad (10)$$

where $\{A\}$ is the column vector of unknown vertex values of field function A, $\{S\}$ the column vector of actual and equivalent current densities, which is a function of ν in permanent-magnet zone and $[M]$ the

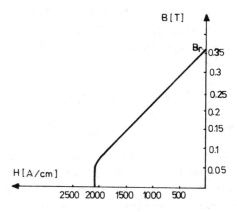

Figure 3. Demagnetization curve of strontium-ferrite permanent-magnet.

global coefficient matrix obtained from the elemental matrices as in (8). $[M]$ is a square, symmetric, band-structured sparse matrix and includes the reluctivity ν as a function of the magnetic flux density and thereby of the vector potential. The matrix $[M]$ and the system of equations (10) are thus nonlinear. The magnetic vector potential at each node of discretization and consecutively the magnetic field distribution

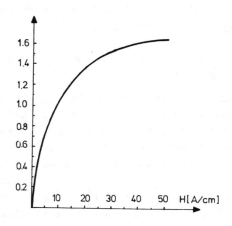

Figure 4. Mean magnetization curve of iron material.

in the field region are obtained by solving the set of nonlinear equations (10) by means of an iterative technique [2]. In each iteration the resulting linear system for the up-to-date values of ν is solved by Gaussian elimination.

For the investigated d.c. tachogenerator, the permanent magnet represents an anisotropic, radially magnetised strontium-ferrite, which has : $\nu_x = \nu_y = \nu(B)$ and $B_{rx} = B_r \cos\varphi$, $B_{ry} = B_r \sin\varphi$, where φ is the angulare coordinate of each triangle centroid in the permanent-magnet zone mesh. B_r and $\nu(B)$ are both obtained from the corresponding stable demagnetization curve given in Figure 3.

In iron parts of the tachogenerator, $\nu = \nu(B)$ and results from the single-valued magnetization characteristic reproduced in Figure 4. Both B-H curves were tabulated to take the form of $\nu = \nu$ (B) and modelled by piece wise cubic spline interpolation [2].

For the finite-element analysed permanent-magnet d.c. tachogenerator, the no-load magnetic field distribution in the quadrant cross-section of the machine is given in

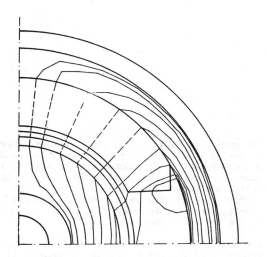

Figure 5. Magnetic field distribution
in the quadrant cross-section of
the permanent-magnet d.c. tachogenerator at no-load condition.

Figure 5. The field plot was obtained by
joining equipotential points with straight
lines. The corresponding air-gap magnetic
flux density waveforms are represented in
Figure 6.

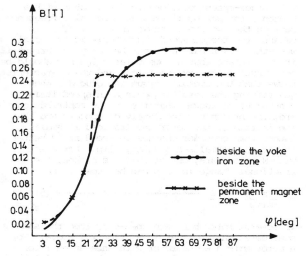

Figure 6. Air-gap magnetic flux density waveforms at no-load.

4   CONCLUSIONS

The essential components of a finite
element solution of the two-dimensional non-
linear permanent-magnet field problem were
introduced. This approach was applied to a
strontium-ferrite permanent-magnet d.c.
tachogenerator. The magnetic field distribution and air-gap flux density waveforms
at no-load condition were obtained.

In conclusion, the authors like to
suggest that the finite element method is
sufficiently advanced to allow interactive
magnetic circuit design to be carried out
for small permanent-magnet machines.

5   ACKNOWLEDGMENT

The authors with to acknowledge the
work of Dr. M. G. Munteanu from the University of Braşov in developing and programming
the finite element algorithms.

6   REFERENCES

[1]   Binns, K.J., Jabbar, M.A., Barnard,
W.R., "Computation of the magnetic
field of permanent magnets in iron
cores", Proc. IEE, 122 (1975), 12,
pp. 1377-1381.

[2]   Mîndru, G., Rădulescu, M.M., "Numerical analysis of the electromagnetic
field", vol. I (in Romanian), Polytechnic Institute of Cluj-Napoca, 1982.

[3]   Stoia, D., Rădulescu, M.M., "Design of
permanent-magnet d.c. servomotors for
incremental motion", 1980 Digests of
the INTERMAG Conference, Boston,
p. 29-7.

THE DETECTION OF ROTOR DEFECTS IN INDUCTION MOTORS

C.Hargis, B.G.Gaydon and K.Kamash

Central Electricity Generating Board, UK

1. INTRODUCTION

Where rotor bar fracture is suspected in an induction motor a method is needed for determining the extent and nature of damage to facilitate potentially expensive maintenance decisions. Several techniques have evolved in different situations in an attempt to meet the need for a fast and convenient method of diagnosis.

Ideally an instant result would be available without stopping the machine, allowing differentiation between fractured rotor bars, bars of anomalous resistance, magnetic anisotropy and load fluctuations; all of which may cause the characteristic ammeter swing which normally arouses the suspicions of maintenance staff. Furthermore, physical access to the machine may be difficult.

The most readily available parameters are stator current, shaft speed and frame vibration, each of which is influenced by an electromagnetically irregular rotor.

2. PRINCIPLES

2.1 Current

Consider a regular cage rotor with an even number, N, of slots rotating with angular frequency ω_R. The impedance as seen from a stator winding varies with a fundamental frequency of $N\omega_R$. If the rotor is irregular then the fundamental becomes $2\omega_R$.

For a stator winding with p pole-pairs and supply frequency ω, the fundamental m.m.f. at mechanical angle θ is represented by

$$m_1 = M_1 \sin (\omega t - p\theta) \quad\text{------------------ (1)}$$

The rotor m.m.f. will be subject to modulation by the impedance variation. Considering only fundamentals, and referring to the stator, irregularity will generate m.m.f. components given by

$$m_2 = M_2 [\sin \omega t(3-2s) - 3 p\theta-\lambda$$
$$+ \sin \omega t(1-2s) - p\theta-\lambda] \quad\text{------------------- (2)}$$

where s represents slip.

The second of these terms alone results in stator winding e.m.f. and a current in the supply which is a direct measure of rotor non-uniformity.

It may be shown that if a contiguous group of bars subtending electrical angle α is open circuit, and the machine speed remains constant, the ratio of the magnitude of this component of current to that of the supply current is given approximately by

$$R_s \underset{\sim}{\sim} \frac{\sin \alpha}{2p(2\pi - \alpha)} \quad\text{------------------ (3)}$$

$$\text{where } \alpha = \frac{2 \pi n p}{N} \quad\text{------------------- (4)}$$

for n broken contiguous bars, where $n \ll N$.

The cyclic variation in current produces a torque variation at twice slip frequency. This results in a speed variation dependent upon the system inertia, which is generally not negligible. Consequently there is a reduction in the magnitude of the current component at $\omega(1-2s)$ and a component appears at $\omega(1+2s)$, enhanced by modulation of the third time-harmonic flux in the stator.

The stator current inherently reflects the overall condition of the rotor, and is not capable of providing information on the configuration of non-contiguous broken bars. In the limit, a pair of faulty bars spaced by an electrical angle of $\pi/2$ radians would produce no $\omega(1-2s)$ term. It is widely observed in practice however that bars tend to fail in groups, since a single broken bar causes an increased current to flow in its neighbours (1).

Similarly, it is unlikely that current analysis would be able to discriminate the effects of a broken bar from those of a group of bars with anomalous resistance.

2.2 Speed

The torque-speed relationship for a motor with a broken rotor bar oscillates at twice slip frequency between the two limits shown in Fig.1. This is because the torque-speed characteristic is normal when the broken bar would not be carrying current if it were intact, but a moment later the bar should be contributing its maximum torque and the characteristic shows that the overall torque is reduced. When quantifying the resulting change in speed it is convenient to assume that the torque contribution from the broken bar completely disappears and that the inertia of the motor and its load is small. Rather than consider changes in speed it is better to use the normalised quantity slip. For a motor with N rotor bars, one of which is broken, the fractional change in slip can be shown to be

$$\frac{\Delta \text{ slip}}{\text{slip}} = \frac{2}{N} \quad\text{------------------------- (5)}$$

If several rotor bars are open-circuited the same considerations apply as in section 2.1 above. For a motor with a wound rotor with unbalanced rotor currents (such as would be caused by unequal liquid resistors in the external rotor circuit), the equivalent expression is

$$\frac{\Delta \text{ slip}}{\text{slip}} = \frac{2 I_n}{I_p} \quad\text{-------------------- (6)}$$

2.3 Vibration

The vibration of an induction machine has been described, for instance by Binns and Barnard (2). A frame-mounted accelerometer responds to vibration at all the principal frequencies, although no meaningful measurement of relative magnitudes can be made without knowledge of the transfer function of the path between the stator teeth and the frame.

The predominant vibration frequencies are in the series $2\omega k$ $(k = 1,2,3 \text{-----})$ and $\omega[N(1-s) \pm 2K]$ $(k = 0,1,2,3 \text{------})$ which arise from the cross-products of the fundamental flux wave with itself and its harmonics and with rotor-slot components.

An electromagnetic irregularity in the rotor causes modulation of the vibration by a function periodic at the rotational speed. The function is strong in harmonics in the case of a discontinuity such as a broken bar because of the high flux density around that bar. Since the spectrum for a healthy motor contains lines spaced at intervals of 2ω, the addition of a multitude of lines at intervals $\omega(1-s)$ is clearly visible.

The accelerometer on the frame measures the net effect of the force distribution throughout the stator. In a typical machine of 5MW rating, the frequencies of interest are around 2.6KHz, with pole numbers around 104. Some idea of the dynamic response of the stator may be gained from the fact that the lowest shell mode of vibration is in the region of 200 Hz.

No attempt has been made at a full analysis, but there is some experimental evidence that the effect of individual rotor slots may be discerned.

3. APPLICATION

3.1 Current Analysis

Current is particularly easy to monitor, even where the motor is inaccessible or in a hazardous environment, since a current-transformer circuit (for protection and/or measurement) is usually located in a non-hazardous situation.

Normal procedure is to make a tape recording of the current in one phase for later analysis with a proprietary high resolution spectrum analyser. The inevitable nonlinearity of measurement does not significantly affect the results.

Fig.2 shows spectra for two machines of identical design, one of which has a rotor defect corresponding to three fractured bars. In this case the lower sideband is clearly discernible and easily measured relative to the fundamental.

In the case of Fig.2 the load was a fan fitted directly to the shaft, providing a steady load torque. Fig.3 shows a spectrum for a coal pulverising mill with two stages of reduction gearing, some under-damped flexible couplings and a randomly fluctuating load (because of the pulverising action). Several 'sidebands' are present at frequencies such as 0.3Hz, 2.7Hz and 7.5Hz, and the 50Hz line is broad because of the random torque fluctuations. It is clearly important to identify the exact slip frequency if rotor anomalies are to be identified. Assuming that an independent slip frequency measurement is not available, it is normally possible to deduce an accurate value of speed by measuring the frequency of the principal rotor slot products, $\omega(N\pm1)$.

In the machine of Fig.3 the slip frequency was 0.4Hz so a rotor anomaly would generate a line 0.8Hz below 50Hz, absent in this case.

Current analysis also has application in mechanical condition monitoring, since load disturbances may be quantified from measurement of current modulation and a knowledge of mechanical parameters.

There is no obvious method for distinguishing between the various possible rotor anomalies.

Cases of a group of rotor bars with abnormal resistivity have been encountered; although undesirable there may not be a significant risk of consequential damage.

3.2 Speed Measurement

Fluctuations in motor speed at twice slip frequency are indicative of rotor defects. Two instruments have been developed to measure any twice slip frequency component in rotational speed, both of which require a once-per-revolution pulse from a tachometer sensor and a 50Hz mains reference signal.

The simpler instrument, called the Spirostrobe, uses analogue techniques to generate a polar display on a storage oscilloscope. A defective rotor is indicated by the display having a peanut shape (actually a second-order cardioid) instead of being circular, as shown in Fig.4.

The trace is drawn during one slip period, and each point on the trace represents the time for a shaft rotation. The polar angle Θ represents the phase of the slip cycle, and the radius R depends on the slowness of rotation (increasing with slip).

A more sophisticated instrument has been developed which uses signal averaging techniques to provide accurate measurements even in the presence of random speed fluctuations. This instrument is based on a proprietary mini-computer mounted on a trolley. Fig.5 shows the computer display of two cycles of speed fluctuations during one slip cycle, and its Fourier transform which quantifies the amplitude of the twice slip frequency component of speed fluctuation. To avoid the difficulty of transportation, it is technically feasible to use a simple analogue telephone link between a shaft pulse generator and the remote computer. In this way any motor connected to the National supply can be tested from a single location, using only a shaft pulse generator and a telephone interface beside the motor.

Several hundred speed fluctuation measurements have been made on motors in the C.E.G.B. and S.S.E.B., and some of the motors identified as being defective had been thought to be in good condition. In most circumstances the presence of a single defective rotor bar can be detected. When a tachometer sensor is not already fitted it is usually easy to clamp an optical sensor close to the shaft to monitor a painted stripe. Although it is easier to paint a stationary shaft, it has proved possible to mark the shafts of motors under load.

3.3 Vibration Analysis

Vibration monitoring is used within the C.E.G.B. for mechanical condition monitoring of important motors. An extension of the technique to include electrical rotor condition monitoring is therefore attractive.

The motors whose current spectra are shown in Fig.2 have accelerometers fitted to their frames measuring radial acceleration. They are two-pole machines with 52 rotor slots running at a nominal speed of 2970 r.p.m. on full load, so rotor slot-derived vibration is centred on 2574 Hz. Fig.6 shows the result of spectral analysis over a 25 Hz band around the main rotor-slot frequency, and shows that the presence of three broken bars has a dramatic effect which is easily recognised by non-specialist staff as related to a rotor defect.

The spectrum is difficult to interpret further, and time-domain analysis is a potentially useful alternative. Fig.7 was produced from the same pair of machines as Fig.6 by superimposing successive acceleration traces synchronously with shaft rotation. The defective rotor produces a clear group of high-amplitude peaks, repeated rather less than 180° later.

This effect would not occur with a magnetically anisotropic rotor which causes a relatively small disturbance in flux density. In the case of bars fractured at intervals of $\pi/2$ electrical radians, when no significant current or speed variation occurs, only vibration analysis will expose the defect.

4. CONCLUSIONS

Several practical techniques have been presented for determining the condition of an induction machine rotor. The effect of electromagnetic irregularity may be quantified by either speed or current analysis: or both where confirmation is important. Either technique may be used to monitor the progress of a defect. Both are liable to under-estimate the number of bars broken and may, under certain rare circumstances, fail to detect a defect. They are complementary to one another since the high inertia load which maximises current modulation also mini-mises speed variation, and vice-versa.

Vibration analysis is different since it does not summate the overall effect of rotor condition, but separates the effects of individual slots. At the present state of development it is useful as part of an overall condition monitoring programme. It excludes the effect of magnetic anisotropy and detects broken bars in configurations which cause no speed or current fluctuation, but it is not capable of quantitative results.

All of these techniques may be applied quickly under site conditions, without stopping the machine. Where the machine is inaccessible and neither shaft pulse generators nor frame vibration transducers are available, current analysis is the only viable technique.

5. REFERENCES

1. M.Jufer and M.Abedelaziz. Influence d'une Rupture de Barre ou d'un Anneau sur les Caractéristiques Externes d'un Moteur Asynchrone à Cage. Bull. SEV/VSE 69 (1978) 17, 9 September.

2. K.J.Binns and W.R.Barnard. Some Aspects of the use of Flux and Vibration Spectra in Electrical Machines. Conference on Applications of Time-Series Analysis, University of Southampton, Sept.1977 pp 17.1 - 17.12.

6. ACKNOWLEDGEMENTS

The authors are grateful to the Central Electricity Generating Board for permission to publish this paper.

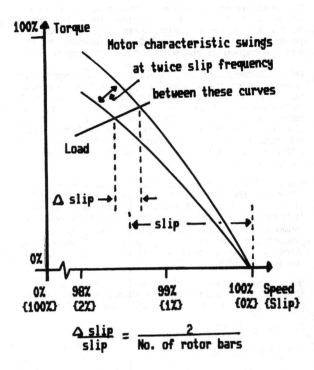

$$\frac{\Delta \text{ slip}}{\text{slip}} = \frac{2}{\text{No. of rotor bars}}$$

Fig.1   Torque-speed characteristic

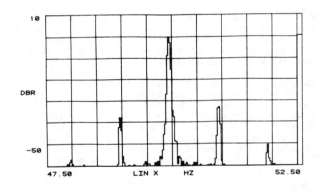

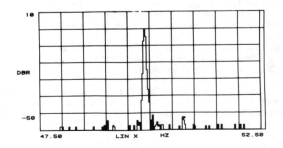

Fig.2   Stator current spectra
upper : three contiguous broken bars
lower : no broken bars

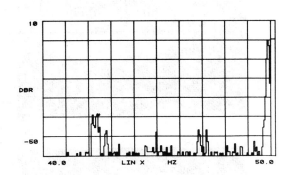

Fig.3   Stator current spectrum for coal
         pulverising mill motor, no
         broken bars

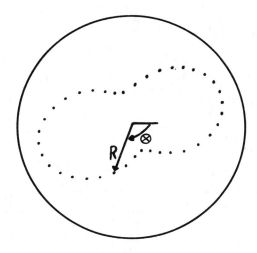

⊗ = phase of slip cycle

R ∝ instantaneous slip

Fig.4   Spirostrobe display

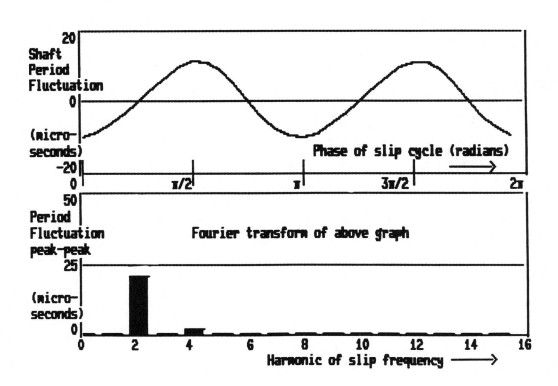

Fig.5   Computer analysis of speed fluctuation

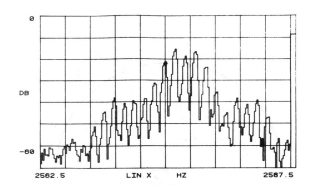

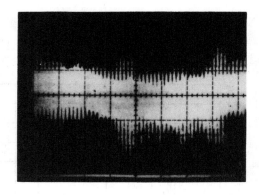

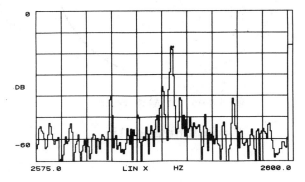

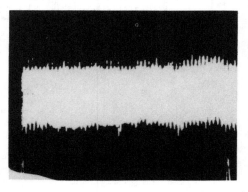

Fig.6   Frame acceleration spectra
        upper : three contiguous broken bars
        lower : no broken bars

Fig.7   Frame acceleration vs. time
        upper : three contiguous broken bars
        lower : no broken bars

MEASURING TECHNIQUES FOR IDENTIFYING PARTIAL DISCHARGES IN STATOR WINDINGS OF ELECTRICAL MACHINES

R. Miller, W.K. Hogg and I.A. Black

Department of Electrical and Electronic Engineering, Brighton Polytechnic, Brighton, BN2 4GJ, UK

INTRODUCTION

High-power electrical machine insulation failures are both costly and time-consuming to the user and the ability to be able to identify and possibly locate the source of such faults is economically advantageous. Core monitor devices (1) will sense certain faults before any extensive damage occurs within the machine; however, they do not provide any indication as to the fault location. The use of compounds (2) for coding particular areas within a machine, when used with condition monitor systems, could provide a more positive location as to the position of a particular fault. However a continuous minor fault may develop quite rapidly into a major fault, causing extensive damage to the machine before the above sensors could operate. The inability to detect such faults can be attributed to the fact that the thermal insertion of insulating particles or coding compounds are insufficient to activate the condition monitor. Hence, fast reacting, electronic early warning of the development of a potential fault is economically viable. Radio frequency techniques (3) appear to be the most probable methods to give an early warning of localised faults. These methods rely upon the fact that electrical discharges emit high-frequency pulses, the spectra of which can be analysed. In addition to this, any discharges such as those occurring within the bulk of the stator insulation, will have magnitudes and spectral signatures different from those of, say, slot discharges between coil surfaces and the stator core.

The pulse spectral analysis technique (4) which is described in this paper, is in the relatively early stage of development. However the results demonstrate that the method can be employed to detect, locate and identify the source of a particular discharge. The results also indicate that this method of analysis could be used in acceptance and quality control testing of stator bars and high-voltage machine windings. Once fully developed, there is also the possibility of using the technique in association with condition monitors for a continual assessment of the condition of a machine on load. In this paper the theory and application of special analysis techniques is outlined and discussed.

THEORY OF PULSE SPECTRAL ANALYSIS

Electrical discharge sources, associated with high-power electrical machines, can be broadly divided into two categories, namely those taking place within stator winding insulation systems and discharges and noise outside the machine. For the purposes of this paper, only simulated stator discharges will be considered. These discharges can also be divided into a number of different types, each having its own typical range of magnitude and frequency; some of these are listed below :

(a) Partial discharges within the stator bar insulation. These will have magnitudes possibly up to 10,000 pC and a frequency of typically 25 MHz. The discharge pattern is reasonably symmetrical.

(b) Slot discharges between the stator bar insulation and the stator core. Usually the magnitudes are well in excess of 10,000 pC, but the frequency spectrum will be similar to that quoted in (a) above. However, the discharge pattern will not be symmetrical.

(c) Surface discharges over the end winding region. The magnitudes would generally be of the same order as quoted in (a), but the frequency would be about 2 MHz. The discharge pattern would again be unsymmetrical.

(d) Electrical discharges between broken strands. In this case the magnitudes would be in excess of those of (a), possibly by two orders of magnitude. Since the frequency is related to the resonant frequency of the winding, it would not be in excess of 500 kHz.

It is to be appreciated that large generators and high power high-voltage machines are normally star connected, consequently line end coils are at much greater risk from the above type of deterioration mechanisms in service than those further down the winding. However, if the technique to be described is used for acceptance or quality control tests, each bar would be tested at the phase voltage.

To demonstrate how the various simulated discharge pulses propagate, it is necessary to consider the high-frequency equivalent circuit of a stator winding. Figure 1 shows one phase of a typical winding arrangement having 7 coils in series per parallel path, one upper bar and one lower bar for each stator slot. This simplified circuit may be used because the outer stator bar insulation surface is coated with a semiconducting layer which is effectively grounded through the stator core. Thus the capacitance between adjacent coils will be negligible, as will be the mutual inductance between coils sharing the same slot. Hence the only effective components which have to be considered are the capacitance to earth and the series inductance of each coil. The circuit of Fig. 1 can be further simplified by considering each phase to consist only of the total capacitance to ground and the total series inductance. It should also be appreciated that if a neutral grounding transformer is in use, then at the pulse frequencies being considered, its capacitive reactance would approach the characteristic impedance of the winding. The overall effect of this could help to reduce the effect of reflections, due to the high-frequency pulse.

MEASUREMENT AND INSTRUMENTATION

Figure 2 illustrates the measurement system for applying simulated discharge pulses to a stator bar and analysing the partial discharge frequency characteristics. The minicomputer controls the magnitude, frequency, polarity and initial slope of the simulated discharges. This control system also enables a sequence of positive pulses followed by a negative group to be applied to the bar, at a rate equal to the test frequency, thus making the test conditions as near practical as possible. The separation between consecutive pulses (double or alternate polarity) can be varied, with a minimum spacing of 2 μsec.

The pulses in the bars are monitored at each end by high-frequency pulse amplifiers. These have a 200 MHz gain-bandwidth product, an input impedance of 10^7 Ω and an output impedance of 50 Ω, suitable for driving the long lengths of cable between the amplifier at the ends of the bar and the oscilloscope outside the high-voltage test area. Having recorded the discharge pulse shapes on the oscilloscope, these are then transferred to the minicomputer. This stores and evaluates the magnitudes of the various harmonic components and their respective phase-angles relative to the fundamental frequency of the pulse being studied.

By considering the phase angle of the (n^{th}) harmonic relative to its fundamental frequency, together with a knowledge of the insulation system employed, the position of the discharge source may be predicted. The particular harmonic (n^{th}) selected for analysis of the discharge position is the one whose magnitude is significantly higher than the next higher harmonic $((n+1)^{th})$.

STATOR BAR TEST ARRANGEMENT

When setting up the laboratory model to study the transmission of discharge pulses along stator bars of electrical machines, it was important to represent the return path through the core plates by a suitable conductor arrangement. The depth of penetration of the pulse currents and the resistance of the earth return path at various frequencies were therefore considered. The measurements showed that for a frequency component as low as 200 kHz, the depth of penetration of pulse current into an iron core plate is approximately 20 μm. Since this frequency is well below the effective frequency of a discharge pulse, the pulse current penetration into the iron core is even less than this. Due to the severely restricted current penetration into the core plate, aluminium sheet 2 mm thick could be used to represent the stator earthing system in the laboratory model. Although the depth of pulse current penetration into aluminium is considerably greater than that into iron, the effects are negligible compared with the characteristic impedance of the stator bars. The aluminium laboratory model which is shown in Fig. 3 is therefore a suitable representation of an actual stator core for the purpose of this study.

EXPERIMENTS WITH INJECTED PULSES

Initial measurements were undertaken on a single bar prior to its installation in the stator core model. This enabled the characteristic impedance and attenuation characteristics at various frequencies to be determined for the stator configuration under test. Here the partial discharge pulses were represented by a fast rise pulse generator (5 nsecs, ±50 V) connected between the stator bar and earth via a 20 pF capacitor to give an injected discharge simulation of 1000 pico-coulombs (pC). The initial measurements required that the characteristic impedance be evaluated so that the stator bar could be correctly terminated for this range of tests. This enabled the various types of pulse to be identified without having to consider the effects of reflected waves. The results demonstrated that the characteristic impedance is approximately 20 Ω and the fundamental pulse frequency varied from 18MHz at the position of signal injection into the stator bar, down to 9 MHz after 10 m of travel. After 60 m of travel (down six bars in series) the output pulse frequency was down to 500 kHz and the peak magnitude was only 0.5% of the input signal.

A further consideration in the initial measurements was the need to study the effective change of capacitance per unit length of stator bar for signals at various frequencies. In this particular case, when the frequency was increased from 1 kHz to 50 MHz, the stator bar capacitance reduced from 1350 pF/m to 295 pF/m. The reduction is due to a change in the permittivity of the insulation, which is frequency dependent and results from a variation in the fundamental frequency of the signal being applied to the stator bar insulation.

Using the aluminium test arrangement in Fig. 3, the 1000 pC simulated discharge pulse was applied to all conductor strands of the stator bar. The frequency spectrum of the pulse observed at the far end of the bar, via the capacitive coupling, together with the input pulse spectrum, are shown in Fig. 4. From this it is observed that there is a sharp reduction in the pulse current magnitude at frequencies higher than the third harmonic. This harmonic corresponds to a frequency of 18 MHz, which is the fundamental frequency of the input pulse. Relating the phase angle of this third harmonic to the distance the pulse travelled, showed that the discharge source was about 10 m from the capacitive coupling. Figure 4 also shows the frequency response for pulses transmitted into the lower bar and adjacent slot, near the capacitive-coupling end of the test rig. It is observed that the percentage of third harmonic present in adjacent slots is around 1% of that measured at the capacitive coupling, whilst there is about 12% present in the lower bar.

In order to simulate a slot discharge, a similar pulse was injected between the bar and core at one third of the way along the stator bar. This showed that the fundamental output pulse has a frequency of around 9 MHz. Evaluating the phase angle of this pulse indicated correctly that the source of the possible discharge site was about 7 m from the capacitive coupling.

Surface discharges over the end winding region were simulated by injecting a 1000 pC discharge pulse at a point beyond the stress grading paint and arranging that the rise time of the signal was increased to about

100 nsec. The fundamental frequency of this injected pulse was 2·5 MHz. However, by the time the pulse reached the capacitive coupling, it had a fundamental frequency of only 1 MHz. As the second harmonic of this pulse contained 20% more signal than the third, the phase angle of the second harmonic was evaluated which in turn indicated correctly that the source of the discharge site was about 9·5 m from the capacitive coupling.

FUTURE APPLICATIONS AND CONCLUSIONS

A new method of detecting discharges within stator bar insulation has been described. The results have demonstrated for simulated faults, that by considering the various harmonic components of the discharge pulse, in relation to its fundamental frequency and magnitude, it is possible to identify and locate the source of a particular type of discharge.

Future developments of the technique are to apply it to testing of individual stator bars at high-voltage, thus enabling it to be used in association with other techniques for acceptance and quality control tests. It is envisaged that the method will be particularly useful with very-low-frequency (0·1 Hz) diagnostic testing, as the discharge pulses have the same shape as those at power frequency, but the resolution time between consecutive pulses is increased.

The ultimate aim of the development is to employ the spectral analysis technique, in association with condition monitor systems, to continually assess the condition of a machine whilst it is on load.

ACKNOWLEDGEMENTS

The authors wish to thank Brighton Polytechnic for providing laboratory facilities and the S.E.R.C. for providing a research grant to enable this work to proceed. They are also grateful to Mr. R. Grahame, Mr. D.G. Poulter and Mr. R. Gooders for their technical assistance. Finally they wish to thank the Scientific Services of C.E.G.B. Harrogate, and particularly Mr. K.G. Burnley, for providing the stator bars for this investigation.

REFERENCES

1. Wood, J.W., Ryder, D.M. and Ryan, M.J., 1980, "Turbogenerator condition monitoring instruments, operational procedure and assessment of indicators", Canadian Elec. Ass.Int.Conf. on Generator Insulation Tests, 60-66.

2. Hogg, W.K., Ryder, D.M. and Wood, J.W., 1981, "The feasability of identifying and locating thermal mechanisms in large machines by remote sensing", CEIDP Conf., Whitehaven, Penn., USA.

3. Sawada, F.H., Barton, S.C. and Gunnoe, G.H., 1972, "Early detection and warning of excessive brush arcing", IEEE Trans. on PAS. Vol.91m 167-171.

4. Miller, R., Black, I.A and Hogg, W.K., 1982, "Development of techniques for detecting and locating the source of partial discharges in stator windings of electrical machines", BEAMA Conf., Brighton, England.

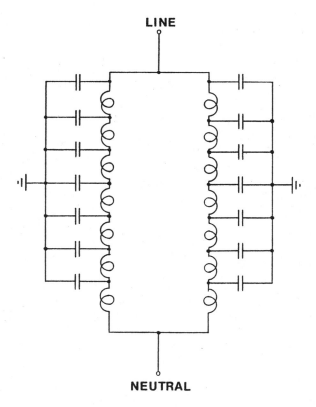

Figure 1   High-frequency equivalent
circuit of one phase of a
stator winding

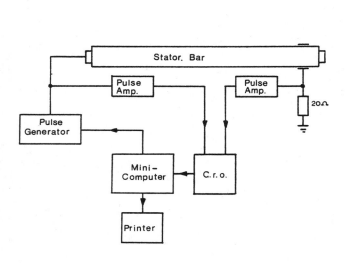

Figure 2   Discharge simulation and pulse
measurement system

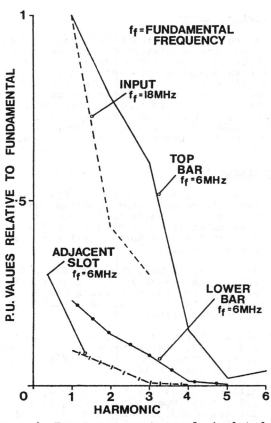

Figure 3   Experimental stator bar test
rig arrangement

Figure 4   Frequency spectrum of simulated
discharge pulses

PERFORMANCE OF THIRD-HARMONIC GROUND FAULT PROTECTION SCHEMES FOR GENERATOR STATOR WINDINGS

G.W. Buckley   R.L. Schlake

The Detroit Edison Company, U.S.A.   Westinghouse Electric Corporation, U.S.A.

INTRODUCTION

The reliability requirements placed on modern power systems demand increasingly complete protection of the generator. Generator failure statistics indicate that the three primary failure modes of generator stator windings are ground faults, interturn short circuits and excessive stator currents, in that order. These three failure modes account for more than 95% of the total generator repair costs. Stator ground faults and interturn short circuits account for more than 60% of all stator winding failures. (1)

Since generator ground faults are the largest single cause of stator winding damage, protection of the generator from them has become a major concern for modern utility companies. Currents flowing as a result of such a fault can cause extensive damage to both the stator winding and stator core, depending on the type of fault and on the design of the generator's ground fault protection scheme. The major causes of stator ground faults include:

1. Mechanical stresses resulting from thermal cycling of stator conductors.

2. Movement of end-winding bracing.

3. External faults.

4. Defects in cooling systems.

5. Electrolysis effects.

Because the major causes are electromechnical stresses and local insulation deterioration, the locations of ground faults on the stator cannot be predicted a priori. Thus the entire stator winding (neutral end included) must be considered when designing schemes for protection against ground faults.

The conventional unit type generator step-up transformer has the neutral stabilized by a resistance loaded distribution type transformer, see Fig. 1. The load resistor is sized to limit the in-phase component of line-to-ground fault current to a value not less than the total charging currents of the capacitances-to-ground of the generator winding and the associated isolated phase bus, transformers and leads. This value of neutral effective resistance has evolved over the years and results in moderate ground fault currents, generally under 15 amperes for a solid phase-to-ground fault at the generator terminals. Currents of this magnitude generally do not cause serious damage to the core steel. It is, therefore, unnecessary to use high speed detection for ground faults, although good industry practice requires it.

Small 60 Hz ground currents may flow under normal conditions, possibly due to generator winding imbalances or to faults on the secondaries of the generator potential transformers. Under these conditions the generator should not be removed from service.

For a single ground fault near the neutral end of the winding, there will be proportionately less voltage induced in the winding shorted to ground, resulting in a low fault current and a low neutral bus displacement voltage. At the lower limit, a fault on the neutral bus will result in no fault current or displacement voltage at all. Because the setting of the standard 60 Hz relay scheme is designed to ignore these low level, but normal ground currents, ground faults in the lower portion of the winding cannot be detedted. Such a fault is illustrated in Fig. 1.

To allow for the aforementioned small ground currents under normal condition, trip settings for over-voltage ground relays are generally set to protect 90 to 95% of the generator winding. The potential hazard of an undetected ground fault in the lower portion of the winding, where the neutral bus displacement voltage is below the ground relay trip setting, therefore arises. Moreover, a fault at the neutral end of a generator phase winding will effectively short circuit the neutral ground transformer. Under these conditions the conventional ground fault protection scheme will be totally inoperable, with potentially catastrophic results.

If a ground fault occurs and remains undetected because of its location or otherwise, the probability of a second fault occurring is much greater. This second fault may result from insulation deterioration caused by transient over-voltages due to erratic, low current, unstable arcing at the first fault point. This second fault may yield currents of devastating magnitudes.

The present paper describes an investigation into the feasibility of utilizing the third harmonic (180 Hz) emf, induced in the stator phase windings of all large generators, to give ground fault protection in the lower 10-15% of the winding. In conjunction with the conventional 60 Hz scheme, which relies on a resistance loaded distribution transformer to limit ground fault currents, this can be designed to give ground fault protection over 100% of the stator phase winding. In addition to the above, the paper also highlights a number of other operational advantages of the scheme and investigates its range of validity. A further major advantage of the scheme is its simplicity and low cost. The scheme can also be easily retrofitted on existing installations.

DISCUSSION

Typical Unit Connected System

A three-phase circuit model of a typical unit connected generating station is shown in Fig. 1. Normally the potential transformer (P.T.) neutral is directly grounded, although some power companies have adopted the practice of connecting the neutral point of the P.T. primary winding to the generator neutral, as shown.

When providing protection for the generator

stator winding, it is important to consider the winding neutral for several reasons. After high potential testing of the stator winding it is necessary to attach safety grounds to the generator neutral. Other conditions occasionally require disconnecting the generator neutral and leaving the neutral open. There are many recorded cases of these grounds not being removed when the generator is returned to service or alternatively, the generator neutral to grounding transformer connection is not made. This is a potentially dangerous situation, both for the machine, and also for plant personnel. In addition, the presence of the cable which connects the generator neutral bus and the potential transformer primary neutral increases the exposure of this neutral to ground faults. If a ground occurs in this cable, the neutral grounding transformer is short circuited.

The third harmonic relay will detect all of these conditions.

The Problem

The relay scheme consists of two relays in parallel with the load resistor, as shown in Fig. 1. A regular over-voltage relay, (59N1), operating at the fundamental generator frequency of 60 Hz, protects the upper 90 to 95% of the stator winding as explained earlier. The lower 10% (neutral end) of the winding is protected by a relay which detects a reduction in the third harmonic, or 180 Hz component of the neutral bus voltage following a fault.

No 180 Hz component of line-to-line voltage appears in either delta or wye connected machines. However, most generators are connected in wye to eliminate 180 Hz circulating currents which can cause undesirable heating. This voltage causes 180 Hz current to flow, through the various leakage capacitances to ground, returning to the generator neutral bus through the neutral grounding transformer. This current will cause a 180 Hz voltage drop across the load resistor. If a ground fault occurs in the lower end of the generator winding or on the neutral bus (see Fig. 1), the grounding transformer will be effectively short circuited and this 180 Hz current will bypass the ground transformer. This will cause a reduction in the 180 Hz load resistor voltage. Thus a ground fault in the lower 10% of the generator winding may be detected by a marked reduction in the 180 Hz neutral bus displacement voltage.

In developing a method for determining the applicability of this relay scheme for a typical unit-connected generator, the standard 60 Hz scheme of Fig. 1 is assumed appropriate for the upper 90 to 95% of the winding. The applicability of the package thus depends on the proper operation of the 180 Hz (27N3) relay. There are two problems associated with the operation of the 180 Hz relay.

1. **180 Hz Neutral Bus Voltage.** The applicability of the protection scheme depends on the magnitude of the 180 Hz neutral bus voltage under all expected operating and fault conditions. The unfaulted 180 Hz neutral bus voltage must be within the relay's operating range. In addition, for a fault in the lower 5 to 10% of the winding, the resulting reduction in the 180 Hz neutral bus voltage must be sufficient to cause the 180 Hz relay to trip and indicate the presence of the fault.

A method had to be developed to calculate the 180 Hz neutral bus voltage under all expected load and fault conditions. These estimates could then be used to determine the resulting 180 Hz neutral bus displacement voltage range for a given machine.

2. **Effect of the P.T. Connections.** The second objective of this project was to determine the effect of the P.T. connection described previously on the applicability of the relay package. The performance of the 180 Hz relay depends on all of the generated 180 Hz current returning to the generator neutral through the neutral bus grounding transformer. This P.T. connection provides a second current path in parallel with the neutral bus grounding transformer. This current path might bleed enough of the 180 Hz current around the grounding transformer to limit the range of applicability of the relay package. Thus a method for determining the 180 Hz currents flowing through the P.T. primary windings was also desired.

The 180 Hz neutral bus displacement voltage is directly proportional to the 180 Hz current flowing through the grounding transformer primary winding. Thus both of the problems associated with the operation of the 180 Hz relay can be solved by determining the distribution of the 180 Hz currents in the third harmonic, generating station impedance network.

Method of Solution

As part of the present work, a simple but extremely versatile computer program named GTHAP was written to fully model the machine on a coil by coil basis, together with its externally connected apparatus such as the isolated phase bus, main generator step-up transformer, generator potential transformers, unit auxiliary transformer, etc. This program is used to estimate the 180 Hz circulating ground current for any given machine based on either a calculated or measured third harmonic voltage value. Thus the applicability of the third harmonic scheme, and its range of protection for a given machine, can be determined.

Since the third harmonic voltage acts as a zero sequence component, no third harmonic currents flow in the low voltage delta windings of the unit and auxiliary transformers. This means no 180 Hz voltage appears on the wye connected, high voltage side of the unit transformer. Thus the main power system appears as an open circuit in the third harmonic current network.

Using the assumed method of connecting the potential transformer (P.T.) primary neutral to the generator neutral, see Fig. 1, there are two parallel paths external to the generator through which 180 Hz current is driven. One of these paths is through the various machine capacitances to ground, returning to the generator through the neutral grounding transformer. The second path is through the Y-Y connected P.T. primary windings and back to the generator neutral. However, initial calculations and subsequent simulations with GTHAP have shown that the 180 Hz series impedance of these P.T. windings is very large. Thus the effect of this second current path on the relay performance is almost undetectable and it can safely be neglected in evaluation of the relay scheme.

Large generators often contain several parallel paths in each phase winding, so the precise path for the third harmonic current depends on whether the machine winding is faulted or unfaulted. The precise equivalent circuits for each case are described in Ref. 2.

General Outline

Each of the circuit models yields a set of mesh current equations and GTHAP was developed to solve any of these sets of equations for any fault point and fault resistance.

180 Hz Circuit Models

The unfaulted system is of primary importance in determining the normal 180 Hz current distribution. Under faulted conditions, two types of circuit models are relevant. A faulted, single path per phase model must be used when there is only one current path per phase. When there are two or more parallel current paths per phase, another circuit model is needed. For these reasons three cases must be simulated. Because of space limitations, however, only the most common circuit arrangement will be considered here, that of two circuits per phase. Detailed assumptions used in the derivation of this model are set out in Ref. 2.

The circuit model for the faulted case with two parallel current paths per phase is shown in Fig. 2.

Only one fault is considered at a time. This fault is placed in Phase A as shown. Phases B and C are modelled in a slightly simpler form. The voltage sources in the unfaulted current path are the normal 180 Hz induced voltages, E_1, E_2, E_3, etc. The sum of the voltages e_{a1} and e_{a2} in the faulted path is equal to the coil voltage, the individual voltages being obtained from the percentage of the coil faulted.

If the generator winding contains two parallel current paths per phase, the faulted and unfaulted paths in Phase A must be modelled separately. The capacitance per path will be one-half of the total dapacitance per phase. The series impedance per path will be twice the total series impedance per phase. Again, simple circuit theory is used to solve for the current flowing through the grounding transformer.

A faulted machine with more than two parallel paths per phase may be modelled as a two path machine by approximating the unfaulted paths by one equivalent winding. The faulted path must then be modelled separately.

Calculation of 180 Hz Faulted Phase emf's

In order to calculate the individual third harmonic coil emf's for a particular machine, the number of slots, poles and parallel winding paths must be known. Either a measured or calculated 3rd-harmonic rms line to neutral voltage must also be known. A conventional coil voltage phasor diagram for the particular machine can then be constructed as shown in Fig. 3. The relationship between the nth harmonic phase-to-neutral voltage, E_{rn}, (measured or calculated) and the nth harmonic coil voltage, E_{rn}, is given by

$$qE_{cn}K_{dn} = E_{rn} \qquad \ldots (1)$$

where K_{dn} is the nth harmonic distribution factor. For a three phase winding:

$$K_{dn} = \sin(n\pi/6)/q\sin(n\pi/6q) \qquad \ldots (2)$$

where q = number of slots/pole/phase for the fundamental.

To illustrate the manner in which the partial coil voltages, e_{a1} and e_{a2}, shown earlier in Fig. 2 is obtained, Fig. 3 shows a case for a fault part of the way into the first coil. It should be noted that each coil emf, including those in the faulted coil, is used with its correct in-phase and quadrature components to determine the correct ground path and leakage current. Similar constructions are used for other fault points and winding configurations.

Effect of Load and Power Factor on Generated Third Harmonic Voltage

The major sources of third harmonic voltage are due to the rotor ampere-turn distribution and saturation of the rotor core and rotor teeth. The former component varies with the field current, while the latter varies with machine voltage and real reactive power. Reference 2 explains these in more detail.

The combination of these effects renders the third harmonic terminal voltage dependent on the excitation level, the load and the power factor at the generator terminals. The curves of Fig. 4 illustrate the behavior of the third harmonic terminal voltage for a typical machine under varying load conditions. The exact relationships governing the interactions of the sources of third harmonic terminal-to-neutral voltage, discussed above, are extremely complicated, and beyond the scope of this present paper.

EXPERIMENTAL VERIFICATION OF THE MODEL

Reliability of the Model for Unfaulted Machines

Measurements of the neutral grounding transformer and potential transformer 180 Hz secondary voltages were made at various output power levels on the chosen test unit as an aid to determining the reliability of the mathematical model.

The 180 Hz neutral grounding transformer secondary voltage was measured under generator start-up conditions. The voltage was recorded for 75 hours during which time the machine was off line five times. The maximum power output attained was 400 MW, which was 0.5 p.u. on the generator MW base.

Knowing the 180 Hz voltage on the secondary of the neutral grounding transformer and the load resistance, the transformer's 180 Hz secondary current was calculated at various generator output levels. The unfaulted system simulation was then computed using the 180 Hz generator terminal-to-neutral voltage measured at each power level.

The tested generator's load resistance is rated at 0.588 ohms when a maximum current of 307 amperes is flowing through it. This current corresponds to a solid phase-to-ground fault at the machine terminals. The resistor was measured at 0.498 ohms, prior to installation, with no current flowing through it. The effects of small changes in resistance due to heating from current flow are negligible as shown in Ref. 2. The comparisons of the estimated and measured 180 Hz neutral grounding transformer primary currents are shown in Table 1.

As indicated in Table 1, the error encountered in predicting the 180 Hz grounding transformer current was approximately 20 to 30%. There are several possible sources of this error but most relate to either experimental or data errors. Fortunately errors of this magnitude can be tolerated in making a determination of the applicability of this protection scheme to a particular generator. It is believed that the errors arise from faulty data as to winding-to-ground capacitances, and to the somewhat uncontrolled conditions under which third harmonic voltages were measured.

Predicted Reduction of the 180 Hz Grounding Transformer Currents under Various Fault Conditions

The third area of investigation is an example of the method used to determine the applicability of the relay package for a specific generator. This method entails determining the expected reduction of the 180 Hz neutral grounding transformer current under various fault conditions.

The 180 Hz terminal line-to-neutral voltage is assumed to be 730V in this experiment (730V was an actual measured voltage, see Table 1). In an actual application of this program, the smallest expected voltage would be used since this would produce the smallest magnitude of unfaulted grounding transformer current and the smallest reduction in this current when it is reduced to zero. This experiment considers a two parallel path per phase winding machine.

First, the unfaulted case was run to determine the expected 180 Hz grounding transformer current with a given 180 Hz terminal line-to-neutral voltage level. Simulations were then run with hypothetical faults placed on the machine. Six different fault resistances were placed at each of six fault locations in the lower 10% of the winding. The cases were all run with the grounding transformer load resistor equal to the resistor's value measured prior to installation. The resulting 180 Hz grounding transformer current magnitudes and percent reductions are shown in Fig. 5. Fig. 5 shows that the scheme is most sensitive for fault resistances in the range 0 to 1000 Ω.

Percentage of Winding Protected

The only questions which now remain to be answered are, firstly, what percentage of the stator winding can be effectively protected by the third harmonic scheme?, and secondly, how can we determine this?

Under normal circumstance with no faults present, a certain amount of third harmonic voltage will be measurable at the neutral bus. If the neutral bus suffers a fault, then this voltage will fall to zero because the neutral grounding transformer is short-circuited. At the other extreme, if a zero resistance short circuit is applied to the machine terminals, then the level of third-harmonic current flowing through the grounding transformer will increase because the current can flow through this fault as opposed to flowing through the leakage capacitances of the circuit. This increased current will raise the neutral bus voltage above the unfaulted level. Between these two extremes, there exists a position on the winding at which, if a zero resistance ground fault were to occur there, there would be no reduction in the third harmonic bus voltage, thus the third harmonic relay would not detect the fault. It is obviously important that this position is above the lower point protected by the conventional 60 Hz relay!

The above questions can be answered very simply by simulating a fault at progressively different points along the stator winding. Zero re-

sistance faults in the range 10 to 80% in steps of 10% were simulated and the results are shown in Table 2. As we move out from the neutral bus, zero resistance faults will result in a reduction in the third harmonic neutral bus voltage, until some position is reached where an increase is noticed. A finite resistance short circuit will alter this position somewhat and it is possible to construct a family of curves from an extension of Tabel 2 which would depict the variation of third harmonic neutral voltage as a function of fault location with various resistance values as a perameter.

On a practical note however, because we are attempting to protect the lower portion of the stator winding, the liklihood of a high or medium resistance short caused by insulation cracking, surface tracking or discharges is small because the available voltage is small. It is much more likely that such a fault would be as the result of mechanical damage such as fretting caused by relative motion of the stator winding and the stator core and therefore be of very low resistance. According to Table 2, theoretically, a zero resistance ground fault at the 45% position would be undetectable on this particular machine. Practically though, the relay would typically be set to detect a 50% reduction in neutral bus displacement voltage, then Table 2 shows that the 180 Hz scheme will protect at least 20% of the winding, giving good overlap with the conventional 60 Hz scheme.

USE OF ARMING RELAYS

A major disadvantage of the scheme described herein is that the range of protection is, in effect, a function of the minimum third harmonic voltage reached during normal operation. For a typical machine, this might be about 50% of the open-circuit value, although the precise variation is very much machine dependent and will not necessarily follow the shape of Fig. 4. However, if Fig. 4 is used as a typical example, this voltage might be expected to vary between 50 and 250% of the open-circuit value while the load ranges from open-circuit to full load. In order to ignore the minimum at about 15% load, the 27N3 relay pickup must be set below the 50% value, say at 40%. Thus, when at full load, the voltage has to fall from 250% to 40% in order for the relay to indicate a problem, i.e. a reduction in the 180 Hz voltage of 85% at full load. By referring to Table 2, it can be seen that the range of protection achieved is very small for such large changes in voltage, perhaps only 5%. Finite resistance shorts would reduce this figure even more. It is important, therefore, to be able to ascertain what this minimum value is before applying such a relaying scheme in an unmodified form. It is therefore recommended that this information is requested from the manufacturer as part of the generator specification.

The above problem can be avoided quite easily by employing a further relay to arm the third harmonic system above say 60% load. The amount of time spent below 60% load on a fossil or nuclear unit is insignificant and it avoids the very low voltage seen at low loads.

The relay pickup is then set at, say 80% of the 60% load value. Using Fig. 4 and Table 2, the range of protection can then be increased to over 20% of the winding, giving good overlap with the 59N1 60 Hz relay.

CONCLUSIONS

The following conclusions can be reached as a result of this investigation.

1. Calculations indicate that the additional loop provided by connection of the P.T. neutral to the generator neutral does not bleed sufficient current away from the ground path for the effectiveness of the scheme to be impaired.

2. Good coverage, typically 20% of the winding, can be obtained with the third harmonic relay package.

3. Preliminary studies given in Fig. 5 show that the most significant reductions in third harmonic grounding transformer current are produced for fault resistances in the range 0 to 1000 ohms. This applies for all fault positions between 0.01 and 10.0% of the stator winding.

4. The combined relay package can provide 100% stator ground protection if sufficient third harmonic voltage is generated. However, it should be pointed out that, even though 100% of the generator winding is protected, no backup protection is provided.

5. Due to the fact that at certain low load conditions, see Fig. 4, the third harmonic voltage passes through a minimum, the 180 Hz relay may operate at this low voltage if this reduction is greater than the relay setting. For this reason, it is advised that the 180 Hz relay only be used to alarm or an arming scheme employed. The normal 60 Hz relay in the package should be used to trip the machine as usual.

TABLE 1 - Error in predicting the 180 Hz grounding transformer current
Assuming the load resistor = 0.498 ohms

Load		Terminal-to-Neutral 180 Hz r.m.s. voltage	Grounding Transformer			Primary 180 Hz Current	Computer Estimate 180 Hz Current	Error	
				Secondary					
MW	MVAR		Load Resistor	180 Hz Volts	180 Hz Current			mag.	%
607	59	730 V	0.498 Ω	4.6 V	9.24 A	0.111 A	0.138 A	0.027 A	20
404	30	605 V	0.498 Ω	3.3 V	6.63 A	0.080 A	0.114 A	0.034 A	30
224	6	437 V	0.498 Ω	2.4 V	4.82 A	0.058 A	0.083 A	0.025 A	30
234	-2	440 V	0.498 Ω	2.5 V	5.02 A	0.060 A	0.083 A	0.023 A	28
380	25	590 V	0.498 Ω	3.2 V	6.43 A	0.077 A	0.111 A	0.034 A	30

TABLE 2 - Determination of range of protection

Driving Voltage	Fault Resistance	Fault Position %	I_3 Amps	% Reduction in Current
730	0	10	0.033	76
730	0	20	0.065	53
730	0	30	0.095	31
730	0	40	0.123	11
730	0	50	0.150	-9
730	0	60	0.169	-22
730	0	70	0.187	-36
730	0	80	0.199	-44

Unfaulted base case. $V_3 = 730$, $I_3 = 0.138$ amps

ACKNOWLEDGEMENTS

The authors are grateful to the IEEE for permission to reproduce parts of reference 2 by Schlake, Buckley, and McPherson in this paper.

REFERENCES

1. IEEE Power Sys. Relay in Comm. Rep., 1972, IEEE Trans on PAS, PAS-91, 24-28.

2. Schlake, R. L. et al, 1981, IEEE Trans on PAS, PAS-100, 3195-3199.

3. Ilar Metal, 1979, Protect. Rel. Conf., Georgia Inst. Tech.

4. Stien, M. and Linders, J. R., 1977, Fourth Ann. Western Protective Ref. Conf.

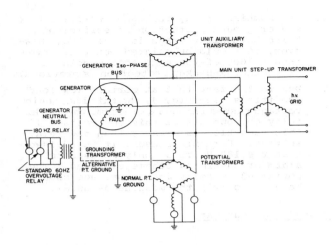

Figure 1 Typical unit-connected system

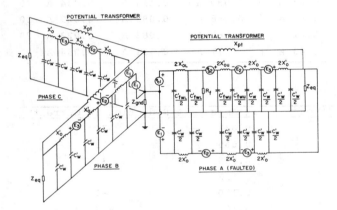

Figure 2 Circuit diagram for two-circuit wye with fault

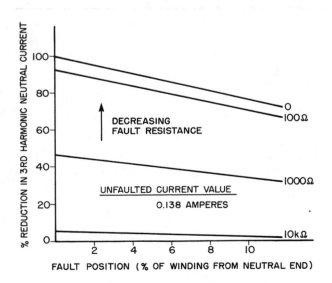

Figure 5 Effect of fault resistance on current reduction

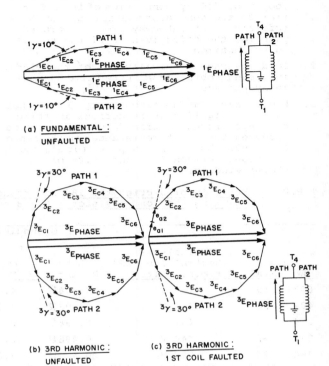

Figure 3 Coil emf diagram

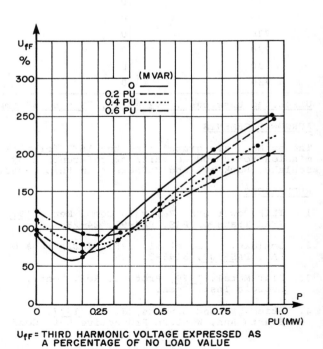

U_{fF} = THIRD HARMONIC VOLTAGE EXPRESSED AS A PERCENTAGE OF NO LOAD VALUE

PU = PER UNIT POWER OUTPUT

Figure 4 Variation of third-harmonic voltage with load for a typical generator

AN ELECTRICAL METHOD FOR CONDITION MONITORING OF MOTORS

M.E. Steele, R.A. Ashen and L.G. Knight

Standard Telecommunication Laboratories Ltd., UK.

INTRODUCTION

Condition monitoring of electrical drives is an important aid to the prevention of expensive plant breakdowns since it provides warning of incipient failure. At present, vibration or noise techniques are used to monitor most mechanical defects in electrical drives (Neale (1)). The majority of these defects are associated with rolling-element bearings and special techniques have been developed to monitor them, the most significant being acoustic emission monitoring (Balderston (2)), shock pulse monitoring (Thomson and Sharp (3)), and the kurtosis method (Dyer and Stewart (4)).

Vibration monitoring techniques require access to the motor for the location of transducers. The technique described in this paper is analogous to the mechanical vibration method, but electrical line quantities, typically current, are monitored instead. Hence, direct access to the motor is no longer necessary, which may be a significant advantage for remote applications such as mines or submersibles.

The theory of the method is outlined and the prototype equipment described. Some practical examples of its use are presented, and an indication given of how the equipment might be realised in a commercial form.

IMPLEMENTATION OF TECHNIQUE

Theory of Method

A qualitative explanation is that noise/vibration and other effects in a motor dissipate power, with components at certain dominant frequencies, in addition to the main supply of power absorbed directly in driving the shaft against a steady load. Measurement of the electrical spectra at the input to the motor can provide an indication of the mechanical/noise spectra. The electrical spectra can therefore provide useful information on motor condition and detection of incipient failure.

Prototype Equipment

The experimental measuring equipment used was designed to provide spectra signals for voltage, current, and power over a wide range of operating values and to display other general information (Steele and Barker (5)).

One phase of the basic sensing circuit is shown in Figure 1. Amplifier A1, with its floating supply provides a sizable current signal with negligible insertion loss which is passed to A2 via the potential divider chains R3-R4 and R5-R6. Amplifier A3 produces a signal proportional to the voltage difference between the phase voltage Vph and Vref. (Vref will usually be the neutral or common point.) The output from multiplier M1 is therefore the resultant phase power signal which is combined with those of other phases

into a final summing amplifier.

The selected signal (phase current, phase voltage, phase power or total power) is then passed to the metering/display circuit which provides scaling and digital display, with options of average/r.m.s. and linear/dB values. Additional circuitry provides calibration, amplifier overload detection, etc. A conventional spectrum analyser is used to process the selected signal.

EXPERIMENTAL RESULTS

In the present work, constant voltage supplies with low source impedance were used exclusively and so only the current was monitored. Further, for three phase systems, only one phase was monitored to avoid the cancellation effects which would occur in monitoring a balanced system.

For signal processing a Fast Fourier Transform spectrum analyser was used with a frequency range of 0-20 kHz. For many purposes spectrum analysis may be adequate. However, when the record shows a large number of harmonics or sidebands it may be difficult to interpret. It is sometimes possible to simplify the record pattern by further signal processing. This involves taking the logarithm of the spectrum and performing a Fourier analysis on the result to obtain a cepstrum (Bogert et al (6)). The cepstrum has the effect of separating the sidebands from the source spectrum or differentiating between sets of harmonics or sidebands. The cepstrum was calculated in the present instance with a desktop computer working in conjunction with the spectrum analyser.

A variety of drive units have been tested with various component faults and this testing was largely restricted to simple comparisons between normal and defective units. The detailed interpretation of spectra and cepstra and their eventual use as fault 'signatures' is planned to follow the present work. More prolonged, elaborate testing and evaluation will be required to establish the necessary fault signature confidence levels for an individual fault and drive unit type.

Centrifugal Pump

The pump used was of the submersible type with a single vane impeller, driven by a 3 phase, 50 Hz, squirrel cage induction motor. It was rated at 2.6 kW at 1400 rpm.

General Effects of Load. A normal pumping spectrum over the frequency range 0-200 Hz is shown in Figure 2(a) and Figure 2(b) shows the spectrum when the pump is running dry. Marked differences are apparent.

In Figure 2(a), peaks occur at the 50 Hz supply frequency, 100 Hz, 150 Hz, and sidebands spaced at the pump motor rotation frequency.

Defective Top Bearing. A bearing fault was simulated by drilling through the bearing cage to damage the ball element surface. The spectrum obtained a few minutes before the defective unlubricated top bearing failed is shown in Figure 3(b). This may be compared with a normal pumping spectrum (Figure 3(a)), and the increase in the spectral component amplitudes caused by the defective bearing noted.

Broken Rotor Bar. The effect of a broken bar in a squirrel cage rotor is to produce torque fluctuations at twice the slip frequency (Gaydon (7)). The torque fluctuations result in modulation of the supply current so that sidebands are produced about the supply frequency (Williamson and Smith (8)). The detection of these sidebands was abandoned in reference (7) since the fluctuations were said to be difficult to detect in the presence of random load fluctuations.

For the tests, a broken rotor bar fault was introduced by drilling through a rotor bar/ endring connection. A 0-100 Hz current spectrum for a pump with a broken rotor bar is shown in Figure 4(b) and this may be compared with the normal pumping spectrum in Figure 4(a). Estimation of the slip frequency from the rotational frequency sideband spacing in Figure 4(b) gives twice the slip frequency as 5 Hz so that the current spectrum should have spectral components at 45 and 55 Hz. Inspection of Figure 4(b) shows peaks at approximately these frequencies. These peaks are non-existent in Figure 4(a). To confirm the findings, the tests were repeated on the following day and the results agreed to within 2 dB. It is worth noting that the 45 Hz peak is 6 dB greater or a factor of 2 larger than the normal pump spectrum amplitude at this frequency. A further test was performed with a reduced bandwidth, 0-50 Hz and this revealed a component at approximately 45 Hz which is non-existent in the normal pumping spectrum.

Other Bearing Tests. The defective top bearing was an example of catastrophic failure producing a widely different pump spectrum from the normal. Further tests have been done with the pump's lower bearing slightly damaged. Figure 5(a) shows the normal pumping spectrum which may be compared with the spectrum for the defective lower bearing in Figure 5(b). The defective bearing spectrum shows significantly larger amplitudes at 300, 350, and 400 Hz and a smaller component at 150 Hz.

Further work is in progress to establish the method's sensitivity to specific bearing faults.

Windscreen Wiper Motor

The motor used was of the conventional 2 pole permanent magnet type with a worm gear drive. The worm material was mild steel and the gear wheel material was nylon with 55 teeth. The commutator had 12 segments.

From Figure 6(a) for a nominal output shaft speed of 30 rpm, the predominant peak in the current spectrum occurs at 347.5 Hz. Assuming this to be the commutator ripple frequency implies the true output shaft speed to be 31.6 rpm. The validity of this assumption is confirmed by referring to the cepstrum of this result, Figure 9(a), which has a principal low order component at 34.3 ms or 29.2 Hz. This is the input shaft rotation frequency,

implying an output shaft speed of 31.8 rpm. Hence, the principal components of the spectrum are the commutator ripple frequency and sidebands with shaft rotation frequency spacing.

The effect on the spectrum of damaging the gear teeth can be seen by comparison of Figure 6(b) with Figure 6(a). Figure 6(b) was obtained at the same speed but with four gear teeth removed. This gives an overall increase in spectrum amplitude plus a considerable increase about the commutator ripple frequency. The corresponding cepstra, Figures 9(a) and 9(b), also show considerable differences. In Figure 9(b) the higher frequency components are larger, the 34.3 ms component, corresponding to the rotation frequency, is smaller and the rotation frequency sub-harmonics have changed in amplitude. It should be noted that these sub-harmonics, which show up clearly in the cepstrum, are not readily distinguishable in the basic spectrum.

Printed Motor with Out-of-Balance Load

The motor had a continuous torque rating of 0.177 Nm at a full load current of 4.7 A with a 24 V supply. It was loaded with an out-of-balance weight producing a static out-of-balance torque of 0.037 Nm.

Running the motor with a balanced disc inertial load produced the current spectrum shown in Figure 7(a). The peak spacings are equivalent to the rotation frequency.

For the out-of-balance load case, shown in Figure 7(b), the general spectrum level is raised by about 30 dB, so that the inherent peaks disappear, apart from a few at the low frequency end.

Cam Timer System (Motor, Gearbox and Cam Unit)

The drive used a 230 V, 50 Hz synchronous motor with a power consumption of 2.5 W. The motor speed was 500 rpm and the plastic gears produced one revolution every three seconds.

Figure 8(a) shows the current spectrum with normal gears and Figure 8(b) the corresponding spectrum for gears with three adjacent teeth missing. The main differences are an increase in the spectra amplitudes about 89 Hz and the appearance of some peaks at 9, 189, 211, 290, and 390 Hz. Calculations suggest that the highest tooth meshing frequency at a speed of 500 rpm should be 83 Hz with harmonics at 166, 249, 332 Hz, etc.

Three Bladed Three Speed Fan

Tests on this unit showed the progressive frequency shift of spectra with changes in speed. In addition to monitoring, it is thought that these results could have a useful control application.

COMMERCIAL SYSTEM REALISATION

The prototype form of the equipment is not suitable as a commercial instrument and consideration has been given to the final form of the system. It is possible to replace current-sense resistors by Hall effect devices, to produce an isolated monitoring system. The spectrum analyser is to be replaced by a system comprising A to D convertors, signal processor chip and appropriate memory. A suitable portion of signal will be digitised and a Fast Fourier Transform implemented by the signal processor. The normalised spectrum will be compared with a permanently-stored signature spectrum to identify significant condition changes and, after further processing, activate alarms and warnings.

Installations using many identical motors might be monitored by sequentially interrogating a sensor in each motor's supply via a multiplexer.

CONCLUSIONS

An electrical condition monitoring technique for motors has been presented. A representative selection of a large number of test results for induction motor and permanent magnet d.c. motor drives with faults has been given. Although the method's potential has been demonstrated, much further work is required, both to fully explain the spectra obtained, and to produce a commercially viable system.

In particular, the use of the technique with inverter supplies, and its use with other types of electrical machine, remains to be investigated.

ACKNOWLEDGEMENTS

This development stems from work on motor noise initiated by G.F. Barker. The authors gratefully acknowledge the permission of Standard Telecommunication Laboratories Ltd. to publish the paper.

REFERENCES

1. Neale, M., and Associates, 1979, "A Guide to the Condition Monitoring of Machinery", HMSO, London, England.

2. Balderston, H.L., 1969, Materials Evaluation, June, 121-128.

3. Thomson, T., and Sharp, D., 1978, IEE Colloquium on "The Design Application and Maintenance of Large Industrial Drives", Conference Publication No. 170, November, 45-51.

4. Dyer, D., and Stewart, R.M., 1977, "ASME Paper No. 77-DET-83 for meeting, Chicago, Illinois, Sept. 26-30.

5. Steele, M.E., and Barker, G.F., 1981, British Patent Application No. 8 111 815.

6. Bogert, B.P., Healy, M.J.R., and Tukey, J.W., 1963, Proceedings of the Symposium on Time Series Analysis, John Wiley and Sons, New York, 209-243.

7. Gaydon, B.G., 1979, Conference on Electronic Test and Measuring Instrumentation, Testmex 79 Conference Papers, 5-8.

8. Williamson, S. and Smith, A.C., "Steady-State Analysis of Three Phase Cage Motors with Rotor Bar and End-ring Faults", to be published in Proc IEE-8, EPA.

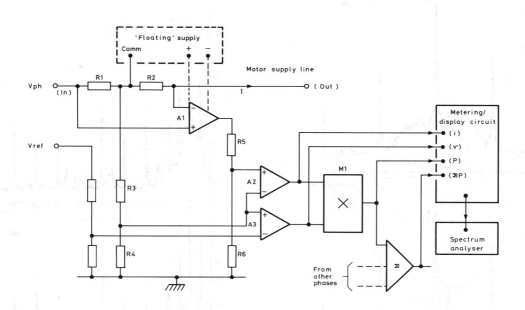

Fig. 1   Condition monitor circuit.

234

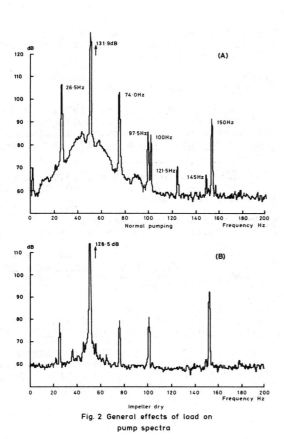

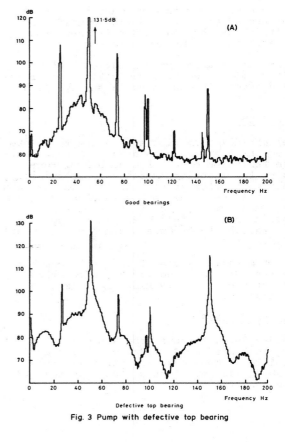

Fig. 2 General effects of load on
pump spectra

Fig. 3 Pump with defective top bearing

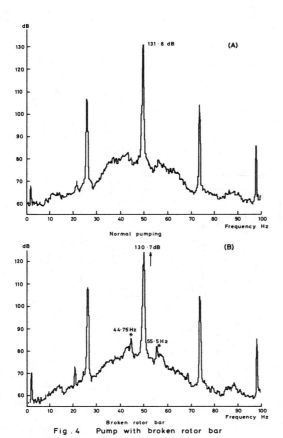

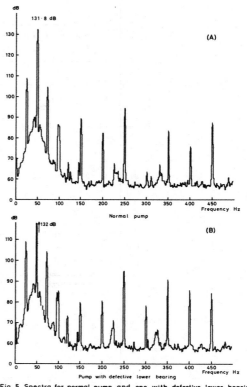

Fig. 4   Pump with broken rotor bar

Fig. 5 Spectra for normal pump and one with defective lower bearing.

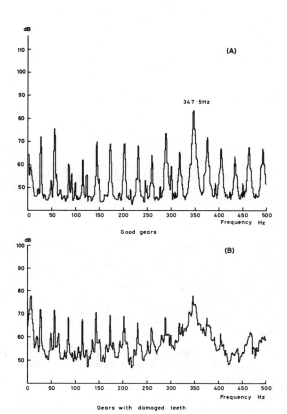

Fig. 6   Windscreen wiper motor with damaged gears.

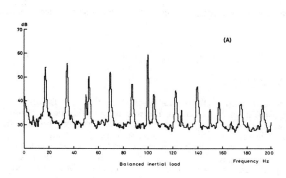

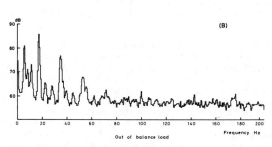

Fig. 7 Printed motor with out of balance torque

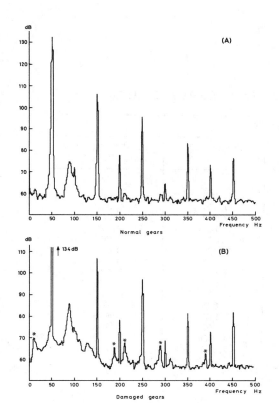

Fig. 8   Cam timer system (motor, gear box and cam unit.)

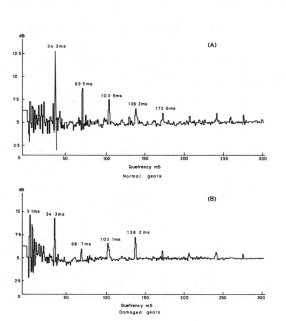

Fig. 9 Windscreen wiper motor cepstra

SOME ASPECTS OF SELF-STARTING PERMANENT-MAGNET MACHINES

K. J. Binns, T. M. Wong and *M. A. Jabbar

University of Southampton, UK   *Qualcast (Lawn Mowers Division)UK

INTRODUCTION

In recent years there has been a most significant development in permanent magnet a.c. machines. The reasons are not too hard to assess; first, permanent magnet machines can have a higher output than induction motors in the same frame; secondly, there may be no magnetising current and they can operate close to unity power factor; thirdly, there are no significant field losses, and finally they are easier to control, having no slip and not being inherently prone to hunting.

However, because of the obvious appeal of permanent magnet motors some designs have emerged which do not take full advantage of the permanent magnet materials used. This is particularly true of machines involving rare-earth magnets which are inevitably fairly expensive. A salient magnet adjacent to the air-gap and having a pole arc/pole pitch ratio of say 0.6 inevitably has a gap density well below the level of the working point of the magnet. However, it is possible to have a working density in the air-gap above that in the magnet and thereby use less magnet material at the same time. Some form of flux density increase from inside the magnet material to the air-gap is vital to the efficient utilisation of material.

This paper concentrates primarily on a particular geometry which can be effectively used either with rare-earth or ceramic magnets. The configuration is shown in Fig. 1 and the machine can be operated synchronously either at leading or lagging power factor. This feature is not found in any conventional machine but is interesting and not necessarily disadvantageous. The rotor laminations have a profile which needs to be carefully optimised. A high pull-out torque can be achieved but the main requirement is a torque which is high (for example, when compared to an induction machine in the same frame) and an efficient use of magnet material particularly if this be rare-earth.

If a machine is intended to be self-starting without feedback it must incorporate a cage and the optimum design is a compromise between synchronous and asynchronous operation. Machines of the type to be discussed can also operate with a feedback loop as a variable speed drive. Alternatively they can operate on open loop provided the design is such that the pull-in and pull-out torque are appropriate to the application.

A class of rotor configuration is shown in Fig. 1 and this is suitable for use either with rare-earth or ceramic magnets. Some results indicating the synchronous performance recently achieved from such machines is shown in Table 1 for a machine having a core length of 82 mm and a rotor diameter of 93 mm. These sample results are chosen for a voltage at which the power factor changes from leading to lagging as load is applied. At two-thirds of the pull-out torque the power factor is 0.995 lagging and the efficiency is 86%. The pull-out power is greater than 2.8 kW at the relevant supply voltage.

TABLE 1   Measured performance characteristic of a samarium-cobalt synchronous motor.

Synchronous performance at 220V, 50 Hz. Pull-out = 2843 W					
CURRENT	OUTPUT	POWER FACTOR		EFFICIENCY	POWER FACTOR x EFFICIENCY
A	W				
1.04	20	0.565	lead	0.105	0.059
1.36	177	0.723	lead	0.529	0.382
1.68	344	0.821	lead	0.689	0.566
2.0	491	0.886	lead	0.762	0.675
2.35	648	0.934	lead	0.815	0.761
2.72	805	0.959	lead	0.835	0.801
3.15	962	0.975	lead	0.837	0.816
3.49	1120	0.990	lead	0.858	0.849
3.89	1277	0.994	lead	0.874	0.869
4.36	1434	0.998	lead	0.877	0.875
4.81	1591	1.0		0.865	0.865
5.38	1748	0.999	lag	0.861	0.860
5.85	1905	0.995	lag	0.860	0.856
6.55	2062	0.991	lag	0.840	0.832
7.21	2219	0.987	lag	0.810	0.799

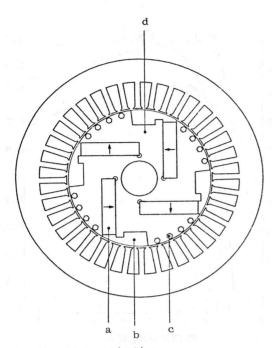

→ Direction of magnetisation

a magnet   b conducting material
c cage bar   d rotor iron

Figure 1 Configuration of high field self-starting
         motor

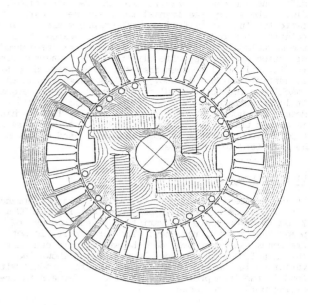

Figure 2 Computed flux distribution for rotor with
         rare-earth magnets

COMPUTATION

Field computation is vital if effective use is to be
made of the magnet material and the design is to be
close to an optimal solution. A method has been
described for obtaining the two-dimensional field of
permanent magnets in the presence of saturable iron.
More recently this method has been refined and second
order as well as first order elements are used in a
routine way. Fig. 2 shows the flux distribution of a
rotor within the slotted stator of a machine operating
just below full load.

It is evident that the peak gap density is considerably
higher than that in the magnet itself. Also virtually
all of the magnet flux crosses the air gap and is therefore useful flux.

A 3-dimensional analysis has also been accomplished
using a finite element program (TOSCA) for which carefully discretised geometries in three-dimensions were
analysed. The efficient use of three-dimensional
finite element programs is essential for the computation
to be economical. Fig. 3 shows the computed torque-
current curve, making use both of a two and a three-
dimensional analysis compared with experimental results.
The comparison shows that both analytical methods are
reasonable but the three-dimensional analysis give a
very close approximation to the measured performance
up to full load.

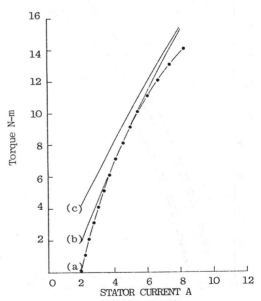

a measured result   b 3-D analysis

c 2-D analysis

Figure 3 The comparison of torque evaluation using
         2-D and 3-D finite element analyses with
         measured results

DIRECTION OF ROTATION

Because the configuration is not symmetrical in the direction of rotation there is an interesting but small difference in characteristics for the two directions. Fig. 4 shows the experimental torque-current characteristic for the two directions. The magnets are inclined relative to a radius and the direction towards which the magnets are inclined will be called the 'preferred' direction and the opposite direction the 'non-preferred'. In Fig. 1 it will be seen that the 'preferred' direction is anti-clockwise. At 250V, a voltage higher than the 'back' emf, the 'preferred' direction has higher torque. At lower voltage, 180V, the comparison is less clearly described though the difference is small. This machine is almost unique in the way it departs from symmetry in a pole-pitch and this is no disadvantage and can even be exploited to advantage.

VARIABLE FREQUENCY PERFORMANCE

It is interesting to study the variation in performance with frequency and results have been obtained at 30 and 75 Hz to demonstrate the variation in efficiency and power factor with frequency. The gap density is not frequency dependent provided the stator core can carry the main flux without undue loss. Fig. 5 shows the variation in the efficiency x power factor product with load in the 'non-preferred' direction. Certain interesting points are shown:

1. The efficiency x power factor product is almost identical at the two frequencies at appreciable load.

2. The points at which the two power-factor curves reach unity are quite different though the voltages are approximately proportional to frequency.

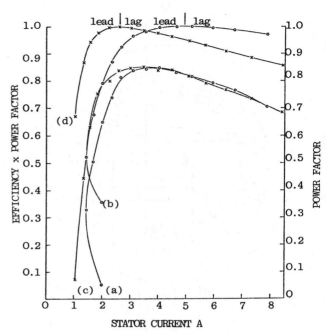

a Efficiency x power factor (30 Hz)
b Power factor (30 Hz)
c Efficiency x power factor (75 Hz)
d Power factor (75 Hz)

Figure 5 The variation of the efficiency and power factor with frequency

CONCLUSIONS

It is shown that the configuration shown can be optimised to produce an excellent synchronous performance. Field analysis making use of computer programs is virtually essential for the development of optimal designs and a three-dimensional analysis has advantages when economic. The comparison between computed and measured performance is good.

ACKNOWLEDGMENTS

The authors wish to thank those manufacturers who have collaborated in the development of these machines. They would also wish to acknowledge the co-operation of the Rutherford & Appleton laboratory in the use of the TOSCA computer program.

REFERENCES

1. Binns, K.J., and Jabbar, M.A., 1981, "High-field self starting permanent magnet synchronous motor", Proc. IEE, 128, (3) 157-160.

2. Binns, K.J., and Jabbar, M.A., 1981, "A comparison of performance characteristics of a class of high field permanent magnet machines for different magnet materials", IEE Conference on Small and Special Electrical Machines, London.

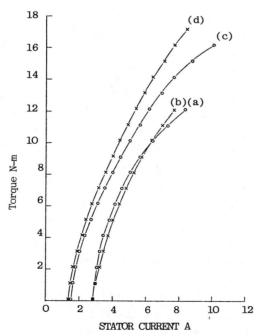

a 180V (non-preferred direction)
b 180V (preferred direction)
c 250V (non-preferred direction)
d 250V (preferred direction)

Figure 4 Torque-current characteristic for the two directions of rotation

THE FEASIBILITY OF HIGH-SPEED MOTORS (40,000 RPM, 50 KW) WITH SIGNIFICANTLY REDUCED ROTOR LOSSES

U.V. Frank and E.F. Fuchs

University of Colorado, USA

INTRODUCTION

Despite the advantages of the designs of high-speed machines, their application at ratings of 50 kW or more is still unusual. This is due to the fact that there are several serious difficulties inherent in a motor designed for use at high speeds:

-- At about 40,000 rpm, centrifugal forces become excessive. Special rotor designs and constructions are required to master the mechanical stresses.
-- The angular speed in connection with shaft diameters of two centimeters or more require bearings having no contact with the rotating shaft at operating speed. Foil bearings, lobed journal bearings, magnetic or tilting pad gas bearings could be applied. The most promising approach is the use of magnetic bearings discussed by Habermann et al. (1).
-- A small clearance of about 20 μm is common to all of the above bearing types. Therefore, vibrations caused by magnetic forces or improper balancing are critical issues. A short stack length and large shaft diameters are suitable to tune critical speeds outside the operating speed range as discussed by Keidel (2). The spring constant of the bearing mounts will also be of influence.
-- Windage losses at 40,000 rpm are very high for salient rotors at non-evacuated airgaps.
-- Pole face losses as they occur in synchronous motors are due to pulsations of the flux density on the rotor's surface and can be quite large if open or semi-open stator slots are employed.
-- An evacuated airgap or a liquid cooled rotor necessitates seals. The durability of carbon shaft seals in some of the designs has been unsatisfactory.
-- At high speeds, a low torque results in a comparatively large power output. Therefore, rotor and overall motor dimensions will be small, resulting in a smaller surface area. At the given high speeds, motor cooling by a shaft-mounted fan can be discarded because of the inherent noise level, mechanical complications and increased windage losses. Large windage losses and pulsation losses are likely to require direct rotor cooling, which is extremely difficult and expensive at the considered speeds.
-- A variable frequency inverter or amplifier will be necessary to start up the motor. Time constants and the commutating reactance of the motor must be small in order to guarantee a good operational behavior of the frequency converter. The stator leakage reactance of a motor is the major part of this commutating or subtransient reactance and thus must be as small as possible (3).

Taking into account the above problem areas, the design of a high-speed motor is likely to become rather expensive. The most promising approach to reduce costs is to avoid direct rotor cooling by minimizing the rotor's iron and windage losses without obstructing the heat transfer between rotor and stator. The design decisions of this paper will be influenced by these considerations.

Reluctance motor designs are suitable to reduce iron losses. Since neither the claw pole nor the homopolar motor carries a winding on the rotating member, both will be considered as possible candidates. The investigation of the mechanical properties will show that a claw pole type is not feasible for large power ratings at 40,000 rpm.

A homopolar motor will be designed which minimizes windage losses--without requiring a vacuum in the working airgap of the motor--by employing a cylindrical sleeve covering the salient rotor and a canned stator. The anticipated windage losses will be calculated on the basis of characteristic Reynolds numbers. The iron losses will be reduced by using nearly closed stator slots, slitted rotor poles and short circuit windings in the stator reducing leakage.

Numerical field calculations are performed for the final design, approximating the three-dimensional flux distribution. A combination of innovations will reduce rotor losses significantly, and direct rotor cooling can be avoided by reducing the rotor losses at the expense of increased stator losses which can be dealt with more easily.

POSSIBLE ROTOR CONFIGURATIONS FOR HIGH SPEED MOTORS

Induction Motors

The earliest commercial ultra-high speed motor design (60,000 rpm, 5 kW) known to the authors was performed in 1952 by AEG (2). Since then, both theoretical and experimental attempts have been made to design high-speed motors at high power ratings (> 100 HP); none of them has been very successful. The above reference describes a two-pole, squirrel cage induction motor operated at frequencies from 145 Hz to 1,000 Hz. Reaching tip speeds of up to 170 m/s, the laminated rotor core was reinforced with steel end rings. Non-laminated rotors for induction machines are possible and structurally highly desirable for high speed operation. However, the generally low power factor raises the kVA ratings of the inverter units, thus increasing costs considerably. Due to its nature of operation, the induction motor also causes eddy current losses in the rotor. The goal of the design of this paper is to avoid direct rotor cooling and its inherent problems and, therefore, a synchronous reluctance motor design seems to be the better approach.

Claw-Pole Motor (CPM)

Claw-pole motors are mainly used at medium speeds. They represent a special version of salient pole synchronous motors. The flux patterns within a claw-pole motor are shown in Fig. 1. The stator houses a three-phase winding on a laminated iron core. The field winding(s) can be placed on the stator. A typical rotor assembly consists of three parts: a non-magnetic shaft supports two magnetic steel members forming the claws. Friction or electron beam welding or shrink fit for low torques are potential jointing techniques. The overall stiffness of a claw-pole assembly will be less than for the homopolar motor discussed below. This is also due to inferior mechanical properties of non-magnetic steel as compared to magnetic steel used for the homopolar design. The supply frequency necessary to drive a CPM at n revolutions per minute is

$$f = p \frac{n}{120} \text{ [Hz]} \tag{1}$$

where p is the total number of claws. From an electromagnetic point of view, a claw-pole geometry of Fig. 2 is advantageous. The claw form facing the working airgap is of trapezoidal shape, and the surface facing the shaft is parabolic, yielding a constant flux density in the airgap. The base of the trapezoidal is chosen slightly smaller than the pole pitch length, while the tip of the claw should be about the width of one stator tooth. This results in a skewing of the stator slots relative to the claw's edge. This design reduces the mechanical vibrations caused by magnetic forces. The frequency f_N at which the vibrations will occur is given by Inagaki et al. (4),

$$f_N = 0.1 \cdot p \cdot n \text{ [Hz]} . \tag{2}$$

Homopolar Synchronous Motor (HSM)

The rotor of a homopolar motor is shown in Fig. 3a. It can be manufactured as a solid one-piece iron forging capable of withstanding high rotational speeds. The stator of the machine houses a three-phase winding similar to an induction motor stator. The iron core, however, is subdivided into two parts, as can be seen from Fig. 3b. The field winding has the form of a solenoidal coil, located in between the two laminated stator cores. At n revolutions per minute, a supply frequency as described by Eq. 1 is required, where p is the total number of rotor poles.

The advantage of the HSM is its robust construction. The flux pattern allows a larger shaft diameter for a given rotor radius than the claw pole rotor. Sensitivity to vibrations and magnetic saturation in the shaft of the HSM are thus decreased. The moderate amplitude of the flux modulation in the working airgap results in a relatively low utilization at low frequencies as compared to CPM's. The stator iron is operated below the B-H characteristic of the iron core. This disadvantage diminishes at frequencies above 1,000 Hz since the flux excursion in the stator iron of any machine has to be reduced at higher frequencies in order to avoid large iron losses.

CALCULATION OF MECHANICAL STRESSES

Claw-Pole Motor

From a mechanical point of view, the differences between the two outlined rotor constructions of Figs. 1, 3 are limited to the form of the saliencies and the three-part assembly versus the solid body. The rotor of the homopolar design can be treated as a special case of a claw-pole configuration. A subdivision of the rotor system into a cylindrical shaft, hollow disk and claws as sketched in Fig. 4 leads to a simple model. The claws are partitioned into three segments--B_1, B_2 and B_3-- roughly approximating the shape of the claws. The mechanical stresses on the disk caused by the claws can then be modeled by the plane stress theory (5).

Minimum Shaft Radius

The task of the shaft is to support the overall rotor structure and to transmit the motor torque. From (6) follows

$$r = \sqrt[3]{\frac{M_T}{0.785\ \tau}} \tag{3}$$

and one obtains the minimum shaft radii of Table 1 for different motor ratings.

TABLE 1 - Minimum shaft radii for different motor ratings

Rating [kW]	Torque [Nm]	Maximum Shear Stress τ [N/m^2]	Shaft radii [cm]
50	11.9	8.2×10^7	0.55
75	17.9	8.2×10^7	0.65
100	22.4	8.2×10^7	0.70

The final selection of the shaft diameter will also be a trade-off between susceptibility to vibrations and increasing stresses on the inner surface of the hollow disk for increasing shaft diameters.

Maximum Stress at the Inner Surface of the Disk. The stresses in a rotating disk can be modeled by the plane stress theory (5). If R_i and R_a are the inner and outer radii of the disk, p_a the stress at radius R_a originating from the claws, ρ is the density of the material, one obtains for the radial and tangential stresses at radius r for the mechanical speed ω:

$$S_{rad}(r) = \frac{R_a^2}{R_a^2 - R_i^2} p_a \left(1 - \frac{R_i^2}{r^2}\right)$$

$$+ \frac{3+\nu}{8} \rho\omega^2 (R_a^2 + R_i^2 - \frac{R_a^2 R_i^2}{r^2} - r^2) \tag{4}$$

and

$$S_{tan}(r) = \frac{R_a^2}{R_a^2 - R_i^2} p_a \left(1 + \frac{R_i^2}{r^2}\right)$$

$$+ \frac{3+\nu}{8} \rho\omega^2 (R_a^2 + R_i^2 + \frac{R_a^2 R_i^2}{r^2} - \frac{1+3\nu}{3+\nu} r^2) \tag{5}$$

By inspection, one notes that $S_{tan}(r)$ is always larger than $S_{rad}(r)$ if $\nu < 1$. Actually, ν varies between 0 and $\frac{1}{2}$ for all materials. It can be shown that the largest value for S_{tan} occurs at the inner cylindrical surface. At radius R_i, Eq. 5 can be reduced to

$$S_{tan|max} = S_{tan}(R_i) = \frac{2R_a^2 p_a}{R_a^2 - R_i^2}$$

$$+ \frac{3+\nu}{4} \rho \omega^2 \left(R_a^2 + R_i^2 \left(\frac{1-\nu}{3+\nu} \right) \right) \tag{6}$$

Eq. 6 enables us to compute the maximum stress within the rotating disk taking into account given stresses p_a on the outer surface.

Determination of the Boundary Conditions on the Outer Disk Surface. The boundary conditions on the outer disk surface describe the influence of the claws on the disk. The appropriate surface stresses p_a are determined by centrifugal forces and bending moments caused by the claws. The following analysis is based on a subdivision of a claw in sections B_1, B_2 and B_3 as shown in Fig. 4. Section B_1 puts a normal stress σ_{B1} on the disk given by

$$\sigma_{B1} = \frac{F_{c1}}{A_1} \tag{7}$$

where F_{c1} is the centrifugal force caused by section B_1 and A_1 is the base area of a claw. Sections B_2 and B_3 cause additional bending moments at the base's cross-section. Since the centrifugal forces F_{ci} $(i = 2,3)$ act on the centers of gravity of sections B_2 and B_3, the moments M_i $(i = 2,3)$ can be computed from

$$M_i = F_{ci} \cdot r_{ci} \quad \text{for} \quad i = 2,3 \tag{8}$$

where r_{ci} is the horizontal distance between the appropriate center of gravity and geometric center of the base of the claw (Fig. 5).

According to Bernoulli's theory of the distribution of normal stresses during bending (6), the stresses σ_M in a cross-section of a claw at a distance z from the geometric center line (Fig. 5) is given by

$$\sigma_{M_i}(z) = \frac{M_i}{J_y} \cdot z \quad \text{for} \quad i = 2,3 \tag{9}$$

where J_y is the polar moment of the base's cross-section with regard to the y-axis. For a rectangular area of the claw's base-- as it applies to normal stresses--at the disk's outer surface radius R_a (of angular width α radians and axial length ℓ_1) the polar moment is

$$J_y = \frac{\alpha \cdot \ell_1^3 \cdot R_a}{12} \quad . \tag{10}$$

From Fig. 5, it can be seen that the largest additional bending stress occurs at the edge of the base facing the cantilevered part of the claw. Therefore,

$$\sigma_{M_i \, max} = \sigma_{M_i} \left(z = \frac{\ell_1}{2} \right) \quad \text{for} \quad i = 2,3 \tag{11}$$

Superposing the stresses σ_{B1}, $\sigma_{M2} \left(z = \frac{\ell_1}{2} \right)$, $\sigma_{M3} \left(z = \frac{\ell_1}{2} \right)$ at point A of Fig. 5 results in the appropriate boundary condition p_a of Eq. 6.

Computation of Rotor Dimensions and the Associated Stresses. A computer program was written (7) and the rotor stresses were calculated based on Eqs. 3 to 11. As a result, then one obtains (Fig. 6) the minimum value of the disk radius R_a versus the tensile strength σ_T, and Fig. 7 illustrates the maximum claw length versus the base radius R_B. Summarizing the results shown in Figs. 6,7, one can note that a claw pole design is not feasible at the given speed of 40,000 rpm

and required rotor dimensions. The maximum achievable claw length does not result in truly interlacing claws.

The above calculations are done without taking into account safety factors common to all mechanical designs, which will further reduce the allowable claw length. Note that the tensile strength of a material--taken as the basis of all mechanical stress calculations--is also larger than the yield strength describing the range of elastic deformations.

Since the electromagnetic advantages of the feasible claw pole geometry does not balance the mechanical disadvantages as compared to a homopolar motor, the latter will be chosen for the design.

Homopolar Motor

From a mechanical point of view, the homopolar motor is a simple version of a claw pole motor. The claws are reduced to poles without sections B_2 and B_3 of Fig. 5. More importantly, the rotor can be manufactured as a solid one-piece forging.

The homopolar rotor is modeled by a solid disk and its appropriate surface stresses due to section B_1 of Fig. 5 and the stress equations are now

$$S_{rad}(r) = p_a + \frac{3+\nu}{8} \rho \omega^2 (R_2^2 - r^2) \tag{12}$$

and

$$S_{tan}(r) = p_a + \frac{3+\nu}{8} \rho \omega^2 \left(R_a^2 - \frac{1+3\nu}{3+\nu} r^2 \right) \tag{13}$$

Note that the stresses in a hollow disk are more than twice the stresses in a solid disk. For steel, $\nu = 0.31$ and

$$\frac{1+3\nu}{3+\nu} = 0.58 < 1 \quad . \tag{14}$$

Therefore, the tangential stress in the disk is always larger or equal to the radial stress. The maximum stress in either direction is given by

$$S_{rad|max} = S_{tan|max} = p_a + \frac{3+\nu}{8} \rho \omega^2 R_a^2 \tag{15}$$

or replacing p_a by

$$\sigma_{B1} = \frac{\rho \omega^2}{3 R_a} (R_R^3 - R_a^3) \tag{16}$$

one obtains

$$S_{tan|max} = \rho \omega^2 \left(\frac{R_R^3 - R_a^3}{3 R_a} + \frac{3+\nu}{8} R_a^2 \right) \tag{17}$$

Table 2 shows the minimum disk radius R_a as a function of the rotor radius R_R. This table illustrates the mechanical superiority of a solid rotor homopolar machine. The disk radius, which is equal to the shaft radius, will finally be selected according to electromagnetic requirements.

HOMOPOLAR MOTOR WITH NEARLY CLOSED STATOR SLOTS AND SHORT CIRCUIT WINDINGS

All conventional heteropolar and homopolar electrical machines have magnetically open or semi-open stator slots in order to limit the leakage flux of the three-phase stator winding. Such open or semi-open stator slots modulate the airgap flux density with slot frequency and cause pulsation losses on the rotor pole surfaces. Magnetically nearly closed stator slots with unsaturated slot wedges reduce these pulsation losses of the

TABLE 2 - Minimum disk radii as a function of the rotor radii for a tensile strength of steel of $\sigma_T = 9 \times 10^8$ N/m^2

Disk Radius R_a [cm]	Rotor Radius R_R [cm]
1.2	6.0
1.5	6.5
1.8	7.0
2.7	8.0

rotor significantly but increase the leakage flux of the stator winding. To reduce this leakage flux, a short circuit winding for each stator slot is employed which reduces this leakage flux. This reduction depends upon the coupling coefficient between the three-phase stator winding and the short circuit windings. The arrangement (8) of the nearly closed stator slots, the three-phase stator winding, and the short circuit windings is schematically shown in Figs. 8,9.

The magnetically nearly closed stator slots can be manufactured either by a wedge which is an integral part of the stator core lamination--as shown in Fig. 8--or by closing the stator slot by a non-conducting magnetic composite wedge.

In order to reduce the slot leakage flux around the three-phase and short circuit windings, a small additional radial airgap between stator core and stator backiron is required, as shown in Figs. 8,9. As a result, using magnetically nearly closed stator slots the slot harmonics of the working airgap flux density can be made small enough to virtually eliminate any pulsation losses on the surface of the rotor poles.

ANTICIPATED WINDAGE LOSSES OF THE ROTOR

Windage losses can become a major problem in the design of high-speed motors. They depend largely on the dimensions of the rotor. A feasible solution well-suited for small rotor sizes might be completely impractical for larger ones. Windage losses can be substantially reduced by smoothing the stator bore and the rotor surface. A cylindrical sleeve around the rotor and disks covering both rotor ends presents such an approach and is discussed in Ref. 7.

RESULTS OF NUMERICAL FIELD ANALYSIS

A numerical solution of the given three-dimensional vector potential problem is presently not possible because of the size of the resulting system of equations, the required computer memory and the large computing times necessary. In the case under consideration, however, it is possible to calculate the DC excitation requirements and the induced voltage separately in axial and coaxial cross-sections, respectively. Fig. 10 shows the flux distribution within the adjusted (7) axial cross-section for a DC excitation of 10 kAt. A typical flux distribution at full load for nearly closed slots--with a slot opening of 0.5 mm--is shown in Fig. 11. Flux densities at no-load on the surface of the rotor poles are given for nearly closed slots in Fig. 12. Note that the flux pulsations are reduced significantly for nearly closed slots. The total pulsation

losses of the 8 poles are for open stator slots 16.7 kW and for nearly closed slots 25 W. The analysis in Ref. 7 indicates that the leakage reactances are approximately the same for both (open and nearly closed slots) configurations.

CONCLUSIONS

In this paper, two techniques were introduced and investigated, reducing the rotor losses significantly. Cylindrical sleeves covering the rotor and stator are proposed reducing the windage losses. Nearly closed stator slots combined with short circuit windings are used to minimize pulsation losses on the rotor poles. These methods appear to be sufficient for a limitation of the rotor losses to an extent that direct rotor cooling could be avoided.

REFERENCES

1. H. Habermann, G.L. Liard, 1979, "Practical Magnetic Bearings," *IEEE Spectrum*, 16, 26-30.

2. E. Keidel, 1952, "Ein neuer hochtouriger Motor," *AEG-Mitteilungen*, 42, Jahrgang Heft 11/12, Berlin.

3. K.F. Schenk, 1970, "Optimization of Non-linear Homopolar Inductor Alternators," Ph.D. Dissertation, Univ. of Colo.

4. Inagaki et al., 1978, Wechselstromgenerator, *Deutsches Patentamt*, Offenlegungsschrift DE 2830883 A1.

5. Ch. R. Mischke, 1963, *Elements of Mechanical Analysis*, Addison-Wesley Pub. Co., Inc., Palo Alto, Calif.

6. L. Levison, 1965, *Fundamentals of Engineering Mechanics*, Gordon & Breach, New York.

7. U.V. Frank, 1981, "The Feasibility of Ultra-High-Speed Motors at 40,000 RPM and 75 kW with Significantly Reduced Rotor Losses," M.S. Thesis, Univ. of Colo.

8. E.F. Fuchs, U.V. Frank, 1981, "Reduction of Pulsation Losses of Homopolar Machine Rotors by Means of Magnetically Closed or Nearly Closed Stator Slots and Compensation Windings Reducing the Leakage Flux of the Polyphase Stator Winding," Patent Application.

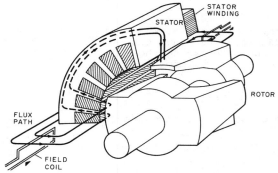

Fig. 1. Schematic of claw pole motor and flux pattern

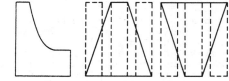

Fig. 2. Standard claw pole geometry

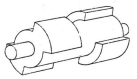

Fig. 3a. Solid Rotor of a homopolar synchronous motor

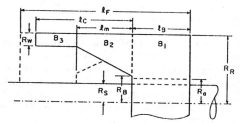

Fig. 4. Parameters and geometry of claw pole rotor

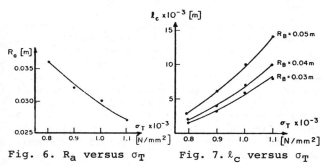

Fig. 6. R_a versus σ_T Fig. 7. ℓ_c versus σ_T

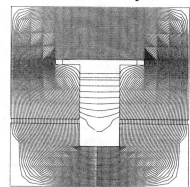

Fig.8. Cross section in $r\theta$-plane

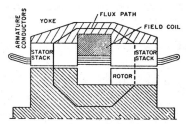

Fig. 3b. Coaxial cross-section of a homopolar synchronous motor

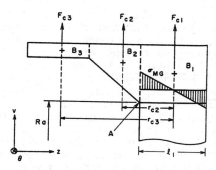

Fig. 5. Influence of sections B_2, B_3 on stress distribution

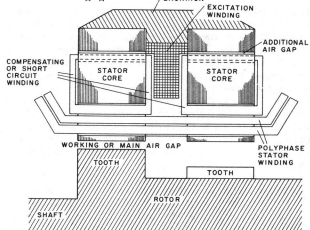

Fig. 9. Cross-section in rz-plane

Fig. 11. Flux distribution at rated load of the HSM with nearly closed stator slots (P = 64kW, I_{ph} = 80 A, V_t = 350 V, cos φ = 0.913 leading)

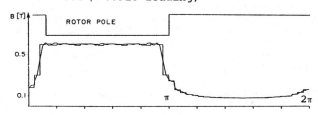

Fig. 12. Flux density at no-load on the rotor surface for nearly closed stator slots (slot opening 0.5 mm).

Fig. 10. Flux distribution in the axial cross-section at I_f = 10kAt. Geometry is adjusted in order to take into account real saturation (7)

PERFORMANCE PREDICTION OF ASYNCHRONOUS MOTORS WITH A SHORT-CIRCUITED STATOR PHASE

A. Consoli - C. Cavallaro

University of Catania, Italy

INTRODUCTION

The sudden change of operating conditions that induction motors experience when asymmetrical stator phase connections are intentionally or accidentally introduced, produces a transient situation during which instantaneous values of currents and torque may considerably increase. One of the most interesting cases of unbalanced conditions of operation is when one phase of the motor is short-circuited to the neutral point of the machine. In this case it is important to estimate the stress imposed on the motor in order to enhance understanding of the machine both at the design and at the operating stage.

Many analysis techniques have been proposed for studying the problem, which is characterized by the presence of the zero sequence component, so that a correct evaluation of its effects is necessary in order to predict the performance of the machine. From the approach suggested by Brown and Butler (1) and also applied by Lyon (2), to the recent paper by Murter and al. (3), the basis of the proposed methods is the symmetrical component theory, which has been more recently extended in the form of instantaneous symmetrical components in order to include the issue of transient behavior of the machine.

A recent paper (4) has demonstrated the possibility of applying the approach of the generalized theory of electrical machines to study the problems associated with asymmetrical connections of induction motors. The method has as a key step the definition of three separate groups of equations independent from each other, the first one regarding the relations between source voltages and phase voltages of the motor, the second one the transformation of phase voltages in d-q-0 voltages and the third one relating to the equations which describe the dynamic behavior of the machine in the d-q-0 components. While the last two groups of equations are unchanged for a fixed reference frame, the first group, which defines the constraints imposed by the source to the terminals of the motor, depends on the particular connection of the stator phases. With these assumptions, the approach leads to a simple, straightforward simulation process, which can be easily implemented both in analog and digital computer for a wide variety of asymmetric operating conditions.

The present paper examines the problems involved by the short circuit of one phase of the motor. The asymmetric connection is experimentally created on an asynchronous 10 HP

motor and the results of the digital simulation based on the suggested method, are compared to the experimental traces. A close correlation of experimental and computer traces demonstrates the validity of the method for predicting the unusual operating condition which has been considered.

ORTHOGONAL AXIS MODEL FOR ASYMMETRIC CONNECTIONS

The short circuit to neutral of one phase of the motor is schematically represented in Fig. 1. The stator phases are normally connected to a three-phase system of source voltages, whose internal impedance is also considered for each phase. The considered short circuit on the phase a of the motor results in a sudden and asymmetric connection of the phase itself to the neutral point of the machine. In order to simulate the behaviour of the machine both in transient and steady-state conditions, the approach suggested in (4) can be followed, whose essential steps are here applied to the connection at hand.

Assuming that the source voltages e_{ag}, e_{bg}, e_{cg} are known and sinusoidal, the voltages v_{as}, v_{bs}, v_{cs} applied to each phase of the motor during balanced working conditions are:

$$v_{as} = \frac{2}{3} e_{ag} - \frac{1}{3} e_{bg} - \frac{1}{3} e_{cg} \qquad (1)$$

$$v_{bs} = -\frac{1}{3} e_{ag} + \frac{2}{3} e_{bg} - \frac{1}{3} e_{cg} \qquad (2)$$

$$v_{cs} = -\frac{1}{3} e_{ag} - \frac{1}{3} e_{bg} + \frac{2}{3} e_{cg} \qquad (3)$$

when the phase a of the motor is short-circuited, the phase voltages are expressed by:

$$v_{as} = 0 \qquad (4)$$

$$v_{bs} = \frac{1}{2} (e_{bg} - e_{cg}) + \frac{1}{2} (r_s i_{as} + L_{ls} \frac{di_{as}}{dt}) \qquad (5)$$

$$v_{cs} = \frac{1}{2} (e_{cg} - e_{bg}) + \frac{1}{2} (r_s i_{as} + L_{ls} \frac{di_{as}}{dt}) \qquad (6)$$

As it is demonstrated in (4), the generalized theory of electrical machines, which is generally the preferred approach for studying almost all types of transient and steady-state phenomena of the machines, can also be extended to the problems involving asymmetric connections of induction motors. The basic assumption of this theory is that it is possible to transform all three-phase 120° degrees spaced quantities in an orthogonal coordinate system d - q - 0, which can be chosen rotating or stationary. In a stationary reference frame, the equations of transformation relating d-q-0 stator voltages to the actual phase voltages are:

$$v_{qs} = \frac{2}{3} v_{as} - \frac{1}{3} v_{bs} - \frac{1}{3} v_{cs} \qquad (7)$$

$$v_{ds} = -\frac{1}{\sqrt{3}} (v_{bs} - v_{cs}) \qquad (8)$$

$$v_{0s} = \frac{\sqrt{2}}{3} (v_{as} + v_{bs} + v_{cs}) \qquad (9)$$

Equs.7 - 9 clearly show that the zero-component of the voltage is present only in case of asymmetries of the phase voltages of the motor, as for the short-circuit represented by Equs.4 - 6.

In fact, the expressions for the d - q - 0 voltages in this case are:

$$v_{qs} = -\frac{r_s}{2} i_{qs} - \frac{L_{ls}}{2} \frac{di_{qs}}{dt} \qquad (10)$$

$$v_{ds} = -\frac{1}{\sqrt{3}} (e_{bg} - e_{cg}) \qquad (11)$$

$$v_{0s} = -\sqrt{2} \, v_{qs} \qquad (12)$$

Equs.10 - 12 suggest two important conclusions about tha short-circuit of the phase a. First of all, the q and the 0 components are mutualy coupled, while the d component remains unchanged with respect to the balanced working conditions. Moreover, the q voltage appears to be independent from the source voltages, as if it were short circuited with additional resistances and inductances.

By transforming all the variables in the stationary reference frame, the equations which describe the dynamic behavior of the motor in the d - q - 0 components can be written in the form:

$$\begin{vmatrix} v_{qs} \\ v_{ds} \\ v_{0s} \\ v_{qr} \\ v_{dr} \\ v_{0r} \end{vmatrix} = \begin{vmatrix} r_s + L_s p & 0 & 0 & L_m p & 0 & 0 \\ 0 & r_s + L_s p & 0 & 0 & L_m p & 0 \\ 0 & 0 & r_s + L_{ls} p & 0 & 0 & 0 \\ L_m p & -\omega_r L_m & 0 & r_r + L_r p & -\omega_r L_r & 0 \\ \omega_r L_m & L_m p & 0 & \omega_r L_r & r_r + L_r p & 0 \\ 0 & 0 & 0 & 0 & 0 & r_r + L_{lr} p \end{vmatrix} \begin{vmatrix} i_{qs} \\ i_{ds} \\ i_{0s} \\ i_{qr} \\ i_{dr} \\ i_{0r} \end{vmatrix}$$

$$(13)$$

where r_s and r_r are the stator and rotor resistances, L_{ls} and L_{lr} are the stator and rotor leakage inductances and L_m is the magnetizing inductance of the machine. Also, ω_r is the rotor electrical speed, $p = d/dt$ and $L_s = L_{ls} + L_m$, $L_r = L_{lr} + L_m$. Finally, note that rotor voltages are generally zero and that all rotor quantities are referred to the stator by the turns ratio.

Equs.10-13 completely represent the short circuit of the phase a, as it results from the equivalent circuits of Figure 2. They permit the calculation of the d-q-0 components of the currents, from which the phase currents of the machine can be deduced by:

$$i_{as} = i_{qs} + \frac{1}{\sqrt{2}} i_{0s} \qquad (14)$$

$$i_{bs} = \frac{1}{2} i_{qs} - \frac{\sqrt{3}}{2} i_{ds} + \frac{1}{\sqrt{2}} i_{0s} \qquad (15)$$

$$i_{cs} = -\frac{1}{2} i_{qs} + \frac{\sqrt{3}}{2} i_{ds} + \frac{1}{\sqrt{2}} i_{0s} \qquad (16)$$

COMPUTER APPLICATION

A digital computer program has been implemented in order to simulate the phase short circuit of a motor having the following parameters: stator and rotor resistances $r_s = 0.412 \, \Omega$, $r_r = 0.3601 \, \Omega$, magnetizing reactance $X_m = 12.28 \, \Omega$ (unsaturated), stator and rotor reactances $X_{ls} = 0.85 \, \Omega$, $X_{lr} = 0.85 \, \Omega$, bus internal reactance and resistance $X_i = 0.45 \, \Omega$, $r_i = 0.0 \, \Omega$, rotor inertia $J = 0.12 \, kgm^2$. The machine is rated at 380 volts, 50 Hz, 8.3 kW, $\bar{p} = 2$.

Due to the particular connection of the motor which takes into account the source impedance, calculations of the phase voltages v_{as}, v_{bs}, v_{cs} must be implemented by considering the source voltage drops. This can be accomplished by lumping the source impedance with the motor stator impedance. Also, since the derivative of the stator current on the q-axis is needed to calculate the stator voltage during short-circuit, Equs.13 have been manipulated in order to obtain the following equation system:

$$pi = Ai + \omega_r Bi + Cv \qquad (17)$$

where v and i are the voltage and current vectors defined in the Equs.13.

In order to completely simulate the motor, the following electromechanical equations must be added to Equs.17:

$$p\omega_r = \frac{\bar{p}}{J}(T_e - T_1) \qquad (18)$$

$$T_e = \bar{p} \, \frac{3}{2} L_m (i_{qs} i_{dr} - i_{ds} i_{qr}) \qquad (19)$$

where T_e and T_1 are the electromagnetic and the load torque, and $\bar{p}$ is the number of pole pairs.

EXPERIMENTAL AND COMPUTED RESULTS

Figure 3a shows the experimental trace of stator line current measured with an analog recorder when the machine was accelerated from rest at 380 V without load. It can be noted that due to the relatively low value of the inertia, the acceleration of the motor is very rapid. The same trace shows the stator line current when the phase a is connected according to Figure 1, while Figure 3b shows the line current of the phase b of the motor during the short circuit of the phase a. Figure 4a shows the digital computer traces of the two currents, calculated for the above conditions using the proposed simulation model given by Equs.1-16. A close correlation of experimental and computed traces is clearly evident. For the sake of completeness, Fig. 5 and

6 show the computer traces of the electromagnetic torque and rotor speed of the motor
during the whole transient. It is interesting to note that, as was experimentally
observed, the motor holds its speed while
torque and current values change and oscilla-
te due to the unbalanced connection.

CONCLUSION

A practical asymmetrical connection of induction motors has been investigated in order to
calculate transient and steady state behavior
of the machine. The sudden phase to neutral
short circuit of the motor can be considered
a sufficiently high possibility of fault for
the machine that it seems important to
find simulation methods useful for its analysis. This paper has experimentally demonstrated the validity of a new method for predicting the unusual operating conditions of the
motor with this connection. The method is
based on the orthogonal axis theory of electrical machines and is believed to involve a minimum of computer computational charge. The
versatility of the method for the analysis of
any type of induction machine connections and
for different modes of operation has been
outlined, so that both the design and the
operation stages of the motors could be helped
by performance predictions obtained through
the proposed procedure.

ACKNOWLEDGEMENTS

This work has been supported by the Electrical
Machines Group of the Italian National Research Council.

REFERENCES

1. Brown, J.E., and Butler, O.I., 1953,
   "A general method of analysis of 3-phase
   induction motors with asymmetrical primary connections", Proc. IEE, 100, 25-34.

2. Lyon, W.V., 1954, "Transient Analysis of
   alternating-current machinery", (book),
   J.Wiley & Sons, New York.

3. Murthy S.S., Singh, B. and Tandon, A.K.,
   1981, "Dynamic Models for the transient
   analysis of induction machines with asymmetrical winding connections", Electric
   Machines and Electromechanics, 6, 479-492.

4. Consoli, A., Lipo, T.A., 1982, "Orthogonal
   axis models for asymmetrically connected
   induction machines", IEEE PES Winter
   Meeting, New York, paper 82 WM 230-1.

5. Jones, C.V., 1967, "The unified theory
   of electrical machines", (book), Plenum
   Press, 183-194.

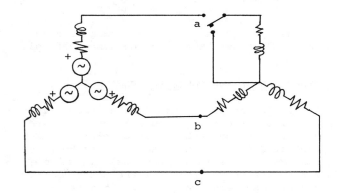

Figure 1 Phase to neutral short circuit

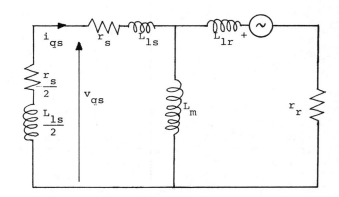

Figure 2 Equivalent circuit of the considered
asymmetrical connection

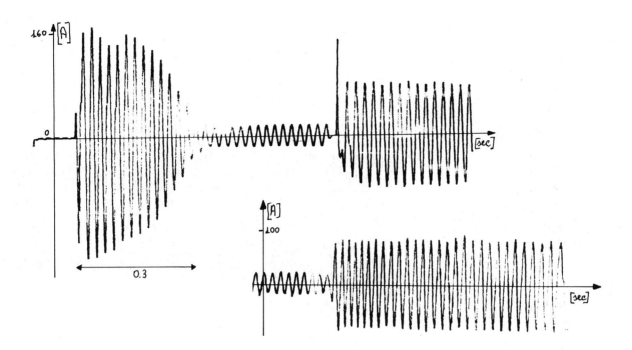

Figure 3 Measured stator current of test machine:
(a) phase a during free acceleration and short circuit of phase a
(b) phase b during short circuit of the phase a

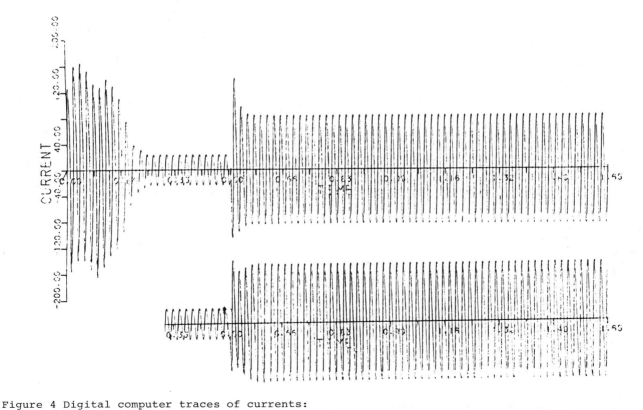

Figure 4 Digital computer traces of currents:
(a) phase a during free acceleration and short circuit of the phase itself
(b) phase b during short circuit of the phase a

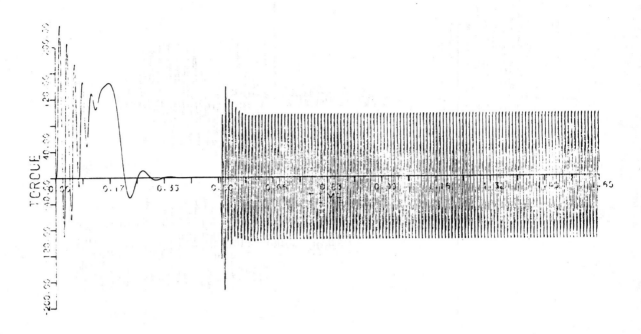

Figure 5 Computer traces of electromagnetic torque during acceleration and short circuit of the phase a

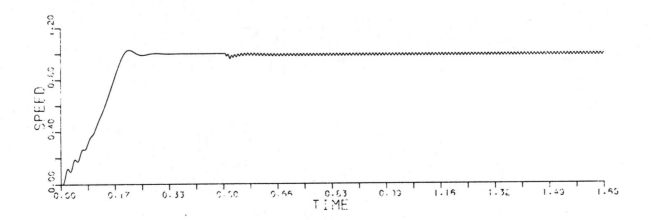

Figure 6 Computer traces of speed during acceleration and short circuit of the phase a

INFLUENCE OF THYRISTOR-SUPPLY TO THE DESIGN OF D.C. AND A.C. MOTORS

Peter-Klaus Budig

Technische Hochschule Karl-Marx-Stadt, GDR.

Summary

Speed-control for electric drives is realised by means of static converters. These are voltage-controlled rectifiers for d.c. motors or voltage controlled or voltage-frequency controlled for a.c. motors. For d.c. motors, in addition to the d.c. voltage, additional a.c.-components arise, whilst for a.c. motors there are also a series of harmonic voltages and currents. This leads to new effects in the motors and their operational behaviour.

1. Speed-controlled d.c. motors

In Figure 1 some rectifier-schemes are illustrated which can be used for voltage-control to control motor-speed. Depending on the number of pulses of the rectifier the output-voltage and the corresponding d.c.-current now consists of a d.c.-component and a summation of a.c. harmonics. This is called a "ripple-current" (r.c.) and in most cases it is sufficient to consider only the first harmonic. The ripple-factor, see Figure 2, is given by,

$$w = \frac{i_{max} - i_{mini}}{i_{max} + i_{mini}} \qquad (1)$$

The a.c.-component of the current can be written

$$i = w \cdot I_o \qquad (2)$$

where I_o is the d.c. component.

Important quantities are given in the following equations.

rms value of current $\quad I = I_o \sqrt{1 + \Sigma w^2} \qquad (3)$

segment-bar-voltage $\quad E = (1+K) \dfrac{U_{max} 2pf}{\alpha k} \leqslant 40 \text{ V} \quad (4)$

reactance-voltage $\quad E_r = \sqrt{E_{ro}^2 + \Delta E^2} \leqslant 0.8 \text{ V} \qquad (5)$

It is generally known that d.c. motors for thyristor supplies are designed with laminated magnetic yokes, to avoid the appearance of eddy-currents in the magnetic parts of the motor. In Figure 3 are shown locus diagrams for the magnetic flux for massive, partial massive and laminated magnetic yokes. Amplitude and phase are significantly influenced by the construction of the yoke.

Considering the magnetic flux in the air-gap and the r.c. in the armature-winding the following equation can be derived for the torque.

$$m(t) = c\Phi_o I_o + cI_o \hat{\Phi}_\mu \sin(\mu\omega t + \psi) + c\Phi_o \hat{I}_\nu \sin(\nu\omega t)$$

$$+ c\hat{I}_\nu \hat{\Phi}_\mu \sin(\nu\omega t) \cdot \sin(\mu\omega t + \psi) \qquad (6)$$

and

$$i = I_o + \hat{I}_\nu \sin(\nu\omega t);$$

$$\Phi = \Phi_o + \Phi_\mu \sin(\mu\omega t + \psi)$$

The average value is:

$$\bar{m} = c\Phi_o I_o (1 + w_i w_\Phi \cos \psi) \qquad (7)$$

The result of a practical example is shown in Table 1.

Table 1   Ripple-factor, phase-angle and average-torque for d.c. motor with massive and laminated yoke

w_i	w	ρ	$\bar{m}$
.3	.05	30°	$1,01.M_o$
.3	.25	10°	$1,074 M_o$

Besides a small increase of torque which can equalize a part of the output-reduction caused by the increase of the rms-value of current there also occur pulsating torques which can cause resonance in the driving system. The lamination of the yoke not only improves the motor behaviour with a thyristor-supply but also its dynamic properties by decreasing the total time-constant.

2. Speed-controlled a.c. motors

Only asynchronous motors are considered here to control speed, voltage-frequency-control is applied. In this case the magnetic flux-linkage for the stator remains constant. The dependence of voltage upon frequency is shown in Figure 4 for different rotor-frequencies. Motor-speed and magnetizing current are given by the following equations.

$$n = \frac{f}{p} \qquad (8)$$

$$I_\mu = \frac{U_1}{R_1 + jX_1} \qquad (9)$$

In Figure 5 are shown the inverters which can be used for v.-f. control. The numbers of necessary components (capacitors C, inductors L, diodes D, thyristors Th, transistors T, transformers Tr) are listed in Figure 5. The shape of current and voltage for the current-, voltage- and pulse-inverter are shown in Figure 6. In the following voltage- and pulse-inverters are considered. In Figure 7 are plotted the amplitude of the voltage-harmonics for different frequencies. Whilst for the voltage-inverter (vi) the amplitude rapidly reduces with increasing frequency toward "O" the pulse-inverter (pi) shows a wide spectrum of harmonics causing currents of rather a high frequency. Although the current-harmonics are proportional to

1/f they can produce I^2R losses of remarkable amplitude. This shows in Figure 8 for both types of inverters. Additional losses, compared with sine-wave-supply, occur in iron and copper. The first are rather small because of the high value of the mutual-inductance in Figure 8. Copper losses are to be considered in the stator and rotor as well. Because of the high frequencies of the harmonic currents skin-effect is to be taken into account. For the motors considered, no skin-effect occurs in the stator because of the circular shape of the conductors. This is not the case for the rotor-conductors. In Figure 9 are plotted the a.c. resistance against the frequency. For constant torque the losses (iron, copper, mechanical) are plotted against the frequency. This is done for the pulse inverter. With decreasing speed, i.e. decreasing frequency, the losses of harmonics are remarkably increased so that for f < 10 Hz these losses are so high that already under no-load conditions the motor becomes too hot. The rotor-circuit is a short-circuit for the mutual-inductance. Therefore the harmonic losses here do not depend on the torque. This is shown in Figure 10. For practical use it is necessary to know the output which is to be achieved with the thyristor or transistor-supplied a.c. motor. This is shown in Figure 11. The pulse-pattern for the pulse inverter was realised with 5, 7 or 9 pulses per half-wave. By variation of this pattern it is possible to decrease the number of harmonics and their amplitudes. Significant improvements can be expected with the application of power-transistors. In this case much higher frequencies can be used. The advantages for the motor are paid for with higher losses in the inverter, because losses in the inverter components in thyristors, diodes and transistors are frequency dependent too. This is shown in Figure 12.

Last but not least the design of an a.c.-drive is a question of optimisation for motor and inverter-losses to minimize the total losses. According to the above considerations the permissible torque of the normal a.c.-motor is given in Figure 13. This is valid for a normal a.c. series motor. These motors are typical mass-production machines and the design is unlikely to be changed to achieve a percentage improvement of less than 10% for speed-controlled application. This is different for motors of higher output. Here more or less individual motors are to be produced. They can be designed from the point of view of an inverter supply. However the range of freedom is limited.

The ampere-coverage in stator and rotor are unique

$$A_{st} \sim A_r \qquad (10)$$

The number of slots in the stator are given by

$$N_1 = 2p\,m\,q \qquad (11)$$

They are chosen from considerations of the smallest possible slot-pitch, and the ratio N_1/N_2. With this ratio the rotor slot-pitch is fixed. They can only be varied by varying the cross-section of the rotor-bars as shown in Figure 14, and the upper portion of the slot which is responsible for the leakage-reactance of the rotor. Speed-controlled motors do not need a high starting torque. That means they can be started with their pull-out-torque as shown in Figure 15. The diameter of the stator current locus diagram can be decreased. By the increase of the rotor leakage-reactance the amplitude of the harmonic-currents can be influenced whilst on the other hand there are no disadvantages in the starting behaviour. Changing the shape of rotor-bars involves having a more or less rectangular

cross-section to vary the height. To keep the current density constant, it is necessary to make them wider. This is limited by the minimum cross-section of the rotor teeth according to the magnetic flux density. Finally the critical conductor height is to be taken into account. Figure 16 shows h_k to be dependent on rotor frequency. It is to be seen that for higher frequencies the height of the rotor bar can never be as small as would be necessary to minimize the losses, but merely approaches the optimum value. To achieve this it is necessary to have knowledge of the specific inverter to be used. That tends to show that the design of an inverter controlled a.c. motor is best achieved in close cooperation with both motor and inverter specialists.

3. Conclusion

The design of thyristor or transistor-supplied d.c. or a.c. drives makes it necessary to take into consideration the operational conditions for the motor, the total losses, the overall-efficiency and the permissible torques. A carefully matching between motor and rectifier or inverter is necessary. It is only for motors that are not mass produced or special purpose 'one off' machines that special "converter designs" can be made. D.c. motors are now thyristor proofed by the lamination of the magnetic yoke.

4. References

Budig, P.K. Beanspruchung elektrischer Maschinen bei Thyristor und Transistorspeisung. Wissensch. Kolloquium der TU Dresden 1981.

Budig, P.K. Die Bedeutung der Eletronik und neuer Magnetmaterialien fur Energie und Material-okonomie in geregelten elektrischen Antrieben. Informationen aus Wissenschaft und Technik der AdW der DDR 12/1981.

Muller G. Diskussionsbeitrag zum Wissenschaft Kolloquium der TU Dresden.

Budig, P.K. Thyristorgespeiste, dynamisch hochwertige Gleichstrom-maschinen Teil 1, 2 und 3. Eletrie 1979 Heft 5, 6 und 7.

F. de Buck Losses and parasitic torques in electric motors subjected to PWM waveforms. IEEE Trans. (IAS) Vol. IA 15, No. 1 Jan./Feb. 1979.

Weninger, R. Einfluss der Maschinenparameter auf Zusatzverluste, Momentenoberschwingungen und Kommutierung bei der Umrichterspeisung von Asynchronmaschinen. AfE. 1981 (63) S.19 ff.

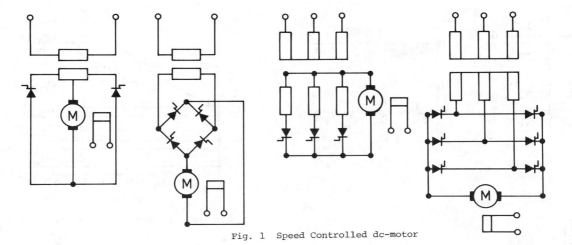

Fig. 1 Speed Controlled dc-motor

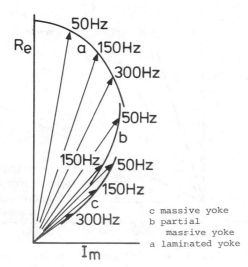

Fig. 2 Ripple-current (rc)

Fig. 3 Locus-diagram

c massive yoke
b partial
    massive yoke
a laminated yoke

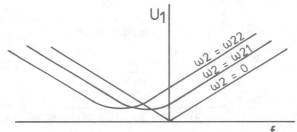

Fig. 4 Voltage against frequency for
constant magnetic stator flux

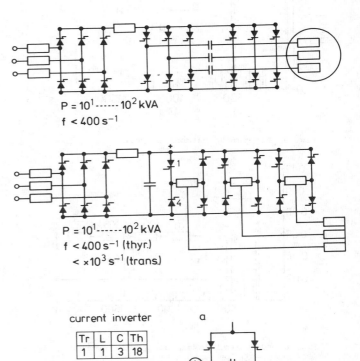

$P = 10^1 \text{------} 10^2 \, kVA$
$f < 400 \, s^{-1}$

$P = 10^1 \text{------} 10^2 \, kVA$
$f < 400 \, s^{-1}$ (thyr.)
$< \times 10^3 \, s^{-1}$ (trans.)

current inverter

Tr	L	C	Th
1	1	3	18

voltage inverter

Tr	L	C	Th	D	T	
1	1+3	6+1	12	12	–	a
1	1+3	6+1	30	6	–	b
1	1+3	1	–	6	12	c

a
b
c with transistors

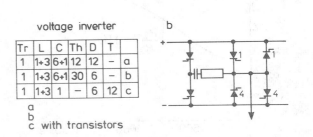

Fig. 5 Inverters for speed-controlled
ac-motors

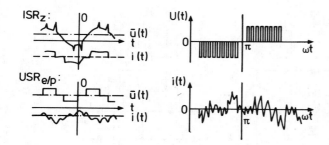

Fig. 6 Waveform of voltage and current

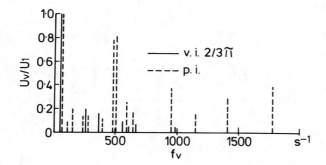

Fig. 7 Diagram of harmonics (volt.)

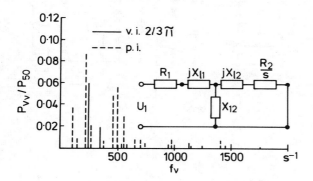

Fig. 8 Additional losses due to the current harmonics

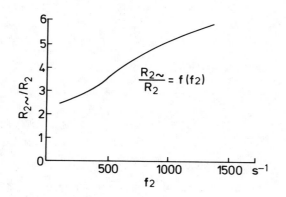

Fig.9 ac.ohmic resistance against frequency

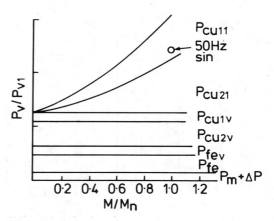

Fig.10 Losses above torque of pi-supplied ac motor.

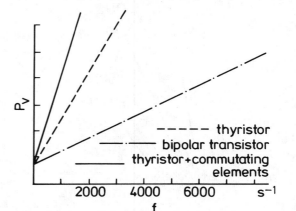

Fig. 11 Losses against frequency for pi.

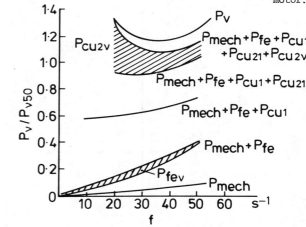

Fig.12 Losses of power-electronic elements above freq.

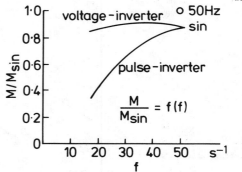

Fig.13 Permissible torque above stator-frequency

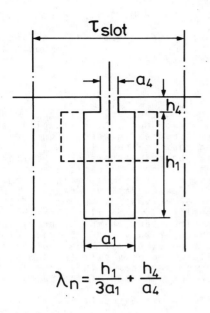

$$\lambda_n = \frac{h_1}{3a_1} + \frac{h_4}{a_4}$$

Fig. 14   Rotor slot-pitch

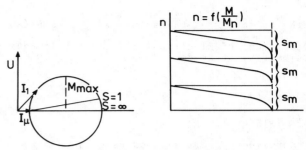

Fig. 15   Stator-current locus-dia. and speed torque curve.

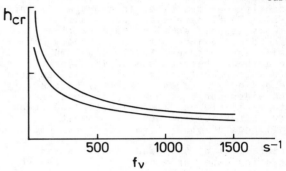

Fig. 16   Critical height of rotor-bar above frequency.

SOME RECENT EXPERIENCE WITH SWITCHED RELUCTANCE MOTOR DRIVES

N.N. Fulton, P.J. Lawrenson, J.M. Stephenson

Department of Electrical and Electronic Engineering
University of Leeds, UK.

R.J. Blake, R.M. Davis, W.F. Ray

Department of Electrical and Electronic Engineering,
University of Nottingham, UK.

1) INTRODUCTION

Controlled-speed, switched reluctance motor drive systems and aspects of the motors and power electronic converters involved have recently been described in a number of papers (1-5). There have also been a number of patents associated with the work (6-10) and more detailed information on aspects of motor design are described in (11-14). Much of the emphasis has been on the application of these drives to road traction but it has become increasingly apparent that they have a very much wider application and, indeed, are of potential interest in any controlled-speed drive situation in industry, domestic appliances or other forms of transportation.

In the light of this and of design and operating experience over the last two years, the present paper offers a brief review of the properties and status of switched reluctance motor drives for controlled-speed applications. This is attempted with particular reference to the inverter-fed induction motor where comparisons can be made most directly. The position vis-a-vis thyristor-fed, dc machines is also touched upon.

2) Principles of Operation

The switched reluctance (SR) motor, one of the earliest forms of electric motor, is closely related to various forms of stepping motor and also, of course, to conventional forms of reluctance motor with rotating fields, and the renewed interest in it during the last decade grew out of work on these forms of machine. As shown diagrammatically in Fig.1, the machine has a salient pole rotor and a salient pole stator, the number of poles on rotor and stator being different, with a number of different combinations being of practical importance. The machine as shown has 8 stator poles and 6 rotor poles. There are no windings of any type on the rotor, which consists only of laminations; and the stator has simple, concentrated windings around the poles with diametrically opposite windings connected in series to form a single 'phase'. The rotor incorporates a position sensor which is used to provide basic signals which switch currents into the phase windings so as to produce continuous rotation.

There are two points of fundamental importance to be made about the properties of such a motor. The first of these is that, contrary to what has been received opinion for many years, such reluctance machines are capable of achieving specific power outputs at least rivalling those of conventional machines, both ac and dc. The second point, which is of major practical importance, is that the machine operates equally well with positive or negative current flow in the phase windings, so that, in designing a power electronic converter to operate with it, there is no need to provide for current reversal during the cycle (as in the inverter for an induction motor, for example), and important economies in the design and the associated cost follow. The switches in the diagram may be transistors or thyristors as appropriate to the application, and the elementary form of circuit illustrated provides for regeneration, which is a normal feature of SR drives. In several of the earlier publications bifilar types of winding have been discussed, which, by providing close-coupled primary and secondary windings around each pole, permit regeneration to take place while using only half the number of semiconductor switches. They are clearly attractive for a number of applications.

In a system in which the timing of the current pulses is fixed in relation to the rotor position, the torque/speed characteristic of the motor is that of a dc series-excited motor. However, by suitable adjustments in the timing of the pulses superimposed on the basic dependence on rotor position, it is possible to produce any desired shape of torque or power characteristic as a function of speed (as may be required by a particular application). In this sense, therefore, the SR drive can be properly thought of as the equivalent of a fully-controlled, dc-motor drive and this includes inherent 4-quadrant operation, given the capability of the dc supply to absorb as well as supply power. For example, in the applications to road-traction systems described earlier, the required operating characteristic involved a lower speed region, up to base speed, at constant torque, followed by a constant power region to three times base speed, followed thereafter by the natural series characteristic. Such a characteristic is well within the capability of the system.

3) Design and Cost Comparison

Hardware comparison with conventional machines is most readily made with induction motors fed from inverters. So far as the motor itself is concerned, the construction has all of the robustness and simplicity which is associated with the squirrel-cage induction motor and indeed the SR motor has the important advantage of eliminating the need for any rotor winding and, hence, those problems which can occur due to imperfect casting or fatigue faults in the cage, and possibly speed limitations. As compared with the induction motor stator, the SR motor has a particularly simple and robust construction. Some form of position sensor has to be incorporated but experience of these in many applications now shows them to be cheap and reliable. During the last two years there have been a number of cost studies carried out on SR motors and as a result it is now possible to predict that manufacturing costs of SR motors will be even lower than those of cage induction machines.

Comparing the SR motor power converter with a

typical induction motor inverter, advantages in terms of the count and cost of major components arise from the point already noted, viz that current does not have to be reversed but, in addition, as described particularly in Reference 5, original configurations have been developed which offer important economies over the inverter in various ways. These include the use of a single commutating circuit to service all the main power switches, or, in other configurations, the use of dormant motor windings as resonant reversal inductors. Overall, therefore, the converter is both simpler and, since the main power devices for given power are of essentially the same size, cheaper than the inverter for equivalent duty.

The SR drive system therefore has significant advantage both in simplicity and cost in comparison with the inverter-fed induction motor. Reliability also goes in hand with simplicity and a point which has emerged as of particular significance is the fact that the converter does not have a low-impedance 'shoot-through' path because a motor winding is always in series with a main device. This has led, under operating conditions, to considerable benefits. Again the economy and the general nature of the converter design result in it achieving very high efficiencies.

4) Performance Comparison

Comparing the performance of the SR drive with that of the induction motor, experience with a number of systems has now confirmed that the SR system is certainly capable of equalling the output power of an induction motor in a given frame and, in many instances, is capable of comfortably exceeding the output power of the induction motor. This capability is, of course, associated with the efficiency and thermal properties of the motor, both of which are unusually good.

The advantageous thermal properties arise from two features. Firstly, losses in the rotor are very small indeed (being restricted to iron loss in the laminations) and rotor cooling poses no problem at all. Secondly, and by the same token, the great bulk of all the heat generated occurs in the stator core and in the coils, which are easily cooled both because they are easily ventilated and because they are at the outside of the machine.

The unusually high efficiencies achieved by the system are shown in Fig.2(a) and (b). Fig.2(a) shows the output power against speed for the traction drive as discussed earlier. Efficiencies are recorded at different points on this characteristic. Note that these efficiency values include the loss in the converter. These results relate to a motor in a 180M frame. The cooling is by through-ventilation of the converter and the machine (in series) at a rate of approximately 0.08 m³/s.

For comparison, the manufacturer's full-load efficiencies for C180M, 3-phase, sine-wave-fed, 50-Hz, 8-, 6- and 4-pole induction motors are given in Table 1 with the corresponding efficiencies for a single 180M prototype SR motor operating over the same range of speeds. To complete the comparison, Table 2 shows the results of heat runs on the same SR motor to establish the given Class B continuous ratings at 750, 1000 and 1500 rev/min.

In Fig.2(b) the contours of constant efficiency for the SR drive over a range of speeds and powers are shown. These further emphasize the above point about high efficiency over wide ranges of speed and load - e.g. the efficiency is 86% or above at 1500 rev/min between 6 and 22.5 kW output and at 12.5 kW output between 750 and 3000 rev/min. By contrast, Table 1 shows that only one of the induction motors reaches 86% efficiency, and even that at a single speed. It will be appreciated, of course, that when the comparisons are made with an induction motor operating under variable-speed conditions the results are much more favourable still to the SR motor. The authors know of no induction motor variable-speed drive which produces comparable figures.

A point which is often raised concerns the stability of the 'system'. As is well known, variable-frequency-fed induction motors exhibit, particularly at low frequencies, unstable and oscillatory behaviour which is an inherent property of the motor's characteristics, independent of any external feedback loops or dynamics of the coupled system. This form of behaviour does not occur at all with the SR system, a fact consistent with the operating mode and characteristics of the system being identical to those of a dc machine.

The results given in Fig.2 are for a machine with a bifilar winding constructed some 1½/2 years ago. The conclusions to which they lead have been confirmed more recently by motors manufactured in industry to our designs. For example, a non-bifilar wound machine in a D132M TEFC frame, develops 7.5 kW at 1500 rev/min within Class B temperature rise and can be continuously rated at full torque without separate ventilation down to below half speed.

5) Non-Linearities

In the foregoing, the emphasis has been placed on simplicity and economy of the SR drive system. This simplicity in relation to manu-facturing and operating conditions is in marked contrast with the rather complex strategies of analysis and design which have to be invoked. Inevitably, of course, the voltages and currents required for the system's operation are wholly non-sinusoidal and Fig.3 shows an example of a typical low-speed current waveform. Both the height and shape of this waveform are critically dependent upon the saturation level of the machine and serve as one illustration of the tight interdependence of the design between motor on the one hand and power electronics on the other, which, on both sides of the design, pose non-trivial problems. All aspects of the machines are crucially dependent upon the non-linear properties of the magnetic material and a method of handling the non-linear interrelationships between flux-linkage, current and angle has been outlined previously [11]. From a power electronics viewpoint, the problems of design, especially those relating to snubbing and leakage reactance effects, are strongly influenced by the non-linear characteristics of the machine.

In connection with the non-linear behaviour, it is to be emphasised that in the designs of machine now available and for which results are here presented, no attempt is made to exploit 'unnatural' levels of saturation as recommended by Jarret and others.

7) Current Status

At the present time a variety of machines in the range from 10W at 10,000 rev/min to 50 kW (peak) at 750 rev/min have been made. A recent 50 kW machine is shown in Fig.4 where the length of the scale is 25cm. Detailed design studies have been made for machines up to 220 kW and other designs have been projected up to 1MW and these confirm the general properties and qualities of the SR system as outlined above. Indeed, there is evidence, at least up to the sizes studied, that the relative performance of the machine improves further with respect to its established rivals with the increase in size.

Attention should be drawn to two possible weaknesses of the system, namely acoustic noise and the potentially large number of connecting leads between motor and converter. Inevitably, of course, the basic mode of operation of the motor is a source of noise and resonances at particular frequencies can be troublesome. Nonetheless, experience to date has shown that at least for a substantial number of applications this problem is not critical and further improvements in noise level can confidently be expected. So far as the number of leads is concerned, this is strongly influenced by whether or not a bifilar winding is chosen. Bifilar systems can involve many connections and therefore an integral construction (see Fig.4) is particularly appropriate. In singly-wound motors the number of connections is not a problem because the number of power leads can be as low as 5.

Overall, therefore, the SR drive appears to offer a combination of high specific output and high system efficiency covering wide ranges of both speed and power; robustness; reliability; simplicity of manufacture; suitability for hazardous environments and flexibility of control, all of which make it potentially attractive for a very wide range of applications in addition to those of a road vehicle system. The comparison above with the induction motor suggests a clear advantage for the SR system which does not appear to be significantly eroded even when noise considerations are taken into account, because it has to be borne in mind that inverter-fed induction motors are very far from being quiet.

No point-by-point comparison is attempted here with regard to DC machines but those involved will be familiar with the relative advantages of controlled-dc and induction-motor drives and, given the current increasing competitiveness of the induction motor, it will be apparent that the SR system is likely to be a serious competitor of the dc motor system. In this context, apart from the speed, thermal and environmental advantages of the SR machine, it is important to note that future changes in cost trends are likely to favour the SR system. At the present time much the greater part of the cost of the dc system is in the motor itself and the cost in this area is likely to increase from an already high level. On the other hand, the greater part of the cost of the SR system is in the power and control electronics where cost reductions should lead to a progressive shift in favour of the SR system.

8) Acknowledgements

Thanks are due to Chloride Technical Ltd for its sponsorship of the project on road traction.

The authors also wish to acknowledge the use of the facilities of their respective universities.

9) REFERENCES

1. RAY, W.F., and DAVIS, R.M. 'Inverter drive for doubly salient reluctance motor: its fundamental behaviour, linear analysis and cost implications', IEE J. Electr. Power Appl., 1979, 2, (6), pp. 185-193.

2. LAWRENSON, P.J., STEPHENSON, J.M., BLENKINSOP, P.T., CORDA, J., and FULTON, N.N. 'Variable-speed switched reluctance motors', IEE Proc. B. Electr. Power Appl., 1980, 127, (4), pp. 253-265.

3. LAWRENSON, P.J., STEPHENSON, J.M., FULTON, N.N., and CORDA, J. 'Switched reluctance motors for traction drives', International conference on electrical machines, Athens, Sept., 1980.

4. DAVIS, R.M., RAY, W.F., and BLAKE, R.J. 'An inverter drive for a switched reluctance motor', ibid.

5. DAVIS, R.M., RAY, W.F., and BLAKE, R.J. 'Inverter drive for switched reluctance motor: circuits and component ratings', IEE Proc., Vol. 128, Pt. B, No. 2, pp. 126-136.

6. DAVIS, R.M., and RAY, W.F. British Patent 13415, 1977.

7. DAVIS, R.M., and RAY, W.F. British Patent 13416, 1977.

8. STEPHENSON, J.M. British Patent 22891, 1978.

9. DAVIS, R.M., and RAY, W.F. British Patent 22892, 1978.

10. DAVIS, R.M., and RAY, W.F. British Patent 22893, 1978.

11. STEPHENSON, J.M., and CORDA, J. 'Computation of torque and current in doubly salient reluctance motors from nonlinear magnetisation data'. Proc. IEE, Vol. 126, No. 5, 1979, pp. 393-396.

12. CORDA, J., and STEPHENSON, J.M. 'An analytical estimation of the minimum and maximum inductances of a double-salient motor'. Proc. Int. Conf. on Stepping Motors and Systems, University of Leeds, 1979, pp. 50-59.

13. BLENKINSOP, P.T. 'A novel, self-commutating, singly-excited motor', PhD Thesis, University of Leeds, 1976.

14. CORDA, J. 'Switched reluctance machine as a variable-speed drive', PhD Thesis, University of Leeds, 1979.

TABLE 1 - Powers, speeds and efficiencies for three C180M, Class B, Drip-Proof, Sine-Wave-Fed
Induction Motors and a Prototype Variable-Speed, 180M, Through-Ventilated SR Motor.

Power (kW)	11	15	22
Speed (rev/min)	720	960	1460
Induction motor efficiency (%)	85	85	86
SR motor efficiency (%)	86	88	86

TABLE 2 - Continuous ratings for three C180M, Class B, Drip-Proof, Sine-Wave-Fed Induction Motors
and a Prototype Variable-Speed, 180M, Through-Ventilated SR Motor (0.08 m³/sec airflow).

Speed (rev/min)	720	750	960	1000	1460	1500
Induction motor output (kW)	11	-	15	-	22	-
SR motor output (kW)	-	12.75	-	18	-	22

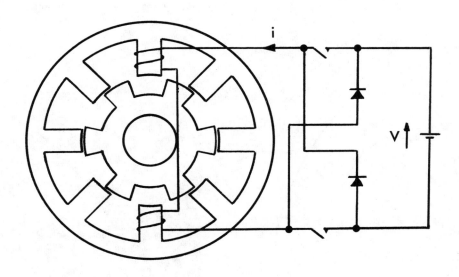

Fig.1: Motor and drive circuit

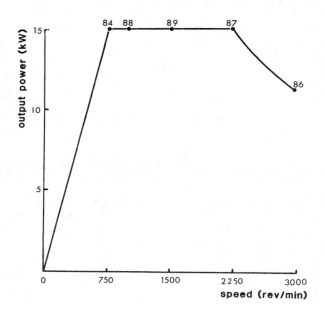

Fig.2(a): Output power/speed characteristic with
efficiencies (%)
180M frame SR motor.

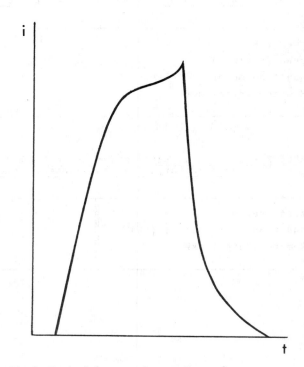

Fig.3: Typical low-speed current waveform.

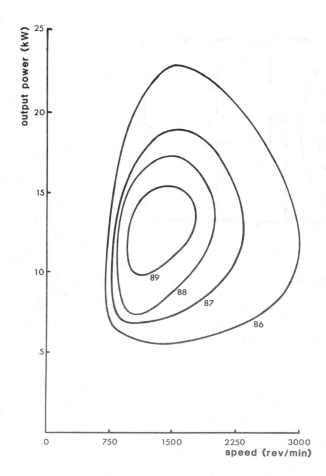

Fig.2(b): Contours of constant efficiency.
180M frame SR motor.

Fig.4: Integrated 50kW traction drive.

AN EXPERIMENTAL VERIFICATION OF A THERMAL-ELECTRICAL ANALOGUE OF A SINGLE PHASE SERIES COMMUTATOR MOTOR

W.K. Yeung and K.J. Overshott

Department of Electrical and Electronic Engineering, University College, Cardiff, UK

INTRODUCTION

The single phase a.c. series commutator motor is used in many modern domestic appliances, e.g. washing machines. This motor suffers armature overheating at low speeds and therefore the lowest operating speed of the motor depends on the maximum allowable loss of the armature. This restriction in operating speed dictates the washing speed of a domestic washing machine which uses a single phase a.c. series commutator machine. Hence, the optimum washing speed may not be achievable. An investigation has been carried out to develop a thermal-electrical analogue of the motor and to identify the major causes of the armature temperature rise in the low speed range and hence to suggest methods of reducing the armature temperature rise at a given output power.

In this paper, a heat transfer block diagram of the single phase a.c. series commutator motor is presented and a thermal-electric analogue is constructed from physical dimensions and thermal properties. The temperature rises at three different locations in the motor have been measured and good agreement with the theoretical temperature rises derived from the analogue has been obtained. An experimental verification of the analogue is achieved. The results show that there is no significant difference in the ventilation conditions within the speed range of the motor and therefore the losses must be reduced if a lower operating speed is required.

It can also be shown that a modification of the analogue enables the temperature rises under load conditions over the whole speed range to be predicted. This approach has enabled the thermal design and machine design, particularly brush performance, to be optimised (1).

THERMAL NETWORK OF THE A.C. COMMUTATOR MOTOR

Heat conduction in a material is proportional to the temperature difference between its two ends and its thermal conductivity. A current, flowing in a material, is proportional to the voltage difference between its two ends and the electrical conductivity of the material. Therefore there are similarities between the heat transfer equation and Ohm's Law. This similarity enables the possibility of representing the thermal network of an electrical machine by a lumped electrical analogue equivalent circuit in which current is analogous to heat flow, voltage to temperature, thermal conductance to electrical conductance and thermal capacity to electrical capacitance. The thermal conductances of the parts of the machine can be calculated from their physical dimensions and properties.

The storage of heat is represented by a capacitor, C, in the electrical analogue circuit.

$$C = H.V \text{ w-sec } K^{-1}$$

where H = thermal capacity
V = volume
and the rate of heat storage = $C \dfrac{d\theta}{dt}$

where θ is the temperature rise.

The presence of the capacitor facilitates the calculation of transient heat flow or transient temperature rise, as the heat storage is changing. For steady state heat flow conditions, the capacitor can be neglected.

In a small commutator motor, the major losses during low speed operation are the core losses and the ohmic, I^2R, losses. These losses are the heat sources in the armature and stator.

The thermal conduction between armature coils and the armature stack is good, so that they can be considered to have the same temperature. The heat produced by the total losses in the armature is removed through the shaft, the armature winding overhang and by the air turbulence in the air gap.

The thermal conduction between the stator coil and the stator stack can not be neglected because the heat is mainly removed from the surface of the stator stack to its surroundings.

Experimental results show that the temperature difference between the stator and armature is only a few degrees, and a large error does not occur if it is assumed that they have the same temperature rise.

It is assumed that no heat from the armature can pass through the commutator. The temperature rise of the commutator and brush may be very high, but are considered as independent thermal circuits. The thermal paths between the commutator and the armature are through the insulation between the commutator segments and shaft, and through the end terminals of each armature coil. The thermal conductivity of the insulation is low and the cross sectional area of the armature conductors is very small, therefore these thermal path conductances are very small, and the heat from the commutator is removed through the air.

Using the assumptions and simplifications above a thermal block diagram can be developed, Fig. 1. The electrical analogue circuit of this thermal block diagram which can be developed from Fig. 1 is shown in Fig. 2.

THERMAL-ELECTRICAL ANALOGUE CIRCUIT

In the electrical circuit, Fig. 2, the stator and armature are assumed to have the same thermal potential, so that there is no heat flowing between them. It is assumed that the core losses of the whole magnetic circuit are equally divided between the stator and armature and since their winding resistances are nearly equal, the total losses in the stator and armature are nearly equal. The maximum temperature of the motor is 90°C (class E insulation) and therefore within the permissible temperature rise it is possible to represent radiation and convection by equivalent conductances which are regarded as constants. Fig. 2 can be simplified as shown in Fig. 3 and the application of Kirchhoff's current law to each junction gives:

$$W_1 = (\theta_1 - \theta_2) G_1 + G_5 \theta_1 + C_1 \frac{d\theta_1}{dt} \quad \ldots \ldots (1)$$

$$W_2' = \theta_2 G_2' + (\theta_2 - \theta_1) G_1 + C_2' \frac{d\theta_2}{dt} \quad \ldots \ldots (2)$$

where W_1 = stator copper loss, w
W_2 = stator core loss, w
W_3 = total armature loss (core losses and ohmic loss), w
$W_2' = W_2 + W_3$
θ_1 = stator field winding temperature, °C
θ_2 = stator and armature temperature, °C
C_1 = thermal capacitance of field winding
C_2 = thermal capacitance of stator
C_3 = thermal capacitance of whole armature
G_n = thermal conductances

t = heating time in minutes

The solution of equations 1 and 2 and the substitution of the measured and calculated values of the constants for the experimental machine gives:

$$\theta_1 = (0.645 W_1 + 0.523 W_2')$$
$$- (0.504 W_1 + 0.539 W_2') e^{-\frac{t}{21.38}}$$
$$- (0.141 W_1 - 0.016 W_2') e^{-\frac{t}{0.65}}$$

$$\theta_2 = (0.523 W_2 + 0.55 W_2')$$
$$- (0.539 W_1 + 0.549 W_2') e^{-\frac{t}{21.38}}$$
$$+ (0.016 W_1 - 0.002 W_2') e^{-\frac{t}{0.65}}$$

The values of the stator copper loss, stator core loss and total armature loss have been measured for a range of values of field current, I_f, and these values can be substituted in the equations for stator field winding temperature and armature temperature.

If I_f = 3.5 amps then

$$\theta_1 = 51.9 - 49.3 e^{-\frac{t}{21.38}} - 2.4 e^{-\frac{t}{0.65}}$$
$$\theta_2 = 50.8 - 51.1 e^{-\frac{t}{21.38}} + 0.3 e^{-\frac{t}{0.65}}$$

which may be simplified for the experimental heating and cooling time range of 0 to 50 minutes to:

$$\theta_1 = 51.9 (1 - 0.95 e^{-\frac{t}{21.38}}),$$
$$\theta_2 = 50.8 (1 - e^{-\frac{t}{21.38}})$$

Similarly, when I_f = 2.5 amps,

$$\theta_1 = 29.2 (1 - 0.96 e^{-\frac{t}{21.38}})$$
$$\theta_2 = 28.8 (1 - e^{-\frac{t}{21.38}})$$

From these theoretical equations derived from the thermal-electric analogue network it can be seen that the heating curve is exponential. The temperature rises derived from the thermal analogue network only indicates the average value irrespective of speed, because all of the conductances, derived in the network, are assumed to be constant and independent of speed and hence the estimation of hot-spot temperatures can not be obtained.

The theoretical temperature rises and time constants derived from the analysis of the thermal analogue circuit are shown in Table 1 and experimental measurements have been made which will be compared to the values shown in Table 1.

TABLE 1 - Theoretical temperature rises and time constant derived from thermal analogue circuit

	Armature and Stator		Field Winding	
Field Current	3.5A	2.5A	3.5A	2.5A
Final Steady State Temp. Rise	50.8	28.8	28.8	29.2
Final Temp. Rise per Watt	0.74	0.71	2.12	2.34
Temp. Rise After 50 min.	45.9	26.0	47.1	26.5
Temp. Rise per Watt	0.67	0.64	1.92	2.12
Thermal Time Constant	21.38	21.38	21.38	21.38

EXPERIMENTAL MEASUREMENTS

The temperature rises at three different locations in the motor, namely armature, pole tip and field winding, have been measured when only the field winding is energised, with all of the brushes lifted out, and the armature is driven at various speeds.

The experimental heating and cooling curves are exponential and the experimental parameters of the heating of the motor can be derived from these curves and are shown in Table 2.

The final steady state temperature and the temperature rise after 50 mins. of the armature decrease with increasing armature speed, Table 2, due mainly to air turbulence. The heating curves follow closely the Theory of heating of a homogeneous body, since they can be represented by exponential expressions which are derived from expressions based on this Theory. The thermocouple is embedded in the armature slot, i.e. among the armature windings, and the heat from the armature core loss passes from the armature stack to the armature windings. From the experimental results the actual heating curves can be represented by a single thermal time constant, which means that the thermal conductance

TABLE 2 - Tabulation of experimental temperature rise results with only the field circuit energised and the armature driven at various speeds

Field Current	Armature		Pole Tip		Field Winding		Armature		Pole Tip		Field Winding	
	3.5	2.5	3.5	2.5	3.5	2.5	3.5	2.5	3.5	2.5	3.5	2.5
	Zero r.p.m.						390 r.p.m.					
Final Steady Temperature	6.6	47.3	49	33	57.5	31	56	36.7	39.3	30.3	53.6	32.1
Final Temp. Rise per Watt	0.79	0.88	0.73	0.58	2.34	2.48	0.77	0.79	0.98	0.70	2.19	2.54
Temp. Rise After 50 min.	56	38.7	39.2	26.9	51.6	28	48.7	31.3	34.9	25	48.4	26.9
Temp. Rise Per Watt	0.67	0.72	0.58	0.48	2.10	2.24	0.67	0.67	0.87	0.57	1.97	2.16
Thermal Time Constant	26.4	28.5	31	29.5	22	21	24.3	25	28.4	21.4	27.5	
	600 r.p.m.						990 r.p.m.					
Final Steady Temperature	50.7	34.6	44.8	28.5	54.4	31.5	51.3	33	45.3	23.8	53.5	30.4
Final Temp. Rise Per Watt	0.66	0.81	0.66	0.66	2.20	2.52	0.68	0.66	0.67	0.53	21.8	2.43
Temp. Rise After 50 min.	45.7	30.5	38	23.6	48.8	28	44.5	30	39.3	21	47.4	26.9
Temp. Rise Per Watt	0.60	0.72	0.56	0.54	1.99	2.24	0.59	0.60	0.58	0.47	1.93	2.15
Thermal Time Constant	21.4	23.4	26.4	28.4	22	22.4	24.8	21.6	24.7	23.3	23	23.2

between the armature stack and the armature winding is very large and hence the stack and winding can be treated as a unit body which is the assumption made in the development of the thermal analogue network. During cooling the temperature drops more rapidly at the beginning of the cooling period than the expressions predict. This difference shows the marked effect of convection on the rate of heat removal and is proportional to (temperature)[1.25].

The thermal time constant and the temperature rise per watt are appreciably larger for standstill conditions than for rotating armature conditions, which shows that the rate of heat removal increases when the armature rotates, but there are no significant differences between the temperature rise when the armature is driven at various speeds in the range, 0 to 990 r.p.m. Hence the final steady state temperature rise of the rotating armature is lower than for standstill conditions.

The experimental temperature rise and heating curves for the thermocouple situated on a pole tip also closely follows the Theory of heating of a homogeneous body. Convection influences the cooling condition which is expected since the thermal path is mainly in the iron, i.e. within the stator stack. From the experimental results, the temperature rise of the pole tip is lower than that of the armature, which is expected since the pole tip should have a temperature rise lower than that of the pole body and the yoke of the stator. The rotating armature does not have a marked influence on the temperature rise of the pole tip, which implies that there is no significant increase in the rate of heat dissipation within the speed range considered.

The temperature distribution of the field winding is not uniform and the middle of the winding has the highest temperature rise and the rise decreases towards both sides. The thermocouple was situated on the surface of the field winding near the overhang region, therefore the temperature measured is lower than the average temperature rise of the field winding. There is found to be a considerable discrepancy between the initial part of the actual heating curves and those derived from the network, and the discrepancy becomes more prominent at higher values of the power loss. The actual heating curves of the field winding seem more accurately represented by two exponential terms, one with a small time constant and the other with a large time constant. The small time constant may be due to the presence of insulation between the field winding and the stator stack because when the field winding is initially energised heat passes from the field winding to the stator stack which has a larger thermal capacitance than the field winding. The temperature rise equations derived from the thermal analogue circuit has two time constants but the coefficients of the small time constant terms are small and therefore these terms are neglected. The large time constant of the temperature rise equations is similar to the values obtained from the actual heating curves, but the small time constant values from the experimental and theoretical methods are different. This difference may be due to the over-estimation in the network of the conductance between the field winding and the stator stack because the effective contact areas between the field winding/insulation and insulation/stator stack may be very small, i.e. point contacts. From the experimental cooling curves it is clearly shown that the rate of heat dissipated is not linearly proportional to temperature because the thermocouple was situated on the field winding surface near its overhang region, therefore convection and radiation should be more pronounced.

COMPARISON OF THEORETICAL PREDICTION AND EXPERIMENTAL RESULTS

The comparison of the temperature rises and time constant of the experimental results for

TABLE 3 - Comparison of the temperature rises and time constant of experimental results with values derived from thermal analogue network

| Field Current | Armature | | | | | | Field Winding | | | | | |
| | 3.5A | | | 2.5A | | | 3.5A | | | 2.5A | | |
	A	B	C	A	B	C	A	B	C	A	B	C
Final Steady Temp. Rise	66	52.3	50.8	47.3	33.9	28.8	57.5	53.5	51.9	31.0	31.5	29.2
Final Temp. Rise per Watt	0.79	0.70	0.74	0.88	0.74	0.71	2.34	2.18	2.12	2.48	2.51	2.34
Temp. Rise After 50 min.	56	46	45.9	38.7	30	26	51.6	48.2	47.1	28.0	27.4	26.5
Temp. Rise After 50 min. per Watt	0.67	0.62	0.67	0.72	0.66	0.64	2.10	1.97	1.92	2.24	2.19	2.12
Thermal Time Constant	26.4	23.4	21.4	28.6	23.0	21.4	22.0	21.6	21.4	21	24.5	21.4

A - Experimental values with stationary armature
B - Average experimental values with rotating armature
C - Theoretical values derived from thermal-analogue circuit

the armature and field winding with values derived from the thermal analogue network is shown in Table 3. It can be seen that the theoretically predicted values are acceptably close to the experimental values for all values of field current and over the whole speed range. The predicted values are in general lower than the experimental results but a more accurate assessment of the conductance could reduce this difference.

The average temperature rise of the field winding for 50 min. excitation are, by the resistance method, 52°C and 32°C for field currents of 3.5A and 2.5A respectively. These values are close to the experimental and predicted value.

A detailed consideration of Table 3 demonstrates that a simple thermal-electrical analogue network can be used to adequately predict the temperature rises and time constant of a single-phase a.c. series commutator motor.

CONCLUSIONS

The prediction of the temperature rise of electrical machines is still a difficult problem, because of the number of uncertainties, such as conditions of ambient surroundings and uneven distribution of power losses. An approximate estimation of the temperature rise is valuable to a machine designer who has to choose the most suitable insulation and cooling system for the machine. Usually the prediction of the temperature rise involves solving a heat flow equation which is complicated and tedious. The alternative is to construct a thermal analogue network and to calculate the corresponding thermal analogue parameters, then the temperature rise can be obtained by analysing the network. The thermal analogue network appeals to the machine designer, since it is much simpler.

In this work, a thermal-electrical analogue network of single phase a.c. series commutator motor has been developed and this network has been verified by comparison with experimental results. The use of this thermal analogue network should be beneficial to the designer of small motors for domestic appliances.

REFERENCES

1. Yeung, W.K., 1980, Ph.D. Thesis, University of Wales.

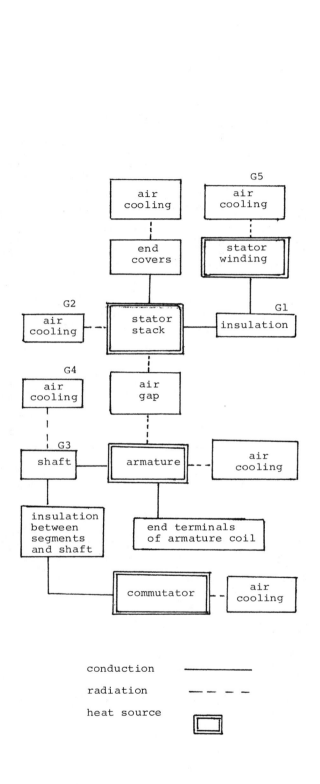

Figure 1 Block Diagram of Commutator Motor Showing Thermal Sources and Paths

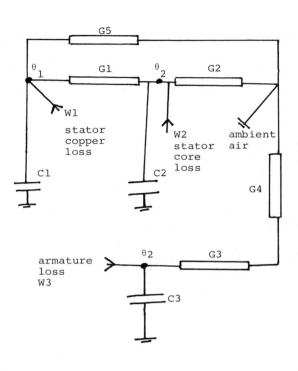

Figure 2 Thermal Electrical Analogue Circuit

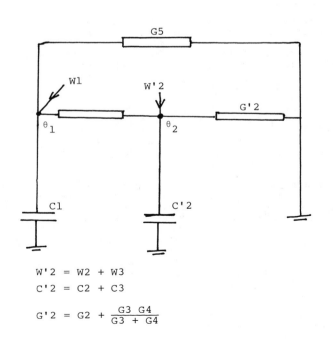

$$W'2 = W2 + W3$$
$$C'2 = C2 + C3$$
$$G'2 = G2 + \frac{G3\ G4}{G3\ +\ G4}$$

Figure 3 Simplified Thermal Analogue Circuit

UTILIZATION OF DEEP BAR CONCEPT IN IMPROVING THE STARTING PERFORMANCE OF RELUCTANCE MOTORS

S. A. Hassan[*]   A. L. Mohamadein[**]   A. M. F. Osheiba[*]

* Faculty of Engineering & Technology, University of Monoufia, EGYPT
**Faculty of Engineering, University of Alexandria, Alexandria, EGYPT.

ABSTRACT

Starting and synchronization of three phase reluctance motors presents an important feature which should be taken good care of when designing this type of motor. The deep-bar winding concept can then be employed success - fully to improve the starting as well as synchronizing performances.

This paper presents an experimental investiga- tion for making use of this concept. Four rotors were built, having the same construct- ional features, and maintaining the same volume of cage winding material. Transient runup and synchronization of the motors is recorded experimentally and predicted theoret- ically.

Changes in starting performance versus differ- ent values of bar depth/bar width (of the cage) were measured. It was found that an optimum ratio exists which yields the highest starting torque, lowest starting current and shortest starting up period.

The effect of employment of this concept on a motor's steady state performance is also investigated and evaluated both experimentally and theoretically. Useful conclusions regarding the way in which deep bar windings could be utilized are given.

INTRODUCTION

Reluctance motors have been considered as an attractive solution for the constant speed problem of certain drives. The merits offered by this type of motor such as speed constancy, robustness and absence of current collection gears, are partially offset by the associated poor performance obtained.

Research was then focussed on two main areas. Firstly, to improve the steady state performa- nce by increasing the saliency ratio, which in turn led to higher pull out torque and power factor. Several designs appeared to achieve such a goal(1,2,3).

Regarding motor dynamic performance during the run up and pulling into synchronism period, less attention was paid. Few papers(4,5) dealt with this topic and emphasis was laid on the importance of damper winding arrangements and their relevant axes parameters. In conclusion, it was found that better asynchro- nous performance could be achieved by increas- ing the starting torque as well as the rate of change of torque with slip near the synchronous speed.

It is thought worthwhile to investigate the effect of utilizing the skin effect phenomenon to improve the asynchronous performance of conventional type salient pole reluctance motors. Also, the influence of such utilizat- ion on the steady state performance is evaluated.

DESIGN DETAILS OF EXPERIMENTAL ROTORS

In order to investigate the effect of cage winding shapes on the starting performance, four salient pole rotors were built and tested. The rotors have the same configurations regar- ding their dimensions. The damper bars fitt- ed in the pole face of the different rotors have the same cross-sectional area with differ- ent bar height/bar width ratios as shown in Fig(1). The interpolar space of the different rotors is also filled with the same conducting material used for the bars, to ensure suffici- ent direct axis damping circuit.

The dimensions of the rotors are so chosen as to fit in a three phase stator used originally for an induction motor, squirrel cage type rated at 220/380 V, Δ/Y, 0.75 hp, 2.78/1.61 A, 4 poles, 50 Hz, 1430 rpm, p.f.= 0.75.

The bar dimensions and depth to width ratios for the different rotors are listed in the following table:

TABLE (1)

Rotor Designation	h_s	b_s	h_s/b_s
A1	6 mm	6 mm	1
A2	12	3	4
A3	18	2	9
A4	20	1.8	11

The reluctance motor was tested and loaded by a DC machine, while the load angle (δ) was measured by the conventional method of strobo- scope and protractors.

Regarding the evaluation of the transient performance, a torque transducer, tachogenera- tor and X-Y recorder were used.

Results regarding both steady and transient performances are given in the following sectio- ns.

EFFECT OF DEEP BAR CAGE WINDINGS ON MOTOR PARAMETERS

The dependence of motor performance on its associated parameters makes its evaluation, both experimentally as well as theoretically worthwhile, as a first step towards explaining the different performance characteristics obtained by different rotors.

Axes Reactances & Saliency Ratios

In estimating axes reactances, the method presented in ref(5) was employed and the results obtained theoretically and experimentally are listed in table(2).

Regarding the saliency ratio, the stator leakage reactance was measured (found to be equal to 10 ohms), then X_d and X_q were calculated. The saliency ratio of rotor Al was found to be equal to 3.21, while that of rotor A2 was 3.27, rotor A3 was 3.38, and finally for rotor A4 the saliency ratio was 3.42.

The variation of axes reactances, and saliency ratio versus (h_s/b_s) is shown in Fig(2), where it could be observed that direct axis reactance increases with the increase in (h_s/b_s) while the quadrature axis reactance decreases. As a result the saliency ratio increases by the increase of bar height to width ratio. This behaviour is attributed to the effect of the bar channel in the pole face associated with the distribution of flux density for the same m.m.f. wave.

TABLE (2)

Rotor Designation	X_{md} (Ω) Computed	Test	X_{mq} (Ω) Computed	Test
Al	133.0	130.0	35.0	33.6
A2	135.0	132.4	34.0	33.5
A3	136.0	134.3	33.5	32.7
A4	138.0	135.5	33.0	32.5

Deep-Bar Damper Winding Impedance

The referred values of rotor damper winding parameters were measured by the locked rotor test. The variation of these quantities in the two axes versus (h_s/b_s) is shown in Fig(3). It can be observed that quadrature axis damper winding parameters increase as bar height to width ratio increases. Also, direct axis damper winding parameters increase slightly as (h_s/b_s) is increased. This is due to the uneven distribution of current in the deep bars and its liability to concentrate at the surface.

To demonstrate the variations occuring in the damper bars during asynchronous operation, rotor parameters were evaluated at different values of rotor frequency. The variation of these parameters versus slip is shown in Fig(4), where it can be observed that rotor A4 experiences more pronounced skin effect than A3, A2 and A1.

RESULTS

Transient Performance

In evaluating the transient performance of each rotor, the stator was instantaneously conn ected to the AC supply, after which the speed, torque and input stator current versus time were recorded.

Theoretical evaluation of transient state was done by representing stator and rotor circuits in two perpendicular axes, namely direct and quadrature. Solution of the associated five non-linear differential equations was done using the Runge-Kutta method.

Speed/time variations of the four rotors are shown in Fig(5), both experimentally and theoretically. Also, the variation of starting runup period versus (h_s/b_s) is shown in Fig(6). It can be observed that a ratio of bar depth to width of 9 possessed by rotor A3 yielded the shortest runup period and for further increases in that ratio the starting period

begins to increase with inferior starting characteristics.

This aforementioned behaviour can be regarded as a direct consequence of the relative magnitudes of steady starting torque of the different rotors as measured by a steady state performance test and shown in Fig(6).

Synchronous Performance

The synchronous performance of the four rotors as predicted theoretically and evaluated experimentally is shown in Fig(7); namely, torque and apparent efficiency versus δ. It is clear that A4 yielded the best performance followed by A3 then A2 and finally Al. Fig(8) summarises the main performance criteria obtained versus (h_s/b_s).

It should be pointed out that the performance figures shown in Fig(8) are a reflection of the effect of motor saliency ratio.

EFFECT OF BAR DEPTH/WIDTH RATIO ON MOTOR PERFORMANCE

The results shown in Figs(6 & 8) give quite a clear idea about motor behaviour at different values of (h_s/b_s).

Regarding transient runup time, the shortest was yielded by a specific ratio of bar depth/width which resulted in rotor cage parameters of appropriate values such that highest starting torque was obtained. So, in calculating rotor parameters, emphasis should be laid on the value of asynchronous starting torque.

On the other hand, the presence of rotor cage windings especially in the pole face affects the flux density distribution in the direct axis. The greater the bar width, the lower the fundamental flux density component will be, and lower X_{md} will result as has been indicated in table(2). Moreover, as a consequence of the drop in the value of X_{md}, the saliency ratio will decrease and inferior steady state performance characteristics such as full load torque, efficiency, power factor and apparent efficiency will be obtained.

It is then necessary to choose a proper value of (h_s/b_s) such that optimum starting conditions could be achieved, bearing in mind that higher values of this ratio are desirable for better asynchronous performance.

CONCLUSIONS

From the foregoing discussion, it can be concluded that for the same volume of damper winding material, the choice of this winding's proportions is of prime importance for achieving the best possible performance.

Higher ratios of (h_s/b_s) were observed to produce the following effects :

a)- Pronounced skin effect leading to variation in damper winding parameters. A certain ratio will lead to the highest possible starting torque and hence the lowest starting time.
b)- Better synchronous performance due to decreased flux distortion especially in the direct axis with a resulting higher X_{md} and higher saliency ratio.

REFERENCES

1. Lawrenson, P.J. & Agu, L.A.;"Developments in the performance and theory of segmental

rotor reluctance motors"; Proc. IEE,
1967, pp 645 - 653, Vol. 114

2.   Chalmers, B.J. & Mulki, A.S.;"Design
      and performance of reluctance motors
      with unlaminated rotors"; ibid, Vol.
      119, 1972, pp 1562 - 1569

3.   Cruickshank, A.J.O., Anderson, A.F.&
      Menzies, R.W.;"Theory and Performance
      of reluctance motors with axially
      laminated anisotropic rotors"; ibid,
      Vol. 118, 1971, pp 888 - 893

4.   Douglas, J.F.H.;"Pull-in criterion for
      reluctance motors"; AIEE Trans., Vol.
      79, July 1960, pp 139 - 142

5.   Lawrenson, P.J., Mathur, R.M. &
      Stephenson, J.M.;"Transient Performance
      of reluctance motors"; Proc. IEE, Vol.
      118, No 6, June 1971, pp 777 - 783

6.   Hassan, S.A., Osheiba, A.M.F. &
      Mohamadein, A.L.;"A generalized Appro-
      ach for the evaluation of reluctance
      motor reactances;" Electric Machines &
      Electromechanics, Vol. 5., No 2, pp
      155 - 168.

LIST OF SYMBOLS

h_s	Bar depth of cage windings.
b_s	Bar width of cage windings
R_D	Cage windings referred direct axis resistance.
R_Q	Cage windings referred quadrature axis resistance.
X_D	Cage windings referred direct axis leak-age reactance.
X_Q	Cage windings referred quadrature axis leakage reactance.
X_{md}	Direct axis magnetizing reactance.
X_{mq}	Quadrature axis magnetizing reactance.
X_d	Direct axis reactance.
X_q	Quadrature axis reactance.
T	Developed electromagnetic torque.
T_{st}	Asynchronous starting torque.
t_s	Starting up time in seconds.
I_{fl}	Full load current.
$\cos(\phi)$	Power factor.
η	Efficiency.
$\eta \cdot \cos(\phi)$	Apparent efficiency.
δ	Load angle in elect. degr.

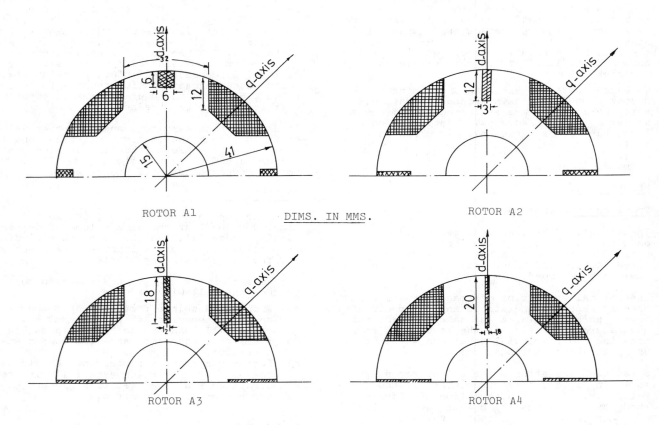

Figure 1 Salient Pole rotors with different (h_s/b_s) ratios.

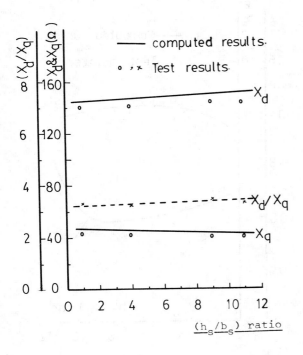

Figure 2 Variation of axes reactances (X_d & X_q) & saliency ratio (X_d/X_q) versus (h_s/b_s) ratio.

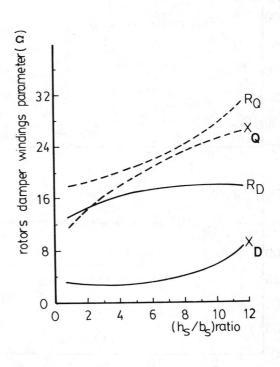

Figure 3 Variation of damper winding parameters versus (h_s/b_s)

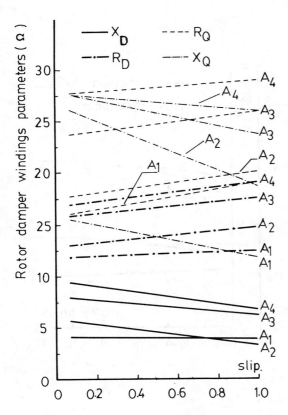

Figure 4 Variation of damper winding parameters versus rotor slip

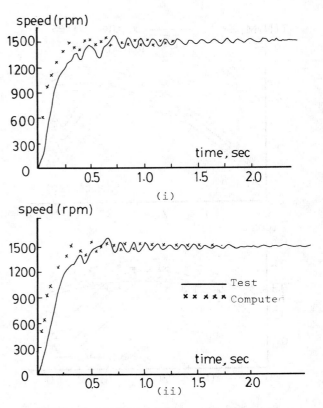

Figure 5.a. Speed/time variations for rotors: (i) A1 & (ii) A2

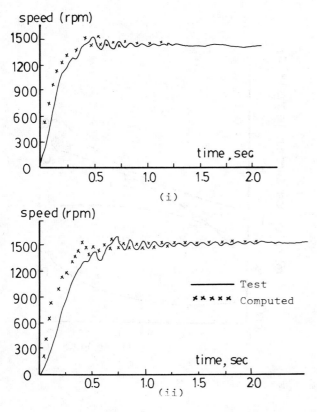

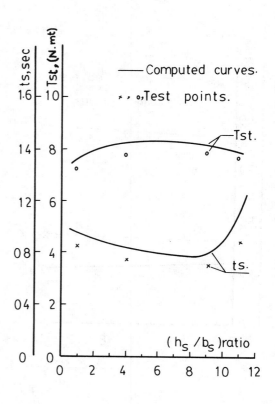

Figure 5.b. Speed/time variations of rotors : (i) A3 & (ii) A4

Figure 6 Variation of starting runup time and torque versus (h_s/b_s) ratio.

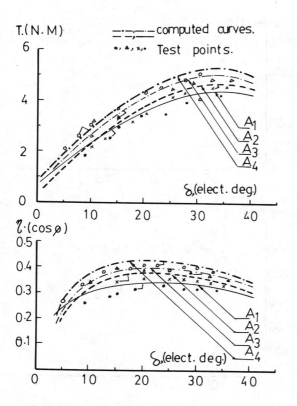

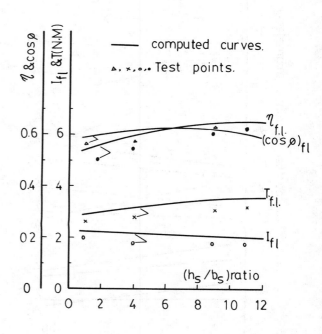

Figure 7 Synchronous performance of the different rotors versus (δ)

Figure 8 Variation of performance criteria versus (h_s/b_s).

ANALYTICAL DETERMINATION OF THE AXIAL VARIATION OF AIRGAP FLUX DENSITY IN A SKEWED-ROTOR INDUCTION MOTOR

A.C. Smith and S. Williamson

University of Aberdeen, U.K.; Imperial College, London, U.K.

INTRODUCTION

Whilst it has been demonstrated that an appropriate choice of slot numbers can eliminate the effects of cogging, the fact remains that motor manufacturers still employ slot skew as a method of minimising harmonic and cogging torques. This is particularly the case in fractional horsepower machines. One unattractive side-effect of skew is the introduction of axial airgap flux variations with a resulting increase in rotor losses and axial forces. An extensive experimental investigation by Binns et al (1) has demonstrated that skewing of the rotor cage can produce axial variations in the airgap flux density as large as 1.5:1. A reliable method of predicting the airgap flux variations due to rotor skew could therefore be an asset in the preliminary assessment of a new machine design.

The field analysis described in this paper was developed over a number of years (see introduction of Reference 6), and is based upon a direct solution of Maxwell's equations in an idealised model of the machine. Recently, however, several authors (2,3,4) have reformulated and extended the basic theory to produce a versatile and convenient system of analysis. In general, the basic principle lies in the replacement of the real machine by a stack of homogeneous layers (see figure 1). The physical properties of these layers reflect those of the parts of the real machine they represent. A feature of this model was the replacement of the rotor cage by a continuous layer of uniform conductivity. For this reason, 'layer theory' found its widest application in the field of linear motors, where there were obvious physical similarities with the multi-layer model. One of the obstacles which prevented a more widespread use of the field analysis, was its basic inability to simulate the slotting effects produced by the rotor cage of a standard induction machine. More recently however, a new form of field analysis was proposed (5) which allowed the rotor bar currents to flow in discrete paths, and which was therefore applicable to rotating induction machines. The theory was developed further (6) to enable the effects of skew to be included directly, and in its final form represented a general field-based analysis capable of modelling cage induction motors incorporating skew. A useful feature of this type of analysis is the ease with which airgap fields can be determined. This alone makes the analysis an attractive method for the analytical determination of the axial airgap flux variations present in a skewed cage induction motor.

Analytical Determination of Airgap Flux Density

The stator of an induction machine is normally unskewed and consequently, when excited, produces magnetic fields which are invariant in the axial direction. On the other hand the currents flowing in a skewed rotor result in the production of a field which has axial variations in addition to the normal circumferential variations. It is apparent therefore, that two distinct forms of field variation exist within the machine. However, one-dimensional field variation may be regarded as a specific case of two-dimensional variation, so that the field analysis may be developed in a two-dimensional form to obtain a generally applicable formulation. All field quantities are resolved into double harmonic series using standard Fourier techniques, the harmonic components are investigated individually and subsequently superimposed. This, of course, assumes that the effects of saturation are negligible. The notation for any field quantity is therefore of the form

$$b = \text{Re}\left\{ \sum_{\ell} \sum_{m} \bar{B}^{k\ell m}(z) \; e^{j(s^k \omega t - \ell y - mx)} \right\} \qquad (1)$$

in which k and ℓ are circumferential harmonic wave numbers, m is the axial harmonic wave number, and sinusoidal time variation has been assumed. s^k is included as a general parameter which is interpreted as fractional slip for the harmonic rotor fields.

For the specified field variation along two coordinate axes (x,y) and with time, Maxwell's equations are solved to determine the field variation along the remaining third axis (z). Solution for the magnetic field strength in any layer gives the following relationships

$$\bar{H}^{k\ell m}_x = \frac{m}{\ell} \; \bar{H}^{k\ell m}_y \qquad (2)$$

$$\bar{H}^{k\ell m}_y = C \cosh \varepsilon z + D \sinh \varepsilon z \qquad (3)$$

$$\bar{H}^{k\ell m}_z = \frac{j}{\ell} \left\{ \bar{J}^{k\ell m}_x + \varepsilon (C \sinh \varepsilon z + D \cosh \varepsilon z) \right\} \qquad (4)$$

in which ε is a propagation constant given by

$$\varepsilon = \sqrt{m^2 \frac{\mu_x}{\mu_z} + \ell^2 \frac{\mu_y}{\mu_z}} \qquad (5)$$

and C and D are constants of integration. μ_x, μ_y and μ_z are the appropriate magnetic permeabilities of the layer along the three coordinates axes (see figure 1). These equations are valid for any layer within the model, producing twice as many constants of integration as there are layers in the model.

In a normal machine analysis however, the determination of these constants is superfluous, it being sufficient to relate the field values at one boundary of any layer to those at the other, using a transfer matrix equation (2). Successive use of the transfer matrix throughout the regions in the model enables surface impedances looking "up" and "down" from any general excitation layer to be evaluated. These impedances together with the transfer matrix principle allows the fields produced by any excited winding to be determined on a harmonic by harmonic basis at all region boundaries within the model.

The machine is considered as a series of coupled circuits, with each distinct stator winding constituting a single circuit. In the rotor however, induced emfs differ in frequency, distribution and amplitude with harmonic order. It is necessary, therefore, to regard the rotor current distributions, each flowing in its own well-defined circuit. A single rotor bar is used to typify each rotor circuit, as is common practice. Each individual circuit is assumed, in turn, to be excited with unit current and the resulting fields within the model are determined by employing the procedures described earlier. Standard techniques allow the induced emfs to be determined in all circuits, enabling coupling impedances to be calculated. These coupling impedances are assembled into an impedance matrix (5) relating the applied winding voltages to the unknown winding and harmonic bar currents for a voltage-forced solution. The unknown currents are then readily determined by solution of this matrix equation.

It is apparent that the calculation of boundary surface fields for unit bar or winding currents is an integral part of any machine solution. The actual boundary fields are therefore determined with ease by simple superposition of individual current components, scaled by the actual bar or winding currents. The boundary field values can then be substituted into equations (2)-(4) to solve for the constants of integration, so that the field values within the airgap of the motor can be determined.

The average flux density measured by a search coil situation on the stator surface at position $y = Y_o$, $x = X_o$ is obtained by integrating the flux density over the domain of the search coil and dividing by its area,

$$b_{av} = \text{Re}\left\{ \bar{B}\, K_\delta\, K_\beta\, e^{j(\omega t - \ell Y_o - m X_o)} \right\} \qquad (6)$$

where
$$K_\delta = \frac{\sin\frac{\ell\delta}{2}}{\frac{\ell\delta}{2}} \qquad (7)$$

and
$$K_\beta = \frac{\sin\frac{m\beta}{2}}{\frac{m\beta}{2}} \qquad (8)$$

K_δ and K_β are search coil width and breadth factors respectively.

As mentioned previously, equation (6) can be used to determine both the stator and rotor driven fields by appropriate substitution for the circumferential and axial harmonic wave numbers ℓ and m. The flux variations within the airgap of an induction machine can therefore be predicted by the field analysis, in which the stator winding harmonics (denoted by k, $m = 0$) are considered, and the principal rotor slot-harmonic fields ($\ell = k,m$) only are considered. The effect of the remaining rotor slot-harmonic fields ($\ell \neq k$) were ignored since they induce non-line-frequency emfs in any search coils mounted on the stator. The total flux density therefore, measured by the n-th axial search coil at position $x = X_n$ and $y = Y_n$, is

$$b_{av}^n = \text{Re}\left\{ \sum_{k=-\infty}^{+\infty} \left[\bar{B}_{ST}^k\, K_\delta^k \right. \right.$$

$$\left. \left. + \sum_{m=-\infty}^{+\infty} \bar{B}_{RT}^{-km}\, K_\delta^k\, K_\beta^m\, e^{-jmX_n} \right] e^{j(\omega t - kY_n)} \right\} \qquad (9)$$

Experimental Procedure

Of all induction machines the single-phase fractional-horsepower range commonly display extensive amounts of rotor skew. For this reason experimental measurements were performed on a standard production, 240 Volt, 1/3 horsepower, single-phase induction motor, with a rotor skew of 1.5 slots. The stator winding consists of a 4-pole, concentric winding, with three series-connected coils per pole.

Measurements of the airgap flux density within the motor were obtained from a series of search coils mounted on the inner surface of the stator. Five sets of search coils were utilised, spanning one complete pole-pitch, with each set consisting of five coils uniformly distributed along the axial machine length. Figure 2 illustrates the exact positioning of these coil sets in relation to the stator winding. The search coils were finally connected through a multi-selector switch to a low-pass active filter, which amplified the signal and removed the high frequency components, such as slot ripple.

Discussion of Results

The experimental measurements of airgap flux density obtained from the five sets of search coils, labelled A to E in accordance with figure 2, are illustrated in figures 3-6. These are shown together with the airgap flux variations predicted by the field analysis for two different rotor speeds, corresponding to slip values of 50% and 0.66% respectively.

Inspection of figure 2 reveals that coil sets A and E are positioned one circumferential pole-pitch apart. The magnetic symmetry of these coil sets is reflected in figure 3 and is thought to be sufficient indication of the validity of the measurement system. The overall correlation between measured and computed values (figures 3-6) is also believed by the authors to be acceptable considering the practical uncertainties associated with search coil measurements. It is clear from figures 3-6 that the major discrepancies occur in axial positions where large flux-density gradients exist. In these regions however, exact positioning of the search coil in the axial sense becomes of increasing importance to the accuracy of the analytical results. A preliminary computer investigation also revealed that the axial flux variations were sensitive to relatively minor changes in rotor skew. It is thought that a combination of both of these effects accounts to an unknown extent for the difference between the experimental and analytical results. In general however, the results are good, and verify the ability of the field analysis to model the airgap field of a skewed-rotor induction motor with accuracy.

Inspection of figures 3-6 also indicates the presence of axial flux variations in the airgap as large as 5:1, particularly at the lower speed. These large flux variations are especially noticeable in the inter-coil position (B) of the stator winding, compared to a relatively constant axial flux in the coil-axis position (D). This type of axial discontinuity along the circumferential direction has also been demonstrated by Linkous (7), using a graphical method to illustrate typical airgap flux variations due to rotor skew.

Conclusions

The field-based analysis described in this paper has been shown to be capable of modelling to a reasonable degree of accuracy the axial variations of airgap flux density within an induction motor with a skewed rotor cage. As such, it represents a useful tool to the designer interested in a preliminary assessment of the airgap field variations produced by a new machine design, and their influence upon machine performance.

REFERENCES

1. Binns, K.J., Hindmarch, R., and Short, B.P.:
   "Effect of skewing slots on flux distribution
   in induction machines", Proc. I.E.E., 1971, 118,
   (3/4), pp. 543-549.

2. Grieg, J., and Freeman, E.M.: "Travelling-wave
   problem in electrical machines", ibid, 114, (11),
   1967, pp. 1681-1683.

3. Freeman, E.M.: "Travelling waves in induction
   machines: input impedance and equivalent
   circuits", ibid, 115, (12), 1968, pp. 1772-1776.

4. Williamson S.: "The anisotropic layer theory of
   induction machines and induction devices",
   J. Inst. Maths. Applics., 1976, Vol. 17, No. 1,
   pp. 69-84.

5. Williamson, S., and Smith, A.C.: "Layer theory
   analysis for integral-bar induction devices",
   2nd Compumag Conference, Grenoble, Sept. 1978.

6. Williamson, S., and Smith, A.C.: "Field
   analysis for rotating induction machines and its
   relationship to the equivalent-circuit method",
   Proc. I.E.E., 1980, 127 Part B, (2), pp. 83-90.

7. Linkous, C.E.: "Effect of skew on induction
   motor magnetic fields", Trans. A.I.E.E., 1955,
   74, (3), pp. 760-765.

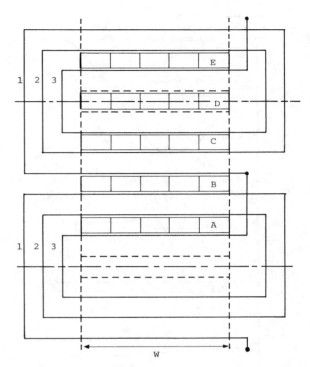

Coil 1 = 69 turns; Coil 2 = 59 turns;
Coil 3 = 39 turns

Figure 2 Winding connection diagram showing
relative positions of search coil sets
A-E

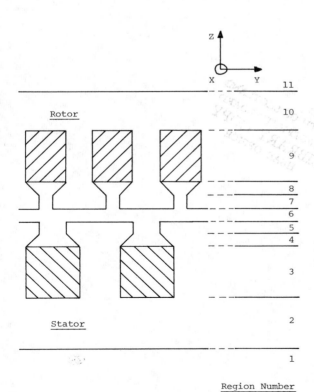

Figure 1 Development of the multi-layer model

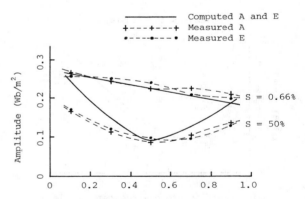

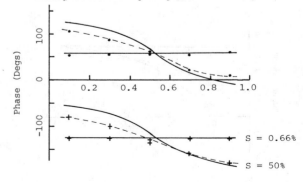

Figure 3 Variation of airgap flux density for
search coil sets A and E

272

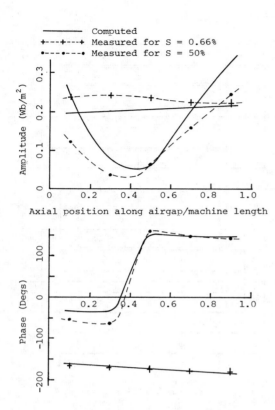

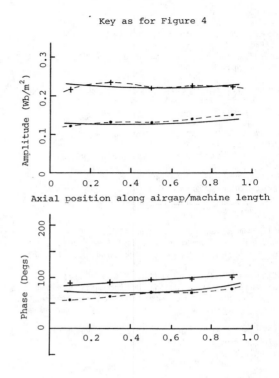

Figure 4 Variation of airgap flux density for search coil set B

Figure 6 Variation of airgap flux density for search coil set D

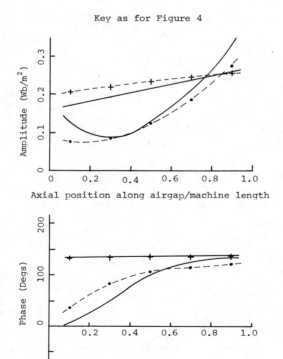

Figure 5 Variation of airgap flux density of search coil set C